TOUGH-MINDED CHRISTIANITY

Honoring the Legacy *of* **JOHN WARWICK MONTGOMERY**

Edited by

WILLIAM DEMBSKI :: THOMAS SCHIRRMACHER

ACADEMIC

Nashville, Tennessee

ISBN: 978-0-8054-4783-5

Published by B&H Publishing Group
Nashville, Tennessee

Dewey Decimal Classification: 239
Subject Heading: APOLOGETICS\
MONTGOMERY, JOHN W.\THEOLOGY

Printed in the United States of America
1 2 3 4 5 6 7 8 9 10 11 12 ✦ 17 16 15 14 13 12 11 10 09
VP

Part III

DOCTRINAL INTEGRITY

Part IV

DEFENDING THE FAITH

Part V

LAW, ETHICS, SOCIETY

Part VI

TRIBUTE

Renaissance Apologist

JOHN WARWICK MONTGOMERY
AND THE RESTORATION OF CLARITY
TO CHRISTIAN THINKING

Paige Patterson

*From these conclusions it is but a short step to the cen-
tral claim of this paper: that the current attempt to
maintain a divinely inspired but non-inerrant Bible is
as analytically nonsensical as are the dualistic and existential assumptions upon which the attempt rests.*[1]

Those words from John Warwick Montgomery were as invigo-
rating to a third-year theology student at New Orleans Baptist
Theological Seminary as the discovery of an unexpected oasis for a
famished traveler in the Kalahari Desert of Botswana. I thank God
for Christian parents and for the vibrant, vital church of my youth.
Both implanted deep within my soul a profound love for God and
respect for His Word. In my home and church, I was taught that
people who did not experience the regenerating grace of God in
Christ would be lost forever and spend eternity in a horrible place
called hell. I was also taught, however, that God's grace and love were
revealed to the world in the person of His Son, Jesus Christ, who in
His incarnation, substitutionary death and victorious resurrection,
provided the means by which any individual could be saved from
his sin and an eternal hell and could experience instead the presence of God in heaven forever. I was further instructed that God
had even gone a step further, and through the witness of the apostles
and prophets in a book, which we know as "The Bible," God had revealed His character and ways and had done so in such a way as to be

fully trustworthy. I cannot recall my pastor father specifically using the word *inerrant* or even infallible to describe the Scriptures, but I do know this beyond any shadow of doubt: Dad and Mother both taught me that the Bible had no mistakes and would always provide the counsel I needed for life and eternity.

From that sheltered environment full of love for Christ and for the lost of the world, I enthusiastically drove my aging Chevrolet across Texas from Dallas to Abilene to begin my college education. In both college and later in seminary, I was stunned to discover that in the very institutions supported by my home church and thousands others like it, the sacred truths, which were highlighted in the preaching and the teaching I heard in my youth, were suddenly the focus of criticism. My father had prepared me to some degree and had even gone so far as to suggest that it was appropriate to seek truth diligently wherever that led and that, in the pursuit of such truth, the theology of my youth would doubtless be challenged. "You must know these challenges, son, in order to be able to be confident in your own faith and to meet the doubts coming from the social order with the liberating news of the Gospel."

In college and seminary, I studied with good men and women. Some of them believed and taught in concert with what I had been taught in the home and church. Others simply raised doubts about the validity of many concepts that were a part of the "orthodox consensus." However, some seemed to delight in generating doubt in student minds. These professors apparently felt a compulsion to destroy more than to encourage the faith of the student. Still others were not so adept at generating questions as they were overt in their denials of such ideas as the inerrancy of God's Word and even of other doctrines, such as the bodily resurrection of Jesus. Perhaps the most damaging part of this whole enterprise, however, was not the dissemination of doubt or the avowal of error in Scripture but the siren song of academia to which some listened more often than they did to our school song. This anthem of unbelief established a new priesthood in the Christian faith. The priesthood of the biblical scholar operated within the holy of holies in the academic community. These men and women who had secured ultimate academic credentialing believed that they knew more than the relatively untutored pastors of the suburban and country churches, which dotted the landscape. There is indeed freedom in America to believe the "simple and homely faith" of the popular religion; but if one wished to be a member of the intelligentsia, if he wished to function in the world of the "scientifically real," then he would not only have to read the scholars with all of their doubts but would also eventually endorse their construction of a new faith for modernity.

Somehow this academic hymn did not ring true to my mind, but it did ring endlessly and with such consistency that inadvertently I had arrived at the position somewhat as follows: Bible-believing people are simple primarily because they lack the intellectual rigor of the classical liberal and neoorthodox thinkers who are writing the majority of the books in the field of religion. Clinging to the hope that the Scriptures were in fact true, I stumbled through my educational Kalahari experience wondering how Scripture could be true while most of the scholars writing in the field disavowed it. In the frustration of that experience, I said to one of my professors at New Orleans Baptist Theological Seminary, "Are there no members of the intellectual community who affirm the precise truthfulness of the word of God?" Reaching into his briefcase, the professor handed me a copy of John Warwick Montgomery's *Crisis in Lutheran Theology*. The professor said, "I know you are not a Lutheran, and I think your position on the Bible is wrong. However, I have just been reading this book; and the author, Montgomery, didn't fall off a load of watermelons on his way into town this morning. The case he argues is impressive."

Eagerly I took the book, went immediately to my room, and literally devoured its contents in an hour's time. I discovered that the faith once delivered to the saints was indeed a faith that was capable not only of saving our souls but also of generating arguments and understandings even more profound than those of the critics whom I had been reading. The logic of the work was to my mind irresistible. The love for Christ and for the Word of God exhibited therein and the humility of the author before God were apparent. Imagine my further surprise when I discovered that he was a graduate of the prestigious Cornell University, the University of California at Berkley, Wittenberg University, the University of Chicago, and the

University of Strasbourg. With Th.D. and Ph.D. degrees, both from universities that could hardly be styled as fundamentalist centers of indoctrination, Montgomery increased my confidence in the future of evangelical scholarship.

In 1970, I discovered a new volume by the perceptive Montgomery. *The Suicide of Christian Theology* was more profoundly helpful to me as a Ph.D. student than even *Crisis in Lutheran Theology* had been. Employing his famous analogy of the two men on the teeter-totter poised at the edge of the cliff, he pointed out that the man who was teetering over the edge of the cliff, were he to shoot his companion on the other side, would perhaps inadvertently, but nonetheless just as thoroughly, seal his own fate. Montgomery further suggested that this was exactly what modern theology had done. In the remainder of the book, Montgomery addressed all of the theologies with which I had been challenged. Beginning with Bishop Pike, progressing to the theological morticians, and moving on to Barth and numerous others, Montgomery, with impeccable logic and commanding but humble authority, demonstrated the abject vacuity of the theologies of modernity and to a large degree even anticipated the advance of postmodernity. Once again I found these assessments to be liberating and wondered quietly if any of the theologians addressed ever bothered to read Montgomery's assessment of their theology.

The following years witnessed the development of a confrontation within the life of the Southern Baptist Convention, that ecclesiastical Zion of which I have been a part all of my life. The issue was clearly the inerrancy of God's Word. A host of others from outside the denomination were helpful to those of us fighting what seemed to be in those days an impossible skirmish. Forever, I am grateful for the encouragement of Presbyterian philosopher Francis Schaeffer, professor Robert Preus of the Lutheran Church (Missouri Synod), and for a host of others, including all those who made up the executive committee of the International Council on Biblical Inerrancy, on which I was privileged and honored to serve. These theologians provided the matrix to generate the understandings of the inerrancy of God's Word, which was needed in Southern Baptist life.

Southern Baptists overwhelmingly had always believed in the inerrancy of God's Word; and some, such as the great Greek scholar,

A. T. Robertson, had even used the word. But in the era immediately following World War II, Southern Baptists became much less isolated and were therefore subject to the inroads of historical-critical methodology in a way that they had been able to avoid until then. Our six theological seminaries[2] were inhabited largely by neoorthodox theologians and some classical liberals. Indeed a few of the six would not have been able to point to a single professor who still embraced the concept of the inerrancy of God's Word. The twenty-five-year battle that ensued was intense and sometimes debilitating. Unquestionably, mistakes were made on both sides, but one of those sides could claim historically to be the faith of the fathers; and once that was established, it remained only to show that the position of biblical inerrancy was totally defensible on intellectual and biblical grounds and that it should be the position of any evangelical Christian, including Southern Baptists.

The degree to which that conflict became determinative for Southern Baptists can be observed in the fact that today, only a little more than twenty-five years later, not one scholar, to my knowledge, in any one of our six seminaries does not embrace the doctrine of the inerrancy of God's Word. Moreover, the Baptist Faith and Message was revised in the year 2000. While the article on Scripture still did not make use of the term *inerrancy*, all the neoorthodox language that had existed in the document was removed, and the final article on Scripture leaves no question in anyone's mind that the Bible is in fact the inerrant and infallible Word of God:

ARTICLE I. THE SCRIPTURES

The Holy Bible was written by men divinely inspired and is God's revelation of Himself to man. It is a perfect treasure of divine instruction. It has God for its author, salvation for its end, and truth, without any mixture of error, for its matter. Therefore, all Scripture is totally true and trustworthy. It reveals the principles by which God judges us, and therefore is, and will remain to the end of the world, the true center of Christian union, and the supreme standard by which all human conduct, creeds, and religious

opinions should be tried. All Scripture is a testimony to
Christ, who is Himself the focus of divine revelation.

Imagine then my joy when I was approached by my colleague, William Dembski, and asked to write a foreword to this volume honoring Dr. Montgomery. Like Montgomery's own work, the volume that follows does not have the narrow scope of a single issue but rather encompasses not only an assessment of Montgomery's own views of such things as the occult and the contemporary movement of intelligent design but also addresses a host of other subjects, such as environmental education, the Gospel of Judas, the proper function of natural reason, an analysis of Montgomery's debate with unbelievers, and numerous other subjects listed in the table of contents. The chapters are written by many of the finest evangelical scholars of our churches today: Edwin Yamauchi, Vernon Grounds, Norman Geisler, William Dembski, well-known apologists John Ankerberg and Gary Habermas, and a host of younger scholars. All have been influenced by the life and work of this substantive thinker, John Warwick Montgomery.

In the end, that a movement among Southern Baptists to return to the faith of their fathers would have been spawned by a Lutheran theologian may seem strange to many. Indeed, that would be an overstatement since the forces converging to bring about one of the few cases in history when a denomination drifting to the left then returned to the faith of its founding fathers were certainly not limited to a single Lutheran theologian or a single student in a Louisiana seminary. But what could be said is that Montgomery's impact on that one student and subsequently on students and professors throughout the Southern Baptist Convention was a central factor in bringing about that Bible-believing renaissance in a denomination to which Montgomery did not belong. The blended prowess of his intellectual grasp and his heart for God provided the example that so many of us needed. We not only learned at his feet and heard him occasionally with great profit; but also, inspired by his example, we fought the noble fight for the inerrancy of God's Word among Southern Baptists.

There is a sense then in which John Warwick Montgomery can be counted as a major source in the revival of orthodoxy among Southern Baptists, and in every way I must offer to God my personal thanksgiving for him. I will remember almost as vividly as I do the day of my conversion that day when the professor handed me *Crisis in Lutheran Theology*. On that day I learned that the faith of our fathers is intellectually defensible, a fact that was confirmed hundreds of times over in the years to come by a host of other faithful scholars. I will always be grateful for John Warwick Montgomery and the insight that he provided.

This volume, which you hold in your hand, honors this wonderful professor who has given so much to so many; but it is more than just a volume honoring Montgomery. It is, as he would have it to be, a further exercise in intellectual endeavor for the glory of God. May God bless the book, and may God bless John Warwick Montgomery.

Paige Patterson, President
Southwestern Baptist Theological Seminary
Forth Worth, Texas

Endnotes

1 John Warwick Montgomery, *Crisis in Lutheran Theology* (Minneapolis, MN: Bethany Fellowship, 1967), 33.

2 Golden Gate Baptist Theological Seminary, Midwestern Baptist Theological Seminary, New Orleans Baptist Theological Seminary, Southern Baptist Theological Seminary, Southeastern Baptist Theological Seminary, and Southwestern Baptist Theological Seminary.

Preface

William A. Dembski and Thomas Schirrmacher

Rare thinkers exhibit such intellectual vitality that they do not merely add to the thought of an age but radically transform it. John Warwick Montgomery is such a thinker. By the middle of the twentieth century, theological liberalism and scientific materialism had become so entrenched among Western intellectuals that a robust Christian theism no longer seemed tenable. Serious Christian thinkers saw themselves as needing to accommodate secular thought at every turn. Yet rather than preserve faith, this strategy of accommodation led to its steady erosion. By the 1960s, one would be hard-pressed to find a theologian at a mainstream seminary or divinity school who did not hide behind metaphor to deny the biblical miracles or invoke advances in philosophy to question core Christian doctrines. Intellectual integrity seemed to require abandoning Christian orthodoxy.

Enter John Warwick Montgomery. Bursting on the intellectual scene of the 1960s like a meteor, he was a theologian with an attitude. Christian orthodoxy was for him not just true. Nor was it merely defensible, as though it were but one among many credible intellectual options. For Montgomery, Christian orthodoxy could be and needed to be vindicated. And with unstoppable energy he was going to make that happen. Not only did he begin a furious publication schedule (see the bibliography at the end of this volume), but he also took his assault on secularism as well as the vindication of Christian orthodoxy right into the belly of the beast—to the highest levels of an academy that had spurned Christianity.

In our day, when debates in academic venues between evangelical Christians and secular thinkers are common fare, to characterize Montgomery's engagement of secularism in such revolutionary terms may sound overblown. But if we think that, we forget that such debates are now common fare precisely because of Montgomery. He blazed the trail. Things only seem easy in retrospect. It took Montgomery to get in there and mix it up with the theologians who proclaimed that God is dead or with the philosophers who embraced situation ethics and its underlying moral relativism.

Montgomery, as a Lutheran theologian, enjoyed the plain speaking of Martin Luther. In debating situation ethics, for instance, he could analyze its philosophical problems as well as anyone. But in debating situation ethicists before a live audience, he would also point out that situation ethics places no premium on truth, with the result that situation ethicists are "morally obligated" to lie to their audience if the situation demands it. So why should the audience trust anything his interlocutor was saying at this moment?

Such in-your-face challenges by Montgomery did not endear him to the academy's wine-and-cheese intellectuals who prefer collegiality to honesty and respectability to honor. But Montgomery decided early in his career that Dale Carnegie's approach to winning friends and influencing people was inadequate for handling the theological disarray of his time. Stronger medicine was required.

Notwithstanding, anyone who knows Montgomery recognizes in him a lover of life and people. If he stepped on toes, it's because toes needed stepping on. If people got angry with him, it's because they were covering up things that he was rightly exposing. Montgomery epitomizes Terence's dictum *homo sum humani a me nihil alienum puto*. Nothing human is alien to him. Moreover, for Montgomery, Christianity is the key to humanity's full flowering. Thus, when people saw the tough side of Montgomery in vindicating Christianity, it was because he saw false ideologies as suffocating the human spirit and needing to be debunked. We might say that Montgomery's apologetics consisted of opening windows in stuffy deoxygenated rooms.

Montgomery is a radical thinker in the true sense of the word; his program of cultural engagement cuts to the very *root* of what it means for evangelicals to be intellectually responsible. Yet to achieve the impact he did, Montgomery needed to be more than just radical. He needed to span an array of disciplines that had been infested with false ideology and then to work skillfully for their renewal. This required a long education, to which Montgomery's long list of earned academic degrees attests. And yet Montgomery was never a dilettante. In whatever field he set his mind to master, he achieved world-class scholarship and recognition.

Thus we find that Montgomery is a world-renowned man of law and practices at some of the highest courts in the world. At the same time he has a long-standing ministry of research, academic teaching, and writing. It's hard to believe that one and the same man could achieve in two worlds what others typically do not reach in one. But, as this volume demonstrates, at the heart is the same one person, who, with the mind of a lawyer and the faith of a theologian, has become one of the most brilliant thinkers in defending the Christian faith. For Montgomery, to act vigorously in the practical world and to think with logical precision in the intellectual world form a coherent whole, one that is necessary for affirming God as both creator and redeemer.

This volume celebrates John Warwick Montgomery's life and legacy. The chapter contributions are not merely by fans but by thinkers whose intellectual and spiritual journey Montgomery profoundly impacted. Indeed, some of us would have veered off the path of truth but for God's grace working through Montgomery. Although it is impossible to capture the full range and depths of Montgomery's thought in a single volume, here is as close an approximation as you will find. We offer this volume as tribute to a man mightily gifted and used by God.

We want to thank B&H Publishing Group for their integrity and vision in publishing this work. We also want to thank Jim Lutzweiler, Ron Kubsch, Bill Youngmark, and Craig Freeman for their diligence in handling so many of the details required to bring a work like this from conception to birth. Finally, we want to thank John Warwick Montgomery himself for his wisdom and insights at all stages of this project. Thank you, John!

William A. Dembski

Thomas Schirrmacher

Contributors

John Ankerberg is president and founder of The Ankerberg Theological Research Institute as well as producer and host of the nationally televised *John Ankerberg Show*, a half-hour internationally seen program that examines challenges to the Christian faith. He received his B.A. from the University of Illinois and his M.A. and M.Div. from Trinity Evangelical Divinity School, overlapping with John Warwick Montgomery while he was a professor there. In 1992 Ankerberg was awarded The Television Program Producer of the Year Award by the National Religious Broadcasters. He has authored and edited more than seventy books. Married to Darlene, he is father of one daughter, Michelle.

John A. Bloom received his B.A. from Grinnell College and M.Div. from Biblical Theological Seminary. He holds a doctorate in physics from Cornell University and a second doctorate in ancient near eastern studies from the Annenberg Research Institute. He is professor of physics and director of the Science and Religion Program at Biola University in La Mirada, California. He has published articles on human origins and on fulfilled prophecy. His interest in viable alternative energy sources is not merely academic: he recently equipped his home with photovoltaic solar panels that supply most of its electrical needs. Bloom lives in La Mirada with his wife and son.

The late *Harold O. J. Brown* was for many years professor of biblical and systematic theology at Trinity Evangelical Divinity School in Deerfield, Illinois. Brown earned his four degrees from Harvard University: B.A. (Germanic languages and biochemistry), B.D., M.Th. (church history), and Ph.D. (Reformation studies). With former United States Surgeon General C. Everett Koop, Brown co-founded the Christian Action Council, a leading evangelical pro-life action group. *Christianity Today* described "Brown's most prominent work" as "helping form and intellectually arm the pro-life movement." A prolific writer, Brown was intensely interested in training the next generation of Christian leaders. He was always challenging his students with the question, "How do we impact this culture for Jesus Christ?"

Bruce Burgess holds a master of theology degree from Morling College as well as a bachelor of laws degree from the University of Sydney. He is the national director of PeaceWise (www.peacewise. org.au), a cross-denominational ministry dedicated to helping people learn to use biblical principles so that they may respond better to the challenge of conflict. Bruce's work spans disputes involving schools, workplace conflict, church-based conflict and victim-offender cases. Bruce leads PeaceWise's national training program each year. He is the coauthor with Rev. Kel Willis of *The Challenge of the Da Vinci Code* and lives in Sydney with his wife, Helen, and two children, Lachlan and Ariel.

The late **L. Russ Bush** was born in 1944 and spent his life serving the Southern Baptist Convention. Most recently he served as the academic dean of Southeastern Baptist Theological Seminary in Wake Forest, North Carolina, as the director of the L. Russ Bush Center for Faith and Culture and as distinguished professor of philosophy of religion. He earned his graduate degrees at Southwestern Baptist Theological Seminary in Fort Worth, Texas. With his friend and colleague, Tom Nettles, he authored *Baptists and the Bible* (Moody Press, 1980), a book calling for the return of the SBC to biblical inerrancy as a core doctrine. Bush also served as a president of the Evangelical Theological Society.

Ross Clifford is principal of Morling Theological College, Sydney. Prior to entering the Baptist ministry, he practiced law. He holds a doctorate in theology (Australian College of Theology) and an M.Th. (University of Sydney). He is the author of eight books including *John Warwick Montgomery's Legal Apologetic*. He also has his own top-rated Sunday night radio program and copioneered outreaches into Mind.Body.Spirit festivals. He is president of the Baptist Union of Australia and former president of the NSW Council of Churches. He is chair of the Australian Lausanne Committee and the Commission on Christian Ethics, Baptist World Alliance.

David Cullen (d. théol., Strasbourg, France) is currently an instructor in humanities, logic, geometry, and physics at the Classical School of Wichita (Kansas). He has taught at university and secondary school levels in California and Kansas in the fields of ancient history, ancient and modern literature, logic, and philosophy. He has been a newspaper columnist and is presently at work on three novels. Active in community affairs and historic preservation in Wichita, he is also happy to be married to Nancy Hancock Cullen, an air traffic safety specialist for the Federal Aviation Administration.

Robert Duncan Culver is a retired professor of theology who taught at Wheaton College and Trinity Evangelical Divinity School. He received his A.B. from Heidelberg College and B.D., Th.M., and Th.D. from Grace Theological Seminary. He has been a special or visiting lecturer in Canada, several states in the United States, Jordan, Hong Kong, France, Holland, and Argentina. Author of *Systematic Theology: Biblical and Historical* (Christian Focus Publications), Culver has written other books including *Daniel and the Latter Days* (Revell, Moody) and also *Daniel* (Wycliffe Commentary Series), both of which have been in print since the 1960s. He has preached twice on most Sundays since 1937. He enjoys being a "hobby farmer" of 120 acres.

William A. Dembski holds doctorates in mathematics (University of Chicago) and in philosophy (University of Illinois at Chicago). He is research professor in philosophy at Southwestern Seminary in Fort Worth, Texas, and senior fellow with Discovery Institute's Center for Science and Culture. He has authored and edited more than a dozen books, including the first book on intelligent design to be published by a major university press, *The Design Inference* (Cambridge University Press, 1998). He lectures around the globe on intelligent design and has appeared on numerous radio and television programs, including ABC's *Nightline* and Jon Stewart's *The Daily Show*.

James Dietz has worked in the passenger rail transportation industry for 30 years. He holds a B.S. in electrical engineering from the University of Maryland and is a member of Eta Kappa Nu. Jim spent 10 years working for General Electric in Erie, Pennsylvania, where he designed propulsion and auxiliary control systems for rail vehicles. For the last 20 years, Jim has worked as a senior consultant on many rail vehicle projects for major cities throughout the U.S. Jim is a fellow of the International Academy of Apologetics, Evangelism and Human Rights, with a special interest in engineers who are bewildered that some technical people actually believe in Jesus.

George Wolfgang Forell joined the faculty of the School of Religion at the University of Iowa in 1954. Except for occasional semesters lecturing in universities and seminaries in Europe, Asia, and Africa, as well as in America, his career has been centered in Iowa City. Director of the School of Religion from 1966 to 1971, he was named Carver Distinguished Professor of Religion in 1973. His national and international reputation is based on his work in the field of Christian ethics, especially in the period of the Protestant Reformation. His many publications include *Faith Active in Love: The History of Christian Ethics, The Augsburg Confession: A Contemporary Commentary, Christian Social Teachings: The Proclamation of the Gospel in a Pluralistic World*, and *The Luther Legacy*.

Norman Geisler (www.normgeisler.com) has taught at the college and graduate level for 50 years, including Trinity Evangelical Divinity School, Dallas Theological Seminary, and Southern Evangelical Seminary, which he cofounded and for which he has served as longtime dean. He has authored 70 books and 200 articles. Dr. Geisler was the founder and first president of The Evangelical Philosophical Society, the president of the Evangelical Theological Society, and the founder and first president of the International Society of Christian Apologetics. He holds a B.A. and an M.A. from Wheaton College and Graduate School, a Th.B. from William Tyndale College, and a Ph.D. (in philosophy) from Loyola University in Chicago.

Colonel (Retired) **David Stott Gordon** holds A.B. and J.D. degrees from the University of Georgia and the M.A. (church history) from Trinity Evangelical Divinity School, where he was Dr. Montgomery's assistant. He retired after 30 years' active and reserve U.S. Army service. He was the Rule of Law Officer for the Office of Military Cooperation—Afghanistan, an attorney at the Peacekeeping and Stability Operations Institute, Army War College, and the Rule of Law Program Director, Army Civil Affairs and Psychological Operations Command. He is a rule of law consultant to civilian and military agencies.

Vernon C. Grounds, chancellor of Denver Seminary and its former president, has had an extensive preaching, teaching, and counseling ministry. A Phi Beta Kappa graduate, Grounds received his B.A. from Rutgers, B.D. from Faith Theological Seminary, and Ph.D. from Drew University. Wheaton College awarded him an honorary D.D. and Gordon College an L.H.D. in recognition of his long service as a Christian educator and leader. Grounds has traveled widely, preaching in hundreds of churches and lecturing at colleges, universities, and seminaries across the country as well as Europe and Latin America. Besides regularly contributing devotionals to *Our Daily Bread*, he has also written many magazine articles and books, including *Evangelicalism and Social Responsibility* as well as *Revolution and the Christian Faith*.

Gary R. Habermas (Ph.D., Michigan State University) is distinguished research professor and chair of the Department of Philosophy and Theology at Liberty University, where he teaches in the Ph.D. program in Theology and Apologetics. He has published 34 books (17 on Jesus' resurrection), such as *The Risen Jesus and Future Hope* (Rowman and Littlefield, 2003). He has also contributed more than 50 chapters or articles to other volumes, plus more than 100 articles or reviews for periodicals. In recent years he has been adjunct or visiting professor at 15 different graduate schools and seminaries in the U.S. and abroad.

Craig J. Hazen is a professor of comparative religion and Christian apologetics at Biola University and founder/director of the master of arts program in Christian Apologetics. He holds a Ph.D. in religious studies from the University of California and has won research awards from both the American Association for the Advancement of Science and the American Academy of Religion. He is the author of the breakout new novel *Five Sacred Crossings* and the monograph *The Village Enlightenment in America*. Hazen is also the editor of *Philosophia Christi*, which is now one of the top-circulating philosophy of religion journals in the world.

Irving Hexham is professor of religious studies at the University of Calgary, Alberta, Canada. He holds a B.A. in religious studies from the University of Lancaster, England, where he studied with professors Ninian Smart and Edward Conze. He was awarded his M.A., with distinction, and Ph.D. by the University of Bristol, England, and has published over 30 books and numerous articles. His Festschrift, "Border Crossing," edited by Dr. Ulrich van der Heyden and Dr. Andreas Feldtkeller, was published by the Franz Steiner Verlag of Stuttgart in 2008.

W. Howard Hoffman, M.D., is a pathologist with Associated Pathologists and Quest Diagnostics in Las Vegas, Nevada, where he has practiced since 1978. He is certified in anatomic pathology and clinical pathology (laboratory medicine) by the American Board of Pathology. He is certified in the subspecialty of dermatopathology by the American Boards of Pathology and Dermatology. Dr. Hoffman has an undergraduate degree in chemistry from Texas Tech and an M.D. from Southwestern Medical School of the University of Texas. He is a long time friend of Dr. Montgomery and has studied his theological works. He has a strong interest in philosophy and theology as being important for understanding and presenting Christian teachings to others. He and his wife, Jane, have four children.

Michael S. Horton (Ph.D., University of Coventry and Wycliffe Hall, Oxford) is J. Gresham Machen Professor of Systematic Theology and Apologetics at Westminster Seminary, California. The author of 20 books, his most recent are *People and Place: A Covenant Ecclesiology* (WJK, 2008) and *Christless Christianity: On the American Captivity of the Church* (Baker, 2008). He is also associate pastor of Christ United Reformed Church (Santee), the editor of *Modern Reformation* magazine and a host of the White Horse Inn radio broadcast; and he lives with his wife and four children near San Diego, California.

Willy Humbert received his Ph.D. in biological sciences from the Louis Pasteur University in Strasbourg, France. He worked in a number of different and emerging scientific fields for many years while employed at the National Center for Scientific Research in Strasbourg. Dr. Humbert's research was largely devoted to the field of ecophysiology and calcifications in both the animal and human worlds. He is the author of over 60 articles in scientific journals and books and has presented his findings at numerous scientific and scholarly conferences throughout the world. Dr. Humbert is also an accomplished and avid mountaineer and skier.

Philip Johnson, B.A., B.D. (University of Sydney), M.Th. (Australian College of Theology) is a visiting lecturer in apologetics and alternative religious movements at Morling College, Sydney, Australia. He has coauthored several books including *Beyond Prediction* (Lion, 2001), *Jesus and the Gods of the New Age* (Lion, 2001), and *Beyond the Burning Times* (Lion, 2008), and contributed three chapters to *Encountering New Religious Movements* (Kregel, 2004). He is a cofounding editor of the e-journal *Sacred Tribes Journal*, and had essays published in *Australian Religion Studies Review*, *Lutheran Theological Journal*, and *Missiology*.

Thomas K. Johnson, M.Div. (MCL), A.C.P.E., Ph.D., vice president for research and professor of philosophy, Martin Bucer Seminary and director of the associated Comenius Institute (Prague), was a church planter in the U.S., a visiting professor of philosophy at the dissident European Humanities University (Minsk, Belarus), taught philosophy for eight years at Charles University (Prague), and lectured in 10 countries. He has written about 80 articles, reviews, and essays; this essay began as a Bible study related to his book *Natural Law Ethics* (Bonn: VKW, 2005). He has two books forthcoming: one on the Trinity and one on human rights. He is married with three adult children.

Mary H. Korte, associate professor of natural sciences and director of the Graduate Program in Environmental Education at Concordia University Wisconsin, graduated Phi Beta Kappa from the College of William and Mary. She holds a master of science (Southern Illinois University) and a doctorate in Christian education (Trinity College and Seminary). Dr. Korte also holds the diplôme from the International Academy of Apologetics and Human Rights in Strasbourg, France, for her thesis, "The Secularization of Lutheran Higher Education and the Promise of Evidential Apologetics."

Erwin Lutzer, senior pastor of The Moody Church in Chicago, was born and reared near Regina, Saskatchewan, Canada. He received his B.A. from Winnipeg Bible College, Th.M. from Dallas Theological Seminary, M.A. from Loyola University (Chicago), and

LL.D. from Simon Greenleaf School of Law. Lutzer is an award-winning author of numerous books, a celebrated international conference speaker, and the featured speaker on three radio programs: *The Moody Church Hour, Songs in the Night,* and *Running to Win.* These programs are available through the Moody Broadcasting Network, the Bible Broadcasting Network, Trans World Radio, and many Christian radio stations around the world. He and his wife, Rebecca, live in the Chicago area and are the parents of three married children.

James Lutzweiler is the archivist at Southeastern Baptist Theological Seminary. He holds the B.A. in biblical languages from Pillsbury College, the M.Div. from Central Baptist Theological Seminary in Minneapolis, and the M.A. in American history from North Carolina State University. He operates a microfilm business specializing in the preservation of historic fundamentalist and evangelical periodicals (e.g., Arno Gaebelein's *Our Hope* and Moody's *The Record of Christian Work*) and manuscript collections (e.g., the papers of Lyman Stewart, Wilbur Smith, and E. Y. Mullins). With Dwain Waldrep he is coediting *The Faces of Fundamentalism,* a biographical dictionary of the contributors to *The Fundamentals.* He has published 12 monographs on *The Roots of Billy Graham.*

I. Howard Marshall holds degrees in classics (University of Aberdeen) and theology (Universities of Aberdeen and Cambridge). He has spent most of his working life (1964–99) in Aberdeen where he is now an honorary research professor. He has supervised many postgraduate students from all over the world and lectured in several countries. His published works include commentaries on Luke and the Pastoral Epistles and a *New Testament Theology.* He is a former chair of the Tyndale Fellowship and the Fellowship of European Evangelical Theologians. He belongs to the Methodist Church and is a regular preacher.

Edward N. Martin received his B.A. at Hillsdale College in 1988, his M.A. from Trinity Evangelical Divinity School in 1990 (under John Feinberg), and Ph.D. from Purdue University in 1995 (under William Rowe). He is professor and cochair of philosophy and theology at Liberty University in Lynchburg, Virginia, and associate editor with Dr. Montgomery of the e-journal *Global Journal of Classical Theology*. He is author of several journal articles and reviews appearing in *Sorites*, *International Journal for Philosophy of Religion*, and *Global Journal*, and has contributed essays to various publications including ones from InterVarsity and Wiley-Blackwell.

Angus J. L. Menuge is professor of philosophy at Concordia University Wisconsin. Born in England, he became an American citizen in 2005. Menuge has written articles on the vocation of scientist, intelligent design, philosophy of mind and apologetics. He is the author of *Agents Under Fire: Materialism and the Rationality of Science* (Rowman and Littlefield, 2004) and editor of *Reading God's World: The Vocation of Scientist* (Concordia Publishing House, 2004).

The Honourable **Dallas K. Miller** holds degrees in history, religious studies, and law, as well as an M.A. in philosophy and apologetics (Trinity Seminary). He is a fellow of the International Academy of Christian Apologetics in Strasbourg, France. In his legal practice Dallas has handled cases at all levels of court including the supreme court of Canada and has advocated on behalf of the family throughout Canada and internationally. His legal skills were recognized when he was made Queen's Counsel in 1998. After almost 25 years in legal practice, Dallas was appointed as a justice of the Court of Queen's Bench of Alberta by Canada's minister of justice in December 2006.

Will Moore is a graduate of the Universities of Saskatchewan and Alberta with degrees in Canadian history, archival science, and education. He is president of the Canadian Institute of Law, Theology, and Public Policy, Inc., the publisher of a number of John Warwick Montgomery's books and recordings of lectures and courses. He is a former board member of the Canadian Real Estate Association and the Alberta Real Estate Association. He is a member of the Anglican Church of Canada and a former rector's warden.

Roger R. Nicole, emeritus professor of theology at Reformed Theological Seminary, is a native Swiss Reformed theologian. He holds an M.A. from Sorbonne, a Th.D. from Gordon Divinity School, and a Ph.D. from Harvard University. Nicole has long been regarded as one of the preeminent theologians in America. He was an associate editor for the *New Geneva Study Bible* and a corresponding editor for *Christianity Today*. He assisted in the translation of the NIV Bible, is a past president of the Evangelical Theological Society, and was a founding member of the International Council on Biblical Inerrancy. He has written over 100 articles and contributed to 50 books and reference works. Students esteem him highly for his approachability and wisdom.

William Beadon Norman was born in London and educated at Eton and Cambridge. After receiving his B.A. (1st) in law from Cambridge University, he became a barrister at Lincoln's Inn. Subsequently he returned to Cambridge University to receive his M.A. He was ordained a deacon in 1952 and then a priest in 1953. From 1955 to 1965 he was tutor and then acting principal at Buwalasi Theological College in Uganda. Returning to Great Britain, he served as a vicar in Yorkshire and a rector in Birmingham. He retired in 1991 and was preacher at Lincoln's Inn from 1994 to 2006.

Robert S. Ove holds a B.A. in English and psychology (Carthage College), one year of media studies (University of Iowa), and an M.Div. (Wittenberg University). He owned a motion picture business in California filming all TV appearances of Gov. Knight plus films for Sacramento State College. He served parishes in eight states plus Mazatlan, Mexico. He wrote weekly religious columns in Philadelphia, Pennsylvania, and Cheyenne, Wyoming, and produced a weekly TV program in Helena, Montana. He served as seminary professor in Nepal before retiring to New Mexico. He published *Geronimo's Kids* (Texas A&M Press, 1997).

James I. Packer received degrees in classics and theology and also his D.Phil. from Oxford University. He served 17 years in English seminary education, punctuated by eight years directing a study center in Oxford, after which he moved in 1979 to Regent College, Vancouver, Canada, where he has been successively professor of historical and systematic theology, Sangwoo Youtong Chee Professor of Theology, and Board of Governors Professor of Theology, a position he continues to hold. He has published many books, including the best seller *Knowing God*, and was named by *Time* magazine as one of North America's 25 most influential Christian teachers.

Craig Parton is a trial lawyer and partner with the oldest law firm in the Western United States—Price, Postel, and Parma of Santa Barbara, California. On graduating from college, he spent seven years on staff with Campus Crusade for Christ, the last four of which were spent as national lecturer for Crusade. Parton traveled to over 100 universities and colleges across the country defending the Christian faith through lectures and debates. He received his masters in Christian apologetics under John Warwick Montgomery at the Simon Greenleaf School of Law. He then earned his J.D. from the University of California, Hastings Law School in San Francisco. Parton is the United States director of the International Academy of Apologetics, Evangelism, and Human Rights in Strasbourg, France (www.apologeticsacademy.eu). His latest book is titled *The Defense Never Rests: A Lawyer's Quest for the Gospel.*

Paige Patterson, a graduate of Hardin-Simmons University, completed Th.M. and Ph.D. degrees in theology from New Orleans Baptist Theological Seminary. He was twice elected president of the Southern Baptist Convention, serving in that capacity from 1998 to 2000. During those years he appointed a committee to revise the Baptist Faith and Message, the confession most widely employed by Southern Baptists. Patterson played a pivotal role in the conservative resurgence among Southern Baptists, which unseated the theological liberalism that had previously dominated Southern Baptist education. Patterson is an evangelist, writer, and world traveler. He assumed the presidency of Southwestern Baptist Theological Seminary (Fort Worth) in 2003, having previously served as president of Criswell College (Dallas) and Southeastern Baptist Theological Seminary (Wake Forest).

The Honourable *Andrew Phang*, Senior Counsel, LL.B. (National University of Singapore), LL.M., S.J.D. (Harvard), Advocate & Solicitor (Singapore), was professor of law at the Singapore Management University at the time his essay for this volume was written. He has since been appointed a judge of the supreme court of Singapore. Phang was in legal academia for over two decades and has published many books, book chapters, and articles. Author of *Basic Principles of Singapore Business Law*, his works have been cited by Singapore and

Malaysian courts as well as by the Australian High Court and the New South Wales courts.

Robert Rodgers holds seven degrees in theology and education. He is research professor of the history of Christian thought in Miskolc, Hungary. There he established the University Department of Christian Studies, the first in any former Communist country. He lectures throughout Central and Eastern Europe and the United States. He has edited several major books and authored *The Life and Work of Robert Watts* and *The Incarnation of the Antithesis: The Educational Philosophy of Abraham Kuyper Viewed from a Theological Perspective.* His doctoral thesis on the theology of Robert Watts (Faculte Libre Theologie Reformee, Aix-en-Provence, France) provides the only full study of that subject. The work on Kuyper's educational philosophy has been recognized as the first of its kind.

Michael Saward has written over a hundred hymns and worked closely with the Hymn Society of Great Britain and Ireland as well as the Jubilate Group, for which he served as director until 2001. Educated at Eltham College and Bristol University, where he studied theology, he was ordained to the Anglican priesthood at Canterbury Cathedral. After serving as curate outside London and working with the Liverpool Council of Churches, be became the Radio and Television Officer for Archbishop Michael Ramsey. As a member of the Church of England Evangelical Council, he served as chair for the Billy Graham London Mission 1989 Media Task Group. He has held a Winston Churchill Travelling Fellowship and is a member of London's Athenaeum. Saward's best known hymn is "Christ Triumphant, Ever Reigning."

Christine Schirrmacher, M.A. and Ph.D. in Islamic studies, is presently professor of Islamic studies at the Evangelisch-Theologische Faculteit (Protestant University) in Leuven/Belgium and head of the Institut für Islamfragen (Institute of Islamic Studies) of the German Evangelical Alliance as well as an official speaker and advisor on Islam for the World Evangelical Alliance (WEA). She lectures on Islam and security issues, serves in continuing education programs related to politics, and is a consultant to different advisory bodies in Germany.

Thomas Schirrmacher holds four doctoral degrees: Dr.theol. (Ecumenical Theology, TU Kampen, Netherlands), Ph.D. (Cultural Anthropology, PWU, Los Angeles), Th.D. (Ethics, WTS, Lakeland, Florida), Dr.phil. (Sociology of Religion, State University, Bonn, Germany) and received two honorary doctorates: D.D. (Cranmer Theological House, Shreveport), D.D. (ACTS University, Bangalore, India). He is professor of ethics and rector of Martin Bucer Theological Seminary (Bonn, Berlin, Zurich, Innsbruck, Prague, Istanbul, Ankara), professor of the sociology of religion at the State University of Oradea, Romania, and professor of international development at ACTS University in Bangalore, India. He is also director of the International Institute for Religious Freedom of the World Evangelical Alliance.

Alvin J. Schmidt was born and raised in Western Canada. He is a former member of the Royal Canadian Mounted Police, holds the B.A., M.Div., M.A., and Ph.D. degrees, and has authored eight books. His book *Fraternal Organizations* (1980) received the award of Outstanding Reference Work of 1980 from the American Library Association. He has published *The Menace of Multiculturalism: Trojan Horse in America* (1997); *The Great Divide: Failure of Islam and the Triumph of the West* (2004); *How Christianity Changed the World* (2004); and *Dust to Dust or Ashes to Ashes: A Biblical Examination of Cremation* (2005). He and his wife, Carol, have two grown sons.

Edwin M. Yamauchi received his B.A. in Hebrew and Hellenistics from Shelton College in 1960. He later earned both his M.A. and Ph.D. in Mediterranean studies from Brandeis University. He is currently the professor of history emeritus at Miami University in Oxford, Ohio. Throughout his productive writing career, Yamauchi has authored 17 books, written chapters for 34 books, and crafted 172 articles in 36 reference works, 89 journal articles, and 107 reviews in 27 journals. Yamauchi serves as a high-ranking officer in five different scholarly societies, including the Evangelical Theological Society. Featured in Lee Strobel's *The Case for Christ*, Yamauchi is a leading evangelical thinker.

Peter Zöller-Greer was born in 1956 in Mannheim, Germany. He studied mathematics and theoretical physics in Siegen and

Heidelberg. In 1981 he received his M.A. in mathematics from the University of Heidelberg. In 1990 he received his Ph.D. from the University of Mannheim for a mathematical solution to a quantum mechanical problem. From 1981 on he worked as a computer researcher at ABB Mannheim and as a lecturer at several colleges. Since 1993, he has been professor of mathematics and computer science at the State University of Applied Sciences in Frankfurt am Main, Germany.

TOUGH-MINDED
CHRISTIANITY

Part I

THE CHRISTIAN WORLDVIEW

Paul Against Pluralism

THE RELEVANCE OF THE ATHENIAN SPEECH TODAY

J. I. Packer

Our Pluralist Culture

The modern Western world is pluralistic to its fingertips. Pluralism has become foundational to contemporary culture. Pluralism is a sociopolitical ideology, an aggressive viewpoint that holds forth guidelines and parameters, a trajectory and sense of direction, and a definite goal and purpose, for the entire human community of which we are part. The viewpoint is that personal freedom is the supreme value; the goal is that freedom be maximized up to the limit; and the guidelines are that those who govern, manage, educate, and control others should not impose any one view of reality but should let all views coexist as options in life's smorgasbord display so that we each may choose what appeals without any convictional cards being forced upon us. Free from the guidance and restraint of universally accepted principles, we may all now live by our own values and ideals without hindrance. What is expected is that this freedom, plus the material prosperity and bodily well-being that today's technology reckons to provide, will ensure everyone's happiness. Though rarely displayed in its pure form, pluralism is a miasma that infects governmental, social, and educational policies constantly, and no modern Westerner escapes its influence.

Clearly post-Christian, postliberal, post-Marxist, and postmodern—and reflecting skepticism about every world-and-life view from the past, whether religious, philosophical, scientific, or romantic—today's pluralism directs that public policy be based not on public acknowledgment of universal truth and standards but on a purpose of enabling everyone to pursue personal options. Pluralism knows that the global village that we call the world is full of metanarratives, that is, accounts of reality that claim to make sense of the human story and to declare the meaning of human life; every religion has one, and

2

antireligious viewpoints like Marxism and evolutionism have them too. Pluralism professes to tolerate and, other things being equal, to protect all these views, but it throws a dark canopy of uncommitted-ness over them and thus reduces them to private interests that must not be allowed to rock, let alone steer, the community boat. This is a huge break with how things have been everywhere up to now, or at least until a generation ago, and what will come of it remains to be seen.

How long publicly established pluralism can last is a serious ques-tion. In the past Western society has been held together culturally and behaviorally by public commitment to some form of Christian belief about God. Thus medieval Christendom saw God as guaran-teeing the world's ongoing stability; Reformation Christendom saw him as executing an ecclesiastical and political spring-cleaning; Vic-torian Christendom saw him as generating universal progress; all had good hope for the future because it was in God's beneficent hands. Pluralism, however, has no such hope. Shaped by revolt against all forms of what it sees as totalitarianism, including Christian civili-zation, and functioning in society as a form of practical atheism, it produces short-term optimism as triumphant technology keeps wid-ening our range of options, but the optimism is framed by long-term pessimism about how things will finally turn out. Cognitive disso-nance as to how our ongoing rape of the planet and destabilizing of the climate can square with a universal advancement of human wel-fare abounds. It is almost a case of "let us eat and drink, for we don't know how soon all mankind may die." Pop culture, when not alien-ated, is absorbed in, and euphoric about, the present; meanwhile, in-tellectuals wring their hands in despair about the future. Welcome to our modern Western world!

Christians cannot but be saddened at these developments in our culture, but we should not be surprised at them. We know, or at least we should know, that fallen human nature on its own is incapable of choosing a path that leads to real happiness; all paths that sin-ful humans, left to themselves, actually choose lead to disillusion-ment, more or less. We know that when people are encouraged to be egocentric, and to live their own lives and do their own thing in their own way, the result is a compound of pride and misery and cosmic resentment that may well find expression in antisocial behavior. Though pluralism itself is blind to this, I think we can already see that today's pluralistic culture is actually producing more misery, alienation, social instability, and personal hurt, than were there before. We know, too, that this is itself the beginning of divine judgment on us and that more catastrophic disasters await us if there is not community repentance and return to God. But we cannot pursue that theme now.

A Pluralist View of Religion

Our present task is to look more closely at what we may call the "in-church" version of this pluralism that we meet among the theological liberals. Liberalism as a flow of thought in the church today is in my view really bankrupt, but it constantly refinances itself by taking into itself what is uppermost in the culture, according to its operative principle that the world under God has the wisdom and the church must always be playing catch-up; and this is the case in point. During the past century liberal theologians have developed a pluralistic account of world religions, which sees them as quests for the same goal, ways up the same mountain, partners in countering hedonism and materialism, resources to enrich and encourage one another in a common task, and avenues leading finally to the same eternal happiness. This is the academic version of the world's idea that "religions are all the same really." Academically this idea sprang from the world of Friedrich Schleiermacher; it was given as a boost by the 1893 World Parliament of Religions and is sustained today by the globalistic relativism of many thought leaders. But the thesis is vulnerable to three major criticisms.

First, it embodies a false *modesty*. Forswearing all modes of religious imperialism, Christian pluralism presents itself as humble: humble in insisting, as all liberals do, that no formulation of the faith is final, nor is any question of faith ever finally resolved; humble, therefore, in insisting that discussion must go on, and that it is spiritually obtuse to treat any sort of creedal definitions as fixed points for thought; humble, too, in now elevating non-Christian faiths to the same level as Christianity. All liberals see the positions they hold

4

at present as provisional, being relative to other proposals today and whatever ideas may appear tomorrow, and liberal pluralists in theology extend this to cover what other significant religions may have to say. But in thus seeing religious thought as an ongoing exploration rather than following an established track, and in being open to augmentation and redirection from non-Christian sources, cultural, and religious, the pluralism we are considering expresses arrogance rather than modesty and pride rather than humility, for its method excludes treating clear and unambiguous Bible teaching as the abiding word and unchanging truth of God. That is bad; and if it is compounded, as it frequently is, by assuming an attitude of superiority—intellectual, theological, and spiritual—toward those who treat Bible doctrine as divine and definitive, bad becomes worse. And should this arrogance of heart prompt aggressive response when it is pointed out that the pluralist position is unfaithful to Christ, to the gospel, and to the church's world mission, bad becomes worse still; it is then not far from sin against the Holy Spirit. There is no true humility or modesty here, just the reverse.

Second, the pluralist thesis expresses a false *charity*. It is well-known that, understandably, since Christianity is so directly salvation oriented, discussions of non-Christian religions have kept revolving around the question, whether they mediate the same salvation that Christians receive—that is, salvation through the historical death and resurrection of Christ and the action of the Holy Spirit leading us to faith in Him and fellowship with Him. As we all know, three answers have been given to that question. The exclusivist answer is that in this life there must be conscious faith in a known Christ for salvation to be ours hereafter. The inclusivist answer is that this is not the whole truth; additionally, some who lived and died ignorant of Christ, but who sought God as they conceived Him and strove for what they thought was good, will find in a future life that they have been saved by grace through Christ nonetheless. And the universalist answer is that this is not the whole truth either; for whatever our view of reality, whatever we may affirm or deny about God, and whatever our behavior or misbehavior in this life, God's grace in Christ will triumph by finally bringing us all without exception to the same happy heaven. Expositors of pluralism divide as to whether they give answers two or three, while the New Testament seems clearly to give answer one. But that being so, answers two and three, with their affirmation of non-Christian religions as so many ways of salvation, over and above Christianity, express a false charity since their zeal to extend the sphere of saving grace and the number of the saved leads them to part company with the apostolic Scriptures. The apostolic account of non-Christian religions, as we shall see in a moment, is that though they are shot through with true inklings about God alongside many distortions, they neither present a true concept of salvation nor mediate the reality of it, and their ideas about God are idolatrous to a degree. Pluralists, however, turn their backs on this teaching and insinuate, if they do not actually declare, that those who hold it thereby show a lack of charity toward most of the world's inhabitants. A sight gag used twice in Buster Keaton movies is a life belt that sinks the moment it hits the water; Bible believers have reason to regard all Christless faiths in similar terms. Pluralism's unhappy move at this point leads us on to our final criticism.

Third, the pluralist thesis involves false *belief*: mistaken notions, that is, about how world religions relate to one another. The closer one gets to them, the more obvious become the specific differences between them, as well as the differences between them all and Christianity, and the less plausible becomes the idea that they are "all the same really." Two things must be noted about how they all differ from the Christian faith. To start with, there is a huge contrast between the way of salvation from evil, however that evil is understood, in all non-Christian faiths as compared with biblical Christianity. They point to behavioral options in daily life and say, "Do"; biblical Christianity points to Calvary and says, "Done." They say, "Work, and gain salvation from evil by your own effort"; the Christian gospel says, "Receive salvation from the God who by rights would condemn and reject you, by his own amazing grace, through faith in His Son, Jesus Christ." Then, too, the Christian concept of salvation, first to last, and supremely at its destination point, is Jesus centered. The essence of it is fellowship with, and worship of, Christ in His glory; and at the heart of our adoring vision of God in heaven will be our adoring vision of Jesus, the divine Son, our Savior, the slain Lamb now exalted to share His Father's throne. Glorified believers will be loving and serving Him, and He will be loving and enriching them, to all eternity. Heaven will be a world of love; mutual outpourings of love between the Lord and His people will be at its center. And whatever inclusivists and pluralists offer as to how knowledge of Christ will come after death to those who lacked it when alive, it remains untrue to claim that non-Christian faiths as such—some of which (Judaism and Islam most notably) explicitly deny Jesus' divinity and savior-hood—have in view anything like the love relationship, the ongoing doxology, and the endless joy of final salvation according to the gospel. To say that all world religions are climbing the same mountain is simply false, both to the self-understanding of each one of them and to the biblical revelation of reality. The assimilation of world faiths to one another at which academic pluralists like John Hick aim is impossible intellectually and disastrous pastorally. Any who doubt this should read Harold Netland's learned book *Dissonant Voices* (Leicester: Apollos, 1991), which is cogent indeed on this matter.

Paul and First-Century Pluralism: Polytheism at Athens

To confirm what has just been said, we shall now look at the way in which the apostle Paul responded to the pluralism he found at Athens on his pioneer missionary visit to Europe. Luke records this for us in Acts 17:16–34. Acts, as we know, is Luke's second volume on Christ and Christian beginnings. Jesus' ascension is the dividing point between them, and while this book is canonically titled Acts of the Apostles, it could equally well be called Acts of the Holy Spirit, or (even better) Acts of the Enthroned Lord. It tracks the gospel from Jerusalem to Rome and en route gives samples of the various kinds of evangelistic communication that the apostles addressed to various audiences.

Luke's purpose, being evidently apologetic and catechetical as well as simply narrational, required of him factual accuracy; doubly so if, as seems virtually certain, he was writing his two-volume work in the early sixties of the first century, when many witnesses of all that he records were still alive. He claims to be presenting facts that he has researched, that he knows well, and that he is qualified to relay with precision (Luke 1:1–4); and the hypothesis that he is entirely truthful and worthy, therefore, of our trust has stood up successfully to all the many skeptical queryings that the past 200 years have brought forth. To be sure, his account of Paul at Athens, as of most of the events he narrates, is compressed; and his summary of Paul's address, which he casts into direct speech, according to the conventions of Greco-Roman historical writing, can be read aloud in two minutes. But there is every reason to treat the whole story as authentic, no reason to doubt any aspect of it, and we shall draw on it accordingly.

First-century Athens, though long bereft of its former glory, still was thought of (and thought of itself) in Oxford-and-Cambridge, Harvard-and-Yale terms as the cream of the cream brain-wise, the intellectual capital of the world; and Athenian religion was a distinctive and highly sophisticated compound of manipulative polytheism in a frame of argumentative philosophizing about life's true values. From verses 16–21 we learn how Paul reacted to all this. He was "provoked," Luke tells us—moved, that is, to grief and indignation on God's behalf—by the polytheism to which multiple shrines bore witness. The civic religion at Athens, a free city within the Roman Empire, was worship of the goddess Athena, who set Athens going, and of the god Apollo, the city's patron, and with them Athenians worshipped at their discretion a range of what were in essence nature gods—Poseidon the sea god; Demeter the harvest goddess; Bacchus, god of wine and energy; and so on. In all polytheistic systems each deity has some aspect of the natural order under his or her control, and one must do homage to the proper god or gods in order to get the help one needs in life's various involvements. Slavish attempts to manipulate the gods, wheedling favors from them by special efforts to please them, is the spirit of all polytheism everywhere. Here, then, was the religious substratum of Athenian life.

But there were philosophers there too: Epicureans and Stoics, the former committed to a withdrawn lifestyle, tranquil, unattached, and free as far as possible from all forms of business and trouble, including all worship of the gods, the latter embracing a stern elitist moralism in which reason and fate, pantheistically conceived, were the ultimate realities and fortitude the ultimate virtue. Athenians welcomed traveling teachers and loved novelties so Paul easily got into discussion with philosophers of both sorts. Some (Epicureans?) dismissed him as a "babbler," that is, a picker-up of ill-considered trifles, an intellectual charlatan not to be taken seriously. Others (Stoics?) thought he was wanting to add two foreign deities, a god named Jesus and a goddess named Anastasis ("resurrection"), to Athens's already overcrowded pantheon. Foreignness would be a reason for rejecting these additions so there was some coolness toward Paul. But curiosity triumphed, and so he found himself summoned to Athens's most prestigious debating chamber to answer the question, "May we know what this new teaching is that you are presenting?" (v. 19). Luke now summarizes the points Paul made in reply.

Paul's appearance before the Areopagus had the nature of an official hearing, for the Areopagus was the legal body that would screen all proposals to introduce new gods into the Athenian pantheon. It has indeed been powerfully argued that the question cited above from verse 19 is actually a statement that should be translated, "We possess the legal right to make a judgment about" what this new teaching amounts to. At all events it was a situation calling for both courtesy and clarity as Paul sought to challenge and correct the polytheistic frame of thought on which the hearing was based, and what Luke shows us is Paul rising brilliantly to an almost impossible combination of demands upon him.

A time-honored mistake is to suppose that in his Areopagus address Paul was trying to show off as a philosopher among the philosophers, that the relatively small number of converts at the end of the day was God's way of indicating that he should not have done so, and that his declaration that when he moved on from Athens to Corinth, "I decided to know nothing among you except Jesus Christ and him crucified" (1 Cor 2:2), was a renouncing of his Athenian style and method. This is totally wrong, as all modern commentaries acknowledge. Paul began where he had to begin with the mixed bag of polytheists and philosophers that he was talking to. First he gave them a lesson in basic theism, introducing them to the one real God whose existence they acknowledge despite their ignorance about Him, and who will break one day into history to judge the world. Next, he laid before them the truth about man, displaying to them their own present plight under God's judgment. The gospel message as Paul preached, taught, and defended it can be summarized under six heads for which the keywords are God, *man, history, salvation, fellowship,* and *heaven;* we may, I think, be sure Paul was trying to turn this legal hearing into an evangelistic occasion and that, having spoken of God and of man, he would have gone on to complete his account of saving history by speaking of Christ's atoning death on the cross prior to His resurrection and would then have explained the way of salvation in precise terms, as he did elsewhere (Acts 13:38–39; 16:31; Rom 3:23–26; 10:9–13). But before he could do that, he was howled down (that is what "mocked" really means); when his hearers realized that he was seriously affirming that a man had been raised from death by the power of God, cries (in Greek) that were the equivalent of the English "Boo," "Yah," "Rubbish," "Nonsense," "Poppycock," "Stop it," "Sit down and shut up," broke out; the noise was such that Paul could not go on speaking; and the meeting broke up in confusion. Some, however, met with Paul again to hear more, and the small church that he left behind him included at least one Areopagite of standing. Luke seems to be telling us as the chapter closes that even in Athens, the toughest nut to crack evangelistically in all Greece, the gospel achieved real if qualified success.

Now look in more detail at what Paul said before he had to stop talking.

What did he tell them about *God?* In verses 23–25 we learn that he told them the following: (1) By their own admission (the altar to the Unknown God), they do not know the one true God, whatever gestures of worship they may make in his direction. (2) This God is their Creator, to whom they owe their present and continued existence. (3) He is the sovereign Lord, God in charge of the world He has made. (4) He is infinite and omnipresent, not therefore localized, and not to be thought of as inhabiting buildings specially set apart for Him. (5) He is eternally self-sufficient and self-sustaining and does not depend on our gifts and sacrifices to keep Him going, for He never runs out of vitality or energy. (The theologians' term for this is aseity, which means the quality of drawing your life continually and endlessly from within yourself. It is a word worth learning.) (6) He is the source of every good thing we have or ever receive, so that (Paul implies) constant thanksgiving to Him would be in order (cf. Acts 14:15–17), and any lack of thankfulness would be a disorder (cf. Rom 1:21).

What did Paul then tell them about *man?* In verses 26–30 we learn that he laid before them the following truths: (1) The unity of the human race through a common ancestor is a fact. (2) The sovereignty of God in human history, geography, and all of everyone's affairs, is a further fact. (3) The purpose of the Creator was that we should, through intentionally seeking God, find him; in other words, knowing God is the true purpose of human life. (4) The dignity of each human being lies in the fact that we live in and through God as his offspring. Being God's image bearer (this was Paul's thought, whether or not he used that phrase) brings great dignity, though it brings responsibility too. (5) Since Greek poets, whom Greeks everywhere venerate as oracular wiseacres (they all did, and Paul builds on that), have testified to this human relationship to God, it is inexcusable to imagine God in the form of an idol, a process that means, first, scaling Him down to the level of His creatures, and then reducing Him further to the level of our own image of this creature or that. (Mental as well as metal images come under the lash of Paul's words here.) (6) God holds us all guilty for not worshipping and serving Him according to the highest we know of Him, and directs us to repent of—that is, to turn our back on—everything that has so far kept us from worthy worship.

And what, after all that, did Paul go on to tell them about history, before their booing and catcalling silenced him? From verse 31 we learn that he was able to set forth just four facts: (1) The era in which God shows forbearance toward our willful disregard of him is coming to an end. (2) God has fixed the day on which He will stop the flow of space-time history in order to bring us all to judgment and deal with us all as we deserve for our shortcomings toward both Him and other people. (3) God's executive agent in that judgment will be the man called Jesus, whom He has designated for that purpose. (4) God has given the world a public proof and pledge of this by resurrecting Jesus after he was put to death. As 1 Corinthians 15:3–8 also shows, Paul was ready to deploy testimony to the reality of Jesus' bodily resurrection whenever there was need; Luke's summary does not however enable us to know how much of that, if any, He did here.

How long had Paul been speaking before he was shouted down? This, too, is something we cannot tell. But we can safely guess that anger had been mounting steadily among the Areopagites since he began, so that his asserting of Jesus' resurrection was for them the last straw. By affirming the unity of the human race he, a visiting Jew, had challenged the elitism and racism that, as we know, were built into the Athenians' standard view of themselves compared with others. By declaring God's sovereignty, he had shown them that the true God cannot be manipulated and that we have no independent standing before him—always an unsettling notion when a person first meets it. By what he said about idols, he had in effect declared that Athenian religiosity, about which he had sounded affirmative at first (v. 22, the word translated "religious" can have a positive meaning), was misguided from start to finish; the gods of the polytheistic system in which the Athenians generally, Epicureans and Stoics included, invested their hopes were no gods at all. By quoting their own poets to them (Epimenides and Aratus, for the record [v. 28]), he had implied that Athenians were blameworthy for not worshipping the one true God. By speaking of final judgment, he had torpedoed the common Greek view of world history as endless cycles of events repeating themselves. By relaying God's call for repentance, he had in effect directed his learned listeners, Athens's brightest and best, to change their whole religion and lifestyle in a radical and upsetting way. And now for him to say of a particular dead man, not that his soul was immortal (which most, if not all, of them believed already), but that as a matter, not of mythology or legend, but of space-time, this-world, real-life fact he had been reanimated and somehow refashioned in the process, so that embodied existence, which to Greeks was a lower form of existence anyway, would never end for him, and to speak of this as something wonderful—well, it was just too much, and they were not going to listen to any more of it! Paul was talking offensive nonsense, and it was high time they shut him up. So they did.

Pluralism Ancient and Modern

What relevance has all this to our present concern? Its relevance lies in the fact that the Athenians were religious pluralists, and Paul was responding to their pluralism. There were, to be sure, many differences between the polytheistic pluralism of Athens, typical as it was of the ancient world, and the monotheistic or, rather, post-monotheistic and post-Christian, immanentist, cognitively skeptical pluralism that breaks surface among today's liberal theologians. But the essential pluralist position, that all responsible religions and cults are on a par with one another, that there is room for them all, and that they are all friends in that none really counters or contradicts either the theology or the promise of any other, was and is the same. Pluralism exists wherever it is thought good, for whatever reason, to sanction and endorse a plurality of rival beliefs and cults, and that is what we see here. Certainly, the theoretical grounds on which the position rests in the two cases are very different: Athenian pluralism, in the manner of polytheistic systems generally, was a superstitious system that rested on the idea of distinct spheres of power for a wide array of gods about whom horrific legends were circulated; today's Western pluralism is a sophisticated ideology that rests on the belief that the human mind, being finite, is fallible at a deeper level than it can know. Prone to misconceptions and misperceptions as we are, and lacking power to discern the fullness of ultimate truth, we must not wonder (so it is said) that different religions, and different experts within those religions, give different accounts of divine and/or transcendent things. We really are like the six blind men in the Hindu parable who touched different parts of the elephant and came back with six different and seemingly irreconcilable stories about it. Humble realism about ourselves, so it is argued, requires a high level of agnosticism about the ultimate, and the way to project the fundamental unity of religions is to practice that form of intellectual self-denial that refuses to treat one's own present understanding as in any way definitive.

The *attraction* of this view is, of course, its openness and friendliness to other faiths. It is always a pleasure to proclaim peace and play host. The *problem* with it is, however, that no consistent form of it ever appears, since all its advocates prove on inspection to be commending, not consistent distrust of all human religious definitives as such but only consistent distrust of all human religious definitives except for the defined viewpoint of the teachers themselves (Blatavsky, Besant, Steiner, Campbell, Radhakrishnan, Hick, Coomaraswamy, Schuon, whoever); and logically it does not appear how it can ever be otherwise, for it is the nature of teachers to project, explicitly or implicitly, what they think they know, and this will come across, willy-nilly, as a positive option for learners to embrace. According to pluralist theory, for instance, the fact that one religion sees God as personal, another does not, and a third is atheistic; or that one religion anticipates a future existence with God in love and joy, another foresees gloom and diminution for all, and a third hopes only for nonexistence—pain ended because one is no longer there to feel it—should be explained somehow (there are different ways of doing this) in terms of the incompetence of human minds to discern and conceptualize ultimate realities. But teachers explaining this will have a personal view on both these matters and will be unable to conceal or refrain from commending it if only by the way they critique other opinions and options; and the very fact that they teach will seem to be saying that their views are likely to be wiser than those of others—certainly, than those of the persons under their instruction. The guru syndrome has historically been noticeably strong among advocates of religious pluralism, just as it has among liberal theologians generally, and the reason is obvious: having moved beyond both biblical and church authority, their only authority is now themselves.

And the *unhappiness* of the pluralist view is precisely that it is so decisively post-Christian and sub-Christian, the fruit of falling back from the apostolic gospel that announces the sufficiency, finality, cosmic dominion, and universal claim of Jesus Christ, our crucified Savior and risen Lord. The humility of mind for which pluralists call is actually unbelief of the Bible and ignorance of the Holy Spirit, who spoke by the prophets, inspired the Scriptures, interprets them to us so that we know the truth about God and Jesus, and through that knowledge sets us in a vital, saving relationship with the Father, the Son, and the Spirit Himself. So, too, the openness to non-Christian religious wisdom for which pluralists plead regularly involves disregard of Bible truth about world religions, and thus is in effect unbelief once more. What, therefore, we must do today in relation to the pluralism we face matches what Paul did, courteously but firmly, in relation to the pluralism he found at Athens: stand against strategies of assimilation, affirm the biblical view of God, man, and Christ in its fullness, and set it, not in syncretistic synthesis with, but in categorical contrast to, all other teachings, so that the insufficiency of non-Christian religions is clearly seen.

Relating to Other Faiths

What view then should we take of non-Christian religions today? And how should we relate to their adherents, with whom in these days of immigration we rub shoulders constantly? First, let us learn to distinguish things that differ in our own backyard, starting with the liberals in the church who find pluralism so attractive. In 1924 the Presbyterian J. Gresham Machen, in his book *Christianity and Liberalism*, argued that there were two distinct religions side by side in the Protestant world. In 1998 the Canadian Anglican George Eves, in his book *Two Religions One Church: Division and Destiny in the Anglican Church of Canada*, argued similarly within an Anglican frame. Clarity and truth forbid us to pretend that here are merely minor variants on a single theme. Five centuries of Western thought have shrunk the God of the Bible by discounting His sovereignty, His holiness, and His use of language to reveal Himself to us; at the same time, they have inflated man by soft-pedaling original sin and seeing us as evolving toward intellectual and managerial omnicompetence in a world that is all ours, and they have robbed the church of vision and vigor by setting out, as we noted earlier, to play catchup to the world. In the churches of the Reformation, great confusion and uncertainty have resulted from all this, and it is no wonder that we now find it hard to think clearly about the crosscurrents of belief and behavior that flow from the presence among us of people of other faiths. The weight of generations of muddle, compromise, uncertainty, and cultivated vagueness lies heavy upon us. Before we can relate Christianity to persons of other faiths, who are often more clearheaded about their religion than we are about ours, we need to sort ourselves out.

Our confusion is often made worse by the wide spectrum of ways in which Protestants use the Bible. Let it be said at once that there is only one right way to interpret "God's Word written," as Anglican Article 20 calls it: that is, first, to practice grammatical-historical, common-sense exegesis on each biblical book, treating it as written not to mystify but to be understood, and second, to let Scripture illuminate Scripture by its own internal links and cross-references. The combination of these two procedures is nowadays called canonical interpretation; Christ centered and life centered, as the entire Bible is, it yields results that in theological substance differ surprisingly little from what Christians found in the Bible from the start. Reformation exegesis and biblical criticism are often said to have transformed Bible study, and in terms of technique that is true, but in terms of content almost the whole story is that precision has been given to what men like Augustine and Chrysostom already knew. The selective impressionism and straining after novelty, which mark so much liberal exegesis and leave ordinary Christians feeling that biblical interpretation is much too difficult for any save experts to attempt, is a modern aberration. Biblical authority means the direction is given, and the limits set, by the Bible properly interpreted, and proper interpretation means canonical interpretation, and there is a heritage of canonical interpretation going right back to the apostolic age, a heritage whose essential correctness has been vindicated by critical examination time and time again. Canonical interpretation, clear and cogent in its fidelity to the whole Bible, yields the doctrines of the ecumenical creeds and Reformation confessions and classic catechisms and latter-day statements of evangelical faith. It dispels confusion and anchors Christian minds in a simple, straightforward grasp of the Christian faith; and thus it orients us for the relationships through which we are now to think our way.

Assuming, then, that we are clear in our minds as to the central realities of the historic biblical faith of which we are both beneficiaries and trustees, what principles (we ask) should guide us as we discuss religion with neighbors and friends of other faiths, and as we consider invitations to involve ourselves in interfaith and multifaith services and joint activities that bring the religions together? Taking my cue directly from Paul's Areopagus address, I suggest that three principles should guide us constantly: recognize what non-Christian faiths have; identify what they lack; and highlight the unique Savior and salvation that Christians have, and that everyone needs. Let me, as I close, develop that.

Recognize what non-Christian faiths have. The Bible view of non-Christian religions (Judaism and modern Islam excluded, as being latter-day special cases) is that they are the product, first, of universal ongoing revelation—*general* revelation, scholars call it—whereby God generates in everyone some inklings of His own reality, of the reality of moral standards, and of retributive judgment to come, and then, second, of the distorting of these awarenesses by inroads of idolatrous superstition (desiring gods man can manipulate and manage is the root of idolatry), and by various self-affirming techniques for getting one's god or gods to meet present and future felt needs. The story differs with each religion, just as the religion itself does: each is distinct. But all religions have in them some awe and respect toward the transcendent powers, personal or impersonal, from whom or through which they hope to receive good, some real morality that commands the conscience, some pattern of prayer and/or meditation, and some heartfelt hopes for the future, and we should surely be interested in exploring all these aspects, looking throughout for streaks and flashes of undistorted God light and trying to discern why and how the religion of our conversation partners came to its present shape. Out of such explorations can come not only understanding but also friendship, and in all informal evangelism, as we know, friendship is a major factor.

Identify what non-Christian faiths lack. A just appreciation of anything takes note of what is missing as well as of what is present, and that is as true in the realm of religion as anywhere. Comparison of the various non-Christian faiths with Christianity shows that the God who addresses us in His Word and who fellowships with us on the basis of promises He has made, who loves redemptively and whose gift of His Son to die on the cross for our sins is the measure and pledge of His love, who adopts and recreates us as His children and heirs, and who holds out to us a hope of supreme unending joy with Him beyond this world, is a God with whom our non-Christian conversation partners are not acquainted. Our thoughts, and when appropriate our words too, should focus on this lack rather than fudge it. General revelation may convey some sense of the Creator's everyday generosity (cf. Acts 14:16–17; Rom 2:4) but gives no knowledge of him as the Redeemer of lost and guilty sinners. It is here that Christianity stands apart from all other world faiths, and in conversation we should keep this difference constantly in view.

Highlight the unique Savior and salvation that Christians have and that everyone needs. When Paul began to do this at Athens, the Areopagus closed ranks against him; to have the established religious pluralism of Athens challenged as this wandering Jew was challenging it was more than they could bear, no matter how respectfully and persuasively Paul phrased what he had to say. Today Christians are often invited to share in interfaith and multifaith activities—books of essays, combined worship services, multifaith meetings to promote united interests—and it becomes a crunch-point question whether to say yes or no. If the organizers want only gestures of unity and rule out anything more, nonparticipation may be the wisest as well as the most honest course. We cannot honor God by pretending to be closer to others in theology and spiritual identity than we really are. But if witness to the divine Christ and salvation in and through Him, which is the constitutive core of Christianity, may be borne, alongside whatever witness to the constitutive core of other religions may also be given, then accepting involvement may be the proper thing to do. The Areopagus story shows that Paul, for one, were he in our shoes, would certainly think so. Every opportunity of highlighting the reality of God's love, the reality of our personal Savior, and the reality of the Christian hope of resurrection and joy should be taken, and if the implication that there is really no place for faiths that are not faith in Jesus Christ gives offence, as it did at Athens, we like Paul must bear it. The key elements of the Christian calling are transcultural and unchanging, and this is one of them. Everyone needs to be confronted with God's call to repent and put faith in the Lord Jesus Christ because of the coming day of judgment; and all forms of pluralism, whether polytheistic, superstitious, and idolatrous as at Athens or postmodern, secular, and ideological as in the modern world, must be challenged and critiqued in the name of Jesus Christ for the sake of God's kingdom and the salvation of souls. Cultures may change, but this is an obligation that remains.

This essay, which it is my pleasure to present to Dr. Montgomery, is a revision of a public address. No attempt has been made to change its spoken-word style.

"Ever Hearing but Never Understanding"

A Response to Mark Hutchins's Critique of John Warwick Montgomery's Historical Apologetics

Craig J. Hazen
Graduate Program in Christian Apologetics
Biola University
La Mirada, California, USA

Nearly 10 years ago I attended a scholarly symposium at a state university in southern California that featured a number of luminaries in the fields of religious studies and philosophy. The capstone paper to the symposium was one that I was really looking forward to because I knew that it would be utterly out of place at such a meeting. I knew in advance that it would be provocative because the presenter was an influential former professor of mine, John Warwick Montgomery. I doubt very much that many of the mainstream religion and philosophy scholars in attendance knew his name or had read any of his works, but the lecture hall was packed—probably due to the stimulating title of the paper: "The Search for Absolutes: A Sherlockian Inquiry."[1] In a very creative presentation, Montgomery made his arguments about discovering religious truth through the voices of Sherlock Holmes and Dr. Watson—as if he were reading a long lost manuscript penned by Sir Arthur Conan Doyle. Of course, as one might imagine, Holmes was working his way through these important questions utilizing the factual and logical approaches for which this character is famous.

As the presentation went forward, however, some in the audience were visibly disturbed. One local religious studies professor sitting right across the aisle from me was a fair-skinned fellow whose ear-lobes I noticed were turning various shades of purple. The lecture was obviously raising his blood pressure, but I was anxious to find out exactly why it was causing him so much difficulty. He didn't let me wonder for long because the moment the formal lecture was finished he jumped to his feet—even before time for questions was officially opened—and blurted out, "Dr. Montgomery, you do tremendous damage to *religion!*"

Now, what exactly had Montgomery done to "damage religion" in this person's mind? Montgomery had subjected religious questions and claims—those about ultimate reality and ultimate human concerns—to methodologies available to all of us. He employed techniques by which we all attempt to examine mundane questions and claims in everyday life. This local religious studies professor had clearly represented the sentiments of a number of people in the room that evening who were also decidedly uncomfortable to hear this approach to their field of study. If the tools and methods of the scientist, the historian, the lawyer, or the sleuth could legitimately be brought to bear on the actual truth claims made by the vast variety of religious groups around the world, the very ethos of an entire discipline would implode. Like matter and antimatter, faith and fact cannot come into real contact without destroying something. Indeed, the reason faith and fact are usually kept in separate, hermetically sealed compartments in the academy is twofold. First, it is postulated that, *à la* Immanuel Kant, facts and faith simply have no point of interaction by definition—to force them to deal with one another is simply a category mistake. Second, and I believe far more important because it is used to justify the irrationality of the first, it is fundamentally *immoral* to allow such interaction because it undermines the sacrosanct agenda of religious pluralism. After all, if the academy were to sanction the idea that facts, evidence, and rationality can play a legitimate role in deciding ultimate religious questions, some beliefs or entire religious traditions would be in serious jeopardy. There was palpable moral outrage in the lecture hall that evening, because Sherlock Holmes was snooping around in areas that were morally off-limits to him according to the rulebook of pluralistic ideology.

If Montgomery attracted the ire of the religious studies establishment on that occasion, it is no wonder the apostle Paul has become such an onerous figure in the recent wave of studies in Christian origins. Paul's overt linking of faith and fact makes Montgomery's look rather tame and nuanced. In what I consider to be one of the most bizarre passages in any of the sacred texts of the great religious traditions (I mean bizarre given the predisposition of religious studies folk against such notions and that the passage is unique in its message), Paul wrote, "If Christ has not been raised, then our preaching is vain, your faith also is vain." And just to make sure his readers in Corinth were not confused on this point, the apostle reiterated it several lines later, writing, "If Christ has not been raised, your faith is worthless" (1 Cor 15:14,17). This bald-faced linking of an entire historical and global religious tradition to a single fact of history would not only unnerve religious pluralists in the mainstream academy, but it would also unfortunately surprise and unnerve most Christian clergy today. For those of us willing to admit that Paul's New Testament writings speak authoritatively for the Christian tradition, we will simply have to come to terms with the fact that Christianity is indeed testable—a religion for which evidence and reason count in a dramatic way. But God does not appear to be the least bit insecure amid the controversy, not hesitating to inspire His apostle to throw down the gauntlet and not only unlock the door but to throw it open and invite investigation of this remarkable event.

* * *

Nearly 40 years ago, John Warwick Montgomery published a small but very influential book entitled simply *History and Christianity*. The book had its origin as a set of lectures delivered at the University of British Columbia in January 1963. Soon thereafter the material was published as a series of four magazine articles and finally in book form. This little volume may have garnered most of its original notoriety because it was quoted so often in the wildly popular books in the 1970s by the ubiquitous Christian apologist from Campus Crusade, Josh McDowell.[2] A great deal of anti-Christian attention has been paid to the popular-level material from McDowell. This makes perfect sense since McDowell's were the publications that lay-Christian apologists were quoting to the skeptics around the country. However, on occasion a more sophisticated skeptic has attempted to refute one of the scholarly sources of McDowell's material, such as the works of Montgomery, which can be a much more difficult proposition.

One such attempt to examine critically Montgomery's work has been floating on the Internet for several years. The title of this piece is "Faith and History: A Critique of John Warwick Montgomery's [sic] Apologetics" by Mark Hutchins.[3] It is not a deep scholarly analysis, but it is illustrative of the kinds of popular criticism traditional historical apologetics has faced in the last half of the twentieth century. Hutchins's essay also provides a good opportunity to look back and reevaluate the basic arguments of Montgomery's influential little book to see if they are still sound and useful after almost 40 years in print and 40 years of critical attention.

Hutchins begins with an outline of Montgomery's case, a case that Hutchins may not know has been rehearsed in one form or another in powerful ways since the time of the Enlightenment and the Deist controversies of the eighteenth century. These are not new arguments and have weathered far more sophisticated critiques than the one Hutchins assembles. Montgomery, a prolific scholar and author of over 40 books and hundreds of articles, has produced several variations of his case for the life, death, resurrection, and divinity of the historical Jesus.[4] Indeed, one can certainly not conclude that one has overturned Montgomery's position until one has dealt with much more than *History and Christianity*. Nevertheless, Hutchins does describe the case provided in this early work with a fair degree of accuracy. In brief, Montgomery argues the following points (my summary, not Hutchins's):

1. Using standard tests derived from "general historiography and literary criticism," the New Testament documents "must be regarded as reliable sources of information" and "contain testimony to the life and claims of Jesus."[5]

2. Upon a careful and objective reading of these trustworthy documents, "a consistent portrait of Jesus emerges": He is a "divine being on whom our personal destiny depends."[6]

3. After logical consideration of the possible interpretations of the New Testament data about His identity,
   "we are brought to affirm Jesus' deity not only as a
   claim, but also as a fact."[7]
4. In addition, "the factual character of the resurrection
   provided the disciples with the final proof of the truth
   of Jesus' claim to deity and it provides the historian
   the only adequate explanation of the conquering
   power of Christianity after the death of its founder."[8]
5. Although the resurrection is certainly a miracle, "the
   only way we can know whether an event can occur
   is to see whether in fact it has occurred." Miracles
   cannot be ruled out because of "an *a priori* causal
   schema."[9]
6. Finally, "the weight of historical probability lies on
   the side of the validity of Jesus' claim to be God incarnate," and "if probability does in fact support these
   claims . . . then we must act in behalf of them." You
   truly have "nothing to lose and everything to gain."[10]

Before getting into the details of Hutchins's responses to Montgomery, I must first point out a general impression that his essay left
with me. I must say that it is hard to take a critique like this seriously
when one of the key critical methodologies is unabashed straw-man-
ism. Hutchins has found that caricatures of Montgomery's arguments
are much easier to knock down than the real thing. Out of scholarly
charity I would have let this slide had it occurred once, but because
it is so pervasive, I felt obliged to point it out. Consider a sampling of
such statements. Montgomery has a "reverent, almost naïve trust in
the idea that history always gives us the truth."[11] (Why then would
Montgomery insist on objective and reasonable standards by which
to make judgments about what is accurate historically?[12]) "Montgomery's desire is to have us read the New Testament as though it is
a collection of instantaneous bulletins, reporting the news of Jesus
as it happened." (Why then would he admit that the earliest original written material about these events derives from A. D. 51–62?[13])
"Montgomery implies . . . that the evangelists were somehow capable

of being present every time such amazing phenomena occurred, and recorded these events with infallible accuracy." (Why then would he again and again take such care to make the much more limited claim that based on objective criteria, these documents should be considered "reliable sources of information?"[14])

Perhaps the strongest piece of evidence that Hutchins was not the least bit interested in Montgomery's actual argument, but rather a much weaker one of Hutchins's own making, is when he equates Montgomery with the following "common circular defense of Christianity." "I believe the Bible, because the Bible is the word of God. How do I know? Because it says so. . . . But why do I believe what it says? Because God wouldn't lie, and it's his word." One cannot let this mistake of Hutchins slide for three reasons: (1) Montgomery does not commit this fallacy, (2) Montgomery recognizes this fallacy when it is committed by others and says at the outset that he will take great pains to avoid this ("We won't naively assume the 'inspiration' or 'infallibility' of the New Testament records and then by circular reasoning attempt to prove what we have previously assumed"[15]), and (3) properly avoiding this particular fallacy is a theme throughout all of Montgomery's apologetic work—the only way to miss it is through gross negligence or intentional disregard on the part of an investigator. Unfortunately, this kind of straw-manism irrevocably taints the rest of Hutchins's essay. One simply cannot trust a "critique" of another's work if the critic has not had the courtesy to get right the arguments that are under review. Hutchins is not alone in this scholarly *modus operandi*. Many of the essays found on Internet sites such as the "Internet Infidels" are rife with such problems. The situation cries out for a peer-review system at sites that contain essays like these so that such fundamental errors are not committed— errors that discredit the whole genre and the sites to which the essays are attached. We don't mind if the writings of Christian scholars are critiqued; that is part of the academic enterprise. But at least critique the arguments we are offering and not a defective, manufactured version. (This, of course, is an admonition to Christians as well not to make similar mistakes in critiquing non-Christian arguments.)

I shall now address a few of the more specific problems that Hutchins finds in Montgomery's *History and Christianity*. Hutchins, like many thoughtful critics of Christianity, properly recognizes if one wants to pull the plug on historical apologetics most quickly, one must defeat the Christian case for the reliability of the New Testament documents. If one can successfully call the documents into question as reliable sources of information, one has stopped most lines of apologetic argumentation dead in their tracks. No reliable testimony, no reliable picture of Jesus. No reliable picture of Jesus, no good reason to believe He was a divine being and resurrected savior of humankind. Hence, although Hutchins deals with other aspects of Montgomery's arguments in *History and Christianity*, in this essay I will focus primarily on responding to Hutchins's critique of Montgomery's defense of the integrity of the New Testament witness to Christ.

Following Montgomery's outline, Hutchins first goes after the reliability of the documents by calling into question the "bibliographical test" that Montgomery applies to them. This standard test measures such things as the time interval between the original writing of a document (the autograph) and the earliest extant manuscript as well as the number of manuscript copies available to modern investigators. In other words, it examines "the textual tradition by which a[n ancient] document reaches us."[16] Based on the objective demonstrations provided by textual scholars such as Sir Fredric G. Kenyon, A. T. Robertson, and F. F. Bruce, Montgomery concludes that "to be skeptical of the resultant text of the New Testament is to allow all of classical antiquity to slip into obscurity, for no documents of the ancient period are as well attested bibliographically as the New Testament."[17] After reviewing this test, Hutchins concludes that Montgomery "comes short of proving anything." Such a statement seems odd in that a more objective demonstration would be difficult to imagine. Based on a scientific examination of the textual tradition, there are far more manuscripts available (indeed, the comparison with other ancient documents is almost unfair), and the time between actual authorship and key extant manuscripts is miniscule compared to other works of antiquity. It is not controversial in the slightest to say, based on this measurement, that the New Testament documents rise to the top of the heap on comparative analysis. Isn't that at least proving something? Yes, and something enormously valuable to scholars who study ancient documents of all kinds, not just religious texts.

Hutchins then writes that Montgomery "tells us that the earliest copies that have been found are closer to the original writings than the copies of classical literature." "This is an interesting point," Hutchins continues, "but it has no direct bearing upon the question of whether the authors wrote, or even intended to write, fact or fiction, or a mixture of both." Hutchins is exactly right on this point. These data do not tell us anything about the intent of the authors. But Hutchins has himself missed the intent of the author (Montgomery) in that Montgomery's argument on bibliographical data has nothing to do with author intent. The bibliographical test is an objective way to measure the relative integrity of the textual tradition. Whether the evangelists got the story right is another question—one that Montgomery takes up in logical order, that is, *after* the documents are found to be at least worthy of being admitted into evidence. Given Montgomery's clear delineation of the logical steps, one wonders if this objection by Hutchins is not simply another species of straw-man-ism.

On a related note, one other issue bothers Hutchins about the dating of the original autographs. He thinks that the time interval between the "supposed" events of Jesus' life and the recording of the events by the various New Testament writers "provides a generous period of time for numerous creative efforts on the part of the new Church leaders." "Consequently," he concludes, "numerous versions of Jesus showed up after a generation or two. A serious study of the New Testament, the 'apocryphal' Gospels, and other extra-biblical writings proves this point." The idea that Jesus legends took hold that early is problematic (and by legend I mean a persistent and inflated picture of Jesus that was carried forward in a strong tradition). As to the time intervals, even Hutchins admits that the documents were written as early as 35 years after the crucifixion, which means there were some still alive who had personal contact with these events while these documents were circulating—a difficult environment in which to incubate legends. However, the interval could actually have been as little as 17 years if Jesus died in AD 33 and Paul wrote his first epistle (1 Thessalonians) in AD 50—a thoroughly plausible date in scholarly circles.[18] Is a 17- to 35-year interval enough time for legendary material to develop? Not according to the evidence we have for the genesis of such material. The perennially quoted scholar of first-century Greco-Roman history, A. N. Sherwin-White, measured such developments and concluded with regard to the NT materials that if they contained legendary accounts they would have had to accumulate at an utterly "unbelievable" rate.[19] In another comparative example of just how short an interval we are talking about with regard to the NT and the events it records, the relatively reliable biographers of Alexander the Great—Plutarch and Arrian—wrote more than 400 years after Alexander's death in 323 BC. But, as historian Robin L. Fox pointed out, most of what we have come to know as legendary did not come about until hundreds of years after the work of Plutarch and Arrian.[20] The one necessary ingredient for the fermentation of legends is time and lots of it. In the case of the various accounts of the life of Jesus, that ingredient is sorely missing.

The existence of apocryphal (perhaps more accurately termed pseudepigraphal) pictures of Jesus that Hutchins believes are examples of legendary development is in reality an example of just the opposite. That is, the existence of such literature is an example of how legendary development is *kept at bay* for years and years just as in the case of Alexander. When books such as the so-called *Gospel of Thomas, Gospel of Peter,* the *Gospel of the Hebrews,* the *Gospel of Truth,* and so on, circulated in the early Church they were examined and *rejected* as inauthentic or nonauthoritative. But why? Because the Church was concerned about making sure they had an authentic picture of Jesus and turned away hundreds of other writings that had no connection to the apostles or to apostolic authority. I am not here trying to make a general case for canonicity but simply pointing out that the early Church was concerned with false accounts about Jesus, had tools for identifying them, and rejected them when they were discovered. Inauthentic Jesus stories certainly existed very early, but they did not develop into legends. They were revealed for what they were at the time and could never gain a foothold because of the diligence of Church leaders in rooting out what Eusebius of Caesarea called "totally absurd" religious lore. The hundreds of rejected "gospels" that litter the first few centuries of the Church are a testimony to the careful authentication practices of the early Christians. They put a premium value on the writings of those who were known to have direct connections with the events.

Hutchins next turns his attention to the "internal test" Montgomery used to help establish the reliability of the NT documents. The internal test simply looks to the documents themselves to see if there is good evidence in the text that the purported author was the actual writer and had a connection to the events described. Montgomery quotes several relevant passages to demonstrate this, but Hutchins objects saying that passages such as "1 John 1:1–4 alludes to a personal acquaintance with the 'word of life.' But the wording here refers more to a mystical relationship with Christ, than a flesh-and-blood encounter." One wonders exactly how Hutchins would know the proper interpretation of this passage given his utter skepticism concerning the text, but that is another issue. As for a refutation, one simply needs to quote the passage. Hutchins quotes only the phrase "word of life," but the passage as a whole shows exactly the kind of internal evidence Montgomery believes is relevant. I shall only quote two of the four verses to demonstrate: "That which was from the beginning, which we have heard, which we have seen with our eyes, which we have looked at and our hands have touched—this we proclaim concerning the Word of life" (1 John 1:1–2 NIV). I know from Hutchins perspective this passage might not be impressive. However, having myself done a doctorate in religious studies and having had an opportunity to study and compare most of the sacred texts of the great religious traditions, I find these kinds of passages in the New Testament utterly compelling. You simply do not find this kind of empirical, verificationist language in the *Bhagavad-Gita*, the *Granth*, the *Tripitaka*, or the *Qur'an*. The writers of the New Testament were obsessed with this kind of language because something astounding had happened right in their midst, in broad daylight for all to see. From this standpoint this kind of language sets the New Testament apart as a unique type of religious literature—spiritually edifying *and empirically testable.*

Another objection is raised by Hutchins to the final test that Montgomery employs—the "external test." Montgomery describes the test in this way: "Do other historical materials confirm or deny the internal testimony provided by the documents?" Montgomery then proceeds to quote archaeologist Sir William Ramsay to establish the accuracy of Luke-Acts, and two prominent early Church Fathers, Papias and Irenaeus, to attest to the fact that the other authors of the Gospels had contact with the events they recorded. Hutchins's only response to this is an offensive comment and a self-refuting point: "to use the early Church Fathers as objective corroboration is like calling upon Joseph Goebbels to give a neutral opinion about his führer . . . use of these ecclesiastics ignores the fact that all of them write from the standpoint of their own presumed convictions about Christ." I shall ignore the offensive comment, but I shall not ignore the fact that Hutchins too writes from the standpoint of his own presumed convictions about Christ. That is why apologists like Montgomery focus on the evidence, so that people might be able to get beyond their own presumed convictions and arrive at conclusions that are clearly more objective. Ironically, the "presumed convictions about Christ" that Papias and Irenaeus may have been carrying had very little to do with their comments. In context, their comments do not display that they were at a critical juncture in a religious argument or in a description of a miraculous event in which an overflowing of their own "faith experience" might have been persuasive. In a rather mundane statement, Papias was simply reporting what he learned from the apostle John himself about who wrote the Gospels, while Irenaeus was reporting what Polycarp knew about the Gospel authorship. And since Polycarp likewise studied at the feet of the aged apostle John, their reports provide astounding external attestation as to the authorship of the Gospels.

At the end of his case against the reliability of the New Testament, Hutchins engages in what I shall call here "kitchen-sink-ism"—that is, after using his entire repertoire, he tosses in the kitchen sink as a last resort. Quoting Michael Grant quoting A. J. P. Taylor (with no source references for either), Hutchins exults in the following factoid: "No man can recall past events without being affected by what has happened in between and . . . there is no reason why the evangelists should be expected to escape this tendency." He then concludes from this that "faith necessarily colored all of their writing." I think this statement tells us much more about Hutchins's views of Christian scholarship than anything about the New Testament writers. Perhaps he thinks a Christian apologist would not agree with such a point? Hence, to clear up any confusion, I want to let him know that I do agree.[21] People's views of history, including the Gospel writers', are colored by faith, environment, facts, and a whole assortment of experiences. This is obvious and hence tells us nothing. The real issue is this: *To what extent are the views colored?* Again, why should we believe any of Hutchins's conclusions about NT reliability and authorship since his views are likewise colored by his own faith and experience? I have little doubt that Hutchins's own faith commitment to the naturalistic worldview dramatically colors his assessment of what *could* have happened in the life of Jesus and the early Church. Is Hutchins therefore incapable of knowing or expressing what actually happened based on the evidence? Certainly not. But what he does say must be in principle open to investigation so that we can know it is something more than his own subjective expression. Throwing blanket condemnations over the statements of early Christians by saying that all of their writing was "necessarily colored" is just the kind of presuppositionalism that Christian scholars like Montgomery have been arguing against.

Obviously I do not think that Mark Hutchins succeeded in undermining Montgomery's case for the historical reliability of the New Testament witness to Christ. Indeed, I don't think on many key points he even understood it. Since by clear and objective testing the documents are shown to be authentic and accurate renditions of the life, work, and person of Jesus, the conclusion that Montgomery reached in *History and Christianity* nearly 40 years ago still stands: "Jesus did rise, and thereby validated his claim to divinity. He was neither charlatan nor lunatic, and his followers were not fablemongers; they were witnesses to the incarnation of God, and Jesus was the God to whom they witnessed."[22]

Endnotes

1 This essay can be found in John Warwick Montgomery, *The Transcendent Holmes* (Ashcroft, British Columbia: Calabash Press, 2000).

2 These books include *Evidence that Demands a Verdict* (San Bernardino, CA: Campus Crusade for Christ, 1972), *More Evidence that Demands a Verdict* (San Bernardino, CA: Campus Crusade for Christ, 1975), and *More Than a Carpenter* (Wheaton, IL: Tyndale House, 1977), of which well over one million copies have been printed.

3 This essay can be found at two Internet sites: "The Non-Believer's Page" at www.dcd.net/NBP/fandh1.html_and on the "Internet Infidels" Web site at www.infidels.org/library/modern/mark_hutchins/faith_and_history.html. In addition, there are links to this essay from a range of humanist Web sites and even from one Muslim site.

4 For a complete list of Montgomery's writings up to 1996, see *Bibliography of Dr. John Warwick Montgomery's Writings* (Edmonton, Alberta: Canadian Institute for Law, Theology and Public Policy, 1996).

5 John Warwick Montgomery, *History and Christianity* (Downers Grove, IL: InterVarsity Press, 1971; reprint, Minneapolis, MN: Bethany House Publishers, 1986), 26, 43.

6 Ibid., 57–58.

7 Ibid., 61.

8 Ibid., 74.

9 Ibid., 75–76.

10 Ibid., 78–79.

11 All quotes from Hutchins are from his internet article "Faith and History." Unfortunately, no pagination is available for this electronic publication.

12 See Montgomery, *History and Christianity*, 25–26.

13 Ibid., 50.

14 See for instance, ibid., 43.

15 Ibid., 25.

16 Ibid., 26.

17 Ibid., 29.

18 For just a few examples from recent scholarship, see Donald Guthrie, *New Testament Introduction*, rev. ed. (Downers Grove, IL: InterVarsity Press, 1990); D. A. Carson, Douglas J. Moo, and Leon Morris, *An Introduction to the New Testament* (Grand Rapids, MI: Zondervan, 1992); and Paul Barnett, *Is the New Testament Reliable? A Look at the Historical Evidence* (Downers Grove, IL: InterVarsity Press, 1986).

19 A. N. Sherwin-White, *Roman Society and Roman Law in the New Testament* (Oxford: Clarendon, 1963), 188–91.

20 Robin L. Fox, *The Search for Alexander* (Boston: Little, 1980).

21 Montgomery himself agreed with this long ago. See his *The Shape of the Past: A Christian Response to Secular Philosophies of History* (Minneapolis, MN: Bethany Fellowship, 1962), 241.

22 Montgomery, *History and Christianity*, 78.

John Warwick Montgomery

GOD'S UNIVERSAL MAN

David Stott Gordon

While others in this book will address Dr. Montgomery's numerous contributions to theology, history, apologetics, and law, I would like to comment on his contribution to the practice of being human.

I first met Dr. Montgomery in 1972 when I enrolled in his class on the Renaissance at Trinity Evangelical Divinity School. I quickly discerned that this class was not merely an analysis of long-past thoughts and events but was an exploration of what we as Christians might and should be in the contemporary world. I learned early that Dr. Montgomery was not merely a teacher about the Renaissance but was also a dedicated practitioner of the Renaissance life. Not only were Luther, Castiglione, Erasmus, and Sidney Montgomery's academic subjects, but they were his compatriots, companions, and comrades in arms. For Montgomery taught us that these  great men had done in the past was by no means to be left in the past but that their ideas could bring about transformation in individual lives and in the life of our civilization.[1]

In reviewing his biography in *Who's Who in the World*, I found that Dr. Montgomery has done numerous things as an academician: he has earned multiple degrees, has written numerous scholarly works, and has held many appointments in a formidable array of academic institutions. But he has also done many other things in his life that take him beyond the narrowly academic. He has written numerous books and articles on a wide range of topics, including church history, theology, the occult, apologetics, jurisprudence, contemporary social issues, fantasy literature, and Sherlock Holmes. He is a gourmet, for many years a member of the *Chaîne des Rôtisseurs* and the prestigious *Académie Internationale des Gourmets et des Traditions Gastronomiques* in Paris.[2] He has debated in public *fora* many of the major thinkers of twentieth-century liberalism. He has climbed Mt. Ararat in search of Noah's ark. He has become a practicing lawyer in the United States and a barrister of note in England. He has tried significant human rights cases before national and international tribunals. He has collected antiquarian books and antique automobiles. He is styled the "Compte de St Germain de Montgommery" in France and "Baron of Kiltartan" in Ireland. Indeed, several of my more pietist friends at Trinity looked askance at Montgomery's various *personae* and wondered aloud if his activities were compatible with sound theology and the godly life. However, all the aspects of Montgomery's life—his interest in law and human rights, his active engagement with contemporary culture in the apologetic endeavor, even his interests in gourmet cookery, antique cars, and Sherlock Holmes—are a working out of his theology.

While I am almost hesitant to use the often-abused phrase "Renaissance man,"[3] Dr. Montgomery has consistently embodied that concept as it was described by Burckhardt in his famous *The Civilization of the Renaissance in Italy*.[4] While the idea (and ideal) of the "universal man" was identified by later historians such as Burckhardt and Kelso[5] as one of the defining characteristics of the Renaissance, it is by no means a construction made long after the fact. Rather, the concept of a man who could fight battles, write poetry, paint and sculpt, sing and play music, and discuss all manner of subjects ancient and modern was an ideal consciously adopted and articulated by numerous writers in the period, of whom Baldasarre Castiglione (1478–1529) is the most well-known.

Castiglione's *Book of the Courtier*[6] is in the form of a series of colloquies between a group of noble men and women at the court of Urbino. The book describes in detail how the men of the Renaissance formulated their conception of the characteristics of the model gentleman. The Renaissance courtier was to be an individual, and an exceptional individual at that. Throughout the entire discussion the emphasis was on personal development, not the development of men to serve as mass-produced cogs in the ponderous and creaking mechanism of society. For the men of the Renaissance, there was never any talk of becoming the perfect team but rather of perfecting the individual. There was no idea of producing equality among men but rather of producing individual excellence.

Hence, the courtier was to be a good warrior and athlete, a musician and painter, and a man of *belles lettres*. He was to press forward for the prize of fame and renown, but he was to do so in a seemingly effortless manner. He was to seek to stand out in all that he undertook. He was to place his strongest efforts into the profession of arms, which was his main occupation, but he was also to engage in many diverse activities. The courtier was not to be as the man who considered himself to be only a fighter, with all other activities being useless frivolities to him. Castiglione's characters considered such a man to be a boor who should have himself "well-greased and stored away in a cupboard" so that he would become no rustier than he already was.[7]

Castiglione's courtier was not portrayed as being a fashionable socialite who did nothing other than pursue amusement and pleasure but rather as a man of purpose who possessed definite priorities in his different activities. The first duty of the courtier was to serve his prince properly. He was to excel in his primary occupation of warfare, be loyal to his master in all his undertakings, and be honest and respectful in his dealings with his lord. The courtier was to consider all his other courtly activities, such as music-making, athletics, and literary pursuits, as serving to adorn his service to his prince.[8]

Castiglione thought it quite appropriate for the courtier to expect and seek recognition for his accomplishments. Often Christians have thought that such a desire for preeminence is of the flesh and therefore to be shunned in all circumstances. However, it was a very common view during the fifteenth and sixteenth centuries that the active seeking of the highest positions was a laudable, and indeed commanded, pursuit for the Christian. Calvin's comments on Matthew 19:30, "And many that are first shall be last, and the last first," are illustrative:

The apostles, though they had scarcely begun the course, were hastening to gain the prize. . . . But Christ exhorts those who have begun well (Gal iii.3,7) to vigorous perseverance, and at the same time gives warning, that it will be of no avail to runners to have begun with alacrity, if they lose courage in the midst of the course. In like manner Paul . . . exhorts believers, by referring to his own example, to forget those things which are behind, and press forward to the remaining portion of their course (Phil iii 13,14). As often, therefore, as we call to mind the heavenly crown, we ought, as it were, to feel the application of fresh spurs, that we may not be more indolent for the future.[9]

Calvin's comments, written in the early part of the sixteenth century, support the view that it was appropriate for the Christian to seek the reward God offers to those who strive for excellence. As Castiglione points out, the successes of the courtier redound to the honor of his prince; as a man or a woman in the service of Christ, the Great Prince, the Christian's deeds of worth are added to Christ's glory in the eyes of all the world. Christians of the period would have acknowledged that they accomplished their works only by the power and presence of their Lord. The origin of their good works and achievements lay in God's grace, as did their creation and redemption, yet God would give his servants the blessing and the reward for what they accomplished.

Clearly, the resemblance between Castiglione's courtier and Dr. Montgomery are more than passing or chance. Both are formed by and exist in a world resting on similar propositions; the underpinnings of Castiglione's Renaissance and Montgomery's world are inherently theological. For Montgomery, his Renaissance pursuits express his theology of creation, incarnation, man as the image of God, redemption, and revelation.

In his lectures on the Renaissance, Montgomery compared and contrasted the medieval, modern, and Renaissance views of the world. The medieval age was theocentric and communal, with everyone having his or her place in society, whereas the modern age is atheistic, rationalistic, and centered on self-interest. The Renaissance encompassed the humanistic and individualistic—man in his innumerable possibilities—while still retaining the most central principle that both man and the world were under God. Montgomery did not and does not believe that the Renaissance worldview inevitably had to lead to modern secularism. In his class he posed the question: what if the elements of medieval society which were sociological (i. e., the life of the individual as being subordinate and determined) were seen as such, and were in fact not necessary in the Christian scheme? It would be possible to have both the revelation and the individual, with God having spoken to men, who were thereby free to be themselves as unique individuals who stand before and serve the God who had become a man himself, and glorify him by the infinite variety of their expressions of his image.

In the Renaissance course Montgomery pointed out that the differences between the medieval, Renaissance, and modern world views could be seen clearly in art. Medieval art depicts human beings as being symbolic of mankind. Renaissance art seeks the essence of the individual, but the individual is not an autonomous being; rather, he is shown as standing before God, his Creator. Medieval art springs directly to universals; in Renaissance art, the universal principles are resident in the particulars. Modern art, having abandoned universals, leaves us only with particulars. In medieval art there is a sense of order in which everything and everyone has its place; in

Renaissance art, everything is not strictly ordered; there is a sense of mystery. There is room for the expression of the individual, but that expression is still within the broader order of the Christian world-view. According to Montgomery, the Renaissance says, "The world is mine"; the Reformation affirms that the God who created the world and gave it to humankind is knowable by individuals in a personal manner.

For Montgomery individual freedom is designed by God for the glory of God. Two concepts Montgomery stressed in the class on the Renaissance were the ideas of man as the *imago Dei* (man as the image of God) and man *coram Deo* (man before God). He has continued to return to these concepts over the years.[10] The first is the basis for his view of the nature of humankind. We are created in the image of God (Gen 1:26–27; 2:7; 5:1–2); from that fact we see that both corporate humanity and each individual person have

great significance. God has made us for himself; even with the fall, the image of the living God still remains and was of such great importance to him that he chose to become one of us in the incarnation and to redeem us through his death. Montgomery aptly quotes Karl Barth's famous statement, "From the moment God himself became man, man is the measure of all things."[11] The individual has worth because of Christ's intervening in human history.[12]

The second, interrelated, concept of *coram Deo* relates to his view of how we should live our lives, given that we bear the *imago Dei* and that we have been redeemed through the death of Christ. In our redemption, we have been restored to right relation with God, and have been freed to carry out our original mandate to subdue the earth.[13]

It is not surprising that Montgomery considers all aspects of culture as being encompassed by the Christian's mandate. All the universe is properly God's, for God is the Creator of all. God has spoken to us in his creation through Christ the living Word and the Scripture as the written Word. Neither the living Word nor the written Word exist in some manner separate from the world of quantum physics or physical geography but are part of the same world; there is not, and cannot be, a division. As Montgomery states: "From the incarnational perspective of the Bible itself, all dualisms of 'spiritual' and 'secular,' however defined, are rejected. The epistemological theme of Scripture is not 'the Word disembodied,' or 'the Word' (like Ivory Soap?) floating 'spiritually,' but 'the Word *made flesh*.'" He then quotes the famous line of the Roman Terence, "*Homo sum, humani nihil a me alienum puto*" (I am a man, and nothing human can be alien to me), as summing up what is perhaps his most fundamental principle of living life.[14] For the redeemed man, climbing mountains, appreciating good food, enjoying imaginative literature, and arguing human rights cases are all part of life in the world God has created and given to us, that we may glorify him.

Montgomery sees as a Renaissance motif the concept of the baptism of this world, a hallowing of common everyday experience. The Renaissance emphasizes the doctrine of creation rather than the doctrine of redemption; if this emphasis is carried to an extreme, creation and the Creator drop out, and naturalism prevails, as was the case in the eighteenth century. However, the Renaissance properly brought back the biblical doctrine that "the heavens declare the glory of God" (Ps 19:1).

For Montgomery the Renaissance is incomplete without the Reformation. The Renaissance and the Reformation are related phenomena, in that both desired to rediscover the basic sources of Western life (*ad fontes*). The Renaissance looked to recover the written sources of classical culture by discovering the writings of the ancient Romans and Greeks; the Reformation looked to recover the written sources

of Christian faith by returning to the written Word of the Bible. The Renaissance focused on the individual and his glory; the "Reformation concerned itself with the individual in the presence of God."[15]

The Reformation continued and completed the Renaissance by going to the bedrock beneath the foundations of the Western world and uncovering the written revelation of God, which underlies all truth and all true civilization. As Montgomery said in the class, "In a sinful world everything that is not revelatory eventually begins to cloy"; without the Revelation of God found in Christ and in the written Word, all the glories of the world discovered by the Renaissance eventually become dimmed and disintegrate to dust.

The Reformation also went beyond the self-centeredness of the Renaissance man to the redeemed nature of the man in whom God dwells. For the secularist an individual seeks self-fulfillment because that is all there is; life ultimately comes to an end, and there is nothing further. The Christian seeks perfection of his individuality because his very individuality and its achievements are an offering to God; the Christian asserts and claims his individuality precisely because he is a child of God, redeemed by Christ, and fashioned to be a unique creation of God.

The very fact that we bear the image of the Eternal One and that our image of him is restored by Christ's redemptive act allows us to focus our lives on the service of our heavenly Prince. Having our

Creator dwell within us frees us to be the individuals he intended us to be: "Only when one has been liberated from self-centeredness is there freedom to serve the needs and protect the rights of others.... Again to use Luther's felicitous expression, the redeemed man becomes a 'Little Christ' to his neighbor."[16]

Bearing the *imago Dei* is not a matter of becoming identical with other Christians and certainly does not require the suppression of individual desires or aspirations. Rather, we become like the one who *is* creativity, the one by whom all things are made.[17] We become like Christ in different ways that reflect the *imago Dei* in myriad variations.

Montgomery has baptized *panache* and made it a Christian virtue. He has brought Castiglione's courtier into the court of the Prince of peace. Who he is as an individual is a unique masterpiece of his Creator. He is the great example of the *homo universalis coram Deo*—the universal man, standing before God.

Endnotes

1   The major sources for this paper are my notes from the 1972 Renaissance class and the paper on Castiglione's *Book of the Courtier* I wrote for it. The class was a major watershed for me; as a result, I went to law school and became an army officer—both very Renaissance activities!

2   Dining with the professor is a transcendental experience rarely matched on the earth.

3   The movie *Renaissance Man*, with Danny DeVito, is a prime example of how this phrase has passed into common parlance.

4   Jacob Burckhardt, *The Civilization of the Renaissance in Italy*, vol. 1, trans. by S. G. C. Middlemore (New York: Harper & Row, 1958). This was one of the required readings in the 1972 Renaissance class.

5   Ruth Kelso, *The Doctrine of the English Gentleman in the Sixteenth Century* (Gloucester, MA: Peter Smith, 1964).

6   Various translations and editions; the most famous and influential being the English translation done by Sir Thomas Hoby and published in 1561.

7   Baldassare Castiglione, *The Book of the Courtier*, trans. and ed. George Bull (Baltimore: Penguin Books, 1967), 61–63, 95–96, 90–92, 66–68, 58.

8   Ibid., 131.

9   John Calvin, *Calvin's Commentaries*, vol. 7, *The Gospels* (Reprint Grand Rapids: Associated Publishers & Authors, 1972), 389.

10 John Warwick Montgomery, *Human Rights and Human Dignity* (Edmonton, Alberta: Canadian Institute for Law, Theology, and Public Policy, 1995), 208–10.

11 Ibid., 215.

12 Cf. John Warwick Montgomery, *Giant in Chains* (Milton Keynes, England: Nelson Word, 1994), 80.

13 Montgomery, *Human Rights*, 210.

14 John Warwick Montgomery, "Biblical Inerrancy: What Is at Stake," in *God's Inerrant Word*, ed. John Warwick Montgomery (Minneapolis: Bethany Fellowship, 1974), 25.

15 John Warwick Montgomery, *The Shape of the Past: An Introduction to Philosophical Historiography* (Ann Arbor: Edwards Brothers, 1962), 50.

16 Montgomery, *Human Rights*, 216.

17 Cf. John Warwick Montgomery, "The Chronicles of Narnia and the Adolescent Reader," in *Myth, Allegory and Gospel*, ed. John Warwick Montgomery (Minneapolis: Bethany Fellowship, 1974), 106.

Evangelicalism and Social Responsibility

Vernon Grounds

We are living in a revolutionary era. Philosophically, technologically, politically, ethically, and religiously, our world is in the throes of change. That well-known line from Marc Connelly's *Green Pastures* grows more and more relevant, "Everything nailed down is coming loose." It is imperative, then, that as evangelicals we engage in some hard thinking about our social responsibility. Are we faithfully obeying God's will as it has been disclosed in God's Word? Are we communicating and implementing a full-orbed Gospel? Is our version of Christianity truncated, perhaps emasculated, and therefore something far less than the dynamic it ought to be? Are we reading the Bible through the dark glasses of tradition, failing to see what it actually teaches and how it actually bears upon every dimension of life? Granted that Scripture is no more a compendium of sociology than it is of science, as evangelicals we affirm that it is, nevertheless, our infallible rule of faith and practice, and practice certainly includes all of our relationships, internationally no less than interpersonally.

We must not forget, either, that critics of evangelicalism—some within our own ranks as well as many outside our churches—find fault with American evangelicalism because of its apathy with respect to this-worldly concerns, its social indifference, and ineffectiveness. More specifically, evangelicalism is criticized, first, for its *conservatism*. Quite invariably, we are told, biblicists not only stand far right of center; they are also stubbornly reactionary, fighting against any change, supporting and sanctifying the *status quo*.

In the second place, evangelicalism is criticized for its *quietism*. We are told that it insists on remaining piously aloof from politics and economics, naively trusting that an inscrutable providence in its own time will remedy oppression and injustice.

Evangelicals, we are therefore told, cannot honestly sing:

> Rise up, O men of God,
> Have done with lesser things;
> Give heart and mind and
>   soul and strength
> To serve the King of Kings.

No, evangelicals, if they are going to be honest, ought to sing:

> Sit down, O men of God;
> His Kingdom He will bring
> Whenever it may please His
>   will.
> You cannot do a thing!

In the third place, evangelicalism is criticized for its *pietism*. Inner purity, we are told, is its major concern; hence evangelicals are grossly egocentric, devoting attention inordinately to the state of their own souls, so busily taking their own spiritual temperatures and maintaining their own status before God that they have little time for the problems of society and little interest in the concrete needs of their neighbors

In the fourth place, evangelicalism is criticized for its *perfectionism*. We are told that it operates unrealistically on the all-or-nothing principle: every situation must be brought into absolute conformity with biblical norms; anything less than precise alignment with the will of God is compromise, a betrayal of the faith. Because of this, the only consistent stance for a biblicist is a sort of extramural monasticism, a refusal to soil his holy hands with the dirty realities of political action. How can he do so and still be loyal to his inflexible standards of righteousness?

In the fifth place, evangelicalism is criticized for its *legalism*. We are told that it equates righteousness with undeviating adherence to a set of taboos: spirituality is gauged by abstinence from bad language, tobacco, playing cards, and perhaps mixed bathing. Evangelicals, we are likewise told, grow indignant when an English teacher assigns a high school class J. D. Salinger's *Catcher in the Rye*; yet they fail to rebuke churchmen who pay inadequate wages, rent rat-infested tenements to poverty-stricken people, and practice *de facto* segregation.

Once more, evangelicalism is criticized for its *nationalism*. We are told that evangelicals are really chauvinistic: they advocate a patriotism which is fiercely parochial, a prejudiced tribalism which declares, "My country may she always be right, but right or wrong my country!" Evangelicals therefore are indiscriminating nationalists who reduce Christianity to a folk religion and thus deny the global genius of the gospel.

Last of all, evangelicalism is criticized for its *pessimism*. It usually teaches, we are told, a rigid system of eschatology; its understanding of God's future program for history eliminates any possibility of ameliorating social evils, any prospect for or hope of cultural renewal. Instead, it necessitates the belief that society must inevitably grow more and more corrupt until it falls under divine judgment. Consequently, all attempts to improve man's life and lot in this world, all long-range attempts to promote justice, are as futile as dropping an aspirin in the Pacific to quiet its turbulence.

We shall not stop here and now to consider the legitimacy of these criticisms; we shall merely remark that some evangelicals at any rate appear to merit such rebuke. Unwittingly they lend substance to the communist indictment of religion as an opiate, a drug that induces hallucinatory dreams, causing its addicts to forget the harsh circumstances around them. Some evangelicals, it cannot be denied, propagate a version of Christianity that turns its back on the world, counsels resignation no matter how unjust the prevailing order of things may be, advocates submission to the edicts of whatever powers control a government, and consoles afflicted people with the assurance of "pie in the sky, by and by."

I.

In approaching the problem of Christian social responsibility, let us mention two polar orientations. Obviously many other positions lie somewhere between these extremes, but for the sake of both brevity and clarity we are going to ignore important distinctions and significant nuances. Suppose we say that on the one end of the spectrum we find a policy of *indirect influence*, while on the other extreme we have a policy of *direct involvement*. The policy of indirect influence argues that the gospel is the good news of a post-temporal salvation: it is a message addressed to the individual in his sinful need, a message designed to bring him by faith unto a right relationship with God, a Message that is therefore only incidentally social in its application and outworking. Years ago this policy was rather classically stated by a Southern Baptist editor, whom Rufus Spain quotes as a representative spokesman for traditional evangelicalism:

> The true church is not to deal directly with communities, States and nations, but with the individual. . . . Our future and eternal interests are as far above our present fleshly interests as the heavens are above the earth. The great question is not how to get ready to live here, but to live hereafter; to go to be with Jesus when we die and to stand acquitted in the day of final judgment.
>
> (Christ favored social reform but) he waited for it as a necessary fruit of the blessed gospel received into men's hearts.
>
> If we follow the teachings and example of Christ and the apostles, instead of the instruction and example of many modern reformers, we will act upon the principle that the regeneration of men by the Holy Spirit through the preaching of the word is the basis and surety of all true reform. It is of little use to make the outside of the platter clean when the inside is corrupt.
>
> "Glory to God in the highest" first, and then "Peace on earth, good-will among men."[1]

Antithetical to this stands the policy of direct involvement, arguing that the gospel is essentially social in its application and outworking, a message unquestionably designed to bring the individual into a right relationship with God, consequently—yes, inevitably—a message just as unquestionably designed to bring the individual into a sustained struggle for right relationships in all other areas and dimensions of life; a message which demands that the love of God be expressed and embodied not alone in family and church and neighborhood but in business and government, in politics and economics, internationally as well as interpersonally. George McLeod, the founder of the Iona Community in Scotland, has affirmed this position powerfully:

I am recovering the claim that Jesus was not crucified in a cathedral between two candles, but out on a cross between two thieves: on the town garbage heap . . . at the kind of place where cynics talk smut, and thieves curse, and soldiers gamble. Because that is where He died. And that is what He died about. And that is where churchmen should be and what churchmanship should be about.[2]

The policy of indirect influence is by no means a puerile position, a feeble pushover. On the contrary, an impressive phalanx of tests can be marshaled in its support. Let us review them hastily. (All Scripture passages in this essay are HCSB.)

1. "My kingdom is not of this world," said Jesus. "If My kingdom were of this world, My servants would fight, so that I wouldn't be handed over to the Jews. As it is, My kingdom does not have its origin here" (John 18:36).
2. Be saved from this corrupt generation! (Acts 2:40).
3. Therefore, brothers, by the mercies of God, I urge you to present your bodies as a living sacrifice, holy and pleasing to God; this is your spiritual worship. Do not be conformed to this age, but be transformed by the renewing of your mind, so that you may discern what is the good, pleasing, and perfect will of God (Rom 12:1–2).
4. Do not be mismatched with unbelievers. For what partnership is there between righteousness and lawlessness? Or what fellowship does light have with darkness? What agreement does Christ have with Belial? Or what does a believer have in common with an unbeliever? And what agreement does God's sanctuary have with idols? For we are the sanctuary of the living God, as God said: I will dwell among them and walk among them, and I will be their God, and they will be My people (2 Cor 6:14–16).
5. [Jesus Christ] gave Himself for our sins to rescue us from this present evil age, according to the will of our God and Father (Gal 1:4).
6. Pure and undefiled religion before our God and Father is this: to look after orphans and widows in their distress and

to keep oneself unstained by the world. . . . Adulteresses!
Do you not know that friendship with the world is hostility
toward God? So whoever wants to be the world's friend becomes God's enemy (Jas 1:27; 4:4).

7. Do not love the world or the things that belong to the world.
If anyone loves the world, love for the Father is not in him. For
everything that belongs to the world—the lust of the flesh,
the lust of the eyes, and the pride in one's lifestyle—is not
from the Father, but is from the world (1 John 2:15–16).

Though these texts obviously require intensive study and careful
interpretation, we shall allow them to stand without comment except
for a few remarks on the concluding passage. The apostle is pointing
out the principles that underlie our entire world-system, that enor-
mous complex which we know as civilization, a fallen structure contrary to the mind and will of God. John mentions the lust of the flesh,
which is sensualism; the lust of the eyes, which is materialism; and the
pride of life, which is egotism. These, he maintains, are the structural
principles that underlie and animate the world-system—sensualism,
materialism, and egotism. Needless to remark, any order of life that
is informed by such principles is necessarily contrary to the mind and
will of God. Thus John's delineation of the world-system helps us to
understand better the antagonism brought out emphatically in the
fourth Gospel. Take, for example, this passage:

> If the world hates you, understand that it hated Me before
> it hated you. If you were of the world, the world would
> love you as its own. However, because you are not of the
> world, but I have chosen you out of it, the world hates you.
> Remember the word I spoke to you: "A slave is not greater
> than his master. If they persecuted Me, they will also per-
> secute you. If they kept My word, they will also keep yours"
> (John 15:18–20).

The Johannine analysis of the world-system helps us, furthermore,
to understand a hymn that grates on the sensibilities of our socially
involved contemporaries:

Are there no foes for me to face?
Must I not stem the flood?
Is this vile world a friend of grace
To help me on to God?

But is the policy of indirect influence the scriptural viewpoint? Admittedly, it seems to be. Does it nevertheless move too exclusively on the surface, appealing uncritically to such texts as have been mentioned? Does it, however, plumb the depths and express the demands of revelation? To answer these questions we must analyze the biblical data.

As Christians, we in no way minimize the inspiration and authority of the Old Testament, although we believe that the New Testament clarifies and consummates the Old Testament disclosure of God's nature, purpose, and will. Before turning to the New Testament, then, we need to remind ourselves of what the Old Testament teaches in this area, and indisputably the Old Testament teaches a social ethic that stands as an abiding challenge to any policy of quietistic withdrawal from the rough-and-tumble of politics. In God's name the Old Testament demands that injustice be fought, righteousness be established in society, and the orphan, the widow, the stranger, the poor, and the oppressed be made the objects of protection and provision. Consider a passage like Amos 5:10–15,20–21:

> They hate the one who convicts the guilty at the city gate
> and despise the one who speaks with integrity. Therefore,
> because you trample on the poor and exact a grain tax from
> him, you will never live in the houses of cut stone you have
> built; you will never drink the wine from the lush vineyards
> you have planted. For I know your crimes are many
> and your sins innumerable. They oppress the righteous,
> take a bribe, and deprive the poor of justice at the gates.
> Therefore, the wise person will keep silent at such a time,
> for the days are evil.
>   Seek good and not evil so that you may live, and the
> Lord, the God of Hosts, will be with you, as you have
> claimed. Hate evil and love good; establish justice in the

gate. Perhaps the LORD, the God of Hosts, will be gracious
to the remnant of Joseph.

. . .

Won't the Day of the LORD be darkness rather than
light, even gloom without any brightness in it? I hate, I
despise your feasts! I can't stand the stench of your solemn
assemblies. There we have the Old Testament stance from
Genesis through Malachi: religion divorced from social justice is a blasphemous mockery; true spirituality manifests
itself in a concern for the needs and rights of people.

Consider also the passage that was one of our Lord's favorite texts,
Hosea 6:6, a text that He evidently quoted again and again: "For I
desired mercy, and not sacrifice; and the knowledge of God more
than burnt offerings" (KJV). Here again we have the Old Testament
insistence that genuine religion issues in concern for social justice.
Indeed, Jehovah does not accept a man's sacrifice unless that man is
doing justice and mercy. What, according to Hosea, is the knowledge
of God? In this text the knowledge of God is equated with mercy, and
mercy is an inexhaustibly rich Hebrew term signifying an attitude of
care and compassion akin to God's own compassion and care.

Hosea's assertion is explained by a passage in Jeremiah 22:16,
where once more reference is made to the knowledge of God: "He
took up the case of the poor and needy, then it went well. Is this not
what it means to know Me? This is the LORD's declaration." So what
is it to know God? To know God is to be like God. To know God is
to render justice and fair judgment. To know God is to share God's
compassion and care for the concrete needs of His people.

Consider also a passage like Isaiah 1:10–18.

Hear the word of the LORD, you rulers of Sodom! Listen
to the instruction of our God, you people of Gomorrah!
"What are all your sacrifices to Me?" asks the LORD. "I have
had enough of burnt offerings and rams and the fat of well-
fed cattle; I have no desire for the blood of bulls, lambs,
or male goats. When you come to appear before Me, who
requires this from you—this trampling of My courts? Stop
bringing useless offerings. Your incense is detestable to

Me. New Moons and Sabbaths, and the calling of solemn assemblies—I cannot stand iniquity with a festival. I hate your New Moons and prescribed festivals. They have become a burden to Me; I am tired of putting up with them. When you lift up your hands in prayer, I will refuse to look at you; even if you offer countless prayers, I will not listen. Your hands are covered with blood.

"Wash yourselves. Cleanse yourselves. Remove your evil deeds from My sight. Stop doing evil. Learn to do what is good. Seek justice. Correct the oppressor. Defend the rights of the fatherless. Plead the widow's cause.

"Come, let us discuss this," says the Lord. "Though your sins are like scarlet, they will be as white as snow; though they are as red as crimson, they will be like wool."

How emphatic this is! God fulminates that He abhors worship carried on by people who tolerate social injustice. Observe Jehovah's explicit directive in verse 17: "Learn to do what is good. Seek justice. Correct the oppressor. Defend the rights of the fatherless. Plead the widow's cause." No doubt the eighteenth verse is susceptible of an evangelistic application; in its context, however, that eighteenth verse is exclusively social: "'Come, let us discuss this,' says the Lord. 'Though your sins are like scarlet, they will be as white as snow; though they are as red as crimson, they will be like wool.'"

Consider, further, a passage like Isaiah 58:1–10; and despite its length, the entire passage must be taken into account.

Cry out loudly, don't hold back! Raise your voice like a trumpet. Tell My people their transgression and the house of Jacob their sins. They seek Me day after day and delight to know My ways, like a nation that does what is right and does not abandon the justice of their God. They ask Me for righteous judgments; they delight in the nearness of God.

"Why have we fasted, but You have not seen? We have denied ourselves, but You haven't noticed!"

Look, you do as you please on the day of your fast, and oppress all your workers. You fast with contention and strife to strike viciously with your fist. You cannot fast as you do today, hoping to make your voice heard on high. Will the fast I choose be like this: A day for a person to deny himself, to bow his head like a reed, and to spread out sackcloth and ashes? Will you call this a fast and a day acceptable to the LORD? Isn't the fast I choose: To break the chains of wickedness, to untie the ropes of the yoke, to set the oppressed free, and to tear off every yoke? Is it not to share your bread with the hungry, to bring the poor and homeless into your house, to clothe the naked when you see him, and not to ignore your own flesh and blood? Then your light will appear like the dawn, and your recovery will come quickly. Your righteousness will go before you, and the LORD's glory will be your rearguard. At that time, when you call, the LORD will answer; when you cry out, He will say: Here I am. If you get rid of the yoke among you, the finger-pointing and malicious speaking, and if you offer yourself to the hungry, and satisfy the afflicted one, then your light will shine in the darkness, and your night will be like noonday.

Whatever our interpretation of this passage prophetically, we cannot evade its thrust ethically. Isaiah depicts a people who relish worship, a people who love theological discussion, debating the will of God abstractly. Such is the burden of verse 2: "They seek Me day after day and delight to know My ways, like a nation that does what is right and does not abandon the justice of their God. They ask Me for righteous judgments; they delight in the nearness of God." But God fiercely rebukes His hypocritical people, a people who imagine that ritualistic worship and theological discussion are acceptable substitutes for social justice! God Himself defines acceptable worship in terms of specific acts of charity and justice:

Isn't the fast I choose: To break the chains of wickedness, to untie the ropes of the yoke, to set the oppressed free, and to tear off every yoke? Is it not to share your bread with the hungry, to bring the poor and homeless into your house, to clothe the naked when you see him, and not to ignore your own flesh and blood? (Isa 58:6–7).

Unquestionably, therefore, the Old Testament insists on social justice. Passionately it affirms that the evidence of a right relationship with God is a right relationship with one's neighbor—and this implies a willingness to struggle for his rights.

Now the New Testament, of course, does not negate the Old Testament; it fulfills and intensifies the disclosures and demands of Hebrew revelation. Though it centers in a spiritual kingdom rather than in a space-and-time theocracy, the New Testament in no way cancels out God's demand for social justice. Instead, it adds a new dynamic and a new dimension to that demand. This will become evident as we examine briefly some of the major strands of truth woven into the fabric of the New Testament.

What, to start with, are the implications of the *theological* motif that runs through the New Testament? What can we deduce from its disclosure of God's own nature and purpose? Building on the Old Testament foundation, the New Testament asserts that God is both holy and loving; it asserts that God, the self-existent Source and Sovereign of all reality, is the triune person of holy love, perfect in holiness and love, creating, sustaining, governing, judging, and reconciling in infinite holiness, which is the obverse of infinite love, and in infinite love, which is the obverse of infinite holiness. As John declares in his first epistle, God is love and God is light. Hence all God does He does in holy love. His nature is holy love; His purpose, accordingly, is a purpose of holy love: His will, moreover, is always a will of holy love. God's will for man, consequently, is a life of holy love, a life that in the totality of its relationships is governed by God's holy love. Paul, for example, compendiously exhorts his readers in 1 Corinthians 10:31, "Therefore, whether you eat or drink, or whatever you do, do everything for God's glory." But the glory of God is precisely the glory of holy love. In short, human existence is to reflect the very nature of God. And plainly the ethical and social implications of holy love baffle adequate exposition.

What next about the *Christological* motif that runs through the New Testament, a motif inextricably knit together with the theological motif? The nature and purpose and will of God are explicated in the whole Christ-event. The sovereign Creator stands self-revealed in the person of our Lord Jesus, who said concerning

Himself, "The one who has seen Me has seen the Father" (John 14:9). Jesus Christ is God become man, God who accordingly is for man, the man who accordingly is for God, the God-man who is entirely the Man-for-others.

Thus, according to Luke's Gospel, the Man-for-others says at the outset of His public ministry: "The Spirit of the Lord is on Me, because He has anointed Me to preach good news to the poor. He has sent Me to proclaim freedom to the captives and recovery of sight to the blind, to set free the oppressed, to proclaim the year of the Lord's favor" (Luke 4:18–19).

Thus according to the tenth chapter of Luke's Gospel, in the unforgettable parade of the Good Samaritan, the Man-for-others teaches that the next-and-nearest-person-in-need whom a disciple meets is his neighbor and has a claim upon loving ministry, even if that ministry must overleap the barrier of racial prejudice and be carried on at the cost of danger and delay, to say nothing of money that will never be repaid.

Thus according to Matthew 5:44–48, the Man-for-others declares:

> But I tell you, love your enemies and pray for those who
> persecute you, so that you may be sons of your Father in
> heaven. For He causes His sun to rise on the evil and the
> good, and sends rain on the righteous and the unrighteous.
> For if you love those who love you, what reward will you
> have? Don't even the tax collectors do the same? And if
> you greet only your brothers, what are you doing out of the
> ordinary? Don't even the Gentiles do the same? Be perfect,
> therefore, as your heavenly Father is perfect.

Thus according to Matthew 22:37–39 the Man-for-others declares further in a masterful simplification of religion and ethics: "Love the Lord your God with all your heart, with all your soul, and with all your mind. This is the greatest and most important commandment. The second is like it: Love your neighbor as yourself."

Thus according to that disturbing vision of judgment in Matthew 25:35–36, the Man-for-others insists that we are to minister to the widow and the poor and the hungry and sick and the imprisoned and the naked, putting love into action. "For I was hungry and you gave Me something to eat; I was thirsty and you gave Me something to drink; I was a stranger and you took Me in; I was naked and you clothed Me; I was sick and you took care of Me; I was in prison and you visited Me." He can insist on this because He personally ministered to people in their need. Nor must we forget that this ministering love, inspired by Christ's example, includes enemies no less than friends. In contemporary terms it includes militant Muslims and homosexuals and convicted felons and gang members.

But supremely, of course, on Calvary the Man-for-others revealed His Father's holy love. As Paul writes in Romans 5:6–10:

> For while we were still helpless, at the appointed moment, Christ died for the ungodly. For rarely will someone die for a just person—though for a good person perhaps someone might even dare to die. But God proves His own love for us in that while we were still sinners, Christ died for us! Much more then, since we have now been declared righteous by His blood, we will be saved through Him from wrath. For if, while we were enemies, we were reconciled to God through the death of His Son, then how much more, having been reconciled, will we be saved by His life!

Thus Calvary is the definitive exegesis of *agape*, that holy love that satisfies its own demands by a self-giving without any limit.

In Jesus Christ, therefore, the New Testament discloses God's character as well as man's obligation and possibility. Hence the New Testament ethic is an imitation of Jesus Christ, an ethic of gratitude and faith and obedience, all grounded in love and issuing in love. It is an ethic that Peter sums up succinctly in Acts 10:38: "[You know] how God anointed Jesus of Nazareth with the Holy Spirit and with power, and how He went about doing good and healing all who were under the tyranny of the Devil, because God was with Him." How simple that is! Simple? Yes—but measurelessly demanding! Indeed, the only dynamic that can enable the Christian do-gooder to meet this demand is the dynamic of a bloody cross and the indwelling Holy Spirit. The imitation of Jesus Christ, Calvary inspired and Spirit enabled, means a life of service and sacrifice, a life of sensitive caring, a life of identification with the oppressed and disinherited and needy, a life of constructive revolution against any political and religious *status quo* that in the name of God is frustrating the will of God.

What, in the third place, about the *anthropological* motif? The New Testament doctrine concerning man is inextricably knit together with the Christological motif. For the God-Man, as we have already noticed, reveals our human obligation and possibility: what you and I ought to be and can be.

Like the Old Testament the New Testament affirms that man, God created, is inescapably God related. Made supernaturally in God's image, man has a supernatural dignity despite his depravity. But in his depravity man must undergo a supernatural recreation in order to bear once again in unblemished splendor the image of his Maker. This is the quintessential truth about human nature.

The New Testament also affirms that man, God created and God relied, is not a disembodied spirit. He is a flesh-and-blood being who needs bread as well as truth, shelter here as well as heaven hereafter, clothes for his body as well as the robe of righteousness for his soul. He is the being bound together with his neighbors in the bundle of life. In short, the New Testament like the Old Testament affirms that man is a social being, a creature-in-community, a person-in-relationship, a being who can find fulfillment only in fellowship, a being who can find fulfillment only as through faith he experiences existence-in-love. So the New Testament affirms that, when by faith man enters into a new orientation to God, he enters into a new orientation with his neighbor, as we read in John's First Epistle:

> Dear friends, let us love one another, because love is from God, and everyone who loves has been born of God and knows God. . . . If anyone says, "I love God," yet hates his brother, he is a liar. For the person who does not love his brother he has seen cannot love the God he has not seen. And we have this command from Him: the one who loves God must also love his brother (1 John 4:7,20–21).

What, in the fourth place, about the *ecclesiological* motif? What about that new society of which Jesus Christ is the Head, that pilot model of human life as it can and eventually will be? According to the

New Testament, the church is the community of faith and love that confesses, embodies, and implements the saviorhood and lordship of God-in-Christ. It is that community that in worship and evangelism and service seeks to share the truth of God's reconciling love in Jesus Christ by the power of the Holy Spirit. It is that community in which each member assumes unlimited liability for all members. It is that community that lives under the law of love. It is that community that takes the apostolic directives with utmost seriousness:

1. Do not owe anyone anything, except to love one another, for the one who loves another has fulfilled the law. The commandments: Do not commit adultery; do not murder; do not steal; do not covet; and whatever other commandment— all are summed up by this: Love your neighbor as yourself. Love does no wrong to a neighbor. Love, therefore, is the fulfillment of the law (Rom 13:8–10).

2. For in Christ Jesus neither circumcision nor uncircumcision accomplishes anything; what matters is faith working through love. For you were called to be free, brothers; only don't use this freedom as an opportunity for the flesh, but serve one another through love (Gal 5:6,13).

3. Therefore, as we have opportunity, we must work for the good of all, especially for those who belong to the household of faith (Gal 6:10).

4. And may the Lord cause you to increase and overflow with love for one another and for everyone, just as we also do for you (1 Thess 3:12).

5. And may the Lord cause you to increase and overflow with love for one another and for everyone, just as we also do for you (1 Thess 5:14–15).

6. Indeed, if you keep the royal law prescribed in Scripture, Love your neighbor as yourself, you are doing well. But if you show favoritism, you commit sin and are convicted by the law as transgressors. For whoever keeps the entire law, yet fails in one point, is guilty of breaking it all. For He who said, Do not commit adultery, also said, Do not murder. So if you do not commit adultery, but you do murder, you are a lawbreaker.

Speak and act as those who will be judged by the law of freedom. For judgment is without mercy to the one who hasn't
shown mercy. Mercy triumphs over judgment. What good is
it, my brothers, if someone says he has faith but does not have
works? Can his faith save him? If a brother or sister is without
clothes and lacks daily food and one of you says to them, "Go
in peace, keep warm, and eat well," but you don't give them
what the body needs, what good is it? (Jas 2:8–16).

The church, then, is that community which prayerfully struggles
to translate Paul's eulogy of love in 1 Corinthians 13 from poetry into
practice. It is that community which prayerfully struggles to function
as light and salt and yeast in the midst of society, bringing individuals
into the life and likeness of holy love. It is that community, as the old
Anabaptist definition has it, of those who not only believe truly but
who live and love aright.

What, in the fifth place, about the *sociological* motif, the consequences of Christian faith as they are worked out in the whole orbit
of a believer's relationship? For man, as the New Testament sees him,
is being-in-the-world, the conscious nexus of a bewildering network
of relationships, a being inextricably enmeshed in the processes of
nature, the movements of history, and the structures of culture—all
those aspects of existence that are the proper province of sociology.
According to the New Testament, then, on becoming a believer a
man is not abstracted from the world with its organizations and its
obligations. Rather, he is realigned to the world.

For example, the New Testament has much to say regarding human government, a worldly structure indeed. Our Lord Himself lays
down an all-inclusive principle in Matthew 22:21: "Therefore, give
back to Caesar the things that are Caesar's, and to God the things
that are God's." This imperative imposes upon us the necessity of a
God-centered relationship to human government, and this relationship includes a fivefold obligation.

We owe the state the duty of honor (Rom 13:7; 1 Pet 3:17). And
honor means the recognition of the divine source of any state, glimps-
ing behind its faltering justice and misused authority the impeccable
justice and equitable authority of God (cf. Ps 82:6).

We owe the state the duty of prayer (1 Tim 2:1–2). And prayer means the faithful ministry of intercession for all officials because providentially and perhaps unconsciously they are subserving God's redemptive purposes (Isa 45:5).

We owe the state the duty of support (Mark 12:13–17; Rom 13:6). And support means quite simply the payment of taxes that are legally demanded even if the state funds are not disbursed in ways of which a Christian can heartily approve. Better to have order than anarchy, and taxes are the cost of order, the price of a stable framework of life.

We owe the state the duty of service (Titus 3:1). And service means the glad performance of every ministry that a Christian can conscientiously render.

We owe the state the duty of obedience (Rom 13:1–7; Titus 3:1; 1 Pet 2:13–16). And obedience means a hearty compliance with the laws that have been duly enacted. Notice the threefold motive assigned for the performance of this duty: (a) for wrath's sake; (b) for conscience's sake; (c) for the Lord's sake. But notice also the limits of civil obedience. It is by no means unqualified. What if the state does not fulfill its function? What if, instead of being a minister of God, it becomes unmistakably a tool of the devil? What if, as John pictures a tyrannical government in Revelation 13–15, it degenerates into a monstrous beast, energized by demonic powers? What if it punishes good and rewards evil? What if it enslaves conscience? Suppose it idolatrously puts itself in the place of God. And the apostolic picture of idolatrous totalitarianism is relevant in our century when Nazism and Communism, to say nothing of nationalism, have demanded unqualified allegiance. What then? Obedience must stop whenever the edicts of the state conflict with the supreme duty of rendering to God the things that are God's. Our final allegiance is to our Creator: every secular loyalty must be subordinate to that (Exod 20:3: Dan 3:8–28; Acts 4:19; 5:29). But precisely how shall a Christian register his disapproval of constituted authority? By passive disobedience (1 Pet 2:19), by acts of nonviolence, or by even bloody revolution?

However these problems may be resolved, a Christian is obviously very much enmeshed in the structures of his society. He can no more escape participation in politics than he can divest himself of his own epidermis.

II.

Having cursorily examined the biblical data, let us revert to our original question. What guidance does the Word of God, especially the New Testament, offer us in fashioning and following a social ethic? Does it furnish us with perspectives and directives as we relate ourselves to the world? Does it supply guidelines and goals for saints in society? Does it sanction direct involvement no less than indirect influence?

Suppose we flatly lay down some evangelical affirmations, recognizing that they are open to criticism and possible amendment.

I. We can and must affirm that the Church's primary task is that of personal evangelism. Whatever methodology we employ—perhaps, for example, the technique of a mass crusade—our task is that of bringing individuals one by one into a redemptive encounter with Jesus Christ. We can and must affirm that personal evangelism and social concern are two sides of the same coin. This is not a case of either-or; it is rather a case of both-and. We can and must affirm that social concern and personal evangelism are not a dichotomy; they are a both-and duality blanketed as our Lord's word in Luke 11:42: "But woe to you Pharisees! You give a tenth of mint, rue, and every kind of herb, and you bypass justice and love for God. These things you should have done without neglecting the others."

II. We can and must affirm that the Church has the responsibility of nurturing and judging the ethos of our political and economic life. Its responsibility is that of improving the moral climate of society, elevating standards and sensitizing consciences. In his own turgid style Paul Ramsey expresses this forcibly:

> Radical steps need to be taken in ecumenical ethics if
> ever we are to correct the pretense that we are makers
> of political policy and get on with our proper task of
> nourishing, judging, and repairing the moral and political
> *ethos* of our time.

To pay attention to the distinctive and basic features of Christian social ethics would as a consequence lead to much greater reticence in reaching particular conclusions. It would make for a proper hesitation in faulting the consciences of our fellow Christians, or in instructing them too narrowly, by pronouncements issued by official and semiofficial conferences of churchmen on policy questions concerning which there may be legitimate differences in practical, prudential judgment. To eschew the latter would also focus our attention upon the former, more fundamental work of clarifying the church's address to the world.[3]

To say the same thing metaphorically, the church is to be a thermostat instead of a thermometer. It is not simply to register the ethical temperature of its environing society; it is to keep that temperature from falling. Let us confess, however, that through much of its history the church has been more like a thermometer than a thermostat. Concluding his study of Southern Baptists, Rufus Spain writes (and the same thing would incontestably be true of any denomination):

> Southern Baptists defended the status quo. Their attitudes toward political, social, economic, and other problems of Southern society coincided with the prevailing attitudes of Southerners in general. The degree of influence which Baptists exerted on society cannot be measured, but whatever influence they had was overwhelmingly in support of existing conditions. Is this to suggest that society molded Baptists? Or that Baptists molded society? It would be a serious indictment indeed to hold Baptists responsible for fashioning Southern society as it was in the late nineteenth century. Granted that morals and mores are relative to time and place, by any standard—either in comparison with the best thinking of that day or of a later day—the society of the South between 1865 and 1900 hardly conformed either to high ethical standards or to Christian principles. The conclusion then must be that Baptists conformed to the society in which they lived. Their significance in Southern life consisted not in their power to mold their

environment to conform to their standards. Rather their importance as a social force was in supporting and per-petuating the standards prevailing in society at large. Only on matters involving personal conduct or narrow religious principles did Baptists diverge noticeably from prevailing Southern views. This study, therefore, verifies the sociolo-gists' contention that institutionalized religions respond more amenably to social pressures than to their "heavenly visions." Christ said of His disciples, "These are in the world . . . but not of the world." But in their attitudes to-ward social conditions in the South, Baptists insisted on being both *in* and *of* the world.[4]

III. We can and must affirm that the church, a supernatural fel-lowship living under the law of holy love, is divinely obligated to maximize love by maximizing justice. In so affirming, we recognize the limits of individual concern and private charity. That is why we can and must insist on the necessity of Christian political action. Agitation and legislation, we can and must unhesitatingly argue, are sometimes imperative. Certainly we must seek to increase the num-ber of regenerate citizens. Certainly we must seek to instruct and inspire these regenerate citizens. But let us be honest in our appraisal of the impact that regenerate citizens have made and are likely to make on society. Let us face frankly four factors which render politi-cal action imperative.

First, regenerate people are often sadly slothful, selfish, and spine-less. They can be slaves of the *status quo*, bound by chains of pride and prejudice. We know this because, while we testify personally to the experience of regeneration, we are doubtless appalled by our own limited sanctification and by the microscopic impact that we have been making on our *milieu*.

Second, bad political and economic structures can prevent regen-erate people from doing the good that they otherwise might do.

Third, conversely, good political and economic structures can pre-vent unregenerate—and sometimes regenerate—people from doing the evil they otherwise might do.

For still another thing, some problems today in our technological, urbanized, more and more depersonalized society are so complicated, so far-reaching, so deep-rooted, so massive that they baffle the resources of individual action and private charity. They require governmental intervention on a mammoth scale: and this means the use of legislative and administrative apparatus. We must confess that frightening evils, persistent needs, and emergency situations make it impossible for persons to control their own destinies and even provide the essentials of life. Evangelicals today must therefore be directly involved in politics. Why not? John Calvin and Abraham Kuyper, to cite only two examples, saw no incompatibility between proclamation and legislation. Will anyone argue that the good Samaritan would have abandoned his role of loving neighbor if he had decided to agitate for an augmented police force on the Jericho Road, or to advocate the installation of electric lights, or to run against the corrupt officials at city hall who were pocketing the taxes that should have been allotted to pay for more policemen and a better lighting system? Direct involvement in politics does not mean that one is abandoning the role of the Good Samaritan; it may mean that he is fulfilling that role.

IV. We can and must affirm that political action as a legitimate expression of Christian love is a self-justifying expression of redemptive love. It is not merely a circuitous method of proselytizing, a technique for obtaining some sort of commitment, an activity that Christians must discontinue if it fails to produce decisions. At the risk of misunderstanding, we can and must affirm that social action as an expression of redemptive love is an autonomous activity that does not demand any end beyond itself.

V. We can and must declare that the church *qua* church ought not enter the political arena. Its function is that of instructing and inspiring its members either individually or unitedly to undertake whatever political activity neighbor-love may demand. We can keep on asserting that nobody and no organization is authorized to speak for the church *qua* church. To borrow the words of Paul Ramsey,

> Let the church be the church and let the magistrate be the magistrate. Let both keep their distances. May there be less

confusion of these roles. Let the President advance policies without playing priest-king to the people in exercising his ruling under God's overruling. Let the churches advise the magistrates under their care in less specific terms, while always renewing in them the perspectives—*all* the perspectives—upon the political order that Christianity affords. And let us pray more for those in authority (not the churches as such) who must shape the future by what they decree, and who in doing so must step creatively into an uncertain future beyond the range of any light that has been or can ever be thrown upon their pathway.[5]

But at the same time we can and must affirm that the Christian pastor is free to express his own considered understanding of social issues as they are illuminated, endorsed, or judged by biblical norms. After all, the pastor is God's prophet and in that role has the responsibility of speaking *against* his people as well as *to* them. In a *Saturday Review* article on "New and Future Clergy," Theodore C. Sorensen reminds us of this all-too-often obscured responsibility.

> I have no credentials or desire to argue church structure. But I question whether the minister of any church is simply a hired hand, wholly the creature of his superiors or parishioners, wholly bound to accept their dictates and doctrines on matters unrelated to dogma, wholly unable to act in accordance with his own conscience and sense of justice.
>
> To be sure, he should not purport to speak for them. He should not deliberately pressure or embarrass them. But surely there is a 2,000-year-old precedent for a preacher's going beyond good words to good deeds, and then going beyond those good deeds to a direct challenge of both religious and secular authorities, and then going beyond even that direct challenge to enduring imprisonment and violence in order to alter man's ways.
>
> Most men of the cloth, one critic has recently charged, are not competent to deal with such issues. But who among us *is* competent to solve the problems of Vietnam or Watts. The

stakes are too great to leave war to the generals, or civil rights to the professionals, or poverty to the social workers. And why should moral battles to right old wrongs in scriptural fashion be left to the laymen of the church? Clergymen, like all the rest of us, must learn by doing, by involving themselves in the practical problems of men. The Civil Rights Bill of 1961, according to Senator Russell of Georgia, passed because "those damned preachers had got the idea it was a moral issue." Indeed they had—and indeed it was.[6]

VI. We can and must affirm that great caution be employed in order to present the identification of some transient issue with the eternal will of God. Paul Ramsey, to cite him once more, offers just such counsel in his critique of the 1966 Geneva Conference:

> It is not the church's business to recommend but only to clarify the grounds upon which the statesman must put forth his own particular decree. Christian political ethics cannot say what should or must be done but only what may be done. It can only try to make sure that false doctrine does not unnecessarily trammel policy choices or preclude decisions that might better shape and govern events.
>
> In politics the church is only a *theoretician*. The religious communities as such should be concerned with *perspectives* upon politics, with political doctrine, with the direction and structures of the common life, not with specific directives. They should seek to clarify and keep wide open the legitimate options for choice, and thus nurture the moral and political ethos of the nation. Their task is not the determination of policy. Their special orientation upon politics is, in a sense, an exceedingly limited one; yet an exceedingly important one.[7]

VII. We can and must affirm that the concrete application of love calls for competence and know-how as well as disinterested goodwill. In other words, disinterested goodwill, even if it ultimately springs from Calvary, is no substitute for competence and know-how, *expertise* if one prefers that term. More than love is demanded, unless by love we mean, as C. F. Andrews defined it, an accurate estimate and supply of someone else's need. As evangelicals we can borrow approvingly a page from the Pastoral Constitution on the Church adopted by the Second Vatican Council.

> Laymen should . . . know that it is generally the function
> of their well-formed Christian conscience to see that the
> divine law is inscribed in the life of the earthly city. . . . Let
> the layman not imagine that his pastors are always such
> experts, that to every problem which arises, however com-
> plicated, they can readily give him a concrete solution, *or
> even that such is their mission.*[8]

VIII. We can and must affirm that every Christian has his own vocation and so needs to determine before God what responsibilities and tasks the lordship of his Savior lays upon himself as an obedient disciple. We can and must emphasize the principles set down in the fourteenth chapter of Romans. Vocationally some Christians may be called to political agitation and action; others may be called to a ministry in which politics will figure only incidentally. Hence we can and must guard against judging our brethren. Instead, we can and must urge them to engage heartily in their God-assigned vocations even if their vocations involve not only evangelistic crusades and spiritual retreats but also protest marches and pacifist rallies. We can and we must encourage a conscientious diversity of opinion and operation among evangelicals. We can and we must urge Christians to heed the balanced warning that Jack Boozer and William A. Beardslee give in their book *Faith to Act*:

> Every citizen is under obligation to involve himself in some
> way in the effort to achieve justice for all citizens. But every
> citizen is also under obligation to respect another person
> in a decision for a course of action different from his own.
> It is very easy for one to condemn the persons who demon-
> strate at voting places, restaurants, hotels, swimming pools,
> just as it is easy for one to condemn a conscientious objec-
> tor. The fact that one does not himself feel called to that
> particular position is no warrant to condemn those who

do so act. The Christian, then, will not only act, but he will be extremely careful about how he speaks of those who act differently. Differences in judgment, in comprehension of an issue, and in courage, are seldom sharp enough to justify the too easy remark that another who acts differently is a Communist, a subversive, or one engaging in un-American activities. Indeed, it is un-American to presume one's guilt before he is proved innocent. Thus, while we are called to be vigilant as to the security of our nation, we are also called to exercise a healthy and flexible reserve in dealing with those with whom we do not agree.[9]

We can and we must affirm that it is worse than un-American to condemn a fellow believer who follows a course of political action different from our own: it is un-Christian.

IX. We can and must affirm that the New Testament warns against Utopianism, any romantic illusions about sweeping and permanent reforms. We can and must remind Christian activists that human beings are infested with sinful self-interest, which means that all social structures will be more or less corrupt until the end of history. Hence we can and must counsel Christians to attack specific evils, devoting their energies to specific causes and programs rather than grandiose schemes for the transformation of culture once for all. We can and must assert that a tolerable balance of conflicting egoisms is the best man will ever achieve in a fallen world.

X. We can and must affirm that, though blessed with divine revelation, we do not have all the answers, perhaps even many of the answers, to the problems of society. But we can and must refuse to be intimidated into irresponsible passivity by our undeniable ignorance. We can and must urge that evangelicals study, discuss, reflect, think, pray, and act. Yes, we can and must urge that all of us act in keeping with the insight and knowledge we now possess. We can and we must urge that all of us pursue the policy of direct intervention as well as the policy of indirect influence.

In conclusion, then, let us listen to an antagonist of Christianity, Bertrand Russell, who in his *Autobiography* speaks movingly about the master-motives in his career:

Three passions, simple but overwhelmingly strong,
have governed my life: the longing for love, the search
for knowledge, and unbearable pity for the suffering of
mankind. These passions, like great winds, have blown me
hither and thither, in a wayward course, over a deep ocean
of anguish, reaching to the very verge of despair.

Love and knowledge, so far as they were possible, led upward toward the heavens. But always pity brought me back
to earth. Echoes of cries of pain reverberate in my heart.
Children in famine, victims tortured by oppressors, help-
less old people a hated burden to their sons, and the whole
world of loneliness, poverty, and pain make a mockery of
what human life should be. I long to alleviate the evil, but I
cannot, and I too suffer.[10]

God forbid that the children of darkness put to shame the children of life!

Endnotes

1   Rufus B. Spain, *At Ease in Zion: A Social History of Southern Baptists* (Nash-
    ville, TN: Vanderbilt University Press, 1967), 209.

2   George F. MacLeod, *Only One Way Left* (Glasgow, Scotland: The Iona Com-
    munity, 1956), 38.

3   Paul Ramsey, *Who Speaks for the Church?* (Nashville, TN, and New York:
    Abingdon Press, 1967), 23.

4   Spain, *At Ease in Zion*, 213–14.

5   Ramsey, *Who Speaks for the Church?*, 157.

6   Theodore C. Sorensen, "New and Future Clergy," *Saturday Review* (April 30,
    1966), 24.

7   Ramsey, *Who Speaks for the Church?*, 152.

8   Quoted ibid., 131.

9   Jack Stewart Boozer and William A. Beardslee, *Faith to Act: An Essay on the
    Meaning of Christian Existence* (Nashville, TN: Abingdon Press, 1967), 213.

10 Bertrand Russell, *Autobiography, 1872–1914* (Boston: Little, Brown, n.d.),
    3–4.

Trashing Evangelical Christians

THE LEGACY OF JAMES BARR'S FUNDAMENTALISM

Irving Hexham

Introduction

Beginning in the 1960s, John Warwick Montgomery established a presence as one of the leading Evangelical Christian apologists of modern times. His clear thinking and careful rational discussions enabled him to devastate the arguments of opponents while presenting a reasonable alternative to modern scepticism based on logical analysis and empirical evidence. Avoiding academic fads, from Christian discussions of worldview analysis to secular postmodernism, he promoted traditional Christian orthodoxy through a mastery of argument and evidence. Today, however, the historic orthodoxy of Evangelical Christianity is increasingly dismissed without any discussion of the facts or available evidence. Instead, homonym slurs are used that avoid careful thought by labelling orthodox Christians as fundamentalist fanatics. This chapter examines the roots of such labelling and the academic text used to promote it.

An example of the type of labelling of Evangelical Christians that avoids serious discussion yet presents a serious challenge to Christian orthodoxy can be seen in remarks made by Dr. Antje Vollmer, who at the time was the vice president of the German Parliament and a leading member of the Green Party in Germany. Recently she spoke out about what she identified as the dangers of Evangelical Christianity. In Ms. Vollmer's mind Evangelical Christians embrace "aggressive mission programs" that promote fundamentalist views similar to those of radical Islam. Therefore, both Evangelical Christians and radical Muslims are equally dangerous to a well-organized civil society like modern Germany (*Idea Spektrum*, 20, 2004:14–15). Similar views to those of Ms. Vollmer were expressed in April 2000 by the Rev. Stephen Parsons following the reports of "cult suicides" in Uganda. He is reported to have said, "The press has termed

Kanungu a cult. I would rather term Kanungu the tragic outcome of a combination of extreme American fundamentalist beliefs with African poverty and despair" (*Church of England Newspaper Online*, April 7, 2000).

Such a comment shows a profound ignorance of Islam, African religions, American fundamentalism, and Evangelical Christianity. The African side of this discussion and the true significance of the Uganda murders are dealt with elsewhere (Hexham 2000). Here I want to examine the background to the attitudes expressed by people like Ms. Voller and the Rev. Parson when they attack Christian fundamentalism and Evangelical Christianity. To do this I will examine James Barr's work *Fundamentalism* (1977, second edition 1981).

Although over 30 years old, James Barr's book *Fundamentalism* remains a key text in shaping both public and academic attitudes to both Christian fundamentalism and Evangelical Christianity. Anyone who doubts this and the continuing influence of Barr's views on fundamentalism and Evangelical Christianity has only to check the bibliography of standard reference works in various countries. For example, dictionaries of religions or theology such as *Die Religion in Geschichte und Gegenwart, Evangelisches Kirchenlexikon*, or encyclopedias such as *The Canadian Encyclopedia* and similar sources, particularly those published outside the United States America, all cite Barr. Further, anyone who checks the footnotes of more recent writings on these subjects soon discovers that most of the authors either rely directly on Barr's formulations or use them second-hand by relying on books that developed Barr's views. Thus while there is no mention of Barr in Steve Brouwer, Paul Gifford, and Susan D. Rose's *Exporting the American Gospel* (1996), his work plays a prominent role in Gifford's *The Religious Right in Southern Africa* (1988).

Probably because of Barr's high status as Professor of Hebrew at Oxford University, Barr's work carried an authority that less scholarly works lacked (cf. Conway and Siegelman 1984; Haiven 1984). Further, it continues to play an important role in setting the tone of subsequent literature on the subject worldwide (e.g., Engel, Kamphausen, and Linz 1993; Schnabel 1998).

Consequently, a discussion of Barr's book is relevant today, even though it was published so long ago, because it has prejudiced many readers throughout the world against various individuals and groups, including Evangelical Christians, by labelling them "fundamentalist." Therefore, this chapter examines the arguments Barr presents in *Fundamentalism* (1981) pointing out that for all of its scholarly trappings his work is just as propagandistic and lacking in scholarly merit as similar popular works that fail to receive the respect accorded to Barr's book. Most of the arguments presented here also apply to later scholarly works on the topic that continue Barr's savage attack on Christians who maintain traditional orthodox beliefs.

This chapter will focus on seven issues that illustrate this point: (1) Barr's understanding of fundamentalism; (2) the problem of biblical interpretation; (3) the importance of metonym; (4) Christian conversion and the appeal of metonymic thought; (5) interpretation and common sense; (6) Barr's attack on K. A. Kitchen; and (7) the slur of political reaction; and conclusion.

1. Barr's "Fundamentalism"

Throughout his book Barr stresses that it was written "with the goal of understanding" fundamentalism (Barr 1981:8) and that his book was "not written for the sake of controversy with fundamentalists" or to encourage them to "change their minds." Rather he repeatedly says that his aim is to "understand fundamentalism as a religious and intellectual structure" and "attempt a theological analysis" (Barr 1981:9). This claim linked with his insistence that "most Christians" reject fundamentalism is extraordinary and shows that Barr lacks the sensitivity of Ernst Troeltsch, who clearly recognized, and had the honesty to admit in 1906, that the majority of laymen embrace fundamentalist types of religion (Troeltsch 1991:112).

The more sophisticated Christians, whom Barr believes represent "most Christians," are in fact a small minority of university professors and highly educated clergy (Finke and Stark 1992:237–75; Kelly 1986:1–35). Therefore, Barr's initial claim is misleading. If he really wanted to "understand" the people he calls fundamentalists, he ought to admit that they make up the majority of practicing Church members and accept their self-definition as "conservative Evangelicals," not impose what he admits is a pejorative term on them. This is normal scholarly practice. But, as we will see, Barr is not interested in understanding. He seeks to destroy a movement he cannot tolerate. Thus, Barr begins *Fundamentalism* (1981) by explaining:

Fundamentalism . . . is a group of characteristics which most Christians do not approve of or like. . . . The most pronounced characteristics are the following:

a. a strong emphasis on the inerrancy of the Bible, the absence from it of any sort of error;
b. a strong hostility to modern theology and to the methods, results and implications of modern critical study of the Bible;
c. an assurance that those who do not share their religious viewpoint are not really 'true Christians' at all. (Barr 1981:1)

Barr explains that because "fundamentalism is a bad word: the people to whom it is applied do not like to be so called. It is often felt to be a hostile and opprobrious term, suggesting narrowness, bigotry, obscurantism and sectarianism" (Barr 1981:2). Most British fundamentalists prefer to be called "Conservative Evangelicals." But he offers a variety of reasons for rejecting this and similar alternative descriptions because he believes that the "suggestions of narrowness," etc., are "true and just" (Barr 1981:3).

Consequently, Barr says, "As a practical course of procedure within this book, I shall continue to use the term 'fundamentalism' for a certain basic personal religious and existential attitude" (Barr 1981:5). He also notes that many Eastern Orthodox and Roman Catholic Christians share these characteristics but argues that they are not really "fundamentalists" in the sense that he is using the word (Barr 1981:7–8). For Barr, fundamentalism proper is an attitude found "*within Protestantism*" (Barr 1981:7) associated with groups like the InterVarsity Christian Fellowship (Barr 1981:21).

Barr observes, "The core of fundamentalism resides not in the Bible but in a particular kind of religion. Fundamentalists indeed suppose that this kind of religion is theirs because it follows as a necessary consequence from the acceptance of biblical authority. But here we have to disagree and say that the reverse is true" (Barr 1981:11). Thus, it is a particular type of "religious experience," which Barr argues originated during the eighteenth century Evangelical revivals, that created the tradition he labels "fundamentalism" (Barr 1981:11).

He outlines the core doctrines that he describes as fundamentalist, which include an emphasis on conversion (Barr 1981:17) and the acceptance of various beliefs that turn out to be fairly traditional Christian beliefs, including such as the physical resurrection of Christ (Barr 1981:12–33) and the practice of personal prayer. "The centrality of prayer," he argues, "is such that it creates 'the whole milieu' in which fundamentalists live, including their attitude to the Bible." "Even the Bible," he writes, "is not read rightly or understood rightly except with prayer; seen in all its infallibility, it is only when it is read prayerfully and with the presence of the Holy Spirit that it acts upon the heart" (Barr 1981:31–33).

The problem with this extended discussion of Evangelical and fundamentalist religion is that, despite all his attempts to argue otherwise, it is not significantly different from any other form of traditional Christianity, be it Anglicanism, Roman Catholicism, or Eastern Orthodoxy, all of which contain core movements that emphasize conversion, traditional doctrines, and prayer.

2. The Problem of Biblical Interpretation

Barr argues that fundamentalist Christians espouse a form of biblical interpretation that allows them to flip-flop between literal and other forms of interpretation at will without embracing an overarching scientific principle that provides them with a coherent approach to hermeneutics. He writes: "It is thus certainly wrong to say . . . that for fundamentalists the literal is the only sense of truth. . . . Literality, though it might well be deserving of criticism, would at least be a somewhat consistent interpretative principle." (Barr 1981:49).

According to Barr, fundamentalist attempts to interpret the Bible are to be rejected not because fundamentalists take the Bible literally but because they lack a guiding "principle of interpretation" (Barr 1981:49). Instead of interpreting the Bible in a consistent manner, Barr argues, fundamentalists rely on the naïve belief that "veracity as correspondence with empirical actuality has precedence over veracity as significance" (Barr 1981:49).

What Barr fails to recognize here is that he has actually identified the key interpretative device used by fundamentalist Christians. This device is the use of metonym. Although he does not use the term, J. I. Packer makes this clear in his introductory essay on "Revelation and Inspiration" in the *New Bible Commentary Revised*, which is the focus of much of Barr's criticism. Here Packer clearly states that "it is by the use of the faculty of faith that we discern God's Word for what it is. Faith sees the real nature of that at which it looks. This has been the church's experience down the ages. Since it is the Spirit who implants faith and works in believers their acts of faith, the presence of this conviction is termed the Spirit's witness" (Guthrie and Motyer 1979:17).

In other words, for fundamentalists and most ordinary people the experience of the Christian in relation to the Bible is the determining factor in understanding the meaning of Scripture. Thus, C. E. Graham Swift, whom Barr explicitly criticizes, appeals to the experience of his readers with evil when he comments on the cleansing of the temple to justify his view that there were two cleansings. Swift writes, "There is nothing improbable about this; indeed it is likely that evil would revive after a first cleansing" (Guthrie and Motyer 1979:875). This argument is rooted in the tradition of metonymic interpretation that is a respectable hermeneutical device.

Unfortunately, few people are aware of, let alone trained in, classical rhetoric. Therefore, the significance of statements like this, which abound in both the *New Bible Commentary* and *New Bible Commentary Revised*, is often overlooked and certainly not seen as a legitimate and time-honoured mode of interpretation. Nor is it recognized that in rejecting this type of interpretation Barr and like-minded theologians privilege metaphor over metonym in a manner that ignores the importance of the preceding acts of symbolisation upon which both metaphor and metonym are based. Consequently, the issue is not, as Barr claims, one of consistency of approach. Rather it is of preferring one rhetorical technique to another. To understand the significance of this, we need to look more closely at the theory of metonym and its role in conservative interpretations of the Bible.

3. The Importance of Metonym

The following argument, which was originally developed by Karla Poewe, helps explain the logic of fundamentalist biblical interpretation and its basis in metonymic thought (Poewe 1994:28–29; 234–58; and 1989). She begins by noting that according to the late Edmond Leach in *Culture & Communication: The Logic by Which Symbols Are Connected* (1976:15), humans posses a deep structure or symbolising ability that is somewhat analogous to grammar in speech. This human ability to symbolise consists of using (1) symbol relationships, which are arbitrary but habitual or conventional, and (2) sign relationships, which are contiguous but in a relationship of a part to a whole, as well as (3) signal relationships, which are causal. In other words, to symbolise, the human being relies on his inborn ability to recognise and work with things we call metaphor and metonymy, not, as many modern scholars have it, by metaphor and related genres alone.

To understand the significance of this observation it is important to define what we mean by these important terms. Metaphor exists when A stands for B by arbitrary association. The association can be habitual, conventional, private, or one of planned resemblance as in an icon. Metonymy on the other hand includes the use of something that Leach calls a sign, natural index, or signal. In the first, A stands for B as part for a whole; in the second, A indicates B; in the third, A triggers B so that the relationship between A and B is mechanical and automatic. Metonym is a figure of speech (a way of saying something), which allows one to interpret an event or a happening as a sign that the whole of which this event is a part also caused it.

This understanding of metonym is based on the theory of rhetoric which argues that rhetoric is most effective when it imitates life or nature, or when figures *"demonstrate* feeling" and are "signs of a state of mind in the speaker" (Vickers 1989:304, 303). As Cicero purportedly said: "For nature has assigned to every emotion a particular look and tone of voice and bearing of its own" (quoted in Vickers 1989:66).

For example, when charismatic Christians are prayed over and fall down, which is referred to as "resting in the spirit," this event is interpreted as a sign that the Holy Spirit who caused their falling is working in their spirit and life. This small event is therefore *a part of* and *caused by* a much larger whole, namely God's presence. The causal aspect, which is important to what we call metonymic pattern of thought, is usually ignored, yet it provides the framework for understanding the unity of conservative Evangelical interpretations of the Bible, which assume that behind the written Word stands the living God (Poewe 1989).

Once this fact is recognized, it becomes clear that Barr is wrong when he dismisses fundamentalist modes of interpretation as lacking coherence. The coherence is there; Barr failed to see it. For the fundamentalist the metonymic structure of Christian experience is such that events in the Bible both mirror and trigger events in daily life. Therefore, when fundamentalists read the Bible, they expect the stories they read to reflect the essential structure of their own experience.

Poewe observed, based on fieldwork and numerous interviews with Christians, that most people do not carefully distinguish between sign, index, and signal. This means that in practice A stands for and indicates B, while B is seen to cause A. Such a generalised use of metonym we believe lies behind fundamentalist movements and is not necessarily bad. Indeed, it can be freeing and highly creative. On the other hand, emphasising literary theories can lead researchers into academic gamesmanship and a retreat from empirical evidence.

By embracing metonym rather than metaphor as their primary mode of interpretation fundamentalist Christians show a preference for experiential and restorative religion that strongly emphasizes the use of metonymic patterns of thought. Actually this is something that Barr implicitly acknowledges (Barr 1981:52). But instead of admitting that fundamentalists are using metonym as their prime mode of interpretation and that this is indeed a legitimate approach to the Bible, he attempts to discredit metonymic thinking by identifying it with the doctrine of biblical inerrancy to make it appear dogmatic and arbitrary (Barr 1981:52).

The question Barr never answers is why anyone adopts a belief in inerrancy in the first place. All that Barr does is assert that it is there and speculates that this belief explains fundamentalist attitudes to Scripture, including their theological statements about the inspiration and inerrancy of the Bible itself (Barr 1981:75). But this argument is circular and actually explains nothing.

On the other hand, recognising that metonymic modes of interpretation arise out of the conversion experience of Christians enables the observer to appreciate why fundamentalists interpret the Bible in the way they do and why they embrace doctrines like the inspiration and inerrancy of Scripture. Fundamentalist attitudes toward the Bible are a result of the conversion experiences that are triggered by reading the Bible itself. These experiences are essentially metonymic and predispose the Christian to read the Bible, consciously or more likely unconsciously, through the lens of metonymic interpretations. Thus, the adoption of metonym as the prime mode of interpretation is a natural event in the life of converts because it arises out of their conversion experiences.

4. Christian Conversion and the Appeal of Metonymic Thought

To understand dynamic between conversion and metonymic thought, it is useful to look at the work of Johann Georg Hamann (1730–1788). Hamann was an eighteenth century Lutheran Pietist, empiricist, and philosopher, compatriot and adversary of Kant. His work is widely recognised as a turning point for eighteenth century philosophy (Metzke 1967; Berlin 1997). Hamann's reflections are very useful because they can help us understand why many people today do not regard reading the Bible in a way that takes it at face value to be illusory. Instead, such people see uncomplicated Bible reading as the anchor or foundation of their knowledge.

According to Metzke (1967), the key to Hamann's thought is a specific happening or proleptic experience. Hamann himself called it *Bekehrung* or conversion and argued that it gave a permanent direction to his life and view. This happening is the source of the peculiar constitution of Hamann's understanding of Being and the world. While some people see Hamann as having deliberately set himself against the Enlightenment for the sake of argument (Unger 1968), Metzke insists that Hamann's outlook is the result of a positive disclosure. His outlook on life, the constitution of his thought, has its source in a specific *Bekehrung* experience. His intentions cannot be understood as having their source in the thought world of his immediate environment. They have their source, emphasizes Metzke (1967:3), in the totality of his own new experience.

The atheistic intellectus of the late twentieth century is rooted in the antisystem thinking and the radical relativism of postmodernism (Richardson 1967). This thinking takes place largely within the categories of being, body, life, and metonym. The source of Hamann's intellectus (Metzke 1967:3) and of fundamentalist Christians who take the Bible fairly literally is a radical breakthrough to a new experience, perception, and conception of *reality* triggered by the Bible itself. This trigger action, which is metonymic in structure, explains the often unconscious adoption of metonym as the prime mode of interpretation by fundamentalists.

Hamann argues that the very specific happening of a conversion is central to human existence, gives it meaning, and, most important for his thought, provides the key to our perceptions of reality (Metzke 1967:6). According to Hamann, and here we are loosely translating and paraphrasing Metzke's explication (1967:6–7), a *Bekehrung* is not just any happening. It is not a random happening that does not affect the substance of the person's life. Rather, it is a crisis-driven shattering through which a human being becomes another from what he was. The change is radical. It changes not only the meaning, belief, or dealings of a person, but his or her very being. It is becoming a new person. It does not, of course, change the material nature of the person. Instead, it is a turning of one's whole life history and way of life (Poewe 1994: 243–44).

For our purposes Hamann is important because he witnesses to the fact that conversion is a proleptic experience which centres one's thought and life. It is not an experience that frees one of the problem of good and evil, nor does it produce instantaneous holiness. In the fundamentalist understanding of religion, the major Christian act is that of baring the self in order to restore the individual's relationship with God and to make it the central axis of his or her existence. Thus, conversion is the *Urerfahrung*, the original, most basic, or grounding experience that informs the life and thought of the individual thereafter. It is a proleptic or assumption-changing experience. Fundamentalist Christians are quite aware that it centres their existence, gives them meaning, and, importantly, provides the key to their perceptions of reality, to their ontology. If there is a danger here, it is the unwillingness of people to endure this baring. Consequently, some Christians, as well as observing scholars, prefer to ignore conversion experiences both in practice and in print.

Augustine's *Confessions* remind us that intellectualism has very little to do with the process of a person's conversion experience. But having achieved that state of being, and after the climax of conversion, the intellect, now inspired by a right source, or simply by a new source, works in full boldness among human beings to manage the affairs of life. Indeed, the whole of *Confessions* is a carefully structured anagogical testimony the skeleton of which is based on the effective use of metonyms. There is, first, the *premonitory curing* of Alypius signifying that God worked through Augustine (Blaiklock 1983:137) and foreshadowing Augustine's own healing and healing of others. Such premonitory healings are usually the first event that starts believers on a new path. In numerous interviews with converts to Christianity we were told again and again that some form of healing led them to take the Bible seriously.

Second, there is the phenomenon of the *smiting word*. Again in *Confessions* it happens first to Alypius (with Augustine the instrument) and later to Augustine himself (Blaiklock 1983:137). Alypius is cured of his love of the racecourse after listening to one of Augustine's lectures in which the latter used the racecourse as a convenient illustration. Alypius, however, was convinced that what Augustine said was said on Alypius's account alone.

While "smiting words" have very much to do with coincidence—with that point in a person's development where they are ready to hear precisely that which is being said—the occurrence of this event when the person least expects it is crucial. "The word," in other words, is all the more powerful now because God chooses the time and place. "It is God's appointment" with the individual. Above all, it is God's initiative and this distinguishes it from magic.

Third, Augustine places events, encounters, and appointments so that they reveal God's plan for the individual. Thus Alypius's encounter with the market police (Blaiklock 1983:139) who mistook him for a thief is described as being part of God's plan for Alypius. It gave Alypius a knowledge he could not afford to be without. The later meeting between Ambrose and Augustine, "divine coincidences" or "divine appointments," fits the same pattern. Thus, the testimonial structure of Augustine's *Confessions* makes important use of metonym as a rhetorical device.

Fourth, we see in a subtle form in Augustine's *Confessions* the explicit transformation of *failure* into God's *closing some doors in order to open others*: the failure of his mother to find him an appropriate bride (Blaiklock 1983:146), with the failure of the commune (Blaiklock 1983:147), with the break-up of his common-law marriage (Blaiklock 1983:148), and so on. The importance of a counterbalancing *victory* is also present in Augustine's work. He was converted and became a Catholic bishop—for this, and this alone, the door was open.

Fifth, Augustine assigns equal significance to listening to other people's testimonies especially prior to their own conversion and/or crossing of other ritual milestones. Augustine records several in *Confessions* starting with the story of Victorinus's conversion (Blaiklock 1983:186–94). These testimonies are full of metonymic signs so that listeners become sensitive to detecting them in their own lives.

Sixth, at the height of the conversion drama, between the point of "snapping" and the "light of confidence," emotions come thick and fast. Despite the great intensity of emotion, however, three intellectual heralding events stand out: (1) the crystallization of reality into two opposing forces (at the point of conversion); (2) the sharp mental concentration at the sound of a voice (at the point of "divine intervention"); (3) the instant recognition that the "smiting words" state his new being (at the point of climax). The divine intervention is described by Augustine when he wrote of the Bible that "I seized it, opened it and immediately read in silence the paragraph on which my eyes first fell. . . . I did not want to read on. There was no need. Instantly at the end of this sentence, as if a light of confidence had been poured into my heart, all the darkness of my doubt fled away" (Blaiklock 1983:204).

It is this type of conversion experience based on a metonymic reality that provides the impetus for fundamentalists consciously or unconsciously to make metonym their prime mode of interpretation when approaching the Bible. They do this not because, as Barr suggests, of some rationalistic impulse (Barr 1981:53) but because such a method of understanding the Bible echoes their own life experience.

5. Interpretation and Common Sense

When Barr attempts to illustrate what he sees as the folly of fundamentalist approaches to Scripture, he takes as a major example the "harmonizing of biblical passages which appear to refer to the same realities but to say something different about them" (Barr 1981:56). This practice, Barr claims, "is the most thoroughly laughable of all devices of interpretation" (Barr 1981:57) and is, therefore, unhistorical. Barr writes:

> The most striking example (of harmonization) is the famous incident of the cleansing of the Temple by Jesus. In the synoptic gospels this is narrated at the very end of the ministry of Jesus, at the beginning of passion week (Matt 21:10–17; Mark 11:15–19; Luke 19:45–48), while John has it right at the beginning of the ministry (John 2:13–17). The New Bible Commentary Revised (on Mark, C. E. Graham Swift, p. 875b) gives us the simple but ludicrous harmonization: "By far the most satisfactory solution is that Jesus cleansed the Temple twice" (Barr 1981:56).

Instead of explaining why this is "ludicrous," Barr distracts his readers from observing the metonymic structure of Swift's approach by asking, "Why should the ascension of Jesus to heaven not have taken place twice?" (Barr 1981:56). He then launches into a lengthy discussion of apparent discrepancies in the ascension accounts between the narrative in Luke's Gospel and that of Acts (Barr 1981:56–57). After stating that some conservative commentators have suggested that Jesus ascended into heaven twice, Barr notes that in the New Bible Commentary Revised, I. H. Marshall "achieves harmonization by taking the Acts account literally . . . and holding that the Luke account is telescoped" (Barr 1981:57). For Barr, this proves the inconsistency of conservative commentators because

> what never enters the head of the conservative interpreter is that there was no certain knowledge of the temporal sequence, or that quite contradictory accounts existed, or that some source represented the events in such and such a way not because that was the way it happened but because that was important for the theological message of a particular source (Barr 1981:57).

Barr's arguments and caustic comments come so thick and fast that they seem to make perfect sense. Consequently, the reader is easily convinced that conservative commentators, like Marshall, are unscholarly individuals unworthy of serious consideration. When one sits back and reflects on Barr's work, however, the rhetorical nature of his argument becomes clear. Rather than deal with real issues, Barr sets up men of straw, which allows him to prejudice his readers against other scholars whom he labels "fundamentalist." From his scornful comments one would never guess that Professor I. H. Marshall held the New Testament chair at the University of Aberdeen that is at least as prestigious as Barr's own chair in Oxford.

Actually, Marshall's conclusion that Luke telescoped his account of the resurrection and ascension does not involve the arbitrary and unsystematic interpretation adopted to preserve a preconceived theological stance that Barr suggests. Like most commentators, including many otherwise radical critics, Marshall accepts that the author of Luke's Gospel was also the author of the Acts of the Apostles. Therefore, for him it makes prefect sense that when winding down a long narrative that the author intends to continue in a second volume, he telescopes some events at the end of the first volume that are more fully explained at the beginning of the second. This is what authors do.

Harmonization, far from being an unhistorical attempt to explain discrepancies, is precisely what most traditional historians do every time they discover conflicting accounts in the archival record (Gottschalk 1963:132). Of course, one has to be alert for bias, forgery, and the intent of the writer, etc. Nevertheless, unless there is strong evidence to the contrary, minor discrepancies do not cause historians to reject the essential historicity of manuscript evidence. With regard to the cleansing of the temple, W. F. Albright and C. S. Mann point out, "We have no external evidence as to whether the event recorded happened once, twice, or even three times, and at present the whole matter is beyond our investigation" (Albright 1971:257). Even so they think that the similarities in the Greek indicate one event rather than two. On the other hand Alfred Edersheim argued that the differences in detail are so great that there must have been two events (Edersheim 1915), a viewpoint shared by R. V. G. Tasker (1960:60–63). The problem here is not the dogmatism of conservative scholars but Barr's own narrow theological focus that forces him to assert that his interpretation is true while other possibilities are false.

This is why many well-educated people, including professional historians, who have not been socialized into the tortured hermeneutics of modern critical biblical scholarship, accept most biblical accounts at face value just as they accept other historical biographies. It is also why laymen see the "problems" encountered by biblical scholars as nonproblems. It seems to us that many biblical critics read the gospels as a particular genre of religious literature in such a way that creates problems where they do not exist for the average reader who approaches the Gospels like any other book.

The issue of harmonization and possible parallel accounts is a case in point. Anyone who has read several biographies of someone like Adolf Hitler knows that parallel events are the norm not the exception. Every major event in Hitler's career—be it the Munich Beer Hall Putch, the Night of the Long Knives, Crystal Night, or the Wannsee Conference—has at least one parallel. When read in detailed biographies, these events are clearly differentiated. But when reduced to the bare facts in more general history books, they are either omitted or appear remarkably similar.

Such discrepancies do not trouble the average reader because they know that authors have to make choices and therefore exclude some events while including others. When the layman or even professional historians, who are used to this way of reading history, turn to the Gospels they naturally assume that the discrepancies which trouble professional theologians are similar to those they find in other books. Therefore, the act of harmonization makes perfect sense especially to someone using a metonymic framework of interpretation that sees biblical events in terms of the experiences of everyday life.

Further, normal experience for most people contains numerous seemingly inexplicable coincidences and apparently parallel events that, if written in biographical form several hundred years in the future, would seem fictitious. For example as a child Karla Poewe escaped death several times crossing the fragmented borders of Europe where she was a refugee, or "displaced person" as they were called at the time. Years later she had similar experiences as an anthropologist in Zambia. Such events easily blur and could be seen by future investigators as confused versions of the same event. Similarly, as a small child, during World War II, Irving Hexham played with the daughter of a Chinese medical doctor from the Caribbean in the remote Cumbrian town of Whitehaven. At the end of the war, the girl and her family returned to the Caribbean and Irving's family moved to Yorkshire and later to Manchester. Years later the same girl studied at the University of Manchester where she and Irving became friends without knowing that they had met almost 20 years earlier. Only when his aunts, who still lived in Whitehaven, recognized the girl's name did they discover the almost unbelievable fact that they had met as very young children and that her father had in fact worked in Whitehaven during World War II.

Such real-life coincidences are not different from stories found in the Gospels and other parts of the Bible that biblical scholars routinely dismiss as literary inventions or duplicate accounts of the same event. Yet because people experience such events in real life, it is not hard to see why many people have no difficulty in accepting such stories as unique events when they read them in the Bible. Taking the text of the Bible at face value is not as foolish or simplistic as Barr and many other scholars like to argue.

6. Barr's Attack on K. A. Kitchen

The nature of Barr's book as a propaganda tract is further exemplified by his attacks on K. A. Kitchen, who he admits is a scholar of "distinction in Egyptology" (Barr 1981:221). Writing about Ken Kitchen's *Ancient Orient and Old Testament* (1966), Barr claims, "There is perhaps not a single book among the conservative Evangelical works read in the research for this study . . . that so fully breathes the spirit of total fundamentalism as does Kitchen's work" (Barr 1981:131). Once again, instead of addressing specific arguments, Barr sets up a series of straw men without giving any indication that Kitchen is a well-respected archaeologist and leading Egyptologist.

First, Barr begins by mocking Kitchen's statement that in his book "no appeal whatsoever has been made to any theological starting point" (Kitchen 1966:172) with the comment, "But the personal sense of intellectual contempt held by the writer towards critical scholars shines through everything that he writes" (Barr 1981:131). This prejudicial statement diverts attention from Kitchen's appeal to factual evidence in a totally inaccurate manner. It is Barr who calls his opponents names, not Kitchen, who is respectful toward people with whom he strongly disagrees. For example, Barr repeatedly refers to Kitchen as "polemicist" (cf. Barr 1981:145 and 221), while Kitchen makes factual claims, which are open to refutation, devoid of personal animosity, such as "Old Testament scholarship has made only superficial use of Ancient Near Eastern date" (Kitchen 1966:24). Barr, however, makes no attempt to refute Kitchen's evidence, preferring instead to attack Kitchen personally by labelling him a fundamentalist who he implies uses violence to beat his opponents (Barr 1981:143, 147, 221).

The only extended discussion of Kitchen's work in Barr's book comes on pages 145–49, which begins with the statement, "Polemicists like Kitchen and Harrison represent the scholars who worked out the critical analysis of the Pentateuch, or similarly of other parts of the Old Testament, as entirely controlled by a framework of philosophical presuppositions. . . . Merely to hear this about Wellhausen or other such critics is sufficient to persuade the conservative reader that such people are not worth reading. . . . Now according to this criticism, the customary critical analysis of the Pentateuch was built upon an intellectual foundation that was (a) evolutionistic and (b) Hegelian" (Barr 1981:145–46).

Barr then argues that this viewpoint is completely wrong because "no good evidence for Wellhausen's Hegelianism has ever been produced.... Conservative students say that Wellhausen was a Hegelian without looking at his writings at all: they simply find the accusation in Kitchen" (Barr 1981:148). But, as Barr shows, Wellhausen was not a Hegelian, therefore it seems that he has demonstrated that Kitchen is fundamentally wrong in one of his major assumptions.

The astonishing thing about this diatribe is that nowhere in his book does Kitchen argue that Wellhausen was a Hegelian as Barr claims. All that Kitchen actually says is that during the nineteenth century "the role of *theory* is predominant" and, in a well-documented footnote, that one can see "the influence of such developmental philosophy upon Welhausen" (Kitchen 1966:18). In other words Barr prejudices his readers against Kitchen's work by misinforming them about the tone of Kitchen's book and the nature of his arguments. This is pure propaganda, not scholarship.

7. The Slur of Political Reaction

Another example of Barr's abuse of evidence to prejudice his readers against conservative Evangelical religion is his comment that "many observers have noted that fundamentalism, which takes a very conservative position in matters of religion, is commonly accompanied by very conservative social and political opinions" (Barr 1981:108). Although he modifies this statement by cautioning that fundamentalism is "not monolithic," Barr specifically claims, "This does not alter the fact that the overwhelming preponderance of opinion among fundamentalists falls on the political right and often on the extreme right. This is most obvious in the United States" (Barr 1981:109). As a matter of fact this is *not* obvious at all. George Gallup and numerous other sociologists have shown conservative Evangelicals in the United States are a very diverse group politically and certainly not biased toward the extreme right. Even after the triumph of George Bush, the relationship between Evangelicals and the political right is not as clear as most journalists think, with about one-third of Evangelicals voting Democrat (cf. Gallup 1989:219–50; Berlet 2003).

The fact is that, while many Evangelical and Fundamentalist Christians support the "Religious Right," a large number, by some estimates around 50 percent overall and often more on specific

"Religious Right" issues, do not support these positions politically. Therefore, the sweeping generalization Barr and others make about the right wing agenda of Evangelical and Fundamentalist Christians is not supported by survey and other evidence gathered by political scientists (Wilcox 1996; *Election Focus*, 6 June 2004; *The Economist*, 11 November 2004). Equally significant is the realization that while American Christians tend to support right-wing political causes, such an alignment is missing in places like Britain and Canada (Bibby 2004:66; Northcott 2004)

Specifically, Barr objects to Sir Fred Catherwood's suggestion that "the ineffectiveness of German church resistance against Hitler" was promoted by "doubts about the authority of faith (which the German higher-critical movement had certainly encouraged)," commenting that "illusions of these dimensions are past the possibility of confuting" (Barr 1981:117). Once again Catherwood's argument is not as absurd as Barr makes it sound. The acid test of German religion came during the Nazi era when liberal and radical theologians flocked to the Nazi banner by joining movements like the pro-Nazi *Deutsche Christen* and neo-pagan *Deutsche Glaubensbewegung* (Poewe 2005). Anyone who reads the literature of the time or journals like *Deutscher Glaube* soon encounters references to the pioneering work of Wellhausen and von Harnack in freeing Christians from the clutches of Hebrew religion and biblical literalness. Conservative Christians, on the other hand, avoided such movements like the plague because they denied the essential teachings of Scripture.

To admit this is not to say that the conservatives fared well during the Nazi tyranny. Instead of vigorously resisting the Nazis, most people whom Barr would identify as fundamentalists remained relatively silent. Andrea Strübind points out the tragic failures of Christians in her excellent *Die unfreie Freikirche* (1991) and John Conway (1968) has shown that, with few exceptions, Christians generally did not resist the Nazis very strongly at all. But the failure of ordinary pastors to display heroics should not lead us to draw the mistaken conclusion that theology played no part in the reaction of individuals to Nazi ideology. Fundamentalist Christians were already a small and often despised minority within German society. Therefore, to protest too strongly would have simply meant deportation to concentration camps, which would have served no real purpose. Nevertheless, they did avoid the pro-Nazi stance of most of their contemporaries.

Apart from mentioning the US and Germany, Barr can't resist tarring Evangelicals with the apartheid brush when he states,

> this sort of relation between evangelical religion and politics is not unique to America . . . the situation in South Africa is perhaps in some ways parallel, although there are also many differences, since the traditional and dogmatic Calvinist tradition of South Africa has important dissimilarities from Anglo-Saxon evangelicalism (Barr 1981:110).

It is easy to condemn conservatives for not speaking out strongly enough against apartheid. But the fact remains that it was the liberal, even radical, Afrikaans theologians, not traditional Evangelical or dogmatic Calvinist Afrikaners, who most strongly supported, and even created, apartheid. Thus General Hertzog, who created the National Party, was an agnostic whose spiritual hero was the ultraliberal anti-Christian mystic Count Keyserling (van den Heever 1946:297). The South African prime minister who introduced apartheid was the Reverend Dr. D. F. Malan, who obtained his doctorate in the best traditions of theological liberalism from the University of Utrecht (Booyens 1969:66–69). Unfortunately, Hendrick Verwoerd, the evil genius of apartheid, gives no indication of this intellectual heritage in his various writings or Ph.D. thesis. All that can be said with certainty is that he was not a conservative Christian and appears to have been some sort of freethinker. But Nico Diedrichs, another of the main architects of apartheid and later state president, clearly rejected a biblical perspective in favour of a volkish ideology with German roots, as can be seen from his Ph.D. thesis (1930) and various books like *Nasionalism as Lewensbeskouing* (1936). Diedrichs also maintained a strong interest in Buddhism (Conze 1979:1.9; 2.66–69). Here again it was the "dogmatic Calvinist tradition" of theologically conservative groups like the *Gereformeerde Kerk*, to which President de Klerk belonged, that provided the strongest internal criticism of apartheid; and Evangelicals in the tradition of Andrew Murray, like Beyers Naud, campaigned for years against the unbiblical nature of apartheid ideology.

Conclusion

This brief examination of Barr's *Fundamentalism* (1981) serves to illustrate the slur campaign waged against Evangelical and Fundamentalist Christians by many academics. Close examination of Barr's work shows that *Fundamentalism* is essentially a propaganda piece rich in rhetorical argument that presents Evangelical and Fundamentalist Christians in the worst possible light. Like all religious movements, members of Evangelical and Fundamentalist Christian groups have their faults. But they are not the anti-intellectual, reactionary monsters of Barr's overheated imagination.

If we are to understand the appeal of contemporary religious movements, including African Independent Churches and other movements that are all too often labelled "Fundamentalist," it is necessary to shed the cultural blinkers imposed by Barr's framework and begin by looking at them afresh. Only when this is done will we begin to understand the appeal of Evangelical and Fundamentalist Christianity worldwide. If we do this, we can begin to recognize the true dynamic of these movements instead of continuing to misinterpret them by viewing them through the worn-out prejudicial spectacles Barr created so long ago.

Department of Religious Studies, University of Calgary, Calgary, AB, Canada, T3G 3B4, e-mail: hexham@ucalgary.ca.

Bibliography

Albright, W. F., and Mann, C. S., *The Anchor Bible: Matthew*, New York: Doubleday, 1971.

Barr, James, *Fundamentalism*, London: SCM, 1981, first published 1977.

Berlet, Chris, "Religion and Politics in the United States: Nuances You Should Know," *Public Eye Magazine*, Summer 2003, found on the Internet at: http://www.publiceye.org/magazine/v17n2/evangelical-demographics.html

Bibby, Reginald, *Restless Gods: The Renaissance of Religion in Canada*, Ottawa: Novalis, 2004.

Blaiklock, E. M., *The Confessions of St. Augustine*, New York: Thomas Nelson, 1983.

Booyens, Prof. Bun, *Die Lewe van D. F. Malan*, Cape Town: Tafelberg, 1969.

Brouwer, Steve, Gifford, Paul and Rose, Susan D., *Exporting the American Gospel*, New York and London: Routledge, 1996.

Conway, Flo., and Siegelman, Jim, *Holy Terror*, New York: Dell, 1984.

Conway, J. S., *The Nazi Persecution of the Churches*, Toronto: The Ryerson Press, 1968.

Conze, Edward, *The Memoirs of a Modern Gnostic*, Sherborne: Samizdat, Vols. 1 and 2, 1979.

Edersheim, Alfred, *The Life and Times of Jesus the Messiah*, London: Longmans Green, and Co., 1915, first published 1883.

Election Focus, US Department of State, 16 June 2004, Issue 1, Number 13.

Engel, Lothar, Kamphausen, Erhard, Linz, Johanna, *Fundamentalismus in Afrika und Amerika*, Hamburg: Evangelisches Missionswerk, 1993.

Finke, Roger, and Stark, Rodney, *The Churching of America, 1776–1990*, New Jersey: Rutgers University Press, 1992.

Gallup, George, Jr., and Castelli, Jim, *The People's Religion: American Faith in the '90's*, New York: Macmillan, 1989.

Gifford, Paul, *The Religious Right in Southern Africa*, Harare: University of Zimbabwe Press, 1988.

Gottschalk, Louis, *Understanding History*, New York: Alfred A. Knopf, 1963.

Guthrie, D., and Motyer, J. A., eds., *The New Bible Commentary Revised*, Grand Rapids: Eerdmans, 1979, first published London: InterVarsity Press, 1970.

Haiven, Judith, *Faith Hope No Charity*, Vancouver: New Star Books, 1984.

Hexham, Irving, "An Analysis of Press Reports of Recent 'Cult' Murders in Uganda," for *Religion in the News*, forthcoming.

Idea Spektrum, 20, 2004.

Kelly, Dean M., *Why Conservative Churches Are Growing*, Macon: Mercer University Press, 1986.

Kitchen, K. A., *Ancient Orient and Old Testament*, Downers Grove: Inter Varsity Press, 1975, first published, London, InterVarsity Press, 1966.

Leach, Edmund, *Culture & Communication: The Logic by Which Symbols Are Connected*. Cambridge: Cambridge University Press, 1976.

Metzke, Erwin, *J. G. Hamanns Stellung in der Philosophie des 18. Jahrhunderts* (J. G. Hamann and Eighteenth-Century Philosophy), Darmstadt: Wissenschaftliche Buchgesellschaft, 1967.

Northcott, Michael, "Reflections on the Apocalypse," *Third Way*, London, November 2004:22–24.

Poewe, Karla, ed., *Charismatic Christianity as a Global Culture*, Columbia, SC: University of South Carolina Press, 1994.

Poewe, Karla, "On the Metonymic Structure of Religious Experiences: The Example of Charismatic Christianity," in *Cultural Dynamics* (Amsterdam), 1989, Vol. II, No. 4, 361–80.

Richardson, Herbert, *Toward an American Theology*, New York: Harper & Row, 1967.

Schnabel, Eckhard J., *Sind Evangelikale Fundamentalisten?* Wuppertal: R. Brockhaus, 1998.

Strübind, Andra, *Die unfreie Freikirche*, Neukirchen: Neukirchener Verlag, 1991.

Sundkler, Bengt, *Zulu Zion and Some Swazi Zionists*, Oxford: Oxford University Press, 1975.

The Economist, "The triumph of the religious right," 11 November 2004, found on the internet at: http://www.economist.com/displaystory.cfm?story_id=3375543

Troeltsch, Ernst, "The Separation of Church and State and the Teaching of Religion," in *Religion in History*, Minneapolis: Fortress Press, 1991, first published as "Die Trennung von Staat und Kirche, der staatliche Religionsunterricht und die theologischen Fakultäten," in *Heidelberger Akademische Rede*, Tübingen, 1906.

Unger, Rudolf, *Hamann Und Die Aufklärung* (Hamann and the Enlightenment), Tübingen: Max Niemeyer Verlag, 1968.

Van den Heever, C. M., *General J. B. M. Hertzog*, Johannesburg: A.P.B. Bookstore, 1946.

Vickers, Brian, *In Defence of Rhetoric*, Oxford: Clarendon Press, 1989.

Welbourn, F. B., *East African Rebels*, London: SCM, 1961.

Wells, Jonathan, *Charles Hodge's Critique of Darwinism*, Lewiston: Edwin Mellen Press, 1988.

Wilcox, Clyde, *Onward Christian Soldiers? The Religious Right in American Politics*, Boulder: Westview Press, 1996.

The Transcendent Incarnate

J. W. Montgomery's Defense of a Christocentric Weltanschauung

Dr. Angus J. L. Menuge
Dept. of Philosophy, Concordia University, Wisconsin

1. Introduction

Where should the construction of a theistic worldview begin? Many philosophers suppose we should begin at the top, with an analysis of the character of the religion's god or gods. One example of this is classical apologetics, which offers various proofs for the existence of God and, in the process, identifies important divine attributes. Yet, granted that some of these arguments are successful, they have important limitations. Showing that there is a divine X with attribute A does not establish who X is, nor which of many competing religions that agree that God is A, is true. For example, showing that the divine being is necessary, a first cause and the architect of the universe, does not decide between Christianity, Islam, and Judaism.

Further, to suppose that there is a generic place to start the process of developing a theistic worldview overlooks the contrasting claims particular theistic religions make about how we know the divine. For example, in Islam, Allah is said to be fundamentally unknowable. One can know lots of things *about* Allah—that Allah has certain attributes and what Allah's will is for one's life as revealed in the Qur'an—but there is no such thing as knowing Allah personally because of Allah's radical transcendence. Islam's emphasis on impersonal knowledge of God may provide the Muslim apologist with a good motivation for classical apologetics and the development of a religious worldview based on natural reason. But Christianity makes the unique claim that we come to have a personal relationship with God the Father through His incarnate Son, Jesus Christ (John 14:8–9). It is not by starting at the top, with God's attributes, but by starting at the bottom, with the man Jesus Christ, that we are best able to understand God. This is why Luther held that Christian thought should begin with the incarnation rather than the natural theology preferred by Thomas Aquinas.

But what difference does it make if one constructs a Christian worldview from the bottom, starting with the transcendent incarnate, rather than from the top, starting with pure transcendence? In his prolific contributions to Christian thought, John Warwick Montgomery has provided one of the most sustained and wide-ranging answers.

This goal of this paper is threefold. First, we will flesh out why Luther preferred an incarnational foundation for a Christian worldview. Second, we will consider Montgomery's application of this insight in developing a distinctive, Christocentric methodology for apologetics. Third, we will see how Montgomery uses the same approach to shed light on seemingly intractable problems in religious epistemology, the philosophy of history, ethics, and the legal theory of human rights.

2. Starting with This Man Jesus

Martin Luther is sometimes cast as an irrationalist or fideist, because of his famous remark that reason is the devil's whore. However, the context of Luther's remarks was the rejection of all modes of auto-salvation. While affirming that reason is a precious gift in our daily vocations and the earthly sphere, Luther denies that reason, or anything else, can reach up to God and recreate the relationship with Him that was broken by the fall. Reason is not above God's special revelation, so it should not act magisterially, rejecting the mysteries and paradoxes of the faith because we cannot establish or fully comprehend them starting from earthbound rational categories. However, Luther did not deny the ministerial value of reason as a servant that could help us see and apply the implications of God's revelation in our life and worldview.

Luther reminds us that what we can know of God is limited to what God has chosen to reveal in humanly accessible terms and argues that Christian thought is therefore well advised to begin by contemplating the divine in human form: the man Jesus Christ. In the final version of his commentary on Galatians, Luther writes:

> Paul ... wants to teach us the Christian religion, which does not begin at the top, as all other religions do, but at the very bottom. ... [I]f you would think or treat of your salvation, you must stop speculating about the majesty of God; you must forget all thoughts of good works, tradition, philosophy, and even the divine Law. Hasten to the stable and the lap of the mother and apprehend this infant Son of the Virgin. Look at Him being born, nursed, and growing up, walking among men, teaching, dying, returning from the dead, and being exalted above all the heavens.[1]

If we try to build our picture of God from the top, we overlook the fact that many truths about God are either hidden from us, or when revealed, revealed as mysteries that we cannot fully comprehend. For Luther this "amounts to building the roof before you have laid the foundation,"[2] of supposing that we can reconnect with God the Father while bypassing the Son, the only means of access (John 14:6). However, starting with God's self-revelation, we have both the written Word, the Bible, where divine truth is communicated in human language, and the Incarnate Word, the Son, where divine wisdom and attributes are shown by the human actions of Christ. God's saving acts and His continuing intentions for our lives are best shown by the scriptural portrait of the life of Jesus. This, Montgomery believes, is also the right place to begin in apologetics and the development of a systematic Christian worldview.

3. Defending the Faith

Proponents of classical apologetics generally concede that arguments establishing the existence and attributes of God are insufficient to develop a faithful portrait of the Christian God because, amongst other things,[3] they do not disclose God's plan of salvation.[4] For this we must leave philosophy and focus on the historical case for the incarnation, crucifixion, and resurrection of Christ. However, it is often claimed that classical apologetics is still crucial because there is a gap—Lessing's famous ditch—between the historical events of Christ's life and their meaning for our salvation. This meaning, it is argued, can only be found via a preexisting theistic perspective. Montgomery cites a number of examples of this viewpoint.

> Theological presuppositionalists Carl F. H. Henry and Ronald H. Nash tell us that there are no self-interpreting facts, and Calvinists John Gerstner and R. C. Sproul, as well as Evangelical neo-Thomist Norman L. Geisler, insist that an independent theistic structure must be established to make any theological sense out of Jesus' resurrection.[5]

If these critics are correct, Luther's insistence on starting with the evidence of Christ's identity and actions is inappropriate for apologetics. For presuppositionalists, "a radical break exists between the worlds of the Christian and the non-Christian—a cleavage so fundamental that the Christian cannot convince the non-Christian of Christian truth." Certain facts about Christ's life may be supported by evidence, but "the non-Christian is incapable of arriving at a proper interpretation of saving truth."[6]

At first sight the critics may seem to have support from the philosophy of science. It is commonplace that the same data can be interpreted differently by different scientific theories, just as the famous duck-rabbit diagram can be seen equally well as a duck or a rabbit. Won't the atheist be able to provide a naturalistic account of the facts about Jesus' life every bit as plausible as the explanation of a believer? Montgomery's answer is a resolute "No," so long as we consider enough facts and impartially compare their competing explanations: "Facts ultimately arbitrate interpretations, not the reverse, at least where good science (and not bad philosophy) is being practiced."[7] Although there are conceivable cases where too few facts are known to decide between rival interpretations, experience shows this is frequently not the case. While a diagram of a duck-rabbit is forever ambiguous, closer investigation of real ducks and rabbits reveals telltale differences. One does not have to be a member of the Gastronomic Society of Paris to detect the difference between *canard à l'orange* and *lapin à l' orange*![8] Working scientists devote a great deal of time and care to devising control experiments capable of isolating the causally operative factors and sometimes devise crucial experiments in which, at least by the standards appropriate to experimental science, rival explanations can be decisively tested against each other because they make mutually exclusive predictions.[9] Likewise, in a court of law, a large body of physical evidence and testimony can exclude some suspects and implicate others beyond a reasonable doubt.

But can such tests take us from the historical facts of Jesus' life to His divinity? Following the great Harvard Law School professor, Simon Greenleaf, Montgomery replies in the affirmative. Evidential apologetics begins by showing that the New Testament documents are a reliable source of information about Christ's life. These documents

> handsomely fulfill the historian's requirement of *transmissional reliability* (their texts have been transmitted accurately from the time of writing to our own day), *internal reliability* (they claim to be primary source documents and ring true as such), and *external reliability* (their authorship and dates are backed up by such solid extrinsic testimony such as that of the early second-century writer Papias, a student of John the evangelist, who was told by him that the first three Gospels were indeed written by their traditional authors).[10]

There is no evidence that the writers of the New Testament suffered from internal (psychological or moral) defects or had anything to gain from fabrication (quite the reverse: all but one died for his consistent proclamation of Christ's actions on our behalf). And perhaps most telling of all, this testimony remained unrefuted despite what amounted to hostile cross-examination by the Jewish authorities.[11]

But if the documents are reliable testimony, that includes their report of the resurrection of Christ. It is the resurrection, Montgomery argues, that establishes the divinity of Christ. This is not simply because the resurrection is *a* miracle, for not all miracles implicate the divine.

> If I were to grow a hair on a billiard ball, would this war-
> rant a claim on my part to deity? Hardly.... [T]he sig-
> nificance of a miracle depends ... on the character of the
> miracle—specifically whether or not it speaks to universal
> human need.[12]

In other words, what matters is not the mere fact that a miracle has occurred but what the particular nature of the miracle tells us about the miracle-worker's character and concern for human beings. Death is the most important existential problem faced by all human beings and, as both the author of Ecclesiastes and apologist William Lane Craig[13] have argued, a finite life terminated by oblivion renders all human projects void of ultimate meaning. The resurrection, like no other miracle, provides evidence that there is a solution to the problem of death: the One who promises us eternal life backs up this promise by showing that He can overcome death.

> The conquest of death for all men is the very predicate
> of deity that a race dead in trespasses and sins can most
> clearly recognize, for it meets man's most basic need to
> transcend the meaninglessness of finite existence. Not to
> worship One who gives you the gift of eternal life is to
> hopelessly misread what the gift tells you about the Giver.[14]

Further, just as someone who aspires to be a high wire walker in the circus will seek advice from someone who can actually perform the feat, humans who are manifestly unable to raise themselves from the dead are well advised to listen to the explanation of the meaning of a resurrection provided by the one who has actually experienced one.[15]

Montgomery argues that once the fact of the resurrection is estab-lished, this fact is not equally well explained by atheistic and theistic theories as the presuppositionalist claims.

> Christ's resurrection can be examined by non-Christians as
> well as Christians. Its factual character, when considered in
> light of the claims of the One raised from the dead, points
> not to a multiplicity of equally possible interpretations, but

to a single "best interpretation" (to an interpretation most consistent with the data), namely the deity of Christ (John 2:18–22).[16]

True, Christ's authoritative, demanding and exclusive claims on people mean that the resurrection may still be rejected.[17] But the apologist can argue that this is a matter of willful rebellion and the natural man's desire for autonomy, not something justified by the evidence.

Further, there is an important advantage to the evidential approach over a presuppositionalist one. Starting at the top, with the divine, the presuppositionalist immediately runs into the problem of religious pluralism. A vast number of competing religions and cults make logically incompatible claims about the divine.[18] All of them can claim that acceptance of their system provides internal and pragmatic benefits. Without a clear, external test to decide which system is true, one is left to "try them out." There are, however, too many religions for this to be psychologically realistic or even healthy. It is likely one will be deceived by a false religion (because it suits one's preferences) or that one will become so disgusted by implausible and manipulative religions that, like the dwarves in C. S. Lewis's *Last Battle*, one ends up refusing to believe in any of them for fear of being taken in again. It is quite possible that Christianity will never be given a fair hearing. Even if someone accepts an argument for a divine X, with no practical way to decide which portrait of God is correct, the individual is likely enough to fashion a god in his or her own image. This is why Luther warned that natural theology can easily lead to idolatry.

Starting at the bottom, however, with the case for Christ, one immediately encounters the striking difference between Christianity and other religions: The central claims of Christianity depend on historical facts that can be independently comfirmed. After all, what makes faith valid is not faith itself but the *object* of faith.[19] The gospel is not merely a subjective feeling or comforting mantra but involves historical events completely external to believers. What is more, as we have seen, these events do not merely point to some divine X: they show us who God is. We are not left to construct a god for ourselves but find ourselves in the presence of a divine person. In this way a Christocentric approach is more likely to put an unbeliever in "harm's way," to expose him to Christ's claims to be Lord of his life. And although only the Holy Spirit can work faith, an apologetic based on Christ's life keeps us focused on the gospel through which we know the Spirit works.

4. A Comprehensive Christian Worldview

Montgomery does not confine his Christocentric approach to apologetics but consistently deploys it in developing a systematic, Christian worldview. We will consider four examples: religious epistemology, the philosophy of history, ethics, and the legal theory of human rights.

4.1 Religious Epistemology

Arguably the most important issue in religious epistemology is the identification of a reliable justification for religious belief. Montgomery argues that all the typical sources of justification fail to discriminate between competing religious claims. For example, none of the following discriminate between true and false religions: common sense, intuition, authority, the "focus" of cultural change, spirituality, religious experience, faith, presuppositions, or any combination of the above.[20] The common failing of all these sources is that they lack an unambiguous link or pointer to the truth about transcendence. At worst these sources are insufficient to overcome the challenge posed by debunking naturalistic explanations. For example, while some arguments from religious experience are more sophisticated, the mere fact that some people claim to have had a religious experience fails to show that the experience is veridical and so fails to rebut the skeptic's counterclaim that the experience has a mundane cultural, genetic, or psychological explanation. At best the sources do have undeniable religious significance, but they lead to a morass of irreconcilable conflict since they can equally well be employed by any number of religions. For example, like the Areopagus of Acts 17, contemporary America is awash in more than 57 varieties of spirituality.

Such sources of religious knowledge may establish the existence of transcendence but fail to identify the transcendent being.

Before C. S. Lewis became a Christian, he complained that if God is like Shakespeare and we are like Hamlet, there is no way we can know our Author. We may reason that there must be such an Author to explain the contingent existence of the play and its marks of design, but this does not tell us who the Author is. When Lewis became a Christian, he realized that Hamlet could know Shakespeare only if Shakespeare revealed himself to Hamlet as a character in the play. He saw that this was the way God had revealed himself to us in the historical person of Christ. In Christ a transcendent person becomes incarnate as a historical human being *yet without losing either His transcendence or His divine personality*. Human actions of the incarnate Christ can therefore reveal the identity of a divine person. "In Christ, God truly entered the human sphere. And if this is the case, the human events of His life objectively display His deity and are not adequately explainable apart from it."[21] (Theologically, we understand this as the communication of Christ's human and divine attributes, so that when Jesus wept, God wept, when Jesus died, God died.) Therefore, Montgomery argues, if what counts as success in religious epistemology is knowing the source of religious truth, Christians should start, not with a nebulous, ambiguous and ultimately inconclusive case for divinity, but with the concrete case for the life of Christ.

4.2 The Philosophy of History

Two of the most fundamental questions in the philosophy of history are: (1) Do world events evidence any discernible pattern or purpose, or are they merely in Henry Ford's words, "the succession of one damned thing after another"? (2) If history does have a direction, what is the underlying dynamic that explains it? Montgomery argues that secular attempts to provide nonskeptical answers to these questions not only fail but are bound to fail because of a common and unavoidable weakness, while Christian revelation succeeds in unlocking the true meaning of history.

In his essay "Where Is History Going?"[22] Montgomery develops this case by examining five representatives of a secular approach to

the philosophy of history: Kant, Hegel, Marx, Spengler, and Toynbee. Kant believed that human history was propelled by a hidden
source of rational self-improvement that would enable human capacities to flourish increasingly. Kant did not deny human greed,
envy, and lust for power but thought even these make people more
industrious, thereby developing their capacities. However, this claim
of inevitable progress requires empirical support that Kant failed to
provide: he "attempts to say something substantial about the plot
of history without investigating the data of historical experience."[23]
Kant showed neither that history has progressed nor that it has done
so in a rational manner. And the idea that selfish desires will still pro-
pel progress "does not take evil seriously,"[24] for it overlooks the possibility that only *some* people flourish by enslaving or annihilating
others, which is hardly progress for mankind as a whole. Fundamentally, Kant failed to show that reason necessitates progress. There is
a horrifyingly exact rationality to the construction of concentration
camps and gulags, yet these atrocities epitomized not human flourishing but man's inhumanity to man.

Hegel's advance over Kant was to provide (1) an empirical sequence of epochs (Oriental, Greek, Roman, and Germanic) in which
each successive epoch is manifestly an advance over the one that preceded it and (2) a causal dynamic of progress, the dialectic of the
"world spirit" of rationality. However, Hegel's identification of epochs
seems arbitrary and chauvinistic. And like Kant, Hegel provided no
justification for the idea that reason inevitably yields progress. The
logic of dialectic does produce change since the synthesis will differ
from both thesis and antithesis, but the change can diminish as well
as improve human flourishing. "Hegelian dialectic is really a formal
principle which neither discloses the goal of a process nor places any
value judgment upon it. The dialectic can describe a continual refinement of evil as well as a continual refinement of good."[25]

Marx took Hegel's idea of a dialectic and provided a materialistic interpretation. He understood progress in economic terms and
believed that revolution would replace the "bourgeois-capitalist"
phase with a proletarian dictatorship, followed by the withering
away of the state and a utopian classless society. Like Hegel, Marx
failed to justify his claim that history was inevitably moving in the

direction he claimed. Improvements in workers' standard of living made revolution unmotivated. And Marx externalized evil in oppressive economic conditions without seeing that this evil originates from human corruption, a corruption that will vitiate any attempt to construct a utopia.

Spengler claimed that the history of civilization does not evince linear progress to any absolute goal, but like living beings human societies are born, mature, decline, and die. Thus Spengler identifies many cases in which barbarism gives way to a civilization that eventually declines. While this pattern is no doubt common, Spengler provided no justification for claiming that societies must resemble living things in this way, so he could not show that this is how the future must unfold. And with no sense of an absolute goal, how is it possible for Spengler even to distinguish the barbaric from the civilized, which clearly involves a value judgment?

Toynbee's theory is the most complex, identifying 34 historical civilizations by their distinctive cultural beliefs. His key idea was that the success or failure of a society can be explained by a "challenge-and-response theory," according to which "no civilization dies because of determinist necessity, but because of inadequate response on its own part to the challenges facing it."[26] Among many difficulties for the view,[27] the most fundamental is that "challenge-and-response" is "little more than a formal principle, like Hegel's dialectic,"[28] which does not tell us anything about the direction of history. A society might survive a challenge by recourse to totalitarianism and a vast slave army, but this would not constitute progress for mankind.

The common flaw of these philosophies of history is that they attempt to provide an absolute perspective on all of history from the limited perspective of a finite being located within history and inevitably conditioned by it. Thus Hegel's suggestion that the Germanic was the highest phase of rational progress, so plausible in the nineteenth century, strikes everyone today as an ethnocentric conceit. And Marx's suggestion of inevitable worldwide revolution seemed much more plausible under the labor conditions prevailing in his day than under those operative today.

Consider: because a man stands in history at a particular place, and cannot see into the future, he cannot possibly demonstrate that his conception of history will have permanent validity. For the same reason—lack of perspective on the human drama as a whole—he cannot in any absolute sense know what is more or less significant or valuable in the total history of mankind. . . . Our historical searchlights are incapable of illuminating all of the path we have traversed, and they continually meet a wall of fog ahead of us.[29]

Other than skepticism, it seems that any way out of this predicament must appeal to some perspective unconditioned by history, capable of surveying it in its entirety, and possessing the authority to pronounce on its overall meaning and goal. In other words, only a god, a transcendent being, could provide a demonstrably valid philosophy of history. But, Montgomery points out, "only if the Transcendent were to communicate with us as to history's meaning would a transcendent answer do us any good."[30] Fortunately,

this is precisely the contention of the Christian religion: that God *did* enter human life—in the person of Jesus the Christ—and *did* reveal to men the nature and significance of history and human life, and *did* bring men into contact with eternal values.[31]

From this revealed Christian perspective, history has three primary dimensions of meaning, centering on creation, redemption, and the last judgment. Because of creation and preservation, historical nihilism can be rejected: "No historical act is too insignificant to be outside the Father's care."[32] By solving the problem of human sin and death, Christ's redemption "becomes the center of history and the criterion of significance for interpreting all other acts."[33] And the last judgment means that there is a time in which the justice that eludes the world will finally be done, and in which the goals of human flourishing in community will be fully realized, providing "the Christian conception of history a direction and an ultimate meaning."[34]

4.3 Ethics and Human Rights

Montgomery's approach to the justification of ethical obligation and human rights is strikingly similar to his treatment of the philosophy of history. He surveys the main secular theories and some leading religious accounts outside Christian revelation and shows that all of them fail to justify ethical absolutes and genuinely inalienable human rights. Then the superiority of a Christocentric, biblical solution is presented.

Perhaps the greatest difficulties facing attempts to provide an ethical foundation for human rights are those of (a) defining human rights, and (b) justifying human rights by means of demonstrably valid ethical principles.

Utilitarians, like Bentham and Mill, looked to social utility to define rights. So-called legal realists, like H. L. A. Hart, suppose that rights can only find their source in "successful appeals to a sense of community"[35] and are justified by a "rule of recognition" arising from a shared morality that is incapable of justification by any higher standard. Similarly, legal positivists, like Hans Kelsen, "can only consider human rights from the standard of an actual or potential structure of positive legal protections, since . . . legal norms are no more than hypothetical statements stipulating that a given sanction ought to be executed under certain conditions."[36]

None of these approaches is adequate because all of them are compatible with state-sponsored human rights abuses. Nazi genocide was useful, appealed to an Aryan sense of community, and was, shockingly enough, quite legal by the standards of positive law. At the Nuremburg trials,

> the most telling defense offered by the accused was that they had simply followed orders or made decisions within the framework of their own legal system, in complete consistency with it, and that they therefore could not be condemned because they deviated from the alien value system of their conquerors.[37]

This argument compelled Robert Jackson, the chief counsel for the United States, to appeal to a higher law, inherent to civilization, that transcends the particular laws of various states. "Thus have the horrors of . . . history forced us to recognize the puerile inadequacy of tying ultimate legal standards to the mores of a particular society."[38]

Perhaps most telling is that the whole idea of a human right is that of an *inalienable entitlement one has in virtue of being a human being*, not a conditional privilege which a state or legal system may grant or deny as it seems best. So if any one of utilitarianism, legal realism, or legal positivism were true, the proper conclusion would have to be that there are no such things as human rights. For this reason other thinkers have tried to identify some ethical source of human rights that is independent of the cultural and legal practices of particular societies. Yet this raises the question, "How exactly can a given society or a given individual transcend the values of the culture so as to arrive at standards of absolute worth?"[39]

Some answers are patently inadequate: intuitionism, situationalism, and contextualism all appeal to standards incapable of giving univocal answers because neither intuitions nor judgments of the most "loving" action in the situation nor decisions justified by the context of a particular community's values or faith have any guaranteed connection to objective truth, as is shown by the fact that they all produce conflicting results. To tolerate this conflict means that a human right may be here today and gone tomorrow because of a change in intuition, situation, or the mood and membership of the community. On the other hand, any means of consistently maintaining human rights would have to resolve the conflict and would therefore necessarily appeal to a higher standard than those in conflict. Fundamentally, none of these theories take seriously the fact that human egocentrism will corrupt our intuitions and preferences allowing genuine entitlements to be denied and spurious entitlements to be insisted on to further the advantage of the individual or the group.[40] This problem remains even if the entire society reaches consensus since "fifty million Frenchmen can be wrong."[41]

Kantian and neo-Kantian solutions at least attempt to overcome egocentrism. For Kant, an action or policy is ethically valid only if it can be willed as a universal law. Kant believes it is possible to reveal the moral equivalence of rational agents and thereby to short-circuit the self-centered desire to violate a moral rule that one sees must bind others. The problem is, however, that egocentric people do not grant their moral equivalence to others but brazenly claim superiority on the grounds of power or privilege.

> Genghis Khan (as representative of the tyrants of this world) would not be persuaded by the categorical imperative to stop raping and pillaging, for he would not agree that he and others are equal members of a common humanity; *they* do not have the strength to rape and pillage *him*, whereas *he* does have the power to treat *them* in such a fashion.[42]

Even though it is true that Genghis Khan cannot will that others treat him as he treats others, he has ample reason to suppose that they cannot do so. One might be able to argue that Genghis Khan ought to be able to see his moral equivalence to others, but a complete ethical theory needs to explain how it is possible for Genghis Khan's perception and motivation to be transformed so that he can see this is true and feel some obligation to act accordingly.

Although more sophisticated, the neo-Kantian theories of Rawls and Gewirth are vulnerable to the same basic objection. Rawls argues that we should accept those principles of justice we would agree to under a veil of ignorance regarding our special advantages. Likewise, Gewirth tries to ground rights in the mere fact that one is a "prospective moral agent" independent of any special characteristics. But notoriously, sinful human beings like Genghis Khan can argue that it is not in their self-interest to act as if ignorant of their special advantages and characteristics.

Human egotism is therefore capable of vitiating even the most enlightened attempts to reach up to an objective basis for ethics and human rights based only on reason. The ethical theorist remains a human being with particular interests that get in the way of discovering a truly disinterested perspective. For this reason Rousseau perceptively observed,

> In order to discover the rules of society best suited to nations, a superior intelligence beholding all the pas-

sions of men without experiencing any of them would be
needed.... It would take gods to give men laws.[43]

Rousseau may have been wrong to insist that the intelligence
must not have experienced the passions, but certainly it would have
to remain uncorrupted by these passions (Heb 4:15). The need for a
source of human rights that transcends the foibles of humans themselves has sparked a renaissance of interest in natural law theory.
C. S. Lewis spoke of a cosmic, transcultural moral order called the
Tao;[44] Jay Budziszewski has explored the moral law that we "can't not
know";[45] J. Daryl Charles calls us to return to the natural law as the
basis for moral "First Things";[46] and many Roman Catholic thinkers
(notably Robert P. George[47]) have tried to restore legal respect for
traditional morality by showing that it can be rationally derived from
human nature.

Although these ideas have considerable merit, just as natural theology provides a blurry indistinct picture of deity, so, Montgomery
argues, "Assertions of natural morality, unassisted by biblical revelation, suffer from such vagueness and ambiguity that they offer little
assistance in dealing with practical ethical issues."[48] One example of
natural law that might be claimed to have universal validity is the
Justinian code: "Live honestly, harm no one, give to each his own."
Unfortunately, this code does not specify the kinds of specific actions that uphold or transgress it and so leaves itself open to perverse
interpretations. "The third part of the Justinian definition ... was inscribed by the Nazis on the gate leading into the death camp at Bu-
chenwald: *Jedem das Seine.*"[49]

Of course, defenders of natural law will claim that more specific
moral obligations can be defended yet in practice seem unable to
reach agreement. For example, natural law arguments are used to
defend and critique contraception, the death penalty, and even same-
sex marriage.[50] While it is fair to protest that one side of these disputes is simply wrong about the natural law, these debates reveal that
attempting to base ethics on human nature is difficult because sin
has infected that nature, making it easy to confuse what sinful people
would prefer with God's intentions for humankind.

The author of humankind is going to be the one best placed to write its instruction manual. This is why Wittgenstein despaired of human beings discovering their own ethics from within the world. "If a man could write a book on Ethics which really was a book on Ethics, this book would, with an explosion, destroy all the other books in the world."[51]

Again, Montgomery's solution to the dilemma is that a perspicuous objective morality is delivered to us from above, that the "Holy Scriptures constitute that 'explosive book' of transcendent origin for which Wittgenstein sought in vain."[52] Not only do the Bible and Jesus' exposition of its meaning in His life and teachings sharpen, clarify, and give an internal understanding of the moral law, they also provide a sufficient basis to justify genuine human rights.

> The Bible includes in its ethical teachings the foundations
> for inalienable human rights—both so-called "first genera-
> tion" rights (civil and political freedoms), "second genera-
> tion" guarantees (social and economic rights), and even
> newer rights of the "third generation."[53]

Montgomery shows there is clear scriptural precedent for such fundamental human rights as Procedural Due Process, Substantive Due Process, or Nondiscrimination, life, freedom from torture and slavery, freedom of thought, social and economic development, education, fair remuneration, personal reputation and environmental rights, as well as many others.[54] Of course, the secular world will quickly complain that the Bible is only a matter of some people's private faith and cannot be demonstrated to have objective validity. However, as we have seen, the reliability of the Scriptures can be defended with independent argument accessible to the nonbeliever. Thus, quite against the grain of our times, Montgomery resolutely rejects the idea that biblical truth cannot be applied in the public square because, he argues, that truth is available to public reason and not merely to the private conscience of the faithful.

What is more, Montgomery notes, the gospel is not merely an intellectually defensible creed. It has the power to transform hearts and produce self-forgetful actions of love. In this way the gospel also addresses the fundamental problem of human motivation in a realistic way. Not rational argument but a change of heart can open the eyes of the Genghis Khans of this world to the existence of human rights.

> Only when an individual has been liberated from self-centeredness is there freedom to serve the needs and protect the rights of others. . . . God's grace in Christ touches the world at the point of the redeemed sinner, and spreads out from him to those whose God-given rights have been violated and whose wounds need to be bound up.[55]

5. Conclusion

Obviously, Montgomery's stance is controversial and alien to the typical practices of philosophers of religion. However, it seems to me that Montgomery succeeds in showing some important advantages to constructing a Christian worldview from the bottom, with Christ and the biblical revelation, rather than from the top, with a rational analysis of deity. Starting at the top, one encounters the inevitable limitations of natural theology, finite reason, and human egoism, which lead to vague or distorted answers to fundamental questions of who God is, how we know Him, the meaning of history, and the ethical foundations of human rights. Starting at the bottom, although it requires an arduous evidential apologetic, promises to deliver more accurate, objective, and universal answers. Perhaps not only theologians but also Christian philosophers, historians, ethicists, and human rights activists could benefit from laying the foundation before building the roof.

Angus J. L. Menuge, Ph.D
Professor of Philosophy
Concordia University Wisconsin

Endnotes

1   *WA*, XL, Part 1 (published in 1535 and 1538), 79. Quoted in John Warwick Montgomery, "The Incarnate Christ: The Apologetic Thrust of Lutheran Theology," *Modern Reformation*, Volume 7, Number 1, January/February

1998, 10, and in "Lutheran Theology and Defense of Biblical Faith," in *Faith Founded on Fact: Essays in Evidential Apologetics* (Edmonton, AB, Canada: Canadian Institute for Law, Theology, and Public Policy, Inc., 2001), 142–43.

2   *WA*, XXXVI, 61 (Sermon of 6 Jan. 1532, on Mic 5:1). Quoted in John Warwick Montgomery, "The Incarnate Christ: The Apologetic Thrust of Lutheran Theology," 11 and in "Lutheran Theology and Defense of Biblical Faith," in *Faith Founded on Fact*, 143.

3   Although reason can draw important conclusions about what it means to have a triune God, reason seems incapable of demonstrating the necessity of the Trinity.

4   Pure reason cannot show that God had to save us at all since our salvation is a free gift of love, not an entitlement; nor, *a fortiori*, can pure reason show how God would save us.

5   John Warwick Montgomery, *Human Rights and Human Dignity* (Dallas, TX: Probe, 1986), 156.

6   Montgomery, "The Place of Reason in Christian Witness," in *Faith Founded on Fact*, 32.

7   John Warwick Montgomery, Introduction to *Faith Founded on Fact*, xxii.

8   Lest any reckless person should venture to test this claim, please be advised that the *canard* (duck) is much to be preferred to the *lapin* (rabbit).

9   True, a single test is not decisive, since a false auxiliary assumption about the experimental setup may explain a failed prediction. But scientists can do additional tests to show that the auxiliary assumptions are most likely not to blame. The fact, emphasized by Duhem and Quine, that strict logic allows one to retain a hypothesis in the face of any evidence no matter how recalcitrant, because something other than the hypothesis *might* be to blame, does not prevent one showing a strong probability that the hypothesis is mistaken.

10   Montgomery, *Human Rights and Human Dignity*, 137.

11   Ibid., 148. Montgomery draws on the legal theory of cross-examination to show just how difficult it is to maintain a false story in the presence of hostile witnesses.

12   Montgomery, "Science, Theology, and the Miraculous," in *Faith Founded on Fact*, 59–60.

13   William Lane Craig, "The Absurdity of Life Without God," in *Reasonable Faith*, Second Edition (Wheaton, IL: Crossway, 1994).

14   Montgomery, "Science, Theology, and the Miraculous," in *Faith Founded on Fact*, 61.

15   Ibid., 62–63.

16   Montgomery, "The Place of Reason in Christian Witness," in *Faith Founded on Fact*, 34.

17   At the conference held in honor of Keith Yandell at Madison, WI, September 15–17, 2005, keynote speaker Paul K. Moser argued that much religious skepticism is not rationally defensible because at some point or other, it crucially depends on a willful rejection of Christ's lordship for which no argument is ever given. If Moser is correct, and I believe that he is, we must expect

that even the best apologetics will meet with resistance which only the Holy Spirit can break down.

18 See the aphorisms following proposition 1 in Montgomery's *Tractatus Logico-Theologicus* (Bonn, Germany: Verlag für Kultur und Wissenschaft, 2002).

19 Ibid., aphorisms 2.17ff.

20 Ibid., aphorisms 2.1 to 2.1834.

21 Montgomery, "The Place of Reason in Christian Witness," in *Faith Founded on Fact*, 34.

22 John Warwick Montgomery, "Where Is History Going?" in *Where Is History Going? A Christian Response to Secular Philosophies of History* (Minneapolis, MN: Bethany House, 1969; reprinted by the Canadian Institute for Law Theology, and Public Policy, Inc.), 15–36.

23 Ibid., 18.

24 Ibid.

25 Ibid., 19.

26 Ibid., 24.

27 Montgomery lists 6 in ibid., 25–26.

28 Ibid., 26.

29 Ibid., 30–31.

30 Montgomery, *Tractatus Logico-Theologicus*, aphorism 5.282.

31 Montgomery, "Where Is History Going?" 31.

32 Ibid., 32.

33 Ibid., 33.

34 Ibid., 34.

35 Montgomery, *Human Rights and Human Dignity*, 83.

36 Ibid., 84.

37 John Warwick Montgomery, *Law Above the Law* (Bloomington, MN: Bethany House, 1975), 24.

38 Ibid., 26.

39 Ibid., 33–34.

40 For a fuller discussion, see Montgomery's *Tractatus Logico-Theologicus*, aphorisms 5.4ff.

41 Ibid., aphorism 5.3412.

42 Ibid., aphorism 5.542.

43 Jean-Jacques Rousseau, *The Social Contract*, bk. 2, ch. 7, quoted in Montgomery, *The Law Above the Law*, 36–37.

44 C. S. Lewis, *The Abolition of Man* (New York: Macmillan, 1995).

45 Jay Budziszewski, *What We Can't Not Know: A Guide* (Dallas, TX: Spence, 2004).

46 J. Daryl Charles, "Returning to Moral 'First Things,'" *Philosophia Christi*, vol. 6, no. 1 (2004), 59–76.

47 See for example Robert P. George's *The Clash of Orthodoxies: Law, Religion, and Morality in Crisis* (Wilmington, DE: ISI Books, 2001).

48 Montgomery, *Tractatus Logico-Theologicus*, aphorism 5.33.

49 Ibid., aphorism 5.3312.

50 See "The Same Sex Marriage Debate," featuring articles by Marvin Ellison, J. Budziszewski, Francis Beckwith, and Ronald Long, in *Philosophia Christi*, vol. 7, no. 1 (2005).

51 Ludwig Wittgenstein, "A Lecture on Ethics," *Philosophical Review* 74 (January 1965), 7.

52 Montgomery, *Tractatus Logico-Theologicus*, aphorism 5.8.

53 Ibid., aphorism 5.83. The "third generation" of human rights "at least include national self-determination, the right to economic and social development, the right to benefit from the 'common heritage of mankind'. . . , the right to a healthy environment, the right to peace, and the right to humanitarian disaster relief" [Montgomery, *Human Rights and Human Dignity*, 28].

54 For a comprehensive table of biblically warranted human rights, see Montgomery', *Human Rights and Human Dignity*, Figure 7, 168–69.

55 Ibid., 216.

Preventing Theological Suicide

JOHN WARWICK MONTGOMERY'S
QUEST IN THE 1970S

L. Russ Bush

Whether it is shaping America,[1] teaching us about the higher law,[2] collecting evidence for faith,[3] or asking some of the tough questions,[4] Montgomery has been a virtual fountain of ideas and creative ways to defend the faith within the intellectual framework in which he finds himself at any given time. A recent example of this is his creative play with Wittgenstein.[5] Montgomery's *Tractatus* effectively argues that world religions are incompatible, thus the issue is "What is truth?" The historical validation of Christian faith yields an inerrant, perspicuous, and univocal written revelation. The meaning of human existence finds its resolution in Christian revelation, which satisfies the deepest longings of the human heart. Whereof one can speak, thereof one must not be silent.

The book that most influenced me, however, was published the year I received my M.Div. and began my doctoral studies, 1970. The title was *The Suicide of Christian Theology* (Minneapolis: Bethany, 1970). The book contains seven major introductory essays (including "Why Churches Decline," "The Death of the 'Death of God'," "Theological Education Today," and the essay that names the book). A second section models how a theologian should report relevant current events ("Barth in Chicago," "Vidler at Strasbourg") and produce reviews ("James A. Pike," "Martin Marty," "Georgia Harknes"). Then, finally, the book contains 10 creative essays—not analytical studies of the work of others but essays that set forth original proposals. This part of the book was never given the credit it deserved.

The essay "95 Theses for the 450th Anniversary of the Reformation" should be read every year on Reformation Sunday (a day most Baptists probably could not identify). His essay on "Politics and Religion" was ahead of its time and is especially relevant today. With all the anti-God literature flooding the market, Montgomery again was ahead of his time with "Is Man His Own God?" and "The Descent and Ascent of God," which should be read Christmas and Ascension Sunday (another day most Baptists probably could not identify).

Three of these final essays buried themselves in my young theologically sponge-like mind. First was "Renewal and Contemporary Theology." Gerhard Szczesny had challenged Christian theologians by claiming that the period of widespread unbelief would simply be prolonged as long as we Christians continued to insist that salvation depends upon acceptance of Christian postulates as true. Montgomery showed why that dog won't hunt.

The initial elements of the so-called renewal movement were the substitution of nonverbal art forms, modern liturgical dance, and drama in place of the verbal proclamation of biblical truth. This was the beginning of the so-called seeker churches, and it fed the contemporary worship styles that are still dividing churches today.[6] Freshness and creativity are not offensive; loss of all tradition is. Doctrine is important, but so much of the praise and worship methodology oversimplifies the vast range of New Testament truth. It weakens the church, but it is very popular, and the number of attendees remains one of the most important evaluative criteria. That is not really the case, but that seems to be the case. As Joel Osteen says, he doesn't talk much about the exclusivity of Christ. He just wants people to learn to love one another and come to church. But narrow is the way that leads to life; broad is the way that leads to destruction.

Nevertheless, in the contemporary postmodern congregation, dialog replaces exposition of Scripture, contemporaneity replaces all historical forms of worship, and the focus is on personal spiritual needs or desires and less on appropriate means for approaching God. For the first time in history, the biblical Divine Being is thought of as enjoying seeing His worshippers jump, wave their arms, swallow phallic-shaped microphones, wear tight clothing, sing with both eyes closed, and regularly call out to the crowd to join in rhythmic clapping and pelvic rotations. What is the "image of God" unbelievers receive from such "renewals" in worship? Is this what God desires? If so, has the church been a constant displeasure to God for 2,000 years? The praise and worship style is a legitimate alternative to traditional worship, but it seems to be taking on a life of its own that has no room for historic worship forms. That is a great weakness.

A second renewal Montgomery saw that he felt was potentially a loss for the church was the desire to identify worship with secular involvement. All of this calls for doctrinal reconstruction, but often this effort does not restore historic orthodoxy. The issue is not motive. We can grant the motives, but we do not often see the spiritual results the modern church leadership has been seeking for the past 35 years. We simply cannot make the Christian message fit the desires of unregenerate secular humanistic man. Moreover, why have you heard from the modern pulpit so few prophetic messages against nuclear aggression or against economic or social policies that punish the poor? For sure, our individual sermons alone do not change foreign policy or national social policies (nor is that our proper focus), but Christian faith is not neutral on these issues. Just as the gospel transforms the mind, so it should be understood as a faith that impacts all of life.

Montgomery's extended essay on biblical authority (*Suicide*, 384ff) was my first introduction to inductive inerrancy, a position I soon adopted and have held throughout my career. The essay that is probably Montgomery's most significant (though it is today virtually forgotten) is "The Theologian's Craft." What do theologians do, and how do they do it? As a new theological Ph.D. student, I was hungry for essays like this one in the early 1970s.

This essay, however, focuses on what is probably one of Montgomery's less remembered essays yet one that I have never forgotten: "The Suicide of Christian Theology and a Modest Proposal for Its Resurrection." Two men are standing on a teeter-totter. The midpoint is on the edge of the abyss. One man stands over the land, the other on the end sticking out over the abyss. The man standing over nothing on his end of the board claims he is standing on faith alone, and the man over the land claims to be resting on well-grounded truths. The "faith alone" man has a gun aimed at the "traditional historical fact-based man." After much discussion the faith alone man becomes frustrated and pulls the trigger to rid himself of this old Fundy, and the bullet hits the mark. The grounded man stands for a while because he is strong, but the bullet strikes at a vulnerable place, and the old preacher weakens and falls. "Hooray!" the modern theologian cries. "The New Testament is now known to be unreliable.

Fundamentalism is dead. Now we can move on"—at which time the shooter begins to feel a little movement, as his end of the board, having nothing to rest upon, slowly sinks and collapses beneath him. His fall is especially devastating to his many followers who think they should take the leap of faith behind him, which they do to their own death as well.

When modern theologians fire what they think are fatal shots at Christian orthodoxy, they discover that they are in the process of eliminating the *raison d'être* for their own existence. Do liberals arise from nothing? No! Like Bart Ehrman, they often previously held to inerrancy and fundamentalist doctrine. I do not remember having a liberal professor that did not testify about having come from the conservative right. Dale Moody grew up with his later discarded Scofield Bible. John Hick and Clark Pinnock are further examples. Not all fit this model, but many do.

Montgomery had no problem illustrating the loss of meaning from *avant-garde* film. He also composed his famous "Parable of the Engineers" that revealed what really came from Barth, Bultmann, Tillich, Secular Theology, and Bishop Pike. Eventually the cathedral they thought they were building collapsed, killing them and all of those who had been visiting the construction site.

These names are no longer even recognized by many modern theological students, but the principles remain in the academic community. Modern theologians continue to destroy their own systems because they deny the full trustworthiness of the biblical revelation, which is the foundation of true faith. With graphic intensity, Montgomery argues that the gun was loaded in the eighteenth century, placed against the head in the nineteenth century, and first fired in the twentieth century.

Naturalistic Deism presented itself first as a counter religion. Hume, Lessing, and Thomas Paine shifted to natural law rather than biblical revelation as evidence for God's existence. Biblical revelation was considered superfluous. Man's moral nature was considered sufficient to reveal God's moral perfections.

Man's optimistic confidence grew in the nineteenth century by leaps and bounds in light of the new Darwinian versions of evolution. Evolution seemed to be scientifically established and therefore was more reliable than any ancient (prescientific) teaching claiming to be divine revelation.

Hume, Lessing, and Paine had no irrefutable arguments, and nineteenth century theologians apparently did not read or understand Hawthorne or Melville. The twentieth century, then, felt free to develop a new religion (though for most of the century it continued to call itself Christianity). It was evolutionary and willing to dismember Old and New Testament texts based on no textual evidence at all but based strictly on what the modernist thought was a reasonable stylistic analysis. It was relativistic and humanistic to the core.

Thus, triggers were pulled. Some, like Barth, gave first aid, but it was insufficient since Barth's evidence was existential. Barth conceded that science overwhelmed the miraculous claims of the Bible, and Bultmann then found room to argue that in order to save Christian faith it had to be demythologized. The gospel became "authentic self-understanding." But how does that relate to the Bible's version of authenticity? Where is the biblical version of self and self-understanding? Neatly, Tillich stepped in to propose "ultimate concern," and God as the "ground of being." It was all so simple in those days. A few more rounds and the dead would be down. Modern theology would commit suicide, which it did; God simply became "Being Itself."

Montgomery's 1970 article never saw it coming, though it is obvious today that Montgomery was on target. Within the decade of the 1980s, twentieth century theology transitioned into "postmodernism" and "new age" spirituality. By the twenty-first century, we don't seem to have any accurate descriptive names.

Theology today is evolutionary for the most part. It has adopted many aspects of naturalism in an effort to remain "credible" with the historians and philosophers in the secular universities. Biblical exposition is considered irrelevant. Exposition means to explain what the miracle-ridden text teaches (which is not evolutionary or naturalistic). Exposition assumes that an absolute set of values could be extracted from the biblical teaching and communicated to the people in the church and in the world. Exposition expects the reader to seek out the historical context, find the historic meaning, and apply that meaning to the new historical situation without misrepresentation.

Evangelicals all talk about exposition and write books on exposition, but in fact they teach topically, preach topically, and give their sermons and even their church activities topical names using non-historical, nonspecific language. This is our fellowship hall. Rev up the music, let's worship! This is our "worship center," recognized by video screens, sound equipment, and a wide stage at the front, with a few banners maybe but few if any Christian symbols on display in the building, especially no stained-glass images. Here is our Vacation Bible School. Kids are going to learn about the farm this year and space next year. Let me introduce you to our worship leader. Here is a copy of our pastor's latest book on sex and the good life. Here is our snack bar; we call it the Manna House.

Near the end of Montgomery's essay, he offered a proposal for a resurrected theology. Had he been heard, we would not be in the state of theological confusion in which the modern church finds itself. "The only hope for a resurrected theology lies in a recovery of confidence in the historic Christ and in the Scriptures He stamped with approval as God's Word" (p. 37).

Montgomery's apologetic method has remained consistent through the years. First establish the authenticity and general integrity of the biblical documents, then defend the historical accounts of the resurrection. Today we have Kenneth Kitchen's magisterial contribution, *On the Reliability of the Old Testament* (Grand Rapids: Eerdmans, 2003), and we have many titles that confirm and go beyond F. F. Bruce's classic *New Testament Documents: Are They Reliable?* (Grand Rapids: Eerdmans, 1960): for example, Josh McDowell, *New Evidence That Demands a Verdict* (Nashville: Thomas Nelson, 1999), and Gary Habermas, *The Historical Jesus* (Joplin: College Press, 1996). Numerous other Christian works confirm from every angle the undeniability of the resurrection of Christ. See also the more comprehensive work by Norman Geisler, *Christian Apologetics* (Grand Rapids: Baker, 1988).

Does the factual evidence still stand? Yes, the facts themselves still stand though they have been severely challenged in our day through the Jesus Seminar and other skeptical scholarly groups. Can we really believe in a literal resurrection? Naturalistic science would say no, but naturalism is not an absolute, and there is much to commend the reality of this historical claim. Has our science not broken the back of our evidence? Has our historical skepticism not overruled our literalistic faith? No and no! Naturalism is a philosophical method, and objective historical claims, if sufficiently well grounded, need not be overruled by naturalistic assumptions.

A summary of the evidence for the resurrection may seem unnecessary to some, but every generation must be retaught. Knowledge does not pass down through the genes. Without trying to be simplistic, a review of the evidence will be helpful to those who have forgotten how strong the evidence is and to those who never heard a rational case made for the resurrection. Many of our children made professions of faith based on personal experience under passionate pastoral and/or parental pleas. The emotion fades over time, however, and people begin to wonder just how literal they are expected to be regarding the resurrection. The Bible's case is very literal, however. Jesus literally died on the cross, was buried, and rose from the grave on the third day, being seen alive in His body by many witnesses. This is the heart of all true Christian witnesses. If this is not true, Paul says Christian faith is in vain. The evidence can be classified under seven categories. I have briefly summarized that evidence below:

The Fact of the Unique Resurrection of Jesus:

1. *Jesus died.*
   a. Romans did not make mistakes regarding death by crucifixion.
   b. Many who knew Jesus personally stood at the foot of the cross and reported the events.
   c. Mary his mother was there. She would have recognized the supposed fraud as claimed by Islam. Mothers will recognize their children.
   d. The man on the cross never denies that he is Jesus, nor does he resist the crucifixion.
   e. The man on the cross is concerned about the welfare of Mary and asks John to care for her. Who else but Jesus would have had such concerns?

    f.   The man on the cross sought forgiveness for the soldiers. Who but Jesus would do that?

    g.   The man on the cross offered paradise to the believing thief. Who but Jesus?

    h.   His legs were not broken, his side was pierced, and his issue of blood and water (from the lungs and the enlarged sac around the heart) indicate certain death.

    i.   Pilate was skeptical and had the death verified before agreeing to release the body to Joseph and Nicodemus.

2. *Jesus was buried.*

    a.   Joseph of Arimathea offered a new tomb with no other bones in it.

    b.   Nicodemus, a respected Pharisee, was also there.

    c.   Romans guarded the tomb until the first day of the week. They knew what happened, and their lie about the body being stolen was never very convincing.

    d.   Orthodox Jews then and now are greatly concerned about proper burial. The women were up early to complete the burial process. There is no way the location of this tomb would be lost. If in fact it had not been empty on the first day of the week, the location would have become a memorial site.

    e.   Jesus was laid out and buried on a ledge under spices and a shroud. The body was not broken up and put in an ossuary. This may have been what the women would have wanted to do eventually, after the decay process was complete, but they reported that they did not find the body. Angels reported His resurrection, and the women reported what they had seen and heard, including personal encounters with the risen Jesus.

3. *The tomb of Jesus on the first day of the week was empty.*

    a.   The round stone that had sealed the tomb had been rolled away so that visitors could see inside and go inside.

    b.   The place where the body of Jesus had been laid was empty. Only the linen grave clothes remained. The body was gone. The testimony here is virtually unanimous. It was a new tomb. There were no old bones or old bodies or old ossuaries in this tomb.

   c.   Contrary to the type of testimony one might expect, the earliest witnesses were women. This is not to be taken as evidence based on supposed claims that women were untrustworthy. These women were known personally by the disciples. Their testimony was considered to be trustworthy. The point is not that prejudice would have caused the women's testimony to be discounted because they were women. Jesus certainly would not have taught his disciples to hold such views about women. It is just the opposite. The women were first due to their love for Jesus and their concern for cleaning and caring for the body. It was a gracious honor for them to be the first believing witnesses (the unbelieving soldiers were the first humans to see what had happened). The fact that it was believing women (not believing men) who gave the first testimony is irrelevant to the gender debates. The women were first because they were physically there first. The story as we have it does have a significance we have almost always overlooked, however. It proves that the disciples did not expect the resurrection. It was a surprise, not a plot to deceive. The Gospels record the women's initial testimony because of its factual character and later confirmed nature. Had they expected the resurrection, the disciples would have gone with the women at dawn (as they did later in the morning), only becoming convinced when they saw the evidence for themselves. The tomb was empty.

4.   *Jesus was seen alive by those who knew Him prior to the crucifixion.*
   a.   He met with His disciples in the upper room twice, on the road to Emmaus, and in Galilee.
   b.   He verified His wounds for Thomas.
   c.   He revealed Himself to men and women.
   d.   Hundreds of people saw Him in Galilee apparently at the same time, but the context excludes mass

> hallucination. The profound Great Commission comes out of these testimonies regarding His appearances and His postresurrection teachings.

e. He traveled from Jerusalem to Galilee and back, perhaps more than once.

f. He ate real food (fish, honeycomb) with His disciples more than once. He had fellowship with them in intimate, personal settings. There was no deceit here. Over and over it was confirmed that Jesus Himself was sitting or standing before them (indoors and outdoors).

g. Over more than a month He continually taught the disciples how best to explain His earlier teachings. These meaningful explanations are found throughout the rest of the New Testament and are evidences of His identity.

5. *Jesus ascended bodily into heaven.*

a. This event was visible to the disciples and was reported in detail in the first chapters of Acts. Scripture does not explicitly say, but the story reads so literally (a clear narrative with dialogue) that it is not unlikely that even non-disciples could have seen the ascension if they had been nearby).

b. None of this was ever denied by the disciples, even under persecution.

c. The church soon began to worship on the first day of the week.

   i. This is in commemoration of the resurrection.

   ii. This is in spite of the strong Jewish (Sabbath) traditions in the early Christian community.

d. A promise of His return to earth was made at the time of His ascension. This continues to be a precious and believable promise.

e. Luke, in Acts 1, mentions the physical location of the ascension. The Mount of Olives remains part of the Jerusalem landscape today. The event was outdoors in a public area. The disciples (excepting Judas Iscariot) all saw the same event and heard the same angel's words.

6. *Christ appears even after His ascension.*
    a. To Stephen at his stoning in Jerusalem.
    b. To Paul in the blinding light on the Damascus Road.
    c. To John in his glorious vision on the isle of Patmos.
    d. Others had personal postascension encounters as well. Peter saw the animals in his vision and heard the heavenly voice. Paul, blind in Damascus, was visited by a believer who revealed to him the true message of the gospel. Phillip was led to the Ethiopian.

7. *Christian testimony confirms the living presence of Christ over the past 20 centuries.*
    a. This is an ongoing personal relationship, not simply a personal experience.
    b. This is the result of personal promises made to the disciples by Christ Himself: "Lo, I will be with you always, even unto the end of the world."
    c. This relationship is sealed by the Holy Spirit.

This is Montgomery's message. This is the Christian claim. It is literal to the core. Does any other religion make such claims and then encourage you to test them? Christianity is not afraid of the truth. Jesus is the way, the truth, and the life. Is this what you believe? Denying or giving up this living, historical faith is suicide. John Warwick Montgomery gave the largest part of his intellectual career to preventing the suicide of theology. May he find a host of young apologists to join him in his quest. The evidence is sufficient. It only needs to be collected and presented to the skeptical and opinionated juries of the world with earnest prayer that the Holy Spirit will turn the hearts of men to believe.

L. Russ Bush, Director
Center for Faith and Culture
Southeastern Baptist Theological Seminary

Endnotes

1   John Warwick Montgomery, *The Shaping of America* (Minneapolis: Bethany Fellowship, 1976), which by the way listed 31 published works as of 30 years

ago. The current list I found at www.jwm.christendom.co.uk_shows him as author of 41 titles and editor of 13 titles.

2   John Warwick Montgomery, *The Law Above the Law* (Minneapolis: Bethany Fellowship, 1975): why the law needs biblical foundations, and how legal thought supports Christian truth.

3   John W. Montgomery, ed., *Evidence for Faith* (Dallas: Word; Probe, 1991), a wide-ranging collection.

4   John Warwick Montgomery, *Where Is History Going?* (Grand Rapids: Zondervan, 1969), a book that led me to select Montgomery as one of the theologians/historians to whom I dedicated a chapter in my dissertation.

5   John Warwick Montgomery, *Tractatus Logico-Theologicus* (Bonn: Culture and Science Publications, 2005), a Christian version of Wittgenstein's *Tractatus*.

6   How "renewal" can justify dividing devout believers so severely is beyond me. Praise and worship styles show the power of music and emotion. Modern praise songs demonstrate the worship sensibilities of the current generation, but they do not improve biblical literacy or doctrinal knowledge. How then can this be theological renewal?

Part II

THE NATURE OF NATURE

Nature and Nature's God

DISAPPEARING TOGETHER?

Harold O. J. Brown

"In the middle of my life," wrote Dante, "I found myself in the middle of a dark wood."[1] At 35, he was still young and vigorous, but he could sense old age approaching. Where are we in the West, particularly in my United States, not yet two and one-half centuries old as a nation? Is America in the prime of life, or *al fine?*

At the beginning of our national history, Americans knew that "all men are created equal, and endowed by their Creator with certain unalienable rights." Do we still believe that? For many, perhaps for most, that confidence is still there. How long will it last if the new generations are persuaded that there is no Creator to have endowed us? With no Creator, from whence will our rights come? Will we plunge into the madness extolled by Nietzsche, himself on the verge of insanity, to be ruled by the will to power? Or will we drift into the pathetic abandonment of purpose implied by Jean-Paul Sartre's statement that man is nothing but a useless passion, *une passion inutile?*

The concept of creation, that we human beings were created by the infinite and all-wise God with a purpose and with a destiny, is being levered out of the minds of the young by the relentless promotion of a concept of evolution, praised as pure science that denies every alternative. From the six times 24 hours of creation that emerge from a strictly literal interpretation of the first chapter of Genesis, the first book in the Bible, to the inference that biological life itself requires us to think of intelligent design, every alternative to a materialistic evolution is resolutely condemned by a vociferous majority of scientists, by the educational establishment, and of course by the American Civil Liberties Union, People for the American Way, and all the other usual suspects, to borrow a word from the *commissaire de police* in *Casablanca.*

The eminent biologist Richard Dawkins boasts that evolution is the total and complete explanation of life on earth, happily liberating us from the superstitious veneration of the supposed Creator. Only a few other scientists go so far as to assert that their knowledge puts God out of the picture. Very few others, especially the educators, and certainly none of the civil libertarians, are willing to concede, much less to boast, that they are making God superfluous. What they do is draw up in line of battle to ward off even the moderate suggestion that living beings, from the cell to the whale, bear evidence of intelligent design. Such design would inevitably suggest not merely great intelligence but something resembling omniscience, a quality to be found only in God. It is difficult to see the vigorous denunciations of even the mildest efforts to suggest intelligent design as an alternative to naturalistic evolution as anything but the effort to banish all thoughts of the Creator from the minds of the public.

The Divided Field of Truth

Most scientists and educators, with few exceptions, will protest that they do not exclude the possibility that God is real. They simply say that that is a religious question. People have a right to be religious, but they must not confuse religion with science. This creates what we call the divided field of truth. Certain things are true scientifically: that we know. Others may be true in the religious realm, but that is not science. It is faith. We understand nature through science, and we leave religion to faith. We live and breathe, eat and sleep, grow and eventually die in the realm of nature. We know those things to be true. Are we wise when we think of another, independent realm, accessible only to faith, or are we being foolish and self-deluded? How we answer this question is relevant to the question with which we began, whether we are in the middle or at the end, for if there is no reality beyond that which evolutionary science can show us, there is no difference between the scientist and the high priest, no difference between the king and the subject, the banker and the beggar, the athlete and the couch potato. All will die and be forgotten. The earth will die too, whether by cold or in the heart of an exploding sun.

Extinction and ultimate meaninglessness is not what the evolutionists want us to think. If some of us turn to God in prayer, and that makes us happy, they are willing to leave us in that comforting illusion. But we must not claim to see any connection between the prayers of religion and the reality of biological life.

Did the reader notice this claim of the most strident voices of evolutionary science, that there is no connection between what science knows, namely how life has evolved, and what religion asserts, namely that God created it? The militant evolutionists claim that there is no life that cannot be explained by what they call science alone, excluding all possibilities lying outside of the reach of its instruments. The claim of advocates of intelligent design is that true science will be open to examine things in nature that seem to point beyond mere biological process to prior design, and of course ultimately to a Designer. The late German theologian Paul Althaus contended that God has deliberately revealed Himself in nature, first by constructing it so that principles of His design are evident, and then by endowing us, His creatures, with minds that can discern them. In other words, there is something there that the Creator intends for us to find. Althaus calls it God's self-disclosure in nature. It is precisely this that the naturalistic evolutionist will not tolerate.

The struggle between evolution and intelligent design can be won by the naturalistic evolutionists only if they can maintain an absolute division in the field of truth. The advocates of intelligent design argue that the complexity of biological life points to something beyond it, to design and by implication to a Designer. The ardent partisans of naturalistic evolution say that the complexity, which they acknowledge to be there, points back behind itself to the first cell, behind that to the first molecules, to the first atoms, to the first instant of reality, to the Big Bang.

The advocates of evolution as the explanation for everything accuse their opponents of seeing visions, of dreaming of images without solid feet on the ground of reality. The defenders of intelligent design know that they are being confronted not by commendable scientific skepticism but by a presupposition, by the denial that there is anything there to see. This is a persistent refusal to look beyond what they think they know to see things, if they are really there, that point to something they do not want to see, to design, to a Designer. Natural science in general, and naturalistic evolution in particular, refuses to see that in its zeal to discover how things came to be, it fails to answer, or even to ask, the questions of First Cause and Final Cause. What or who caused the chain of events they seek to understand, and to what end was it caused?

The question of First Cause cannot be answered by natural science, but it can at least be asked. That is precisely what the currently reigning evolutionists and educators refuse to do, and what they do not want their students to dare. But if there is no First Cause, there is no Final Cause. As to the future of the United States, or of Western Civilization, or of the entire inhabited earth, it makes little difference whether we are still at the beginning, at the middle, or at the end.

If we in the United States, the strongest and richest power of the West, lose our confidence in intelligent design, that is to say, if we no longer believe that we are created for a purpose and have a dignity conferred by our Creator, will we be able to stand against the terrorists with whom we wage war? Without a Creator and without a Judge, *homo homini lupus*, man is a wolf to man. Where there is no vision, the Proverb says, the people perish (Prov 29:18). If we wish to have a future as a nation, not merely as a mass of biological specimens, we must have a vision that looks beyond the self-explaining cell to its Designer.

How Long Can America Survive?

Nations are not like people. Human years, biblically speaking, are three score and ten. Few are they who live much longer. Some cities, by contrast, seem to endure almost eternally: *Roma aeterna* was born in 753 B.C. It was still flourishing as the capital of an Empire a thousand years later. Britain's glory days lasted less than two centuries, and Hitler's New Order only a dozen years. The great seal of the United States, still visible on the back side of the one-dollar bill, contains the Latin words, NOVUS ORDO SECLORUM: the New Order of the Ages. How well is our new order holding up? After her hard-fought victory in the Second Punic War, Rome rose to dazzling heights and endured as an empire for six centuries. Half a century after our glorious victories in World War II, we may well ask whether our power shall last longer than Britain's.

Our society is rich, our stores full, our celebrations lavish. In the "holiday season" of 2005, the name of which was not pronounced, new records were reached. We wallow in luxuries—not every one of us but enough to make the picture accurate. Our stores are full; in Charlotte even grocery stores offer wines from hundreds of vineyards all around the world. Yes, there is poverty; yes, there are millions without health insurance; yes, some are homeless. Nevertheless, the vision of the United States at the beginning of the new millennium reveals a society surfeited with dainties, as Calvin put it.

In Eric Maria Remarque's *Arch of Triumph* (1945), the madam of a Paris brothel evokes the apprehensive mood of the summer of 1939: "Even the French are drinking champagne." Our stores are full of champagne, even the real thing at $40 a bottle and dozens of imitations from the wonderful to that which can at best be called bubbly. Do we have the answer to the question raised by Sorokin on the last page of *The Crisis of Our Age* (1941): Will we receive the grace of understanding and have the courage to make the right decisions to continue man's divine creative vision on earth? Or shall we experience instead the *dies irae*, the fiery day of wrath in which the earth dissolves in ashes?

After the Victories

In the third quarter of the last century, the United States had achieved total victory over two of the greatest and most malevolent war machines that the earth had known. Great Britain, also victorious, did not outlast her success. The powerful Soviet Union grew alarmingly strong and increasingly menacing. Until the last decade of the century, it was deemed entirely possible, and by a few inevitable, that the Great Powers would destroy each other and the earth would *solvere in favilla*, dissolve in ashes. Now we no longer fear that. The threat has receded but changed, not disappeared. We continue to wallow in our wealth, but we are not at ease for "We are at war!" It is not a war like those we have won in the past, against Nazi Germany or Imperial Japan. We face mysterious adversaries who strike from the shadows: terrorists.

This new kind of war began when 3,000 human beings were callously murdered on one September morning. We seek to protect ourselves, not with general mobilization or self-sacrifice but with selected engagements overseas and the Patriot Act at home. We certainly lack the zeal of 1917 or 1941. More and more of us are like those described in the Epistle to the Hebrews: "Through fear of death all our life long subject to slavery." Unlike the unknown author of Hebrews, we do not know anyone who can render powerless those who have the power of death (Heb 2:14–15). And so we are ill at ease. Rome was still wealthy when the barbarians began to swarm over her frontiers. Is it possible that our marvelous society—with its wealth, its weapons, its medical miracles, its glittering towers—can go down into the ash heap of history like the Rome of the Caesars?

In *The Camp of the Saints*, Jean Raspail envisages hundreds of thousands of the wretched of the earth crossing the seas to invade the Mediterranean coast of France, where the rich were basking in the beauty of nature and the comforts of their wealth. No one knows what to do. The French military, the navy first and then the army, refuse to fight against the pitiful wretches who are flooding their land. The intellectuals and the churches preach brotherhood, unable to grasp that they are laying their lands over to destruction. Whom does the French military attack? It destroys a tiny group of men trying to defend themselves against the mob.

Looking at the Rome of the fourth century, rich and powerful, we may ask why their leaders did not react with measures that would help save the empire while they still had the resources with which to do it. Looking at ourselves in the twenty-first century, one may well ask why we see that what the terrorists are doing to our towers and to our soldiers is but nibbles compared to what we are doing to ourselves.

Having Eyes, We See Not

On September 11, 2001 3,000 perished in the World Trade towers. Millions across the country saw that as it was happening on network television. Hundreds of millions around the world have now seen it. That same September day, 4,000 perished in America's hospitals and abortion clinics, 4,000 who would never see the sun or hear a song. Four thousand also perished the day before and the day after. We were told when the two thousandth American was killed in Iraq and when the thousandth convicted murderer was executed in America, but we do not know the day in 2001 when the millionth baby that year was aborted, nor the day in 2002, nor in any other year since *Roe v. Wade* (1973).

The terrorists kill by the dozens, by the hundreds, by the thousands. Our leaders tell us that they hate us, and that may be so. They kill us, motivated by a religious rage, the source and nature of which we do not dare to examine. Is this a danger? Indeed, it would be stupid to deny it. But how many terrorist attacks would it take to do to us in a year what we do to ourselves in a month? We ourselves, motivated by no passion, kill members, or would-have-been members, of our next generation by the hundreds of thousands, by the millions. That is the situation into which the people of the United States are plunging, in a stupor only momentarily relieved by the gaiety of a new "holiday" season. How can we fail to see the contradiction inherent in going to war for the sake of 3,000 killed, while at the same time bleeding ourselves to death by millions of abortions?

Whatever one may think about abortion, whether or when it is justifiable, can anyone of sound mind believe that it is good for a nation to kill, "safely and legally," as President Clinton used to say, one-quarter to one-third of every new generation? Can the members of Congress, as they stand on the steps of the Capitol to sing "God Bless America," not see the contradiction in asking the Deity to protect them from those who killed 3,000 of ours while they endorse killing 4,000 more every day?

Forgetting God, Forgetting Man

In his 1978 Harvard commencement address, published as *A World Split Apart*, Aleksandr Solzhenitsyn cried, "Men have forgotten God." Great trouble is associated with the forgetting. "It is he that hath made us, and not we ourselves," says the psalmist (Ps 100:3 KJV). The story of creation by God fills the first two chapters of the Hebrew Scriptures. Faith in God the Creator is the first declaration of the classical creeds of Christendom: "Creator of heaven and earth," says the Apostles' Creed, "and of all things visible and invisible," adds the Nicene Creed. How can we, in a nation where three-fourths of the people profess Christianity, forget the Creator and the act of creation that begins the Bible and the great creeds? For a century and a half we have been putting forward views that make the creation a process of uncreated nature, not an act of God.

Denial of creation means denial of the Creator and thereby deprives human beings of their greatest dignity, namely that they are made in His image (Gen 1:26). The principle of the origin of species by survival of the fittest would lead us logically to suppose that there are differences between the human races and from that to think that certain races may be fitter and others less fit for survival. The doctrine that we are all made in the image of the Creator is the only solid basis for teaching the equality of all human beings, of all of the races of man. It is not yet apparent how far denial of that creation may take us in the transformation of our world. Today we have abortions for many reasons, or for any reason at all, as the late Justice Byron White warned in his dissent in *Roe v. Wade*. Is the day far away when we begin to breed humans for quality and selectively weed out those who are less than the best?[2]

In this land where in moments of fear we sing "God Bless America" and address Him in song as "Great God, our King," few will dare to say, "There is no God." The question is, why do we then act *etsi Deus non daretur*, as though God were not there?[3] We have no one to have created us. We just happened. The dignity of being made in the image of God is gone. As Sorokin wrote, we are stripped of our invisible armor and can deal with one another just as we please.

We do not hate our human nature, at least not consciously. But we act as though we do. Why do we not understand what we are doing to ourselves? Why do we acquiesce in the loss of the dignity we once shared, of Sorokin's "invisible armor" that made us worthier of protection than the animals? Forgetting God, we forget that we were made and did not just happen. To forget God means ultimately to forget man. Rejection of the concept of creation (not necessarily six times 24 hour creation, as I shall discuss below) does not mean to forget that man exists but to forget who he is and for what he exists.

In the years when the great Roman Empire was crumbling, Augustine, bishop of a small city in North Africa, prayed to God, "Thou has made us for thyself, and our hearts know no rest until they rest in thee." That knowledge offered comfort when Roman towers were falling. Today, with ever-increasing energy, we are telling all those who will listen that No One has made us and that where our hearts may rest we cannot imagine.

Denial of Reality

If the universe was created and we are designed and created with a purpose, as Americans used to take for granted, then to deny intelligent design and with it every possibility of creation is to move from the real world into a world of imagination. The struggle between evolution in the absolute sense—in which there is no Creator, no plan, no design, and no purpose—and even the most moderate suggestion of intelligent design is not a scientific struggle: it is a spiritual or metaphysical one. As naturalistic evolution tries to tell us *how* all that is came to be, it does not only not tell us *who* and *why*; it tells us not to ask. It is not the advocates of intelligent design who seek to suppress inquiry but its opponents.

Among their other logical flaws, they beg the question, presupposing the desired result. Science, that is to say naturalistic evolution (just "evolution," its advocates say), has no room for intelligent design because intelligent design is not scientific. It is religious, and science and religion must be kept separate. In this divided field of truth, there must be no crossover between science and religion. The study of living organisms is what science does. Intelligent design suggests that within living organisms we find signs that point beyond them, to design. Is it scientific to exclude, permanently and *a priori*, that possibility? We are not to think such a thing because, in effect, it would be unscientific to suppose that there is anything science does not know and cannot eventually find out.

Religion and science must be kept separate, and a designer of any kind, not to mention the Divine Designer who is surely suggested, means the interference of religion in science. Science is by definition not religious, so finding a place of interaction between the two is not scientific. To say this is to presuppose *a priori* that the thing we do not accept does not exist. This will not help us find it. If Paul Althaus's suggestion is true, that it is the intention of the Creator that we should find evidence of Him in the world of reality, to refuse to look is not science; it is rebellion.

Darwin and the Terrorists

In the nineteenth century, Charles Darwin discovered the method by which he believed species might evolve from lower orders to higher, the survival of the fittest by natural selection. If he is correct in every respect, then the terrorists we fear are merely trying to prove themselves fitter than we are, which is precisely what they ought to do if they are to evolve, and culture with them. We should honor them even as we fight them in the next stage of the struggle for survival. It is at this point impossible to say that they are wrong and we are right or that they are evil and we are less so. We simply must wait to see who wins.

Darwin's insight fed materialists such as Ludwig Feuerbach, for whom man is nothing but the sum of all of the matter of which he is made: *Man ist, was man isst* (one is what one eats). God is a projection of human ideals, and theology is really anthropology. God is dead, Nietzsche wrote, and man is his own master. He died in 1900, when the world looked bright, *la belle époque*. Two decades later Europe began an orgy of self-destruction in World War I. France emerged victorious, aided at the crucial moment by the United States. Fifty years after Nietzsche, when France lay under the feet of Hitler's *Wehrmacht*, the existentialist Jean-Paul Sartre drew the logical conclusion of forgetting God: man is nothing but a useless passion, *une passion inutile*.

Unlike so many of our scientists, the terrorists have not forgotten God as they conceive Him. They see in us idolaters or unbelievers. It is probably more correct to say that they hold us in contempt than in hatred. We do well to fear them, at least to be aware of the danger that they bring. We would do better to be even more aware that we are becoming our own worst enemies. The terrorists kill by the dozens; we kill ourselves by the millions. Few in number, the terrorists can wound us but cannot destroy us.

Far worse than what terrorists can do to us is what we shall do to ourselves when, consciously or unconsciously, we see ourselves as nothing but *passions inutiles*. Certainly the terrorists do not respect us, our values, our civilization. Their contempt is a danger but not the worst. We are moving by degrees, ever more rapidly, to a state of mind in which first we no longer respect ourselves, our civilization, our culture, and—alas—our God. What good will it then do us to stand on the steps of our federal buildings singing "God Bless America"?

A Worse Nihilism

As Pascal Bruckner writes in *The Sob of the White Man* (*Le sanglot de l'homme blanc*, 1986), we heirs of Western Christendom are teaching our children disrespect for us and ultimately for themselves. We may never reach the point of hating ourselves, but if we teach our children that those who built our society—dead, white, and male, most of them—deserve no respect, we might as well hate ourselves. The result will be the same. This is what Bruckner laments the French are doing, and we are doing it as well. If we can see no good in the society we have built, we can see no evil in terrorism, even when it destroys towers and decapitates prisoners. We must ask ourselves not, "What are they doing?" not, "How can we stop them?" Instead, our question should be, "What have we done to deserve this?"

This is precisely where the French are now. They are now feeling the vicious blows of people who cannot respect them even as they do not respect themselves. And their intellectuals cannot see the evil in it. Years ago, long before the recent riots in France, the French philosopher Alain Finkelkraut wrote, "The worst of all nihilisms is that which pretends that evil does not exist." If the hands of the clock cannot indicate midnight, they cannot indicate the daylight hours. In the wake of the worst civil disturbances that France has had since the French Revolution, President Jacques Chirac, far from calling evil by its name, has offered to do more to help the rebels integrate into France. Commenting on this, M. Finkelkraut asked: How it is possible to acculturate people to a culture that no longer exists? The Sob of the White Man? Our problem, as Aleksandr Solzhenitsyn said in his 1978 Harvard University commencement address, is that "men have forgotten God." This is not the work of a few dictators or philosophers alone. It is promoted by the scientists who see nothing but blind nature and by the lawyers who find any other suggestion an attempt to establish religion. Darwin did not cause all that; it had already begun. He gave it a powerful thrust forward with his substitution of natural selection for any divine design.

Loss of Dignity, Loss of Purpose

Our best and brightest continue to imagine that we are on the road to progress, led by them, hampered only by the ignorance of religious believers and moral conservatives. We cannot speak for the whole human race or for the whole earth. Others think differently than we do, with different priorities. This the suicide bombers show us. They are willing to die for an ideal, or more precisely for a vision of God, which we do not understand. Will our vision of progress, if it is all that we have, outlast their vision of jihad?

Let us speak for ourselves, we the sobbing white men—and women—of our Western, increasingly post-Christian civilization in Europe and North America. Do we have a vision that will stand up to theirs? Or, with the loss of design, have we forgotten our own *raison d'etre*, our reason for being? The evolutionists are telling our children we are only mildew on the clock of time. Forget God, as the Soviet Union did so energetically, and we shall soon find that He has forgotten us.

In the West we have not necessarily swallowed all the science of Darwin or of the far more advanced scientists who succeed him, but we certainly have swallowed the implications. Ultimately man has no more dignity than any other animal: to be fed and cared for when productive, to be eliminated when useless or dangerous. Those implications were anticipated but only vaguely in evidence in the Victorian England of Darwin's day. Today they are present everywhere in the West, even in the United States. Here there still seems to be a residue of strength and sense of purpose. Give us another generation of forgetting God, and the consequences will be undeniable and inescapable.

For 16 centuries, since the beginning of the Christianization of Europe, men and women had accepted the thought that they are made in the image of God the Creator, "to know, love, and serve Him in this world and to be happy with Him forever in the next," as the old *Baltimore Catechism* (Roman Catholic) says. That idea, in the various forms it was expressed, gave to human beings dignity, purpose, and promise. "For what is a man profited, if he shall gain the whole world, and lose his own soul?" Jesus asked his disciples (Matt 16:26 KJV). Those who determined to follow him could accept destitution in this world because of their hope of heaven. Martin Luther wrote, "Let goods and kindred go, this mortal life also; the body they may kill, God's truth abideth still; His kingdom is forever." All this our evolutionists and educators would have us forget, dreams of a world that no longer exists except in the minds of the dreamers.

Victory or Death

Will the Darwinians win? Will human beings learn to think of themselves as nothing more than intermediate beings in a biological process without cause or purpose? If we see our dignity in having developed from the lesser primates, from the various *homines* who preceded *homo sapiens*, will we then realize that we are only way stations on the road to greater progress, to races that will be as far superior to us as we are to the apes, or to the chipmunks? If we give in to the present widespread pattern that this is the voice of science and reason, it will be because we did not examine it thoroughly enough. We are not being persuaded that naturalistic evolution is the total and complete answer but are having it forced upon us by rhetoric based on logical flaws.

To point this out is not to answer the question whether naturalistic evolution is the only truth but rather to ask why it is being forced on us at the expense of logic and common sense. Do its advocates not give the general public credit for being able to spot logical flaws? It is true that in the new world of TV spots, the Internet, and blogs, logic is not prized. Still the flaws should be pointed out. If we believed that there is no answer other than naturalistic evolution, it would be appropriate to submit to its advocates. But if we notice that, rather than examining the alternatives, they reject them out of hand, riding roughshod over the logical inconsistencies in their arguments, we must wonder if they are fighting, not for truth but for their faith, or rather for their counterfeit for faith, the doctrine that we explain everything.

First, the whole presupposition not of evolution itself but of the evolutionists' case for suppressing intelligent design begs the question. Intelligent design must not be taught or even examined in science classes because it is not science. Science is confined to those things that are capable of investigation and proof by the normal methods of science, and intelligent design is only an inference from evidence. It cannot be tested and verified and therefore is not scientific. The difficulty with that position is that evolution itself is not a science by that standard. It was not observed and it cannot be repeated. If an evolutionary process could be repeated under controlled conditions in a laboratory, it would only prove that under certain circumstances, namely those provided by intelligent scientists, it can occur. It would prove neither that it can occur without intelligence creating the conditions, nor that, even if it could have, it did occur in the far distant past. If a detective establishes the possibility that a suspect could have committed a murder, the possibility does not prove that he did commit it. To state that what cannot be observed or verified by scientific proof is not science destroys the claim that evolution is scientific.

Evolution is a theory derived from myriad observations, measurements, and interpretations of data. Let us say, a very good theory, especially if we presuppose that there is no outside force, and certainly no supernatural force, that could possibly have influenced it. But that presupposition excludes *a priori* any evidence that might appear to point to an outside force and hence any evidence for intelligent design. One may accept evolution because one believes that the evidence is persuasive; but in the absence of proof, one must not insist that no other process can be considered.

Why do the evolutionists neglect this evident weakness in their case and proceed energetically to attack the alternative? They do so because they are apparently under the influence of two logical flaws: the false continuum and the false dichotomy. The rhetoric of the evolutionists and their legal representatives assumes a total dichotomy between naturalistic evolution and all other possible interpretations. If one does not hold to the evolutionary position, it makes no difference to what position one does hold, one is off of the playing field. This is rather like saying on the abortion issue that one must either accept abortion as a right at any time during pregnancy and for any reason or condemn every abortionist and woman procuring an abortion as murderers. There are many levels of crime between innocence and first-degree murder. Another false dichotomy is that proposed between totally legal abortion and millions of back-alley abortions. Either the unplanned baby will be aborted safely and legally, in a clinic, or the mother will risk her life in a back-alley abortion. This does not take into account that women not granted a legal abortion might simply decide to bring the child to birth.

To the false dichotomy, either evolution or creation, they then add a false continuum, or the fallacy of the undistributed mean. If one is an antievolutionist, then one is essentially the same as those who teach that the world was created quite recently in six times 24 hours. Just as the aggressive evolutionist will not admit that there are any scientific positions other than one that does not exclude design, he assumes that there is no alternative to evolution that does not teach the literal interpretation of the Genesis account is true and that to accept it as the Word of God and therefore true means accepting six times 24 hours as the time span of creation.

Not all of those who think that evolution occurred are evolutionists in this sense, and not all of those who believe that God created are creationists in the sense of six-day creation. It is reasonable to call people who believe in creation creationists, but it creates a false continuum to say that they all believe that everything happened in 144 hours.

An even deadlier aspect of the false continuum is the assertion (a) that those who believe in creation want to impose religion, especially fundamentalist Christianity, and (b) that part of their design is to create a theocracy, a state ruled by God, or by His agents, the church, and her priests. It actually makes at least as much sense, if not more, to say that those who want only evolution taught as science want to destroy Christianity and every theistic religion with it. That is, or should be, a false continuum. Indeed, there are believers in the process of evolution who also believe in God. Recently the Vatican pronounced that creation and evolution are compatible with each other.

Will a statement such as this satisfy the evolutionists? It would, if the defense of their theory were their only goal. From the ongoing debates it should be clear that it is not. Their goal, implicit for some and explicit for others, is the denial of creation, and with it of the Creator. It might be reasonable for the courts to rule that schools may not teach intelligent design as science, but only if they also rule that they may not teach evolution as science, but only as the religion, or antireligion, of atheism.

Where are we as a nation? In the middle or at the end? If material nature is all there is and naturalistic evolution is the total explanation, whether we deny creation or not will make little difference. The world will go on in its course and our nation with it. If on the other hand we are created, as our Declaration of Independence asserts, and we choose as a matter of principle to deny it and to prevent it from being taught in school, we may find that the Creator will not listen when we sing "God Bless America." Why should He?

Endnotes

1 *Inferno I*, canto 2.
2 The Chinese now weed out many unborn girls. Our own extreme feminists would like to weed out boys. Perhaps in a nightmare future that could lead to a Chinese-American war between the sexes.
3 Dietrich Bonhoeffer (1906–1945) wrote this in the years of total Nazi control of Germany. By it he meant that we should act responsibly and not depend on God's coming to pull us out of a hole into which we had plunged ourselves. He certainly did not mean to deny God. What we are doing today is to act irresponsibly, as though there were no God to judge us.

Evolution as Alchemy

William A. Dembski

In its heyday alchemy was a comprehensive theory of change. It described not only changes of base into precious metals but also changes of the soul up and down the great chain of being. Alchemy was not just a physics but also a metaphysics. Alchemy as metaphysics attracts interest to this day, as in Carl Jung's writings about the soul and personal identity. As he noted,

> The alchemists sought for that effect which would heal not only the disharmonies of the physical world but inner psychic conflict as well, the "affliction of the soul," and they called this effect the *lapis philosophorum* [i.e., the philosopher's stone]. In order to obtain it, they had to loosen the age-old attachment of the soul to the body and thus make conscious the conflict between the purely natural and the spiritual man.[1]

Alchemy's metaphysical aspirations aside, to include alchemy as part of the natural sciences is nowadays regarded as hopelessly misguided. The scientific community rejects alchemy as superstition and commends itself for having successfully debunked it. For scientists the problem with alchemy is that it fails to specify the processes by which transmutations are supposed to take place. An overused Sidney Harris cartoon illustrates the point. The cartoon shows two scientists viewing a chalkboard. The chalkboard displays some fancy equations, a gap, and then some more fancy equations. In the gap are written the words: "Then a miracle occurs." Pointing to the gap, one scientist remarks to the other, "I think you should be more explicit here." This is the problem with alchemy. To characterize a transformation scientifically, it needs to be specified explicitly. Alchemy never did this. Instead, it continually offered promissory notes, promising that some day it would make the transformation explicit. None of the promissory notes was ever redeemed. Indeed, the much sought-after philosopher's stone remains to be found.[2]

Officially the scientific community rejects alchemy and has rejected it since the rise of modern science.[3] Unofficially, however, the scientific community has had a much harder time eradicating it. Indeed, I will argue that alchemical thinking pervades the fields of chemical and biological evolution.[4] This is not to deny that biological systems evolve. But unless the process by which one organism evolves into another (or by which nonliving chemicals organize into a first living form) is specified, evolution remains an empty word. And given that such specificity is often lacking, much (though not all) of what currently falls under evolutionary theory is alchemy by another name.

Alchemy followed a certain logic, and it is important to see the fallacy inherent in that logic. The problem with alchemy was not its failure to understand the causal process responsible for a transformation. It is not alchemy, for instance, to assert that a certain one-dimensional polypeptide (i.e., a properly linked chain of amino acids) will fold into the three-dimensional shape thereby yielding a functional protein. How polypeptides fold to form proteins is an open problem in biology. Three-dimensional proteins "evolve," one might say (in the literal etymological sense of the word as in *unrolling the potentialities inherent in a thing*), from suitably arranged one-dimensional polypeptides in suitable cellular contexts. This happens repeatedly and reliably. We can describe the transformation, but as yet we cannot explain how the transformation takes place. Ignorance about the underlying mechanism responsible for a transformation does not make the transformation alchemical.

Things transform into other things. Sometimes we can explain the process by which the transformation takes place; at other times we cannot. Sometimes the process requires an intelligent agent; sometimes no intelligent agent is required. Thus, a process that arranges randomly strewn Scrabble pieces into meaningful English sentences requires a guiding intelligence. On the other hand, the process by which water crystallizes into ice requires no guiding intelligence; lowering the temperature sufficiently is all that is needed. It is not alchemy that transforms water into ice. Nor is it alchemy that transforms randomly strewn Scrabble pieces into meaningful sentences. Nor, for that matter, is it alchemy that transforms a one-dimensional polypeptide into a functional protein, and that despite our ignorance about the precise mechanisms governing protein folding.

What, then, is the problem with alchemy? Alchemy's problem is its *lack of causal specificity*. Causal specificity means specifying a cause sufficient to account for an effect in question. Often we can specify the cause of an effect even if we cannot explain how the cause produces the effect. For instance, I may know from experience that shaking a closed container filled with a gas will cause the temperature of the gas to rise. Thus, by specifying the causal antecedents (i.e., a closed container filled with gas and my shaking it), I account for the container's rise in temperature. Nonetheless, I may have no idea why the temperature rises. Boltzmann's kinetic theory tells me that the temperature of the gas rises because temperature corresponds to average kinetic energy of the particles constituting the gas, and by shaking the container I impart additional kinetic energy to the particles. Boltzmann's theory enables me to explain why the temperature goes up. Even so, I do not need Boltzmann's theory to specify a cause that accounts for the temperature going up. For that, it is enough that I specify the causal antecedents (i.e., a closed container filled with gas and my shaking it).

Alchemy eschews causal specificity. Consider the standard example of alchemical transformation, the transmutation of lead into gold. No logical impossibility prevents potions and furnaces from acting on lead and turning it into gold. It may just be that we have overlooked some property of lead that, in combination with the right ingredients, allows it to be transformed into gold. But the alchemists of old never specified the precise causal antecedents that would bring about this transformation. Consequently, they lacked any compelling evidence that the transformation was even possible. Note: modern-day particle physicists can, in principle, transform lead into gold with their particle accelerators, smashing the lead into more elementary constituents and then reconstituting them as gold. But here the causal antecedents are specified and differ plainly from those considered by the alchemists (particle accelerators were not part of the alchemists' tool chest).

Causal specificity was evident in the examples considered earlier: Water cooled below zero degrees Celsius is sufficient to account for its turning to ice. A random collection of Scrabble pieces left in the hands of a literate, nonhandicapped English speaker is sufficient to account for the Scrabble pieces spelling a coherent English sentence. A given sequence of l-amino acids joined by peptide bonds within a cellular context is sufficient to account for it folding into a functional protein (for instance, the protein cytochrome c). In each of these cases the causal antecedent is specified and accounts for the effect in question. We may not be able to explain how the cause that was specified produces its effect, but we know that it does so nonetheless.

But how do we get from causal antecedents like lead, potions, and furnaces and end up with gold? The alchemists' conviction was that if one could find just the right ingredients to combine with lead, lead would transform into gold. Thereafter the transformation could be performed at will, and the alchemist who discovered the secret of transmutation would be rich (until, that is, the secret got out and gold became so common that it too became a base metal). Discovering the secret of transmutation was the alchemist's deepest hope. The interesting question for us, however, is the alchemist's reason for that hope. Why were alchemists so confident that the transmutation from base into precious metals could even be effected? From our vantage we judge their enterprise a failure and one that had no possibility of success (contemporary solid state physics giving the *coup de grâce*). But why were they unshaken in their conviction that with the few paltry means at their disposal (particle accelerators not being among them), they could transform base into precious metals? Put another way, why, lacking causal specificity, did they think the transformation could be effected at all?

Without causal specificity one has no empirical justification for affirming that a transformation can be effected. At the same time, without causal specificity, one has no empirical justification for denying that a transformation can be effected. There is no way to demonstrate with complete certainty that Dr. Jekyll cannot transform into Mr. Hyde by some unspecified process. Lack of causal specificity leaves one without the means to judge whether a desired transformation can or cannot be effected. Any conviction about the desired transformation being possible, much less inevitable, must therefore derive from considerations other than a causal analysis. But from where?

Enter metaphysics. The motivation behind alchemy was never scientific (as we use the term nowadays) but metaphysical. Alchemy is a corollary of Neoplatonic metaphysics. Neoplatonism held to a great chain of being in which all reality emanates from God (conceived as the One) and ultimately returns to God. The great chain of being is strictly hierarchical, so for any two distinct items in the chain, one is higher than the other. Now consider lead and gold. Gold is higher on the chain than lead (lead is a base metal; gold is a precious metal). Moreover, since everything is returning to God, lead is returning to God and on its way to God will pass through gold. Consequently, there is a natural pull for lead to pass through gold on its way to God. The alchemist's task is therefore not to violate nature but simply to help nature along. All lead needs is a small suitable catalyst to achieve gold. The modest means by which alchemists hoped to achieve the transformation of lead into gold thus seemed entirely reasonable (in particular, no particle accelerators would be required).

Here, then, is the fallacy in alchemy's logic. Alchemy relinquishes causal specificity yet confidently asserts that an unspecified process will yield a desired transformation. Lacking causal specificity, the alchemist has no empirical grounds for holding that the desired transformation can be effected. Even so, the alchemist remains convinced that the transformation can be effected because prior metaphysical beliefs ensure that some process, though for now unspecified, must effect the desired transformation. In short, metaphysics guarantees the transformation even if the empirical evidence is against it.

Alchemy continues to flourish to this day in the fields of chemical and biological evolution. Whereas classical alchemy was concerned with transforming base into precious metals, evolution is concerned with transforming batches of chemicals into organisms (i.e., chemical evolution) and then organisms into other organisms (i.e., biological evolution). Now, I do not want to give the impression that evolution is a completely disreputable concept. The concept has applications that are entirely innocent. Consider, for instance, finches evolving stronger beaks to break harder nuts or insects developing insecticide resistance. Evolution in such cases is nonproblematic. Why? Because of causal specificity. Microevolutionary changes like this happen repeatedly and reliably. Given certain organisms placed in certain environments with certain selective pressures, certain predictable changes will result. We may not understand the precise biochemical factors that make such microevolutionary changes possible, but the causal antecedents that produce microevolutionary changes are clearly specified. So long as we have causal specificity, evolution is a perfectly legitimate concept.

But what about evolution without causal specificity? Consider, for instance, chemical evolution as an explanation for the origin of life. For much of the scientific community, the presumption is that life organized itself via undirected chemical pathways and thus apart from any designing intelligence. Yet, unlike the causal specificity that obtains for microevolutionary processes, origin-of-life researchers have yet to specify the chemical pathways that supposedly originated life. For instance, Francis Collins, former head of the Human Genome Project, admits that "no serious scientist would currently claim that a naturalistic explanation for the origin of life is at hand."[5] Self-organizational theorist Stuart Kauffman is bolder yet: "Anyone who tells you that he or she knows how life started on the earth some 3.45 billion years ago is a fool or a knave. Nobody knows."[6]

Despite a vast literature on the origin of life, causally specific proposals for just what those chemical pathways might be are sorely absent. Which is not to say that there have not been any proposals. In fact, there are too many of them. RNA worlds, clay templates, hydrothermal vents, and numerous other materialistic scenarios have all been proposed to account for the chemical evolution of life. Yet none of these scenarios is detailed enough to be seriously criticized or tested. In short, they all lack causal specificity.[7]

In the absence of causal specificity, the logic of evolution parallels the logic of alchemy. Evolution, like alchemical transformation, is a relational notion. Alchemy never said that gold just magically materializes. Rather, it said that there are antecedents (lead, potions, furnaces) from which it materializes. So too evolution does not say that organisms just magically materialize. Rather, it says that there are antecedents (in the case of the origin of life, it posits RNA worlds, clay templates, hydrothermal vents, etc.) from which life materializes. Thus, to say that something evolves is to say what it evolves from: just as for the alchemist gold "evolves" (again, in its literal etymological sense) from lead plus some other (unspecified) things, so for the contemporary origin-of-life researcher organisms "evolve" from suitable (albeit unspecified) batches of prebiotic chemicals.

"X evolves" is therefore an incomplete sentence. It needs to be completed by reading "X evolves from Y." Moreover, the claim that X evolves from Y remains vacuous until one specifies Y and can demonstrate that Y is sufficient to account for X. Lowering the temperature of water below zero degrees Celsius is causally specific and adequately accounts for the freezing of water. On the other hand, a complete set of the building materials for a house does not suffice to account for a house—additionally what is needed is an architectural plan (drawn up by an architect) as well as assembly instructions (executed by a contractor) to implement the plan. Likewise, with the origin of life, it does no good simply to have the building blocks for life (e.g., nucleotide bases or amino acids). The means for organizing those building blocks into a coherent system (i.e., a living organism) need to be specified as well.

Given the pervasive lack of causal specificity in origin-of-life studies, why are so many origin-of-life researchers supremely confident that material causes are even up to the task of originating life? (By a material cause I mean, not in the Aristotelian but in the modern scientific sense, a cause reducible to matter, energy, and their law-determined interactions, with these interactions being, in principle, describable by physics and chemistry.) The singular lack of success of science in elucidating the origin-of-life problem makes this overweening confidence all the more puzzling if we try to understand it in light of the skepticism and tentativeness with which the scientific method tells us to approach hypotheses.

On the other hand, if, as I am suggesting, there is a precise parallel between evolution and alchemy, then this confidence is perfectly understandable because in that case it flows from a prior metaphysical commitment that for many scientists has become inviolable and nonnegotiable. What prior metaphysical commitment ensures that material causes, though for now unspecified, must effect the desired evolutionary transformations? In the case of alchemy, the prior metaphysical commitment was Neoplatonism. In the case of chemical and biological evolution, the prior metaphysical commitment is, obviously, materialism. Materialism is the view that material causes at base govern the world. Given materialism as a prior metaphysical commitment, it follows that life must evolve through purely material causes. But that commitment, like the alchemists' commitment to Neoplatonism, is highly problematic.

Proponents of materialism are, at this point, apt to note that life is here, life was not always here, and so some transformation from non-life to life had to occur. Life has come about by a process of chemical evolution even if we cannot quite spell out the precise causal antecedents for life. The origin of life is a great unsolved problem, and origin-of-life researchers are valiantly trying to resolve it. For me to compare chemical evolution with alchemy will therefore strike the committed materialist as misconceived if not catty and churlish.

To see why this dismissal of my position is itself misconceived, consider what it means to say that life has, as the materialist claims, originated from purely material causes. Because the origin of life is an open problem, the reference to "purely material causes" lacks, to be sure, causal specificity. But there is a deeper problem, and that is the imposition of an arbitrary restriction. The problem with claiming that life has emerged from purely material causes is not that it admits ignorance about an unsolved problem but that *it artificially restricts the range of possible solutions to that problem;* namely, it requires that solutions limit themselves to purely material causes. This is an arbitrary and metaphysically driven restriction. Life has emerged via purely material causes. How do we know that? In general, to hypothesize that X results from Y remains pure speculation until the process that brings about X from Y is causally specified. Until then, to impose restrictions on the types of causal factors that may or may not be employed in Y to bring about X is arbitrary and certain to frustrate scientific inquiry.

In this respect evolution is even more culpable than alchemy. Alchemy sought to transform lead into gold but left open the means by which the transformation could be effected (though in practice alchemists hoped the transformation could be effected through the modest technical means at their disposal). Evolution, on the other hand, seeks to transform nonlife into life and then life into increasingly complex forms of life but, when biased by materialism, excludes any place for intelligence or teleology in the transformation. Such a restriction is gratuitous given evolution's lack of causal specificity in accounting for not only the origin of life but also the macroevolutionary changes supposedly responsible for life's subsequent diversification.

People are free to hope (or delude themselves into thinking) that materialism will eventually be vindicated and that the great open problems of evolution will submit to purely materialistic solutions. But in the absence of clearly delineated evolutionary pathways (i.e., causal specificity), there is no reason to let materialism place such restrictions on scientific theorizing. Restrictions like these—typically unspoken, metaphysically motivated, and at odds with free scientific inquiry—need to be resisted and exposed. Science must not degenerate into applied materialistic philosophy. But this is exactly what it does at the hands of today's alchemists, namely, the materialistic evolutionists who hold their views not because of empirical evidence but because of a prior metaphysical commitment to materialism.

Science needs to be a free inquiry into all the possibilities that might operate in nature. One of these possibilities, clearly, is design. Indeed, the great contribution of the intelligent design movement is to open up such inquiry.[8] Unlike Darwinian evolution, whose hostility toward Christian theism has been evident from the start, intelligent design creates conceptual room for Christian theism. In consequence, it benefits both Christianity and science, removing barriers that science supposedly has erected against Christianity and freeing science from the false ideology of materialism.

Endnotes

1   Carl G. Jung, *Mysterium Coniunctionis: An Inquiry into the Separation and Synthesis of Psychic Opposites in Alchemy*, in *Collected Works of C. G. Jung*, vol. 14 (Princeton: Princeton University Press, 1963), 114.

2   Not only has alchemy failed as a scientific project, but as a metaphysical project it seems not to be in a much better state. Consider the following admission by Carl Jung toward the end of his life: "I observe myself in the stillness of Bollingen, with the experience of almost eight decades now, and I have to admit that I have found no plain answer to myself. I am in doubt about myself as ever, the more I try to say something definite. It is even as though through familiarity with oneself one became still more alienated." Quoted in Gerhard Wehr, *Jung: A Biography*, trans. D. M. Weeks (Boston: Shambhala,

1987), 416. According to Jung's biographer (407), Jung regarded it as speaking well for the honesty of alchemists that "after years of continuing toil they were able to produce neither gold nor the highly praised philosopher's stone and openly admitted this. To these men, failures in the popular sense, Jung compared himself. He too had in the end been unable to solve the riddle of the mysterium coniunctionis."

3   Even so, it is worth remembering that Isaac Newton devoted a full half of his writings to theology and alchemy. See the introduction by Brad Gregory to Baruch Spinoza, *Tractatus Theologico-Politicus*, trans. S. Shirley, intro. B. S. Gregory (1670; reprint, Leiden: Brill, 1989), 9.

4   Chemical evolution denotes origin of life studies—specifically, how prelife chemicals might organize themselves into living forms. Biological evolution denotes how life has changed once it is here—usually with a heavy emphasis on the Darwinian mechanism of natural selection acting on random variations.

5   Francis S. Collins, *The Language of God: A Scientist Presents Evidence for Belief* (New York: Free Press, 2006), 92.

6   Stuart Kauffman, *At Home in the Universe: The Search for the Laws of Self-Organization and Complexity* (New York: Oxford University Press, 1995), 31.

7   To appreciate this failure of chemical evolution, see the following critique of origin-of-life studies: William A. Dembski and Jonathan Wells, *How to Be an Intellectually Fulfilled Atheist—Or Not* (Wilmington, DE: ISI Books, 2008). The title of this book keys off of Richard Dawkins's widely publicized claim that Darwin made it possible to be an intellectually fulfilled atheist. Darwin's theory, however, presupposes the origin of life, which poses deeply vexing challenges for biology. Thus, unless the origin-of-life problem is satisfactorily resolved in materialist terms, Darwin is in no position to provide atheists with intellectual fulfillment; his theory has a gaping hole at the very place it begins.

8   For an overview of intelligent design, see William A. Dembski and Sean McDowell, *Understanding Intelligent Design: Everything You Need to Know in Plain Language* (Eugene, OR: Harvest House, 2008). The foreword by Josh McDowell makes clear why intelligent design is so crucial to understanding creation and thus to forming a coherent Christian worldview.

Does Intelligent Design Theory Help Christian Apologetics?

John A. Bloom, Ph.D., Ph.D.
Professor of Physics
Director, M.A. Program in Science and Religion
Biola University

ABSTRACT

Intelligent Design (ID) theory attempts to demonstrate that an intelligent agent has acted in the natural world by seeking examples of specified complexity that cannot be explained through the mere action of law and chance. Some Christian apologists have criticized ID because it makes too weak a claim; specifically, it does not seek to identify who the designer is.

I will suggest that the claim of "mere design," although admittedly weak, is of tremendous value in apologetics for countering two roadblocks to saving faith: (1) a two-tier model of God and nature wherein God is so removed that he does not, or even cannot, interact with the material world in any substantive manner; (2) the prevailing sense in much of our culture that naturalism offers adequate explanations for all of reality.

I will further suggest that ID's openness regarding the identity of the designer is an important scientific demarcation. Given that modern science focuses on efficient cause, the contemporary scientific community relegates questions of final cause to the disciplines of philosophy and theology. Thus it is appropriate for the question of agency to be addressed as a strictly scientific question but for questions about the nature of the agent to require an interdisciplinary approach that is beyond the bounds of most research programs in the natural sciences.

The goal of Christian apologetics, to borrow the analogy of John Warwick Montgomery,[1] is to remove roadblocks in the path to genuine faith. Unfortunately, contemporary Western thought places two major impediments there by asserting that

1. the sciences offer the most—and perhaps only—reliable public source of truth;
2. the sciences assure us that everything can (or will) be explained solely through naturalistic processes.

These cultural norms have their roots in the Enlightenment, where the objective appeal to Reason and Experience was skillfully employed to erode confidence in Revelation and in God's interaction with the natural world.

Add to this situation a third roadblock from liberal theology, which teaches that God is so transcendent that he does not, or cannot, act in a tangible way in the physical world (e.g., a video camera in Jesus' tomb on Easter morning would have seen nothing unusual), and it is no wonder that many scholars today think that God is not relevant or necessary.

These attitudes extend far beyond the scientific and broader academic community. In most coffee shops one can overhear comments like: "Everyone knows that science has shown that the Bible is wrong." "Religion is just a way to talk about emotional experiences; it has no real factual or historical basis." Or most bluntly: "Religious people are stupid."

It comes as no surprise then that Christian apologists have appealed to science itself to overcome these "scientific" and "theological" roadblocks. Given its cultural authority and claim to seek truth, scientific warrant and credibility are seen as necessary preconditions for justified belief.

Over the past decade a new movement among scientists and philosophers has crystalized, which I believe is a helpful ally in taming the claims of modern science and liberal theology. Known as "Intelligent Design," "ID," or "Intelligent Design Theory" (and as "Intelligent Design Creationism" by its detractors who try to dismiss it as merely a religious view), the approach is simple enough: To quote Bill Dembski, "Intelligent design is the science that studies signs of intelligence."[2]

Were ID only to apply itself to archaeology, cryptography, murder trials, and insurance claim settlements, it would hardly be controversial. In all of these situations, patterns are sought to infer whether the artifact or event occurred naturally, or whether the action of an agent is involved. However, ID looks at *biological* systems and claims to find evidence that nonhuman agents had a hand in their development.

How so? ID looks for objects in nature that cannot be explained through the simple actions of law and chance (the only two causal mechanisms that naturalists allow in the physical world). Designed objects exhibit what Dembski calls *specified complexity*. They have too complex a pattern to be the likely result of chance, and they are specified: their pattern serves a purpose or has a function that is independent of the object itself. Standard illustrations of specified complexity that involve human agents are the faces of the presidents on Mount Rushmore or a paragraph of writing in a book. Biological examples include the bacterial flagella and other molecular machines.

Dembski argues that specified complexity is equivalent to information and has proposed that information can only be created by intelligent agents, not by chance and necessity alone. If Dembski were speaking of natural agents (humans, squirrels, etc.), there would be little problem with his approach because for all the talk from naturalists about there being only law and chance mechanisms, agent-action is recognized in the sciences whenever it is evident. For example, the actions of Hendrik Schön to substitute and fabricate data at Bell Labs were detected because his results were too precise or in violation of known physical laws.[3] The actions of mice who chew through wires and short-circuit equipment can sometimes perturb experiments also. Natural agents are recognized routinely, but when Dembski thinks outside the box of naturalism, the sparks start to fly.

Specified complexity is seen in more than biological systems. Hugh Ross[4] and more recently Guillermo Gonzalez[5] argue that the fine-tuning of the physical constants that shaped our universe to be life friendly, as well as the uniqueness of our earth and its local environment, are further examples of intelligent design in nature. Once again we see the same bias: SETI, the search for extraterrestrial intelligence, is a valid scientific project because it seeks material agents, but looking for possible signs of nonmaterial intelligence is not considered science.

The mere possibility of a causally open material universe is obviously threatening to naturalists and atheists, so it is not surprising that Dembski's views are attacked with a McCarthy-like zeal from those quarters.[6] However, some evangelical Christian scientists and philosophers have voiced concerns that intelligent design theorists are claiming that science can detect God.

This is a critical question: Has God done anything that modern science can detect? Before we try to answer that question, we have to stop and ask another: "How does one define 'modern science,' and what are its goals?" Phil Johnson and many others have noted that the current definition of science requires that all "scientific" explanations be naturalistic, physical ones. Since God is nonphysical, science by definition cannot detect God. Because of this restriction, any observation in nature which suggests that God might exist must be given a naturalistic explanation, no matter how strange that explanation seems (i.e., a multiverse model "explains" our improbable life-friendly universe without evoking a Creator who made it that way. Apparently faith in the existence of an unknowable, actual infinite number of other universes is a more acceptable faith than simply believing in a transcendent, infinite God).

Here is the first significant way, then, that ID is helping Christian apologetics: it challenges this comfortable, naturalistic definition of science that makes the world safe for atheists (such as Richard Dawkins and Steven Weinberg). Methodological naturalism may be an important *simplifying assumption* for scientists to use when trying to explain how things work, like physicists may model the behavior of a gas by assuming that atoms bounce off each other like perfect billiard balls. Simplifying assumptions must be recognized as what they are: imposed *assumptions* that may need to be discarded or modified later if the data warrant it. Recognizing the limits imposed by one's assumptions is one of the more challenging aspects of science, but it happens often enough. Engineers generally work very well within the assumptions of Newtonian mechanics, but atomic-level phenomena require an additional tool kit: quantum mechanics.

Thus ID is critical for exposing this metaphysical presumption about the world that modern science incorporates and that some scientists cling to despite suggestive data otherwise. By opening up the mere possibility of something significant beyond the natural, and pointing out this blind spot in the goals of modern science, ID can help science refocus on the search for truth (how things really work and how they came to be), instead of allowing science to continue being a game of finding clever, peer-reviewed naturalistic schemes to explain away some of nature's most interesting and profound phenomena.

But someone might say, "Wait, it is called 'natural science,' so one can understand why it should restrict itself to naturalistic answers." True, and if scientists and the media were careful to present their results (in public school textbooks and elsewhere) as "the best *naturalistic* explanation for what we see," it would help. It would help even more if they added, "Of course, there are broader perspectives that may explain things better, but we have chosen to focus only on possible mechanical causes rather than look beyond them to ultimate or final causes." With these disclaimers the public would be warned of the possible limited value of naturalistic-only explanations for answering the big questions of life. Instead, most scientists do not use disclaimers and present their results as "the best *scientific* explanation for what we see," which to most people means that the explanation is true and logical and that any other explanation would be nonscientific, hence illogical and false. Moreover, some scientists and media assert with an evangelistic zeal that "our answers prove that there *is* nothing beyond natural causes." So something here has to change: Either the public trust that scientists seek truth should change to the postmodernist notion that scientists are one of many communities of belief which has no right to impose its views on others, or the definition of what counts as a scientific answer needs to include some notion like ID. I think it is better to broaden "what counts as a scientific answer" and retain the possibility of discerning truth than to change the cultural impression of what science does—but perhaps I am mistaken on that.

If we grant that modern science should explain—rather than explain away—what we observe in the universe, and if we permit it to be open to the possibility of nonphysical causes, then the question, "Can modern science detect God?" is truly interesting. Personally, I think that the answer is "Yes" and that a number of Bible passages imply it. Paul tells us in Romans 1:20 that God's power and divine nature are clearly seen in what He has made. However, Paul also notes that this evidence will not be universally accepted prior to Jesus' return. Given the current naturalistic bias in our culture, ID theorists must cite scientific examples of agent causation that are clearly beyond the power of law and chance to produce. This is one of Mike Behe's goals in his concept of irreducible complexity: showing that scientists do not have a clue how some molecular machines could have evolved by a gradual Darwinian mechanism that is governed only by law and chance.[7]

To a Reformed theologian, looking for "clear examples of agent causation" in nature sounds strange because they believe that everything is under God's control. There is no "chance" to God, and the laws of nature are simply God's regular way of doing things. Thus all of nature is intelligently designed and even guided! True enough, but ID theorists are not talking to conservative theologians but to a scientific community who accepts the laws of nature as brute facts. There is some argument among scientists over chance—is anything truly random, or is "chance" simply a placeholder for human ignorance—but whatever it is, chance also works on its own. There is no mastermind behind it all. That was the whole point of Darwin's evolutionary model (as Julia Wedgwood informed Asa Gray).[8] In order to convince skeptics, ID theorists must detect design in very clear examples and avoid *false positives*—avoid making the claim that an agent is required only to have a naturalistic mechanism that can produce the result discovered later. Isaac Newton's comment that God needed occasionally to tweak the positions of planets orbiting the sun in order to keep them in their places is one famous example of a false positive, or "god of the gaps" fallacy, that LaPlace was later able to refute using more sophisticated mathematical models.

Since nobody today appears to be a prophet, how do you know when you have found an example of intelligent design (such as irreducible complexity) that will stand forever? Well, you don't, but you can use good examples to make some points. First, you can note that the sciences commit a "naturalism of the gaps" fallacy whenever they face an intractable problem, and you can suggest that causality should not be presumed in open questions. It is not fair to let naturalism be the default position until all naturalistic explanations are proven to be impossible.

Darwin himself played off a "god of the gaps" fear when he commented, "If it could be demonstrated that any complex organ existed which could not possibly have been formed by numerous, successive, slight modifications, my theory would absolutely break down."[9] Note that Darwin requires his detractors to prove a universal negative—that it is impossible to form a complex system by gradual means—in order to defeat his theory. Since this can never be shown, naturalism can, therefore, bridge all gaps in nature.

Despite its apparent generosity, Darwin's "prove that there must be gaps" argument is logically equivalent to the village atheist's tease, "Can God create a stone so heavy that he can't lift it?" Forcing ID to carry the burden of proving a universal negative about the physical world, and then claiming that naturalism wins by default, is a logical trick that we as apologists should be sharp enough to catch. Why assume Darwin is correct unless proven wrong? Instead, we must place the burden of proof back on Darwin, as Mike Behe does, and require that Darwinists demonstrate that molecular machines and other complex systems *actually have* "been formed by numerous, successive, slight modifications."

Another powerful feature of ID theory is that it recognizes design without requiring gaps or otherwise specifying how the agent acted. A designed object need not be produced through a miracle or violation of natural law; and the means that the agent used to create the object may be open to scientific study. In other words, a complete string of mechanical causes does not discount a possible final cause and agent influence. For example, a potter makes a coffee mug entirely by natural means, yet the final product is obviously designed. Thus ID theory is not as susceptible to the "god of the gaps" fallacy because it does not evoke miracle as the only vehicle the agent can use; if the result is extremely unlikely and fits an independent pattern, this is sufficient grounds to postulate that an agent may be involved. One does not require miracles in order to conclude that an object is designed; one only needs to show that the finished product is not the result of law and chance *only*.

Some apologists find fault with ID in that it does not identify who the designer is. If there really is a Designer, "Who is he?" is certainly the next logical question to ask, and it would be nice to try to answer it. But here ID theorists recognize a fault in natural theology—that of trying to infer too much about God, or the Designer, from nature alone. To continue the mug example, we can recognize that it is designed, but what can we infer about the age, gender, height, or personality of the potter simply by studying the mug? Artists and authors have often commented that their critics are totally wrong in assigning motives to their works; if we find it hard to figure out what a human agent was thinking by only looking at his works, why should it be any easier with a cosmic Designer? Thus ID theorists may have an opinion about who they think the designer is, but this opinion is informed by more than nature. Staying strictly within the scientific disciplines and studying the physical world, we cannot go further—unless we find John 3:16 encoded in the human genome or occurring as a background signal in the cosmic background radiation.

ID theorists and researchers grant that the jury is still out on the question, Can clear evidence of design be found in nature? If it can, the payoff for Christian apologetics is huge—we would have evidence of nonhuman agents. Thus, (a) naturalism is inadequate, and (b) the two-tier model that has dominated liberal theology since Kant is wrong. If a designer can influence the natural world, then we cannot rule out revelation and the miraculous *a priori*. Perhaps the tomb was empty on Easter morning after all! While the confirmation of design would not remove every roadblock to the cross ("Who is the Designer?" is still an open question), it would make great headway.

But what if ID fails to find even one clear example of nonhuman agent causation? Can we safely use ID in apologetics while ID is still in its infancy?

I believe the answer is an unqualified "Yes." Even if ID does nothing more, it has already won a major point—exposing the naturalistic bias in the goals of modern science. This is newsworthy. The sciences do NOT always seek truth but give naturalistic explanations for things *no matter what*. "Scientific" answers are not the neutral, objective, and unbiased conclusions that most of us thought they were. If in the future the sciences want to stay intentionally blind to possible nonmechanistic causes, then the sciences lose their authority to speak in any case where the cause may possibly be nonmechanistic. If we want to know if something beyond the material world exists, we are learning that we cannot turn to science for the answer, unless it chooses to pursue truth and is open to the possibility of thinking outside the materialistic box. Thankfully many scientists are willing to follow the evidence wherever it leads, and hopefully they can free the discipline from this snare.

If we ask blind people to tell us what a sunset is like, they can describe the fading warmth on their skin, the shift in the wind, and the change in the sounds from birds and other animals, but they cannot describe the most significant aspects of the transition from day to night! As apologists we can enhance the credibility of the gospel by pointing out this voluntary blindness of materialism in most current scientific practice and by asking scientists to remove the scales from their eyes and enjoy the view.

Endnotes

1 Like Dr. Montgomery, I also was strongly influenced by the ministry of Herman J. Eckelmann during my time at Cornell University. This paper was presented at the 2005 Evangelical Theological Society Conference in both Montgomery's and the late Pastor Eck's honor.

2 William Dembski, *The Design Revolution* (Downers Grove: InterVarsity Press, 2004), 25.

3 Independent committee report available from http://www.lucent.com/ news_events/researchreview.html, accessed November 12, 2005.

4 Hugh Ross, *The Creator and the Cosmos* (Colorado Springs: NavPress, 2001).

5 Guillermo Gonzalez and Jay Richards, *The Privileged Planet* (Washington, DC: Regnery, 2004).

6 See for example, Barbara Forrest and Paul Gross, *Creationism's Trojan Horse* (New York: Oxford University Press, 2003).

7 Michael Behe, *Darwin's Black Box* (New York: Free Press, 1998).

8 A. Hunter Dupree, "Christianity and the Scientific Community in the Age of Darwin," in *God and Nature*, edited by David C. Lindberg and Ronald L. Numbers (Berkeley: University of California Press, 1986), 362.

9 Charles Darwin, *Origin of Species*, 6th ed. (1872), 154.

The Imaginative Embrace

JOHN WARWICK MONTGOMERY AND THE DOOR TO THE INSIDE OF THE WORLD

David Cullen

One typically attributes to the writings of John Montgomery an analytical and empirical nature at once well crafted and persuasive. This is certainly true of his work in apologetics (whose subjective, or imaginative, facet will be under the lens in this essay) and doctrinal studies; but it is, of course, equally true of his polymathic endeavors elsewhere: the law, philosophy of history, human rights—one might say he makes gold from lead at every turn.

Thus, while acknowledging differences in personal and professional habit and certain interests, one could easily say of John Montgomery something akin to what Dr. Johnson said of Oliver Goldsmith in the inscription for Goldsmith's tomb in Westminster Abbey: *Qui nullum ferè scribendi genus non tetigit, nullum quod tetigit non ornavit.*[1] One is assured by the grace of God that a good many years remain to be counted before the stone will be thus engraved, but surely a similar epitaph is merited by Montgomery in light of the variety, quantity, and quality of his published work.

Quite real, though naïve, is the temptation cleanly to categorize Montgomery's thought along lines suggested by the titles of his books. *Crisis in Lutheran Theology* would seem to have a narrow focus, as would *Repression of Evangelism in Greece*. Even *Computers, Cultural Change, and the Christ*, barely on the radar screen in the field of "Montgomery Studies" (yet a little marvel of prophetic insight, on its way to fulfillment in the age of the Internet), looks to have a limited appeal at first glance. What such an approach lacks, of course, is the recognition of the dominant theme that overlays the entirety of Montgomery's work and has a particularly apt application to the topic of this essay, as will be seen.

In brief, that theme is the acknowledgement of the presence of Christ in seen and unseen worlds, everywhere and always, and the influence and effects of that presence in terms of how it brings meaning to every human activity. This theme forms the foundation of Montgomery's work in law, human rights, and history, subjects not under direct consideration in this essay but a study of which would easily verify this insight. Certainly, it is woven brightly into his objective apologetic and doctrinal studies where it is rooted in the historically reliable Scriptures. In its apologetic and doctrinal settings, the theme has a particular phrasing that focuses on the historicity of the biblical documents, proper interpretation of statements within those documents, and existential encounter with the One in the documents whose coming, or Presence, is therein announced. Supporting citations from a number of Montgomery's books could demonstrate the centrality of this theme in relation to his apologetic and doctrinal work; but, guided by the principle of parsimony, a few examples from one source will suffice.

"[T]he revelational content [of Christianity] is wedded to historical manifestations of Divine power. The pivot of Christian theology is the biblical affirmation that . . . God Himself came to earth—entered man's empirical sphere—in Jesus Christ." Another: "From the first verse of the Bible to the last God's *contact* with man's world is affirmed." More to the point yet: "The truths of which God's revelation is composed are legion . . . but they all center upon the great truth which serves as the axis and focal point of the revelation as a whole: the Word become flesh, who died for the sins of the world and rose again for its justification." The essay from which these citations are extracted, "The Theologian's Craft," sums up Montgomery's vision of the task of the systematic theologian in a way that clearly shows the apologetic base for the work of the theologian. Without an inerrant Scripture—the demonstration of which is surely part of the apologist's craft—the true theologian would be unable fully to trust his source and would end in the fog of the "methodological reductionisms" Montgomery so clearly delineates in the essay. Montgomery concludes the essay with a "structural model of theological explanation" that sweeps away that fog and replaces it with the clear air of a biblically based methodology. This tri-level model highlights the relationship in Christian theological thinking between facts (the scientific level, per Montgomery); subjective (or personal) interaction with, and commitment to, the systematized, exegetically based interpretation of said facts (the artistic level); and consequent elevation to "the realm of the Sacred, where both the impersonal 'it' of science and the subjective 'I' of the humanities stand on holy ground, in the presence of the living God." Montgomery continues: "Lost in wonder, then, does theological theorizing find its fulfilment [sic]." This dynamic conjunction of facts and response, the tie between words and experience, between head and heart, is reminiscent of what Walker Percy called "the union of the knower and the thing known," and it is the final step in the quest of the systematic theologian for ultimate meaning (as it should indeed be for everyone who names the Name). As well, it provides a transition to the remainder of this essay being that it is allied with the goals of the imaginative, or subjective, apologetic which moves toward the same destination as the objective form (that of the presence of Christ active in the universe) but from a different direction. That is, it shares the principal theme but casts upon it a light all its own. Rather than beginning with science (level one "facts"), this apologetic begins with the imagination but also moves through the artistic level of Montgomery's tri-level "cone of illumination" to the subsequent personal encounter with the sacred. Such an apologetic is not a denial of the need for facts, but it approaches the "realm of the sacred" and its existential imperative by way of a path that parallels facts without directly focusing on them.

Striking in the way it blends in certain aspects of his objective apologetic, Montgomery's imaginative apologetic is an aspect of his work often overlooked on the grounds that it is "just Montgomery; he likes that sort of thing." *Cross and Crucible, Demon Possession, Principalities and Powers, Myth, Allegory, and Gospel, The Transcendent Holmes*—all are evidence of a doppelgänger at work, regaling readers with investigations of spirits, hobgoblins, nursery bogies, the Tarot, alchemy, fictional detectives, elves, dwarfs, and hobbits. Although his deerstalker and Inverness should have offered evidence enough that such a twin existed, the finding cannot but be strengthened by the rumor that Montgomery's library of multiple thousands of volumes is watched over by Paddington Bear in a Harrah's suit.

Bear in mind that this "imaginative apologetic" has nothing to do with fabricating or falsifying justifications for Christian belief, nor does it allow room for any departure from orthodox Christian doctrine. Neither is it an alleyway by which Montgomery smuggles counterfeit goods into the storehouse of God. Rather, it is a term that describes the apologetic use of literary forms such as myth and the modern novel, and of means other than the strictly objective (such as symbols and images), by which the presence of Christ, in seen and unseen worlds, may be acknowledged. The intention of imaginative apologetics is "to reflect the Christian story in its objective sense and trigger conscious acceptance of it," but not by beginning with the objective or scientific. (In the end, of course, such an apologetic cannot be separated from facts, as it can be successfully undertaken only when its symbol-making reflects accurately the facts of the Christian faith.) But why the need for such an apologetic? Montgomery replies, "The on-going, self-perpetuating juggernaut of scientific technology has alienated many in our society from the ideals of scientific objectivity. Objectivity seems for them . . . the source of pollution [and] depersonalization. . . . They seek another kind of answer—an answer perhaps hidden in the subjective depths of their own souls." Another reason for an imaginative apologetic is suggested by a recurrent theme in the work of C. S. Lewis. Lewis, in his autobiography, writes of a nearly inexpressible hunger for an experience that eludes him; he names this hunger *Sehnsucht*, a word that denotes a deep yearning for something beyond oneself. Following his reading of George MacDonald's *Phantastes*, he recalls the approach of the thing for which he yearned: Joy. He writes, "It was as though the voice which had called to me from the world's end was now speaking at my side." Transformed by reading this tale filled with the elements of great myth, Lewis says his imagination was baptized.

"Imagination," used here, is a faculty of the human mind that creates (as well as responds to) analogical or metaphorical structures designed to mirror cognitively apprehended, and typically abstract, data (e.g., the content of the scientific level of Montgomery's "cone of illumination"). Thus, there is an initial separation between the objective and subjective with respect to the form in which fact is encountered, but an eventual return to a single stream at the artistic level, en route to the sacred, where one may discover the existential outworking of Montgomery's central theme—union with the revealed presence of Christ.

This union figures prominently in Montgomery's rigorous and fascinating treatment of Lutheran alchemist Johann Valentin Andreae in *Cross and Crucible*. The task of the true alchemist, Montgomery writes, is to unite the macrocosm (that which is external to man; heaven) and the microcosm (man himself; earth). The goal of such a union is to arrive at "a unified, harmonized conception of the created universe." Drawing on insights from Valentin Weigel, Montgomery states that the union of the macrocosm and microcosm points toward the providential activity of God throughout His created universe—in the heavens as well as in man—this echoing the petition in the Lord's Prayer that His will would be done on earth as it is in heaven. The macrocosm and microcosm thus conjoined, one recognizes "Christ's centrality in both, and thereby [the infusion] of all of created reality with the truth of the Gospel." Surely this is Montgomery's unifying principle and the foundation of his apologetic, objective as well as subjective: Christ present in all, transforming all human activity and making it an instrument of discovery. The resemblance of macrocosm and microcosm to the sacred realm of Montgomery's methodological cone ought not to be a surprise, for the goal of both is a transcendent unity, a meeting of heaven and earth, of God and man. Christian Rosencreutz, Andreae's protagonist in *Chymical Wedding*, himself enters "an existential union with God on the microcosmic level" by virtue of the reception of stigmata in his feet.

The vision of Christ's centrality, not focused in one specialization but reaching across a wide range of interests such as science and literature, is crucial because it leads to "ultimate purpose and meaning [which] are the very substance of the universe." Such substance obtains, according to Montgomery, because Christ *is* present in everything.

He confronts man in every moment and in every place. His desire is for union and His presence in the created order provides a framework for that union to occur. But how is it man can enter into such a union?

"[E]very created thing is, in its degree, an image of God, and the ordinate and faithful appreciation of that thing a clue which, truly followed, will lead back to Him." Thus did C. S. Lewis describe the spiritual maxim that he called "the affirmation of images" in the work of fellow writer Charles Williams. Mary McDermott Shideler, no stranger to Williams's work, writes of the habit of the "imagist . . . to whom imagery is a natural mode of thinking and perceiving," and states that the method of imagery draws on "the declaration . . . that persons and events which in themselves are local, immediate, and material can reveal transcendent glories and convey that glory into the most ordinary aspects of our lives."

Montgomery informs his reader, as noted previously, that the task of the alchemist is to unite heaven and earth with the goal of providing "a unified, harmonized conception of the created universe," which includes the existential, divine encounter in the sacred realm. Granting that Williams is correct, that the things of the created order are themselves images of God which, when properly appreciated, will lead back to God, one better understands the conjoining of the macrocosm and the microcosm. Affirming the images—the things of creation—is to recognize that Christ is truly present in all. That this is tantamount to the core of Shideler's declaration is evident. As well, it has resonances in Percy's "union of the knower and the thing known." The object-subject relationship of Percy; the "affirmation of images" of Lewis-Williams; Shideler's revelation of "transcendent glories"; Montgomery's "harmonized conception" of the created order: all speak of union, of life in the presence of Christ, of ultimate meaning in the universe.

The use of the imagination to arrive at such union is imperative. Montgomery points out the error, among others, of reducing the artistic and the sacral to the scientific: its end is dead orthodoxy. Dorothy Sayers remarked that "[t]o forbid the making of pictures about God would be to forbid thinking about God at all, for man is so made that he has no way to think except in pictures." Rather than discouraging the imaginative, then, one ought to be encouraging it, as does Gene Veith, who praises imagination as a curative for modern people so "impoverished that they cannot even begin to conceive of anything spiritual." Montgomery brings together the objective and imaginative apologetic tasks when he writes, "The genuine historicity of the Gospel does not prevent it from being at the same time genuinely mythical—in the special sense of a story that cuts to the heart of man's subjective need."

Such is the nature of Montgomery's methodological cone, a journey through either facts or symbols toward the sacred. The linking of picture making to experience to knowledge is surely another way of describing Montgomery's "cone of illumination," particularly in relation to the imaginative apologetic. One seizes upon an image or symbol (e.g., a lion, a symbolic "fact"), engages that image subjectively (interpreting it by way of revelation and experience), and consequently comes to the point of "immediate knowledge" of the reality behind the image (in this case, to the point of knowing at the deepest existential level a certain Lion). "Lost in wonder," indeed! Montgomery notes that "the myths and legends and tales of the world that give symbolic expression to man's fundamental needs . . . serve as pointers to the reality of the Christian message in which they are historically fulfilled." As a guarantee that a given symbol will not lead one astray, one is forced to return, even after an "imaginative conversion," to facts—to check one's symbol set against the revelational content of Holy Scripture. In this venture Montgomery is an excellent guide.

Summing up the governing principle of Andreae's thought, Montgomery writes,

> [A] science without the illumination of the Gospel inevitably obtains an elevated, false conception of itself, and comes to think that even eternity exists only to serve its purposes; the result is a complete inversion of values and a loss of what is most important of all: existential encounter with the Christ and the inestimable privilege of using one's talents to glorify Him.

That this is true as well of John Montgomery, that he has entered into union with Christ and used his talents in His service, is not unknown to any who know him.

Endnotes

---

1 "Who left scarcely any style of writing untouched, and touched nothing that he did not adorn."

To Every Occultist an Answer

ASSESSING JOHN WARWICK MONTGOMERY'S APOLOGETIC CRITIQUE OF THE OCCULT

Philip Johnson

The final decade of the twentieth century and the opening decade of the twenty-first century have evidenced a widespread interest in occult, esoteric, and alternative spiritualities.[1] Such interests abound in the high cultural pursuits of scholars in anthropology, history, religious studies, and the sociology of religion.[2] Academic centres for the study of esotericism now exist at Bathspa University, University of Exeter, and the University of Amsterdam. Journals such as *Aries, The Pomegranate,* and *Nova Religio* also attest to the growing body of new scholarship in these fields. In popular culture these interests are broadly attested in neo-pagan, neo-gnostic and New Age spiritual groups, cultural events such as Burning Man and the Festival for Mind-Body-Spirit, contemporary American television series such as *Medium, Ghost Whisperer,* and *Supernatural,* fantasy and gothic novels, comic books and anime, and on the Internet.[3]

In the midst of this current fascination for the esoteric, evangelicals should recall that John Warwick Montgomery anticipated the apologetic implications of these broad trends several decades ago. As we shall discover, Montgomery is a trail-blazing scholar and creative apologete in charting the missional terrain of the occult. He has provided important analytical guidance for missionary-apologetes who labour among those serious occultists that are seeking both ultimate spiritual experiences and ultimate truth.

Biographical Background

In his own estimation Montgomery feels that he was "born out of due time" relative to today's interests in the occult.[4] As a precocious teenager growing up during World War II in the small town of Warsaw, New York, he collected inexpensive mail-order booklets on occult topics like magic, omens, superstitions, and witchcraft.[5] In

1949 he was an undergraduate student in philosophy and classics at Cornell University and studied Dr. J. B. Rhine's researches into paranormal phenomena.[6] Montgomery also met an engineering student named Herman John Eckelmann who successfully goaded him into examining the case for Christ.[7] Montgomery's conversion to Christ eventually led him to become a confessional Lutheran.[8] Like the archetypal Renaissance scholar he pursued a multifaceted career in librarianship, the humanities, theology, ethics, jurisprudence, human rights, and canon law.[9]

Graduate Studies

Throughout the formative years of his postgraduate studies in the 1950s and early 1960s, Montgomery maintained a keen theological interest in the occult. In 1959 he examined the impact of C. S. Lewis's Narnia stories on adolescent readers particularly in light of its allegorical images and symbols of redemption. It prompted him to develop a fresh apologetics trajectory that is known as the literary or subjective-evidentialist style.[10] In the literary apologetic style it is understood that spiritual needs are expressed symbolically. The recognition of one's redemptive needs can be triggered off subjectively by encountering Christ motifs that appear in various imaginative, symbolic, and mythic contexts. It is the apologete's task to draw attention to these Christ motifs that appear in the mythic archetypes of fantasy literature and detective fiction, in the world's folklore, in psychoanalytic studies of dream symbols, and in the myths and rituals of religious phenomenology.[11]

Two years later Montgomery penned a short ghost story, "God's Devil," that wove a moral around a liberal theological student's doubts about orthodoxy and his radical *volte-face* after a ghostly demonic experience.[12] In 1963 he addressed the Royal Society of Canada on the Lutheran contributions to the rise of science via alchemy and astrology during the Reformation era. The resultant paper formed the introductory chapter of his doctoral dissertation at the University of Strasbourg.[13]

During 1963–1964 he propounded a radical view for the history of seventeenth-century occultism in his dissertation *Cross and Crucible*.[14] It involved challenging an unfavourable image of seventeenth-century Lutheranism as being intellectually and socially sterile. He countered this antipathetic portrait through a careful reappraisal of the career of Johann Valentin Andreae (1586–1654), a Lutheran theologian known for his interests in alchemy and hermeticism. Various negative misunderstandings of Andreae's life and writings have accrued in modern secondary literature. The main allegation is that Andreae was the principal creator of the Rosicrucian manifestos known as the *Fama Fraternitatis* and *Confessio Fraternitatis*. Allied to this is a longstanding hermeneutical tradition that regards Andreae's allegorical romance *Chymische Hochzeit* (*The Chymical Wedding of Christian Rosencreutz*) as a Rosicrucian document. Montgomery argued from the primary sources that Andreae consistently held to orthodox Lutheran beliefs and that he was opposed to the autosoteriology of esoteric Rosicrucian thought. He contended that modern authors had ignored these primary sources and often lacked the intellectual empathy to appreciate Andreae's Lutheran worldview. As he demolished these confusing stereotypes Montgomery rehabilitated Andreae as a creative missionary-apologete whose apostolate was to the hermetic philosophers and followers of Rosicrucian occultism. Here Andreae's *Chymische Hochzeit* was painstakingly reinterpreted in light of Lutheran alchemy and theology as an apologetic work designed to woo esotericists back to Christ.

Death-of-God Controversy

Montgomery then returned to the USA in the halcyon days of the mid-1960s. There were radical theologians proposing the death-of-God, while many baby boomers gravitated toward utopian countercultural political visions and submitted to mystic gurus of new religions.[15] Some death-of-God theologians such as Thomas Altizer relied on Nietzsche's radical criticism of transcendental belief and also used hermeneutical principles that are formative elements in secular postmodernist philosophy. The countercultural interest in new religions and alternate forms of spirituality became the seedbed from which postmodern approaches to spirituality have arisen.[16]

The need for critical dialogue with these nascent forms of emerging postmodern culture drew an immediate response from Montgomery. The radical proposal for theothanatology that was put forward by Altizer goaded Montgomery into a sustained theological analysis that culminated in a formal debate at the University of Chicago in 1967.[17] He excoriated the methodological and philosophical deficiencies in Altizer's theological position, including an uncritical reliance on the anthroposophist Owen Barfield and the Swedenborgian inspired writings of William Blake.[18] He underscored Blake's dubious occult encounters with the spirits of the deceased, and the dire ramifications of accepting anthroposophy.[19]

The theology of the liberal Episcopal Bishop James Pike drew criticism from Montgomery and culminated in a debate in Canada in 1967. As Pike's theology went into serious decline it appeared that he was evidencing signs of mental and spiritual collapse in the wake of his son's suicide. Pike participated in a televised séance to contact his dead son that was conducted by the spiritualist medium Arthur Ford.[20] Montgomery revisited Pike's beliefs some years later when reviewing Richard Woods' book *The Devil*. Woods was a New Shape Catholic theologian who dedicated his book in memory of Pike.[21]

Counterculture and the Esoteric

At the same time Montgomery noted the rising tide of youth interests in altered states of consciousness. Hallucinogenic drug-induced mystical experiences were being regarded as the salvific door through which one could attain what William James once referred to as the "anaesthetic revelation."[22] Montgomery was especially critical of Timothy Leary's experiments with LSD and the monistic mysticism espoused by Aldous Huxley and Alan Watts.[23] He ensured that his theological students did not overlook these trends.[24] On three separate occasions during his 10-year association with Trinity Evangelical Divinity School, Montgomery presented a seminar on "The Theology of Occult and Demonic Phenomena."[25]

During the late 1960s he helped to promote the apologetics ministry of the Christian Research Institute (CRI) in Europe. CRI was founded in 1960 by the countercult apologist Walter R. Martin (1928–1989).[26] Montgomery assisted Martin in designing and collating important apologetics material for a projected computer database network.[27] Years later they collaborated in shaping the apologetics curricula at both Melodyland School of Theology and the Simon Greenleaf School of Law's master of arts programme where the occult was studied in elective courses.[28]

The early 1970s witnessed much interest in astrology, esoteric knowledge, tarot cards, and psychic phenomena.[29] At that time American evangelical analyses of the occult were characterised by a confrontational negative apologetic. In this genre the analysis tended to concentrate on pastoral warnings of demonic deception and biblical prohibitions over occult involvement. Arguments negating occult teachings were buttressed by didactic discussions of biblical texts and Christian doctrines. All occult phenomena and esoteric dogma were theologically condemned with a corresponding appeal to readers to repent and have faith in Christ.[30]

As interest in the occult grew, Montgomery responded with three books that were released in 1973: *Cross and Crucible*, *Principalities and Powers*, and *How Do We Know There Is a God?* It has already been noted that *Cross and Crucible* is addressed to the world of scholars. In the latter two books Montgomery addressed a wider audience, and what he said marked a new kind of evangelical engagement with the occult. *Principalities and Powers* broke new ground by treating the occult as a serious quest for ultimate meaning and refocused discussion on interpretative questions that covered a broad spectrum of occult phenomena: parapsychology, astrology, cabala, hermetic sciences, secret societies, divination, psychic gifts, tarot cards, folklore, lycanthropy, theosophy, witchcraft, and demon possession. Across this topical spectrum Montgomery was less interested in recounting occult phenomena and more concerned about achieving a deeper level of analysis. He therefore did not proceed on the predetermined basis that all occult phenomena is diabolical:

> As evangelicals we present an eternally true gospel embedded in a permanently veracious Scripture, but we refuse to baptize or damn any contemporary cultural expression simply because this is "how we've always felt." Here we have taken no *a priori* stand on the occult—and readers will find that, in the complexity of the subject, positive or negative judgment must always be applied to particular phenomena, never to the entire field as if it were a monolithic entity.[31]

His prefatory remarks also indicated that the theology he was offering readers is "the path that fulfils the occult quest."[32] Thus Montgomery's approach was quite different in style and attitude from the way in which evangelicals had previously presented their doctrinal refutations of occultism. At the outset of his work, he showed an explicit willingness to regard the occult as a spiritual search for ultimate meaning, and he was not committed *a priori* to the stance that all occult phenomena is demonic. He argued that the categories of the supernatural and paranormal are often treated in reductionist ways depending on the analyst's assumptions. Montgomery was unwilling to lump all occult phenomena into the twin reductionist categories of "humbug" and the "demonic." At the heart of Montgomery's research is a strong commitment to a critically informed empirical method that eschews an *a priori* bias in favour of a naturalistic worldview.[33]

In *Principalities and Powers* Montgomery synthesised his work on the subjective-evidential apologetic in relationship to occult symbols, especially those expressed in alchemy, astrology, the cabala, tarot cards, fairies, and monsters. In the course of his analysis, Montgomery pointed to Christ motifs in tarot and fairy symbols and also found significant theological points of contact in the alchemist's and astrologer's quests. He simultaneously followed in the footsteps of his theological mentor Luther by making his apologetic gambits from a Christocentric perspective. Alongside these discussions Montgomery was unqualified in his condemnation of evil, paid serious attention to the reality of the demonic, and argued against the esoteric speculations of theosophic forms of religion. The religious studies specialist Irving Hexham remarked that "the strength of this book lies in its historical analysis and logical criticism."[34]

Two other distinct features undergird this book. One is that Montgomery is not an armchair critic. Instead he has investigated occult claims by meeting adepts and listening to their teachings before engaging in any critical analysis. He acknowledges that while living and studying in Europe he "met many contemporary practitioners of the hermetic arts and members of secret societies."[35] This type of interpersonal contact is consistent with one of the foundational planks of religious studies research and of missiology.[36]

The other feature is that he raised the bibliographical standards on which Christian research into the occult should be based:

> As careful students of occult literature are aware, the quantity of current publishing in this field is no indicator of quality: the vast majority of today's paperback and hardcover occult literature . . . consists of journalistic rehashing of yesterday's unscholarly popular treatments . . . the worthless character of this material can be detected by a very simple test: note the absence of documentation (specific footnote references and specific citation of bibliographical sources) in connection with the accounts of marvels and the recording of occult rituals . . . The present book, however, is grounded in the serious literature of the subject.[37]

Principalities and Powers is richly supported by 27 pages of endnote documentation. The author notes that "all bibliographical materials cited in the present volume are in my personal possession."[38] As a compulsive bibliophile Montgomery's personal collection of some 18,000 volumes includes a substantial number of significant "secondary literature on all branches of the occult sciences," as well as many "Latin, French, and German grimoires or manuals of occult practice" from the sixteenth, seventeenth, and eighteenth centuries.[39] This aspect impressed Hexham who stated that *Principalities and Powers* is "a well-documented confrontation with occult phenomena from the standpoint of an evangelical Lutheran."[40]

In *How Do We Know There Is a God?* Montgomery replied to a list of religious questions that had been submitted to the Sermons from Science Pavilion in Montreal. The list included occult topics such as Edgar Cayce's prophecies, demons, horoscopes, and necromancy.[41] In 1974 the motion picture *The Exorcist* was released in cinemas, and the popular reaction to it prompted Montgomery to explain the topics of exorcism and demonology in the public square.[42] That same year also witnessed the release of his book *Myth, Allegory and Gospel*, which explicated the case for the literary or subjective-evidential apologetic. The following year he revised *Principalities and Powers* to include a fresh collection of articles addressing both practical pastoral problems and theological issues about the demonic and exorcism.[43] It was also in 1975 that 25 scholars studied the problem of the demonic at an interdisciplinary symposium organized by the Christian Medical Association that culminated in the volume *Demon Possession*.[44] In that symposium Montgomery presented two papers. One evaluated the juridical criteria that were employed to justify the late medieval, Renaissance, and post-Reformation witch trials, while the other entailed responding to a colleague's paper concerning depression and the demonic.[45]

New Age and Neo-Pagan surge

Although Montgomery's career from the 1980s onward has been centred in jurisprudence, he continued in his apologetic work alongside the cultural surge into New Age and neo-pagan spiritualities. In 1986 he replied to critics of his thesis on Andreae as a symposium lecturer at the Ritman Library in Amsterdam.[46] In 1993 he participated in a philosophy symposium at California State University and entered into critical discussions with Emily Culpepper on radical feminist theologies. Here Montgomery briefly noted the occult feminist theology of Starhawk who is a prominent figure in American witchcraft.[47] He also examined the role of occult practices in understanding Chinese religions in his book *Giant in Chains*.[48]

The International Academy of Apologetics was created in 1998 under Montgomery's direction with an annual summer intensive programme of courses in Strasbourg. Montgomery has ensured that occult and New Age spiritualities are included as courses presented through the Academy.[49] Similarly, as the editor of the *Global Journal of Classical Theology*, he has published essays on New Age spirituality.[50] Recently, he reiterated the relevance of his subjective-evidential apologetic among occult and new spirituality seekers at the Hope for Europe conference that gathered in Basel in November 2006.

Influence and Assessment

Friends and critics alike have analysed Montgomery's apologetic monographs on the defence of Scripture, historiography, and jurisprudence.[51] However, a comprehensive analysis that integrates the entire corpus of his writings remains as a task for future scholarship. When that exercise is undertaken, his monographs and audiotaped lectures on the occult and subjective-evidential apologetics must be appraised. Without that analysis there cannot be a holistic picture concerning his entire apologetic labours.[52] The following remarks are offered as mere embryonic cells for that future comprehensive work.

Cross and Crucible Controversy

In any assessment of Montgomery's writings, it is *Cross and Crucible* that looms large on the scholar's canvas. Montgomery regards it as his most important piece of scholarship.[53] It is interesting to note that although it was first released 33 years ago the book remains in print.[54] Perhaps the book's durability is explicable because in the words of one reviewer it "is erudite, stimulating, and prolix."[55] Mircea Eliade (1907–1986), the doyen of religious phenomenologists included it in his list of "stimulating recent books on Renaissance and post-Renaissance alchemy."[56]

Cross and Crucible can be regarded as a singularly radical, controversial, and yet influential piece of work inasmuch that it has "turned the world upside down" in scholarship concerning Andreae, the origins of Rosicrucian thought, and long-held negative impressions of seventeenth-century Lutheranism. It is not surprising to discover a spectrum of attitudes concerning this book. The historians William Bouwsma and Charles Kay have agreed with Montgomery that the unfavourable image of early Lutherans being opposed to scientific thought and being intellectually sterile is untenable.[57] Montgomery's evidence helped to goad Robert Westman and John R. Christianson into fresh studies on Lutheran astrology in the rise of modern science.[58] It has also been a helpful source for Hereward Tilton's work on the Lutheran alchemist Michael Maier.[59]

However, the central controversy that ensues concerns Andreae's authorship of the Rosicrucian manifestos. Bouwsma, Christianson, and Kay have accepted Montgomery's demolition of the claim that Andreae supported Rosicrucianism. Bouwsma avers that "Montgomery demonstrates convincingly that, far from advocating Rosicrucianism, his *Chymische Hochzeit* sought to counteract its dangers by reinterpreting the story of Christian Rosencruez in terms of orthodox Lutheranism."[60] Kay accepts that Andreae held at the very least to Lutheran orthodoxy which was framed within a cultural milieu where the hand of God's "magic" abounded.[61]

Christianson concurs:

> If Montgomery is right, Andreae thought of himself as a kind of missionary to those many intellectuals of his generation who had been enticed away from orthodox Christian beliefs by various occult movements. . . . [Montgomery] argues that the *Chymical Wedding* was intended to lead them back to Christian orthodoxy. He wanted, says Montgomery, to transform Christian Rosencreutz from a Magus into "Christian Everyman." This is certainly consistent with Andreae's frontal attacks upon the Rosicrucian movement a few years later.[62]

However, there are other partisan stances. Antoine Faivre draws in part on Montgomery's interpretation of the seven alchemical processes that can be discerned in Andreae's *Chymische Hochzeit*.[63] Faivre believes that Montgomery's interpretation of the *Chymische Hochzeit* favours "the theological level over that of alchemy." He recognises that Montgomery explains the Lutheran pursuit of alchemy using a model of science illuminated by faith rather than favouring a theosophical understanding of the hermetic arts.[64] However, in Faivre's view a point of tension remains in orthodox Lutheran thought where Paracelsus's esoteric nature philosophy is set against the "omnipresence of Christ in the natural world and, in a general way, against the theology of Revelation."[65] Here Faivre seems to favour an understanding of the Christian pilgrimage "from a theosophical standpoint" where grace and gnosis conjoin in "a spiral voyage."[66] This latter option is clearly at odds with Montgomery's position.

Christopher McIntosh believes that Andreae held to a Protestant form of hermetic wisdom and that he may have cowritten the *Fama Fraternitatis*. Yet after arguing his point McIntosh is prepared to acknowledge that there is an alternative perspective found in Montgomery's "fascinating study of Andreae."[67] McIntosh is open to the possibility that Tobias Hess, rather than Andreae, may have been "the chief architect of the manifestos."[68]

Jackson Spielvogel notes that although various authorities have argued for Andreae's authorship of the manifestos he admits in light of Montgomery's work that "this has never been proven."[69] Spielvogel accepts that Andreae was a Lutheran pastor but catastrophically misinterprets Andreae's theology in his book *Christianopolis*. He asserts that "the Hermetic emphasis on pantheism is plainly expressed in *Christianopolis*" and construes Andreae's remark that "the smallest leaf contains the whole lessons" as evidence for it.[70] This is particularly curious since Andreae stood in the tradition of Luther. In *Cross and Crucible* Montgomery specifically discussed Luther's attitude toward the natural world and science as being grounded in the doctrine of Christ's presence in the world. Montgomery even cited Luther's remarks that Christ is "substantially present everywhere" and that presence is found "even in the most insignificant leaf."[71] Spielvogel has confused the biblical view of divine immanence in the creation with pantheism.

Donald Dickson and Roland Edighoffer hold that Andreae's role in composing the manifestos is by no means beyond doubt.[72] Dickson accepts that in his later life Andreae is unquestionably an orthodox Lutheran but believes there is sufficient evidence to suggest some collaboration between the younger Andreae and Tobias Hess on the *Confessio Fraternitatis*.[73] Here Dickson relies on the findings of Edighoffer who in 1981 argued the case for collaboration. Edighoffer maintains that the evidence for collaboration is found in a comparison of Andreae's 1612 book *Cosmoxenus*, and his 1616 book *Theca gladii spiritus*, which was dedicated to Hess who had died in 1614.[74] Edighoffer is at odds with Montgomery's interpretation of the relationship between Hess and Andreae.[75] What scholars must weigh up is the primary source evidence presented by Montgomery and Edighoffer on the Hess-Andreae relationship, and establishing which of the rival interpretations proffered best fits the facts.[76] Beyond that hermeneutical divide it should also be noted that elsewhere Edighoffer argues that Andreae was a Lutheran who wanted to bring the Reformation to fruition but that the key to understanding his work should "be found in religious Hermeticism."[77] The unanswered question here for Edighoffer is whether Andreae's hermetic views were framed in a contextualised orthodox Lutheran theology and apologetic (Montgomery's view) or grounded in an anthropocentric version of Gnostic esotericism.[78]

Lastly *Cross and Crucible* has been the object of some scathing criticism from Adam McLean.[79] McLean admits there has been a long controversy over the authorship of the *Chymische Hochzeit* and notes that Andreae claimed later in life to have been its author. He finds it difficult to accept that Andreae was the author:

> From what we know of Andreae as an orthodox and emi-
> nent Lutheran pastor and academic, it seems unlikely that
> he could have devised such a profoundly esoteric docu-
> ment, which in fact has at its basis many heretical ideas
> even in Protestant terms.[80]

McLean rejects Montgomery's argument that the *Chymische Hochzeit* was a work of orthodox Lutheran apologetics. He bluntly states that "Montgomery's commentary on the *Chemical Wedding* is a perfect, though sad example of biased and blind scholarship, as he insensitively cobbles and pulverizes the text."[81] He maintains that Montgomery misconstrues the alchemical symbolism and fails to grasp the esoteric parts of the book. McLean insists that Andreae's book is "one of the most important Rosicrucian documents" and that it presents allegorical insights "into inner transformation."[82] In his own commentary McLean argues that the *Chymische Hochzeit* con-veys an esoteric Christian message that radically differed from the theology of the cross proffered in the Reformation.[83]

McLean calls attention to the meaning of the Rose on the Cross as "a new symbol in the soul of humanity."[84] He takes this symbol on the cross to be "a symbol of resurrection and transformation" and that the rose is "also a symbol of the feminine placed on the mascu-line cross."[85] McLean believes that the twin masculine-feminine ele-ments reflect the central motif of the "Hermetic androgyne" that was expressed in alchemy.[86] He then articulates this view:

> Rosicrucianism is that esoteric philosophy lying at the
> heart of Western Hermeticism which provides a path for
> the balancing and integration of the masculine and femi-
> nine aspects of our souls, and the inner meeting of the lofty

intellect with the primal earthy energies at the center of our being.[87]

McLean concludes: "The power of our inner transformation, our resurrection and rebirth to the spirit, lies within each of our souls if only we go on our inner quest and participate in the *Chemical Wedding*, to which all of us are eternally invited."[88]

McLean's position is fraught with many critical problems. The first is his reluctance to accept that Andreae as an orthodox Lutheran wrote the *Chymische Hochzeit*. McLean simply creates a problem for his own view because Andreae unequivocally says he wrote the book. The tension that McLean has is, on the one hand, he admits that Andreae was a Lutheran, and on the other hand he wants to retain an esoteric reading of the book. His preference for an esoteric interpretation collides with the clear evidence of Andreae's authorship and orthodoxy. If Andreae wrote the *Chymische Hochzeit*, then one is bound to follow the primary source evidence of Andreae's life and the corpus of writings that attest to his orthodoxy. If the *Chymische Hochzeit* is indeed a contextualised apologia designed to woo esotericists to Christ, then the author's intent must take precedence over what we might like his book to have said or meant. It needs to be reiterated that a contextual apologetic addresses a particular audience in their thought forms, using points of contact and overlap to show how Christ fulfils their human quest for meaning.[89] Thus if the *Chymische Hochzeit* employs the language, thought forms, and concepts of alchemy and hermeticism, this should not appear to be very surprising at all.[90]

Another problem arises from his accusation that Montgomery's interpretation is biased because the same point can be argued back about McLean's interpretation. The question remains whether Montgomery's or McLean's interpretation concurs with Andreae's text and professed worldview. Although McLean regards the rose symbol as one concerning the resurrection, he appears to take this only as an inner symbol for transformation. However the symbol of the rose is traceable back from Andreae's family herald to Luther's own seal. Montgomery photographically reproduced Luther's seal in *Cross and Crucible*.[91]

What is also problematic is that McLean does not integrate into his understanding those dogmas that Andreae believed in about the bodily resurrection of Christ and of humankind in the general resurrection. In the seventeenth century the great debates ensued between orthodox Christian apologists and the Deists over the miracle and historicity of Christ's bodily resurrection.[92] That controversy was not concerned with interior esoteric symbols. Although one can indeed point to symbols, typologies, and analogies of resurrection in myth, literature, and the natural world, the Christian tradition holds these things to be mere shadows of the reality of corporeal resurrection.[93] In neither Andreae's nor Montgomery's theology is there merely an inner or symbolic resurrection. McLean has possibly not realised that in the wider corpus of Montgomery's writings there stands his historical-juridical apologetic for the bodily resurrection of Christ. Montgomery would agree that the inner being of every human needs transforming. However, unlike McLean's apparent advocacy of autosoteriology, the way to transformation and final resurrection that Andreae and Montgomery unswervingly point to is via the unmerited grace of God in Christ that is received in repentance and faith.

A further criticism concerning McLean's commentary is whether it represents a strict reading of alchemy as it was understood in Andreae's day. McLean is correct in pointing to the enigmatic symbol of the androgyne. However, his vocabulary on the masculine and feminine aspect in each soul resembles Carl Gustav Jung's thought. Is McLean offering us an interpretation that is consistent with the way a seventeenth-century alchemist thought? Or are we simply being offered the impressions that Andreae's text has made on the mind of a modern-day esotericist? While Montgomery does employ Jungian categories to explore the *Chymische Hochzeit*, he is careful in staying close to Andreae's theology for hermeneutical purposes. To this it could be added that an appreciation of creation theology could help us understand better the masculine and feminine motifs of Lutheran alchemy. God made human beings, both female and male, in his own image and likeness (Gen 1:26–27). Both genders equally reflect the *Imago Dei*. The resurrected union of believers in Christ does not lead to inner androgyny but to the whole person transformed for eternity in an I and Thou fellowship.

General Influence

Montgomery has taught a generation of students on various campuses about understanding and sensitively responding to seekers who tread the labyrinthine ways of esoteric knowledge and occult phenomena. His campus wisdom has been further disseminated in permanent form through his writings thereby reaching a wider audience. Bibliographically his texts are cited in many different disciplines. The Christian folklore specialist Bill Ellis has relied on Montgomery's sagely insights about the witch trials in analysing modern social panics about Satanic groups.[94] *Demon Possession* is also cited in evangelical literature on exorcism.[95] Elements of Montgomery's literary apologetic have also directly inspired Michael Frost's apologia for recovering the imagination and finding points of contact in popular culture.[96] Montgomery's subjective-evidential apologetic style, as it is applied to the motifs of fantasy literature and occult symbolism, converges in Philip Johnson's proposal for developing mythic apologetics in both secular postmodern and alternate spiritual contexts.[97]

Prominent countercult apologists such as John Ankerberg and John Weldon, James Bjornstad, Douglas Groothuis, Craig Hawkins, Robert Morey, Josh McDowell, and Don Stewart have relied on various parts of Montgomery's work.[98] Among the new generation of missionary-apologetes dealing with the esoteric, New Age, and neo-pagan networks, Montgomery's direct influence can also be found in the writings of John Drane, Ross Clifford, Philip Johnson, Ole Skjerbaek Madsen, Simeon Payne, and John Smulo.[99] The way Montgomery's insights and apologetic styles have been used by these countercult and missionary practitioners is quite varied, and their conclusions should not be attributed to him. However this corpus of literature attests to the broad influence that he has had in evangelical networks worldwide.

Conclusion

Today's missionary-apologete who inhabits the terrain alongside the New Age, neo-pagan, and esoteric seekers in order to make disciples has much to gain from the pioneering example of Montgomery. He provides a model of careful study where the missionary-apologete becomes acquainted with seekers firsthand, making a conscientious effort to listen and understand. His meticulous bibliographical standards serve as a reminder that one must always read the primary sources before taking up any critical response. In *Principalities and Powers* he shows how one can creatively engage the occultist's quest by uncovering areas of common interest, which is a basic step in cross-cultural missionary communication. He unpacks many rich and striking Christ motifs in alchemy, astrology, and tarot cards, while discerning good from evil in all forms of occult phenomena. He further demonstrates that one can bear sensitive witness on intuitive and empirical problems while maintaining an unswerving obedience to the uniqueness and particularity of Christ as saviour. The corpus of his work highlights a high degree of originality as witnessed in *Cross and Crucible* and also in developing his subjective-evidential apologetic gambits. His writings also remind us that both the academy and popular culture require the presence and work of missionary-apologetes. His work has directly inspired contextual forms of mission in New Age festivals in Denmark and Australia.

New religions expert J. Gordon Melton regards Montgomery as one of "the finest evangelical writers on the psychic and paranormal."[100] Melton maintains that both Montgomery and J. Stafford Wright "stand out for their balanced, Christian approach to the occult" and that their books "should satisfy even the most curious mind about the reality, the dangers, and a Christian assessment of what is popularly termed the psychic realm."[101] According to Melton their books can guide average church members through the occult and are valuable because they "strip away the aura of fear ... by a plain and simple divulging of basic information."[102] Such high esteem for his writings is indeed a splendid and apt way of honouring Montgomery's apologia to the occult.

Endnotes

1   On the technical definition of these words see Antoine Faivre and Karen-Claire Voss, "Western Esotericism and the Science of Religions," *Numen*, 42: 1 (January 1995), 48–77. Thomas Robbins, "New Religions and Alternative Religions," *Nova Religio*, 8: 3 (March 2005), 104–11.

2   Edward F. Crangle, ed., *Esotericism and the Control of Knowledge* (Sydney: Department of Studies in Religion The University of Sydney, 2004). Antoine Faivre, *Access to Western Esotericism* (Albany: State University of New York Press, 1994). B. J. Gibbons, *Spirituality and the Occult: From the Renaissance to the Modern Age* (London and New York: Routledge, 2001). Wouter J. Hanegraaff, *New Age Religion and Western Culture: Esotericism in the Mirror of Secular Thought* (Albany: State University of New York Press, 1998). Ronald Hutton, *The Triumph of the Moon: A History of Modern Pagan Witchcraft* (Oxford: Oxford University Press, 1999). Roelof van den Broek and Wouter J. Hanegraaff, ed., *Gnosis and Hermeticism: From Antiquity to Modern Times* (Albany: State University of New York Press, 1998).

3   Douglas E. Cowan, *Cyberhenge: Modern Pagans on the Internet* (New York: Routledge, 2005). Bill Ellis, *Lucifer Ascending: The Occult in Folklore and Popular Culture* (Lexington: The University Press of Kentucky, 2004). Steven Sutcliffe and Marion Bowman, ed., *Beyond New Age: Exploring Alternative Spirituality* (Edinburgh: Edinburgh University Press, 2000), 188–200. Jin Kyu Park, "Creating My Own Cultural and Spiritual Bubble: Case of Cultural Consumption by Spiritual Seeker Anime Fans," *Culture and Religion*, 6: 3 (November 2005), 393–413. Adam Possamai, *Religion and Popular Culture: A Hyper-Real Testament* (Brussels: P.I.E.-Peter Lang, 2005).

4   John Warwick Montgomery, *Principalities and Powers* (Minneapolis: Bethany Fellowship, 1973), 14. This edition was a hardbound text illustrated with photographs. A revised paperback edition was later issued without the photographs see note 20 below. In 1981 Bethany House reissued the original 1973 edition.

5   Ibid., 14.

6   Ibid., 30.

7   Montgomery, "Preface," in *Evidence for Faith: Deciding the God Question*, ed. Montgomery (Dallas: Probe, 1991), 9.

8   See David R. Liefeld, "Lutheran Orthodoxy and Evangelical Ecumenicity in the Writings of John Warwick," *Westminster Theological Journal*, 50 (1988), 103–26.

9   Montgomery's résumé appears on-line at www.jwm.christendom.co.uk/.

10 Montgomery, "The Chronicles of Narnia and the Adolescent Reader," *Religious Education*, 54:5 (September-October 1959), 418–28. Cf. Montgomery, "Neglected Apologetic Styles: The Juridical and the Literary," in *Evangelical Apologetics*, ed. Michael Bauman, David W. Hall, and Robert C. Newman (Camp Hill: Christian Publications, 1996), 119–33.

11 Montgomery, "Introduction: The Apologists of Eucatastrophe," in *Myth, Allegory and Gospel: An Interpretation of J. R. R. Tolkien, C. S. Lewis, G. K. Chesterton, Charles Williams*, ed. Montgomery (Minneapolis: Bethany Fellowship,

1974), 11–31. Montgomery, *The Transcendent Holmes* (Ashcroft: Calabash Press, 2000). Montgomery, *Tractatus Logico-Theologicus* (Bonn: Verlag für Kultur und Wissenschaft, 2003), 184–89.

12 Montgomery, "God's Devil: A Ghost Story with a Moral," *Chiaroscuro*, 4 (1961), and reprinted in *Principalities and Powers*, 151–66.

13 Montgomery, "Lutheran Astrology and Alchemy in the Age of the Reformation," *Ambix: The Journal of the Society for the Study of Alchemy and Early Chemistry*, 11 (June 1963), 65–86.

14 Montgomery, *Cross and Crucible: Johann Valentin Andreae (1586–1654), Phoenix of the Theologians*, 2 vols. (The Hague: Martinus Nijhoff, 1973).

15 Cf. Montgomery, "Back to the Sixties?" *New Oxford Review* (July-August 1994), 25–27.

16 See Paul Heelas, David Martin, and Paul Morris, ed., *Religion, Modernity and Postmodernity* (Oxford and Malden: Blackwell Publishers, 1998). Cf. John Drane, *Do Christians Know How to Be Spiritual? The Rise of New Spirituality and the Mission of the Church* (London: Darton, Longman and Todd, 2005).

17 Montgomery, *The 'Is God Dead?' Controversy* (Grand Rapids: Zondervan, 1966). Montgomery, *The Altizer-Montgomery Dialogue: A Chapter in the God Is Dead Controversy* (Chicago: Inter-Varsity Press, 1967). Montgomery, *Ecumenicity, Evangelicals and Rome* (Grand Rapids: Zondervan, 1969), 97–100. Montgomery, *The Suicide of Christian Theology* (Minneapolis: Bethany Fellowship, 1970).

18 On Swedenborg's influence see Marguerite Block, *The New Church in the New World* (New York: Octagon, 1968). On Anthroposophy see Geoffrey Ahern, *Sun at Midnight: The Rudolf Steiner Movement and the Western Esoteric Tradition* (Wellingborough: Aquarian, 1984).

19 Montgomery, *The Altizer-Montgomery Dialogue*, 43–44 and 48–50.

20 Montgomery, "The Bishop, the Spirits, and the Word," *Christianity Today* (February 16, 1968), 48. Cf. Montgomery, *Principalities and Powers*, 144–46, and *The Suicide of Christian Theology*, 17–61.

21 Montgomery, "An Anti-Ecumenical Devil?" *Christianity Today* (May 24, 1974), 61–62.

22 William James, *The Varieties of Religious Experience* (Glasgow: Fount, 1977), 373–75. Montgomery assessed James' work in *The Shape of the Past*, rev. ed. (Minneapolis: Bethany Fellowship, 1975), 312–40.

23 Montgomery, "The Gospel According to LSD," in *The Suicide of Christian Theology*, 73–75. On the counterculture see Robert S. Ellwood, *The Sixties Spiritual Awakening: American Religion Moving from Modern to Postmodern* (New Brunswick: Rutgers University Press, 1994). Charles Y. Glock and Robert N. Bellah, ed., *The New Religious Consciousness* (Berkeley, Los Angeles, and London: University of California Press, 1976). Timothy Miller, *Hippies and American Values* (Knoxville: University of Tennessee Press, 1991). Theodore Roszak, *The Making of a Counter-Culture* (London: Faber, 1970). On the distinction between "postmodern" and "post-modern" see *Religious and Non-Religious Spirituality in the Western World* ("New Age"), Lausanne Occasional Paper No. 45, available at www.lausanne.org/lcwe/assets/LOP45_IG16 .pdf.

24　See the essays by his students in *Christianity for the Tough-Minded*, ed. Montgomery (Minneapolis: Bethany Fellowship, 1973), 145–55, 193–200, and 215–24.

25　Montgomery, *Principalities and Powers*, 1973 ed., 23. Montgomery taught in the divinity school from 1964–1974.

26　On Martin and the Christian countercult movement see J. Gordon Melton, "The counter-cult monitoring movement in historical perspective," in *Challenging Religion: Essays in Honour of Eileen Barker*, ed. James A. Beckford and James T. Richardson (London and New York: Routledge, 2003), 102–13.

27　Montgomery, "Automating Apologetics in Austria," *Christianity Today* (November 8, 1968), 57–58. Montgomery, *Computers, Cultural Change and the Christ* (Wayne: Christian Research Institute, 1969). Walter R. Martin, "SENT/EAST Electronic Answering Search Technology," *The Christian Librarian*, 14:1 (October 1970), 3–6. Montgomery, "Christian Research Institute," *The Christian Librarian*, 14:1 (October 1970), 15–18.

28　On Montgomery's association with Melodyland, see Montgomery, *Faith Founded on Fact* (Nashville and New York: Thomas Nelson Publishers, 1978), 225–27. On Martin's affiliation with Melodyland, see Richard Quebedeaux, *The Worldly Evangelicals* (New York: Harper and Row, 1978), 66–67.

29　See Martin Marty, "The Occult Establishment," *Social Research*, 2 (Summer 1970), 212–30. Marcello Truzzi, "Astrology as Popular Culture," *Journal of Popular Culture*, 8, 4 (Spring 1975), 906–11. Edward A. Tiryakian, "Toward the Sociology of Esoteric Culture," *American Journal of Sociology*, 78:3 (November 1972), 491–512.

30　For example, Gordon R. Lewis, *Confronting the Cults* (Philadelphia: Presbyterian & Reformed, 1966). Walter R. Martin, *The Kingdom of the Cults* (Grand Rapids: Zondervan, 1965). Roger C. Palms, *The Christian and the Occult* (Valley Forge: Judson Press, 1972). J. Oswald Sanders, *Heresies Ancient and Modern* (London: Marshall, Morgan and Scott, 1948). Cf. John A. Saliba, *Understanding New Religious Movements*, 2nd ed. (Walnut Creek, Lanham, New York and Oxford: Alta Mira Press, 2003), 203–39.

31　Montgomery, *Principalities and Powers*, 20.

32　Ibid., 20.

33　Ibid., 28–46. Cf. Montgomery, *The Suicide of Christian Theology*, 267–313; Montgomery, *Tractatus-Logico-Theologicus*, 23–72; Montgomery, "The Quest for Absolutes: An Historical Argument," in *Jurisprudence: A Book of Readings*, ed. Montgomery (Strasbourg: International Scholarly Publishers, 1980), 523–39.

34　Irving Hexham, "A Bibliographical Guide to Cults, Sects, and New Religious Movements (Part II)," *Update: A Quarterly Journal on New Religious Movements*, 8:1 (March 1984), 43.

35　Montgomery, *Principalities and Powers*, 16.

36　See Terry C. Muck, *The Mysterious Beyond: A Basic Guide to Studying Religion* (Grand Rapids: Baker, 1993). Robert N. Minor, "Understanding as the First Step in an Evangelical Approach to World Religions: Some Methodological Considerations," *Journal of the Evangelical Theological Society*, 19:2 (Spring 1976), 121–28.

37 Montgomery, *Principalities and Powers*, 18–19.

38 Ibid., 15.

39 Ibid., 14–15.

40 Hexham, "A Bibliographical Guide to Cults," 43.

41 Montgomery, *How Do We Know There Is a God? And Other Questions Inappropriate in Polite Society* (Minneapolis: Bethany Fellowship, 1973), 69–70, 72–73, and 76–77.

42 Montgomery, "Exorcism: Is It for Real?" *Christianity Today* (July 26, 1974), 4–8. Montgomery, "The Exorcist: An Interpretation of the Film," *Trinity Journal*, 3 (Spring 1974), 107–10.

43 *Principalities and Powers: The World of the Occult*, rev. ed. (Minneapolis: Dimension Books, 1975), 165–91. This revised paperback edition included the articles in notes 21 and 42, and it further differed from the original hardbound edition with the deletion of photographs that appeared on pp. 10, 64, 69, 72, 98, 100, 130, 133, 145, 148, and 152.

44 Montgomery, ed., *Demon Possession* (Minneapolis: Bethany Fellowship, 1976).

45 "Not Suffering Witches to Live: A Brief Reappraisal of Witch Trial Theory and Practice," and "Commentary on Hysteria and Demons, Depression and Oppression, Good and Evil," in ibid., 91–104 and 232–36.

46 Montgomery, "The World-View of Johann Valentin Andreae," in *Das Erbe des Christian Rosencreutz*, ed. F. A. Janssen (Amsterdam: In de Pelikaan, 1988), 152–69.

47 Montgomery, "Gorgon Theology," *New Oxford Review* (July-August 1993), 20–21.

48 Montgomery, *Giant in Chains: China Today and Tomorrow* (Milton Keynes: Nelson Word, 1994), 102–13.

49 This venture is a successor to an earlier programme in human rights and apologetics that Montgomery created in the 1980s through the Simon Greenleaf School of Law. Cf. Trinity College and Seminary, Newburgh, Indiana www.trinitysem.edu/TrinityDifference/InternationalFocus.html

50 For example, Ben M. Carter, "New Age Thinking About the Soul: The Postmodern Metaphysics of Gary Zukav," *Global Journal of Classical Theology*, 2: 2 (August 2000), available at www.trinitysem.edu/journal/carterpap_v2n2 .html.

51 Start with Kenneth D. Boa and Robert M. Bowman, *Faith Has Its Reasons: An Integrative Approach to Defending Christianity* (Colorado Springs: NAV Press, 2001), 167–246. Ross Clifford, *John Warwick Montgomery's Legal Apologetic: An Apologetic for All Seasons* (Bonn: Verlag für Kultur und Wissenschaft, 2004).

52 Space limitations precluded any discussion of his audio lecture "The Occultic Revolution", which is available from the Canadian Institute for Law Theology and Public Policy see www.ciltpp.com/.

53 See Montgomery, ed., *International Scholars Directory* (Chicago: Marquis Who's Who, 1975), 175. He reaffirmed this fact to me in a private conversation on February 14, 1986 in Sydney, Australia.

54 Kluwer Academic in The Netherlands is the current publisher.

55 J. R. Christianson, *Christian Scholar's Review*, 6:4 (1977), 368.

56 Mircea Eliade, *The Forge and the Crucible: The Origins and Structures of Alchemy*, translated by Stephen Corrin, 2nd ed. (Chicago and London: University of Chicago Press, 1978), 15 and see 190–91. On Eliade see Douglas Allen, *Myth and Religion in Mircea Eliade* (London and New York: Routledge, 2002).

57 William J. Bouwsma, *The Journal of Modern History*, 48 (1976), 161. Charles D. Kay, "The Rise of Modern Science," *Christianity Today* (April 25, 1975), 33–34.

58 Robert S. Westman, "The Astronomer's Role in the Sixteenth Century: A Preliminary Study," *History of Science*, 18 (1980), 105–47. John Robert Christianson, *On Tycho's Island: Tycho Brahe and His Assistants, 1570–1601* (Cambridge: Cambridge University Press, 2000).

59 Hereward Tilton, "The Life and Work of Count Michael Maier (1569–1622): Understanding Christian Alchemy in the German Calvinist States," *Theology and Religion*, 1 (1999), 23–42.

60 Bouwsma, *The Journal of Modern History*, 160.

61 Kay, "The Rise of Modern Science," 34.

62 Christianson, *Christian Scholar's Review*, 368.

63 Faivre, *Access to Western Esotericism*, 167–69.

64 Ibid., 115.

65 Ibid.

66 Ibid., 173 and 175.

67 Christopher McIntosh, *The Rosicrucians: The History, Mythology, and Rituals of an Esoteric Order*, 3rd rev. ed. (York Beach: Samuel Weiser, 1997), 30.

68 Ibid., 30.

69 Jackson Spielvogel, "Reflections on Renaissance Hermeticism and Seventeenth-Century Utopias," in *Utopian Studies 1*, ed. Gordon Beauchamp, Kenneth Roemer, and Nicholas D. Smith (Lanham: University Press of America, 1987), 193.

70 Ibid., 194.

71 Montgomery, *Cross and Crucible*, 6. Cf. Robert D. Preus, *The Theology of Post-Reformation Lutheranism*, vol. 2 (St. Louis: Concordia Publishing House, 1972), 204–5.

72 Donald R. Dickson, "Johann Valentin Andreae's Utopian Brotherhoods," *Renaissance Quarterly*, 49: 4 (Winter 1996), 760–802. Roland Edighoffer, "Rosicrucianism: From the Seventeenth to the Twentieth Century," in *Modern Esoteric Spirituality*, ed. Antoine Faivre, Jacob Needleman, and Karen Voss (New York: Crossroads, 1992), 186–209.

73 Dickson, "Utopian Brotherhoods," 760–61.

74 Roland Edighoffer, "Johann Valentin Andreae. Vom Rosenkreuz zur Pantopie," *Zeitschrift fur mittiere deutsche Literatur*, 10 (1981), 211–39. Cf. Edighoffer, "Rosicrucianism: From the Seventeenth to the Twentieth Century," in *Modern Esoteric Spirituality*, especially 196–203.

75 Montgomery, *Cross and Crucible*, 57–58, 175–76, 201–9, and 233–35.

76 Cf. Montgomery's reply to his critics in "The World-View of Johann Valentin Andreae."

77   Roland Edighoffer, "Hermeticism in Early Rosicrucianism," in *Gnosis and Hermeticism*, 213.

78   On Lutheran theology in the seventeenth century see Robert D. Preus, *The Theology of Post-Reformation Lutheranism*, 2 vols. (St. Louis: Concordia Publishing House, 1970 and 1972). On contextualisation in missionary theology start with Stephen Neill, *A History of Christian Missions* (Harmondsworth: Penguin, 1964). David J. Bosch, *Transforming Mission: Paradigm Shifts in Theology of Mission* (Maryknoll: Orbis, 1991). David J. Hesselgrave, *Communicating Christ Cross-Culturally: An Introduction to Missionary Communication*, 2nd ed. (Grand Rapids: Zondervan, 1991).

79   Adam McLean, *The Chemical Wedding of Christian Rosenkreutz* (Grand Rapids: Phanes, 1991).

80   Ibid., 10.

81   Ibid.

82   Ibid., 11.

83   Ibid., 154–55.

84   Ibid., 155.

85   Ibid.

86   Ibid.

87   Ibid., 156.

88   Ibid., 157.

89   See Harold Netland, "Toward Contextualized Apologetics," *Missiology*, 16: 3 (1988), 289–303.

90   Cf. the contextualised apologetic in John Drane, Ross Clifford, and Philip Johnson, *Beyond Prediction: The Tarot and Your Spirituality* (Oxford: Lion, 2001), where tarot imagery is employed to point to its fulfilment in the gospel and the person of Christ as saviour.

91   Montgomery, *Cross and Crucible*, photographic plate facing p. 200. Cf. Montgomery, *Heraldic Aspects of the German Reformation* (Bonn: Verlag für Kultur und Wissenschaft, 2003).

92   William Lane Craig, *The Historical Argument for the Resurrection of Jesus During the Deist Controversy* (Lewiston and Queenston: Edwin Mellen Press, 1985).

93   See Montgomery, *Myth, Allegory and Gospel*; also Leon McKenzie, *Pagan Resurrection Myths and the Resurrection of Jesus* (Charlottesville: Bookwrights Press, 1997).

94   Bill Ellis, *Raising the Devil: Satanism, New Religions, and the Media* (Lexington: The University Press of Kentucky, 2000), 287–88.

95   C. Fred Dickason, *Demon Possession and the Christian* (Chicago: Moody, 1987). Ken Olson, *Exorcism: Fact or Fiction?* (Nashville: Thomas Nelson, 1992).

96   Michael Frost, *Eyes Wide Open: Seeing God in the Ordinary* (Sutherland: Albatross, 1998), 97–99.

97   Philip Johnson, "Apologetics and Myths: Signs of Salvation in Postmodernity," *Lutheran Theological Journal*, 32: 2 (July 1998), 62–72.

98   John Ankerberg and John Weldon, *Astrology: Do the Heavens Rule Our Destiny?* (Eugene: Harvest House, 1989). Ankerberg and Weldon, *The Coming*

Darkness (Eugene: Harvest House, 1993). James Bjornstad and Shildes Johnson, *Stars, Signs and Salvation in the Age of Aquarius* (Minneapolis: Bethany Fellowship, 1971). Douglas R. Groothuis, *Revealing the New Age Jesus* (Leicester: InterVarsity Press, 1990). Craig S. Hawkins, *Goddess Worship, Witchcraft and Neo-Paganism* (Grand Rapids: Zondervan, 1998). Josh McDowell and Don Stewart, *Understanding the Occult* (San Bernadino: Here's Life, 1982). Robert A. Morey, *Horoscopes and the Christian* (Minneapolis: Bethany House, 1981).

99 Drane, Clifford, and Johnson, *Beyond Prediction*; Ross Clifford and Philip Johnson, *Jesus and the Gods of the New Age* (Oxford: Lion, 2001/Colorado Springs: Victor, 2003). Philip Johnson and Simeon Payne, "Evangelical Countercult Apologists versus Astrology: An Unresolved Conundrum," *Australian Religion Studies Review*, 17: 2 (Spring 2004), 73–97. Philip Johnson and John Smulo, "Reaching Wiccan and Mother Goddess Devotees," in *Encountering New Religious Movements: A Holistic Evangelical Approach* (Grand Rapids: Kregel, 2004), 209–25. Ole Skjerbaek Madsen, "Spiritual Conflict Among Western Seekers," in *Deliver Us From Evil: An Uneasy Frontier in Christian Mission*, ed. A. Scott Moreau, Tokunboh Adeyemo, David G. Burnett, Bryant L. Myers, and Hwa Yung (Selangor: Glad Sounds, 2003), 127–37.

100 Ronald M. Enroth and J. Gordon Melton, *Why Cults Succeed Where the Church Fails* (Elgin: Brethren Press, 1985), 67.

101 Ibid., 107–8.

102 Ibid., 108.

The Decrease of Pineal Production with Age

CAUSES AND CONSEQUENCES

Willy Humbert

Aging has been defined as a general decline in organic functions as well as a decrease in adaptiveness to change and to restore disrupted homeostasis.

In the last few years, it has been established that circadian rhythms observed in *e.g.* endocrine, behavioral, and anatomical processes were a fundamental feature of living organisms (Aschoff, 1981). In addition to the classical concept of homeostasis, it is now recognized that the functional integrity of organisms also depends on the maintenance of relations between various oscillating variables at the cellular level of organs and organ systems.

The suprachiasmatic nuclei (SCN) of the hypothalamus have been established as the circadian pacemaker of the mammalian brain. It has become increasingly clear that a desynchronisation between the activity of the SCN and the activity of the subject, either experimentally or as a result of shift work or jet lag, results in severe cognitive, emotional, and endocrine disturbances (Feteke et al., 1968).

Within this framework, Samis (1968) hypothetized that the gradual and progressive deterioration of functional potential, which is the ubiquitous hallmark of aging, is the loss of coordination among the many interdependent oscillating systems.

Furthermore Pittendrigh and Daan (1974) suggested that a decay of circadian organization may be involved in the programmed physiological deterioration that limits life span.

This hypothesis of "loss of circadian rhythmicity" in aging is supported by numerous animal studies. Little is known, however, about how the central nervous system correlates the senescence-related changes in circadian rhythms. However, it is now established that in mammals the pineal gland by its rhythmic secretion of melatonin and the SCN play an essential role in the regulation of these rhythmic functions; it is probable that the disfunctioning of one of these structures, or both of them, is at the root of these disturbances.

With respect to the pineal gland, reported to be a circadian or seasonal aging clock, aging coincides with several functional and morphological alterations (Boya and Calvo, 1984). Decrease of secretory processes and particularly of nocturnal melatonin synthesis (the pineal hormone) was reported to occur in rodents during aging (Brown et al., 1979; Reiter et al., 1980). Similar results have been observed in humans. A disappearance of day-night rhythm of melatonin in old and Alzheimer's patients has been reported by Skene et al. (1990). The size of the SCN is also decreased in Alzheimer patients.

A decrease of pineal activity, a reduction of adrenergic innervation as well as a reduction of the number of pinealocytes—the melatonin-producing cell type—has been reported in old male rats (Reuss et al. 1990). However the cause of this melatonin reduction is not clear. We reported in a recent paper an increase in the calcium content of pineal glands of aging rats and the appearance of calcium concretions (Humbert and Pévet, 1991). This increase of calcium in old rats appeared to be the consequence of a degenerative state, especially that of dark pinealocytes (Humbert and Pévet, 1992). Increasing permeablity of the membrane to calcium could be followed by a cascade of events which could represent the transition between viablity and cell death. Dark pinealocytes could be cells on the way to degeneration and be a consequence of the leakiness of the cell membrane.

Loss of cells during the course of aging is not an unknown phenomenon and has been reported in the literature. An age-related loss of neurons has been reported in the septal complex of the rat (Sabel and Stein, 1981). Significant loss of pyramidal neurons in the human hippocampus was described by West and Gunderson (1990).

The aging process being characterized by a progressive decline of the circadian organization of some functions, the role of the SCN appears essential. The SCN and the pineal gland are functionally connected. The rhythm of the pineal hormone melatonin is generated in the SCN. Melatonin has also been shown to synchronize free-running locomotor activity in rats and hamsters. The demonstration of melatonin receptors in the SCN suggests that melatonin may be acting at this site. Age effects on pineal function have also been described. A marked reduction in nocturnal pineal melatonin concentrations has been observed in old rats and hamsters; similar results have been obtained in humans. Indeed, it has been observed that the day-night rhythm in melatonin levels in human pineal glands disappear in old and Alzheimer's patients (Skene et al., 1990). The size of the SCN is also reduced in Alzheimer's patients (Swaab et al., 1985).

Conclusions

It appears that the progressive decrease in the number of pinealocytes observed during the process of aging is associated with the increase of dark degenerating pinealocytes and may be the cause of the age-related reduction in melatonin synthesis occuring in pinealocytes. This phenomenon can be linked to the decrease in electrical activity in old rats (Reuss et al, 1986), to the reduction of sympathic innervation in aging animals and to the decline of the density of β-adrenergic receptors on pineal membranes (Reuss et al., 1990) inducing a reduction of the metabolic activity of the gland.

These hypotheses raise also the question of whether, in the course of aging process, the progressive decrease in amplitude of melatonin rhythm is a consequence of changes at the level of the SCN, or whether these changes at the level of the SCN are a consequence of the decreasing melatonin production. Although these questions need further investigations, it appears that the decrease in melatonin synthesis during the aging process might be a consequence of the progressive decrease in the number of pineal cells.

***

John,

You are always the life of the party at our gatherings here in Strasbourg and I believe that your jokes are even more hilarious when told in French than in English!

While my article argues that aging is an irreversible process on this earth, that seems not to be the case with you. I fully expect you to have 75 more wonderful years, regardless of whether you take melatonin or not!

To a continued long and full life marked by good humor, good friends, and good wine . . .

Dieu vous garde!
Willy Humbert
STRASBOURG, FRANCE
Dr ès Sciences, research engineer
University Louis Pasteur and C.N.R.S.
(Centre national de la recherche scientifique)

References

Aschoff, J. "Biological rhythms". In *Handbook of Behavioral Neurobiology*. F. A. King, ed. Vol 4, Plenum Press, New York (1981).

Boya, J. & J. Calvo. "Structure and ultrastructure of the aging rat pineal gland". J. Pinel Res. 1: 83–89 (1984).

Brown, G. M., S. N. Young, S. Gauthier, H. Tsui, & L. J. Grota. "Melatonin in human cerebrospinal fluid in daytime; its origin and variation with time." Life Sci 25: 929–36 (1979).

Feteke, M., J. M. Van Ree, R. J. M. Niesienk, & D. De Wied. "Disrupting circadian rhytms in rats induces retrograde amnesia." Physiol. Behav. 34: 883–87 (1985).

Humbert, W. & P. Pévet. "Calcium content and concretions of pineal glands of young and old rats. A scanning and X- ray microanalytical study." Cell Tissue Res. 263: 593–96 (1991).

Humbert, W. & P. Pévet. "Permeabilty of the pineal gland of the rat to lanthanum: significance of dark pinealocytes." J. Pineal Res. 12: 84–88 (1992).

Pittendrigh, C. S. & S. Daan. "Circadian oscillators in rodents: a systematic increase of their frequency with age." Science 196: 548–50 (1974).

Reiter, R. J., B. A. Richardson, L. Y. Johnson, B. N. Ferguson, & D. T. Din. "Pineal melatonin rhythm: reduction in aging syrian hamsters." Science 210:1372–73 (1980).

Reuss, S., J. Olcese & L. Vollrath. "Electrophysiological and endocrinological aspects of aging in the rat pineal gland." Neuroendocrinology 43: 466–70 (1986).

Reuss, S., C. Spies, H. Schröder, & L. Vollrath. "The aged pineal gland: reduction in pinealocyte number and adrenergic innervation in male rats." Exp. Gerontol. 25: 183–88 (1990).

Sabel, B. A. & D. G. Stein. "Extensive loss of subcortical neurons in the aging rat brain." Exp. Neurol. 73: 507–16 (1981).

Samis, H. V., Jr. "Aging: loss of temporal organisation." Perspect Biol. Med. 3: 95–102 (1968).

Skene, D. J., B. Vivien-Roels, D. L. Sparks, J. C. Hunsacker, P. Pévet, D. Ravid, & D. F. Swaab. "Daily variation in the concentration of melatonin and 5 methoxytryptophol in the human pineal gland: effect of age and Alzheimer disease." Brain Res. 528: 170–74 (1990).

Swaab, D. F., E. Fliers & T. Partiman. "The suprachiasmatic nucleus of the human brain in relation to sex, age and senile dementia." Brain Res. 34: 37–44 (1985).

West, M. J. & H. J. G. Gunderson. "Unbiased stereological estimation of the number of neurons in the hippocampus." J. Comp. Neurol. 29–22 (1990).

Unbelief, General Revelation, and the Gospel

REFLECTIONS ON ROMANS 1

Thomas K. Johnson

Romans 1:16–32 (original translation):

> *I am not ashamed of the gospel, for it is the power of God intended
> for salvation for each person who believes, first for the Jew and then
> for the Greek. (17) In it the righteousness of God is revealed by faith
> and unto faith, as it is written, "The righteous will live by faith."*

(18) For the wrath of God is being revealed from heaven on all the godless-
ness and injustice of men who suppress the truth by means of injustice, (19)
since the knowledge of God is plain in them; for God has made himself
known to them. (20) His invisible characteristics are received into consciousness through the creation of the world, namely his invisible power and divine
nature, so that people are without an apology. (21) Although they knew
God, they did not glorify him or give thanks to him, but became worthless in
their thoughts and their senseless hearts were darkened. (22) Claiming to be
wise, they became foolish and (23) exchanged the glory of the immortal God
for the image of the likeness of mortal man, birds, animals, and reptiles.

(24) Therefore God gave them over by means of the covetous desires of
their hearts unto uncleanness to dishonor their bodies among themselves,
(25) particularly the very people who exchanged the truth of God for a
lie and deified and worshipped the creation in place of the Creator, who is
blessed forever, amen. (26) Therefore, God gave them over unto dishonorable passions; for example, the women exchanged natural sexual relations
for those which are contrary to nature, (27) as also the men left natural
sexual relations with women and burned in their desires for each other,
man for man, contrary to the scheme of nature; and thereby they receive
in themselves the repayment which was necessary for their delusion.

(28) And since they did not recognize the knowledge of God that they had,
God gave them over to a confused state of mind, to do those things which are
inappropriate. (29) They are full of envy, murder, strife, deceit, and malice.
They are gossips, (30) slanderers, God haters, insolent, arrogant, and boast-
ful; they invent ways of doing evil; they disobey their parents; (31) they are

senseless, disloyal, lacking in normal affections, and merciless. (32) They know
the requirement of God that those who do such things are worthy of death,
but they not only do these things, they also approve of those who do them.

Probably many readers of Saint Paul have been deeply impressed by this text.[1] The author displays incredible confidence about both the truth of his message and about the tremendous importance of his message. And this becomes more striking when one remembers that Paul did not live in a ghetto, separated from the various religions and philosophies of his day. The New Testament portrays for us a man who carried on a continual and living dialogue with the literature, ideas, and representatives of various Jewish and Gentile worldviews, beliefs, and cults. This makes an important question unavoidable: where or how did Paul attain this high level of confidence? The answer, very simply, seems to be that Paul attained this confidence from his understanding of the human condition before God. In the following, in a way that should not be very original or very technical, we will try to gain an overview of Paul's understanding of the human condition, which includes parts of a theory of knowledge. This will be followed by some suggestions about how believers today might think about such matters as secular philosophy and the relation between general revelation and the gospel. The goal of this study is to assist believers in understanding the condition of the unbelieving world, thereby increasing our confidence in the gospel and our ability to communicate the biblical message in a secular world.

I. The Human Condition Before God

To understand Paul's conception of human nature before God, one has to be ready to see human knowledge and life as filled with contradictions and tensions. At the center of these contradictions stands the problem that all people have knowledge of God, even though people often do not want to accept or acknowledge that they have a knowledge of God. Though Paul did not give us precise terminology to use, he assumes some type of contrast between two types of knowledge of God, perhaps something like a contrast between a deficient knowledge and a proper knowledge, or a contrast between a rejected knowledge and an accepted knowledge. The first type of knowledge is what all people have by virtue of creation, whether it is called deficient or rejected knowledge of God. The second type of knowledge, whether it is called proper or accepted, comes only by the gospel.

Paul claims that God really is revealing himself through creation to all people on earth, and the language he uses is in the present tense, meaning this is an active, ongoing work of God through all of human history. God did not merely create the world and go into retirement (as some Deists seem to think); he is currently speaking to all men, women, and children, whether or not they want to listen to God or believe in God. To avoid misunderstanding, it may be wise to notice that Paul sees this activity of God as coming before any human interest in knowing God or asking about God. This activity of God has often been called general revelation, natural revelation, or creational revelation by followers of Paul. Each of these terms has certain strengths, since this revelation of God is general (to all people), coming through nature (including human nature) which is always understood to be God's creation.

As Paul describes this general revelation, it is important to notice that it has very significant content. It is not only a vague feeling or awareness of something higher or holy, though this is surely included. At least three distinct aspects of the content of general revelation are specifically mentioned: the power of God, the deity of God (v. 20), and a very significant portion of the moral demands of God's law (v. 32), which fits closely with a natural scheme or pattern for life (v. 27). This content is much of what has often been called "ethical monotheism;" in Paul's way of thinking, ethical monotheism is the pattern of truth proclaimed by God through creation (as well as in the Scriptures).

As a result of this general revelation, there is a very important sense in which all people in all times and places know God. Paul says the knowledge of God is plain to and in all people (v. 19) and this knowledge is taken into the consciousness of all people (v. 20). Of course, there is also an important sense in which many people do not know God; this is what makes the gospel so important. One of the deepest self-contradictions or paradoxes of human experience is that in at least one area, lack of knowledge is based on knowledge, namely in relation to God. How can this be?

People generally do not like knowing God. And for this reason this knowledge is suppressed or repressed, with the result that people can easily say they do not know God, while, at the same time, they really do know God in an important sense. They know a lot about his power, his deity, and his moral law. But they "suppress the truth" (v. 18). In recent centuries psychologists and psychiatrists have sometimes talked about the suppression of memories or truths that are frightening or deeply disturbing, but this is not a new idea. It is already present in the Bible. One can take the account of Adam and Eve hiding from God behind a bush or tree as a metaphor for what many people do much of the time. Or maybe one could think of the way small children imagine that if they cover their eyes so they cannot see other people, other people cannot see them; if people say they do not know God, they imagine that God does not exist or does not see them. Only when we grasp the gospel, that God is so gracious and forgiving that he sent his son to purchase our redemption, can we then begin to recover from this illness of mind and soul that leads us to claim that we do not know God, when in fact all of us do know God.

According to Paul's description of the human condition, much of our predicament is epistemological sin or epistemological injustice. If a witness in a criminal court trial does not tell the court all he or she knows about the crime under consideration, that witness is guilty of an important crime or sin in the realm of knowledge. He or she did not publicly acknowledge all that he or she really knows. We could call this an act of epistemological (related to knowledge) crime or injustice. Something very similar is happening all the time in relation to God. People say they do not know God when they do know God. This is lying. Unbelief always involves sin since unbelief is epistemological sin. One could wonder if unbelief is close to the very core of original sin.

A sin of this magnitude is not without significant results in the entire life of those guilty of the sin. Some of the results that Paul mentions are closely related to the arena in which the sin occurs, that of thinking and the internal life of the mind and soul. He says, "They became worthless in their thoughts and their senseless hearts were darkened. Claiming to be wise, they became foolish" (vv. 21–22). Here one should not confuse cause and effect. Worthless thoughts, darkened senseless hearts, and claims of wisdom that cover up true foolishness are the result, not the cause. The cause is the epistemological sin of unbelief. People claim they do not know God when they really do know God.

These worthless thoughts, darkened hearts, and general foolishness lead to a profound exchange or substitution: People try to replace the Creator God with something he created. In verse 23 he says, "They exchanged the glory of the immortal God for image of the likeness of mortal man, birds, animals, and reptiles." This means that people create substitute gods to try to replace the Creator. Unbelief does not lead to irreligion; unbelief in the Creator leads to all sorts of religions. People are unavoidably religious, even if they may claim not to be religious and even if they claim they cannot or do not know God. People are constantly creating new gods, and Paul's language suggests a wide diversity of substitute religions. Sometimes people imagine gods or goddesses that are images of themselves, as seen in many types of polytheism. Sometimes people imagine a god or gods that are similar to something else in creation, as seen in various nature religions and fertility cults. Whatever the type of substitute religion, unbelief in the known but denied Creator drives people to replace him with something that may seem to promise what only God can provide. Paul claims that human life is filled with self-deception on a scale that few other people have imagined.

This leads us to a second major theme in Paul's thought in this text. Even though many people may deny it, the human confrontation with God is a central, essential characteristic of human existence.

In general, misbelievers are guilty of a twofold substitution or replacement in their confrontation with God. (There are no unbelievers since everyone believes something and has some substitute god.) Verse 25. The first part of this substitution was already mentioned, but it bears repeating. People replace the truth about God with a lie. This is the truth that comes from God and is about God. It includes the knowledge of much about the demands of God's law, the so-called natural moral law. The lie which replaces the truth about God is that one can be wise without God, denying the power of God or his moral demands. The second part of this substitution or replacement is the worship of creation, or some dimension of creation in place of God. If people find themselves almost compelled to worship something, and if they refuse to worship God, it is only natural that people worship something from creation or an imagined image of something created.

In the confrontation with God at the center of every person's life, God does not somehow remain passive or inactive. The God of the Bible is never passive or inactive. God gives people over to their sinful desires, a claim that Paul repeats in similar terms three times over (vv. 24,26,28). This seems to mean that God lets people experience some of the results of repressing their knowledge of God. In verse 24 Paul uses terms that echo the tenth of the Ten Commandments, that which forbids coveting. God lets people go into their own coveting. In verse 26 Paul says that God gives people over to dishonorable passions. In verse 28 Paul says that God gives people over to a confused state of mind. These are probably three complementary descriptions of the same type of act of God. What probably unites these three complementary descriptions is the claim that God repays the act of people dishonoring God (by not accepting their knowledge of him) by allowing people to dishonor themselves. In this way there is pure justice in the repayment. And to bring about this type of justice, God does not need to intervene from outside by a special act; God repays dishonor by allowing people to dishonor themselves. A key assumption in this act of God, which is not always noticed by readers, is that there is proper way for people to honor themselves, namely by recognizing the truth of God and living according to his plan for his creation. When people accept their status as image bearers of the Creator, there is honor for all; when people create god-substitutes in their own image or in the image of some lower part of creation, there is dishonor for all. Much of what Paul says about sinful actions in this text can best be understood as ways in which people dishonor or debase themselves because God lets them do so.

What Paul says on the topic of homosexuality can best be seen as a particular example of self-dishonoring. He claims homosexual desires and actions arise from a darkened heart and mind, a heart and mind deeply alienated from God and God's creation order. There is a knowable scheme or pattern of nature, which means a created order that all people should follow, and this is heterosexual. Actions and desires contrary to this scheme of nature will be self-dishonoring, assuming that actions that correspond to the scheme of nature will be self-honoring. This means there is something deeply honorable about marriage and childbearing, whereas homosexuality is self-dishonorable. Though homosexuality can be described as sin, it can also be described as the self-punishment for the sin of disbelief and rejection of God's created order.

Something similar must be said about the whole list of sins in verses 29 through 31. The confused state of mind and heart resulting from rejecting God leads people to do all sorts of things that are inappropriate, meaning contrary to honor of those who bear the image of the Creator. The problem is not primarily that people do not know that these actions are wrong; people know that many things are wrong and that these actions are condemned by their Creator. But their actions arise from their confused state of mind arising from unbelief, not from what they know (but probably reject) about what is truly right and wrong. But the confused state of people can go so far that they not only do what they know to be wrong; they can sometimes even begin to excuse or condone those wrong actions which they know to be wrong.

Paul's understanding of the human condition before God was closely related to his tremendous confidence in the truth and importance of his gospel. In preaching he assumed that the people to whom he was speaking already had a long history of conflict with the God whom they know, and whose law they know at least in part, but whom they pretend not to know. Rather than being ashamed of the gospel, in a certain sense, Paul was proud of the gospel since the gospel is the message that God has not left the human race in the predicament we have made for ourselves. It is the message of forgiveness and reconciliation with God, leading to the beginning of a new way of life that is marked by a renewed heart and mind, replacing the darkened heart and mind. This new way of life would be in closer conformity with the law of God and the scheme of nature, and for this reason it would also be more honorable. It goes without saying that Paul's assessment of the human condition before God has deep roots in the Old Testament. In addition to being a commentary on the early chapters of Genesis, it also appropriates the claim of the prophets, that the human problem is not primarily that people do not know right and wrong but that people do not want to follow the knowledge of right and wrong that has been given by God to all people.

II. General Revelation, Christian Thought, and Gospel Proclamation

In the previous section I attempted to exposit the message of Romans 1:16–32, putting matters of technical exegesis into the translation itself. Now it is appropriate to try to demonstrate the significance of a Pauline approach to God's general revelation for the interaction of believers with the secular, unbelieving world. The role of believers in the secular world is always missiological since all believers and the body of Christ as a whole have received a missions commission from our Lord, but that missiological commission calls us to reach people who have often grown up in a culture of unbelief which is shaped by various misbelieving philosophies, worldviews, and religions. Therefore, we must ask how a Pauline type of analysis can help us to understand the lives, ideas, and culture of the people who need the gospel. There is no attempt to be original or creative in what follows since most of these ideas are found in the better evangelical theologians and apologists of the last few centuries. But before going further, it is appropriate to notice a few extreme points of view regarding general revelation that should be avoided.

During the Nazi time in Europe, there were some Protestant theologians who combined a seriously confused theory of general revelation with aspects of the Nazi ideology to form the so-called "German Christian Movement." While the sad details of this type of thinking are beyond purview of this essay, the "German Christian" theologians claimed there was a general revelation of God's law through the demands of the Nazi-Germanic people, or alternately there was a general revelation of God's redemption in the work of Adolf Hitler.[2] Few Christians today will be inclined to mix the biblical faith and the National Socialist ideology, but the tragic mistakes of these theologians (and the churches that followed them) stands as a warning for all time; believers must be very careful about how we think about general revelation in its relation to secular ideologies and worldviews.

In reaction to the German Christians, Karl Barth is properly famous for shouting "Nein!" with such volume that his voice is still echoing in parts of the church today. Barth was concerned that talk of general revelation tends to reduce the biblical message to be merely a religious dimension of a particular culture so the church becomes merely the department of religion of a particular society. While many of Barth's concerns are surely right, they probably result from a misunderstanding of general revelation, not from a proper understanding of general revelation. A Pauline understanding of general revelation enables believers and the church to become confident critics of society and proclaimers of a gospel that all people need.

Another extreme point of view is found in the writings of the so-called "Transcendental Thomist" Roman Catholic theologians. The most famous of these writers is probably Karl Rahner. Whether or not it is exactly what these writers intend, one can easily receive the impression from their books that God's general revelation is so complete that people do not need the gospel of Christ, which only comes via special revelation. Talk of a self-giving, forgiving presence of God in general revelation makes one wonder if the gospel is necessary. In stark contrast, Paul's interpretation of general revelation shows why the gospel is so urgently needed.

Sometimes believers have said that the revelation of God in nature makes it possible for us to use rational arguments to infer or prove the existence of God. This is one of the main sources of the long tradition of various types of arguments for the existence of God. According to this way of thinking, our natural knowledge of God (that comes before the gospel) is largely indirect and received by means of rational reflection on creation. On the other hand, other believers have thought that the revelation of God in creation is largely inside ourselves, within the human mind and heart. According to this way of thinking, our natural knowledge of God (that comes before the gospel) is direct and intuitive, perhaps without much reflection and without arguments for the existence of God. But in light of Romans 1, it would not be wise for us exclusively to follow either of these parts of the Christian tradition, without regard for the other part of the Christian tradition. Paul's way of thinking seems to include both a revelation in nature that provides a basis for rational reflection leading to arguments for the existence of God, and also a general revelation of God within human nature, meaning inside the human mind and heart created in the image of God, which leads to a direct or intuitive knowledge of God. God is revealing himself both through nature and through human nature created in his image, with the result that our knowledge of God's coming through creation is multifaceted and received into consciousness in multiple ways.

Paul claims that all people know something about God and his law from general revelation. It is probably also safe to conclude that many other things that all people know come from general revelation. These might be called commonsense ideas, or they might be called the transcendental conditions of human experience. How is it that all people seem to know that we can usually trust our five senses to tell us truth about the everyday world; that two plus two will still equal four tomorrow; that people generally know what love, honesty, justice, and loyalty are? How is it that people know that simple logical deductions somehow correspond to the real world? Why is it that many people will think these questions are almost too stupid to consider? Probably because all people have a lot of knowledge about everyday matters that comes to us from God's general revelation, so that our created minds are in some ways the images of his creating mind. But people often do not want to acknowledge God and therefore do not want to the total extent to which we are dependent on God.

Even though there are traces of God's mercy and kindness in his general revelation, so that his rain falls on the just and the unjust alike, yet there is no clear statement of the gospel of Christ in general revelation. To know that "Christ died for our sins" and that "in Christ, God was reconciling the world to himself," we truly need the special revelation of God in Christ and in the Scriptures. A proper understanding of general revelation will not reduce our sense of need for special revelation; a rich understanding of general revelation will increase our understanding of our deep need for special revelation. Using the traditional evangelical distinction between law and gospel, with caution one can say that general revelation is only in the realm of law, while special revelation contains both law and gospel. And one of the chief functions of God's law is to show our need for the gospel.

One of the slogans of the Protestant Reformation was "*Lex semper accusat*," the law always accuses. God's law accuses us because we are sinful, and if a person does not trust the gospel, that person will have a strong sinful tendency to reject, deny, or suppress the knowledge of God's law that all people have. Only in light of the gospel of forgiveness can we acknowledge the depths of our sin and the depths of our knowledge of God's demand in his law. In a very important way, the gospel of Christ enables us to accept or acknowledge God's general revelation, which we would otherwise want to suppress. When we talk about the gospel with unbelievers, they enter into the discussion feeling accused and maybe condemned by the law of God which they may want to ignore or deny. Whatever method of presentation we might decide to use, they are not objective hearers or observers. They will have deep prejudices that affect what they can accept and believe, even if we think we might be presenting rather objective reasons one should accept the Christian faith. For this reason, it may be necessary to talk about God's mercy and offer of forgiveness before talking about whether God really exists, though this order may seem exactly backwards.

Because we have the difficult task of bringing the gospel to people who may be hiding from God and suppressing their knowledge of God, we should expect some frustrations and many misunderstandings. And the suppressed knowledge of God will tend to lead people to reject our presentation of our reasons we believe the biblical message to be true. Nevertheless, the several ways of presenting why we think the biblical message to be true, e.g., arguments for the existence of God, attempts to prove the resurrection of Jesus, evidence for the historical truthfulness of the Bible, arguments that show the coherence of theism or the incoherence of atheism, all tend to increase the level of cognitive dissonance for the unbeliever. The person who has a suppressed knowledge of God deep within, while claiming to believe something else, has a deep tension within that will probably need to reach a breaking point for him/her to come to faith. The various types of apologetic presentation can each tend to increase the level of tension or dissonance within the unbeliever, which can lead to the breaking point and total change of mind we call repentance and faith.

Since God asked Adam and Eve, "Where are you?" God's speech or general revelation to all people has included questions that seem just to arise in human experience and which need biblical answers. These questions range from "What is the meaning of life?" to "Why do we feel guilty and what is the solution?" to "What happens at death?" For this reason we should say that honest questions require honest biblical answers, though sometimes the questions may need to be slightly corrected to receive biblical answers. But because God is the one who asks the questions via general revelation as a way of driving people to the answers in special revelation, we can expect to find a deep correlation between honest questions and honest biblical answers. In presenting the biblical message we should always be listening to the questions and concerns of the people we address and try to point them to the biblical answers.

When people do not come to an honest faith in the God of the Bible, they have a strong tendency to create a God-substitute which is usually some part or aspect of God's good creation. At the core of such a religion substitute there is normally some promise that speaks to the inner religious needs and questions of men and women. For example, in our time there is a strong tendency to make wealth or prosperity a God-substitute. When Jesus talked about the "deceitfulness of wealth" (Matt 13:22) he was probably thinking that wealth makes a deceitful or deceptive promise to make us happy or secure. This is probably indicative that most God-substitutes contain a deceptive or deceitful promise, meaning that we think we hear a promise from some part of creation when, in fact, only God himself can make such a promise. When people suppress the knowledge of God given in general revelation, they cannot cease to be religious, but their worship gets turned in inappropriate directions.

The suppression of general revelation has multiple extensive effects on academic and educational life. Just a couple examples can be given. Once people select one dimension or aspect of creation as an idol, they have a tendency to interpret all of life and experience in light of that idol, which leads to a series of idolatrous worldviews and philosophies on the pages of history and in our society today. Just a few examples must suffice. The Marxist ideology or philosophy was a result of turning the economic dimension of life into an idol, and then thinking that humans are primarily economic creatures, so that all of life and experience were seen as controlled by economic factors. This philosophy largely controlled the schools, media, and culture of the communist countries with disastrous results. The Nazi ideology was the result of turning blood and race into a God-substitute and then interpreting all of life and society in light of their religion substitute. The ideology was then communicated in every possible means in the society under Nazi control, with results so disastrous they need no further mention. The philosophy of existentialism absolutizes human choice or decision, with a marked tendency to think that individual choices or decisions are all that matter in the world, regardless of what those decisions may be. Like the other worldviews that suppress the general revelation of God, existentialism stands in serious tension with the world that God has made and in which we live. In academic and educational life, one must always ask if the claims one hears and reads are the result of worldviews, ideologies, or philosophies that suppress the general revelation of God or which result from idolatry.

Another effect of the suppression of general revelation in educational and academic life is the tendency for academic theories to absolutize falsely and separate aspects of creation and human experience that properly belong together. Examples can be found in many different academic disciplines, but only a few from the field of the academic study of ethics will be mentioned. In the common secular (meaning God denying or God ignoring) theories about ethics that are not nihilistic (meaning those theories that do think moral truth is unavailable), there are at least four contradictory theories about right and wrong. Each claims to be a total explanation of moral life and experience. The deontological or Kantian ethicists say that ethics is all about our rational duty. The utilitarian or consequentialist ethicists say that ethics is all about the consequences or results of our actions, whether for good or evil, in the lives of other people. The virtue ethics theorists say that ethics is all about what kind of person each of us should become. The social contract ethicists say ethics is all about the formal or informal social agreements that hold society together and prevent social chaos. From a Christian perspective, one can say that each of these ethical theories contains elements of truth that result from God's general revelation. A proper theistic ethic can include these elements within a framework coming from the Bible, while also observing that in everyday experience these proper ethical considerations blend or merge together. But because unbelief tends to lead to false absolutizing, secular ethical theorists have a tendency to isolate these considerations from each other and to see them as totally contradictory. This very brief analysis of the tendency for people falsely to absolutize different aspects of creation in the realm of ethical theory can also be expected in most fields and disciplines of education and academic life. An understanding of general revelation, and the tendency of people to suppress that revelation, helps us to understand and avoid the problem.

The apostle Paul had tremendous confidence in the truth and importance of his message, and this confidence was worked out in the middle of the secular worldviews and multiple religions of his day. This confidence was closely tied to his understanding of the human condition before God which is largely characterized by the rejection and suppression of the knowledge of God which comes from general revelation. For believers in the twenty-first century to find Pauline confidence in the truth and importance of the biblical message, we would do well carefully to consider Paul's teaching.

Endnotes

1   I have decided not to include a bibliography or extensive footnotes with this essay since that would unnecessarily extend its size and make it less accessible to readers. Implicitly this essay is a dialogue with much of the history of Western theology and philosophy, but to make that explicit would require an interaction with hundreds of books and many dozens of articles, for which neither the writer nor the reader may have patience. Some of the relevant information can be found in the bibliography of Thomas K. Johnson, *Natural Law Ethics: An Evangelical Proposal* (Bonn: VKW, 2005), 147–68.

2   More information on the German Christian Movement can be found in Thomas K. Johnson, *Helmut Thielicke's Ethics of Law and Gospel* (Ph.D.

dissertation, University of Iowa, 1987), chapter 1. The footnotes and bibliography provide references to the primary and secondary sources. A lightly revised version of this text may appear as a book, probably from VKW in Bonn, in 2006 or 2007.

Logic, Quantum Physics, Relativism, and Infinity

A RATIONAL APPROACH TO THEISM

Peter Zöller-Greer

Dep. of Computer Science and Engineering, State University of Applied Sciences, Frankfurt am Main, Germany

Come now, let us reason together. (Isa 1:18)

In the beginning was Logic [the logos].
And Logic was with God, and Logic was God.

(John 1:1, most accurately translated by Gordon H. Clark)

In the nineteenth century Nietzsche declared "God is dead." He was inspired by the then new scientific revelations, especially by Charles Darwin's theories. But now, at the beginning of the twenty-first century, naturalistic explanations of our existence seem to be more and more implausible. In this article I describe a rational approach for our existence without any theistic or atheistic bias. This approach is based on new results of contemporary physics and the application of logic and plausibility. Quantum physics—once titled "Christianity's greatest challenge"—gives new insights on reality that may actually help theism.

I. Where Theists and Atheists May Agree

To be independent of theistic or atheistic bias, I will try to point out some premises that should be able to be agreed on by both sides:

1. Logic is an accurate tool to describe our reality (though not necessarily the only one).
2. Mathematically probable explanations are preferred in contrast to improbable ones for physical observations (at least if you don't know otherwise).

3. *"Pluralitas non est ponenda sine neccesitate"* (Occam's Razor), i.e., "Plurality should not be posited without necessity." In other words, when competing theories attempt to explain something, use the "simplest" explanation that has the least assumptions.
4. The law of causality ("Every effect has a cause") is an apodictic property of our physical reality.
5. The contemporary knowledge of science should be included in our philosophical considerations (but not dogmatically).

Let me comment briefly on this. The first premise is (hopefully) agreed on by everyone; otherwise meaningful communication is not possible. Of course, we experience more than logic in our life, e.g., music, art, or feelings. And they may very well be used to describe parts of our reality. But the most unambiguous way to communicate is via logic. Most sentences in this and the other articles in this book are compounded by logical statements, which at least its authors believe to be true. I once heard someone say, "If logic is not true, then...." I interrupted this person at this point and said that without logic there is no "if ... then" because this is a law of logic itself. Hence one can't use an "if ... then" construct if not presuming the validity of logic.

The second premise is sometimes refuted by statements such as the following: "This very situation in this very moment is extremely improbable, since trillions of other possibilities could have been actualized; nevertheless it is happening right now." Such statements expose a deep misunderstanding of how statistic works. What you need beforehand are categories. Take, e.g., a lottery. To determine the mathematical probability of a certain combination of numbers, let's say six out of 49, you find approximately 14 million possibilities of combinations. Every combination is equally (im-)probable: one out of 14 million. But is your lottery ticket worth something only because your personal combination is so special that it may not occur again in the other 14 million (minus one) cases? Of course not. Another thing has to take place: Your combination must be in the winning category! The drawing of lots separates the winners (first category) from the losers (second category). And the probability of being in the first category is what counts because the second category is a kind of "black box" containing all the losers. Therefore the probability that your special number is in the category of the losers is very high. Probability is always connected with categories. And this is also how our common life-decisions work. You would not decide to walk across the street when the traffic light is red because you (at least unconsciously) know that by doing this the mathematical probability to fit the "category of dead people" is very high. You would not consider the walking across the street when the light is red as equivalent to the green light just because both events are surely unique in the universe and therefore equally "improbable."

Then there are people who say that even if an event is most improbable, it nevertheless can happen. It can even occur in the next second, since mathematical improbability doesn't say anything about when it happens. Look at the lottery above: Even if the chances to win are one out of 14 million (approx. $1:10^7$), almost every week people do win. So the improbable does happen! But in terms of science, this is not really a very improbable event. First of all, there are usually more than 14 million people who participate in the lottery; therefore it is highly probable that one should win. And secondly, physicists agree that "really improbable" are events beyond a probability of one out of 10,000,000,000,000,000,000,000,000,000,000,000,000,000 (this is $1 \bullet 10^{40}$). Although mathematically possible, it is absurd to believe that such an event could really happen in our universe (given the life span and the size of our universe).

The third assumption (Occam's razor) is helpful as long as there is no other indication for the validity of any of the competing theories describing a physical phenomenon. Prefer the simplest explanation unless there is a better one.

The law of causality, which is our fourth presumption, is sometimes misunderstood by philosophers and physicists as well. These misunderstandings often have to do with the category or "domain" where this law is applicable. For example, the well-known philosopher Paul Kurtz, coauthor of the *Humanist Manifestos* I and II,[1] asked the question, "Who made God?" during a debate with the Christian apologist Norman Geisler.[2] He pointed out that since God surely is an "effect" he therefore must have a cause. But this is a logical flaw because the law of causality is only applicable within the category of things that come into existence. Since the God of the Bible is defined as to exist eternally, he could not have come into existence. And if something or someone exists and did not come into existence, he is not caused by anything. The cause of his existence must lie within himself. Because of such misunderstandings, it is better to formulate the law of causality in this more "redundant" way: "Everything that comes into existence has a cause." The law of causality refers only to the category of events which come into existence. The God of the Bible does not belong to this category.

There is no violation known of the law of causality. Even the existence of randomness or free will is no violation since randomness or free will concern only the tool for a result. So every freewill decision has a cause, namely the brain which performs it. Every random number has a cause, namely its "generator." The methods may be unclear (e.g., free will), but the law of causality is never violated. Another misunderstanding of the law of causality has to do with time. I will show later that this law is independent of time, it transcends space and time. Some people say that the law of causality is violated, e.g., in quantum physics. But this is not the case as we'll see later.

Last but not least, the fifth premise, namely that our contemporary science is the "best we have" and that it should be taken into account, is also very important. I will focus on this later on. In the following I will try to draw conclusions from the former premises and compare theistic and naturalistic explanations for relevant phenomena.

II. Logic and Logic—or: Where Does Logic Come from?

It is hard to find a naturalistic explanation for the existence of logic since logic is something that undoubtedly exits but is not material. Platonists believe that logic is "out there," and humans fortunately can recognize it. In contrast, naturalists often believe that logic is only created by the human brain in order to be able to coordinate the events we are experiencing in our life. Therefore logic has "evolved." Beside the fact that it is questionable what the survival advantages of mathematicians are, our physical universe seems to operate according to logic, independent of the existence of human beings. Even naturalists believe that the universe "obeyed" certain physical laws long before human brains existed. And these physical laws are logical ones. So the question "Where does logic come from?" is hard to answer since there seem to be only two possibilities: either logic exists from eternity or it came into existence. If it exists from eternity, then it is not caused (premise 4) and the question where it came from is not applicable. If logic *did* come into existence once, it must have been caused. But does the law of causality apply at all to or within a world without logic? Since all our descriptions are logical statements themselves, it seems to be a kind of an endless regress to ask these questions. So let's deal with the evidence that is that logic *is* existing. (By the way, Christians have their explanation in John 1:1—see the quote at the beginning of this article). The most important thing within logic is the notion of truth. Mathematicians start out by *defining* basic truths (see e.g., Tarski's definition of truth). These so-called axioms are premises which cannot be proven true but which are evidently true (e.g., Euclid: "The whole is greater then its parts"). Tarksi's definition of truth (in fact he did not invent these laws but merely collected them) also includes the logical laws for the methods of mathematical proofs and inferring strategies. Mathematicians must not care if these truths are given by God or if they are the result of a two-thirds majority of a mathematicians' congress. But they stick to them, no matter what. This is the reason mathematical laws do not get out of time (in contrast to physical laws). Logic never fails. A friend of mine and advocate of eastern religions, who is a critic of our "Western thinking," once told me: "Everything exists with its opposite—this is the nature of perfection." I answered him that if it is true that everything exists with its opposite, then also does his statement. But the opposite of his statement is: "Not everything exists with its opposite," which must be true also. My partner accused me of leading him into a trap and terminated the conversation.

Conclusion 1: Logic is true (of course!).

III. Logic and Relativism—or: The Illogic of Moral Relativism

I once heard of a survey which says that over 60 percent of people do not believe in absolute truth. As a mathematician I am amazed by this result. I believe that 150 years ago almost 0 percent would believe such a thing (and nobody would have gotten the idea to conduct such a survey at that time). Within logic there is no such thing like "relative truth." The belief in the absence of absolute truth is a logical impossibility because of this: assume for a moment that there is no absolute truth. If there is no absolute truth, the statement itself ("There is no absolute truth") is not absolutely true, too. So it may be false. But in this case its opposite is true: "There *is* absolute truth." Hence we have inferred something with its opposite at the same time. The law of noncontradiction forces us to conclude that the original statement is self-contradictory and therefore false. So only its opposite can be true: there *is* absolute truth. A question for doubters: Is your existence an absolute truth?

This problem stands for an important characteristic of relativism: you end up very often with self-contradicting statements, which cannot logically be true. Consider, e.g., a statement I once heard from a liberal activist: "Since there are no absolute moral values, you ought to tolerate the relative moral values of other cultures." What sounds so nice is a logical flaw: the first part of the sentence presumes that no absolute moral values exist. In the second part you "ought" to do something, namely tolerate other moral values. But this is already a moral value itself! If the request "You ought to tolerate" is not an absolute moral value (according to the premise of the sentence), it must be a relative one. But then its opposite must be tolerated too! Imagine a culture which does not tolerate the moral values of other cultures (such a culture can easily be found). According to the second part of the sentence you ought to tolerate this intolerance, which is a direct contradiction to the statement. And if "ought to" is not a moral absolute, why should I "ought"? So the self-contradiction here is the demand to tolerate, which is an implicit presumed absolute and at the same time the statement says that there are no moral absolutes. To avoid such self-contradictions, you only can assume that there are absolute moral values! This is the only logically consistent way. Otherwise you never could use words like "it is better if . . ." or "you should . . ." etc. accurately because if moral values are relative then these words can only express personal opinions and cannot be imposed on other people. An atheist recently said to me that there could be no "good" God because of all the evil in the world. But since my atheistic friend does not believe in moral absolutes, why is something really evil at all? It may be my friend's opinion that certain things *he* thinks are evil, but without an absolute reference point, why should God consider these things as evil, too? Why impose my own standards on God? Again, the admittance of the existence of evil in the world implies that there is an absolute measure for it.

Some object that a statement like "You are beautiful" is only relatively true since this is a matter of opinion. But this is not so because if two people would agree what the meaning of the word *beautiful* is, e.g., with the help of a long list which defines this word, they surely would also agree about what is beautiful. So this "relativism" is only lack of agreement concerning semantics. They simply don't mean the same thing when talking about "beautiful" things.

Last but not least, there are logical inconsistencies with moral relativism like these: Moral relativists proclaim that they are inclusive and nonpartisan. This, of course, is also a self-contradictory statement because they exclude the party of moral objectivists.

Conclusion 2: Moral relativism is self-destructive, while moral objectivism is logically consistent. There are only absolute truths.

IV. Logic and Quantum Physics

With the development of quantum physics a lot changed. Physical dualism was wrongly applied to philosophy and justifies postmodernism. Some even proclaim that the law of causality is violated. So let's try to straighten this out. First of all, physical theories always are made of three things: (1) physical presuppositions, (2) mathematical descriptions, and (3) logical/physical conclusions. If we assume that no mathematical errors were made, physical theories are wrong only when the presuppositions are wrong. And these presuppositions are based on observable data. If we assume further that the data are measured accurately, then we have two "unchangeable" components in physics: Data and logic (mathematics). These two things are always accurate. How does it happen then that sometimes physical theories go wrong? This is because of additional presuppositions that are added to the measured data. Newton's law of gravity for example was based on accurate measures and accurate mathematics. But Newton assumed in addition that space and time are absolute (he had no chance of detecting otherwise at that time). Einstein used the same data and the same mathematics, but *his* additional presumption was that space and time are not absolute. This led to his famous theory of relativity.

Quantum physics is a mathematical theory which most accurately describes measurements concerning small particles. Since our everyday experiences normally do not recognize quantum-effects, our "commonsense" views the results of quantum physics as very strange. And here is the point where the law of causality comes in. Our premise number 4 says nothing about the order of cause and effect. Our common experience is that first comes the cause, later the effect. But this is not always so. Allan Aspect showed experimentally that cause and effect can occur exactly at the same time.[3] He produced two so-called "Twin-Particles," which are physically "entangled," i.e., they have certain common characteristics and are indistinguishable. Aspect directed these two particles in opposite directions, and the manipulation of one of the particles had instant effects on the other one, without any time delay. So here we have cause and effect with no time loss and independent of space. The quantum physicist Marlan Scully went even further. He proposed an experiment[4] that was carried out later, which showed that even the order of past and present can be changed for cause and effect. I want to give a rough overview here of the Scully experiment, to show how important its results are.

A light beam enters a crystal, which divides every photon in two so-called "twin-photons" with lower intensity (see fig. 1, next page).

The twin photons are directed in separate directions, each of them reflected by a mirror and later "united" by a semitransparent mirror (50 percent of the photons can pass through; the other 50 percent are completely reflected and therefore cannot pass through). Behind this mirror there are two detectors, able to register each photon.

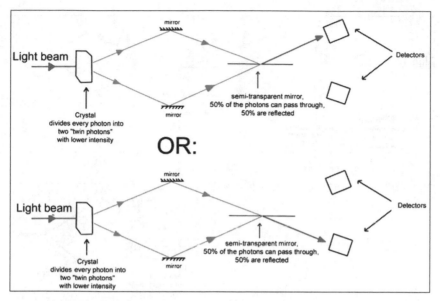

Figure 1: The Scully Experiment

Scully's arrangement of the components is made so that the twin-photons unite in a way, that at one time one of the twin photons is reflected and the other one passes through the semitransparent mirror or vice versa. In either case, as a result, a reunited, "whole" photon (with the original intensity) is detected either at the upper or at the lower detector. This represents the "wave-behavior" of photons and the effect is called "interference." Now the researchers were interested in finding out which one of the two twin-photons took which way before they were reunited at the semitransparent mirror. Therefore they "marked" one of the twin photons with a so-called polarization filter (see fig. 2). This is an optical device, which "twists" the photon-beam a little bit. In doing so, the photons "feel" observed and therefore their wave-behavior is destroyed. Suddenly there are not only "united" photons detected but also "single" twin photons at the upper and the lower detector at the same time.

But what happens if two other polarization filters are set up directly in front of the detectors, which are adjusted in such a way that "behind them" the information of which photon is marked (i.e., polarized) is deleted? (See fig. 3.)

219

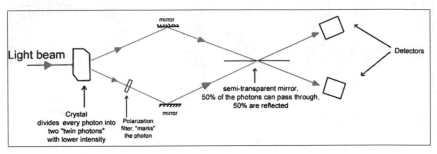

Fig. 2: Marked photons

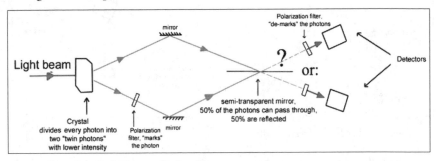

Figure 3: Marked Photons "Deleted"

Here is the amazing result: since the information has been destroyed (concerning *which* photon went which way) the photons no longer "feel" observed and therefore, as in the "undisturbed" experiment (without any polarization filters), there are only reunited twin photons detected, **either** at the upper **or** at the lower detector. So, the twin photons unite once again at the semitransparent mirror in such a way that either the one twin photon is reflected and the other one passes through or vice versa.

But wait a minute—how could the two twin-photons know that **behind** the semitransparent mirror (this means **later** in time) a device is waiting, which destroys the information of the first polarization filter and that for this reason the twin photons reunite at the semitransparent mirror? Can the photons foresee the future? Or does our measurement (i.e., observation) influence the past? If there is an independent reality "out there" (this means, independent from the observer), how could these results be explained? In fact, they couldn't! At least, with no "reasonable" explanations.

Still some scientists tried to do this, for instance, by declaring the existence of so-called "parallel universes" which all exist at the same time and are often very similar to our universe. In this model (founded by Hugh Everett in 1957), according to our experiment, there are (at least) two universes: one where at the semitransparent mirror the twin-photons are reunited and take the upper *or* lower way and one where they stay separated and take both ways. So both universes are supposed to have a true reality and at the moment, when we "look" at the result of our experiment, we decide which of the two universes we are "slipping" into (the one with the appropriate past).

But a lot of scientists feel it is unscientific to invent objects (like multiuniverses) *ad hoc*, which could never be directly observed, only for the purpose to justify a physical model or to explain results of an experiment. Another group of scientists hope, one day, to find so-called "hidden variables" which will connect the observed photons registered at the detectors with the twin photons, which are supposed to unite "in the past" at the semitransparent mirror. The problem with this is that in the whole realm of physics there is not one single example (up to now) of variables, which can "influence" an event in the past from the present. This, too, seems a very "artificial" way, and again it is only justified by the purpose to explain the results of the Scully experiment.

Another point is the "observer-chain." The who-observes-whom problem leads to an infinite regress. In this case, some scientists conclude that there *has* to be an observer "outside" the universe because otherwise the problem of how a universe could exist without an observer is unsolvable. Guess who this outside-the-universe observer could be!

Now, a critic could say, well, the time span between the semi-transparent mirror and the detectors is so short that the influence into the past can be ignored.[5] But this is no real argument because the Scully experiment can be "stretched" to cosmic dimensions! Indeed, there is a cosmic constellation, which destroys this argument.[6]

A so-called "quasar," a pulsating light source, which is "hidden" behind a big galaxy, is visible on earth by "bending" its light around the galaxy, billions of light-years away (see fig. 4). This is possible because according to Einstein's theory of relativity, a large mass (like a galaxy) could work as a gravitational lens and therefore bend the light around itself. So the light of the pulsar is "doubled" by the gravitational lens, i.e., one beam comes from the right side of the galaxy to us, and the other beam comes from the other side. This is similar to our twin-photons in the Scully experiment.

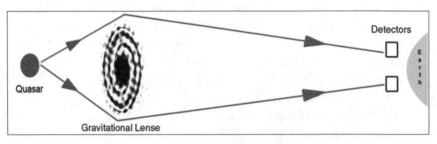

Figure 4: A Cosmological Two-slit Experiment

Without going into too much detail: on the earth an experiment can be made in such a way that it determines, if one photon comes along *either* the right or the left side *or* if it comes along both sides of the gravitational lens at the same time. But how could the photons have known billions of years ago that someday there would be an earth with inhabitants on it, making just this experiment? Or do we "influence" the past "out there" billions of years ago through our observations here in the present? Hardly imaginable! In addition, let's assume that different scientists perform two experiments of this kind at the same time here on the earth. One experiment is arranged in such a manner that the light beams pass both sides of the gravitational lens and the other experiment "forces" the beams to pass either on the one side or the other. So what follows? Are there two different pasts for each observer at the same time? This is *big trouble* for the multiuniverse theory as well as for the "hidden-variables" approach.

Let it be remarked that the older experiment of Alain Aspect was similar, but the question there was not if an observation could "influence" the past but if the observation of one of the two twin-photons could influence the other one through space instantly even at a great distance. The result was that they could with no time loss! But this contradicts Einstein's special theory of relativity, where the speed of light is the absolute speed-barrier. While here some scientist's hope of ghostly "hidden" variables, which are capable of instantly transporting information from one photon to the other, was understandable, the existence of variables, which can transport information back in time, seems ridiculous. So it's no wonder that these scientists now feel a certain angst because of the possible loss of their weltbild.

Some may say that quantum physics, with all its strange results, doesn't matter in the macroscopic world since all the problems described above deal only with elementary particles. And indeed, in the macroscopic world we don't seem to have the problems mentioned here. But this is not *really* so. First, everything in our universe is made out of such elementary particles. And secondly, quantum mechanics is not only applicable to elementary particles; quantum mechanics can also be accurately applied to macroscopic objects. A well-known example of the strange behavior even in our macroscopic world is given by "Schrödingers Cat."[7] And furthermore, phenomena seem to exist in the macroscopic world which are not explainable with classic physics. For instance, some physicists try to explain certain ESP phenomena with quantum physics.[8]

Others say the conscious human is not crucial for the *reality* because a photographic plate could substitute the observer. Of course, this is no valid argument because, as corresponding experiments show, the results come into being (reality) when the photographic plate is observed by a human being. So this is only another example for the already described "observer-chain," since the time-point of the observation is only delayed to the observation of the plate.

According to the results of the Scully experiments, we now know that reality (at least as we observe it) can be a "construct" of our interaction with it, i.e., no one could really say what this reality "looks like" without our observation. And, as we've already seen, this even seems to be true for events that took place in a "past reality." So what can we *really* say about any events of a past, which were not observed by any human being (i.e., before the existence of mankind)? We can only say that our "reconstruction" of the past is an image, which obviously depends on our present observation of it. So the question: "what did the past *really* look like?" cannot be answered accurately as long as no observer was there. Remember, that the Scully experiment teaches us that the past (of the photon's decision, "how" to unite at the semi-transparent mirror) was created during its observation in the present. But we also understand that this reconstruction of the past leads us to more than one possibility. The past's reality "happens" while it is being observed in the present, and the kind of observation even determines what the past looked like.

If one has seen the famous movie *Gone with the Wind*, then she knows which events took place. At first, there was the announcement of the civil war; then there was the war with all its destruction; meanwhile there was a love story going on and after the war the famous "Frankly, my dear, I don't give a . . ." scene took place. But was this *really* the order of the filmed sequences? Of course not! As everybody knows the sequences were filmed in an order, which was suitable to logistic and organizational demands. If, for instance, a person is only to appear three times during the whole movie, let's say at the start, in the middle and somewhere toward the end, then it would be easier (especially if the actor is costing the movie company lots and lots of money!) if all of these scenes were filmed at one time, if this is possible. Later these sequences are inserted at the proper position in the movie even if "years" lay in between (according to the plot).

Or let's take the TV series *Star Trek* (the one with Kirk and Spock, etc.). After this series was on the air, there were book authors who "constructed" a matching past to the series and wrote, e.g., about Spock's youth. So *in the present* a possible, "reasonable" *past* was created for Spock which led to the "reality" of the stories of the series in a logical way. So this reconstruction could be called an "extrapolation" from the present into the past. However there could be more than one possibility for Spock's past which matches the TV series! But remember, in *reality* (in the series) there was no "past" of Spock *at all*. And further Spock "exists" only if someone looks at one or more of the *Star Trek* series or movies. Therefore, in a sense Spock exists only by observation, not in reality! And as we know from the movie *The Truman Show*, even the reality of a "real" person could be a total fake.

Now what do scientists do when they are talking about a past where boldly no man has gone before? They are talking about an extrapolation of the present (of mankind) with three possibilities:

+ The extrapolated past could have *really* happened this way.
+ Another "reasonable" past could have happened.
+ There was no *real* past at all (at least no kind of past that we can imagine).

The Scully experiment is a so-called "delayed choice-experiment" and takes advantage of the fact that every particle in the universe is surrounded by a "cloud" of uncertainty in respect to time and space. Subtle arrangements of certain components on a workbench result in a device, which produces an effect in the past caused by an event in the present. Hence, we can have (1) cause *before* effect, (2) cause and effect at the *same* time, (3) cause *after* effect, and (4) cause and effect independent of space. Evidently the law of causality transcends space and time (since the chronological order of cause and effect can be time independent and independent from the distance).

This has nothing to do with determinism. As Stephen Hawking pointed out, quantum physics does not give up determinism but does reestablish it.[9] Cause and effect is in place, but one cause can produce a given contingent of well-computable effects, and one of these effects is actualized in reality. Why (supposed) identical causes can produce different effects is not all clear. It may be that there is "true" randomness at work or that the causes were not really identical, since we cannot be 100 percent sure what really influences an experiment.

But what we must give up is a "clockwork universe" where one space-time moment of the universe can determine the next in a unique way. All previous and all future states of the universe are "only" one of a contingent of (in principle mathematically calculable) possible states.

Conclusion 3: The law of causality is a "meta-law," i.e., it is independent of space and time.

V. Quantum Physics and Infinity within the Universe—and What Free Will Has to Do with It

When quantum physics arose, more and more physical values turned out to be quantisized. Matter, energy, light, etc.—all have some kind of a "smallest" number possible, and every "lump" is a multitude of this number. Newest results indicate that even "empty" space, and also time, is quanticized. The smallest part of empty space is about 10^{-33} cm "long," and the shortest moment in time lasts 10^{-45} seconds (Planck-length and -time). In school I once learned that irrational numbers do exist "in reality," although they have an infinite number of different decimals, e.g., the square root of 2. The "proof" was the following:

Take an x-y-coordinate system and draw a line between the numbers 1 on the x- and the y-axis (see fig. 5).

Then use a divider with the length of the distance between the

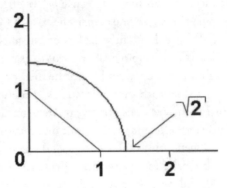

Figure 5: The "Reality" of an Irrational Number

two 1s and draw a circle around zero. The intersection with the x-axis (the real numbers) has the value of $\sqrt{2}$ and seems to exist in reality. But since every piece of space is a multitude of the Planck-length, it is not really possible to adjust the divider so that you can reach a point "within" a Planck-length. Therefore you can never find the exact distance for $\sqrt{2}$ in reality! There is no "infinite small" space in reality. Space is no continuum. The same is true with time. The "flow of time" is more like a movie composed of many single frames, and the time span between two frames is the Planck-time. There is also no infinity detectable on large scales. According to the big bang theory, the universe is expanding, i.e., it is finite at any given point in time. We can speculate if the expansion is going on forever, but there is no evidence of that; we must wait "forever" to be sure.

Scully's and Aspect's experiments show that under special circumstances reality seems to be created while observing it. But things are not as easy like that. One must differentiate what the notion *reality* means. First of all, reality is connected with our cognition. Our cognition tells us something about the reality we live in. This kind of reality I like to call the "physical reality." All that we can measure and perceive belongs to this aspect of reality. The Copenhagen interpretation of quantum physics says that this is the only reality physics can deal with, and it makes no sense to talk about any other sort of reality. The reason for such a statement is that with quantum physics we find another kind of reality, which I would like to call a "mathematical reality." Let's take again for example Schrödinger's famous cat. In this thought experiment the poor cat is caged in a closed box where some radioactive material is the trigger of a poisoning gas. The probability that the radiation activates the release of the gas may be 50 percent. If one describes this scenario with quantum physics, this leads to a mathematical equation, the so-called "Schrödinger equation." The solution of this equation is called a wave function. It shows that the cat is 50-percent alive and 50-percent dead *unless* no one "looks" at the cat. In this unobserved state the wave function is a "superposition" of two mathematical terms, where one term represents the living cat and the other the dead one. If the box is opened, the wave-function "collapses," and one of the two possible states becomes reality (either a dead cat or a living one). Mathematically this corresponds with the vanishing of the "death" or "live" term in the solution of the Schrödinger equation. But what should one make of the superposition of a 50-percent-alive and 50-percent-dead cat? According to human experience we always recognize either dead or living cats. The problem is that we cannot observe this obscure half-alive-half-dead cat since our observation always goes along with the collapse of the wave function, and this means the cat comes out dead or alive. The problem with this "other" kind of (50/50) reality is that no one can say how it looks, since "looking" means destroying this kind of reality (collapse of the wave-function). But what we have is a mathematical description of this kind of reality, and therefore I called it "mathematical reality," since no one knows how it *really* looks, although it can be mathematically described. According to the Copenhagen interpretation statements like "There is no reality below the Heisenberg Uncertainty Limit" always must be understood as: there is no *physical* reality in the sense of my definition above. But there remains what I named the *mathematical* reality since the state of a quantum system could be described mathematically accurate. As I mentioned above, the problem is that no one can understand with "common sense" what kind of reality this should be. For to make an absolute statement like "there *is* really a reality below the Heisenberg Uncertainty Limit" or "there *is not* really a reality below the Heisenberg Uncertainty Limit" would presuppose that we were all-knowing God. So I prefer to state "there *is* a *mathematical* reality below the Heisenberg Uncertainty Limit" and what it *really* looks like—only God can say.

The application of what just was said I called the Divine Anthropic Principle.[10] Quantum physics tells us that the physical reality even of our past may depend on how we look at it at the present. Therefore extrapolations of a possible past before human observers exist is not as certain as it seems to be. We saw that theoretically a large number of different "pasts" is possible, which all could lead to the same "present" we are experiencing now. Of course, physics can accurately extrapolate and it does. But because of the mentioned ambiguity of possible pasts this may lead to different results, depending on the "tools" and theories used for the corresponding extrapolation. Let's illustrate this graphically. If we use any physical law, e.g., the law of entropy (horizontal axis, with a plotting scale so that entropy increases linear), we can demonstrate how large the extrapolation zone is:

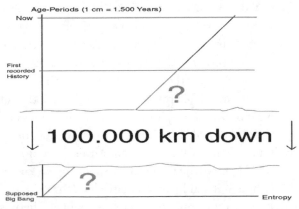

Figure 6: The "Far" Past

In Figure 6 one cm on the vertical axis equates with 1,500 years of time. We assume that the first *recorded* history appeared about 4,500 years ago (middle horizontal line). The lower part of the middle line must be extrapolated. And the relation is as follows: We have 3 cm of recorded history and over 100,000 km of (mathematical) extrapolation. We assume physics does this correctly, but another presupposition is (of course) that there is a *physical* reality "out there" where no man has gone before. On the other hand, the Scully experiments seem to show us that it is possible that how the past "looks" depends on the methods we use to observe this past *today*. Therefore past before mankind at least in part may have the quality of a *mathematical* reality as mentioned above. But is this all we can say? Of course not. The chances are very good that most parts of our calculated past reality are actual real physical ones.

In order to understand this whole issue of an ambiguous past better, let me lay out an analogy (for theists this could be God's perspective since the Bible tells us that God transcends space and time). It may also explain the role of the law of causality, which can be interpreted as a "geometric" property.

We saw that space and time seem to be quantized. Space is a set of little cubes of the size of the Planck-length, and time does not "flow" but "jump" like a set of movie frames with the Planck-time as time span between two "frames." (By the way: The physicist H. W. Beck[11] has good arguments to locate our self-awareness—or call it soul if you like—between the Planck-lengths within our brain). Imagine we could take a snapshot of the whole universe at every Planck-time from the start to the end of the life span of the universe. This would result in a series of snapshots (a kind of "movie of the universe"), which even vary in size (since the universe expands). Let's assume they all lay on a big table with no special order. A little problem is the fact that there are two kinds of reality, the physical one (which *really* happens) and the mathematical one (which we can't imagine with our common sense). The half-dead-half-living cat is such a mathematical reality. As a "working" model we can substitute such cases by thinking of a combination of *two possible alternative* physical realities instead of only *one* half-dead-half-alive reality (this is what the mathematical appearance of the corresponding terms suggests, where in one of these realities the cat is dead and in the other the cat is alive). In fact, Hugh Everett's "Many World Hypothesis" is based on such a conception, but the difference to our model is that Everett believed that these alternative "pasts" have a real physical reality somewhere. To me this is an *ad hoc* hypothesis and not acceptable as a physical theory. Therefore we are talking only of two *possible* physical realties, and they must not really "happen" somewhere out there. In this sense our "movie" of the universe has to be extended by other "possible" movies. These other movies incarnate the physical alternatives according to the mathematical realities as mentioned above.

To simplify matter we assume that the pictures of all the "real" and "possible" movies are lying separated on the table in the following fashion:

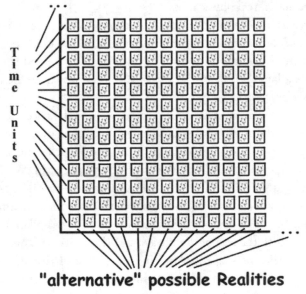

"alternative" possible Realities

Figure. 7: Quantized Space-Time and Alternative Realities

The pictures are lying on the table in such a way that all pictures of possible realities are forming one horizontal line. The next upper line is made of pictures of alternative realities, which we (as human beings) would experience as the next elementary time unit. But remember: this "order" is only for the purpose of a simplified discussion, and it is *not* a necessary one!

In Figure 7 we see the pictures lying on the table (the table would be very huge so we see only a very small outcut). Every little square in Figure 7 is a "snapshot of the universe," which itself is composed of a large number of elementary space-cubes. The columns of Figure 7 represent alternative realities, and the lines represent different time-units. With the creation of physical laws, the set of possible alternative realities is restricted. If we assume that the lines of pictures on the table are arranged in a way that from the bottom to the (far away) top every line represents events, which according to the introduced physical laws are conclusive from time-unit to time-unit, then, e.g., the big bang must be one of the pictures of the bottom line. According to the big bang theory the "first" line at the bottom is probably only one picture of the size of only one elementary cube. If we go further upward more and more pictures appear with increasing size (amounts of elementary cubes) since the universe expands. But for our further considerations this could be neglected.

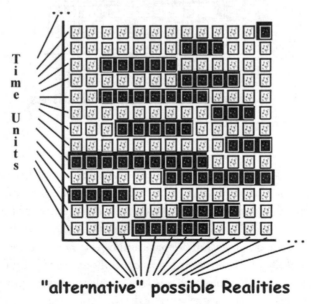

Figure 8: "Associated" Realities (Darkened)

So when physics is there, the collection of possible alternative realities is restricted in every time-unit-line according to the laws of physics and especially of quantum physics. Again only for simplifying matters we assume that such "belonging-together-realities" are lying next to each other.

The blackened areas on Figure 8 represent *mathematical* reality. If we would go along with classical physics, the classical laws of physics would force one to represent the universe as a series of always only one such picture per line (see fig. 9):

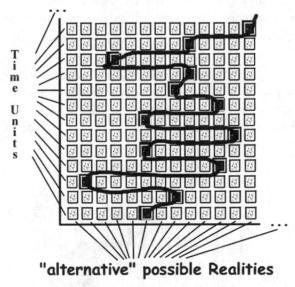

"alternative" possible Realities

Figure 9: "Classical" Realities (Darkened)

Let us call such a line a "path." Within classical physics there would exist only *one* such path. This is the idea of a clockwork universe. This means that with physical laws every state (picture) of the universe is fully determined by the physical laws and the preceding picture (where the quantization of space and time is not necessary since the states of the universe were seen as continuous events). Of course, this leads to a regression where one only needs the first picture (e.g., the big bang) and the "right" physical law, which was called *Weltformel*. It was Einstein's dream to find this *Weltformel*. The idea was that in principle one could calculate all events in the universe with this formula if one would know all the "input parameters." God was seen as the designer of this "clock," and He only had to wind it up, and He left it alone afterwards. But there arises a problem with free will. If the *Weltformel* predetermines *everything*, where is the place for a free will?

But quantum physics shows us a way out of this dilemma. Reality is no longer a predetermined unique path but a collection of possible paths (see fig. 10).

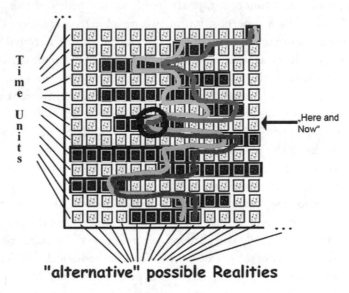

"alternative" possible Realities

Figure 10: "Quantum Physical" with Alternative Paths

In analogy to what we earlier called mathematical reality, we call this collection *mathematical paths*. But what then does correspond to physical reality, the *physical path*? In some odd way the physical path is *not* physically predetermined, i.e., the complete path (from the actual time-unit in the present downward to the beginning of time) can change in dependence of some present and/or future events. Why? Because what *we* see is this: according to Scully's experiments it seems possible that a special *past* path is created at that moment when we perform a certain experiment (like Scully's) in the *present*.

Another drastic example is the cosmological two-slit experiment as mentioned above (see fig. 4): We choose *now* (through our free will by the observation method in the present) how the *past* does look. In figure 10 this is demonstrated by the different paths from present to past.

In accordance to the Copenhagen interpretation of quantum physics, it makes no sense to ask: How did the *physical reality* look in the past (when the light *really* passed the gravitational lens) since this physical past depends on the performance of the cosmological two-slit experiment *today*. The *mathematical reality* of this past is described by a superposition of two possible past realities: One, where a photon passed the right or left side of the gravitational lens (particle-behaviour) and the other one where the photon passes both sides at the same time (wave-behaviour). Unless no one "looks" at the photon, these two possibilities are part of the quantum mechanical description of this problem. This *is* the *mathematical reality*. It represents a gigantic "cloud of probability" of two possibilities. If someone "looks" at the photons, then according to the adjustments of the experiment, the *mathematical reality* "collapses," and one of the two possibilities becomes *physical reality* (remember that this reality concerns the long ago past). Uncertain past collapses into certain past. This is why we sometimes say that the past is created in the present. But this is not exactly true. The past is not created (by us humans), but it's rather "chosen" out of the possible mathematical realities. In a way our free will (e.g., the decision to perform a Scully-like experiment) determines not only (at least parts of) our present and future (as everybody knows), it seems *also* to choose or to determine (at least parts of) our past (which is hard to comprehend by common sense). But the distinction of future and past is only within our human perspective since we are bounded by time. In modification of the saying that our future is uncertain, we can say our past is also! Therefore from our perspective one of the several possible past paths becomes *the* (real) past path.

Thus the law of causality now gains a geometric nature. Like in the movie *Gone with the Wind* (as mentioned above), the series of sequences that determine the events in the movies are "cut" in the "right" order although they may not be filmed in that order. The "geometry" of the frames glued together to a movie by the cutter determines what is causal while watching the movie. And maybe some filmed alternative sequences of a situation were discarded, and (the best) one was eventually actualised. In the same way the "path" of causality in our life may be determined by the geometry (i.e., the order) of the snapshots on the table in figure 10. Humans are limited to change this order only according to their free will within the boundaries of mathematical reality. Free will plus mathematical reality lead to physical reality in accordance with the laws of quantum physics.

In our model God can see all the pictures lying on His workbench. Since God is not bound by time, He sees all the pictures and events at the "same time." For Him the notions "beginning" and "end" have a more geometric quality since the beginning of our universe is associated with the bottom of the table and the end with the top. And somehow God also sees the final path! According to our (restricted) perspective this final path would be *the* real past we would see if we would look back from the very "last" time-unit of the existence of our universe (one of the pictures on the top line of God's table). Then the entire Scully and cosmological two-slit experiments etc. are preformed, and the past is finally determined. But until then the past is a kind of variable which may change (e.g., by future Scully experiments). But not for God. He is "outside" of time and space and therefore "knows the end from the beginning" (Isa 46:10). This is clear, since all events lie stretched out on His table. And not only this. He also "sees" what we called the final path "from the beginning."

A Remark Concerning Miracles

God is all-powerful, and therefore He is able to intervene in our life. This means that He can modify the path of the universe by changing its way. Since He sees "all" possible paths, He can intervene and "correct" the (final) path according to His plans (and perhaps our prayers etc.). To do so, He has the possibility to use a collection of "pictures" even "outside" the realm of what we called the mathematical reality. Or He could use power according to physics (in principle, one could physically "create" thousands of fish out of one or two by gathering molecules of air or sand and change their physical structure; the only problem is that one needs a huge amount of power and energy not feasible to produce by our human technology). Anyway, it's His selection of pictures to modify and create the final path.

A Remark Concerning Free Will

We saw in our analogy that free will is possible since the past, the present, and the future are always a *collection* of possible realities. We further saw that even the past may be influenced by our free will in the present. Nevertheless God sees the results of our decisions since He sees the final path from the beginning (actually, there is no beginning for Him since He is "outside" of time and the word *beginning* is a time-dependent notion). So there is no longer a conflict between a free will and an all-knowing God. In a way this is similar to the possibility of time traveling. If you would have a time machine and you could "jump" a year forward and then back again, you would *know* what will happen next year although this future world is a result of lots of free will decisions. Therefore to *know* the result of a free decision does not mean that there *is* no free decision. The seeming contradiction between human free will and God's predestination is therefore solved, see, e.g., in Ephesians 1:5 (KJV): "*Having predestinated us unto the adoption of children by Jesus Christ to himself, according to the good pleasure of his will.*"

Conclusion 5: Infinity seems not to exist in physical reality; it is probably only a mathematical construct. Amazingly enough, we can "imagine" infinity and even describe it mathematically.

VI. Logic and First Cause

According to the big bang theory space and time (i.e., the universe and all that's in it) had a beginning about 13 billion years ago. We already established that *within* the universe everything that exists has a cause (since everything came into existence). But can the law of causality be extrapolated outside the universe? Since we found out earlier that the law of causality is a "meta-law" (i.e., it is independent of space and time), I would argue that there is no reason the big bang is not also caused (since it undoubtedly came into existence). It seems that the universe was caused by something is at least the more plausible presupposition. But what caused it? There are only two possibilities: Either the cause was never caused itself (then this is the "first cause"), or it was the result of another cause. We can produce a chain by asking again if the cause of the cause was also caused or not. Finally there are only two possibilities: Either the chain of causes stops somewhere at the first cause, or there is an infinite regress of causes and effects. Let's investigate carefully the two possibilities. We look at the latter possibility first.

Theorem

A cause-effect chain can only have a finite number of causes and effects if time passes between cause and effect.

It is clear that an infinite number of even small time-amounts that pass between causes and effects would sum up to an infinite time span, which ultimately avoids our being here now. To illustrate this, imagine a bookshelf with a start but no end (see fig. 11).

If you push the first book (let's assume the beginning is at the left side), then a "domino effect" takes place, and a chain of falling-over

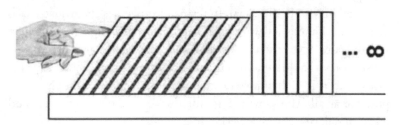

Figure 11: A Bookshelf with a Start, but No End

takes place which never ends (ideal circumstances assumed). This chain of fallings never stops since there is an infinite number of books and a small time span between the fall of every book and its neighbor.

Now let's assume there is a shelf which mirrors the one described, i.e., the shelf is turned 180 degrees to the left. Now we have a bookshelf that reaches from infinity (at the left) and has an end at the right (see fig. 12).

If somehow the falling-over of the books was "started" at infinity on the left, when will the last book on the right fall down? Never, of course, since it would take the same time span as in figure 11,

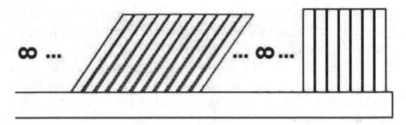

Figure 12: A Bookshelf with No Start but an End

i.e., eternally. If the last book on the right represents our here-and-now in a cause-and-effect-chain, it would never be reached, and you could never read this article.

So if we have an infinite cause-and-effect chain, an infinite number of causes and effects must take place simultaneously, and only a finite number takes place with time. But if we look at the conditions necessary to have a simultaneous cause and effect, we find that this is only possible if the objects are in a quantum physical state of "entanglement" (like twin photons). In terms of universes that caused each other simultaneously, we would need "entangled universes," which is physically never shown possible, and we would need an "outside" cause to start the "de-entanglement" process. This all seems very fantastic, and it is highly questionable if this is logically and physically possible at all. The same is true for the reverse order of cause and effect in delayed-choice experiments.

Another thing: We find physical infinity nowhere in our universe. Why in the world should we assume that there are physically infinite processes outside the universe? This is pure speculation with no evidence anywhere.

So obviously we are "stuck" with the other case: The cause-and-effect chain must be finite and therefore have a start.

Conclusion 6: The existence of a first cause is the most plausible assumption, far more plausible than its opposite.

VII. Logic and Statistics

Although some people think that statistics is the scientific form of a lie, I would argue that statistics is a tremendous tool to pre-calculate probabilities which really take place. That's how we live our life. Since much literature is available, I only will mention two important things briefly: first we have the problem of fine-tuning in the universe. Not only are the basic physical constants *at* the big bang extremely fine-tuned in a way such that other physical values would disable the universe to carry life, but also fine-tuning *within* the universe to enable life is also very carefully chosen. The chance of being in the category of life-sustainable universes is almost zero, at least far beyond $1:10^{40}$, which is the physical "impossibility boundary."[12] Second, there is a thing called "specified complexity." As William Dembski showed, there is a mathematical method to determine if a complex structure is pure chance or if it is designed.[13] Applied to irreducible complex biological systems (like a cell), design seems the only plausible option.

Conclusion 7: The fine-tuning of the universe and irreducible complexity in nature is best explained by design.

VIII. Logic and God

What is more plausible, the assumption that there is no God or the one that there is a God? I would clearly argue that we have more problems if there is no God. According to our premise 3 (Occam's razor), the existence of God is surely the simplest and logically most consistent explanation for our existence. Take, e.g., the existence of moral absolutes (conclusion 1). They couldn't have evolved, since they contradict the "survival of the fittest" (e.g., it is morally "good" to help handicapped people). So where do they come from? And the first cause was the most plausible explanation for our existence. But who or what is the first cause? Because the first cause is not created, it must exist from eternity. Since time and space and matter etc. came into existence with the big bang, this first cause must transcend time, space, and matter and therefore must be spiritual. And if no time passes for this entity, how could it ever start a cause for anything (e.g., our universe)? A "deep frozen" timeless first cause would not cause anything else; how could it? A good explanation I think is the existence of a "will" of the first cause. But this means that the first cause is personal. And very intelligent (to create a universe like ours). If we look at the attributes above of the first cause, we'll find that the God of the Bible is an exact match. Together with other well-documented evidence (e.g., the historicity of the rising of Jesus Christ from the dead[14]), we have a compelling cumulative case for the existence of the Christian-Judaic God.

Almightiness

Since logic is one of the attributes of the God of the Bible, he can only do what is logically possible. Hence there are certain things God cannot do; e.g., he can not lie (see Titus 1:2). The existence of evil in the world has its reason in this since God would have to become illogical to eliminate all evil (among other things this would clash with human free will). Therefore God's almightiness must always be seen in the context of what is logically possible.

Miracles

Because logic is a nonviolable attribute of God, all miracles must be logically possible. But this does not mean that they are also physically possible! As we saw, some events are simply physically impossible because they are very improbable. Take, e.g., the resurrection of a dead person. This is not a violation of logic but a violation of the second law of thermodynamics. If the atoms of a long dead person are re-compounded again in a way that they resemble the once living person exactly, then the resurrection is accomplished. According to the second law of thermodynamics, this cannot happen by normal natural processes because the probability for such an event to happen "on its own" is far beyond $1:10^{40}$, which was the impossibility boundary for events in physics. If it happens, however, we must assume that a non-natural power had intervened, and we call such a thing a miracle.

Conclusion 8: The existence of the God of the Bible is the most plausible and rational explanation for our existence, life, and redemption.

IX. Acknowledgment:

I would like to thank Dr. Warwick Montgomery for his outstanding life-work, which was an important step in my becoming a Christian.

Endnotes

1 Kurtz, Paul et. al. : *Humanist Manifestos I and II*, Prometheus, 1973, und *Humanist Manifesto 2000*, Prometheus, 2000.

2 *The John Ankerberg Show*: "Debate on Christianity vs. Secular Humanism," 1986.

3 Aspect, A. et al. in: *Physical Review Letters* (vol. 49, p. 91) 1982.

4 See Zöller-Greer, P. in: *Perspectives on Science and Christian Faith* (vol. 52, no. 1, pp. 8ff), 2000.

5 Ross, H. in: *The Creation Hypothesis* (p. 158), InterVarsity Press (J. P. Moreland, ed.) 1994.

6 Horgan, J. in: *Spektrum der Wissenschaft* (vol. 9, p. 82) 1992 and Musser, G. in *Scientific American* (vol. 4, p. 18) 1999.

7 Davies, P. C. W. and Brown, J. R. in: *Der Geist im Atom*, Insel Verlag (p. 41–44), 1993.

8 Lucadou, W. von, in: *Experimentelle Untersuchungen zur Beeinflußbarkeit von stochastischen quanten-physikalischen Systemen durch den Beobachter*, Haag + Herchen Verlag 1986.

9 Hawking, Stephen: *Das Universum in der Nußschale*, Hoffman und Campe, 2001, page 114ff.

10 Zöller-Greer, P. in: *Perspectives on Science and Christian Faith* (vol. 52, no. 1, pp. 8ff), 2000.

11 See for example Beck, Horst W.: "Können wir das Alter des Schöpfungskosmos erkunden?" in: *Professorenforum-Journal*, vol. 6, no. 2, 2005.

12 Ross, Hugh: *The Creator and the Cosmos*, Navpress Publishing Group; 3rd edition, 2001.

13 Dembski, William A.: "Irreducible Complexity Revisited," in: *Professorenforum-Journal*, vol 5. no.2.

14 Cf. Zöller-Greer, Peter: "Zur Historizität der Auferstehung Jesus Christus," in: *Professorenforum-Journal*, vol 1. no. 2.

TOUGH-MINDED
CHRISTIANITY

Part III

DOCTRINAL INTEGRITY

Raised for Our Justification

THE SAVING SIGNIFICANCE OF THE RESURRECTION OF CHRIST[1]

I. Howard Marshall

It is a pleasure to offer these thoughts to John Warwick Montgomery in this celebratory volume. Back in 1973 I taught for a fall term at Trinity Evangelical Divinity School where John was listed as a member of the staff. He was reputed to occupy an apartment near to mine. A Citroen car said to belong to him was sometimes parked nearby. Notices appeared announcing lectures that he was to give. Yet somehow I never met him at that time. The man himself was never visible. Staff meetings were held, but he was not there! By Christmas I was declaring that the evidence for the resurrection of Jesus Christ was somewhat stronger than the evidence for the existence of John. I suppose that I should have made a point of going to one of these advertised lectures or knocking on the door of the apartment to see who came to answer. Or I should have believed the testimony of his friends that he was alive and well. Fortunately our paths later crossed at a FEET Conference in Germany, and I was able to satisfy my sceptical mind that he is real and active! After all, somebody had to be the author of all those books and articles. Thank you, John, for your rich contribution to the defence and exposition of the gospel.

It is a remarkable fact that there are many monographs on the theology of the death of Christ but very few by comparison on the theology of his resurrection.[2] Within the latter group of writings, attention has mostly been devoted to the historicity of the resurrection of Christ and to its significance in relation to the future resurrection of believers. Interest also centres on the role of the resurrection in relation to the present new life of believers. But how is it a saving event? Indeed, is it a saving event? Our goal is to understand Romans 4:25 which declares that Jesus our Lord "was delivered over to death for our sins and was raised to life for our justification." Here justification, which we would probably associate closely with the death of Christ, is specifically tied to his resurrection. How can this be so? We shall approach the text indirectly by considering the wider New Testament context of teaching about the resurrection.

The Place of the Resurrection in the Gospel

At the outset we need to recognise that two aspects of what happened to Christ after his death must be distinguished carefully for the sake of theological analysis. One is the resurrection of Christ, namely his being brought back to life after being put to death, and the other is his ascension and subsequent exaltation to sit at the right hand of God. These two actions are integrally connected as aspects of one event, but there is a danger of some confusion because either action can be used as a means of referring to the whole event. The resurrection of Christ is not simply a return to the physical life in this world that he had before his crucifixion but is his reentry into the spiritual life that he enjoyed before the incarnation. Likewise, the language of glorification and exaltation can be used to cover the whole event, and in fact terms referring specifically to the nature of the event as ascension are sparse outside Acts. Only Luke and Acts narrate the story of the ascension as a separate event from the resurrection. The writer to the Hebrews does not refer to the resurrection in the body of his letter although clearly he presupposes it when he writes about Jesus' entering into heaven (e.g., Heb 10:24).

The relative functions of the death and resurrection of Jesus in relation to salvation are variously expressed in the New Testament.

First, in the writings of Paul, on which I focus because they provide the immediate literary context for Romans 4:25, we can observe how there are passages where the dying and rising of Jesus are closely linked together as one saving event (Rom 8:34; 14:9; 1 Cor 15:3–5; 2 Cor 5:15; 1 Thess 4:14).[3]

The fullest text of this kind is the summary of the gospel as it was handed down to Paul and preached by him in 1 Corinthians 15:3–5 according to which "Christ died for our sins according to the Scriptures," followed by a reference to his burial and resurrection. It is universally agreed that here Paul cites a succinct account of the gospel that was shared with other Christians and was not his own idiosyncratic version of it. At first sight the reference to death for our sins is not absolutely essential to the point that he is making, which is primarily a defence of the resurrection. This demonstrates how fundamental the salvific nature of the death of Jesus is for Paul. Paul's point, however, is the crucial one that the death by itself is not sufficient to deal with sins; he goes on to say that "if Christ has not been raised, your faith is futile; you are still in your sins" (1 Cor 15:17). And from what follows, it is clear that human beings are delivered from the death that Paul regards as the wages of sin through being raised to a new life in the same way as Christ was raised; moreover, this resurrection of believers is not simply like the resurrection of Christ but comes about through their being united with Christ. Here, then, it is made absolutely clear that the death of Christ would have no saving efficacy apart from his resurrection.

A second type of material is where the death of Jesus is described as the basis for salvation without any reference to the resurrection. Typical examples of such passages are Romans 3:21–26; 2 Corinthians 5:18–21; Ephesians 1:7; Colossians 1:19–20. Yet even these passages stand in broader contexts where the resurrection is also mentioned.

In a third type of material, it was possible for early Christians to sum up the gospel without mention of the atoning significance of the death of Christ but with some reference to his resurrection or exaltation. Four examples of this can be given.

The first example of this is the important teaching in Romans 10:5–13 about how people are justified and saved. This passage is all the more significant precisely because it stands in the context of the failure of the Jews to achieve righteousness by the works of the law (Rom 10:1–5) and occurs after the long account of how justification comes to believers through the sacrificial death of Christ in chapter 3. Yet when Paul reaches the climax of his statement, he declares that what is required for people to be saved is that they declare verbally "Jesus is Lord" and believe inwardly that God raised him from the dead. He goes on to say, "It is with your heart that you believe and are justified, and it is with your mouth that you confess and are saved." Further, he adds the scriptural support of Joel 2:32 that "everyone who calls on the name of the Lord will be saved" (Rom 10:13).

Being justified and being saved are here two different ways of describing the same event, and consequently Paul means pretty much: "If you believe in your heart and confess with your mouth that Jesus was raised from the dead and is Lord, you will be justified and saved." We might have expected Paul to say, "If you believe that Christ died for your sins, you will be saved," but he doesn't. He is concerned here with the problem of Jews who thought that they could be saved apart from faith in Christ, and therefore his argument is shaped to deal with this point. His argument begins with the fact that the prophet Joel says that it is if you call on the Lord that you will be saved; he takes this to mean that you cannot be saved except by calling on the Lord (rather than by trying to establish your own righteousness). But then he makes the point that the Christ whom God raised from the dead is the Lord, and therefore, even though in the time of Joel people called on Yahweh for salvation, now they must call on the Lord Jesus Christ. The *identity* of the Lord is the crucial issue here. Consequently, the lack of emphasis on the atoning death of Jesus may not be too surprising.

A second relevant passage is 1 Thessalonians 1:9–10. The account of the conversion of the Gentile readers described by Paul relates how they turned to God, the one and only God of the Jews, from their idols, to serve him and to wait for the coming of his Son from heaven, namely Jesus, whom he raised from the dead and who will deliver us from the future wrath at the day of judgment. Here salva - tion (or deliverance) is linked to Jesus, but it is not explained how he is able to deliver people from wrath. The reference to his being raised from the dead explains how it is that he is in heaven, with the implied assumption that a person who has been raised from the dead is able to return from heaven. Elsewhere in the same letter, it is made clear that future salvation is received through our Lord Jesus Christ, who died for us (1 Thess 5:9–10). But, although the connection of salvation to the death of Jesus is made there, the gospel can be sum-marised without reference to it.

A third important passage is Philippians 2:6–11, where the life and death of Jesus are used to form the basis for an appeal to be-lievers to show the same obedience and humility as he did, but the death is not explained as a saving event. Many consider this to be a pre-Pauline composition. However, I think there are good grounds for ascribing it to Paul himself.[4] It is arguable that once we recogn-ise that this passage was probably composed by Paul for its present exemplary purpose, the lack of reference to the saving significance of the death is not especially remarkable. Nevertheless, the text is noteworthy in that Paul did not think it necessary to say anything here about the purpose of Christ's death.[5]

And, finally, in this catalogue, there is a set of passages from the evangelism in Acts, where in the preaching to unbelievers the death of Jesus is never said to be a death for us or for our sins. Rather the death is seen as the obstacle to accepting that Jesus is the Messiah in that not only was he not accepted as such by the Jewish leaders and many Jewish people but also he was actually put to death by them. This obstacle is overcome by pointing to the important fact that God raised him from the dead, thereby undoing the evil act, and at the same time exalting him to his right hand so that he could function as Lord and Messiah. How the death of Jesus is related to this as a saving event is not explained in the evangelistic sermons.

We thus see several ways of presenting the significance of Jesus' death and resurrection. First, both may be mentioned together in a way that shows they were seen as a unity, not surprisingly in view of the temporal proximity of the one to the other and the fact that the resurrection presupposes the death. Second, there may be an exclusive emphasis on the death and its effects in such a way that it might seem that the resurrection has nothing to add to it. Third, there may be mention of the resurrection with little or no reference to the death and its significance.

Although Romans 4:25 belongs formally to the first category of passages where both the death and resurrection are mentioned, it stands close to this third category of passages in that here there is specific emphasis on the place of the resurrection in the saving event.[6] While recognising that Christ was delivered up to death because of our sins (or to do something about them), it relates justification not so much to his death as to his being raised. Here we should also mention Romans 5:10 which appears to make a distinction between reconciliation through the death of Christ and future salvation through his life; here the reference is generally understood to be to his resurrection life.[7]

How, then, are we to understand the place of the resurrection in these specific references to justification and final salvation? And how does Paul's teaching relate to that elsewhere in the New Testament?

We can distinguish this theme from some other related ones.[8] For example, one important aspect of the significance of the resurrection of Jesus as a saving event is the way in which it functions as the guarantee and pattern for the resurrection of believers (1 Cor 15). Consideration of this topic would divert us from our concern with comparatively neglected problems of the relationship of Christ's resurrection to sin and death and the justification of sinners.

The Relationship Between the Death and Resurrection of Jesus

Divine Approval of the Crucified Christ

Perhaps the most common, popular explanation of the connection between the death and resurrection of Jesus is to argue that the resurrection is God's confirmation and acceptance of what Christ did in his death, giving his sacrifice "the stamp of God's approval."[9] There is general recognition that the resurrection is the act of the Father in raising the dead Christ and not the self-raising of Christ. Christ does not raise himself, even though he may be said to have the power to do so (John 10:18).[10] Consequently, as the act of the Father, the resurrection can be understood as his affirmation of the Son openly to the people.

This type of divine action can be seen on a broader scale in Acts 10:38–39, where Jesus was enabled to do his mighty acts because God was with him, and in Acts 2:22 where Jesus is "a man accredited by God to you by miracles, wonders and signs which God did among you through him." Similarly, in Hebrews 2:4 the preaching of the apostles is accompanied by God's testimony by signs, wonders, and various miracles, and by gifts of the Holy Spirit distributed according to his will; although this testimony primarily confirms the message, in fact it demonstrates that salvation comes through Jesus and what he did.

Although the resurrection is not specifically mentioned in these passages, it does figure in this way in the conclusion of the Areopagus address, where the proof that Jesus will be the future judge of the world is the fact that God has raised him from the dead (Acts 17:31).

The resurrection, therefore, although witnessed by only a few people, is proclaimed as God's supreme affirmation of Jesus to all people. Consequently, an important part of early Christian apologetic is the way in which the preaching of the apostles that Jesus is Messiah and Lord is backed up by their witness to the resurrection of Jesus; they have seen and heard the risen Lord.[11]

But the resurrection is more than simply a confirmation of the status and identity of Jesus to a human audience. It is also God's action which undoes what evil human beings and the devil sought to accomplish by putting Jesus to death. They thought to bring his work to an end and to discredit his message by putting him to death. The resurrection is the event in which God undoes what they have done through overcoming death and its effects.

God does so because death could not hold Jesus (Acts 2:24). This means that something about Jesus prevented his death from being permanent. What was it? It was probably the fact that Jesus believed in the God who delivers those who call to him from death and decay, in accordance with the firm statement of David in Scripture that he will not be abandoned to death because God will deliver him. This is a more likely explanation than one which draws conclusions from the divine nature of Jesus as the Son of God.[12] Thus, implicitly rather than explicitly, in Acts the raising of the Messiah is the affirmation of him by God as the Messiah despite human and satanic opposition.

However, this line of argument does not specifically relate the resurrection of Jesus to the achieving of salvation on behalf of sinful humanity. In Acts it is not directly said that Christ dies for sinners[13] and that God accepts this action. The resurrection is not seen as the approval by God of what Christ has done for sinners. Rather, the resurrection is how God undoes the acts of wicked people who put Jesus to death and affirms that he is the Messiah and Lord and thus the author of salvation. This may not be all that Luke-Acts has to say on the matter, as we shall note later, but the interpretation of the resurrection simply as the undoing of the slaying of Jesus does not integrally relate it to the achieving of salvation.

The Heavenly Offering Made by Christ

More promising for our investigation is the path taken in Hebrews. Here the saving action by the Son is seen as having two parts, like the making and offering of a sacrifice. The first stage is the slaying of the sacrificial victim; the second is the offering of the blood to God or the burning of the carcase so that the smoke ascends to God; a gift or offering to God is thus symbolised by these actions (Heb 9:7). The death of Jesus as the victim is followed by the entry of Jesus as high priest bearing the blood of his own sacrifice to God. The writer conceives the heaven into which Jesus enters as being like a temple (or rather it is the antitype of earthly temples)[14] where God is really present, and there he presents his sacrifice to God on the basis of which forgiveness is available to sinners.

The accent thus falls now on the action of the risen Son and High Priest. Two surprising points stand out. First, Hebrews does not use the term "raise" (except in Heb 13:20, a benediction whose language may well rest on tradition rather than being a reflection of the author's distinctive theology). Rather, Jesus passes through the heavens (Heb 4:14; 9:11), enters heaven on our behalf (Heb 6:20; 9:12,24, 25), and sits down when his task is done (Heb 8:1; 10:12; 12:2). The action of God in raising Jesus thus retreats to the background, and the writer simply assumes that, having died, Jesus somehow could have access to heaven.[15] There is no action of God the Father and indeed no mention of resurrection as the mode of entry to heaven.[16] Thus the heavenly entry of Jesus is understood in Hebrews rather more as his own action, contrasted with the way in which God raises him, glorifies him, and honours him in the depictions elsewhere in the New Testament. Here Christ continues to be the agent of salvation in his heavenly activity. Perhaps we should understand this in the light of the appointment of Jesus by God as high priest (Heb 5:5–6), which presumably preceded his entry to heaven; having obtained this delegated authority from God he was able to act on the basis of it.

So the resurrection as such has moved out of the picture. The accent has shifted from the raising of Jesus to his entry into heaven to appear for us in God's presence. But now something else that is also surprising takes place. All that we are told is that Christ appears on behalf of sinners and makes his offering to God, sits down and continues to intercede, but nothing is said about God's acceptance of the offering. No doubt the acceptance can be assumed since the throne that we approach is a throne of grace (Heb 4:16), but it is not part of the story. What Christ has done is accepted by God, but the divine acceptance is not described. Is this because the Old Testament pattern does not contain anything comparable?

A further point should be noted. Hebrews clearly distinguishes two aspects to what Christ does in heaven. The one is the making of the offering to God, and this is stated emphatically to be once for all (Heb 7:27; 9:12, 26, 28; 10:10; cf. 10:14). The sacrifice has been made and offered; then Christ sits down. There is nothing that needs to be repeated.[17]

The other is that from his sitting position he makes intercession for sinners (Heb 7:25). Thus his role as high priest continues, but it is a role of intercession based on the sacrifice once for all made and offered.

It may be noted in passing that Protestant, evangelical Christians have rightly insisted that this way of putting things takes away the need for any further sacrifice or any reenactment of the one sacrifice, specifically in the Roman Catholic understanding of the Mass as in some way a representation of what Christ has done in an elaborate construction whereby the bread and wine become the body and blood of Christ which are then offered by a functionary who is called a priest. Hence popular language refers to "the sacrifice of the mass."[18]

Consequently, Protestants generally have denied any particularly sacrificial role to the minister at the Lord's Supper,[19] although there are tendencies in many rituals to regard the bread and wine as offerings by the people to God which he then takes and uses to be vehicles of salvation to them. This concept of God using what we offer and transforming it is entirely against the spirit of the New Testament in which God is the giver and we are the recipients of sheer grace.[20]

There is nevertheless an ongoing role of intercession. The Son is presented as himself active on behalf of sinners, and the picture is intended to denote the ongoing efficacy of his sacrifice. It avails "for all time," "to the uttermost."

The basic point emerging from all this is that the work of Christ in atonement is not completed until something has been done in heaven that ratifies what has been done on the cross; at that point the sacrifice is complete and Christ has no need to "enter heaven to offer himself again and again" as the Jewish high priest did on his annual visit (Heb 9:25–28). The act of sacrifice and the offering of the sacrifice are theoretically distinguishable, and each must take place. They form a unity, and neither is effective without the other. Here we have possibly some kind of parallel and guide that may help us to understand the somewhat different presentation in Paul.

Victory over the Power of Evil

The resurrection has an important place in the Christus Victor type of understanding of the work of Christ. Here the central thought is that death is, as it were, administered by the devil, who is paying his servants the wages of sin (Heb 2:14; Rom 6:23). The devil seeks to overcome Christ, and the latter succumbs to death. Apparently evil has won the victory. But the resurrection of Jesus shows that death could not overcome him, and he shares this victory with believers. On this view of things one might expect that it would be Christ himself who conquers death, but, as we have seen, the thought is more that God raises him from the dead. Thus, Father and Son are closely united here as the agents of victory and the ensuing salvation. Yet in Hebrews 2:14 it is through death that Jesus destroys the one who has the power of death and sets free his captives. However, we need to be careful how this is understood. Apparently the death of Jesus constitutes the victory over the devil here, and there is no reference to his resurrection. Can it be that the victory over death is rather that what Christ does is to die one death on behalf of all so that the devil can have no power over others because they have in effect already died in the death of Jesus? And is the victory of Jesus to be seen in his gracious willingness to submit to death as compared with the attitude of human beings for whom it is the due punishment for their sins?[21] Or must we not say that no early Christian could have understood the death of Jesus as victory over the devil without closely linking the resurrection to it?

Understanding Romans 4:25

After this survey of other material on the significance of the resurrection, we now come at last to a consideration of Romans 4:25. This verse makes two statements in parallel. Whatever else they convey, these statements emphasise that both Christ's death and his resurrection were for our benefit.[22]

First, Jesus was delivered over [to death] because of our transgressions.

The verb "deliver" is used in three ways elsewhere with reference to the death of Jesus. It can refer to the action of Judas in handing over Jesus to the authorities who crucified him (Mark 3:19; 14:21; cf. 1 Cor 11:23), but it is also used for the action of God who handed over his Son to death (Rom 8:32) or reflexively of the action of Jesus in surrendering himself to death (Gal 2:20; Eph 5:2, 25). In view of the proximity of this verse to Romans 8:32 and the parallelism with the next clause, a reference to the action of God the Father is most probable here. Behind the phrase probably lie such statements as Isaiah 53:12 LXX (his soul was handed over to death) and Isaiah 53:6 (the Lord handed him over for our sins). The statement that it was because of our sins that he was handed over to death agrees with the repeated statements elsewhere in the New Testament that he died "for" our sins.[23] If it had not been for our sins, he would not have died, and hence there is some connection between our sins and his death. The *dia* here is most commonly understood as retrospective and causal although some scholars take it as prospective and interpret it to mean "with a view to doing something about our sins."[24] In any case, this latter sense is surely implied.

Second, in parallelism we are then told that he was raised because of our justification.[25]

In the previous verse Paul states that God will credit righteousness to those who believe in him as the God who raised Jesus our Lord from death. This anticipates and coheres with the statement in Romans 10:9 where justification and salvation are for those who believe that God raised Jesus from the dead. Paul can thus speak both of believing that God raised Jesus from the dead and of believing in the God who raised Jesus. Belief that God did something and believing in the God who did it are two complementary aspects of the single action of faith in which we believe that something is true about what God is and does and put our confident trust in him to act accordingly. The infinitive "to believe" is here linked to its object by the preposition "on" and suggests the idea of confidently resting upon this God and what he has done.[26] So confidence is placed on God in his capacity to raise the dead. The issue is partly the power of God to do the impossible, as is to be seen in the comparison with the action of Abraham in believing that God could give him and Sarah a child despite apparently impossible circumstances. That the impossibility of resurrection was an issue in the first century as also in the twenty-first is clearly apparent from 1 Corinthians 15; Acts 17:32; 26:8. But there is more to it than simply the power of God. God does something impossible in order to achieve a promised goal. In the case of Abraham, the miracle of Isaac's birth took place so that he might become a father of many nations. Consequently, in the case of Christian believers, the raising of Jesus must play some part in the act of justification.

But what is the connection? Here we run into an ambiguity. If we take the prepositional phrase "on account of" in the first clause in verse 25 in a retrospective sense and then interpret the second clause in parallel with it, this would give a statement in which God raised Christ "because our justification had taken place." In that case the resurrection was not part of the action that led to justification but rather something that followed it and simply confirms it. Alternatively, if we take the first clause prospectively to mean that Christ was delivered over to death in order to atone for our trespasses, then we can also take the second clause prospectively: Christ was raised from the dead in order to bring about our justification.

However, whether we take the first clause retrospectively, the second clause by itself can certainly have this prospective sense, namely that Christ was raised from the dead with a view to our justification, i.e., so that we might be justified. This is a standard use of the preposition.[27] With the majority of scholars, I shall assume that this is the correct interpretation.[28]

So we have a statement in which justification is tied in some way to the resurrection of Jesus. This is an interesting shift from Romans 3 where everything rests on the death of Jesus and nothing is said about his resurrection. However, we shall find hints elsewhere that salvation depends on something more than just the death of Jesus.

But in what sense had Christ to be raised so that we might be justified? It is remarkable that some leading commentators barely discuss the issue at all.[29]

1. One possibility, which can be maintained as part of a total interpretation, is that the resurrection is the event through which the new era of salvation comes into existence, so that those who belong to Christ can share in it.[30]

2. From our discussion of contextual material, we might deduce that one function of the resurrection here is to raise Jesus to the right hand of God to intercede for us (Rom 8:34).[31] However, the reference here is to resurrection and not specifically to exaltation to God's right hand or to intercession. This interpretation requires that we read a lot into the verse.

3. Another possibility is that the resurrection places Jesus in the position where he is able to offer and declare forgiveness to sinners, just as in Acts where God raises and exalts him so that he might have this function (Acts 5:31). However, in Paul's usage it is God the Father who offers justification rather than Christ.

4. More promising is the proposal already mentioned that the resurrection offers the essential evidence that God accepted his atoning sacrifice on the basis of which justification is available. However, put in this form the proposal remains vague and needs closer attention.[32]

   a. One possibility is that the resurrection is simply the vindication by God of the death of Jesus and signifies that it has been effective in making justification possible.[33] The resurrection is then a demonstration to human beings that God has accepted what Christ has done.[34] Certainly, this ties in with the apologetic function of the resurrection that we have seen elsewhere, especially in Acts. And it would provide visible evidence of an unseen event. But it seems to confuse the achievement of justification with the corroboration of justification and it rests on what we have seen to be the less likely understanding of the syntax of the phrase.[35] Above all, it is very odd to make confession of belief in the raising of Jesus the ground of salvation if his resurrection is merely the guarantee that his death for us was effective. We would have expected that what was necessary was belief in the fact that he died for our sins as the actual divine basis for our salvation.

b. The other way of taking the statement is to see the vindication as an essential part of the process in which Christ bears the consequences of human sin. God accepts that Christ has borne the penalty of human sin and does so by raising him from the death that he has been suffering on behalf of humanity. The point is put most effectively by W. Künneth:

The resurrection can be the realizing of salvation because it not only enables us to see the death of Jesus as punishment imposed by God, but in awakening Jesus from death remits this punishment, and so liberates from guilt. . . . In the Risen One the new curse-free relationship between God and man is given. In him the new reality of being objectively reconciled with God has taken concrete form. . . . *God justifies the sinner because of the new situation of being reconciled and justified which is created by the raising of the Crucified. In this situation sinful man, in so far as he participates in it through Christ, is qualified as just before God.*[36]

On this view the resurrection is God's release of Christ from the punishment of sin that he is bearing; he remits any continuation of the punishment. Hence there is now the possibility of a new relationship between God and the man whom he has judged in death, and so God can now forgive sinners. This goes beyond the interpretation that sees the resurrection as God's recognition that Christ has paid the penalty for sin; it makes explicit God's granting of the decisive remission of the guilt that Christ has been bearing and makes him the representative Man in whom we can be justified.

Somewhat similar statements are made by other writers.[37] They express in various ways the view that "the resurrection is Christ's justification in which believers participate by faith."[38] It is "a constitutive, transforming action. . . . It is Christ's justification."[39] "God 'justified' Jesus by raising him from the dead: the one verdict has already been given (following the act of obedience on the cross); by faith Christians enter into Christ and are associated with that verdict."[40] "Jesus' resurrection was the divine *vindication* of him as Messiah, 'son of God' in that sense, the representative of Israel and thence of the world. . . . God's raising of Jesus from the dead was therefore the act in which justification—the vindication of all God's people 'in Christ'—was contained in a nutshell."[41]

A particularly influential contribution is that of M. D. Hooker who states that Christ "was raised in order that we might share his acquittal (pronounced at his resurrection)."[42] The argument in Romans 5:12–19 "suggests that the acquittal of the many depends on the acquittal of Christ. This acquittal, which leads to life for the many, would have taken place at the resurrection, an act of vindication which established his righteousness."[43] As Hooker has demonstrated, the *dikaiōma* in Romans 5:18 should have the same sense as in verse 16 and refer to the vindication or acquittal of Christ by God that then results in the *dikaiōsis* or justification of all who are united with him through faith.

Other texts can be drawn into the discussion. Thus we are now in a position to appreciate the brief allusion to the life of Christ in Romans 5:10. The basic thought in the passage is that those who were reconciled to God when they were sinners will *a fortiori* be delivered from the wrath expressed against sinners at the final judgment.[44] The reconciliation is attributed to the death of God's Son but the salvation to his life. Here "saved" refers to deliverance at the final judgment and "life" refers to the resurrection life of Jesus (cf. Rom 6:10). Thus in both parts of the statement final salvation is dependent upon Christ (and not upon ourselves or what we do). Our sins have been dealt with by the death of Christ (with whom we are united); now as those who are united with him in his life we are alive to God and therefore outside the sphere of wrath. Union with the Christ who died and rose for us is the basis of our final salvation.[45]

Gaffin refers to 1 Corinthians 15:17 which states that if Christ has not risen, we are still in our sins. This statement is at least compatible with the view that is being developed: if Christ merely died, the possibility of justification does not exist. For Gaffin the point is that raising to new life is an essential part of justification; and if Christ has not been raised, justification is not possible. Here we are beginning to see that the traditional understanding of justification is possibly too much inclined to the negative side of cancellation of sins and has not done justice to the positive element of creating a new, living relationship with God.[46] Resurrection permeates the theology of Romans.[47]

Somewhat controversial is the interpretation of 1 Timothy 3:16 shared by Gaffin and Bird, according to which Christ was not merely vindicated in the Spirit but specifically justified.[48] There is no doubt that the reference in this phrase is to the resurrection/exaltation of Jesus, but commentators differ whether it vindicates the claims made by Jesus during his lifetime,[49] or demonstrates the righteousness of the One crucified as an evildoer,[50] or is rather a stage further after his manifestation in the flesh in which we have "the eschatological confirmation through God, which brings Jesus' function as mediator to completion in regard to the saving will of God."[51] Gaffin wants to see Jesus here as the second Adam who bears death for human guilt and is now confirmed as righteous, i.e., justified.[52] This reads the verse against a broad background of Adamic Christology and Pauline soteriology (seen in 2 Cor 5:21; Gal 3:13; 4:5) for which I can find no contextual support. A background in the LXX of Isaiah 53:11 (with 50:8) is detected by H. Stettler. Where the MT speaks of the Servant justifying many, the LXX describes how God justifies or vindicates the one who serves many; "after the shame which he has endured he is exalted by God and vindicated."[53] But it would probably be going too far to find a reference to a representative justification in the soteriological sense of Christ here. It is doubtful, then, whether the justification of Christ in this narrow soteriological sense can be said to be taught by this verse, but it certainly refers to God's confirmation of him in broad terms, on the basis of which the missionary preaching and its results in the later part of the verse can take place.

The most that can be said, then, is that these three passages may contain thinking along the same lines as Romans 4:25 and do not constitute an obstacle to our interpretation of it.

It seems to me that here we have a decisive step forward in understanding of the relation of the resurrection to justification. It goes beyond the simple understanding of the resurrection of Christ in terms of God's vindication of him purely as a demonstration to humanity that he was the Messiah after all and that his sacrifice has been effective. Rather, in raising Christ from death after he has taken upon himself the sins of the world and died, God is not so much vindicating what Christ has done and saying that he approves of it, but bringing him back from the dead as the One who is now just and experiencing the new life that God grants to those whose sin has been taken away; and this is happening representatively to Christ so that believers may share in this new life. In the cross God's condemnation of sin is demonstrated and carried out, Christ bears the sin, and so God declares that sin has been taken away and Christ is representatively justified so that those who believe and are united with him share in this justification. Hence the resurrection is essential to the saving act in that it is not merely God saying that Christ has done what is necessary; rather God himself has to carry out the act of pardon on the basis of what Christ has done and he does so. Thus Christ was raised for our justification, and without the raising of Christ we would not be justified.

According to Bird, the death and resurrection have different functions but work in tandem to achieve justification. "In the resurrection God's declaration of vindication and the enactment of it are manifested in the resurrection of Christ."[54] The resurrection is to be seen as the justification of Christ as the last Adam, and consequently our union with Christ "is union with the justified Messiah and the new righteous One."[55]

To put the point slightly differently: on the traditional type of understanding, the death of Christ is the sufficient basis for our justification whether Christ is subsequently raised from the dead, and the resurrection is in danger of being nothing more than a public demonstration that the death of Christ was effective, a sort of sermon in action; on the view that is being developed here, the Pauline teaching is that the death by itself is not sufficient to justify us without the verdict of God expressed in his carrying into effect the result of Christ's death, namely the pardon and enlivening of the sinner who is now brought into the new life of the justified.

The Theological Significance of Romans 4:25

Some significant corollaries follow from this understanding.

Substitution and Representation

First, it follows that in the event of crucifixion and resurrection it is inadequate to think of Christ purely as substitute. Substitution means that Christ acts instead of us[56] and does something that as a result of his doing it we do not need to do. We do not have to bear the eternal consequences of our sin because Christ has done so.[57] But the same cannot be said of resurrection. Christ is not raised instead of us but so that we might share his resurrection. He is raised for us, for our benefit, on our behalf, in order that what has happened in him may be recapitulated in us, by what has happened in him being extended to us as we are joined to him by faith.

Consequently, those theologians are right who assert that representative is the more inclusive term than substitute; substitution is a valid, necessary, and essential category to cover that which Christ does for us so that we do not have to do it, but some such term as representation is necessary to cover that which Christ does for us so that we may share in it.[58] God does something to Christ that is extended to those who are represented by him; compare how a king might make a symbolic presentation of a gift to a representative of his subjects, and the gift is then enjoyed by them all. Alternatively, it may be better to think of Christ as the one in whom we are incorporated or with whom we are identified or in whom (or better, in whose situation) we participate.

Participation and Incorporation in Christ

Romans 6 now speaks of believers being baptised into Christ and hence into his death. Although Paul develops this aspect of his thought primarily in order to indicate that believers should not remain in sin and have the power to overcome its appeal to them, in fact it reveals the underlying rationale of his soteriology. Believers are united with Christ. This is expressed in their baptism, which Paul understands as a baptism into their death. He does not speak of their baptism as being a baptism into his resurrection. This is probably because baptism is understood as symbolising death, in line with the well-known metaphorical use of being plunged into, or deluged with, water. Death delivers the person from sin, meaning its captivity, which includes receiving its wage, namely death. But by the death of Christ, the believer is regarded as having died and therefore no longer standing under the domination of sin. But that can only be half the story. In the case of Jesus, he is resurrected from the dead. He has died once and for all from sin. Now he lives the new life of those who have been raised by God, and it is this life that is shared with believers who are united with him. Thus union with Christ by faith means that believers share in what we can rightly call the justification of Christ as the representative of sinners. They now share in his life, and they are in effect spiritually resurrected with Christ, as the clear statements in Ephesians and Colossians indicate.

Other New Testament modes of expression

1. Hebrews. We can now take a step forward and claim that what Paul is expressing in this way is complementary to what is expressed in Hebrews. In Hebrews the death of Christ as sacrifice is followed by his (resurrection and) entry into heaven to present his sacrifice to God. What we saw as surprisingly absent from Hebrews is any statement that the offering is actually accepted by God! That is taken for granted. Romans, however, sees the acceptance by God as taking place in the resurrection of Jesus and in the intercession that follows. It is emphasised that it is God who justifies sinners (Rom 8:33; cf. 3:26). Thus Romans and Hebrews offer complementary insights that together enable us to grasp more fully the significance of the resurrection and ascension.

2. *Luke-Acts.* In the light of this, the soteriology in Acts merits a fresh examination. The resurrection is here the means by which God exalts Jesus and appoints him to be Lord and Messiah, a Leader and Saviour (Luke 24:26; Acts 3:13; 5:31). Thus a positive value is assigned to the action of resurrection. It is certainly a reversal of what wicked men have done and to that extent a vindication of Jesus to the world, but it is also a public vindication of Jesus because in this action God now seats Jesus beside him as the giver of salvation.[59]

The thought of affirming what Jesus did on the cross may not be so apparent. Yet it remains the case that the death of Jesus, though brought about by evil men, is nevertheless something that was planned and purposed by God, the Messiah had to suffer and then enter into glory. But why was the suffering necessary? It may well be that commentators have generally attached too little significance to Luke 22:37. It is common to deny any vicarious sense in this text, partly because it is urged that this line of thought is not developed elsewhere in Luke-Acts, and that this sense is not required by the present text which is simply stating that it is the lot of Jesus to be treated like a lawless person with the implication that his followers will be treated similarly. L. Morris by contrast says, "Jesus sees his death as one in which he will be one with sinners. This surely points to that death as substitutionary: Jesus will take the place of sinful people."[60] Hence this statement, drawn as it is from the Servant-prophecy in Isaiah 53 and occurring not many verses after the sayings at the Last Supper, may well have a secondary force that there was a divine purpose in the death of Jesus which went beyond simply providing an occasion for God to raise him from the dead. In any case, the thought of Christ dying for sinners is present in the sayings at the Last Supper (Luke 22:19–20).[61]

Even without this thought, it remains the case that the resurrection is the glorification of Jesus as the Messiah, and this is rather more than simply vindicating the one who was crucified as a malefactor. It is his enthronement as Messiah. So for Luke-Acts the resurrection and exaltation has the character of a saving event, the enthronement of Jesus as Leader and Saviour.

The thought in Paul goes further in that Jesus is vindicated as the representative righteous One in whom his people are accepted by

God. Nevertheless, common to Paul and Luke is the belief that in raising Jesus from the dead God *makes* him the one through whom salvation is conferred and does not merely publicly acknowledge him as such.

3. *1 Peter.* Similar things might be said about 1 Peter where both cross and resurrection figure prominently. Here there is no question but that the suffering and death of Jesus on behalf of the unjust, bearing their sins, is clearly taught, and then Peter elaborates that Christ was put to death in the flesh but made alive in the spirit. Of particular significance for our purpose is the statement that baptism now saves through the resurrection of Jesus (1 Pet 3:18, 21; cf. 1:3, 21; 2:24). The precise way in which the resurrection functions in relation to the death of Jesus is not spelled out, but the way in which the resurrection is referred to suggests that it is more than simply ratification or evidence of the saving power of the death but is itself an integral part of the total saving event. Since the purpose of Christ was to bring sinners to God, his resurrection should be seen as the means by which this takes place.

Paradox and mystery

There are various paradoxes in this understanding of things.

1. The death of Jesus is the death of the Son of God[62] and not the death of the Father.[63] Equally, the resurrection is the resurrection of Jesus as man and as Son of God. There is no suggestion that God the Father dies. We thus have, from our later point of view, the paradox of one member of the Trinity dying (and being raised) but not the others. We have the further paradox that the Son of God is capable of death. A solution to these mysteries must take seriously the incarnation of the Son of God as a human being for whom death is a possibility and reality. This is clearly taught in Philippians 2:6–9, although Paul does not stop to consider how it was possible. Neither the Father nor the Spirit became incarnate.

2. The language of intercession and offering envisages the Son requesting pardon for sinners from the Father; nevertheless, the sacrifice and offering are initiated by the Father in his grace, and according to Romans 4:25 he has raised Jesus in order that sinners may be justified; therefore there is no doubt about the outcome of Christ's

intercession. While it could be the case that the Son is portrayed as acting in his capacity as a human being on behalf of human beings with God, nevertheless it is specifically as Son that he intercedes (Rom 8:34 in light of 8:32; 1 John 2:1 in light of 1:7; Heb 7:25 in light of 7:28). Moreover, the gracious saving purpose of God the Father is apparent; note how the love of Christ in Romans 8:35 slides into the love of God in Christ Jesus our Lord in 8:39. The imagery functions to provide both a way for believers to approach the Father on the basis of the One who died for them and an assurance that the sacrifice that he offered avails forever. Thus, all believers share in the priesthood of Christ, in the sense that they have access through and in him to God.[64]

Conclusion

What has emerged from this discussion of the contributions of various recent scholars who have revived an insight from an earlier generation is a persuasive interpretation of Romans 4:25 that integrates the resurrection of Jesus into the saving event on the basis of which we are justified. Jesus Christ, who died bearing our sins and atoning for them, is released from death by God the Father; he has done representatively what was needed for sinful humanity so as to uphold the holiness and righteousness of God, and so he is representatively justified in order that those who believe and are joined to him by baptism into his death for them may share in his representative justification and enter into the new life that has been conferred on him by the Father. Thus the raising of Jesus by God the Father is seen to be an essential part of the saving act and is not simply a way of proclaiming to humanity that the price of sin has been paid. If Christ had not been raised, we would still be in our sins. This way of understanding the significance of the resurrection for Paul corresponds to the reality expressed in a somewhat different imagery in Hebrews, 1 Peter, and Luke-Acts. Moreover, it explains how it is that on occasion the New Testament writers can depict the resurrection and exaltation of Jesus as the saving event without explicit reference to the death of Jesus.

Endnotes

1 The substance of this essay was given as a Theological Society Public Lecture organised by the chaplaincy in the University of Wales Swansea on 23 January 2006; it was also delivered as the second in a series of Chuen King Lectures under the auspices of Chung Chi College, Chinese University of Hong Kong, on 26 February 2006, and as one of a short series of lectures in the Seminari Theoloji Malaysia on 28 February 2006. I am grateful to these institutions for their kind invitations to me and for their hospitality on the occasions of the lectures.

2 W. Künneth, *The Theology of the Resurrection* (London: SCM Press, 1965); R. B. Gaffin, *The Centrality of the Resurrection: A Study in Paul's Soteriology* (Grand Rapids: Baker, 1978); M. J. Harris, *Raised Immortal: The Relation between Resurrection and Immortality in New Testament Teaching* (London: Marshall, Morgan and Scott, 1983); D. M. Stanley, *Christ's Resurrection in Pauline Soteriology* (Rome: Pontifical Biblical Institute, 1961); N. T. Wright, *The Resurrection of the Son of God* (Minneapolis: Fortress, 2003).

3 U. Wilckens, *Der Brief an die Römer* (Zürich: Benziger/Neukirchen: Neukirchener, 1978), I: 280, draws attention to the similar passages in Ignatius, Rom. 6:1; Polycarp, Phil. 9:2.

4 For the former view see R. P. Martin, *Carmen Christi: Philippians ii.5–11 in recent interpretation and in the setting of early Christian worship* (Grand Rapids: Eerdmans, 1983[2]; originally Cambridge: Cambridge University Press, 1967). For the latter see G. D. Fee, *Paul's Letter to the Philippians* (Grand Rapids: Eerdmans, 1995), 43–46.

5 Contrast 1 Pet 2:21–25, where Peter, having begun to give his readers a portrayal of Christ as an example to them in his suffering, just cannot stop himself from going on to express powerfully the saving consequences of those sufferings.

6 In its context this emphasis is undoubtedly related to the preceding verses in which Abraham is presented as believing in the God who raises the dead.

7 E.g. D. Moo, *The Epistle to the Romans* (Grand Rapids: Eerdmans, 1996), 312.

8 Such questions as the historicity of the resurrection of Christ and the nature of his resurrection body lie outside our interest here. Needless to say, the resurrection would have no saving effects if it had not happened.

9 W. Sanday and A. C. Headlam, *A Critical and Exegetical Commentary on the Epistle to the Romans* (Edinburgh: T and T Clark, 1902[5]), 117. So recently (for example), T. R. Schreiner, *Romans* (Grand Rapids: Baker, 1998), 244.

10 I. H. Marshall, "The Resurrection in the Acts of the Apostles," in W. W. Gasque and R. P. Martin (ed.), *Apostolic History and the Gospel: Biblical and Historical Essays Presented to F. F. Bruce* (Exeter: Paternoster, 1970), 101–3.

11 Although the fact of the empty tomb does not figure in the preaching in Acts, the stories in the Gospels were presumably employed for this purpose.

12 In an earlier discussion I said that it was because Jesus was the Messiah and the Messiah could not be held by death. This could be taken to mean that God could not allow death to conquer his agent. It might also be the case that

the Messiah has faith in God to which God is bound to respond. Cf. I. H. Marshall, *The Acts of the Apostles* (Leicester: Inter-Varsity Press, 1980), 76.

13 The thought is, of course, explicit in Luke 22:19–20 and implicit in Acts 20:28.

14 We might be tempted to say that the author pictures heaven on the analogy of the earthly tabernacle, but the writer manifestly thought that the tabernacle was built on the model of the heavenly tabernacle, just as described by God to Moses in Exodus.

15 To be sure, there is reference to the crowning of Jesus (Heb 2:5–9), which implies a divine recognition of Jesus. Also Jesus' session at the right hand of God rests on God's invitation (Heb 1:13).

16 Here the possible contrast between resurrection and heavenly access is most clearly present.

17 A. M. Stibbs, *The Finished Work of Christ* (London: Tyndale Press, 1954).

18 F. Hildebrandt, *I Offered Christ: A Protestant Study of the Mass* (London: Epworth, 1967), has noted how the phrase "to offer Christ," used to describe the action of the priest in the mass was used in a different sense by John Wesley to refer to the offering of salvation to sinners by the preacher.

19 C. J. Collins, "The Eucharist as Christian Sacrifice: How Patristic Authors Can Help Us Read the Bible," *WTJ* 66 (2004), 1–23, argues that the Lord's Supper reflects the Old Testament peace offering and that the ministry of those who lead it constitutes a special priesthood, different from that of the laity.

20 See, for example, *The Methodist Worship Book* (Peterborough: Methodist Publishing House, 1999), where the bread and wine are brought to the table along with the offerings of the people; they are ambiguously referred to in prayer as "these gifts of bread and wine," but whether they are God's gifts or the gifts of the people that God takes and uses is not entirely clear; certainly the prayer on p. 136 suggests the latter, but the prayer on p. 168 clearly indicates the former.

21 Another "Christus Victor" text is Col 2:15. Here Christ either divested himself of the powers or disarmed them and in so doing made a public spectacle of them, i.e., made their defeat clear to all, and he did so "in it" or "in him." The subject of the verb (whether God or Christ) is not clear, and the prepositional phrase could refer to Christ or the cross. Here again the decisive element is the cross, i.e., the death of Christ, rather than the resurrection.

22 See B. A. Lowe, "Oh dear! How is Romans 4:25 to be understood?" (forthcoming, *JTS* ns 57 [2006], unpublished article, kindly sent to me by the author). Lowe finds an echo of the use of the first person plural in Isa 53:4–6.

23 The two prepositions used are *huper* (1 Cor 15:3; Gal 1:4; cf. Heb 10:12) and *peri* (Rom 8:3; 1 Pet 3:18; 1 John 2:2; 4:10; see also Heb 10:6, 8, 18, 26; 13:11 where it is used of OT sacrifices).

24 The sense of *dia* in the two parts of the verse is disputed.

   1. Some take the two prepositional phrases in the same retrospective, broadly causal, way: "He died because we sinned and rose because we were justified"; cf. L. Morris, *The Apostolic Preaching of the Cross* (London: Tyndale Press, 1965[3]), 288–89.

2. Some take the two prepositional phrases in the same prospective way: He died "in order to atone for [our trespasses]" and "to bring about [our justification]"; cf. E. Lohse, *Der Brief an die Römer* (Göttingen: Vandenhoeck und Ruprecht, 2003), 162 n. 19, who says that both must be taken same way as "final" (presumably with a view to dealing with our sins and our justification).

3. Many take the first phrase retrospectively and the second prospectively: "He died because we sinned and rose with a view to our justification"; e.g. C. E. B. Cranfield, *A Critical and Exegetical Commentary on the Epistle to the Romans* (Edinburgh: T and T Clark, 1975) 1:251–52; J. D. G. Dunn, *Romans 1–8* (Dallas: Word, 1988), 224–25.

   It has been suggested that Paul is using the device of parallelism rhetorically to say essentially the same thing in two different ways, so that the meaning is determined by combining what is said in the two clauses. Hence the rendering: "Jesus died and rose again because of our trespasses and justification"; V. Taylor, *The Atonement in New Testament Teaching* (London: Epworth, 1945²), 67. Presumably on this understanding the two occurrences of the preposition are taken to have the same force, whether retrospective or prospective. While this is a true statement (since justification is clearly related to the cross in Rom 3:24–25), it does not do justice to Paul's careful formulation in this verse; cf. M. D. Hooker, "Raised for our acquittal (Rom 4,25)," in R. Bieringer (et al., eds.), *Resurrection in the New Testament: Festschrift J. Lambrecht* (Leuven: Leuven University Press, 2002), 323–41 (323).

25 *Dikaiōsis* is the process of justification; cf. Rom 5:18.

26 Cf. Rom 4:5; 9:33; 1 Tim 1:16; 1 Pet 2:6; Acts 9:42; 16:31; 22:19.

27 Some defenders of the retrospective sense in the first clause argue that the preposition must have the same sense in the second clause. To this objection that it is unlikely that Paul could use the same preposition in two different ways in the same sentence we can reply that in fact he does so elsewhere, and the difference in usage is quite possible despite the parallelism. There are possible cases in Rom 8:10; 11:28; compare the varied uses of *en* in 1 Tim 3:16. Since "sins" and "justification" are terms of two different kinds, a shift in the force of the prepositions governing them is not surprising, perhaps even necessary.

28 See the fuller discussion in M. F. Bird, "Justified by Christ's Resurrection: A Neglected aspect of Paul's Doctrine of Justification," *SBET* 22 (2004), 72–91, here 83–84. I am indebted to Dr. Bird for his helpful comments during the composition of this paper.

29 E.g. Cranfield, 251–52. Dunn, 225 and 240–41 (he notes justifying grace has to be accompanied by life-giving power); Moo, 288–90 (one sentence!); G. R. Osborne, *Romans* (Downers Grove: IVP, 2004), 122–23; B. Witherington III with D. Hyatt, *Paul's Letter to the Romans: A Socio-Rhetorical Commentary* (Grand Rapids: Eerdmans, 2004), 129.

30 Wilckens, *Brief*, 1:278–79, comes within range of this interpretation of Rom 4:25 by seeing the breaking in of the new aeon in the resurrection of Jesus; believers share in this through belonging to Christ.

31 Cf. K. Haacker, *Der Brief des Paulus an die Römer* (Leipzig: Evangelische Verlagsanstalt, 1999), 111, n. 14.
32 Here I am particularly indebted to the recent work of M. F. Bird who helpfully brings together and summarises various suggestions that have been offered before developing one in particular.
33 Harris, *Raised Immortal,* 164–65; J. Stott, *The Cross of Christ* (Leicester: Inter-Varsity Press, 1986), 238–39; Stott is fearful lest anything should detract from the completeness of Christ's sin-bearing on the cross: "The resurrection did not achieve our deliverance from sin and death, but has brought us an assurance of both." Cf. H. Ridderbos, *Paul: An Outline of his Theology* (London: SPCK, 1977), 167.
34 E.g., "His resurrection . . . is the apologetic basis of salvation" (Osborne, *Romans,* 123).
35 It would be a possible interpretation if the prepositional phrase were retrospective, raised because our justification has taken place, i.e., as evidence that it has happened.
36 Künneth, *Theology,* 157–58.
37 D. M. Stanley, *Christ's Resurrection,* 275 holds that Christ becomes the second Adam through his resurrection, but he does not link this to Christ's bearing of the consequences of sin. Cf. Bird, "Justified," 76–77.
38 Bird, "Justified," 79.
39 Gaffin, *Centrality,* 122–24. His point is well summarised in the statement in a later article: "As our substitute, a crucified but unresurrected Christ still bears the guilt of our sins; as long as he remains in a state of death, its penal force continues and he (and believers) are unjustified. The resurrection is his *de facto* justification and so secures the believer's justification. This is the likely sense in Romans 4:25" (R. B. Gaffin, "Atonement in the Pauline Corpus: 'The Scandal of the Cross,'" in C. E. Hill and F. A. James III, *The Glory of the Atonement: Biblical, Historical and Practical Perspectives* [Downers Grove: InterVarsity Press, 2004], 160). Gaffin refers to earlier recognition of the point; cf. H. Heppe, *Reformed Dogmatics* (London: Allen and Unwin, 1950), 498–99, citing Olevian: "Just as by giving the Son to death the Father actually condemned all our sins in him, the Father also by raising Christ up from the dead, acquitted Christ of our sin-guilt and us in Christ."
40 P. M. Head, "Jesus' Resurrection in Pauline Thought: A Study in Romans," in P. M. Head (ed.), *Proclaiming the Resurrection: Papers from the First Oak Hill Annual School of Theology* (Carlisle: Paternoster, 1998), 69 (58–80).
41 Wright, *Resurrection,* 248.
42 M. D. Hooker, *Paul: A Short Introduction* (Oxford: One World, 2003), 94. See especially "Raised for our acquittal."
43 M. D. Hooker, *From Adam to Christ: Essays on Paul* (Cambridge: Cambridge University Press, 1990), 29; cf. 39. Other authors move in the same direction. "[Paul] did not regard the effect of the sacrificial death of Christ as complete in itself. The first part required the ratification of the second. The vindication of Christ was also the vindication of those whom he represented" (J. D. G. Dunn, *The Theology of Paul the Apostle* [Grand Rapids: Eerdmans, 1998], 236). "As Christ's death provides the necessary grounds on which God's

justifying action can proceed, so his resurrection, by vindicating Christ and freeing him forever from the influence of sin (cf. 6:10), provides for the ongoing power over sins experienced by the believer in union with Christ" (Moo, *Romans*, 290). See also M. E. Thrall, *A Critical and Exegetical Commentary on the Second Epistle to the Corinthians* (Edinburgh: T & T Clark, 1994, 2000), 1:439–44, who argues that in 2 Cor 5:21 Christ is vindicated as righteous through the resurrection and it is this righteous status that is shared with sinners.

44 Similarly, in the previous verse, justification is attributed to the blood of Christ, but (future) salvation from wrath simply to him.

45 This encourages the understanding of 2 Cor 5:15 as referring to the Christ "who died-and-was-raised for them."

46 Gaffin, *Centrality*, 123–24; cf. Bird, "Justified," 81.

47 Bird, "Justified," 81–85.

48 Gaffin, *Centrality*, 119–22; Bird, "Justified," 85–89; cf. Hooker, *From Adam to Christ*, 34–35.

49 W. D. Mounce, *Pastoral Epistles* (Nashville: Thomas Nelson, 2000), 227. "Contained in these two lines . . . is the acknowledgment of the truth of the gospel message, that God came among humankind and introduced a new kind of life" (P. H. Towner, *1–2 Timothy and Titus* [Downers Grove: InterVarsity Press, 1994], 99).

50 J. Roloff, *Der erste Brief an Timotheus* (Zürich: Benziger/Neukirchen: Neukirchener, 1988), 205–6. H.-W. Neudorfer, *Der erste Brief des Paulus an Timotheus* (Wuppertal: Brockhaus, 2004), 162, sees it as vindication or justification [same German word] of the one rejected and crucified by men.

51 L. Oberlinner, *Kommentar zum ersten Timotheusbrief* (Freiburg: Herder, 1994), 166.

52 Gaffin, *Centrality*, 123–24. Similarly, Bird, "Justified," 87–88, who wants to trace a background in Isa 53:11, but this verse refers to the Servant vindicating others, not to himself being vindicated/justified.

53 H. Stettler, *Die Christologie der Pastoralbriefe* (Tübingen: Mohr Siebeck, 1998), 96–98. Isa 50:8 refers to God has "he who vindicates me." The presence of allusions to Isa 53:5 in Rom 4:25a and to Isa 53:9, 11 in Rom 5:16 and 19 was detected by J. Jeremias, *TDNT* 5:706. Bird, "Justified," 87–88, also suggested a background in Isa 53:11 for the motif in both Rom 4:25 and 1 Tim 3:16; his case is strengthened by Stettler's observation that the LXX gives better support to this proposal than does the MT.

54 Bird, "Justified," 84.

55 Bird, "Justified," 88.

56 It is something that we cannot do for ourselves, and therefore we need somebody to stand in as our substitute, but that is not the point at issue here.

57 Hooker, *Paul*, 92, insists that Christ's death for us is not substitutionary in regard to physical death or death to sin, both of which we must undergo; this is correct but it does not take into account the fact that Christ bore the consequences of sin, the wrath of God and eternal exclusion from his presence, so that we shall not have to bear them. It is this latter aspect which is unambiguously substitutionary.

58 P. T. Forsyth, *The Work of Christ* (London: Independent Press, 1938²), 182.

59 The term "public" requires some defence. The reference is to an event that takes place before heavenly spectators (cf. 1 Tim 3:16) and which is known by faith to God's people on earth; for them, in the light of scriptural references to the exaltation of the Messiah, the attestation of the resurrection of Jesus to his followers in the empty tomb and the appearances was proof of the heavenly exaltation of Jesus and consequently of his divine vindication.

60 L. Morris, *Luke: An Introduction and Commentary* (Leicester: IVP, 1988²), 339. Other commentators tend to deny that there is any explicit substitutionary reference here.

61 However, the authenticity of Luke 22:19b–20 continues to be debated. For a recent negative verdict see S. McKnight, *Jesus and His Death: Historiography, the Historical Jesus, and Atonement Theory* (Waco: Baylor University Press, 2005), 260 n. 4. Nor should we forget Acts 20:28 where the blood of Christ plays a decisive role in the creation of the new people of God.

62 The death is specifically the death of the Son, Rom 5:10; (8:32); Gal 2:20; implied in Phil 2:6–8; 1 John 1:7; 4:10; John 3:16; 8:35; Heb 6:6. So is the resurrection, 1 Thess 1:10.

63 The hymns of Isaac Watts and Charles Wesley emphasise that it is Jesus Christ as Son of God, himself God, who hangs on the cross and dies.

64 No special priesthood of some believers (ordained ministers) is needed.

The Holy Spirit and Mission

Robert Duncan Culver

This paper proposes that the "mandate for mission," understood as sending out missionaries, is not Matthew 28:19–20 but the events of Pentecost and subsequent developments in the first church at Jerusalem, and the logic of Paul's argument in Romans 10; that a *"greater* commission" is present in Matthew 28:18,20—that of disciples making disciples by taking the gospel along and witnessing by life and word wherever we go. Further, just as the Spirit empowers the mission, so He creates response in the hearers of the message.

Important Contributions of Harry R. Boer and Robert E. Speer

These views found great support in the 1961 book by Henry R. Boer, *Pentecost and Mission* (Grand Rapids: Eerdmans), as shall appear.

Robert E. Speer saw this long ago. I cite this great advocate of mission to the world to help win the sympathetic ear, if not full agreement, for what shall follow. In 1902 he wrote:

> Men who assent to the missionary enterprise on the strength of the last command of Christ alone, or primarily, will give it little support and their interest in it will soon become as formal as the ground on which it rests. The spirit of Christianity is higher than legalism, and it is of the spirit of legalism to press injunctions of courses of action where the underlying principles of action are unseen or unfelt. The men who have done the work of God in the world are men in whom the Spirit of God was at work, and who would have done God's work even in the absence of expressed legislation as to the nature of the work God wanted done (*Missionary Principles and Practice* [New York: Revell, 1902], 9–10).

In an address to the Canadian National Missionary Congress at Toronto, Speer observed, "The last command of Christ, which we call the Great Commission, is not the foundation of the missionary obligation. If those words had never been uttered by our Lord, the missionary obligation of the church would have been in no wise affected thereby" (cited by *Daily Bread*, May 1993).

But Speer's view has either been rejected or forgotten. Most missionary promotion among our churches and students seems to rest on what is taken to be a command of Jesus, especially as reported in Matthew 28:19–20 and Mark 16:15.

Boer's work cited above argues convincingly that there is no trace in the New Testament of a "command" of Jesus in His last meetings with the disciples as authority or motive for mission in the whole New Testament. My reading had convinced me that the same is true of the most active centuries of Christian missionary expansion—the first three centuries. Nor is there any trace of the so-called "Marching Orders of the Church" in the literature and records of medieval or Reformation Christianity and onward until William Carey brought it forward 200 years ago.

The Great Commission's "meaning for and place in the missionary community must," concludes Boer at the end of his chapter on this subject, "be differently construed than is customarily done." How so? According to Boer, it "derives its meaning and power wholly and exclusively from the Pentecost event" (*Pentecost and Mission*, 47).

It is undoubtedly true that in every period of spontaneous expansion the provisions of Matthew's form of the final words of Jesus are being carried out. That is, Christians already in the world are zealously making disciples, baptizing them, and as they do so teaching the new disciples. In the N.T. a disciple is a confessed and baptized believer not the product of a process of postbaptismal "discipling." Discipling as a term for nurture of new believers is of recent coinage. It apparently began in the lectures of a seminary professor at Dallas Seminary.

Problems for the Popular View

If the basis of a mission of "sending" out evangelists with home support is in Matthew 28:19–20, several serious questions arise.

1. Why is there no trace of this in any stage of the first 16 centuries of church history?

2. Why does not the word *send* appear in the commission *somewhere*? The word *go* is there but gets somehow transformed to send in mission promotion.
3. The apostles all heard Jesus speak these words. If it was a command to go or send, why did most of them then stay in Jerusalem for decades until driven out by threat of the Roman siege?
4. Why did Peter fear either to eat nonkosher food or to company with Gentiles if Jesus had commanded the disciples to go to Gentiles to preach?
5. Why did God have to stand Peter on his head, so to speak, to get him to go to the house of Cornelius, a Gentile, at Caesarea?
6. Why was Peter so cautious he took six trusted men along as witnesses?
7. Why were the leaders of the Jerusalem church initially displeased at what Peter did at Caesarea?
8. Why initially did the preachers of the early chapters of Acts address their message to "the people" of Israel, not to the Gentiles, if the now current popular understanding of Matthew 28:19–20 is the same as theirs?
9. And finally, when Paul turned to evangelize Gentiles, why did he always find authority not in dominical command but in Old Testament prophecy—especially in his appeal for help in a ministry to Gentiles in Spain (Rom 15:8–12) or to the simple logic of Romans 10:14–17?

Mission Mandate in Promised and Fulfilled Event

The motive and authority for a going and sending mission is none other than the Holy Spirit Himself. The key to missionary expansion is Pentecost, not the "Great Commission" at a mountain in Galilee. The missionary mandate came in the form of an effusion not a command, as an event not a program. It came as fulfillment of a prediction of what was *going* to happen not of what *ought* to happen. We turn to examination of the critical passage, Acts 1:8.

"But you shall receive power when the Holy Spirit has come upon you; and you shall be My witnesses both in Jerusalem, and in all Judea and Samaria, and even to the remotest part of the earth" (NASB).

Strictly speaking, this sentence is a statement of fact, not a command or commission at all. Perhaps if the word is used loosely, it might be called a "mandate." It is a statement of future fact. Call it either promise or prediction.

In His very last moments with the eleven (see vv. 2,4, and 6), the main interest of the Lord was understandably in the inauguration of the new age of witness. This inauguration was to be accomplished by the special descent of the Holy Spirit "not many days from now" (v. 5). This study will not pause to interpret the phenomena of Pentecost (Ac 2:1–12) or dwell at length on that event, but that is not to suggest it is unimportant. The focus will be on information about the mission itself, yet all must acknowledge the mission would have been powerless without fulfillment of the promise of Pentecost.

At the moment of parting tenderness, Jesus did not command the apostles what they *must* do, or even *should* do. He simply stated what they were *going* to do—be "My witnesses." Granted, there is a certain aura of the imperative about such statements by persons of great authority. However, there is nothing resembling the atmosphere of Sinai in this or any other passage in the New Testament relating to the mission of world evangelism.

"And you shall be My witnesses," or "witnesses unto me" (KJV). Precisely how the genitive "My" is to be taken—whether Christ was what their witness was about or the master of the witnesses—is unimportant. Christ was Lord of those men, and they were to witness about Him. The primitive preachment (the *kerygma*) was about Him. The book of Acts uniformly demonstrates that the content of the witness was to be "of my teaching, actions and life, what ye all have yourselves heard and seen." The most succinct summary is Peter's witness to Cornelius (Acts 10:34–43). Peter did not emphasize teachings. He reported nothing of Jesus' teaching and certainly said nothing at all of "what Jesus did for me," nowadays often considered pure Christian witness. Peter spoke to Cornelius only of *who Jesus was* and *what Jesus did*, that is, the story of redemption. Paul's sermon at Antioch of Pisidia is much the same (Acts 13). C. H. Dodd's summary of the Kerygma delivered by Peter to the Gentiles assembled at Caesarea in Cornelius's house is essentially correct:

> God brought Israel out of Egypt, and gave them David for their king. Of the seed of David Jesus has come as Saviour. He was heralded by John the Baptist. His disciples followed Him from Galilee to Jerusalem. There He was brought to trial by the rulers of the Jews before Pilate, who reluctantly condemned Him. He died according to the Scriptures, and was buried. God raised Him from the dead, according to the Scriptures, and He was seen by witnesses. Through Him forgiveness and justification are offered. Therefore take heed (*The Apostolic Preaching and Its Developments* [New York: Harper, 1936], 29).

The book of Acts shows that "you shall be" means not what the Apostles might occasionally have done or ought to do but what they uninterruptedly were to become: "My witnesses."

When, Where, and How Long

When and where they were to be Christ's witnesses is specified more exactly than at first meets the eye. There is something in Acts 1:8 nearly impossible for any smooth translation to convey: "Both in Jerusalem, and in all Judea and Samaria, and even to the remotest part [literally, end] of the earth" (NASB). RSV omits "both" as does NEB and NIV. "Both" is there in KJV, NASB and ASV. And thereby hangs a tale and the most overlooked point of the passage. In the English language *both* is an adjective and noun designating something common to two items (a pair, as for example, "both men and women," or "both summer and winter"). English has no such word to designate something common to a series of three or more items. The KJV, ASV, and NASB editors chose slightly to misuse "both" to join "Jerusalem, Judea and Samaria, and the remotest parts." RSV, NRSV, and NEB "solved" the problem by simply skipping an important small Greek word altogether, since there is no equivalent in English and something like "not only in Jerusalem but also in all Judea and Samaria and in the remotest parts" is complicated.

The tiny Greek word is *te*. It unites as many items in a series as are there, usually joined by "and" (*kai*). So something true of Jerusalem is true also of Judea and Samaria and the remotest parts. Jesus is not specifically prophesying stages in the spread of Christianity, but an age-long process of witnessing wherever Christians are, however they happened to be there—for employment or business or pleasure or sent by the organized effort of a local congregation or alliance of congregations. It should be simultaneous witnessing, to be addressed shortly.

While not peculiar to Acts, *te* is used there 150 times, more than in all the rest of the New Testament. A clear case of *te* to introduce a series occurs only five verses later (Acts 1:13, KJV). Again, for want of an equivalent term, in most versions translated "both," it introduces the names of the 11 apostles "staying" in an "upper room, where abode both (*te*) Peter, James and John," etc. until all 11 are named. To stay close to the original structure as possible I usually translate, "not only #1 but also #2 and #3," etc.

NIV characteristically loses the simultaneous connection by wiping *te* right out of the text both in 1:8 and 1:13. The very smoothness of the NIV is its defect. The KJV by straining the use of "both" in both verses at least hints at the very great importance of this very small Greek particle *te*. Thus in Acts 1:8 the force of the *te . . . kai . . . kai* construction is that disciples were simultaneously and in some equivalent manner to be Christ's witnesses in Jerusalem, Judea and Samaria, and to the remotest parts. As *disciples*, they do not cease to be *witnesses* in one place when some of them happen to move on to another place. Progress from the center outward took place all right, and the places named anticipate that, but that is not the point of Jesus' declaration. There is to be a *continuing witness wherever* Christians go and are allowed to stay, and as long as they stay. This is what the passage means. A generation later, the epilogue to Mark's Gospel, reflecting on what the first disciples did, says: "And they went out and preached everywhere" (Mark 16:20; cf. Acts 11:19–22). Against official restraint Peter asserted, "We cannot but speak the things which we have seen and heard" (Acts 4:20).

Just as Jesus said it would be, several generations later, when the salt had lost its savor, it was soon fit only to be cast out and trodden under foot. Medieval Islam, for example, did not usually declare Christianity unlawful in the lands it conquered. It only became difficult, especially economically, to remain witnessing Christians. As a result Christendom simply died in most Muslim lands. There are scarcely any Christians today in the Islamic lands of North Africa where in the second to sixth centuries there was a strong Christian population. Many famous ancient Christian saints, including Tertullian, Monica and Augustine were North Africans. Now no places on earth are more resistant to renewed evangelism than the Muslim states of North Africa.

Among the sayings of Jesus about the coming mission of world evangelism, Acts 1:8 is unique and special. He meant that the witness must continue without diminution or interruption in every place Christianity becomes established. The salt must never lose its savor. The light must never be hid under a bushel. Wolves in sheep's clothing must be exposed. Discipline must be exercised in order that the table of the Lord never become extinct or the table of devils!

Matthew's Report from a Mountain in Galilee and Luke's from the Mount of Olives Belong Together

Matthew 28:19–20 and Acts 1:8 belong together. In this way we know how and why the church was to expand throughout the world spontaneously as Christians with Holy Ghost zeal and power preached the Word. The apostles had just asked (Acts 1:6) about restoration of "the kingdom" to Israel. They still had no vision of the mission of evangelism even though Jesus had hinted at it many times and had spoken at length of it on two occasions (Matt 10,13). Acts 1:8 was His answer to the question of the immediate future. Apparently they still thought of the witness as only to Jews scattered throughout the world, as many writers have noted. Their continued lack of understanding revealed how necessary Pentecost really was and the importance of the later revelations to Peter and Paul reported in Acts 9–11 and several of Paul's Epistles.

The last words of Jesus in Matthew, the parting promise of verse 20, are not only a fitting climax but also an unmistakable promise of the presence of Jesus Christ in the witnessing church through the

Holy Spirit. "Lo, I am with you always, even to the end of the age" (NASB). That promise of the continuing presence of the Savior is of a piece with Luke 24:49: "Stay in the city until you are clothed with power from on high," and Acts 1:8: "You shall receive power when the Holy Spirit has come upon you; and you shall be My witnesses." Those promises refer to a truth laid out plainly in the New Testament: the church was constituted a witnessing body by the effusion of the Spirit and "began to speak" (Acts 2:4). Paul said they (and all believers) were "all baptized into one body" (1 Cor 12:13). They have all, so to speak, been speaking in Christian witness ever since. "The Spirit himself testifies with our spirit we are God's children" (Rom 8:16) for our assurance of salvation. "And it is the Spirit who testifies" (1 John 5:7 NIV) to and through us to all who hear the ones who go either spontaneously (as *suggested* by Jesus, Matthew 28:19, and *predicted* by Him, Acts 1:8) or because they are sent (as *argued* by Paul, Rom 10:12–15). The witnessing Spirit caused witnessing to Christ's finished work of redemption to be a law of the very nature of the newly constituted assembly. Herein lies the true foundation of energy for going and sending in the Christian mission. It is part of the essence and being of the church.

Two Constitutional Mandates for Fruitful Multiplication

A teaching found often in recent writings on the theology of mission asserts there are two divine mandates for mankind. The first is for the entire race, announced at the creation of man and reaffirmed after the flood: "Be fruitful and multiply, and fill the earth, and subdue it; and rule over the fish of the sea and over the birds of the sky, and over every living thing that moves on the earth" (Gen 1:28 NASB; cf. 9:1–2). According to Dr. George W. Peters, this "first mandate" was to populate the earth and subdue it. It "was spoken to Adam as representative of the race" (*A Biblical Theology of Missions* [Chicago: Moody, 1972], 166). "The second mandate [the mission of world evangelism] was spoken to the Apostles as representative of the church of Jesus Christ, involving the whole realm of the gospel" carried forward by preaching and the related things that missionaries do.

Boer comments on this teaching in a helpful way as follows:

> Although we have before us here a command [i.e., in Gen
> 1:29], it is no less plain that we are dealing with more than
> *simply* a command. It would be better to say that the com-
> mand we find in Genesis 1 and 9 is a divine and therefore
> *organic law* which enters into the very fiber of man's being,
> which penetrates and permeates his entire constitution. It is
> of the *nature* of man to be reproductive, to subdue the earth,
> and to rule over the animals that inhabit it. This command
> is obeyed, the law is observed, by all men everywhere and
> at all times. Awareness of it is not at all necessary in order
> to obey it. Men observe this law because their nature, their
> whole being, drives them to obey it. . . . It is only when men
> try to evade or escape the law of their natural being that
> this law becomes a command for them. Then they must be
> confronted with the command in order that via obedience
> to the objective imperative they may be brought again to a
> normal observance of the law of their life. The difference
> between command and law . . . is . . . that command has ob-
> jective but no subjective force, whereas law has both. . . . A
> divine law . . . although it has an external origin, carries
> within itself its own effectuation. . . . Understanding com-
> mand [as] a law in this sense, it may be said that God alone
> can make laws, and man can only give commands (Boer,
> *Penteost and Mission*, 121–22).

The men who carried the faith to places where Christ's name had not yet been pronounced in faith—Paul, Ulfilas, the Moravians, Brainerd, Carey, Judson, and all the rest—did not do so primarily because they felt guilty that they had not yet carried out some com- mandments. They had, to the contrary, drunk deeply of the living water and become aware of an inner compulsion to do all they could to be witnesses of Christ, listening first carefully to *all* the instruc- tions, inferences, and arguments of Scripture. They began in the Spirit and certainly did not finish in the flesh.

The analogy between the impulse to multiply the race by procre- ation and the impulse to win men to Christ by evangelism has some limits. The church has not found it in herself to be nearly as vigorous in evangelism as the human race has been in propagating itself. Procreation goes on and hardly even pauses, while evangelism, beyond the realm of professing believers and their families, seems almost to die out for long periods.

For happy results even the procreative impulse needs moral and rational direction and all the practical assistance society can give it. Genesis is very plain about this matter. "Be fruitful and multiply" is severely limited by "leave thy father and mother . . . be joined to his wife . . . and they two [not three or more] shall be one flesh." Society is right now paying the fearful penalties that have come from turning over the relationship of the sexes to natural impulses. The dynamic of propagation is only *furnished* by the inner nature of mankind; it is not properly *directed* by our instinctive impulses.

Similarly, the presence of the Pentecostal effusion of the Spirit of God, perpetual throughout the present age, effectual in every true believer, must be trusted to furnish the motive power of missionary evangelism. Yet the fires of evangelism dampen quickly without careful tending. Energetic promotion of the mission by everyone who finds it even slightly in his heart and mouth to confess Christ where He has not yet been named must be tenderly nourished and systematically promoted.

Wasted Seed?

An aspect of the parable of the four soils and the seed may help to enforce one further, final thought about witnessing: A frightful waste of good seed appears to be a necessary part of the missionary effort. Gospel seed falls in large amounts on waysides where it never germinates. A show of response quickly dies in shallow rocky soil. Even in good earth no fruit is brought forth if the soil is already loaded with seeds of weeds. No permanent fruit comes of it. Yet the sower has faithfully done his best and will not lose his reward. The abundant crop of grain produced in the field of good soils justifies energetic, lavish scattering of seed. Even a cup of cold water given in Jesus' name has some effect for advancement of the kingdom of God and will not fail to be rewarded. The Savior has given His word.

The Witnessing Spirit at Work

I wish now to turn these remarks sharply away from Jesus' seminal promises and predictions in the Gospels and Acts toward framing an abbreviated sketch of the way the witnessing Spirit actually does His work in the mission of evangelism. Herbert Kane makes two points well: "The Resurrection story was so incredible that no man in his right mind would readily believe it. Only as the Spirit of power filled the messengers would they be able to witness effectively (Acts 1:8). *Only as the Spirit of truth illuminated the minds of the hearers would they be able to confess Jesus Christ as Lord* (1 Cor 12:3)" (I have lost the correct documentation of this quote from Dr. Kane and cannot with present resources locate it. I remain quite certain I have correctly represented Kane's thought. See a similar statement under the rubric "God's Dealings with the Sinner" *Christian Missions in Biblical Perspective*, page 103.).

1. We have no less help from the Holy Spirit than Jesus did. Isaiah specifically predicted it would be so (Isa 11:1–3). There is deep mystery about this, but Jesus did not embark upon His career of Messiah's mission—including passion and death—without special enduement of the Holy Spirit, which took place at His baptism (John 1:29–34; Matt 3:16–17). After that "Jesus was led up by the Spirit" through His temptations (Matt 4:1) and everything else He did or endured. There is no record that Jesus performed any miracles until after His special enduement by the Spirit. The best explanation is that the human nature of the Christ was only then enabled to be vehicle of the divine in His redemptive career, especially the passion and death.

Similarly Jesus *gave* the Twelve (minus Judas) a special pre-Pentecostal conferral of the Spirit to support them through six more weeks of patient waiting (John 20:21–23).

On His last night with those "who have been with me from the beginning," i.e., the apostles, He promised the Spirit would bring to remembrance all He had previously said to them. The same Spirit would guide them (the same Twelve) into "the truth"—a truth historical, predictive, doctrinal, complete and final (John 15:26–27; 14:25–26; 16:12–13). This truth was given permanent, unchangeable forms in the New Testament Scriptures (2 Pet 3:15–16).

The written New Testament in a language disciples can read has always been necessary to church planting as acknowledged from Ulfilas to Cameron Townsend. The Holy Spirit not only inspired it but also certified by apostolic miracles, signs and wonders, and "gifts of the Spirit" (Heb 2:2–4) that what those of the first generation who "heard Him" said and wrote was true.

Much has been said about how the Holy Spirit supervised the first known official missionary party from the first known largely Gentile church at Antioch (Acts 13:2ff.). What is not so well canvassed is the fact that the Holy Spirit was the prime motive power in the dispersion of Christians—not by a local church's commission, but by Herod's persecution and by the ordinary course of where Christians went in pursuit of business and pleasure, recreation, and inclination. It is quite specific and extraordinary in the case of Philip the deacon as reported in Acts 8. We do not know how the Spirit spoke to him, but he personally exemplified the witnessing impulse to evangelize "all Judea" in taking the road to Gaza where he joined hard by a prepared heart (Acts 8:26,29) after having already preached in Samaria. He thus in a sense even took the witness to an "uttermost part" indirectly through the Ethiopian eunuch converted on the road to Gaza. This officer of the queen of Ethiopia may indeed be the founder of Christianity in Ethiopia as Eusebius (*History of the Church* II.1) says. Philip is only a sample case of multitudes of similar witnesses. The presence of a church in Rome before being visited by an apostle, the fragmentary report in Acts of the witness of the peripatetic Pricilla and Aquila and innumerable necessary inferences from fragments of written history which come from that epoch are proof of just how intense was the Spirit-driven private, voluntary, missionary activity of the first Christians. There are passages even in the New Testament that hint that already these Holy Spirit-inspired, spontaneous witnesses took the gospel to the limits of the Roman world and beyond (Mark 16:20; Col 1:6). This did not happen simply out of respect for a command to send or to go, but out of conscience to take the gospel with them wherever Providence took them.

2. The success of these common folk as messengers of the kingdom "in all the nations for a witness" came not from extraordinary powers of persuasion. The human hearts that heard their message, then as

now, were "dead in trespasses and sins." Their minds were the natural mind that does not receive the things of the Spirit of God. Such realities were as much foolishness to them as to the evening television news broadcasters today. Edward Gibbon (1737–1794) famously proposed five causes of their success: (1) the zeal of the early Christians, (2) their doctrine of future punishments and rewards, (3) their belief in miracles, (4) their morals, and (5) their organization. To comment on only one—their miracles (which Gibbon didn't really accept): miracles favorably affected only those drawn to Christ by the Spirit of God. The crowd who saw Jesus' miracles crucified Him. They rejected the message of the miracle because they did not believe it; they did not believe because they could not. They could not believe until the Spirit gave the gift of faith. That gift could not become widely distributed until the day of Pentecost had "fully come." This is how I understand the connection between John 7:37–39; 12:37–41; 16:7–11; and 1 Corinthians 12:3 which says, "No man can say that Jesus is the Lord but by the Holy Spirit."

Nothing can crack the crust of unbelief but the Word, accompanied by the invisible, invincible Spirit of God. Abraham Kuyper in his great Christian classic, *The Work of the Holy Spirit* (Grand Rapids: Eerdmans, 1946), after quoting "Whom He did predestinate, them He also called" (Rom 8:30), writes: "In order to hear, the sinner, deaf by nature, must receive hearing ears. 'He that hath ears let him hear what the Spirit saith. . . .' But by nature the sinner has no hearing ear. . . . Hence God's quickening act precedes the sinner's hearing, and thus he becomes able to hear the Word" (p. 338). This was Luther's burden in *The Bondage of the Will* in his rebuttal of Erasmus's moralistic interpretation of the Christian religion.

Not all will agree with these Augustinian and infralapsarian views but all should agree to be taught by Jesus. Let us hear Jesus' own theology of missionary evangelism in the sixth chapter of John. After manifest rejection by the interested but still stiff-necked crowd near the scene of the feeding of 5,000, He declared that the "work of God" is to "believe on him whom [God] hath sent" (v. 29 KJV). Then that crowd who had witnessed the miracle of the bread and fishes, in outrageous, stubborn disbelief, asked for a sign "that we may see, and believe" (v. 30). Then follow, "all that the Father giveth me shall come to me" (v. 37). "No man can come to me, except the Father ... draw him" (v. 44). After that He asserted those who have "heard" and "learned of the Father" do come. And finally, "no man can come unto me, except it were given to him of my Father" (v. 65).

This work, by whatever name—whether awakening grace, calling, prevenient grace, first stage of regeneration, or enlightenment—is something that only the witnessing Spirit can do. As preachers of the Word of the Gospel, we are utterly dependent on Him.

Sovereign Quickening Work of the Witnessing Spirit in Missionary Prayer Letters and the Hymnal

The missionary prayer letters to supporters all seem to imply utter dependence on the work of the Spirit to sustain the missionary in the face of stubborn rejection and to enlighten the darkened consciences of sinful men.

The hymns of all parties to the theological debate imply it. There is remarkable agreement. (I regret more than I can say that most students in my classes under 30 years of age seem to know little and care less about these hymns.)

From the *Methodist Hymnal* (New York: Easton and Mains, 1905) by Charles Wesley:

> 1. Thou Son of God, whose flaming eyes / Our inmost thoughts perceive, / Accept the grateful sacrifice which now to thee we give / ... 3. Is there a soul that knows thee not, / Nor feels his need of thee; / A stranger to the blood which bought / His pardon on the tree? 4. Convince him now of unbelief, / His desperate state explain; / And fill his heart with sacred grief, / And penitential pain. 5. Speak with that voice that wakes the dead, / And bid the sleeper rise, / And bid his guilty conscience dread / The death that never dies (#245, p. 176).

Though Isaac Watts was a third or fourth generation Calvinist Independent minister, the following verses appear in the same Methodist hymnal and somehow seem at home there.

1. How sad our state by nature is! /Our sin, how deep it stains! /And Satan binds our captive souls /Fast in his slavish chains. 2. But there's a voice of sovereign grace / Sounds from the sacred Word: "Ho, ye despairing sinners come, /And trust a faithful Lord." 3. My soul obeys the gracious call, etc. (#268, p. 190).

In the *Lutheran Service Book and Hymnal* (Minneapolis: Concordia, 1958) is a section on "Propagation of the Gospel." The number of verses calling on God to send His Spirit in "awakening grace" is impressive. The first one (#306 of the hymnal) has this line, "Soul without strength inspire with might; Bid mercy triumph over wrath." And this prayer addressed to the third member of the Trinity: "O Spirit of the Lord, prepare /All the round earth her God to meet; / Breathe thou abroad like morning air, /Till hearts of stone begin to beat."

One from the *Psalter-Hymnal* of the Christian Reformed Church (#305, p. 449): "Twas sovereign mercy called me /And taught my opening mind; /The world had else enthralled me, /To heavenly glories blind. /My heart owns none before Thee, /For thy rich grace I thirst; /This knowing, if I love Thee, /Thou has loved me first."

And finally "Amazing Grace," the first, and best-known stanza of which is about as clear a personal acknowledgement of the work of the Holy Spirit in initial awakening grace (special calling, first regeneration, prevenient grace, or by whatever name) as exists. No wonder the spiritually blind journalists of a few years ago were puzzled at its popularity. One of them I read dubbed John Newton a neurotic Anglican cleric. "Amazing grace how sweet the sound, /That saved a wretch like me! /I once was lost, but now am found, /was blind but now I see." Not so amazingly, "Amazing Grace" will be found in almost every collection of hymns.

Trinity and Work

A Critique of the View of Daily Work in Other Religions and in Marxism

Thomas Schirrmacher

This essay outlines a biblical theology of work that shows the importance of the doctrine of the triune God for ethics and for the reconstruction of society.

All employee morals, every work ethic, is an echo of the god of a society and its workers. I want to give some examples of how the nature of the triune God of the Old and New Testament is reflected in the biblical Laws concerning the work of man. Each time we will also ask what we lose if another god or another religion or worldview takes the place of the Creator revealed in the Bible.

Most times I will use the word *triune* instead of *Trinity*. The German word *Dreieinigkeit* (three-oneness, triunity) shows very well that Trinity has two enemies: the *one* stands against polytheism, the *three* against monistic monotheism. Polytheism will vitiate biblical faith as much as nontrinitarian monotheism. The English term *Trinity* does not emphasize this, while "triune" does. *Triunity* would be a good alternative for Trinity.

The Significance of Work Ethics[1]

Wealth cannot be defined merely as a matter of possession in terms of money or other material values. In that sense of the word, Saudi Arabia is immensely wealthy. In terms of the individual's capacity for work, productivity, innovation, or prospects for the future once the oil wells have failed, Saudi Arabia is still extremely poor.[2] George Gilder points to a similar example in European history: seventeenth-century Spain was as wealthy as modern Saudi Arabia. Silver from the Bolivian Potosi mines provided immense riches, but, unable to transform its resources into true wealth, the country soon reverted to its former state of poverty, while seemingly poorer European countries blossomed with industry.[3]

No, wealth is closely related to work and with its profits. For this reason, the morals of labour are an essential element of any economic ethical system or of any economic condition. *Behind all labour is an ethical system, and labour is always the outcome of an ethical conviction.*

The significance of ethics in labour morality can be seen in a few principles of biblical work ethics, which we will investigate more closely later. In the Bible, labour possesses a dignity founded in the fact that man was created in the image of God. Increased responsibility results in increased work. At the same time work is always shared according to the talents involved, for we work for one another. Work is also diverse, for each person has multiple talents.

The proposition of this article can be summarised in the words written by Karl Bernhard Hundeshagen in 1853: "The immeasurable cultural significance of the Christian dogma of the Divine Trinity lies in the fact that this idea provides the prerequisites for the consummation of the idea of humanity."[4]

God Is a God Who Works

1. The triune God is a God who works. In the Bible man's work has a high value because it reflects a God who is working Himself. The triune God had been working prior to men's existence in creation. Because He is triune, He even worked in eternity before creation came into existence. The Persons of the Trinity worked with and for one another.

In the Bible everything good comes from the Trinity. Because the members of the Trinity speak to one another and Jesus is the Word, we can talk to one another. Because the Persons of the Trinity do not live for themselves but live for one another, men can be told to do the same. Because the Persons of the Trinity discuss with one another, not to decide things totally alone is a biblical principle. In the Trinity obedience exists without anybody being forced to do something: love and Law are identical. Communication, love, honouring one another and working to a goal outside of ourselves come from the Trinity. But the Trinity existed before the world was created. So loving, talking, helping, listening, and obedience exist eternally. God does not need men in order to exist or to be good.

For many other adherents of monotheistic religions like the Muslims or those Jews who do not accept that the Trinity is rooted in the Old Testament (I am talking about Jewish theology, not about a biblical view of the Jewish people), this is different. Of course God existed before the world was created. But he can only love creation. There was nobody to love before he created someone. Both religions can only speak about how God deals with creation. Christians have the revelation about how God deals with Himself because He is triune.

Man's work has a *dignity* in the truest sense of the word. In the Ten Commandments work is commanded by God for the following reason: "*You shall labour six days and do all your work, but the seventh day is a Sabbath to the* LORD *your God. . . . For in six days the* LORD *made the heaven and the earth, the sea, and all that is in them, but He rested on the seventh day*" (*Exod 20,9–11*). In fact the Creation Account states that God "*rested from all His work*" (or "*from all His labour*") (*Gen 2,2*) on the seventh day of Creation. The Bible often speaks about the work and labour of God. So David prays for "*the works of your hands*" (*Ps 138,8*), Solomon calls God a wise "*craftsman*" (*Prov 8,30*, similarly *Ps 104,24*) and the psalmist says: "*the one watching over Israel will neither slumber nor sleep*" (*Ps 121,4*).

Work and labour are a major part of the image of God. If man and woman were created in the image and likeness (*Gen 1:26*) of a working God, they must be working themselves.

If a god or the highest authority of a society's law does not work himself, there is no dignity of labour. Buddhism is the best example. The Buddhistic ethic of work is inspired by a god who is demonstrating by his very image as a fat, sitting idol, that the goal of everything is *not* to work but to "*slumber and sleep*," and nevertheless to be rich and well fed. Buddhism does not even have a word for "work," and work is no topic in Buddhist ethics.[5] Buddhism and socialism have a lot in common when it comes to work and economy, as several Buddhist authors have clearly stated.[6]

Two quotations from antiquity will show that the god of a society is the source of its evaluation of labour:

> In Greek society labour was viewed as an inescapable fate imposed by the gods. To be like the gods meant to live free

from labour. In the world of the ancient Orient, labour was viewed as a burden, as slave labor for the gods, who therefore were free from labour. The goal was to withdraw from this service, from this labour as far as possible. Labour was a burden without dignity.[7]

"Classical antiquity assigned the task of labour to the unfree, outlawed classes. It viewed the emancipation from the necessity to work for wages alone being worthy of a human. Thus it dishonoured labour connected with bodily strain."[8]

This view later heavily influenced Christian theology, as another quotation will show:

Thomas Aquinas held the view that only necessity forced people to work. It is no wonder that the Middle Ages saw the use of work in overcoming laziness, in taming the body and in earning one's living. Beside this there is a tendency to be seen to take over the Greek (mainly Aristotelian) view to emphasize contemplative life and to disregard an active life. Thus it was legitimate that the members of the classes of knights and priests were free from bodily labour.[9]

In spite of this heathen influence, we have to agree with Hermann Cremer who adds to his evaluation of the Greek and Roman view of work: "It was only Christendom respectively the religion of revelation, the world has to thank for another view of the nature and value of labour."[10]

Alan Richardson showed how the Reformation revived the biblical view of work:

The Reformers, Luther and Calvin, were the first to use the terms calling and vocation for the daily tasks and positions in life of men. It is important to note that they did this in protest against the use of language in the Middle Ages which was restricted to the call to a monastic life. They wanted to destroy the double standard of ethics and to show that God can be glorified in the world of workdays also.[11]

Christian missions exported this Protestant work ethos to all continents. Gustav Warneck, the German father of Protestant missiology, wrote, "Christian world missions showed, through word and example, that labour (which through slavery carried the stigma of infamy) was based on a commandment of God."[12]

God Is the Hardest Worker Because He Is the Highest Authority

2. The triune God works more than anybody else. Therefore, the more responsibility one carries the more work he has. The example of Buddhism or the Greek and Roman view made clear the goal of these societies to become like their gods, which is to become free of labour. If the one on the very top is not working at all, hard work will be found at the bottom only. The higher you rise, the more people will live by the work of others. Exploitation is unavoidable in such a society.

In the Bible it is just the other way round. We already saw that God *"neither slumbers nor sleeps"* (Ps 121:4). Because the triune God has done and does more than anybody else, He is the example that responsibility means work. Was it not Paul the apostle who wrote twice, *"I laboured more than all the others"* (1 Cor 15:10; 2 Cor 11:23)? This was no boasting, but the natural result of his high responsibility as an apostle. Being an apostle did not mean more leisure time, many servants or greater wealth, but more tears and labor and less sleep. This was the reason Martin Luther, in the beginning of the Reformation, when he still believed in the possibility of changing papalism, wrote a letter to the Pope rebuking him that he should work more toward the well-being of the Church than any monk or priest including Luther himself. He asked the Pope how he could sleep in peace in view of the responsibility of a worldwide church in turmoil. In spite of his responsibility, the Pope spent much time on pleasure and feasts.

If you lose the triune God, the Christian attitude that more responsibility brings more work will change into the humanistic and tyrannical attitude that people in low positions work for people in high positions so that they do not need to work themselves.[13]

Marxism blames society for the exploitation of the lower classes, so it seems to have a negative view of people in high positions who let others work but do not work themselves. But Marxism has no other definition of work. Work is always the exploited work of the lower class. As Marxism only has "matter" and "history" as its gods, there is no way to overcome exploitation. No wonder socialist governments and societies are the best examples for the humanistic principle that the higher you climb, the less hard work you have. No wonder Karl Marx and Friedrich Engels never were workers but lazy employers. Marx himself really earned money only once for a very short time as the owner of a Marxist newspaper. Later on he lived on the money of Engels who was rich because he inherited factories from his father. There is not the slightest hint that Marx or Engels ever had a guilty conscience using the money they had won from the hard work of workers or that Marx was sad about his life which was as unproductive as possible, if you do not take into account some thick books which never got ready in time. Konrad Löw states, "According to their own theory, Marx and Engels always lived by money they did not deserve."[14]

The fact that in communist states the production and the quality of the products continually decline over time is not only the result of statism and wrong state management. A major reason is the employee morals, as the ethic of work is an echo of the atheistic religion. If hard work is seen as exploitation, how will Marxism explain to workers that this is different if the employer is a Marxist state?

"Atheistic capitalism"—as I call a capitalism that denies God's laws and becomes a religion of mammon—soon reaches the same situation as Marxism, Buddhism, and other religions. Many people in Western society have the goal of being rich, in the sense of being free of work. If the results of this growing attitude cannot be seen at once, the reason is that the biblical Protestant ethic of work is still functioning in many areas, although the foundation of it has been lost. A president, chancellor, or prime minister is still expected to work harder than a normal citizen. He would not get many votes if he acted like the kings of absolutism and the enlightenment, who were most of the time engaged in feasting and pleasure (one French king only received diplomats while on the toilet!).

That more power leads to more labour is a unique Christian principle because every authority comes from God—who is the infallible example to everyone in authority—that authority means to work for the good of others. Parents have authority over their children. Does this save work? No, it causes them labour and costs them much sleep. Woe to parents who want authority without labour. Woe to anyone who wants the rights of authority but not its duties! God only delegates authority together with the duty to work!

This is also true of work in general. The duty of men to subdue the earth (*Gen 1:26–30*) was the command to work. The garden of Eden was no land of Cockaigne, no fool's paradise, as the paradise of Marxism or Islam is. In Islam man did not work in Paradise; his work did not come under a curse, and he will not be serving in heaven.[15] "*The* Lord *God took the man and put him in the Garden of Eden to work it and take care of it*" (*Gen 2:15*). (God here names the two sides of every work, which is change and continuity, shape and preserve; humanism always emphasizes one or the other, the Bible keeps them together.) Before the fall we see a variety of work Adam and Eve had to perform. They had to water and grow the plants (*Gen 2:5*), had to get gold and precious stones (*Gen 2:10–13*), had to provide their food (*Gen 2:9*) and had to give a name to every animal (*Gen 2:19–20*). Adam was the first scientific biologist. It is incredible that the creation account states that God gave Adam the right to name the animals and God was to use Adam's names: "*And whatever the man called each living creature, that was its name*" (*Gen 2:19*). Listen to a summary of the Old Testament and Jewish view of work.

> [Work] is not the result or the punishment of sin—according to the unanimous view of Jewish exegetes of Gen 3,17–19, it is only the hardness and the repeated failure which stand in opposition to the ease and freedom from care in Paradise. Bodily labour in general is not despised among the Jews as it was among the Greeks and Romans.[16]

Wilhelm Lütgert similarly writes: "Not work itself, but the disproportion of work and returns or result and pain and toil, which stand in no proportion to the output, are the results of sin."[17]

By the way, according to Isaiah, in the Millennium (see *Isa 65:17–25*) work and labour will no longer be in vain: "They will build houses and dwell in them; they will plant vineyards and eat their fruit. No longer will they build houses and others live in them, or plant and others eat. . . . my chosen ones will long enjoy the works of their hands. They will *not toil in vain*" (*Isa 65,21–23*).

Our heavenly, eternal fellowship with God will be spent in no idle land of Cockaigne but will be filled with praise and service for our Creator, unlike Islam's paradise, in which the believers lie in beds, eat and drink, attended by beautiful virgins. The Islamic paradise has no labouring Adam, no curse of work, and no service in heaven.[18]

God's Work Will Receive Its Wages

In the Bible work has dignity and worth as such whether it is paid or not. But the Law quoted frequently and often referred to, "*The worker deserves his wages*" (*1 Tim 5:18; Luke 10:7*), is the result of this. *Work is not worth something only if it is paid but work is paid because it is worth something.*

How seriously the Bible takes the commandment to pay any work is seen in Jer 22:13: "Woe to him who builds his palace by unrighteousness, his upper rooms by injustice, making his countrymen work for nothing, not paying them for their labour."

Therefore, all work is worth a reward, but this reward need not be money. Every person can decide which reward he wants or renounce earthly rewards. Take, for example, the praise of the good wife in Prov 31. Work payed for and work not payed for directly stand side by side. The work of this housewife is of full value.

God's command to work six days, as we find it in the Ten Commandments, is a general command for men and women. People should not sit around but work, except on Sunday. Work is not merely a natural law and a natural necessity, just because otherwise we would starve, but a created order. Therefore "one of the most severe charges of the prophets is against rich people (e. g. Amos 6,3–6)."[19] You may be rich, but you may not be lazy. It is the will of God, and He has given us creation for this purpose.

Ecclesiastes 5:9–19 contrasts love of money with joy in labour:

> He that loveth silver shall not be satisfied with silver; nor
> he that loveth abundance with increase: this is also vanity.
> When goods increase, they are increased that eat them:
> and what good is there to the owners thereof, saving the
> beholding of them with their eyes? The sleep of a labour-
> ing man is sweet, whether he eat little or much: but the
> abundance of the rich will not suffer him to sleep. There is
> a sore evil which I have seen under the sun, namely, riches
> kept for the owners thereof to their hurt. As he came forth
> of his mother's womb, naked shall he return to go as he
> came, and shall take nothing of his labour, which he may
> carry away in his hand. And this also is a sore evil, that in
> all points as he came, so shall he go: and what profit hath
> he that hath laboured for the wind? All his days also he ea-
> teth in darkness, and he hath much sorrow and wrath with
> his sickness. Behold that which I have seen: it is good and
> comely for one to eat and to drink, and to enjoy the good
> of all his labour that he taketh under the sun all the days of
> his life, which God giveth him: for it is his portion. Every
> man also to whom God hath given riches and wealth, and
> hath given him power to eat thereof, and to take his por-
> tion, and to rejoice in his labour; this is the gift of God. For
> he shall not much remember the days of his life; because
> God answereth him in the joy of his heart.

Wealth can indeed be a good thing to be enjoyed but not when it becomes the highest value of life or destroys the goodness of labour.

What can an unemployed worker do? Work, of course! Although we do not want to play down the problem of unemployment, the unemployed man can do many jobs without wage. He can help his family, the needy, or his church. Lethargy or blaming others is no solution to unemployment.

Excursus on Marxism

What has Marxism to say concerning just wages? Nothing! For Marx in capitalism all wages are unjust, but no one has the right to change this. The difference between a Christian social reformation and a Marxist revolution becomes especially clear in Marx's paper "Critique of the Declaration of Gotha" ("*Kritik des Gothaer Programms*") written when he was an old man and commenting on the party platform of the Social Democratic Party of Germany. The demand of this Socialist Party "that the whole product of work has to belong according to equal right to everybody according to his need while everybody has the duty to work"[20]—in itself full of contradictions—is totally denied by Marx because it is still based on some concept of law and justice. Marx writes: "It is the right of inequality concerning its content as all right is."[21] He goes on: "The equal right here is still, in principle, the bourgeois right."[22] This cannot be accepted because it still "silently accepts a difference of individual gifts and therefore of different efficiency of workers as natural privileges."[23]

Marx studied law at the University of Bonn, and so he knew what he was talking about. He did not want to change any legal positions but wait for his prophecies to become true. His prophecies conclude that the Communist society will not bring immediate results: "But these grievances are unavoidable in the first phase of the Communist society as it has come out of the capitalistic society after long labour pains."[24]

(In German, Marx is here speaking in prophetic perfect, as the prophets of the Old Testament often did!) Engels states it even more directly: "We give up any attempt to make clear to the stubborn jurist, that Marx never demanded the 'right to the full yield of work' and that he never articulates any legal demand of any kind in any of his theoretical writings."[25] He continues, "Marx realizes the historical unavoidability, which is the right of the ancient slave-master, the feudal lord of the Middle Ages etc., as a lever of human development for a certain historical period. He acknowledges the right of exploitation for some time."[26]

No one who thinks that Marx was fighting for the rights of the workers has read Marx or Engels. According to both the worker must submit to the historical necessity and wait until the war of the classes comes to its next stage. Justice cannot be sued for. Marxism blames Christianity for consoling people with a heavenly hope because he does not understand that this hope is the base for changes in this world and for any justice. But Marx himself consoles people with his prophetic vision. But Paradise will come only after the Marxists of today have died. No Marxist has ever gotten anything for his hope, either on earth or in heaven!

For example, Marx fought against the British and German laws against the slavelike work of children. He said laws like this were "reactionary,"[27] because they are incompatible with capitalism and large industries—he was proved wrong by history—and because it slowed down the development of the last phase of capitalism. Marx did not want to help the weak but to see his prophecies come true. Marx did not say any word about the exploited children themselves but saw only the problem that Marxists would lose a major force for revolution if children were to grow up under good conditions.[28]

The boundless disregard of the rights of workers and every act toward a just relationship between employers and employees can be proven by many quotations from Marx and Engels.[29] Marx wrote about the German Parliament: "Because you may use the parliament only as a means of agitation, you never may agitate in it for something reasonable or something being of direct interest for the workers."[30]

Marxism has the same problem as atheistic capitalism. Both call for just labour, but have no law governing this justice. While Marx does not accept any justice put into laws, his capitalistic friends try to put their views into laws. But the religion of Mammon can only realize justice in the form of money. Justice always means getting more money for working less. They forget that justice only can be justice if it regulates every area of life, not just money matters.

God's Work Is Work for God

If the triune God did not work for us, we could not work at all. Although man was created to work and not to be lazy, the command to work is only part of the command to serve God. In the Bible human work is always limited. In spite of its dignity, work is never the first task but always the second. Work is never an end in itself! It is a unique Christian view to combine the highest praise of work as nothing less than working in the image of God, with the limitation of work, so that man is never totally swallowed by work but keeps work under his and God's dominion. Only if you see both sides at the same time can you understand the effective results of a biblical work ethic.

This is the meaning of the Sabbath. The Sabbath reminds man that he can only work on *"the six workdays"* (*Ezek 46:1*) because his Creator works for him and has given him creation for his use. God also knows that to work day and night without exception is not good for man.

Although man was created to work,[31] **the biblical concept of labour always implies limited work.** The individual is not to overwork or to drown in his endeavors. We could also say, "The Bible does not preach work for its own sake. Labour is always secondary to God and to His righteousness" (*Matt 6:33*).

This is the reason for the day of rest. Man is to remember that he can only work for six days (*Ezek 46:1*), because the Creator made him and put the rest of creation at his disposal.

Helmut Thielicke notes that the biblical concept of work lies somewhere "between the ancient Grecian contempt of work, and its modern idealisation."[32] Work is to fill our lives but is not the highest or most decisive value.

We already discussed religions with a low view of hard work. But there are also religions with a high view of labour which miss the correction of work ethics by a whole day without labour. A Japanese lawyer's association states that in Japan 10,000 people die every year through overwork.[33] "Death through overwork" is accepted by the Japanese minister of labour as an official cause of death. There is a special word for death through overwork in the Japanese language, *karoshi.* Death through overwork is said to be the result of too much overtime work and missing recreation. Often "the home is becoming a mere sleeping-place."[34]

The seventh day without work reminds men that without God they could not work at all. *"Unless the LORD builds the house, its builders labour in vain. Unless the LORD watches over the city, the watchmen stand guard in vain. In vain you rise early and stay up late, toiling for food to eat, for He grants sleep to those He loves"* (*Ps 127:1–2*). Prov 10:22 says it even shorter: *"The blessing of the LORD brings wealth, and he adds no trouble to it"* (see also *Matt 6:24–34*). And Jesus tells His disciples: *"for without me you can do nothing"* (*John 15:5*).

Pietistic and liberal exegetes alike see verses like this as referring to religious duties, some spiritual blessing or some symbolical house. The pietist believes that he cannot evangelize without Jesus or cannot grow His Church without Jesus. Of course this is true, but the quoted texts concern *all* work, everything men do, and of course his daily job! According to Exodus 31:2–6 and 35:31 the artists could build the beautiful tabernacle because God had given them His Spirit with the gifts of their crafts.

Therefore, to be thankful is a necessary part of every work. "Isa 28,23–29 says that the outcome of the farmers ploughing, sowing, planting, reaping, threshing, mowing and baking bread go back to God's teaching"[35]: "*His God instructs him and teaches him the right way*" (Isa 28:26).[36]

There are several other instituted ways of expressing the truth that work is not everything and that man needs to thank God for the ability to work. The tithe comes exactly from what a man earns. The tithe is not just a portion of the income, but it is the *firstfruit* of our work to demonstrate that God and thanksgiving comes first before we use the results of our work. The same is true of the sacrifices. Gustav Friedrich Oehler has pointed out that all the plants and animals for sacrifice were "the ordinary food the people would win through their normal work."[37] This can be seen in the first recorded sacrifice in history by Abel and Cain who both offered the firstfruits of their profession. This again shows the close relationship between daily work, service, and thanksgiving to God.

No work is done for oneself or one's family or one's employer but in the last analysis for the supreme employer,[38] God Himself. Thus Paul says: "*And whatever you do whether in word or deed, do it all in the name of the Lord Jesus, giving thanks to God the Father through him*" (Col 3:17). Again this may not be narrowed down in a pietistic sense. This is proved by one of the following verses written to the slaves but valid for everybody: "*Whatever you do, work at it with all your heart, as working for the Lord, not for men, since you know that you will receive an inheritance from the Lord as a reward. It is the Lord Christ you are serving*" (Col 3:23–24). "The nobility of work no longer flows from what you do but from why you do it. Because of the commission to service by God and the service character of work to one's neighbour, the least technical work has the same value as 'intellectual' work."[39]

Many people blame the New Testament because it commands the slaves to be good workers (e. g. *Titus 2:9–11; Eph 6:5–9; Col 3:22–4,1; 1 Tim 6:1–2; 1 Pet 2:18–25; 1 Cor 7:21–24*). We already heard the reason for it. The slave works for God, not for his employer. This is real freedom! *"Slaves, obey your masters in all things not with eye-service or as menpleasers, but with a sincere heart and reverence for the Lord"* (*Col 3:22*). There is no dirty or bad work in the Bible, except those works and professions which are directly forbidden by God like prostitution. The human employer is not the real giver of wages, but the great employer of creation. *Only because God, the general Employer, gives a just wage must human employers do the same.*

The same Paul that tells the slaves to be good workers writes to them: *"Each one should remain in the calling wherein he was called. Were you called being a slave, do not let it trouble you.* **But if you can gain your freedom, do so.** *For he who was a slave when he was called by the Lord is the Lord's freedman; likewise he who was a free man when he was called is Christ's slave. You were bought at a price, do not become slaves of men"* (*1 Cor 7:20–23*). In the letter to Philemon, Paul works toward the release of a slave. Is this a contradiction? No, because Paul says: *"But if you can gain your freedom, do it."* But the slave does not need to wait a life long until he can live a fruitful life. He is called by God, called to His heavenly kingdom, but also called to His work. Not the slave's work for men makes his life worth living but his being called by his Creator and Redeemer.

The penetrating power of the Christian faith in history is based on this fact. The Christian can serve God as a slave without any change of the outward circumstances, and he can obtain freedom and work for release and change the circumstances. He has life in the fullest sense in every situation. Because he has everything already, he can change everything.

In Col 3:25–4:1 we find strict admonitions for the lords of the slaves. They are reminded of their lawful duties because God does not have regard for the person. The Christian slave does not however need to wait until his lord becomes righteous. He can live according to God's will here and now! He does not need to wait until the world has changed totally, as thought in Hinduism, Buddhism, Marxism, and other religions!

For the Marxist, man and work are actually identical. He cannot imagine work apart from man, as he denies a God who could be working also; and he cannot imagine man apart from work, which makes something like the Sabbath, recreation, or a Sunday service impossible. Friedrich Engels writes:

> Work is the source of all wealth, the political economists tell us. Yes, it is, besides nature which offers the material which work changes to wealth. But work is infinitely more than this. It is the first fundamental condition of human life and this in such a measure that we must say in a certain sense: work has created man himself.[40]

That work created men is only another way of saying that man created himself as the following quotation from Karl Marx proves: "Because for Socialist man the whole of so-called world history is nothing else than the begetting of men through human labour, this is the rising of nature through men, he has the vivid and irresistible evidence of his birth through himself, of his own process of origin."[41]

If man and work are identical and work is the highest value of society, this work will not be a positive value approved by all but a tyrannical value hated by all but a few. Because work is not under God's dominion and under the responsibility of man, it becomes a terrible tyranny. Marxism tries to fight without really offering any way to escape. If work and man are identical, how can man escape the tyranny of work without losing himself?

The Toil of Work

Work is always work for God. And one cannot talk about work without talking about God. That is the only reason the curse for the sin of man in the fall was a curse of man's work (*Gen 3:17–19;* *5:29*). Man thought he could have the authority of dominion and work without the One making both possible, namely God. Because of the curse, man is reminded day by day what it means to despise the creator. Whoever wants labour without problems denies the fall and denies that only God can be the source of work that leads to full results and to true rest. Without the sacrifice of the second person of the Trinity, there could be no hope that this situation would ever change. Meanwhile Christians take even the stress and toil of work out of the hand of God. *"What does the worker gain from his toil? I have seen the burden God has laid on to men"* (Eccl 3:9–10). The toil is given by God. Solomon does not come to the conclusion that it is better not to work at all but that we are happy about the results of our work as a gift from God: *"I know that there is nothing better for men than to be happy and do good while they live. That everyone may eat and drink, and find satisfaction in all his toil, this is a gift from God"* (Eccl 3:12–13).

The Bible commands us to take the toil upon ourselves and not to put the burden on others. A thief only puts the burden on others, as does the state, using taxes to redistribute wealth from one to the other. Paul's admonitions do not need long explanations: *"We urge you, brothers and sisters,*[42] *. . . make it your ambition to live quietly, and to do your own business, and to work with your own hands, as we commanded you, so that you walk honestly toward those who are outside and so that you will not be dependent on anybody"* (1 Thess 4:10–12). *"We hear that some among you walk disorderly, working not at all. They are busybodies. Such people we command and urge in the Lord Jesus Christ to work in quietness and to eat their own bread"* (2 Thess 3:11–12). What Paul taught others he and his coworkers did themselves: *"For you yourselves know how you ought to follow our example. We were not disorderly when we were with you, nor did we eat anyone's food without paying for it. On the contrary, we worked day and night, labouring and toiling so that we would not be a burden to any of you"* (2 Thess 3:7–9)

This does not mean, of course, that one may never assist an unemployed person. On the contrary, Paul commands a thief, who has been living at the cost of others, to help others: "Let him that stole steal no more: but rather let him labour, working with *his* hands the thing which is good, that he may have to give to him that needeth" (Eph 4:28). The fact that the former thief is to provide for himself is assumed, not even explicitly mentioned. The main thing is that he now also works for others' sakes.

Basilius the Great[43] (ca. AD 329–379) discusses Christian work ethics by referring to Second Thessalonians, and he emphasized that everyone should work, that work is intended to provide for the poor, and that it is only possible to work, when our final hope is not in work but in God, who makes labour possible.

Again God is the best example. He took the whole sorrow, toil, and pain of the work of redemption on Himself. God gave his only son to redeem us from the fall. He did not put His burden on us but carried our burden to the cross. If theology loses the triune God, it loses God, who carried the burdens of His chosen people. Neither Islam nor Marxism, neither Buddhism nor Statism have anything to offer instead.

Laziness and Industry in the Book of Proverbs

Prov 6:6–11: "Go to the ant, thou sluggard; consider her ways, and be wise: Which having no guide, overseer, or ruler, provideth her meat in the summer, *and* gathereth her food in the harvest. How long wilt thou sleep, O sluggard? when wilt thou arise out of thy sleep? *Yet* a little sleep, a little slumber, a little folding of the hands to sleep: So shall thy poverty come as one that travelleth, and thy want as an armed man."

Prov 10:4: "He becometh poor that dealeth *with* a slack hand: but the hand of the diligent maketh rich."

Prov 10:26: "As vinegar to the teeth, and as smoke to the eyes, so *is* the sluggard to them that send him."

Prov 11:16: "The slothful come to want: but the diligent support themselves with wealth."

Prov 12:24: "The hand of the diligent shall bear rule: but the slothful shall be under tribute."

Prov 12:27: "The slothful *man* roasteth not that which he took in hunting: but the substance of a diligent man *is* precious."

Prov 13:4: "The soul of the sluggard desireth, and *hath* nothing: but the soul of the diligent shall be made fat."

Prov 15:19: "The way of the slothful *man is* as an hedge of thorns: but the way of the righteous *is* made plain."

Prov 18:9: "He also that is slothful in his work is brother to him that is a great waster."

Prov 19:15: "Slothfulness casteth into a deep sleep; and an idle soul shall suffer hunger."

Prov 19:24: "A slothful *man* hideth his hand in *his* bosom, and will not so much as bring it to his mouth again."

Prov 20:4: "The sluggard will not plow by reason of the cold; *therefore* shall he beg in harvest, and *have* nothing."

Prov 20:13: "Love not sleep, lest thou come to poverty; open thine eyes, *and* thou shalt be satisfied with bread."

Prov 21:5: "The thoughts of the diligent *tend* only to plenteousness; but of every one *that is* hasty only to want."

Prov 21:25: "The desire of the slothful killeth him; for his hands refuse to labour."

Prov 22:13: "The slothful *man* saith, *There is* a lion without, I shall be slain in the streets." [He is not willing to take a risk and seeks for excuses to avoid work.]

Prov 26:13: "The slothful *man* saith, *There is* a lion in the way; a lion *is* in the streets."

Prov 24:27: "Prepare thy work without, and make it fit for thyself in the field; and afterwards build thine house."

Prov 24:30–34: "I went by the field of the slothful, and by the vineyard of the man void of understanding; And, lo, it was all grown over with thorns, *and* nettles had covered the face thereof, and the stone wall thereof was broken down. Then I saw, *and* considered *it* well: I looked upon *it, and* received instruction. *Yet* a little sleep, a little slumber, a little folding of the hands to sleep: So shall thy poverty come *as* one that travelleth; and thy want as an armed man."

Prov 24:14–16: "So *shall* the knowledge of wisdom *be* unto thy soul: when thou hast found *it,* then there shall be a reward, and thy expectation shall not be cut off. Lay not wait, O wicked *man,* against the dwelling of the righteous; spoil not his resting place: For a just *man* falleth seven times, and riseth up again: but the wicked shall fall into mischief."

Prov 31:13,18,27: (The virtuous woman) "She seeketh wool, and flax, and worketh willingly with her hands. She perceiveth that her merchandise *is* good: her candle goeth not out by night. She looketh well to the ways of her household, and eateth not the bread of idleness."

Further Texts About Work in Proverbs

Prov 12:11: "He that tilleth his land shall be satisfied with bread: but he that followeth vain *persons is* void of understanding."

Prov 12:14: "Man shall be satisfied with good by the fruit of *his* mouth: and the recompence of a man's hands shall be rendered unto him."

Prov 14:4: "Where no oxen *are*, the crib *is* clean: but much increase *is* by the strength of the ox."

Prov 14:23: "In all labour there is profit: but the talk of the lips *tendeth* only to penury."

Prov 16:26: "He that laboureth laboureth for himself; for his mouth craveth it of him."

Solomon's proverbs often consider the value of labour and the danger and degradation of laziness. "Accordingly, the essential characteristics of indolence are: weak, dishonest excuses (see 22:13), excessive sleep (6:9ff; 19:15; 24:33), laziness even at meals (19:24), overconfidence in one's own abilities. The tendency to surrender to momentary impulses leads to his fall (Prov 21:25)."[44]

God's Work Is Divided Labour

3. The work of the triune God is divided work. The Persons of the triune God divide their labour and do not all have the same task and job, as *1 Cor 12:4–6* clearly shows. Because their work is different yet directed to one goal, the Trinity demonstrates what true fellowship in love and help, word and discussion, plan and fulfillment, means, even prior to creation. This is the infallible *diversity in unity*. Only if you have diversity in unity and unity in diversity, only if you believe in the biblical *God of the uni-verse* (unity in diversity), work can be a way to serve each other. God wants men to serve one another, as the persons of the Trinity serve one another. We depend on one another because we have different callings, different abilities, different gifts, and different tasks. The emphasis on the gifts of the Spirit for the church proves this beyond doubt. God does not want everybody to do the same—except keeping His commands—but wants a diversity of tasks, deeds, and actions in the Church and elsewhere.

The family is an excellent example of the centrality of divided work in life. In the family people learn the difference of the genders, or they do not learn it at all. In the family people learn the different work of parents and children, of old and young people, or they do not learn it at all. In the family people learn how different people are under one common God, or they do not learn to accept that men are different. In the family people learn that life and work means to serve one another, or they never learn it.

It is interesting that Marx saw the division of labour as the fall of mankind, with the immediate result of marriage and private ownership. Man was created through his labour, but the alienation of man from work took place through the division of labour. Exploitation comes through divided work, through marriage, and through private ownership. (By the way, Marx talks about the introduction of divided labour, marriage, and private ownership as the "economic fall" using the German technical term [*Sündenfall*] for the fall of man recorded in Gen 3. He consciously put his "fall" in place of the biblical fall, which would be evidence enough that he founded a rival religion, not just an economic theory. It takes as much faith to believe in the biblical fall as it does to believe in the Marxist fall.)

Marx was right in seeing that there is no marriage and no private ownership without the division of labour. But because he calls sin what the Bible declares to be the good creation of God, he cannot offer any help to overcome exploitation. His only help is his prophecy that one day the division of labour will end. He wrote:

> In a higher phase of the Communist society, after the enslaving submission of individuals under the division of labour and with it the contrast between intellectual and bodily work have disappeared; after work is no longer a means to live but has become itself the first condition of life; after all springs of collective wealth flow fuller through the development of the individuals and his powers of productivity; only then can the narrow bourgeois horizon of justice be crossed and the society can write on its banner: Everyone according to his abilities, everyone according to his needs![45]

Marx never explained how this would be possible without the division of labour. He never answered the question whether the end of divided labour means that everybody has to do the same. He never answered how a society will function without divided labour. He just prophesied his unitarian hope because he hated the triune God, the source of all true diversity.

God's Work Is Service to One Another

Work is never only work for the benefit of the one working. It is always at the same time work for oneself and for others. It is the triune God who makes it possible that work for oneself and work for others do not stand in opposition to each other but always go hand in hand. As God's work toward His own glory is always at the same time work for another person of the Trinity and/or for His creation, so man's work is designed to help himself and to help others.

Work is service. Our languages have taken over this concept under Christian influence. We use the Latin word for servant, *minister*, to name the pastor as well as a politician in a high position. How can the worker in a position of authority get the honorary title *servant*? Because the highest authority, Jesus Christ Himself, is a servant. We talk about "civil service," about military service, about "length of service" and "years of service" instead of years of work.

Therefore the wages are never used for the worker only. "The New Testament does not underestimate the fact that work serves to provide one's own costs of living (Eph 4,28; 1 Thess 4:11; 2 Thess 3:8,12). But on the other side, the wages are not only intended for the one doing the work."[46]

A fixed part of the income, the tithe, belongs to God. The community and the state may lawfully take taxes (even though surely not as much as today). Whoever does not pay for the living of his family, including his parents, is worse than the heathen (*1 Tim 5:8; Mark 7:9–13*). There are other social duties.

The best example is Paul's admonition to former thieves: "*He who has been stealing must steal no longer, but must work, doing something useful with his own hands, that he may have something to share with those in need*" (*Eph 4:28*). Paul even does not mention that the former thief lives on his income, although this is implied. Paul only talks about the possibility to help others if you work.

Divine Providence determines whether man enjoys the fruit of his labour. Christians are grateful when they can use part of their products for their own enjoyment, for they know that "it is good and comely for one to eat and to drink, and to enjoy the good of all his labour that he taketh under the sun all the days of his life, which God giveth him: for it is his portion" (*Eccl 5:18*).

We must recognise two sides of the picture: On the one hand, we are to work in order to provide for ourselves. On the other, our labour is to serve others, either because our efforts are directly for their sakes (for example, the work of a bus driver) because the product serves some purpose (a baby buggy, for example), or because the labourer gives part of his wages to others (to support his family, for example). John Stott calls this "the biblical principle of reciprocity."[47] These two aspects cannot be played off against each other, as a secular scientist, who seems to have understood biblical principles better than some Christians, once wrote: "The belief that others' happiness contributes to one's own wellbeing does not appeal to the human heart. Yet, it is the Golden Rule of the Economy, the key to peace and wealth and the requisite for progress."[48]

Endnotes

1   See: Alfred de Quervain, *Ruhe und Arbeit, Lohn und Eigentum*, Ethik II vol. 3 (Zollikon, Switzerland: Evangelischer Verlag, 1956), 17–112, 149–65; Miroslav Volf, "Arbeit, Geist und Schöpfung," in Hermann Sautter, Miroslav Volf, eds., *Gerechtigkeit, Geist und Schöpfung: Die Oxford-Erklärung zur Frage von Glaube und Wirtschaft* (Wuppertal: Brockhaus, 1992), 32–60; and the excellent summary in Derek Prime, *Biblische Lebenshilfen im Grundriß* (Marburg: Verlag der Francke-Buchhandlung, 1990), 42–43. See also the somewhat critical but important studies in Walther Bienert, *Die Arbeit nach der Lehre der Bibel* (Stuttgart: Evangelisches Verlagswerk, 1954), 414–28 (with an extensive bibliography); Alan Richardson, *Die biblische Lehre von der Arbeit* (Frankfurt: Anker-Verlag, 1953); Udo Krolzik, *Umweltkrise: Folge des Christentums?* (Stuttgart: Kreuz Verlag, 1979), 61–70.
The study closest to my results is Doug Sherman and William Hendricks, *Your Work Matters to God* (Colorado Springs: NavPress, 1990); John Stott, *Christsein in den Brennpunkten unserer Zeit . . . 3 . . . im sozialen Bereich* (Marburg: Francke, 1988 [Engl. 1984]), 11–64; Michael A. Zigarelli, *Christianity 9 to 5: Living Your Faith at Work* (Kansas City: Beacon Hill Press, 1998);

"Arbeit," in *Lexikon der Bioethik*, 3 vols. (Gütersloh: Gütersloher Verlagshaus, 1998), 1:189–204; Walter Künneth, *Moderne Wirtschaft—Christliche Existenz* (München: Claudius, 1959), 6–8, Abschnitt "Arbeit als Stiftung Gottes."

2 See George Gilder, *Reichtum und Armut* (München: dtv, 1983), 64–65.

3 Ibid., p. 65.

4 Karl Bernhard Hundeshagen, *Ueber die Natur und geschichtliche Entwicklung der Humanitätsidee in ihrem Verhältnis zu Kirche und Staat* (Berlin: Verlag von Wiegen und Grieben, 1853), 29 (sic); vgl. die Würdigung des Zitats in Theodor Christlieb. "Carl Bernhard Hundeshagen: Eine Lebensskizze," Deutsche Blätter 1873: 673–700, here p. 698.

5 See Peter Gerlitz, "Buddhismus," 100–18 in Michael Klöcker and Udo Tworuschka (ed.), *Ethik der Religionen—Lehre und Leben*, Arbeit (Munich: Kösel, Göttingen: Vandenhoeck & Ruprecht, 1985), 2:101.

6 See ibid., 112–15.

7 Heiner Ruschhaupt, "Bauen und Bewahren," *Der Navigator* Nr. 13 (Mai/Juni 1987), 2–3.

8 Hermann Cremer, *Arbeit und Eigentum in christlicher Sicht* (Giessen: Brunnen Verlag, 1984), 8.

9 Friedrich Trzaskalik, "Katholizismus," 24–41 in Klöcker and Tworuschka, *Ethik der Religionen*, 2:33.

10 Cremer, *Arbeit und Eigentum*, 8.

11 Richardson, *Die biblische Lehre*, 27.

12 Gustav Warneck, *Die Stellung der evangelischen Mission zur Sklavenfrage* (Gütersloh: C. Bertelsmann, 1889), 67.

13 See the chapter on the ethics of work in my book *Marxismus—Opium für das Volk?* (Berneck: Schwengeler Verlag, 1990).

14 Quoted from Konrad Löw, *Marxismus Quellenlexikon* (Köln: Kölner Universitätsverlag, 1985), 321.

15 See Monika Tworuschka, "Islam," 64–84 in Klöcker and Tworuschka, *Ethik der Religionen*, 2:67, 69.

16 Johannes Wachten, "Judentum," 9–23, cited in ibid., 10.

17 Cremer, *Arbeit und Eigentum*, 9.

18 Cf. Tworuschka, "Islam," 64–84.

19 Richardson, *Die biblische Lehre*, 16.

20 Ursula Schulz (ed.), *Die deutsche Arbeiterbewegung 1848–1919 in Augenzeugenberichten* (Munich: dtv, 1981³), 200.

21 Karl Marx, Friedrich Engels, *Werke*, 42 vol. (Berlin: Dietz Verlag, 1956ff), 19:20.

22 Ibid.

23 Ibid., 19:21.

24 Ibid.

25 Ibid., 21:501.

26 Ibid.; see the whole page.

27 Ibid., 21:32. "Allgemeines Verbot der Kinderarbeit ist unverträglich mit der Existenz der großen Industrie und daher leerer frommer Wunsch. Durchführung desselben—wenn möglich—wäre reaktionär, da, bei strenger Regelung der Arbeitszeit nach den verschiedenen Altersstufen und sonstigen Vorsichtsmaßregeln zum Schutze der Kinder, frühzeitige Verbindung produktiver

Arbeit mit Unterricht eines der mächtigen Umwandlungsmittel der heutigen Gesellschaft ist."

28 We just want to show the position of Marx, not to discuss labour of children or the right of the state to regulate it.

29 Konrad Löw, *Marxismus Quellenlexikon* (Köln: Kölner Universitätsverlag, 1985), 221–22).

30 Marx, Engels, *Werke*, 32:360.

31 However, the postulated correlation between unemployment and the rate of suicide, which is often used to prove that Man was created to work, seems to have been disproved. See:"Kein Zusammenhang zwischen Suizid und Arbeitslosigkeit," Deutsches Ärzteblatt 87 (1990) Nr. 31/32 (6.8.1990), A-2411 as summary of I. K. Crombie, "Trends in Suicide and Unemployment in Scotland 1976–86," *British Medical Journal* 298 (1987), 782–84.

32 Helmut Thielicke, *Theologische Ethik*, 2nd vol. 1st part: Mensch und Welt (Tübingen: J. C. B. Mohr, 1959²), 396–97.

33 D. P.,"Zu Tode gearbeitet," Der Kassenarzt no. 12/1991, 32.

34 Ibid.

35 Richardson, *Die biblische Lehre*, 15.

36 See the details in the context.

37 Gustav Friedrich Oehler, *Theologie des Alten Testaments* (Stuttgart: J. F. Steinkopf, 1891³), 437.

38 In German, "employer" ["Arbeitgeber"] has the meaning of "the workgiver," "the one giving work." In German, we can say that God is the great "Arbeitgeber," the supreme One giving work to men.

39 Emil Brunner, *Das Gebot und die Ordnungen* (Zürich: Zwingli Verlag, 1939⁴), 373.

40 Marx, Engels, *Werke*, 20:444.

41 Ibid., 40:546.

42 In many languages the plural of "brother" or of "sister" is used to group together all male and female children of the same parents. In German the old plural of "sister","Geschwister" is the name for brothers and sisters. Often the Greek plural of "adelphos" ("brother"), "adelphoi" ("brothers" or "brothers and sisters") is used to speak of brothers and sisters at the same time. There is no other word to mark brothers and sisters together. (The plural of sister "adelphai" is only used for sisters.)

43 Basilius der Große,"Ausführliche Regeln" 41, 1–2, in Alfons Heilmann (ed.), *Texte der Kirchenväter*, 5 vols. (München: Kösel, 1964), 3:228–29. See also ibid., 3:224–40, numerous texts by the church fathers on the Christian view of labour. For the position of the early church on labour, see Adolf von Harnack, *Die Mission und Ausbreitung des Christentums in den ersten drei Jahrhunderten* (Wiesbaden: VMA-Verlag, n.d. [reprint 1924]), 197–200.

44 Hans Walter Wolff, *Anthropologie des Alten Testaments* (München: Chr. Kaiser, 1977), 194; see also 192–97 (texts from Proverbs).

45 Marx, Engels, *Werke*, 19:21. (In German the sentence is even more complicated. That is typical of Marx.)

46 Cremer, *Arbeit und Eigentum*, 11.

47 Stott, *Christsein in den Brennpunkten unserer Zeit*, 38–42.

48 Gilder, *Reichtum und Armut*, 19.

Calvin in Strasbourg:
1538–1541

Roger Nicole

When Calvin, together with his mentor Guillaume Farel (1489–1565), was expelled from Geneva (April 25, 1538), it is fairly obvious that they were wronged, as Calvin himself made clear in saying, "Well and good. If we had served men, we would have been ill requited, but we serve a good Master who will reward us." Nevertheless it was also obvious that, at that time at least, their leadership had failed since they were unable to persuade the council of two hundred that to admit scandalous unrepentant sinners at the Lord's table was such a violation of the proper church order that they could not in conscience submit to it. And so they were voted out. Needless to say, both the citizens of Geneva and the reformers must often have reflected over that situation, wondering whether another outcome might have been possible. Geneva, let it be said for their discharge, had the honesty to recognize their mistake and to plead later for Calvin's return. Calvin and Farel never thought that they could even in good conscience admit notable sinners to the Lord's table but must have wondered whether there might have been ways to avoid this head-on confrontation. But God provided for Calvin in Strasbourg a seven-pronged graduate course in Christian leadership that disciplined his effectiveness and was essential to the rest of his life (1541–1564).

1. To Get a Mentor Who Will Temper One's Foibles

Martin Bucer (1491–1551), the second great "Martin" of the Reformation, became Calvin's mentor in the place of Farel. Up to 1540, Farel was undoubtedly the foremost French-speaking reformer, and he had the vision of the importance of associating Calvin to his work in Geneva. Calvin, however, who had a somewhat fiery temperament, needed no one to fan the flames but rather one whose moderation and irenic spirit would temper undue enthusiasm or criticism on the part of others. Bucer was a man of immense erudition who had achieved a position of dominant influence in Strasbourg. The city, situated between France, Germany, and the Swiss cantons, was a place where the Lutheran and Reformed positions were in close contact. Persecution compelled a number of refugees from France to settle here, and Bucer thought that Calvin could readily be a pastor for those people. In 1538 he urged Calvin to settle in Strasbourg. In his efforts to encourage unity in the Reformation, Bucer may have at times appeared to compromise, especially in the debates about the type of the presence of Christ in the Lord's Supper. Undoubtedly his view enriched Calvin's own conception of the Eucharist, and Calvin did reinforce Bucer in the solidity of his Reformed outlook. At a personal level Bucer's influence on Calvin's spirituality was great, and he helped Calvin "cool off" after fits of anger to which he was, alas, subject. What a great blessing for Calvin to have as his mentor a distinguished Christian by 18 years his senior, and whose moderation and generosity enabled him to get along with a great variety of people and to develop for Strasbourg a situation that Calvin had not been able to secure in Geneva. Beside Bucer there was also Wolfgang Capito (1478–1541), a scholar whose mastery of Hebrew Erasmus admired, and whose generosity combined with his strong commitment to Protestant principles was significant in the preparation of the Tetrapolitan Confession (1530) and of the First Helvetic Confession (1536). Strasbourg was also notable for the very capable civic leadership of Jacob Sturm (1489–1553) and for the masterly pedagogue Johann Sturm (1507–1589).

2. To Work in a Church That Is Responsive to Leadership

It was a great joy to preach and minister to the French refugees, a group of people that was growing in numbers and in faith. Some of the practices these people had cultivated for some time were readily adopted by Calvin: they celebrated the Lord's Supper monthly rather than quarterly as in Geneva; they had a habit of the singing of psalms by the congregation, and Calvin arranged to have a songbook with 18 psalms and the Apostles' Creed set to music and French verse. Some of this work had been done by the noted poet Clement Marot, whom Calvin had met in his sojourn in Ferrara, Italy. On the other hand Calvin could use some of the materials for worship, organization, and catechism that had been prepared and tested in Geneva. The buoyancy of the church was kept on by the coming of new arrivals from France, including some young men who desired to prepare themselves for ministry to the French and who came to board in Calvin's home. Calvin's brother Antoine and his stepsister Marie came to Strasbourg. Calvin received the bourgeoisie of Strasbourg as early as 1539. [He had to wait until December 1559 to receive a similar honor in Geneva!] At the head of the city was a notable man, Jacob Sturm, who was *Stettmeister*. Johann Sturm was connected with Calvin's church and has left his mark as a notable pedagogue whose school, the *Gymnasium*, was highly recognized as a model institution. After the harrowing experience in Geneva, Strasbourg was for Calvin as a bath in the true nature of a cooperative Church of Jesus Christ.

3. To Have Time for Serious Publications

a. First of all we need to mention the second edition of *Institutio Religionis Christianae* (1539). Undoubtedly he had thought over additions and modifications since 1535 when the text of the first edition was sent to the printer. The first edition had six chapters on 462 pages in octavo. The second edition, triple in size, had 17 chapters in 434 pages in folio (in the O. C. the difference in size is shown as between 252 col. and some 900 cols.). This edition was later to be developed into the 1559 edition, divided into four books and 80 chapters and occupies some 1,500 pages in the McNeill and Battles English translation. There are those who believe that the 1539 edition is the most excellent because the later editions are mainly tied with the polemic situations in which Calvin was involved after his return to Geneva.

b. Calvin himself took care to translate this work into French, thus showing that it was intended for laypeople as well as for clerics. This appeared in Geneva in 1541 and called for the following comment of Gustave Lanson in his *Histoire de la Litterature Française*: "This translation is one of the masterpieces of the sixteenth century. It is epoch-making" (p. 263). On that account it was reprinted in 1911 and again in 1978. It was also republished by J. Pannier in the collection *Les Belles Lettres* in 4 vols. 1936–39 (1458 pp.).

c. In 1540 Calvin published in Latin his commentary on Romans, the first in a significant series covering Genesis—Joshua, Job—Malachi (except Ezek 21–48) and the New Testament (except 2 John, 3 John, and Revelation). This has been frequently republished and translated. It is widely useful because its aim is to make the text meaningful for the reader rather than to resolve arcane questions or to exhibit the commentator's scholarship. From the very start Calvin proved himself as a first-rate expositor.

d. In 1641 Calvin published *Short Treatise on the Holy Supper*, written in French and advocating a spiritual presence of Christ in the Holy Supper by which "two things are presented to us; Jesus Christ as the source and substance of all good and, second, the fruit and efficacy of his death and passion." In this way, developing what is present in seed form in the *Catechism* and the early *Institutes*, he advocated a position intermediate between Luther's emphasis upon a local presence of Christ in the elements and Zwingli's insistence on a bare memorial by the worshippers of Christ's atoning death. This volume of 73 pages was often republished and translated in several languages.

e. *Letter to Sadoleto*, 1539. See below under 4.

4. To Deal Effectively with Those Who Differ

In rejecting the unjust accusations of Arianism by Peter Caroli in 1537 and again in 1539, Calvin, who was a sound Trinitarian, but who did not like the dryness and repetition of the symbolum "Quicumque," responded with such vigor as to border intemperance. Although Calvin repented with tears of his anger, he did produce in 1545 a very hostile writing entitled *Pro Farello* (1545).

In 1539 the Cardinal Jacques Sadolet (1477–1547), taking advantage of the difficulties in Geneva after the expulsion of Farel and Calvin, attempted to entice this city to return to the Roman Catholic faith through a flattering letter professing great affection for them. Calvin, when requested to answer this text, produced in one week a reply at the same time so courteous and so categorical that it left Sadolet unable to respond. Calvin made such a brilliant summary of the Reformation faith and of the deviation of Catholicism from the position of the primitive church that the responsibility for the separation was dearly placed on the shoulders of Rome. Remarkably Calvin gave no trace of bitterness concerning the poor treatment that he had experienced from Geneva, and his approach must be recognized as a model of effective polemics. Geneva and other Protestants were jubilant. The text published in Latin appeared in French (1540) together with a French translation of Sadolet's letter. Thus the matter was spread before the whole population rather than only the elite. A beautiful edition of these texts was made by I. Backus and C. Chimelli, *La Vraie Piêté* (Geneva: Labor & Fides, 1986).

5. To Develop External Relationship Beyond One's Own Place

The city of Strasbourg had such confidence in Calvin's ability that it appointed him to serve together with M. Bucer, W. Capito, and Johann Sturm as official representatives at the conferences or "diets" called by Charles V in order to establish some unified outlook in his German Empire. These were gathered in Frankfurt (1539), Hagenau (1540), Worms, and Regensburg (1541).

In these meetings Calvin had opportunity to meet and appreciate Phillip Melanchthon (1497–1560) with whom he formed a special friendship. Other Lutherans were present, as were notable Roman Catholic scholars like John Eck (1456–1543) and Gaspard Contarini (1453–1542). This permitted Calvin to know firsthand the approach and arguments of those from whom he differed. At Regensburg, Bucer and Melanchthon managed to frame an ambiguous formulation of the Lord's Supper that could perhaps be acceptable to both Lutherans and Reformed. Calvin did not think that this would resolve their difference because the terms used were vague rather than precise. Calvin turned out to be right, and no progress was made toward unity of the two bodies.

Although Calvin did not know German, he could readily converse in Latin with all theologians at the diets and thus know them and be known of them. This was a tremendous preparation for the international correspondence and ministry that developed in later years.

6. To Maintain Spiritual Development in One's Own Life

While the years in Strasbourg were very positive in their general orientation, some trials afflicted him.

We might mention that he lived in extreme poverty. For several months he did not receive any salary although properly appointed by the city authorities. He had to eke out with pitiful amounts, often constrained to borrow money. He had to sell his library, left in Geneva, in order to pay the rent he owed. Some of his writings did not sell well, and he had difficulty paying the publisher. He had to take lodgers in his home in order to subsist. In a word he lived from hand to mouth but felt obliged to decline offers of help from friends, notably Louis du Tillet, who by that time had reverted to Catholicism.

In Strasbourg, Calvin began to have difficulties with his health. He had frequent headaches, an irregular digestion, and insomnia. This became worse as he aged, and it is well-known that he died early (one month and a half short of 55 years old). It is astonishing that he could accomplish anything under such burden of ill health, and this had started in 1540. His wife was also sickly from the very beginning of their marriage.

Calvin was greatly afflicted by the death of people who were dear to him. Blind Corault, his early colleague, died, perhaps in prison, in 1538. Calvin's cousin Olivetan died in Italy. Then, while Calvin was in Regensburg, the plague struck in Strasbourg; and Claude Ferey, a very promising French student and boarder, died. On the return from Regensburg, Wolfgang Capito also passed away. These deaths so overwhelmed him that he wrote, "I can set no bounds to my grief."

Calvin's "short fuse," as we might call it today, was also a serious problem to him, for which he sought remedy in sanctification. God often harrows the ground from which a great harvest is expected, and we can perceive that this was a part of Calvin's preparation for his future service.

7. To Get Married, if Single

In August 1540 Calvin married Idelette de Bure, the widow of a converted Anabaptist. She joined Calvin with her two children and proved to be a source of wonderful comfort and help to the reformer. He called her "the best companion of my life. Throughout our common life she has been a great help in all my work as a minister. She has never been even in the least a hindrance to me."

The blessing of marriage, which God instituted for the blessing of humanity (Gen 2), certainly was for Calvin a source of comfort, mind broadening, and an avenue for the expression of the rich and tender treasures of his heart. Slightly a year after his marriage Calvin was to return to Geneva, and his wife remained a blessing for him until her death on March 29, 1549.

Conclusion

Because of this seven-pronged course in Christian leadership, the Calvin who returned to Geneva in 1541 was much better prepared for the tasks that were ahead than the man they had dismissed. Indeed, by the singular providence of God, he was deepened, strengthened, enriched, grounded, and equipped for the extraordinary work and influence that he exercised at home and abroad.

Without Strasbourg there would not have been Geneva in the worldwide role that God was pleased to give that city.

Roger Nicole
Birth Citizen of Geneva

Dear John,

I am well aware that you are a confirmed Lutheran, proud of the leadership that God has granted to Luther himself. I, as a confirmed holder of the biblical doctrines of grace as understood in the Reformed communities, can rejoice with you in God's blessing through Luther, and I believe that you can discern with me how God prepared Calvin for his life task.

Bibliography

John Calvin. *Institutio Christianae Religionis*. Strasbourg: W. Rihel, 1539. Folio 434 pp.

_____. *Institution de la Religion Chretienne*. Geneva: M. dvJ Bois, 1541—in–4, 800 pp. Also: Paris: Champion, 1911. 842 pp.

_____. *Short Treatise on the Lord's Supper*. 1541 English Translation in J. R. S. Reid, ed., *Calvin: Theological Treatises*. The Library of Christian Classics. XXII. Philadelphia: Westminster Press, 1954, 140–66.

_____. *Reply to Sadolet*. 1539. English Translation. J. R. S. Reid, ed., 219–56.

Bernard Cottret. *Calvin: A Biography*. Grand Rapids: Eerdmans, 2000, 132–56.

Emile Doumergue. *Jean Calvin, les Hommes et les Choses de son Temps*. 7 vols. 1899–1927, 2:203–649.

Paul Henry. *Das Leben Johann Calvins*. 3 vols. Hamburg: F. Perthes, 1835–1546, 1:210–385.

Thea Van Halsema. *This Was John Calvin*. Grand Rapids: Zondervan, 1959, 83–101.

The Five Points of Lutheranism?

A TENTATIVE PROPOSAL BASED ON THE EXPERIENTIAL THEOLOGY OF MARTIN LUTHER

Robert E. L. Rodgers

Introduction

The famous (or infamous) Five Points of Calvinism have become well established in historical theology and church history. Drawn up by The Synod of Dort in 1618, they were a response to *The Five Points of Arminianism*. The latter were cast in the form of a "Remonstrance" presented to the Dutch Parliament following the death of Jacob Arminius in 1610. Until then, the major Protestant churches in Europe had subscribed to the Belgic and Heidelberg confessions of faith. Recognizing significant differences in their theology, particularly with regard to five key doctrines, the Arminians formulated their protest. The Synod of Dort sat for 154 sessions over a seven-month period before issuing its reaffirmation of the recognized confessional position.

Now, if we have The Five Points of Arminianism and The Five Points of Calvinism, is it possible to speak in terms of The Five Points of Lutheranism? This essay presents an attempt to identify five key doctrines that lie at the heart of Martin Luther's experiential theology. The question mark in the title is important! This is a *tentative* proposal offered by a Calvinistic Baptist for consideration by the outstanding Lutheran scholar, Prof. Dr. John Warwick Montgomery, whom he is honoured to call his friend. Hearty congratulations, Dr. Montgomery, on your seventy-fifth birthday. This is a great occasion!

SOLI DEO GLORIA!

I. The Doctrine of Sin

The Word of God taught Martin Luther his own heart. It stressed his sin. In those early years, between 1505 and 1515, the thing that worried Luther most was not the Church or the need for reform or religion as such. What worried him more than all else was Luther. It was Luther's soul, Luther's sin, and his need of salvation. The Word of God spoke powerfully to his soul, and Romans 1:18 cried out from the printed page. His great and fundamental problem was, *How can I find a gracious God?* Luther knew that his sin had alienated him from God and that sin merits and attracts the wrath of God issuing in eternal punishment. Here, then, was the basic problem—Martin Luther was a sinner!

Such knowledge bore down upon Martin with tremendous force even when he was cloistered. Classified as a Scrupulant, he tried his confessors with the multiplicity of his confessions. He even invented sins to confess in case he had forgotten some he had actually committed. Writes Luther: Though I lived as a monk beyond reproach, I felt that I was a sinner before God with an extremely disturbed conscience. He was driven to despair. No amount of flagellation would bring relief. Often, after whipping himself, he would ask: Who knows whether such things are pleasing to God? He could write, with regard to Galatians 5:17, of his being crucified—constantly crucified by such thoughts as these: You have committed this or that sin. In Luther's emphasis upon and his enumeration and confession of sins of which he felt himself guilty, we may identify a basic problem. That problem, springing from the teaching of the Church of Rome, lay in his failure, at this point, to distinguish between sin inherited and sins committed in thought, word, and deed.

Here, then, emphasis must be placed upon the doctrine of original sin as it is taught in the Word of God. This is markedly different from the teaching of Rome as accepted initially by Luther. According to Rome, original sin does not affect us after baptism but Martin came to see that this is contrary to biblical teaching. Graphic as ever, here is how the Reformer speaks of the fall: "So Adam and Eve were pure and healthy. They had eyes so sharp they could have seen through a wall and ears so good they could have heard anything two miles away. All the animals were obedient to them: even the sun and moon smiled at them. But then the devil came and said, 'You will become just like the gods,' and so on. They reasoned, 'God is patient. What difference would one apple make?' Snap! Snap! And it lay before them. It's hanging us all yet by the neck." There we have Luther's emphasis upon the fall and its consequences. Sin springs from the fall so that the natural man is born in a state of alienation from God. This alienation cannot simply be construed in terms of a passive weakness or a lack of good. It is, rather, a seething rebellion, for this atrocity of sin has vitiated man's entire being. It is an uncontrollable energy that cannot be conquered by ordinary means. The original sin was characterized by two things: unfaith toward God and a reliance upon human reason instead of God's Word. The effects were catastrophic! Here is the plight of man before God—CORAM DEO—and God is the One with whom we have to do.

The unregenerate man stands before God naked and devoid of anything whereby he might hope to commend himself to his Creator. Listen to Luther as he describes man's changed condition. He describes God the Creator as an artist like unto none and his creation as something to inspire our worship and to make it sing, "Glory to God in the highest." This, says Martin, is the very heart of worship, but the natural man has no part in it at all. "For the World, since Adam's fall, knows neither God nor his creatures. Ho, what fine, fair, happy thoughts would man have had were he not fallen! . . . Adam and his children would have gloried in all this; but now, since the pitiable fall, the Creator is dishonoured and reviled." Luther here underlines the difference between root and fruit, between sin and sins. We are not sinners because we sin, but we sin because we are sinners. In the Roman system, however, it was sins that were being remembered, listed, confessed, and forgiven. The emphasis was upon the fruit and not the root. In opposition to this, Luther stressed that sin must first of all be identified in the spiritual realm before we can hope to have it dealt with in its expression as sins in the physical and material realms. This enables Ebeling to write, "Even sin is spiritual in so far as it is recognized in the sight of God as a self-righteousness, as pious self-assertion against God, and as a flight from proclaiming the righteousness of God into self-justification." Increasingly, Luther recognized the differences that existed between the biblical doctrine of sin and the teaching of the Church of Rome. Says Schwiebert, "In the Leipzig Debate he came face-to-face with the orthodox Roman position on sin, grace, justification, the Church, and papal power; and he began to realize how far he had really drifted." With regard to the matter of man's salvation, two of Luther's basic convictions proved to be of fundamental importance. Not only were these two convictions disputed by the Church of Rome, but they were actually anathematized at the Council of Trent. What were they?

1. Until men individually become the subjects of God's special grace, i.e., until God's grace is actually communicated to them in their justification and regeneration, there is nothing in them but what is sinful and deserving of God's displeasure.

In other words, all the actions of unregenerate men are wholly sinful.

2. Even after they have become the subjects of God's justifying and renewing grace, there is still something sinful, and in itself deserving of punishment, about all that they are and all that they do, about every feature of their character and every department of their conduct.

This biblical understanding of the doctrine of sin found powerful expression in Luther's preaching and writings. Says Wood: "Like all true Gospel preaching, Luther's message moved within the twin orbits of Sin and Grace." Mackinnon could state that gospel preaching in the evangelical sense began with Luther. Of the Epistle to the Romans, the Wittenberg professor wrote: "The Sum and Substance of this letter is: to pull down, to pluck up and to destroy all wisdom and righteousness of the flesh ... and to implant, establish and make large the reality of Sin." It need not surprise us, then, what Kooiman says of Luther's lectures on Romans: "The central motif of these lectures is that God's Word causes us to see our sin." This, in turn, enables one authority to say with conviction that Luther's commentary on Romans is a Reform Manifesto. If that be so, and if its central motif concerns the doctrine of Sin, there may be justification in regarding that doctrine as the first of The Five Points of Lutheranism.

II. The Bondage of the Will

"How can I find a gracious God?" That question was paramount on the heart and mind of Martin Luther when the Word of God convinced him of his sin. It taught him that he was a sinner both by nature and by practice. Luther despaired. What added to his despair was the awful fact that there was absolutely nothing he could will or do to gain Salvation. His will was enslaved by sin; his will was bound. Ebeling reminds us, "Luther came to realise the radical bondage of the will . . . as soon as he comprehended the pure gospel." The Word of God spoke powerfully to Martin. The natural man will not come to Christ and, indeed, cannot come. He is in bondage to sin and Satan. Only God in Christ who is the truth can set the prisoner free. Luther saw the idea of free will as asserting itself in opposition to the *free-will* or *determination of God,* and he could not abide such effrontery. Says Luther, "The best and infallible preparation and the sole disposition to grace is the eternal election and predestination of God." Just as man cannot will to come to Christ, Martin would say, neither can he be driven. It is God's work: "God alone does this, coming to dwell beforehand in the heart."

Increasingly, Luther preached and wrote against a doctrine that he regarded as false. In 1516 he said, "The will of man without Grace is not free but enslaved." In 1517, the year of the posting of the Ninety-five Theses, he wrote: "It is not true that the free effort of man is able to decide on either of two opposed courses. Rather, it is not free at all but captive. It is not true that the will is able by nature to follow right guidance." In 1518, at Heidelberg, he emphasized the doctrine again: "To speak of free-will after The Fall is mere words. If it does what lies in its power (i.e. free-will) it commits mortal sin."

Luther's doctrine of the bondage of the will was condemned as heretical in the Papal Bull of Excommunication. Certainly, Martin's ideas were opposed to the teachings of outstanding theologians whose writings were highly regarded in Rome. Peter Lombard, Anselm, Abelard, and Bernard, for example, had refused to accept the unqualified impotence of man's will after the fall. Listen to Luther as he replies to the Pope: "Free-Will is, in reality, a fabrication, a mere turn of phrase without reality." Again, "free-will, which is only apparent with regard to us and to temporal things, disappears in the sight of God." The fact that Luther based his doctrine on Scripture carried no weight with the Pope. Indeed, Pope Hadrian had written to Fredrick the Wise telling him not to be swayed by the fact that Luther quoted Scripture. "So does every heretic," wrote the Pope. Nonetheless, a classic example of Luther's dependence on God's Word is evident in his exposition of such themes as the bondage of the will when he debated at Heidelberg. One authority states that Luther appealed to Scripture "in almost every other sentence of the proofs."

For Luther, this doctrine was not only scriptural but also intensely theological. He refused to place it in the category of metaphysics as others tried to do. Indeed, because it was both scriptural and theological, it was regarded by Luther, and by all the Reformers, as the connecting link between the doctrines of original sin and of divine grace. . . . Martin believed fervently that the whole gospel of God's grace was bound up with this doctrine of the bondage of the will. In his reply to the work of Erasmus, *On the Freedom of the Will*, which had been written expressly in opposition to the German reformer, Luther thanked Erasmus for not bothering him with more extraneous issues, for seeing the hinge on which all turns, and for having aimed at the vital spot. Luther's teaching was biblical, theological, and evangelical. Nevertheless, this vital doctrine was condemned by the Council of Trent, which pronounced an anathema upon all who say that the free will of man was lost and extinguished after the fall of Adam. Luther's reply to Erasmus was entitled *De Servo Arbitrio*, and this has proved to be one of the most enduring monuments of evangelical doctrine, a masterpiece in the realm of polemics, dogmatics, and exegesis. This polemical tour de force not only crushed the specious arguments of the Dutch humanist but also exercised a profound influence upon the doctrine of the Reformation and beyond. Luther, himself, regarded it as his best work and expressed his opinion that the doctrine of the bondage of the will is at the very heart of the gospel. As such, it is involved in the doctrines of original sin, the total depravity of man, the sovereignty of God and human responsibility, the doctrine of predestination, and the scriptural teaching concerning regeneration. Of Luther's masterpiece, H. J. Iwand has written: "Whoever puts this book down without having realized that evangelical theology stands or falls with the doctrine of the bondage of the will has read it in vain." The teaching in *The Bondage of the Will* is absolutely consistent with Luther's doctrine of Christian liberty. The latter was expressed clearly, for example, in his work, *On the Freedom of the Christian*, published in 1520. Nevertheless, in that treatise on freedom, the reformer clearly states: free will is an empty word. This, of course, was consistent with Luther's own experience. In his great struggle with sin, he had been convinced by the Word of God that there was nothing he could will or do to save himself. That word cried out to the sinner, "It is God who worketh in you both to will and to do of his good pleasure." It taught him man's inability in such passages as John 5:40: "Ye will not come to me that ye might have life;" John 6:44,65: "No man can come to Me except the Father who hath sent me draw him."

The doctrine of the will has to do with the basic principles of religion—the nature of God and the nature of man. It is involved in the problem of the ages as Philip Schaff has suggested. Nevertheless, the doctrine of the bondage of the will is asserted in the work of Jonathan Edwards entitled *On the Freedom of the Will*. In connection with the doctrine taught therein, George Marsden says: remove divine sovereignty from the emphasis on individual choice and the whole system would collapse.

It is no wonder, then, that B. B. Warfield should assert that "*The Bondage of the Will* is a dialectic and polemic masterpiece which is, in fact, the embodiment of Luther's reformation conceptions, the nearest thing to a systematic statement of them that he ever made. . . . It is . . . in a true sense, the manifesto of the Reformation. All the Reformers were of one mind concerning this scriptural teaching, which humbles man, strengthens faith, and glorifies God."

On that last point we must allow Gordon Rupp to have the final word. He describes the doctrine as the finest and most powerful Soli Deo Gloria to be sung in the whole period of the Reformation.

III. The Righteousness of God

In the experiential theology of Martin Luther, the doctrine of the righteousness of God occupies a pivotal position. He regarded this teaching as of fundamental importance in the Christian message. Here, we are right at the heart of the gospel. On the one hand, sin. On the other hand, salvation. How could Martin Luther, the sinner, find salvation? How could he find a gracious God? He found that the answer lies in the doctrine of the righteousness of God.

God Against Man?

Before Luther came to faith in Christ, the term *the righteousness of God* troubled him greatly and repeatedly. He had encountered it in his study of the Psalms. There it was, for example, in Psalm 31:1 and again in 71:2. With his heart and mind unenlightened, Luther completely misunderstood the scriptural teaching, and it drove him to distraction. Listen to him as he bears testimony to his reaction to his reading of such passages of the Word of God: "When under the Papacy, I read 'In Thy righteousness deliver me' (Ps 31:1), and, 'in thy truth', I thought at once that this righteousness was an avenging anger, namely, The Wrath of God. I hated Paul with all my heart when I read that the righteousness of God is revealed in the Gospel (Rom 1:16,17)."

Now, if he hated the messenger, he certainly hated the message itself. He tells us how Romans 1:17 "'stood in his way": "For I hated that word 'righteousness of God' which, according to the use and custom of all the teachers, I had been taught to understand philosophically regarding the formal or active righteousness, as they called it, with which God is righteous and punishes the unrighteous sinner." Luther hated the messenger and the message itself, but he also tells us that he hated God whose Word it was. "I hated the righteous God who punishes sinners, and secretly, if not blasphemously, certainly murmuring greatly. I was angry with God and said, 'As if, indeed, it is not enough that miserable sinners, eternally lost through original sin, are crushed by every kind of calamity by the Law of Decalogue, without having God add pain to pain by the Gospel and also by the Gospel threatening us with His righteousness and wrath.'" There, Luther equates "righteousness and wrath" and "law and punishment." He tells us how he "made no distinction between the Law and the Gospel. I regarded both as the same thing and held that there was no difference between Christ and Moses except the times in which they lived and their degrees of perfection."

This struggle of Luther's with regard to the righteousness of God was one of titanic proportions. Instinctively, he related the idea to the Law. He interpreted it in an active sense related to the wrath of God and concluded that the righteous God was against man.

God For Man!

In the grace and mercy of God, Martin was delivered from the bondage of sin. His mind was enlightened, and his eyes were opened so that he realized how he had misinterpreted the Scripture. Romans 1:17, for example, bore a quite different message as he himself explains: "God had mercy on me and I began to understand that the righteousness of God is that gift of God by which a righteous man lives, namely, faith and that this sentence—The Righteousness of God is revealed in The Gospel—is passive, indicating that the merciful God justifies us by faith, as it is written: 'The righteous shall live by faith.' Now I felt that I had been reborn altogether and had entered Paradise."

Now, instead of loathing Romans 1:17, he found that it helped and cheered him: "There I saw what righteousness Paul was talking about. Earlier in the text I read 'righteousness.' I related the abstract ('righteousness') with the concrete ('the righteous One') and became sure of my cause. I learned to distinguish between the righteousness of the Law and the righteousness of the Gospel."

Before his conversion, the term *the righteousness of God* presented to Luther's mind a picture of a Judge and of wrath, but as soon as he was born anew, the Scriptures were opened up to him in a completely new way. "There a totally other face of the entire Scripture showed itself to me. Thereupon I ran through the Scriptures from memory. I also found in other terms an analogy, as, the Work of God, that is, what God does in us; the power of God, with which He makes us strong; the wisdom of God, with which He makes us wise; the strength of God, the salvation of God, the glory of God." His new understanding of this vitally important doctrine opened up for Luther the rest of Scripture. No wonder, then, that one authority says that Luther had obtained the key to the Scriptures.

The Wittenberg professor knew, of course, that this wonderful teaching was contrary to the opinion of all the doctors. Such great truths as the righteousness of God and justification by grace through faith alone were unknown to the academic theology of the Middle Ages. With this, Schwiebert agrees: "there now shines through his expositions the rich soul-experience through which he understood St. Paul better than had been the case for a thousand years."

With what joy did Martin embrace this biblical teaching with regard to the righteousness of God! No longer could he regard God as the Judge sitting upon a rainbow and filled with wrath. No longer could he think in terms of the righteousness of God against man. God in Christ is a gracious Redeemer and Christ is our righteousness as well as our wisdom, sanctification, and redemption (1 Cor 1:30). God against man? No! Now Martin could appreciate as never before that God was for man. Therefore, in his exposition of the Psalms, Luther can rejoice in the believer's riches: Christ is God's grace, mercy, righteousness, truth, wisdom, power, comfort, and salvation, given us of God without any merit. What a tremendous difference this new and correct understanding of a vital doctrine made in the life and ministry of Martin Luther! His lectures now breathed the atmosphere of first-century Christianity. He revelled in preaching this grand truth, and it affected him in every aspect of his being. When he came to the 22nd Psalm, he identified it as relating to Christ. Yet Christ—the holy, spotless, sinless One—is forsaken by the Father. How could this be? One authority tells us that the answer dawned on Luther with the force of a fresh revelation. Christ, who knew no sin, was made to be sin for the sake of sinners.

Christ has taken the sin of believers and has clothed believers with the robe of his righteousness. Luther loved the Savior with all his heart. Christ Jesus not only brought God's righteousness, but also He was God's righteousness. Glory to His name! He praises God repeatedly for this great truth and cries, "Thank God we again have His Word, which pictures and portrays Christ as our righteousness." Martin had discovered that an ocean of grace lies between the concepts of wrath and mercy. His was a comforted despair. This whole experience has been described as Luther's Copernican revolution in theology and as Luther's discovery of a new understanding of the essence of the Christian religion. Gerhard Ebeling could describe it as the fundamental theological perception and the basic Reformation principle. Says Bainton: Luther had come into a new view of Christ and a new view of God. He had come to love the suffering Redeemer and the God unveiled on Calvary.

IV. Justification by Grace Through Faith Alone

In the experiential theology of Martin Luther, there is an inseparable connection between *the righteousness of God* and *justification by grace through faith alone*. The fundamental importance of that connection had dawned upon him when, by God's grace, his mind was enlightened regarding the true import of Romans 1:17. Listen to Luther himself as he bears witness to the grace of God in his heart and life: "Night and day I pondered until I saw the connection between the justice of God and the Statement that 'the just shall live by his faith.' Then I grasped that the justice of God is that righteousness by which through Grace and sheer mercy, God justifies us through faith." That was Luther's gospel! That was the good news that God had called him to proclaim, and proclaim it he did. *If you have a true faith that Christ is your Savior, then at once you have a gracious God, for faith leads you in and opens up God's heart and will, that you should see pure grace and overflowing love.* Here is a gospel worth preaching! It is a gospel where the emphasis is on *grace and sheer mercy* and *pure grace and overflowing love*. Luther had come to realize that justification is an act of God's free grace. It is an *act* and not a *work*. Moreover, Martin realized that Paul had borrowed his terminology from the law courts. Justification is a legal term and demonstrates the fact that God freely pardons our sins and accepts us as righteous in His sight. Luther rejoiced that the *ground* of our justification is not any righteousness inherent, nor our supposed good works, but, rather, the righteousness of the Redeemer imputed to us. Then Martin also realized that the *means* of our justification is faith! We are *justified freely by that faith which receives and rests in Christ only for salvation.*

In his own experience Luther had been convinced of the importance of this tremendous doctrine, and his emphasis upon it shines through in his preaching and teaching, in his commentaries and pastoral counseling, and in his translation of the Bible. When he came to translate Romans 3:28, he added the word *alone*—by faith alone. Greatly criticized then (as now!), Luther replied that a clear and vigorous rendering into German required such an addition. Interestingly, Joachim Jeremias of Göttingen has affirmed that, linguistically and theologically, Luther was correct. We have the same emphasis in Luther's expository lectures on the Epistle to the Romans in 1515/1516. In them justification comes to the fore even as it undergirds the Ninety-Five Theses of 1517. Says Finlayson: Luther had already given his exposition of justification in his lectures on Romans of 1515–1516, and from that time he had been diligently preaching this doctrine from pulpit and chair and had already converted his immediate community to the evangelical faith. In 1517, he nailed his Ninety-Five Theses to the door of the Castle Church in Wittenberg. Superficial readers of the Theses may think that Luther is concerned there only with the matter of indulgences. They fail to note that the doctrine of justification undergirds the Theses throughout. Certainly, Cardinal Cajetan had no difficulty in recognizing the true import of the Theses and actually quoted a papal bull—*Unigenitus*—issued in 1343 by Clement VI, in an attempt to convince Luther of error.

Justification by grace through faith alone was no mere theoretical teaching as far as Luther was concerned. He had been burdened by sin, and his will had been bound. Then he experienced God's grace and mercy and began to rejoice in the doctrines of the righteousness of God and justification. Here was a vibrant faith that brought joy to the heart and peace to the soul.

In justifying the believer, God does not simply overlook man's sin and forgive him. No! Luther emphasized repeatedly the ideas of substitution and imputation. Jesus Christ is our substitute. He has taken upon Himself the sin of the penitent sinner and clothed him with the righteousness of Christ. Listen now to Pastor Martin as he counsels his dear friend, George Spenlein. In a letter to Spenlein, dated 8 April 1516, Luther writes:

Therefore, my dear brother, learn to know Christ and Him crucified. Learn to praise Him and, ceasing to trust in yourself, say to Him, Thou, Lord Jesus, art my righteousness. I am Thy sin. Thou hast taken upon Thee what is mine and given to me what is Thine. Thou hast taken upon thee what Thou were not and given to me what was never mine. . . . Through Him alone, and cheerfully despairing of yourself and your own works, you will find peace.

The Reformer was opposed relentlessly by the Church of Rome, which was implacably opposed to his teaching concerning justification. When the Roman authorities attacked him through an Imperial Edict in 1531, Luther's response was blunt: "I see that the Devil is continually attacking this fundamental doctrine." Referring to himself as an unworthy herald of the gospel, he declared himself determined to preach it all the more.

The Puritan Thomas Watson quotes Luther as saying that, after his death, the doctrine of justification would be corrupted. Such a course must needs be resisted because as Watson says again, "justification is the very hinge and pillar of Christianity. . . . Justification by Christ is a spring of the water of life."

B. B. Warfield writes about a dogma in which is summed up all the teaching of Scripture and identifies it as the sole efficiency of God in salvation. He continues: "This is what we call the material principle of the Reformation. It was not at first known by the name of justification by faith alone, but it was from the first passionately embraced as renunciation of all human works and dependence upon the grace of God alone for salvation. In it the Reformation lived and moved and had its being; in a high sense of the words, it is the Reformation."

James Buchanan also saw justification by faith as the material principle of the Reformation and says, "Martin Luther described the doctrine of Justification by Faith as *articulus stantis vel cadentis ecclesiae*—the article of faith that decides whether the Church is standing or falling."

Let us listen to the pastor, preacher, and professor, as he makes his great confession of faith:

I, Dr. Martin Luther, the unworthy evangelist of the Lord Jesus Christ, thus think and thus affirm, That this article, namely, 'that faith alone, without works, justifies us before God,' can never be overthrown. For Christ alone, the Son of God, died for our sins; but if Christ alone takes away our sins, then men, with all their works are to be excluded from all concurrence in procuring the pardon of sin and justification. Nor can I embrace Christ otherwise than by faith alone. He cannot be apprehended by works. But if faith, before works follow, apprehend the Redeemer, it is undoubtedly true that faith alone, before works and without works, appropriates the benefits of Redemption, which is no other than Justification, or deliverance from sin. This is our doctrine; so The Holy Spirit teaches and the whole Christian church. In this, by the Grace of God, will we stand fast. Amen!

V. The Priesthood of All Believers

That was a glorious day when Martin Luther discovered a copy of the Bible in the library of the monastery at Erfurt. Thomas Carlyle has referred to that as Luther's "most blessed discovery." Among the many treasures he found therein was the doctrine of *The Priesthood of All Believers*. What he learned from the Word of God was contrary to all that he had been taught and had experienced in the Church of Rome. In that sacerdotal system the "laity" was dependent on the priesthood, which was composed of fallen human beings who believed they possessed extraordinary powers. They had been taught that they could change the bread and wine of the Mass into the body and blood of Christ. They could forgive sin and grant absolution. These and other very serious powers were the possessions of men in their vocations as priests.

In Luther's own experience, such ideas terrified him. For example, he experienced tremors whilst officiating at his first Mass, which, according to Rome, is the focal point of the Church's means of grace; here on the altar bread and wine become the flesh and blood of God and the sacrifice of Calvary is reenacted. The priest who performs the miracle of transforming the elements enjoys a power and privilege denied even to angels. The whole difference between the clergy and the laity rests on this.

Martin's early concept of priesthood, therefore, was that taught by the Church of Rome, but he was to experience a profound change in his thinking as a result of his "most blessed discovery." There he discovered that all believers are called upon to present their bodies as living sacrifices unto God (Rom 12:1) and to offer to God the sacrifice of praise (Heb 13:15). Believers have been constituted "a kingdom of priests" (1 Pet 1:9) or *a royal priesthood*. They are living stones and have been "built up a spiritual house, an holy priesthood, to offer up spiritual sacrifices, acceptable to God by Jesus Christ"(1 Pet 2:5). All that, says Luther, is the vocation and the dignity of the humblest believer in Christ. This concept, however, must be construed in terms of all believers' endeavors in life: "A cobbler, a smith, a peasant, whatever he may be, a man has the labour and occupation of his craft and yet all men alike are consecrated bishops and priests." Luther drives the message home as he writes: "A poor servant-girl may say, I cook the meals, I make up the beds, I dust the rooms. Who has bidden me do it? My Master and my Mistress have bidden me. Who has given them the right to command me? God has given it to them. So it is true that I am serving God in Heaven as well as them. How happy can I feel now! It is as if I were in heaven, doing my work for God." The idea of the priesthood of all believers is then, much wider in scope than that of the preaching ministry. It reaches out to the children of God in their daily work and describes that as their *vocation*.

How Luther rejoiced in this doctrine! In his preaching, teaching, and writing, he emphasized this glorious truth—every believer is a priest. On the one hand, Luther could say quite succinctly, "The Office of the Clergy is open to all who are priests—that is—to all Christians." On the other hand, he could write a lovely work entitled *The Freedom of a Christian Man*, which was exceedingly well received. Says one authority: "The work restates the priesthood of all believers and the possessions of the Christian man through faith in such impressive terms that it made a most useful manual of private devotion and as such it enjoyed considerable popularity." For Luther, there was no doubt at all that *what the priest does any Christian may do, if commissioned by the congregation, because all Christians are priests.* In fact, Luther was unhappy with the term *priest* as applied only to the pastor. He had come to the conclusion "that those who presided over the sacraments or the Word among the people neither can or ought to be called priests. . . . According to the Gospel writings, they would be better named Ministers, Deacons, Bishops, Stewards. . . . As Paul says in 1 Corinthians IV: 'we must be regarded as ministers of Christ and Stewards of the mysteries of God.' He does not say 'as priests of Christ,' because he would know that the name and office of priest are the common possessions of all."

Now, whilst every believer enjoys the right and privilege of intercession, not every believer is called to preach. There is, says the Reformer, one common estate (*Stand*) but a variety of offices (*Ämter*) and functions. Yet the community of intercessors, a priesthood of fellow helpers, a family of mutual sharers and burden bearers—that, says Luther, is the *Communio Sanctorum*.

In 1520, Martin Luther published a work entitled *A Treatise on the New Testament*, in which the doctrine of the priesthood of all believers finds admirable expression. Believing with all his heart that the doctrine was true because it was biblical, he wrote, "If faith alone is the true priestly office, then all Christians are priests." Again, he says, "The fact that we are all priests and kings means that each of us Christians may go before God and intercede for the other."

Of course, this teaching was revolutionary and produced the most wonderful results. In fact, Hillerbrand is of the opinion that as far as the economic and social dimensions of society "were concerned, the Protestant Reformation was indirectly revolutionary" and directly conservative. Yet he concedes that Luther's teaching that every job and every profession was "a vocation" and enjoyed a spiritual blessing, "was of immense significance."

In practical terms, the number of people entering monasteries and convents diminished. The man in the street now thought rather differently than previously about what constitutes a vocation. On the other hand, the ranks of teachers, medical doctors, lawyers, and farmers expanded. In pursuing such professions, believers now realized that they were serving God as much as the pastor or preacher. Together, they were priests unto God.

Listen now to Karl Heim as he describes the practical outcome of Luther's teaching: "The workshop became a church, a man's native land a sanctuary; all who were engaged in maintaining human life became consecrated priests in this vast Church of God." This was Luther's new contribution; the conception of a man's calling in the work as service given to God.

Postscript

In this tentative proposal concerning *The Five Points of Lutheranism*, some emphasis has been placed upon the experiential theology of the great reformer, Martin Luther.

That, however, must be understood in the light of his absolute commitment to the Word of God. That Word, for him, was foundational and impregnable. It is on that basis, therefore, that we may hear Luther crying out that the devil was his best professor and that temptation was the best school of theology. At the same time, even though he was an outstanding genius, it is encouraging to hear him say that the best teachers are always learners.

There was nothing coldly academic about Luther's theology and beliefs. Lloyd-Jones could write about this volcanic element, this living element, this experimental element, this experiential element, which lies at the heart and center of the story of Martin Luther and the protestant Reformation. His, therefore, was a heart-felt faith!

Writing about Luther's solution to the antinomy of the Church's teaching, Lindsay says it was "familiar to simple piety although unknown to the academic theology of the middle ages . . . for the theology of the heart is always far in advance of that of the schools." What was Luther's motto?—PECTUS EST QUOD THEOLOGUM FACIT: It is the heart that makes the theologian.

Finally, since a learned Jesuit was of the opinion that the hymns of Luther killed more souls than his sermons, Martin's testimony may be heard again in his lovely hymn "Nun freut euch":

> In devil's dungeon chained I lay
> The pangs of death swept o'er me.

My sin devoured me night and day
In which my mother bore me.
My anguish ever grew more rife,
I took no pleasure in my life
And sin had made me crazy.

Then was the Father troubled sore
To see me ever languish.
The Everlasting Pity swore
To save me from my anguish.
He turned to me his father heart
And chose himself a bitter part,
His Dearest did it cost him.

Thus spoke the Son, "Hold thou to me,
From now on thou wilt make it.
I gave my very life for thee
And for thee I will stake it.
For I am thine and thou art mine,
And where I am our lives entwine,
The Old Fiend cannot shake it."

The Gospel of Judas

A CHEERFULLY TOLD LIE

Erwin Lutzer

"You, Judas, will exceed all of them [i.e., the other disciples].
For you will sacrifice the man that clothes me."

The Gospel of Judas

His name is *Judas*, the Greek translation of the Hebrew *Judah*, which means "praise." It was a name with grand precedent and charged with prophetic hope (cf. Gen 49:8–12). His last name is *Iscariot*, which probably means that he was a man from Kerioth, a town in southern Judah, known for its fruit farms. Whatever *Iscariot* means, it was meant to distinguish him from the other Judas who also was a disciple of Jesus (Luke 6:16; John 14:22; Acts 1:13).

Let's not forget that Judas was, at one time, a teenager, a young man with all of the idealism, fantasies, hopes, and dreams of youth. He was also at one time a baby held in his mother's arms, and he inspired great dreams in her heart.

Imagine the joy in that Jewish home when Judas was chosen as a disciple of Jesus Christ, Israel's bright new hope. Yes, Jesus chose him, but he also had to agree to have Jesus as his teacher and mentor. Judas was now one of the elite, the privileged few (Matt 10:4; Mark 3:19; Luke 6:16). No one could have predicted on that happy day the despair and gloom that would forever be associated with the name *Judas*—no one, that is, except the one that chose him (John 13:11).

Judas was with Jesus, up close and personal. He might have been thinking, *Now at last I will be able to realize the fulfillment of the hopes and dreams I've had as a teenager. What an opportunity! What will the kids I played with think now?* His future was glowing and getting brighter day by day. Hope seemed to have no limits.

Who Was Judas?

But who was this man? The general populace, together with Dante, has long since chained Judas with the devil in the deepest icy regions of hell.[1] From Shakespeare's *Love's Labour's Lost* (Act V, Scene IV) and *Henry VI* (Part III, Act V, Scene VII) to Bob Dylan's "With God on Our Side," his name has long since been synonymous with "traitor." But is it possible that we could have misinterpreted him? What if Judas was not the betrayer of Jesus, but irony of ironies, his confidant and covert operative entrusted with a secret mission?

There have been several books, both in the popular media and in the scholarly press, which have sought to loose Judas from Dante's chains. William Klassen wrote a book suggesting that Judas acted neither as devil nor as saint but as a neutral observer. Klassen insists that Judas did not betray Jesus but just "gave him over" to the appropriate Jewish authorities to evaluate his claims.[2] Judas had difficulty understanding Jesus' course of ministry. Unlike the other disciples, however, Judas thought he would do something about this misunderstanding; he would offer Jesus a helping hand and speed his political reign into motion by handing him over to the Jewish authorities. After all, the Messiah of Israel could never be defeated by pagan overlords! Klassen argues that the Greek word in the Gospels translated as "betray" (*paradidōmi*) means simply to hand over—which is quite neutral; Paul used it when he said, "For I received from the Lord what I also handed on (*paradidōmi*) to you" (1 Cor 11:23).

But there are problems with this cheerfully neutral understanding of Judas's actions. In the Gospel of Luke, he is named last in the list of disciples with this ominous commentary, "Judas Iscariot, who became a traitor" (Luke 6:16). Moreover, the devil is said to have been behind the "handing over" of Jesus (John 13:2). As James M. Robinson has written, "It is very difficult to interpret the canonical gospels as being on Judas' side" (49). Judas, after all, is called the "son of perdition" (John 17:12), the same language used in reference to the "man of lawlessness" in 2 Thessalonians 2:3 (cf. Rev 17:8). Note that Judas and the antichrist share the same description.

Judas was not simply handing Jesus over in a neutral, disinterested manner to be examined. After the deed was done, Judas went back to the chief priests filled with remorse, and tried to return the blood money (Matt 27:3–4). What he says is instructive, "I have sinned, for I have betrayed innocent blood." If Judas merely handed Jesus over in a perfunctory move, why would he confess his sinful act? No, no—Judas was betraying his dear friend, and he knew it.

What, then, of Judas' motives? At a certain level, the motives behind Judas's betrayal of Jesus perished with him. We will never know what he was thinking. What would cause one so close to Jesus to betray him so deeply? Revenge? Misdirected idealism? Money? To display Jesus' final triumph? We don't know for sure.

Enter the Gospel of Judas

The recent discovery of *The Gospel of Judas*, and its popular airing by the National Geographic Society just in time for Easter (2006), have, in the words of op-ed columnist E. J. Dionne Jr., given "the old, sacred story a dramatic new twist."[3] Some say it is one of the most important archaeological finds of the twentieth century, rivaling the discovery of the Dead Sea Scrolls and the Gnostic Gospels of Nag Hammadi. Others say it will change our mind about Judas from villain to hero. Others say it also changes our view about Jesus: he is not the divine Son of God made flesh (John 1:14) but actually an altogether different being, an *aeon* sent from the realm above who only *appeared* to be in human flesh so as to teach the secret truths of salvation.[4] He is a laughing Jesus who mocked the Eucharist and believes in more than one god. In our spiritually crazed society, the gospel has garnered peculiar interest.

According to the Gospel of Judas, he turned Jesus over to the authorities because Jesus wanted him to do so and because Jesus wanted to escape the material world. Jesus wanted to get on with his death, and Judas did him a favor by speeding up the process.

What are the claims being made in *The Gospel of Judas*? Let's introduce the document. Here are several quotes that will give you a synopsis of its teaching.

"The secret account of the revelation that Jesus spoke in conversation with Judas Iscariot during a week, three days before he celebrated the Passover."

"Jesus spoke to his disciples about mysteries beyond the world and what would take place at the end. Often he did not appear to his disciples as himself, but he was found among them as a child."

"One day he was with his disciples in pious observance. When he approached his disciples gathered together and seated and offering a prayer of thanksgiving over the bread, he laughed. The disciples ask why he is laughing and Jesus replies that he is not laughing at them because they are doing the will of their god. When they became angry, Jesus asked anyone among them to bring out the perfect human to stand before him and only Judas was able to stand before him."

Jesus says to Judas, "You will become the thirteenth, and you will be cursed by the other generations—and you will come to rule over them. In the last days they will curse your ascent to the holy generation."

Jesus says to Judas, "Come, that I may teach you about secrets no person has ever seen."

"You will sacrifice the man who clothes me."

This last statement gets to the heart of the Judas Document. Jesus' body was that of a man which masked his true self, namely his spirit. Thus the body must be sacrificed in order to liberate the soul. In betraying Jesus to the authorities, Judas helped Jesus get on with the freedom that would come to his spirit after the crucifixion. Thus Judas did Jesus a favor.

The Teachings of the Judas Document

The Judas document is part of the broader collection of Gnostic literature that has received a great deal of attention in the past few years, especially with the success of *The Da Vinci Code*. Gnosticism, from the Greek word *gnosis* or *knowledge*, refers to the teaching of those who believed that they have hidden knowledge. Gnosticism was an attempt to harmonize Greek mythology with the New Testament. Thus, as a part of this literature, the Gospel of Judas teaches the following:

First, there are many different gods. Indeed Jesus was laughing because they were praying to their god, but he belonged to a different god altogether. The Gnostics couldn't agree on the number of gods but believed it was somewhere between two and 30!

Second, in keeping with Greek mythology, Jesus says at one point, "Your star has led you astray" (31). Again Jesus laughs and explains, "I am not laughing at you but at the error of the stars, because these six stars wander about with these five combatants, and they all will be destroyed along with their creatures" (42). These wandering stars are likely five planets along with the moon. According to ancient astronomical theory, such wandering stars can influence our lives.

Third, this laughing Jesus is not divine except in the sense that all of us are. We are trapped divinities, waiting to escape to return to our distant home. Jesus, some Gnostics believed, was an aeon from the realm above; he was not a man of flesh and blood but only appeared to be human (docetism).

Fourth, the Greeks believed that matter was evil and spirit was good, thanks to various forms of Platonic thought. With that in mind, read this next text carefully: Jesus says to Judas, "But you will exceed all of them. For you will sacrifice the man that clothes me" (43). Let me say again that the notion here is that Jesus' physical body clothed the real Jesus, the spirit, that longed to return to god or gods.

Fifth, there is both an implicit denial of the bodily resurrection and of the church's mission. As already emphasized, the death of Jesus, with the assistance of Judas, is taken to be the liberation of the spiritual person within. The climax of the Judas Document naturally, is the betrayal and Jesus' impending crucifixion—the great release and escape from this world. Resurrection, for the Gnostic, is a return to prison, and if this world is a prison, why would Jesus want to be raised? And, for that matter, why should the church engage in any form of mission? If this world is only a "cesspool of pain, misery, and suffering," then our only hope for salvation is to forsake it.[5] The vision of Christianity according to *The Gospel of Judas*, therefore, is fundamentally at odds with that of biblical Christianity.

The Gnostic teachings have no coherent theology—they contradicted one another in ways great and small. Some taught that there were many gods, others, just two. They could afford to contradict one another because they were simply human musings for which reason and coherence were not important.

An Evaluation of the Judas Document

How, then, should we think of the historical Judas? Should we revise our estimate of who he was in light of recent proposals by the likes of such scholars as Klassen and the wake of the recently released document, *The Gospel of Judas?* What should we make of this document? Does it present credible history, or is this document just more hype? Should it change our opinion of Judas? No, I don't think so.

The Gospel of Judas was written over a hundred years after the historical Jesus and Judas walked the regions of Judea. It is a fictitious account. As Dr. Craig Evans said during the National Geographic Society television special, *The Gospel of Judas* "does not contain any authentic Jesus tradition." Dr. N. T. Wright, bishop of Durham and an authority in historical Jesus research, in a sermon given on 13 April 2006, said, "This document is worthless historically."[6]

In passing, we should note a common misunderstanding. The media has been cheerfully saying that *The Gospel of Judas* is an authentic document. But by that they mean that it was not forged, and probably dates back to the late second century. That is what makes it authentic, not that the events recorded in the document are *historically* authentic.

The Gospel of Judas was known to Irenaeas when he wrote *Against Heresies* around AD 180,[7] wherein he said that the document presents a Judas as one who "alone, knowing the truth as no others did, accomplished the mystery of the betrayal; by him all things, both earthly and heavenly, were thus thrown into confusion. They produce a fabricated work to this effect, which they entitle *The Gospel of Judas.*"[8]

Keep in mind that the Gnostics who wrote this document have no historical or theological connection to either the Old Testament or the books that make up our New Testament. The Gnostics were at war with the Old Testament God, the Creator. They believed that the God of the Old Testament was not the true God to be worshiped but was an ignorant Creator who created the world that we must escape. For many Gnostics their heroes were those who stood against God—Cain, the men of Sodom and Gomorrah—these were the ones who saw the truth and understood the secret necessary for salvation.⁹ The Gnostics vilified the Creator God of the Old Testament—to them a bloody rebel and a fool. Is it any wonder that they chose Judas to be one of their heroes?

Why the hype over this document that was known as fraudulent by the early church and has no basis in fact? Dr. James M. Robinson, the editor of the Nag Hammadi Library, is one of America's leading experts on ancient religious texts. In his book titled *The Secrets of Judas*, he writes:

> The Gospel of Judas, a long-lost second century fictional account that elevated Judas to hero status in the story, has been rediscovered! But it has been kept under wraps until now, to maximize its financial gain for its Swiss owners. The grand expose is being performed by the National Geographic Society, timed for the greatest impact, right at Easter. Those on the inside have been bought off (no doubt with considerably more than thirty pieces of silver), and sworn to silence on a stack of Bibles—or on a stack of papyrus leaves.¹⁰

He goes on to say, "What has gone on in this money-making venture is not a pleasant story—about how all this has been sprung upon us, the reading and viewing public—you have a right to know what has gone on."¹¹

Revisiting the New Testament Account

There is a theological issue we must discuss raised in the Judas Document. Actually, it is a matter that also confronts those of us who believe the New Testament account. In sum, it is this: how could Judas be blamed for betraying Jesus, when Jesus had every intention to go to Jerusalem and die on the cross (Matt 20:19; 26:2)? In the traditional Gospels, Jesus says, "What you do, do quickly" (John 13:27). Does not the Gnostic gospel answer that question by saying that Jesus *wanted* Judas to turn him in so that he could get on with his own liberation, his own freedom from the flesh? To ask it differently: how can Judas be culpable of Jesus' death if he is commanded and foreknown to hand him over?

Stay with me as we probe the heart of Judas and then answer this dilemma.

Despite all that Judas had going for him, and the grand potential that lay ahead, he had some hidden flaws. These were not obvious to the rest of the disciples, but they eventually were brought to the surface when his true intentions were revealed.

When Jesus washed his disciple's feet, he evidently washed the feet of Judas as well. So although his feet were as clean as those of the other disciples (John 13:15), his heart remained calloused and defiled. The feet that Jesus washed had already previously gone to the high priest to find out how much Jesus was worth!

Judas was covetous. In John 12 we have the story of Mary, Martha, and Lazarus entertaining Jesus. When Mary came with a pint of pure nard, an expensive perfume, she poured it on Jesus' feet and wiped them with her hair. The fragrance filled the house with sweetness, and Judas's heart with bitterness. Yet Judas was less than pleased with this expression of gratitude. To him it seemed like a waste, so he pragmatically asked, "Why wasn't this perfume sold and the money given to the poor?" John goes on to tell us that the perfume was worth a year's wages (John 12:5).

Don't be misled to think that Judas had a big heart for the needy. We read, "He did not say this because he cared about the poor but because he was a thief" (John 12:6). He was serving as treasurer and pilfered from what was given for the support of Jesus and His disciples. Under the cloak of religion, he was displaying some of the basest attitudes and motives. He was living a lie.

Judas was a skilled hypocrite. Luke reports that when the disciples gathered together after the Ascension, the apostle Peter commented that Judas had shared in their ministry. Evidently, he had all of the gifts, abilities, and powers granted the other disciples. When they cast out demons, Judas cast out demons. When they healed the sick, Judas healed the sick (cf. Luke 10:17). When they preached a message, so did he; and the disciples never suspected that anything was wrong; they even made him treasurer! Transparently, he must have come off as a trustworthy man.

How was it possible for Judas to do such miracles if he was unconverted? Perhaps demons simply cooperated because they knew that Judas was a fake, and they were helping to hide his true identity. Whatever the case, what was evident was that Judas lacked living faith and trust in God's gospel—Jesus Christ (cf. Jas 2:19; 1 John 2:19). The seeds of covetousness sprouted to become a tree with deep roots, a tree that would eventually hang Judas.

Let's remember that Judas was not the kind of person who slips into a church service late, sits in the back row, and then leaves during the benediction. No, he was discipled by Jesus. He would have volunteered to teach Sunday School; he might have been selected as an excellent deacon or elder or even a pastor. He had the behavior of a saint, though he had the heart of a devil.

Judas apparently was confused and angered by Jesus' lack of political vigor. He lacked the eyes of faith to see the messianic mission of Jesus. He became more like a double agent who was consistently a part and apart of all that Jesus was doing. Although the disciples trusted Judas, Jesus did not. He knew the details of Judas's heart.

According to their custom, they were gathered for the Feast of Passover. As they reclined around the table, Jesus, troubled in spirit, said to them, "One of you shall betray me." To the everlasting credit of the apostles, they never said, "Oh, I think I know who it is! Peter, I've always had some questions about you." No, they did not suspect each other but simply said, "Lord, is it I?" Matthew reveals that even Judas asked the question along with the rest. But he includes a disclaimer, "Surely not I, Rabbi?" (Matt 26:25). He decided to play the game with them; they were genuine, but he was not. He was as smooth as oil.

Trust Peter to have an overwhelming desire to know the identity of the culprit. So he whispered to John, possibly from across the table, "Ask him who it is." John did so, and Jesus whispered to John so that apparently no one else heard who it was, "It is the one to whom I will give this piece of bread when I have dipped it in the dish" (John 13:26).

The custom was for the host to dip a bit of mutton into sauce and give it to the person on his left, the honored guest. At this feast, the honored guest was Judas. So as Jesus dipped the mutton into the sauce and gave it to Judas, who probably was seated to his left, the place of honor, Jesus was in effect saying, "Judas, do you really want to go through with it? This is your last opportunity to back out of your deal. I am now honoring you and giving you acceptance with the disciples."

Judas, I believe, did not blush. Nor did he become pale or nervous. He sat calmly, unperturbed. We read, "As soon as Judas took the bread, Satan entered into him" (John 13:27). Please note in passing that it is possible for Satan to enter a man without a formal invitation. All that you need to do is harden your heart against Jesus and choose to do the devil's work.

Jesus replies, "What you are about to do, do quickly." Here we now address the theological conundrum: this a command or is it simply permission? This command resembles the one issued by Jesus to Judas in the Gethsemane, "Friend, do what you came for" (Matt 26:50). Is Judas simply obeying Jesus, or is he acting on his own accord? And further, why should Judas be faulted when it was Jesus' intention to be betrayed and be crucified?

Literally the command is, "What you are doing, do more quickly," or, "What you are doing, do faster." What this shows is that, rather than being the mere victim of events beyond his control, Jesus was in control (John 10:11,15–18). He knew exactly what was to happen and how the events would unfold. The hour of betrayal was not selected by the Sanhedrin or by Judas. And Judas does work faster, probably because he knew he had been discovered and was likely fearful that the plot would come unraveled if he did not act quickly.

So Jesus only commands him to do what he was already planning to do: to betray the Son of God. Jesus is giving him permission to act and to do so faster. Yes, it is true that it had been prophesied that Judas would betray Jesus, but in the Bible God is always presented as both knowing *and* planning the future. Even the actions of wicked men are a part of his plan.

For example, what shall we make of those who crucified Jesus? Shall we also exonerate them because they did what was prophesied and thus certain to come to pass? They also contributed to the death of Jesus in a way that was an absolute necessity from God's point of view. Yet in the Scriptures those who do evil are guilty, even when they fulfill the predetermined will of God. "This man was handed over to you by God's set purpose and foreknowledge; and you, with the help of wicked men put him to death by nailing him to the cross" (Acts 2:23). Please note: the men who carried out the predetermined will of God are described as wicked!

We must candidly admit that we cannot fully understand how both God's predetermined plan and human responsibility can coexist in the same act, but they do. The dilemma of Judas who helped Jesus carry out his plan to die and yet remains guilty is the same one that is found throughout the Scriptures. No matter how we might try to justify Judas, the Bible consistently finds him guilty, and condemned to an eternity of abandonment. Dante, after all, was right.

We never do God a favor when we do evil, even when God's will is being done. The devil entered Judas to help him make sure that the deed would be accomplished. Then we read, "As soon as Judas had taken the bread, he went out, and it was night" (John 13:30). The darkness of the night matches the darkness of his heart.

The temple guards appeared, led by Judas. Judas embraced Jesus under the pretense of love—the infamous fateful kiss—an outward sign, saying, "I adore You." But by that act he was giving a different message to the temple guards: "He is the man that you have come to arrest. Seize him!" Judas was so smooth that he made great treachery look like loyalty. But in his treachery he showed where his true loyalties laid: with the enemies of God.

Jesus responded with his characteristic gentleness, "Friend, do what you came for" (Matt 26:50). He did not appear to be angry, and, of course, he wasn't surprised. One more domino had fallen into place as Jesus went resolutely to the cross.

When Judas saw that Jesus had been condemned, remorse filled his heart. In a vain attempt to assuage his burning conscience, he threw the money down in the temple, into the inner shrine where only the priests could retrieve it. Then he also confessed the truth, "I have betrayed innocent blood." There was not a single fault in Jesus that Judas had ever detected; if any man deserved *not* to die, it was his Master; if anyone deserved to live and be worshipped, it was his Master.

As he watched Jesus being taken away to Pilate, the full enormity of his treachery finally began to dawn on him as he realized the Jewish leaders did indeed intend to put Jesus to death. He knew that

Pilate would most probably grant permission to have Jesus executed, and now, seeing the full results of what he had done, his conscience was seared. The façade was broken. Judas had enough sensitivity to experience remorse but not enough to experience true repentance.

Judas "repented" but his repentance was not genuine. Knowing that he could never make right what he had done; and knowing that Jesus would be condemned to death, he was led to regret and despair. Perhaps his perverted mind led him to believe that if he died at his own hand he could somehow atone for his own sin. Some Jews believed that there was an atoning element in the taking of one's own life. Two deaths are highlighted in Matthew 27, Judas and Jesus. Both died, but only one was guilty. The other, Jesus, was deemed innocent even by his betrayer.

Judas chose to bear his own remorse and guilt, rather than coming to Jesus for the forgiveness which would have been granted him. Remorse apart from Jesus leads to despair, so Judas was so overcome that he did what 25,000 Americans do every year: he committed suicide.[12] As a fulfillment of prophecy, he was unwilling to lay hold on Jesus Christ's forgiveness (1 John 1:9).

In the "Passion Play 2000," in Oberammergau, Judas is depicted as saying,

> Where can I go to hide my shame, to cast off the agony?
> No place is dark enough. No sea is deep enough. Earth
> open up and devour me! I can be no more. . . . Where
> is another man on whom such guilt rests? I am a
> contemptible traitor. How kind he has been toward
> me! How gently he comforted me when dark dejection
> oppressed my soul! . . . Not a disciple any longer, hated
> everywhere—despised everywhere . . . with this blazing fire
> in my gut!
>
> Everyone curses me. Still, there is one—one whose face I
> wish I could see again—to whom I could cling.
>
> Woe to me, for I am his murderer. Cursed hour in which
> my mother gave birth to me! . . . Here I will bring an end to
> my accursed life . . . Come you serpent, coil yourself around
> my throat and strangle the traitor.

Why did Jesus choose Judas? Possibly it's because Judas represents the whole human race. Jesus wanted to say for generations to come, "This is the heart of man. This is what man is—he has the ability to appear good on the outside, but inside he is rotten." "Christ took [Judas] among the apostles that it might not be a surprise and discouragement to his church if, at any time, the vilest scandals should break out in the best societies" (Henry, 132).

Judas discovered that the gate to hell is next door to the gate of heaven.

Scattered throughout the Scriptures are many epitaphs. Over Judas's grave we would have to write the words of Jesus, "It would have been better for him if he had not been born" (Matt 26:24).

So let us take our cue from the disciples and ask: is it *I*?

Endnotes

1 At the popular level, of course, see *The Last Temptation of Christ*, and *Jesus Christ Superstar*; see, too, John E. Hueter, *Matthew, Mark, Luke, John, Now Judas and His Redemption: In Search of the Real Judas* (Brookline Village, MA: Branden Press, 1983). On the more scholarly side of the printing press, see William Klassen, *Judas: Betrayer or Friend of Jesus* (Minneapolis: Fortress Press, 1996).

2 *Judas: Betrayer or Friend of Jesus.*

3 E. J. Dionne Jr., "A New Twist on Judas: Beyond the Buzz over Gospel's Publication," in *Washington Post*, Friday, April 14, 2006; A17.

4 This, of course, is the ancient heresy called "docetism."

5 Bart D. Ehrman, "Christianity Turned on Its Head: The Alternative Vision of the Gospel of Judas," in *The Gospel of Judas*, ed. Rodolphe Kasser, Marvin Meyer, and Gregor Wurst (Washington D. C.: National Geographic, 2006), 120.

6 See also *Judas and the Gospel Jesus: Have We Missed the Truth About Christianity?* (Grand Rapids: Baker Books, 2006).

7 Also known as *Detection and Overthrew of the False Knowledge.*

8 Gregor Wurst, "Irenaeus of Lyon and the Gospel of Judas," in *The Gospel of Judas*, 123.

9 Cf. Ehrman, "Christianity Turned on Its Head," 90.

10 James M. Robinson, *The Secrets of Judas* (San Francisco: Harper, 2006), vii.

11 Ibid.

12 For a fascinating analysis of this sad phenomenon, see the interesting work of Kay Redfield Jamison, *Night Falls Fast: Understanding Suicide* (New York: Vintage Books, 2000).

The Reconstruction of Jewish Communities During the Persian Empire

Edwin M. Yamauchi

A number of mid-twentieth century popular works—including the British archaeologist John Garstang's *The Story of Jericho* (1940) and the German journalist Werner Keller's *Und die Bibel hat doch Recht* (1955), translated as *The Bible as History* (1956)—spread the notion that "archaeology has confirmed the Bible." Subsequent discoveries and interpretations have proven many of these earlier claims to be unfounded and have led scholars to adopt a more skeptical view.[1] Since the 1970s biblical scholars have moved to a position of radical skepticism about the historical veracity of biblical texts. In what follows, I hope to demonstrate the need, and the possibility, for a more balanced view.

In some judicial systems, as in the United States, the accused is presumed innocent until proven guilty. In other judicial systems, the accused is presumed guilty, and the burden of proof rests on the shoulders of the suspect. Biblical archeology appears to have swung heavily to the latter position in recent decades, and the Bible stands accused of offering, at best, incomplete testimony, or at worst, deception in its account of Jewish history. Scholars often seek proof for biblical texts in an external reference in a nonbiblical document but must always beware of the fallacy of an "argument from silence." Given the fragmentary nature of the archaeological evidence, the mere absence of evidence does not prove that a text is made up of whole cloth. Often the search for truth is hindered by the decay and disintegration of evidence. Except in very dry climates, ancient papyri have disappeared, leaving behind only their clay bullae, or seal impressions. It has been estimated that Egyptian temples used 24 million meters of papyri; of these, only 13 meters from Abusir and a similar length from Ilahun have been preserved. Of the 112 million pay vouchers to the Roman legions, only six and a fragment of a seventh have survived. Of the hundreds of synagogues in Palestine before AD 70, only the remains of three or four have been identified. Of Menander's more than 100 plays, only one complete play has been preserved. Epigraphic or inscriptional evidence of persons mentioned in the Bible surfaces from time to time, including an ossuary of Alexander son of Simon (of Cyrene) in 1941, an inscription of Pontius Pilate in 1961, the ossuary of Caiaphas in 1990, the inscription of the "House of David" in 1993, and the ossuary of "James the son of Joseph, brother of Jesus" in 2002, the authenticity of which is now in dispute.[2]

Assyrian and Babylonian cuneiform texts name many of the Israelite kings from the ninth century BC and later, bullae of Baruch and other figures associated with Jeremiah have also been identified. We still lack attestations of biblical figures who predate David, but it should be remembered that no archive of inscriptions has yet been recovered from ancient Phoenicia or ancient Damascus. No monumental inscriptions have been found from the Hasmonean Dynasty, nor from Herod the Great. To doubt the reality of biblical figures because of the lack of inscriptional corroboration is a non sequitur.

The period of the second temple—that is, the Persian and Hellenistic eras—has received intense recent scholarly attention. According to Paolo Sacchi, today, in contrast to the past, "scholarly interest has come more and more to be focused on the history of the second temple period instead of the history of Israel in general."[3] This shift stems in part from many scholars' conviction that many of the Old Testament texts came from, or were redacted in, the period of the second temple.[4] Other scholars, such as Peter Frei, have argued for the authorization of the Torah by the Persian authorities, noting as a parallel the codification of Egyptian law by Darius I.[5] The argument also results from the claim of revisionist scholars, dubbed "minimalists" by their critics, who credit the late period for the creation of all of the books of the Hebrew Bible, including the Torah, and therefore reject the Hebrew Bible's account of anything earlier than the period of the divided monarchies—that is, they dismiss as fiction all the narratives about the patriarchs, Moses, Joshua, David, and Solomon.[6] The conclusions of these "minimalist" scholars were trumpeted in an article, "False Testament," by Daniel Lazare in the March 2002 issue of *Harper's Magazine*. Lazare based his argument on the claims of a few radical scholars of the Hebrew Bible and depended heavily upon the popular revisionist account *The Bible Unearthed*, written by Israel Finkelstein of Tel Aviv University in collaboration with Neil Asher Silberman.[7] Finkelstein's own revisionism depends on his idiosyncratic redating of pottery, for which he has been criticized by other archaeologists, including Amihai Mazar and Finkelstein's former professor, Anson F. Rainey.[8] William G. Dever, a leading Syro-Palestinian archaeologist, has decried postmodernism's influence on the "minimalist" historians' interpretation of the Bible and archaeology as leading to their radical revisionism.[9] He claims that they reject the Hebrew Bible as a reliable source for the history of the Iron Age "largely because of its predominantly *theological* character, that is, its basic theme of 'salvation-history' (German *Heilsgeschichte*)." Dever sees the problem as one of hypocrisy, arguing that the deconstructionist and new literary critical methods of the minimalists end "by reading out of the texts the specifically *biblical* 'liberation theology' only to replace it with their own, usually quite arbitrary 'liberation theologies,' often sympathizing with Third World Theology."[10]

The Persian Era

The debate about the reliability of competing claims in biblical archeology may only be tested by considering sources, and the history of the Jews during the Persian Empire (539–330) provides an excellent opportunity for such a test. The main primary sources are the biblical books—2 Chronicles, Isaiah, Ezekiel, Daniel, Esther, Ezra, Nehemiah, Haggai, Zechariah, and Malachi—supplemented by important cuneiform texts such as the Babylonian Chronicles, Old Persian inscriptions, the Cyrus Cylinder, the Murashu archive, and archaeological excavations in Palestine, Mesopotamia, and Persia.[11] Some ostraca, seals, and bullae (seal impressions) also corroborate biblical figures.[12] Later Greek sources such as Herodotus, Ctesias, Berossus, and Josephus provide further information, but the biblical texts remain the most important narrative sources.[13] For secondary sources, as Williamson points out, we now have numerous histories of the Persian Empire that have superseded A. T. Olmstead's 1948 classic, *History of the Persian Empire*, notably the comprehensive *The Cambridge History of Iran*, vol. II, *The Median and Achaemenian Periods*, and, on the Jews in the Persian Empire in particular, *The Cambridge History of Judaism*, vol. I, *Introduction; The Persian Period.*[14] Jon L. Berquist has attempted to apply a sociological method to the period in *Judaism in Persia's Shadow.*[15]

The area of Syria, Lebanon, and Palestine, which the Persians called "Beyond the River (i.e., the Euphrates)," is the focus of a new journal, *Transeuphratene*, and a series of essays by Josette Elayi and Jean Sapin, *Beyond the River*. Elayi and Sapin lament that scholars had largely neglected the area during the Persian period, presumably because they were primarily interested in either the earlier civilizations of the Egyptians and Mesopotamians or the later civilizations of the Greeks and Romans.[16] Cyrus, founder of the Persian Empire and the greatest Achaemenid king, reigned from 559 to 530 BC, establishing Persian dominance over the Medes in 550, conquering Lydia and Ionia in 547–546, and capturing Babylon in 539.[17]

Isaiah 44:28 and 45:1 speak of Cyrus as the Lord's "shepherd" and His "anointed."[18] Most scholars believe that Cyrus was an Iranian polytheist, but a number, noting the continuity of religious thought between Cyrus and Darius, have sought to attribute the magnanimity of Cyrus to the teachings of Zoroaster. Whether Cyrus had religious motives, he reversed the policy of his predecessors, the Assyrians and the Babylonians: instead of deporting the people he conquered, he permitted them, including the Jews, to return to their homeland.[19]

During the months following the capture of Babylon, cuneiform texts recorded the Persian king's benefactions to Mesopotamian sanctuaries. Ezra 1:1–4 contains a Hebrew copy of the decree of Cyrus, and a record of the Aramaic memorandum is given in Ezra 6:3–5. Earlier scholars had questioned the authenticity of the decree in Ezra because of the document's Jewish phraseology, but documents and archeological remains from the Persian period have provided convincing evidence of its authenticity.[20] The phrase in Ezra 1:2, "The LORD, the God of heaven, has given me all the kingdoms of the earth," runs parallel to the statement of an inscription of Cyrus from Ur, "The great gods have delivered all the lands into my hand."[21]

Richard Frye notes a distinctive feature of Cyrus's proclamations: "Although his inscriptions are in Akkadian for local consumption, one misses any mention of his own gods in them," and older conquerors in the Near East would characteristically have mentioned them.[22]

The "Verse Account of Nabonidus" and the "Cyrus Cylinder," which indicate that, as one of his first acts as ruler, Cyrus decided to return the gods that Nabonidus had removed from their sanctuaries, impressively corroborate Cyrus's policy of toleration.[23] The latter document relates, "I (also) gathered all their (former) inhabitants and returned (to them) their habitations." A fragment of the Cyrus Cylinder, identified in 1970, states that Cyrus restored Babylon's inner wall and moats.[24] Excavations at Uruk and Ur reveal that Cyrus also worked to restore temples there.[25] More evidence exists of Cyrus's tolerance, which relates directly to the experience of the Jews. Stefan Timm has interpreted some cuneiform tablets to indicate Cyrus's repatriation of Arameans from Neirab in northern Syria to southern Mesopotamia in the early reign of Nebuchadnezzar—providing a striking parallel to the experience of the Jews.[26]

According to the lists in Ezra 2 and Nehemiah 7, about 50,000 responded to Cyrus's offer of an opportunity to return to their homes. Many scholars who question whether such a large group would have joined the initial return under Sheshbazzar have suggested that the totals must include others who came later. Baron observes, "In Ezra's list of those who participated in the first return under Zerubbabel, there are recorded among 'the men of the people of Israel' many descendants of exiles from localities which formerly belonged to the northern kingdom."[27] In particular the names "Pahath-Moab" and "Elam" in Ezra 2:6–7,14, and in Nehemiah 7:11–13,19, may refer to Israelites exiled from Transjordan (1 Chr 5:26) and those settled by the Assyrians in Media (2 Kgs 17:6) and in Elam (Isa 11:11).[28] According to Ezra 6:8, Cyrus not only permitted the Jews to return but also gave them *carte blanche* authorization for funds from the imperial treasury. Since the accounts in Haggai and Zechariah do not speak of support from the Persian treasury, some scholars have questioned the reality of these promises. Extrabiblical evidence, however, leaves no doubt that such authorization was a consistent policy of Persian kings to help restore sanctuaries in their empire. A memorandum written by Bagoas, the Persian governor of Judah, and Delaiah, governor of Samaria, concerning the rebuilding of the Jewish temple at Elephantine, relates their intention: "to rebuild it on its site as it was before, and the meal-offering and incense to be made on that altar as it used to be."[29] Emil Kraeling interprets this passage to mean that this directive presumably suggests "that the rebuilding be done at government expense"—and even hints at government subsidies for the offerings.[30]

Hensley observes, "The gods of the foreign workmen at Persepolis received commodities from the Persepolis treasury equally with the Persian Ahuramazda."[31] Cyrus repaired the Eanna temple at Uruk and the Enunmah at Ur. Cambyses gave funds for the temple at Sais in Egypt.[32] Darius ordered the rebuilding from top to bottom of the temple of Amon at Hibis in the Khargah Oasis, excavated in 1941 by Winlock.[33] Darius also restored the temple of Ptah in Egypt. Both Cyrus's original decree (Ezra 6:7) and Darius's renewal of the permission to rebuild the temple specify that it should be refounded "on its site," which was a matter of special concern in the restoration or rebuilding of ancient temples.

Darius I (522–486), who also appears in Ezra, offers more opportunities to consider biblical and extrabiblical sources pertaining to the position of the Jews under the Persian empire. When opposition to the Jewish attempt to rebuild the temple reached the ears of Tattenai, the governor of the province, he sent a letter to Darius (Ezra 5:7–12) and received a response from the king himself (6:6–12).[34] Some historians have questioned whether the Persian kings would have been personally interested in the affairs of the Jews in far-off Palestine, and whether they would have intervened directly. The publication of the Elamite texts from Persepolis has confirmed that such inquiries were sent directly to the king.

In 1933–1934, several thousand tablets and fragments—known as the Fortification Tablets—were found in the fortification wall of Persepolis, and in 1969, Richard Hallock published two thousand dating from the thirteenth to the twenty-eighth year of Darius (509–494 BC).[35] Between 1936 and 1938, additional Elamite texts, which reveal the king's close attention to minute details, were discovered in the treasury area of Persepolis, and George Cameron published more than one hundred of them in 1948, 1958, and 1965.[36] In an important monograph on the significance of the rebuilding of the temple and the roles of Haggai and Zechariah, P. R. Bedford suggests that Haggai and Zechariah held out expectations that remained unrealized.[37] The completion of the temple did not solve the issue of political autonomy, and Bedford believes that it was "in defence of the continuing eastern diaspora that Ezra-Nehemiah came to be written."[38] According to Haggai 2:3, the older members who could remember the splendor of Solomon's temple were disappointed when they saw the smaller size of Zerubbabel's temple (cf. Ezra 3:12). Yet the second temple, although not as grand as the first, enjoyed a much longer life. The only visible remains of Zerubbabel's building, identified by Kenyon, is a straight joint of stones with heavy bosses about 33 meters north of the southeast corner of the temple. Dunand compared this feature to Persian masonry found in Phoenicia.[39] The Persians collected a great variety of taxes from their subjects (Ezra 4:13)—between $20 million and $35 million annually.[40] Priests and other temple personnel were often given exemptions from enforced labor or taxes (Ezra 7:24). The Gadatas Inscription of Darius I to a governor in Ionia in western Turkey reveals Darius's concern for the priests of Apollo at a temple near Magnesia.[41]

Xerxes (485–465), the Persian king best known for his unsuccessful invasion of Greece in 480–479, appears in the book of Esther as Ahasuerus. The story of Esther has understandably attracted the attention of feminist scholars and others interested in gender issues.[42] In general, these scholars classify Esther as simply an entertaining tale, despite its authentic Persian features corroborated by archaeology, such as a gate at the palace of Susa, and an official named Marduka, who may possibly be Mordecai.[43] The story of how the Jews were saved by God's providence, although He is never explicitly mentioned in the text, has inspired Jews in times of great persecution and is celebrated in the joyous holiday of Purim. Although no copies of Esther have been found at Qumran, fragments of an Aramaic composition labeled "Proto-Esther" have been recovered from Cave IV.[44]

Artaxerxes I (464–424) was nicknamed by the Greeks *Longimanus*. According to Plutarch, "the first Artaxerxes, among all the kings of Persia the most remarkable for a gentle and noble spirit, was surnamed the Long-handed, his right hand being longer than his left, and was the son of Xerxes."[45] When Artaxerxes I came to the throne, he faced a major revolt in Egypt, which was to last a decade. The leaders, Inarus, a Libyan, and Amyrtaeus of Sais, defeated the Persian satrap Achaemenes, the brother of Xerxes, and gained control of much of the Delta region by 462. The Athenians, who had been at war with the Persians since the Persian invasion of Greece in 490 BC, sent 200 ships to aid the rebels.[46] In 459, they helped capture Memphis, the capital of Lower Egypt. Against a background of revolution, the Persians may have found it expedient to support Ezra's return in 458 to secure a loyal buffer state in Palestine.

In 456 Megabyzus, the satrap of Syria, advanced against Egypt with a huge fleet and army.[47] In the course of 18 months, he was able to suppress the revolt and capture Inarus. A fleet of 40 Athenian ships with 6,000 men sailed into a Persian trap. In spite of promises made by Megabyzus, Inarus was impaled in 454 at the instigation of Amestris, the mother of Artaxerxes I. Angered at the betrayal, Megabyzus led a revolt against the king from 449 to 446. If the events of Ezra 4:7–23 took place in the midst of such upheaval, Artaxerxes I would have been suspicious of the building activities in Jerusalem. Why would he have commissioned Nehemiah in 445 to rebuild the walls of the city? By then, both the Egyptian revolt and the rebellion of Megabyzus had been resolved.

Ezra and Nehemiah

The books of Ezra and Nehemiah provide more opportunities to link scriptural and archeological evidence. Kenneth Hoglund has clarified Ezra's mission and Nehemiah's refortification of Jerusalem as part of the imperial Achaemenid strategy against the dangers of Athenian imperialism, which had already drawn the coastal Palestinian city of Dor in its Delian League.[48] Matthew Stolper's recent reexamination of a Babylonian legal text has led him to conclude that the text's parallel reference to the governor and the "scribe-chancellors" "does not undermine the suggestion that Ezra 4:8 f. and 17 were constructed from the subscript of an authentic administrative letter."[49] Richard Steiner disputes David Janzen's claim that the letter authorizing Ezra's mission is not authentic: "In short, the legal component of Ezra's mission and even the term for it fit squarely into the fifth century B.C.E."[50]

Artaxerxes' decision to commission Ezra the scribe to administer the Law to his people has troubled some critics, but it conforms perfectly to Persian policy. Darius's commission to Udjahorresenet, an Egyptian priest and scholar, provides a close parallel. Udjahorresenet had also helped Cambyses, the son of Cyrus, who had conquered Egypt in 525.[51] Darius commanded the codification of the Egyptian laws in Demotic and Aramaic by the chief men of Egypt—a task that required 15 years, from 518 to 503 BC. On the reverse side of the Demotic Chronicle, Darius ordered "that the wise men be assembled . . . from among the warriors, the priests and the scribes of Egypt so that they may set down in writing the ancient laws of Egypt."[52]

Most recent scholars, including H. G. M. Williamson and Joseph Blenkinsopp, have affirmed the traditional order of Ezra before Nehemiah.[53] Nehemiah was sent forth as the governor of Judah. In Nehemiah 5:15, he referred to previous "governors." Kurt Galling believed that Judah did not have governors, and therefore he suggested that the reference here was to governors of Samaria.[54] New archaeological evidence, however, confirms the accuracy of Nehemiah's reference to previous governors of Judah. In 1974, Nahman Avigad observed a collection of about 70 bullae and two seals from an unknown provenance, which provide convincing evidence that there was a series of governors prior to Nehemiah.[55] One of the seals is the first to bear the inscription YHD, the Persian designation of the province of Judah as already known from other seal impressions and coins. Relying on paleography, Avigad dates the seals and bullae to the sixth and early fifth century BC.

The exiles returned to a tiny enclave surrounded by hostile neighbors: the Samaritans to the north, the Ammonites to the east, the Arabs and the Edomites to the south, and the Phoenicians to the west.[56] There had been opposition to the rebuilding of the temple, and when Judah's neighbors learned of Nehemiah's plans, there was even greater concern about the attempt to rebuild the walls. The Samarians' opposition was motivated not primarily by religious differences but by political considerations. A vigorous governor of Judah would threaten the authority of the governor of Samaria. The Persian satraps of neighboring provinces, especially in Anatolia, constantly opposed one another.[57] The book of Nehemiah also chronicles such hostilities.[58] Although Nehemiah does not call Sanballat governor, an important Elephantine papyrus makes his position explicit. A letter dated 407 BC to Bagoas, the governor of Judah, refers to "Delaiah and Shelemiah, the sons of Sanballat the governor (*peha*) of Samaria."[59] The letter offers interesting evidence that Sanballat's sons both bear Yahwistic names, which does not mean that the Samarians were Yahwists but simply indicates the syncretistic character of the Samarian religion.[60]

In 1962 Bedouins found a cave in Wadi ed-Daliyeh, northwest of Jericho, which contained fourth-century BC papyri along with the grim remains of about 200 residents of Samaria—men, women, and children who had tried unsuccessfully to flee from the troops of Alexander the Great.[61] On the basis of papponymy—the recurrence of the same name in alternating generations—Cross has used the data from these Samaria papyri to reconstruct a list of governors over Samaria—one of whom, Tobiah (Neh 1:10), had a name that means "Yahweh is good."[62] He may have been a Judaizing Ammonite, but he was more probably a Yahwist Jew as indicated not only by his own name but also that of his son, Jehohanan (Neh 6:18). Some scholars suggest that Tobiah was descended from an aristocratic family that owned estates in Gilead and was influential in Transjordan and in Jerusalem as early as the eighth century BC.[63] Benjamin Mazar has correlated varying lines of evidence to reconstruct a genealogical table of the Tobiad family.[64]

The region of Ammon was located in Transjordan around the modern capital of Amman. Tobiah is called *'ebed*—literally, "slave" or "servant." The Revised Standard Version of the Bible rendered the term literally as a derisive epithet, "Tobias, the Ammonite, the slave." But *'ebed* was often used both in biblical and in extrabiblical texts to refer to high officials. Tobiah was probably the governor of Ammon under the Persians. A later Tobiah, who is explicitly called "the governor of Ammon," was a leader of the Jewish Hellenizers under Ptolemy II, a relationship that is also illumined by the Zenon papyri.[65]

The site of 'Araq el-Emir ("Caverns of the Prince"), about 11 miles west of Amman, was the center of the Tobiads. The visible remains of a large building, 60 by 120 feet, on top of the hill, Qasr el-'Abd ("Castle of the Slave"), have been interpreted as a Jewish temple built by Tobiah (no. 11). On two halls are inscriptions with the name Tobiah in Aramaic characters. Much dispute surrounds the date of the inscriptions. Mazar favors the sixth or fifth century BC, Naveh the fourth century, and Cross the fourth or third century. Lapp, who reexcavated the site in 1961–1962, favors a date in the third or second century.[66]

Geshem (Neh 1:10), who is also called Gashmu in Nehemiah 6:1, a variant which would have been closer to the original Arabic name, offers an example similar to Tobiah's. *Jasuma,* which means "bulky" or "stout," is found in various Arabic inscriptions, including Safaitic, Lihyanite, Thamudic, and Nabataean. A Lihyanite inscription from Dedan (modern Al-'Ula) in Northwest Arabia reads, "Jashm son of Shahr and 'Abd, governor of Dedan," whom Fredrick Winnett and William Albright identify with the biblical Geshem.[67] In 1947, several silver vessels, some with Aramaic inscriptions dating to the late fifth century BC, were discovered at Tell el-Maskhuta near Ismaila by the Suez Canal. One inscription bore the name "Qaynu the son of Gashmu, the king of Qedar," which also seems to refer to the biblical Geshem. We may conclude that Geshem was in charge of a powerful north Arabian confederacy, which controlled vast areas from northeast Egypt to northern Arabia and southern Palestine. Geshem may have opposed Nehemiah's development of an independent kingdom because he feared that it might interfere with his lucrative trade in myrrh and frankincense. In spite of opposition from without and of dissension from within due to economic problems, Nehemiah was able to galvanize the people by his leadership so that they were able to complete the rebuilding of the walls, which had been in a ruinous state for nearly 150 years, in only 52 days (Neh 6:15).

Life in the Diaspora: Other Exilic Communities

K. L. Younger Jr. and Ran Zadok have compiled onomastic evidence of Israelites deported by the Assyrians and of the Judeans deported by the Babylonians, which indicates that, in a few cases, the Israelites retained their identity for a century.[68] No doubt the exiles were initially saddened and disoriented in their enforced exile, as Psalm 137:1–6 poignantly expressed. Once the exiles were transported to their new homes, however, most were not reduced to a position of abject slavery but enjoyed considerable freedom.[69] Others became dependents of the palace or the temples, and they worked upon lands that belonged to these institutions. Though the Babylonians did use slaves, they had more than enough from natural reproduction.[70]

The Judean exiles settled in various communities in lower Mesopotamia.[71] Judging from the place names, they were settled on the ruins of earlier cities such as at *Tel Abib*, "the mound destroyed by a flood" (Ezek 3:15); *Tel Mela*, "mound of salt"; and *Tel Harsha*, "mound covered with potsherds" (Ezra 2:59). These lists also indicate that the exiles must have maintained some cohesion among members of local communities since those who returned went "each to his own town" (Ezra 2:1 = Neh 7:6). The descendants of the exiles evidently prospered: those who returned brought with them numerous servants and animals and were able to make contributions for the sacred services (Ezra 2:65–69, 8:26–27; Neh 7:70–72).

Ezekiel provides an important source for what life was like in Exile, although his book was subject to much scepticism by earlier scholars.[72] Recent scholarship has restored respect for the integrity and authenticity of the book as an important source for the exile.[73] Ezekiel, who was probably exiled with Jehoiachin, settled on the Kebar River, an irrigation canal near Nippur, where he was married and had his own house.[74] He refers to both the elders of the house of Judah (8:1) and the elders of the house of Israel (14:1; 20:1), who met with him. With the birth of a second and third generation, many Jews established roots in Mesopotamia. But Josephus declared that "many remained in Babylon, being unwilling to leave their possessions."[75] The Murashu Tablets, which were found in a room at Nippur in 1893, shed fascinating light on the Jews in Mesopotamia during the later Persian period. From 1898 to 1912 Hermann V. Hilprecht and Albert T. Clay published 480 of these texts out of a reported total of 730 tablets. In 1974 Matthew Stolper wrote a dissertation using 179 hitherto unpublished Murashu texts from the University Museum in Pennsylvania and four from the British Museum. He reports that the total of texts and fragments that date from the reigns of Artaxerxes I (464–424) and Darius II (423–404), mainly from the years 440 to 414, is now known to be 879—the largest single source for information about conditions in Achaemenid Babylonia.[76]

Murashu and his sons, who managed agricultural land held as estates and fiefs, loaned out money, equipment, and animals and collected taxes and rents. Studies of the names of their clients have demonstrated that some were Jews, and no doubt many Jews, particularly those in official positions, adopted Babylonian names.[77] Extrabiblical evidence indicates that at times those with non-Jewish names gave their children Yahwistic names, and other parents with Yahwistic names gave their children non-Jewish—i.e., Babylonian, West Semitic, and even Iranian—names.[78] Yahwistic names, which end in the theophoric element *Yb/Yw/Yhw* for Yahweh (spelled *ia-a-ma*), are useful for identifying Jews and their families in the Murashu archive.[79] Examples include *Tobyaw*, or Tobiah; *Banayaw*, or Benaiah; and *Zabadyaw*, or Zebadiah. Of those identified as Jews, 38 bore Yahwistic names, 23 West Semitic names, six Akkadian names, and two Iranian names. The Jews, who were from 28 settlements, constituted only about 3 percent of the 2500 individuals named in these records.[80] As these texts deal only with the countryside, they do not yield any information on the possible presence of Jews at Nippur itself.

The Jews appear as contracting parties, agents, witnesses, collectors of taxes, and royal officials. A Gedaliah served as a mounted archer, a Hanani managed the royal poultry farm, and a Jedaiah was an agent of a royal steward.[81] There seem to have been no social or commercial barriers between the Jews and the Babylonians. Their prosperous situation may explain why some chose to remain in Mesopotamia. At the same time their growing confidence may explain why, as Bickerman has shown in his analysis, the proportion of Yahwistic names grew larger in the second generation.[82]

A remarkable cuneiform tablet from the reign of Darius, dated to his 22nd year, has shed new light on a number of Jews listed in a sales contract who lived in *uru ia-a-hu-du*—that is, "the city of Judah."[83] Many of the names in Akkadian can be compared to Hebrew names found in Scriptures: Yahu-azari (Yeho'ezer), Abdu-Yahu (Obadiah), Nadabi-Yama (Nedabiahu), and Nahhum (Nahum).

The Aramaic documents from the mercenary garrison on the Elephantine Island near Aswan provide another important source of extrabiblical information on the Jewish diaspora in Egypt during the exilic period.[84] The Elephantine Community, whose origins are obscure, was a military garrison serving under the Persian occupation of Egypt.[85] Bezalel Porten has pointed out the syncretistic aspects of their religion, while Michael Silverman argues that their religion was more assimilationist than syncretistic.[86] It is clear that, whatever the total numbers of the deported, the upper classes were especially targeted for deportation (Dan 1:3–4), leaving behind most of the poor (2 Kgs 25:12; Jer 39:10; 52:16) to work the vineyards and the fields.[87] The biblical Chronicler (2 Chr 36:17–20) leaves the impression that the deportations had left Palestine essentially desolate. The impression given by the hyperbolic language of Hans Barstad seeks to overturn the "Myth of the Empty Land," but archaeological surveys of Galilee indicate that the Assyrian attacks, beginning with Tiglath-pileser, III did desolate the area.[88] We now have an abundance of epigraphic as well as archaeological evidence for Palestine during the Persian period, during which some limited forms of worship were continued in the ruined area of the temple (Jer 41–5).[89]

The Scriptures themselves pass over developments in Palestine and stress the contribution of the returning exiles from Babylonia. Some have questioned this emphasis. Martin Noth comments that, although "very important developments in life and thought took place among those deported to Babylon. . . . Nevertheless even the Babylonian group represented a mere outpost, whereas Palestine was and remained the central arena of Israel's history."[90] In light of the intellectual and spiritual leaders' deportation, however, the Scriptures may reflect the true historical situation. As Donald Gowan comments, we do not have sufficient evidence or probability "of an active, creative group in the land during the exile, although the continuance of some form of Yahwism is not to be doubted."[91]

Conclusions

Some of the Jewish deportees may have at first been awed by the great ziggurat, the magnificent temple of Marduk, and the 50 other temples in Babylon (Ezek 20:32), but most Jews seem to have dismissed the thousands of idols in Mesopotamia (Isa 46:1–2).[92] Deprived of the temple, the exiles laid emphasis on the observation of the Sabbath, on the laws of purity, on prayer and confession (Dan 9; Ezra 9; Neh 9), and on fasting to commemorate the tragic events of the Babylonian attacks (Zech 7:3,5; 8:19).[93] The exiles placed great stress on studying and expounding the Torah, as we see in the description of Ezra, the scribe as "a teacher well versed in the Law of Moses" (Ezra 7:6).

Many have surmised synagogues probably began in Mesopotamia during the exile, where the gatherings held under the auspices of Ezekiel have been seen as precursors to the synagogue assemblies (Ezek 8:1; 14:1). The reading, interpreting, and possibly the translating of the Scriptures into Aramaic—in important features of the later synagogue service—were part of the great meeting described in Nehemiah 8. Archaeological and inscriptional evidence for synagogues has not been found from the exilic period in Mesopotamia, however; the earliest evidence is from Ptolemaic Egypt.[94]

The Jews were hardly alone in experiencing the hardships of an enforced exile. Nor were they alone in attempting to maintain their identity, inasmuch as groups like the Egyptians tried to do so. But all other exiled communities in Babylonia except the Jews were eventually assimilated and disappeared as recognizable entities. Eph'al remarks, "The outstanding survival of the Jews in Babylonia as an entity-in-exile in the subsequent period—in contrast to the disappearance of all the other foreign ethnic groups there—remains, however, a problem demanding a fuller explanation."[95] No doubt, the key to the Jews' survival was their faith in a God who, although punishing them with exile, remained nonetheless a faithful, covenant-keeping Lord, who would watch over them even in a foreign diaspora and restore them to their Holy Land.

Unlike the fate of the members of the so-called "10 lost tribes," who had already lapsed from the exclusive worship of Yahweh, the exiles transported to Mesopotamia were apparently repulsed by the rampant idolatry they beheld in Babylon. The recovery of over 800 idols from the Assyrian period, half from Jerusalem, indicates that idolatry persisted in Judah despite the fulminations of the prophets. What the prophets could not achieve by their preaching, the trauma of the Babylonian exile accomplished. As Stern observes, "Since the beginning of the Persian period, in all the territories of Judah and Samaria, there is not a single piece of evidence for any pagan cults!"[96]

Endnotes

1 *Newsweek* journalist Jeffrey L. Sheler's *Is the Bible True?* (San Francisco: Harper, 1999), while more balanced, still oversimplifies many complex issues.

2 See recent issues of the *Biblical Archaeology Review* for the ongoing controversy. See also Craig A. Evans, *Jesus and the Ossuaries* (Waco, TX: Baylor University Press, 2003).

3 Paolo Sacchi, *The History of the Second Temple Period* (Sheffield: Sheffield Academic Press, 2000), 9.

4 Joseph Blenkinsopp, "The Social Role of the Prophets," *Journal for the Study of the Old Testament* 93 (2001): 43; "Haggai, Zechariah 1–8, Malachi, Joel, much if not all of Isaiah 54–66, a good part of Isaiah 1–39, and a variably calculated percentage of the material in other prophetic books, depending on who is doing the calculating, are assigned to this period."

5 See Frei's article and responses to his proposal in *Persia and Torah*, ed. James W. Watts (Atlanta: Society of Biblical Literature, 2001).

6 For a sharp critique of minimalist approaches, see William G. Dever, *What Did the Biblical Writers Know & When Did They Know It?* (Grand Rapids: Eerdmans, 2001). Philip R. Davies, *In Search of "Ancient Israel"* (Sheffield: Sheffield Academic Press, 1992), 95, places the birth of "biblical Israel" in the Persian period. Etienne Nodet, *A Search for the Origins of Judaism* (tr. Ed Crowley; Sheffield: Sheffield Academic Press, 1997), 387, opts for the Hellenistic era as the time when the Torah was created. Positive evaluations of the archaeological and inscriptional evidence for the patriarchal period may be found in *Essays on the Patriarchal Narratives*, ed. Alan R. Millard and Donald J. Wiseman (Leicester: Inter-Varsity Press, 1980), and for the exodus in James K. Hoffmeier, *Israel in Egypt* (New York: Oxford University Press, 1997). On Solomon see Alan R. Millard, "Texts and Archaeology: Weigh the Evidence, the Case for King Solomon," *Palestine Exploration Quarterly* 123 (1991): 19–27; and Kenneth A. Kitchen, "How We Know When Solomon

Ruled," *Biblical Archaeology Review* 27.5 (2001): 32–37, 58. The attempt of some revisionist scholars to retranslate or to minimize the "House of David" inscription found at Tel Dan reveals their stubborn inclination to reject any corroborative evidence. See Avraham Biran, *Biblical Dan* (Jerusalem: Israel Exploration Society, 1994); Anson F. Rainey, "The 'House of David' and the House of the Deconstructionists," *Biblical Archaeology Review* 20.6 (1994): 47, commenting on Philip R. Davies, "'House of David' Built on Sand," *Biblical Archaeology Review* 20.4 (1994): 54–55.

7 Lazare based his argument on the work of Keith Whitelam of Stirling University and Phillip R. Davies of Sheffield University, as well as N. P. Lemche and Thomas L. Thompson of the University of Copenhagen, among others. Coincidentally *The New York Times* (March 9, 2002) carried an article "As Rabbis Face Facts, Bible Tales Are Wilting," reporting on the rejection of the historicity of much of the Hebrew Bible reflected in *Etz Hayim* ("The Tree of Life"), a new commentary released by the United Synagogue of Conservative Judaism. Israel Finkelstein and Neil Asher Silberman, *The Bible Unearthed* (New York: Free Press, 2001).

8 Ziony Zevit, "Three Debates About Biblical Archaeology," *Biblica* 83 (2002): 22, observes, "The archaeological community as a whole rejects Finkelstein's ceramic chronology on well argued archaeological grounds." A. F. Rainey, "Stones for Bread: Archaeology versus History," *Near Eastern Archaeology* 64.3 (2001): 140–49.

9 William G. Dever, "Save Us from Postmodern Malarkey," *Biblical Archaeology Review* 26.2 (2000): 28–35, 68–69.

10 Dever, *What Did the Biblical Writers Know and When Did They Know It?*, 262. Though there will continue to be heated controversy over the earlier periods prior to David's reign, there is greater consensus about the later period of Jewish history, during the Babylonian exile and their return from captivity, thanks to the abundance of extrabiblical evidence.

11 For Chronicles, see John W. Kleinig, "Recent Research in Chronicles," *Currents in Research: Biblical Studies* 2 (1994): 43–76. The majority of scholars date the composition of Daniel to the Hellenistic period, due to the close correlation of chapter 11 to the events of the Maccabean Revolt (c. 165 BC), to alleged inaccuracies, and to the presence of three Greek words in the text. The characterization of Daniel as a prophecy after the event was first set forth by Porphyry (AD 233–305), a neo-Platonist critic of Christianity. See M. V. Anastos, "Porphyry's Attack on the Bible," *The Classical Tradition: Literary and Historical Studies in Honor of H. Caplan* (Ithaca, NY: Cornell University Press, 1966), 433–34; and P. M. Casey, "Porphyry and the Origin of the Book of Daniel," *Journal of Theological Studies* 27 (1976): 30–31. Some prominent British scholars of the Near East defend the neo-Babylonian/Persian date of Daniel. See Donald J. Wiseman, et al., *Notes on Some Problems in the Book of Daniel* (London: Tyndale Press, 1965); T. C. Mitchell, "Achaemenid History and the Book of Daniel," in *Mesopotamia and Iran in the Persian Period*, ed. John Curtis (London: British Museum Press, 1997), 68–78. I have argued that in view of the widespread interpenetration of the Greeks in the Near East long before Alexander the Greek words themselves are not conclusive

evidence of a Hellenistic date of compositions. See my *Greece and Babylon* (Grand Rapids: Baker, 1967), and *Persia and the Bible* (Grand Rapids: Baker, 1990), ch. 11, "Persia and the Greeks." See also E. M. Myers, "Second Temple Studies in the Light of Recent Archaeology: Part 1: The Persian and Hellenistic Periods," *Currents in Research: Biblical Studies* 2 (1994), 31; Jane C. Waldbaum, "Early Greek Contacts with the Southern Levant, ca. 1000–600 B.C.: The Eastern Perspective," *Bulletin of the American Schools of Oriental Research* 293 (1994), 67–78; W.-D. Niemeier, "Archaic Greeks in the Orient: Textual and Archaeological Evidence," *Bulletin of the American Schools of Oriental Research* 322 (2001), 11–32. For Nehemiah, see Tamara C. Eskenazi, "Current Perspectives on Ezra-Nehemiah and the Persian Period," *Currents in Research: Biblical Studies* 1 (1993): 59–86; T. Willi, "Zwei Jahrzehnte Forschung an Chronik und Ezra-Nehemia," *Theologische Rundschau* 67 (2002): 61–104; Peter R. Bedford, "Diaspora: Homeland Relations in Ezra-Nehemiah," *Vetus Testamentum* 52 (2002): 147–65.

12   Nachman Avigad, "Seals of the Exiles," *IEJ* 15 (1965): 223–30; idem, "More Evidence on the Judean Post-Exilic Stamps," *IEJ* 24 (1974): 52–58.

13   Daniel Smith, *The Religion of the Landless: The Social Context of the Babylonian Exile* (Bloomington, IN: Meyer Stone Books, 1989), 41; "In sum, we are unable to make definite conclusions about exilic existence apart from the biblical text itself."

14   *The Cambridge History of Iran*, vol. II, *The Median and Achaemenian Periods*, ed. Ehsan Yarshater (Cambridge: Cambridge University Press, 1984). See also Muhammad A. Dandamaev's *A Political History of the Achaemenid Empire* (Leiden: Brill, 1989). See my review in *Bibliotheca Orientalis* 49 (1992): 455–56. An English edition of Pierre Briant's massive *Histoire de l'empire perse* (Paris: Fayard, 1996) has been translated as *From Cyrus to Alexander* (Winona Lake, IN: Eisenbrauns, 2002). William David Davies and Louis Finkelstein, eds., *The Cambridge History of Judaism*, vol. I, *Introduction; The Persian Period* (Cambridge: Cambridge University Press, 1984). See also Lester L. Grabbe, *Judaism from Cyrus to Hadrian* (Minneapolis: Fortress Press, 1992); and Ran Zadok's valuable study of the cuneiform evidence for the exiles, *The Jews in Babylonia during the Chaldean and Achaemenian Periods in the Light of Babylonian Sources* (Haifa: Haifa University Press, 1976, 1979).

15   Jon L. Berquist, *Judaism in Persia's Shadow* (Minneapolis: Fortress Press, 1995).

16   *Beyond the River: New Perspectives on Transeuphratene*, tr. J. Edward Crowley (Sheffield: Sheffield Academic Press, 1998).

17   See Edwin Yamauchi, *Persia and the Bible*, ch. 2.

18   E. Simcox, "The Role of Cyrus in Deutero-Isaiah," *Journal of the American Oriental Society* 57 (1937): 158–71; E. Jenni, "Die Rolle des Kyros bei Deuterojesaja," *Theologische Zeitschrift* 10 (1954): 241–56; M. Smith, "II Isaiah and the Persians," *Journal of the American Oriental Society* 83 (1963): 415–20. The Hebrew name for Cyrus is *Koresh*, which is why the leader of the Branch Davidians at Waco, Vernon Howell, changed his name to "David Koresh." See James D. Tabor and Eugene V. Gallagher, *Why Waco?* (Berkeley, CA: University of California Press, 1995), 40.

19 We know that Cyrus allowed the return of the Jews and one other group, and we may generalize that he did the same for others. The memorandum was found at ancient Ecbatana, or Hamadan (AV. "Achmetha"), the ancient capital of the Medes. See Yamauchi, *Persia and the Bible*, ch. 8. De Vaux observes, "Now we know that it was the custom of the Persian sovereigns to winter in Babylon and depart in the summer to . . . Ecbatana. . . . A forger operating in Palestine without the information which we possess could hardly have been so accurate" (Roland de Vaux, *The Bible and the Ancient Near East*, trans. Damian McHugh [Garden City, NY: Doubleday &Co., 1971], 89). The proclamation in Hebrew of Cyrus's decree and its recording in Aramaic for the repositories is entirely in accord with Persian customs. Darius had copies of his Behistun Inscription sent throughout the empire as copies in Akkadian have been found in Babylon and in Aramaic in Egypt. See David B. Weisberg, *Guild Structure and Political Allegiance in Early Achaemenid Mesopotamia* (New Haven, CT: Yale University Press, 1967), 14–15.

20 Supporters of the authenticity of Cyrus's decree include: Elias J. Bickerman, "The Edict of Cyrus in Ezra 1," *Journal of Biblical Literature* 65 (1946): 249–75; C. G. Cameron, "Ancient Persia," in *The Idea of History in the Ancient Near East*, ed. Robert C. Dentan (New Haven, CT: American Oriental Society, 1955), 85; Peter R. Ackroyd, *Exile and Restoration* (Philadelphia: Westminster Press, 1968), 131; Maurice Meuleau, "Mesopotamia under Persian Rule," in *The Greeks and the Persians*, ed. Hermann Bengtson et al. (London: Weidenfeld & Nicolson, 1970), 378; Geo Widengren, "Persian Period," in *Israelite and Judaean History*, ed. John H. Hayes and J. Maxwell Miller (Philadelphia: Westminster Press, 1977), 519. Lee Hensley, "The Official Persian Documents in the Book of Ezra" (Ph.D. dissertation, University of Liverpool 1977), 233, has examined the seven official documents in Ezra (1:2–4; 4:11–16; 4:17–22; 5:7–17; 6:2b–5; 6:6–12; 7:12–16) in the light of 32 contemporary Persian documents and letters. He concludes, "Linguistically, stylistically, and historically the ED (Ezra Documents) correspond perfectly to the non-Biblical documents of the Achaemenid period."

21 See D. K. Andrews, "Yahweh the God of Heavens," in *The See of Wisdom*, ed. W. S. McCullough (Toronto: University of Toronto Press, 1964), 45–57.

22 A few brief trilingual (Old Persian, Akkadian, Elamite) inscriptions in which Cyrus speaks in the first person have been found at his capital, Pasargadae. See Roland G. Kent, *Old Persian*, 2d ed. (New Haven, CT: American Oriental Society, 1953), 107. See Richard Frye, *The Heritage of Persia* (Cleveland: World Publishing Co., 1963), 82.

23 James B. Pritchard, *Ancient Near Eastern Texts* (Princeton: Princeton University Press, 1955 [hereafter *ANET*]), 312–16. Amelie Kuhrt has studied the antecedents and implications of the Cyrus Cylinder, to illustrate Persian policy ("The Cyrus Cylinder and Achaemenid Imperial Policy," *JSOT* 25 [1983]: 83–94).

24 Janos Harmatta, "The Literary Patterns of the Babylonian Edict of Cyrus," *Acta Antiqua* 19 (1971): 217–31; P. R. Berger, "Der Kyros-Zylinder mit dem Zusatzfragment BIN II Nr. 32 . . . ," *ZA* 64 (1975), 192–234; C. B.

F. Walker, "A Recently Identified Fragment of the Cyrus Cylinder," *Iran* 10 (1972): 158–59.

25 C. Leonard Woolley, *Ur of the Chaldees* (reprint ed., New York: W. W. Norton & Co., 1965), 205; C. L. Woolley and Max E. L. Mallowan, *Ur Excavations IX: The Neo-Babylonian and Persian Periods* (London: British Museum, 1962).

26 S. Timm, "Die Bedeutung der spätbabylonischen Texte aus Nerab für die Rückkehr der Judäer aus dem Exil," in *Meilenstein: Festgabe fur Herbert Donner*, ed. M. Weippert and S. Timm (Wiesbaden: Harrassowitz, 1995), 276–88.

27 Salo W. Baron, *A Social and Religious History of the Jews*, 2nd ed. (New York: Columbia University Press), 1: 343.

28 The hope that the descendants of the 10 northern tribes who had been exiled by the Assyrians would one day be regathered, as prophesied by Jeremiah and Ezekiel, generated the legend of the "the 10 lost tribes," first among Jews and then among Christians. When Columbus first encountered Indians, some thought that they were members of these tribes. See Allen H. Godbey, *The Lost Tribes—a Myth* (New York: KTAV, 1974 reprint of 1930 ed.); H. G. May, "The Ten Lost Tribes," *Biblical Archaeologist* 6 (1943): 55–60; R. H. Popkin, "The Lost Tribes, the Caraites and the English Millenarians," *Journal of Jewish Studies* 37 (1986): 213–27; A. Gross, "The Expulsion and the Search for the Ten Tribes," *Judaism* 41 (1992): 130–47; Shalom Goldman, ed., *Hebrew and the Bible in America* (Hanover: University Press of New England, 1993); S. Gustafson, "Nations of Israelites," *Religion and Literature* 26 (1994): 31–53. On the basis of archaeological surveys, Charles E. Carter has proposed a radically reduced province of Yehud, which raises questions about the figures of returning exiles listed in Ezra 2 and Nehemiah 7, even if one accepts the view that these were cumulative totals. But Carter notes that some Jews lived outside the boundaries of the province. He would estimate the size of Jerusalem in the Persian period as between 130 and 140 dunams, with 80 dunams occupied by the Temple Mount. (A dunam = 1,000 square meters, or about ¼ acre.) Charles E. Carter, "The Province of Yehud in the Post-Exilic Period: Soundings in Site Distribution and Demography," in *Second Temple Studies* II: 129. Carter, on p. 108, suggests that "the population of Yehud ranged from a low of 11,000 in the late-sixth/early-fifth centuries BCE to a high of 17,000 in the fifth/early fourth centuries BCE." On p. 135, Carter estimates the population of Jerusalem at about 1,500. See also Charles E. Carter, *The Emergence of Yehud in the Persian Period* (Sheffield: Sheffield Academic Press, 1999). On various population estimates, see Edwin Yamauchi, "The Archaeological Background of Ezra," *Bibliotheca Sacra* 137 (1980): 185–97.

29 *ANET*, 492.

30 Emil Kraeling, *The Brooklyn Aramaic Papyri* (New Haven, CT: Yale University Press, 1953), 107.

31 Hensley, "The Official Persian Documents," 202.

32 Alan Gardiner, *Egypt of the Pharaohs* (London: Oxford University Press, 1961), 366–67.

33 Mary F. Gyles, *Pharaonic Policies and Administrations 663–323 B.C.* (Chapel Hill, NC: University of North Carolina Press, 1959), 70; R. Parker, "Darius and His Egyptian Campaign," *American Journal of Semitic Languages* 58 (1941): 373–77; George Cameron, "Darius, Egypt and the 'Lands Beyond the Sea,'" *Journal of Near Eastern Studies* 2 (1943): 307–13.

34 See A. F. Rainey, "The Satrapy 'Beyond the River,'" *Australian Journal of Biblical Archaeology* 1 (1969): 51–78.

35 On Persepolis, see Yamauchi, *Persia and the Bible*, ch. 10. Richard T. Hallock, *Persepolis Fortification Tablets* (Chicago: University of Chicago Press, 1969).

36 George C. Cameron, *Persepolis Treasury Tablets* (Chicago: University of Chicago Press, 1948); idem, "Persepolis Treasury Tablets Old and New," *Journal of Near Eastern Studies* 17 (1958): 161–76; idem, "New Tablets from the Persepolis Treasury," *Journal of Near Eastern Studies* 24 (1965): 167–92.

37 Peter R. Bedford, *Temple Restoration in Early Achaemenid Judah* (Leiden: Brill, 2001).

38 Ibid., 309.

39 Kathleen M. Kenyon, *Royal Cities of the Old Testament* (New York: Schocken Books, 1971), 38–41; idem, *Digging Up Jerusalem* (London: Benn, 1974), 111–12, 177–78; M. Dunand, "Byblos, Sidon, Jerusalem," in *Supplements to Vetus Testamentum* 17 (Leiden: Brill, 1969), 64–70.

40 On the terms found in Ezra 4:13 see J. Nicholas Postgate, *Taxation and Conscriptions in the Assyrian Empire* (Rome: Pontifical Biblical Institute, 1974), 119.

41 Cited by A. Burn, *Persia and the Greeks* (New York: St. Martin's Press, 1962), 114.

42 See, for example, Athalya Brenner, *A Feminist Companion to Esther, Judith and Susanna* (Sheffield: Sheffield Academic Press, 1995); and Timothy K. Beal, *The Book of Hiding: Gender, Ethnicity, Annihilation, and Esther* (London: Routledge, 1997).

43 See Edwin Yamauchi, "The Archaeological Background of Esther," *Bibliotheca Sacra* 137 (1980): 99–117; *Persia and the Bible*, ch. 7; and "Mordecai, the Persepolis Tablets, and the Susa Excavations," *Vetus Testamentum* 42 (1992): 272–75.

44 Florentino G. Martinez, *The Dead Sea Scrolls Translated* (Leiden: Brill, 1994), 291–92, 507.

45 Plutarch, *Artaxerxes* 1.1.

46 Thucydides 1.104.

47 Diodorus Siculus 11.77.1–5.

48 Kenneth G. Hoglund, *Achaemenid Imperial Administration in Syria-Palestine and the Missions of Ezra and Nehemiah* (Atlanta: Scholars Press, 1992).

49 Matthew W. Stolper, "The Governor of Babylon and Across-the-River in 486 B.C.," *Journal of Near Eastern Studies* 48 (1989): 300.

50 The letter appears in Ezra 7:12–26. David Janzen, "The 'Mission' of Ezra and the Persian-Period Temple Community," *JBL* 119 (2000): 619–43. Richard C. Steiner, "The *mbqr* at Qumran, the *episkopos* in the Athenian Empire, and the Meaning of *lbqr'* in Ezra 7:14: On the Relation of Ezra's Mission to the Persian Legal Project," *Journal of Biblical Literature* 120 (2001): 630. Cf. J.

Fleishman, "The Investigating Commission of Tattenai: The Purpose of the Investigation and Its Results," *Hebrew Union College Annual* 66 (1995): 81–102.

51 Cambyses is not mentioned in the Hebrew Bible. But the Persian invasion of Egypt in 525 no doubt caused the king to place demands on all provinces, including Judah, for men and supplies. See Yamauchi, *Persia and the Bible*, ch. 3.

52 Gardiner, *Egypt of the Pharaohs*, 366–67.

53 See Edwin Yamauchi, "The Reverse Order of Ezra/Nehemiah Reconsidered," *Themelios* 5.3 (1980): 7–13. H. G. M. Williamson, *Ezra, Nehemiah* (Waco, TX: Word Books, 1985). Joseph Blenkinsopp, *Ezra-Nehemiah* (Philadelphia: Westminster Press, 1988). Luc Dequeker's essay provides an exception ("Nehemiah and the Restoration of the Temple after the Exile," in *Deuteronomy and Deuteronomic Literature*, ed. Marc Vervenne and Johan Lust [Leuven: Peeters, 1997], 547–68). On the basis of a textual emendation, John Bright placed Ezra's arrival in 428 rather than in 458 (*History of Israel* 3rd ed. [Philadelphia: Westminster Press, 1981], Excursus II, "The Date of Ezra's Mission to Jerusalem").

54 Kurt Galling, *Studien zur Geschichte Israels im persischen Zeitalter* (Tubingen: J. C. B. Mohr, 1964).

55 See Nahman Avigad, *Bullae and Seals from a Post-Exilic Judean Archive* (Jerusalem: Hebrew University Press, 1976). In contrast to the rapacity of the earlier governors, Nehemiah acted with compassion in a time of economic and social crisis. See Edwin Yamauchi, "Two Reformers Compared: Solon of Athens and Nehemiah of Jerusalem," in *The Bible World: Essays in Honor of Cyrus H. Gordon*, ed. Gary Rendsburg et al. (New York: KTAV, 1980), 269–92.

56 Though Edomites are not mentioned by name in Ezra-Nehemiah, it is apparent from the harsh condemnation of the Edomites in Scripture (2 Chr 25:11; Ezek 25:12–14; Ps 137:7; Obad; Mal 1:4) that the Edomites took advantage of the Babylonian conquest of Judah. An important confirmation of this enmity comes from an inscription from Arad (early sixth century BC), which reads, "Behold, I have sent to warn you today: [Get] the men to Elisha! Lest Edom should come thither. Send reinforcements to Ramoth-Negeb." See Yohanan Aharoni, "Three Hebrew Ostraca from Arad," *BASOR* 197 (1970): 16–42. By the fourth century BC the Edomites were pushed westward to the region south of Hebron, later known as Idumaea, by the Arab Nabataeans. See K. G. Hoglund, "Edomites," in *Peoples of the Old Testament World*, ed. Alfred Hoerth, Gerald Mattingly, and Edwin Yamauchi (Grand Rapids: Baker, 1994 [hereafter *POTW*]). In the Persian period the coast was occupied by the descendants of the Philistines and by Phoenicians. Ashkelon was under the Tyrians. See W. A. Ward, "Phoenicians," in *POTW*.

57 See O. Leuze, *Die Satrapieneinteilung in Syrien und im Zweistromlande . . .* (Halle: Konigsberger Gelehrten Gesellsschaft, 1935) for the situation in Syria and Mesopotamia.

58 Nehemiah's chief opponent was Sanballat, the Horonite, the governor of Samaria (Neh 2:10, 19; 4:1,7; 6:1–2,5,12,14; 13:28), whose name is derived

from Akkadian *Sin-uballit,* which means, "Sin [the moon god] has given life." His epithet the "Horonite" identifies him as coming from one of three possible areas: (a) Hau-ran east of the Sea of Galilee, (b) Horonaim in Moab (Jer 48:34), or (c) most probably upper or lower Beth-Horon, two key cities located 12 miles northwest of Jerusalem (Josh 10:10; 16:3,5). Mittmann rather dubiously suggests that Tobiah and Sanballat were members of families repatriated with other exiles and then placed by the Persian authorities over Amman and Hauran respectively. See Siegfried Mittmann, "Tobia, Sanballat und die persische Provinz Juda," *Journal of Northwest Semitic Languages* 26 (2000): 1–50.

59   *ANET,* 492.

60   A good portion of the personal names from the Samaria papyri included the names of such deities as Qos (Edomite), SHR (Aramaic), Chemosh (Moabite), Ba'al (Canaanite), and Nebo (Babylonian). Cf. John W. McKay, *Religion in Judah Under the Assyrians* (London: SCM Press, 1973), 69.

61   See Paul W. Lapp and Nancy L. Lapp, eds., *Discoveries in the Waddi ed-Daliyeh* (Cambridge: American Schools of Oriental Research, 1974); Nancy L. Lapp, ed., *The Tale of the Tell: Archaeological Studies by Paul W. Lapp* (Pittsburgh: Pickwick Press, 1975), 66–76; Paul W. Lapp, "Bedouin Find Papyri Three Centuries Older than Dead Sea Scrolls," *BAR* 4 (1978): 16–24; Frank M. Cross, "The Historical Importance of the Samaria Papyri," *BAR* 4 (1978): 25–27; idem, "A Report on the Samaria Papyri," in *The Congress Volume, Jerusalem, 1986,* ed. John A. Emerton (*VT* Sup. 40; Leiden: Brill, 1988), 17–26.

62   Cross, "A Reconstruction of the Judean Restoration," 4–18.

63   B. Oded, "The Historical Background of the Syro-Ephraimite War Reconsidered," *Catholic Biblical Quarterly* 34 (1972): 161.

64   Benjamin Mazar, "The Tobiads," *Israel Exploration Journal* 7 (1957): 137–45, 229–38.

65   Josephus, *Antiquities of the Jews* 12.160. See Martin Hengel, *Judaism and Hellenism* (2 vols.; Philadelphia: Fortress Press, 1974), 1.39–43, 47–56, 2.31–40. For the papyrus which mentions Tobias, see Victor A. Tcherikover and Alexander Fuks, ed., *Corpus Papyrorum Judaicarum* (Cambridge: Harvard University Press, 1975), 1:118 ff.

66   C. C. McCown, "The 'Araq el-Emir and the Tobiads," *Biblical Archaeologist* 20 (1957): 63–76; P. W. Läpp, "Soundings at 'Aräq el-Emir (Jordan)," *Bulletin of the American Schools of Oriental Research* 165 (1962): 16–34; P. W. Läpp, "The Second and Third Campaigns at 'Aräq el-Emir," *Bulletin of the American Schools of Oriental Research* 171 (1963): 8–39; Joseph Naveh, *The Development of the Aramaic Script* (Jerusalem: Israel Academy of Sciences and Humanities, 1970), pp. 62–64; Hengel, *Judaism and Hellenism,* 1:49, 267–77.

67   Fredrick V. Winnett, *A Study of the Lihyanite and Thamudic Inscriptions* (Toronto: University of Toronto Press, 1937), 50–51; William F. Albright, "Dedan," *Geschichte und Altes Testament* (Tübingen: J. C. B. Mohr, 1943), 1–12.

68   K. L. Younger Jr., "The Deportation of the Israelites," *Journal of Biblical Literature* 117 (1998): 201–27. Zadok, *The Jews in Babylonia.*

69   B. Oded, *Mass Deportation* (Wiesbaden: Reichert, 1979), 87.

70 Muhammad A. Dandamaev, *Slavery in Babylonia*, tr. V. A. Powell (Dekalb, Ill: Northern Illinois University press, 1984), 457, 459, 652.

71 B. Oded, "The Settlements of the Israelite and the Judean Exiles in Mesopotamia in the 8th–6th Centuries BCE," in *Studies in Historical Geography and Biblical Historiography*, ed. G. Galil and M. Weinfeld (Leiden: Brill, 2000), 91–103.

72 See L. Allen, *Ezekiel 1–19* (Waco, TX: Word Books, 1990); idem, *Ezekiel 20–48* (Waco, TX: Word Books, 1994); D. I. Block, *Ezekiel, Chs. 1–24* (Grand Rapids: Eerdmans, 1997); idem, *Ezekiel, Chs. 25–48* (Grand Rapids: Eerdmans, 1998). For a review of earlier scholarship, see H . H. Rowley, "The Book of Ezekiel in Modern Study," *Bulletin of the John Rylands Library* 36 (1953): 146–90.

73 Lawrence Boadt, "Ezekiel, Book of," *Anchor Bible Dictionary*, ed. D. N. Freedman (New York: Doubleday, 1992), 2:711–22.

74 Ezekiel 24:18 and 8:1. See Edwin Yamauchi, "Nippur," in *The New International Dictionary of Biblical Archaeology*, ed. E. M. Blaiklock and R. K. Harrison (Grand Rapids: Zondervan, 1983), 339–41.

75 Josephus, *Jewish Antiquities* 9.8.

76 Matthew W. Stolper, *Entrepreneurs and Empire* (Leiden: Nederlands Historisch-Archaeologisch Instituut te Istanbul, 1985), 1. See Guillaume Cardascia, *Les archives des Murašû* (Paris: Imprimerie Nationale, 1951).

77 Such individuals include the leaders Sheshbazar/Shenazzar (Ezra 1:8; 5:14; 1 Chr 3:18) and Zerubbabel (Ezra 3:2), Bilshan (Ezra 2:2), Hattush, Nekoda, Esther (Esth 2:7), and Mordecai (Esth 2:6).

78 E. J. Bickerman, "The Generation of Ezra and Nehemiah," *Studies in Jewish and Christian History* 3 (1986): 316.

79 For studies of comparable Yahwistic names in the Elephantine papyri, see M. H. Silverman, "Hebrew Name-Types in the Elephantine Documents," *Orientalia* 39 (1970): 465–91.

80 Zadok, *The Jews in Babylonia*, 78. Cf. also Zadok, "West Semitic Personal Names in the Murašû Documents," *BASOR* 231 (1978), 73–78, a critical review of Michael D. Coogan, *West Semitic Personal Names in the Murašû Documents* (Missoula: Scholars Press, 1976); G. Wallis, "Jüdische Bürger in Babylonien während der Achämeniden-Zeit," *Persica* 9 (1980): 129–85.

81 Cf. M. D. Coogan, "Life in the Diaspora," *Biblical Archaeologist* 37 (1974): 10.

82 Bickerman, "The Generation of Ezra and Nehemiah," 322: "The break with syncretism occurred in the generation of Ezra, who, probably, was born about 500."

83 F. Joannes and Andre Lemaire, "Trois tablettes cunéformes à onomastique ouestsémitiques (collection Sh. Moussaieff)," Transeuphratene 17 (1999): 17–34. I am indebted to David Weisberg for providing me a copy of this most important article. Shemayahu Talmon, "'Exile' and 'Restoration' in the Conceptual World of Ancient Judaism," in *Restoration*, ed. James M. Scott (Leiden: Brill, 2001), 130, points out that this same expression for Jerusalem was used in a Babylonian chronicle. I am indebted to Kevin Spawn for calling my attention to this important volume.

84 Ibid., 20–24.

85 Egypt was conquered by Cambyses in 525, a Persian king who is not mentioned in the Hebrew Bible. See my *Persia and the Bible*, ch. 3.

86 Bezalel Porten, *Archives from Elephantine* (Berkeley: University of California Press, 1968). Michael Silverman, "The Religion of the Elephantine Jews— a New Approach," in *The Proceedings of the Sixth World Congress of Jewish Studies, 1973*, ed. A. Shin'an (Jerusalem: World Congress of Jewish Studies, 1975), 377–88.

87 J. N. Graham, "'Vinedressers and Plowmen': 2 Kgs 25:12 and Jeremiah 52:16," *Biblical Archaeologist* 47 (1984): 55–58.

88 Hans M. Barstad, *The Myth of the Empty Land: A Study in the History and Archaeology of Judah during the "Exilic" Period* (Oslo: Scandinavian University Press, 1996). Z. Gal, "Israel in Exile," *Biblical Archaeology Review* 24.3 (1998): 49–53.

89 Israel Eph'al, "Changes in Palestine During the Persian Period in Light of Epigraphic Sources," *PEQ* 48 (1998): 106–19.

90 Martin Noth, *The History of Israel* (rev. ed.; New York: Harper & Row, 1960), 296.

91 Donald E. Gowan, *Bridge Between the Testaments* (Pittsburgh: Pickwick Press, 1976), 37.

92 See Donald J. Wiseman, *Nebuchadnezzar and Babylon* (Oxford: Oxford University Press, 1985); cf. Edwin Yamauchi, "Babylon," in *Major Cities of the Biblical World*, ed. Roland K. Harrison (Nashville: Thomas Nelson, 1985), 46–41.

93 The Sabbath is mentioned 15 times in Ezekiel. Individuals named Shabbethai appear in Ezra 10:15 and Neh 8:7, in the Murashu texts (five individuals), and in the Elephantine papyri (three individuals). The latter are fifth-century Aramaic documents from a Jewish military colony on the Elephantine Island in the Upper Nile near Aswan. See Bezalel Porten, *Archives from Elephantine* (Berkeley: University of California Press, 1968), 124, 127. See also Heather A. McKay, *Sabbath and Synagogue* (Leiden: E. J. Brill, 1994).

94 M. Hengel, "Proseuche und Synagoge," in *Tradition und Glaube*, ed. G. Jeremias, et al., (Guttingen: Vandenhoeck & Ruprecht, 1971), 157–84; cf. Edwin Yamauchi, "Synagogue," in *Dictionary of Jesus and the Gospels*, ed. J. B. Green, et al. (Downers Grove, IL: InterVarsity Press, 1992), 781–84.

95 Eph'al, "Western Minorities," 88.

96 Stern, 479. On the often-suggested Persian influence upon Judaism, see my *Persia and the Bible*, ch. 12. Although such a development seems plausible, the problem is that the Persian sources for eschatology and cosmology come from a very late ninth-century date. See also James Barr, "The Question of Religious Influence: The Case of Zoroastrianism, Judaism and Christianity," *Journal of the American Academy of Religion* 53 (1985): 201–33.

TOUGH-MINDED
CHRISTIANITY

Part IV

DEFENDING THE FAITH

Justifying the Faith

BELIEVING AND DEFENDING

Michael Horton

The faith in Christ by which we believe (fides qua creditor) *and the Christian faith that is believed* (fides quae creditor).

These are classic distinctions in Protestant dogmatics, crucial for apologetics as well. While the unbelieving person to whom we bring the good news is "dead in trespasses and sins" (Eph 2:1), incapable of responding to that news in faith apart from God's grace, the Spirit always works through means. As Paul makes clear in Romans 10, there is a correspondence between the way God saves us objectively "then and there" in past history (redemption accomplished, we might say) and the way he brings us subjectively into that reality here and now (redemption applied). Unlike the righteousness that is through works, the righteousness that is through faith does not try to climb up to God but receives him as he has descended to us. That not only refers to the incarnation, however, but also to the entire series of events leading to the justification, sanctification, and glorification of the ungodly. In other words, the Father does not save us by sending the God-Man, his own Son, all the way down to us only to turn around and make us come up and get its benefits. He dispenses or applies Christ's work to us in exactly the same way that he redeemed us in the first place: by condescending to our weakness, by accommodating to our foolishness.

This is why those who do not think they are weak or foolish (i.e., those who follow the righteousness that is by works) miss the point entirely. Later in this passage (Rom 10), Paul explains how this salvation accomplished by Christ is applied to sinners: "So then faith comes by hearing and hearing by the word of Christ. . . . But how shall they hear without a preacher? And how shall they preach unless they are sent?" (vv. 14–15).[1] This is the golden chain that leads from heaven to earth. Just as God saved us by sending his Son in the flesh, so he continues to apply that work to us by sending the gospel of his Son in the flesh, through ministers who speak his word in his name. Thus, they do not send themselves, to announce whatever news they find interesting or useful this week, but are sent by the Christ through his church, to ensure that they are actually coming from God all the way down to us, where we are, in our sin and unbelief. Then the Word and Spirit (always together) do the work—through the humble ministry of sinful saints.

What does this have to do with apologetics? In this chapter honoring someone who has equipped a generation of Christians to respond to the objections of "tough-minded" unbelievers, I would like to elaborate that connection. I will first examine the distinction introduced above, between the act of faith and arguing for the faith, and then apply it to the question of apologetic method after the collapse of modern foundationalism.

Faith Is Certain; Arguments Are Probable

Unlike W. K. Clifford and the positivist philosophers, evidentialism (represented by Old Princeton and J. W. Montgomery) does not maintain that one is only entitled to believe something upon sufficient evidence. One may be a mature believer in Christ without ever having examined the evidence for the resurrection: the fact of the resurrection is independent of the observation; the faith with which one trusts in Christ is distinct from the arguments one might use to defend that faith. Even in the latter case, absolute certainty is not the test of a good argument or evidence. All that history can yield is probability in any case.

G. E. Lessing and the rationalists and idealists of the German Enlightenment were right about that, but their Platonism made it an unbridgeable gulf. I want to suggest that this corresponds to "the righteousness that is by works," a striving for the absolute certainty of the beatific vision—a theology of glory (our ascent, grasping, attaining, controlling, mastering), rather than a theology of the cross (God's descent, giving, serving, accommodating). Rather than demythologize the sagas of religion as expressions of eternal truths clothed in the ornamentation of symbol, the Enlightenment thinkers merely replaced one mythology with another. As in Plato, for these thinkers, the place that is actually occupied by the Triune God was imagined to be filled by abstract principles, such as eternal forms, truths, and ideas. Knowledge of the ideals, attained by steady and earnest contemplation, would finally surrender to the beatific vision—the all-encompassing and enrapturing experience of beholding the Good itself. Of course, this was carried over into Christianity through the monastic tradition as well. Mysticism and rationalism are simply two sides of the same coin.

Lessing's problem was not historical criticism; it was not a question of whether Jesus Christ lived or even whether he rose again. All the evidence in the world would not be sufficient, Lessing held, simply because history is itself inadequate as a conveyor of truth.[2] Updating Plato's "divided line" between the realm of eternal, unchanging, perfect, and intellectual reality and the realm of temporal, mutable, imperfect, and material shadows, Lessing was convinced, on the basis of *a priori* assumptions, that historical arguments and evidences (concerning contingent events in history) are by nature incapable of leading one to any convictions about that which is eternally true (necessary truths of reason). Since, according to rationalists ancient and modern, knowledge (*noesis*) consists of *certainties* and the deliverances of sense-experience upon which historical study rests consist of *probabilities*, there can be no historical knowledge per se. To believe that Jesus lived and even rose again is akin to believing that there was an Alexander who conquered a large piece of real estate in the ancient world, says Lessing. In neither case could historical events lead one to conclude anything concerning the ultimate nature of reality (i.e., metaphysics and ontology). It is simply a *non sequitur*, Lessing claims, to advance willy-nilly from the historical claim that Jesus rose from the dead to the metaphysical conclusion that Jesus is God and Lessing is obligated to confess that he is Lord.[3]

Despite the media circus over an allegedly intrinsic opposition between science and theology, it is the former that has rendered the principal Enlightenment critiques untenable. Were the world as Newtonian physics understood it—as a well-regulated machine with inviolable laws—then the gap between God and the world would indeed be a yawning chasm. History could only be, in Henry Ford's fatalistic account, "one damned thing after another," hardly a realm of freedom and novelty. However, after Einstein, even scientific observation and experimentation assumes *regularities* (equivalent to the historian's probabilities) without *absolutely inviolable laws* (equivalent to the historian's certainties). If probabilities could not convey knowledge, then the history of science is as inexplicable as the historian's craft itself.

But is "probability" all that apologetics can come up with? Can this weak epistemic act qualify as justifying faith? In other words, what is the relation between justification by faith and justification of the faith?

Not surprisingly for a Calvinist, I think that John Calvin was remarkably insightful on this point as others. On one hand, Calvin defined faith, following the New Testament, in the most certain terms. Unlike later pietism he did not think of faith as a human work but as a divine gift. It was certain not because of the level of accurate understanding, resolve, or repentance on the part of the believer but because of the absolute immutability of God's electing grace and redemptive promise. Like the Lutheran tradition, the Reformed emphasize the point that the Spirit creates faith through the preaching of the gospel. In answering the question, "Where does true faith come from?" the Heidelberg Catechism answers, "The Holy Spirit creates it in our hearts by the preaching of the holy gospel and confirms it by the use of the holy sacraments." Justifying faith is not something that wells up or is worked up within the believer; rather, it comes *extra nos*, from outside of us, through the message that is preached (again, Rom 10 is one of the classic passages for this view). True faith comes from God and even the human, earthly means that God uses come from God as well. Faith is certain because the Triune God himself is creating it and sustaining it by his preached gospel and sacraments. In other words, faith in Christ is not established on probability, but the arguments we use for defending the faith, being historical in character, will quite naturally appeal to probabilities. If probabilistic arguments cannot attain the status of epistemic certitude demanded by modern foundationalism, they are nevertheless capable of bearing truth. And because the Necessary Truth is a person and this person became flesh (contingent truth), the gap has been bridged—by God rather than by us. God has accommodated and condescended to us in such a way that we can no longer plead ignorance. "The times of ignorance God overlooked, but now he commands all people every-where to repent, because he has fixed a day on which he will judge the world in righteousness by a man whom he has appointed; and of this he has given assurance to all by raising him from the dead" (Acts 17:30–31). God has made the eternal truth of his existence, charac-ter, and saving purposes available to us in contingent history. Thus, "we make the freely given promise of God the foundation of faith," writes Calvin, "because upon it faith properly rests" (3.2.7).

On the other hand, faith is often assailed by doubts. While our faith is anchored in objective certainties, Calvin and the Reformed tradition assert, with the Lutheran tradition, that the quality of this faith subjectively in the believer is mixed. God's Word does not imagine the sort of faith that is never "violently buffeted hither and thither," even seemingly snuffed out at times (3.2.24). Yet he refused to separate faith and assurance. After all, Scripture says, "Now faith is the assurance of things hoped for, the conviction of things not yet seen" (Heb 11:1). Not only believing in my wife's existence, I trust her. She has proved herself to me time and time again. I do not need to be focally aware of every reason in order to justify my faith in her. At the same time, sometimes I am strengthened in that confidence by arguments and evidences. (Typically, she requires more confirm-ing evidence of my character than I require for hers!) Furthermore, if I am to explain to those who doubt her character for some reason why I have confidence in her, I will have to offer concrete reasons. Even the obstreperous objections of malicious gossips may be offered such counter-testimony for my wife's reputation since by it their re-proaches may at least be recognized as reflecting their bad charac-ter rather than hers. What they do with such counter-testimony, of course, is not in my power to determine.

My own personal faith in my wife is different from the reasons I might give to others. Applied to faith in Christ, the preaching of the gospel that creates faith is distinct from the apologetic task of offer-ing reasons for the hope that we have. Appealing again to our classic categories, there is the faith by which we trust in Christ (*fides qua creditur*) and the faith that we believe (*fides quae creditur*). The former yields a certainty that is nevertheless constantly assaulted by doubts and desires confirmation. This is the truth in Anselm's formula for Christian thought: "faith seeking understanding."

If we fail to recognize this distinction between evangelism and apologetics, conversion and the confirmation and defense of the faith, we will confuse the certainty of God's promise with the certainty of our arguments. In that case, of course, our faith in Christ can hardly rest on probabilities. It must rest on the infallible Word of God alone. We do not believe in the Triune God "as if" he exists (Kant) or as a probable hypothesis (Schleiermacher). At the same time, as Cornelius Van Til recognized, we can have conversations with non-Christians in which we appeal to their own assumptions "for the sake of argument."[4] This recognition assumes behind it the distinction between justifying faith (*fides qua creditur*) and justifying the faith (*fides quae creditur*). Although the verbal difference consists in no more than a vowel, it is not the first time that a crucial distinction has rested on such subtleties (think of the *homoousion* that separates us from the *homoiousion* of the Arians). A similar distinction was made in epistemology by Gottlob Frege, against the psychologism of the idealists; namely, that between *true* and *taking-to-be-true*. I do not require sufficient proofs for believing in Christ in order to be justified in doing so; at the same time, offering arguments and evidence can serve as important confirmations, particularly in the face of specific objections.

The Covenant Lawsuit

Let us go back to that statement of the Heidelberg Catechism: "The Holy Spirit creates faith in our heart by the preaching of the holy gospel and confirms it by the use of the holy sacraments." The sacraments do not confirm God's resolve. They do not make God's Word surer or his promise more valid. Rather, they ratify to our weak faith the assurance that God is gracious toward us in Christ. Similarly, arguments and evidences of God's veracity do not *establish* God's veracity but *confirm* it to us. Is this not an obvious fact throughout the history of revelation? Isn't the Bible one long courtroom drama of testimony, countertestimony, cross-examination of witnesses, presentation of arguments and evidences, with summations in which both God and his people together are vindicated at the final tribunal?

Throughout Israel's history, both Israel and Yahweh are on trial for their fidelity to the covenant. The whole Bible can be read as one long court trial, in fact. Adam is created as God's faithful witness but becomes a false witness in the cosmic courtroom. Israel recapitulates this Adamic trial, failing to fulfill the covenant of law that they had embraced when they said as one person assembled at the foot of Sinai, "All this we will do." Yet in the course of divine judgment, they blame God instead of themselves. All of this leads finally to God, who always has the last word, and the interruption of sin and unbelief by the arrival in time of the God-Man. At last Israel and the nations have their true and faithful witness, the one who perfectly fulfills God's law, the Second Adam who does everything for us and reconciles us to God. He justifies the wicked while remaining just in doing so because the righteousness of Christ is imputed to all who believe.

The point to be made concerning apologetics at this point is that the entire context of the Bible as a covenantal trial is consistent with offering evidences from the concrete events of history for the fidelity of God to his promise. Paul does this, for example, in Romans 9–11, interpreting the prophets, whose role in the old covenant was that of covenant attorneys, prosecuting God's case against the people while also representing the claims of the people to God. Testimony, witness, presenting the case, appealing to historical arguments: the Bible *is* a courtroom drama.

Similar to Lutheran theology, the Reformed tradition emphasizes the point that the Bible is not a collection of timeless, abstract ideas and principles but a history of redemption. No wonder, then, Paul defends the faith against the Epicureans and Stoics in Athens by appealing to the resurrection as evidence of God's claim on humanity. The events upon which the Christian Faith rests its case "were not done in a corner," Paul tells King Agrippa (Acts 26:26). They are public events that are accessible to all. It is not the resurrection itself that is probable but our historical arguments for the event. Of course, the God who offers infallible testimony to the resurrection through the apostles cannot err nor lie. Nevertheless, he condescends to our weakness. To Thomas and the other disciples Jesus offers his resurrected body for inspection. He does not meet our questions with disdain any more than he refused Abram's appeal for greater confirmation of God's promise.

The faith that the Spirit creates in our hearts by the preaching of the gospel may be certain, but the arguments we make for the historical events themselves concern contingent, historical events. As Calvin insists, faith itself does not rest on arguments and evidences, but the latter become crucial for confirming the truth of what has been effectually sealed in and to us by the Spirit through the Word. While the response, "We will hear him more on these things" is hardly satisfying to an evangelist, it satisfies the apologist, whose goal is not to raise Lazarus from the dead so much as to roll away the stone of misunderstanding and misapprehension of the Christian claims themselves. An apologist (at least one working with the assumptions of Reformation theology) will never think that an unbeliever will be converted simply by amassing sufficient evidence any more than that one will be converted simply by more preaching. Nevertheless, God works through means, and preaching and apologetics have their distinct and complementary roles to play in that mission to the world.

Apologetics After the Impossible Dream

There simply are no apologetic methods or arguments that yield absolute certainty. As we are now beginning to realize, such Promethean certitude promised by modernity is the impossible dream—the logic that derives from a theology of glory and "the righteousness that is by works," striving, climbing, grasping, and seeing, rather than by receiving, resting, embracing, and hearing. It is no wonder that apologetics itself has fallen on hard times alongside the demise of modern foundationalism. Already, at the end of the nineteenth century, Abraham Kuyper questioned the value of apologetics: was it not the case that some of the greatest damage to the Christian witness was perpetrated by those who sought to make it intellectually attractive to its "cultured despisers"? Karl Barth and neoorthodoxy deepened this reserve and in a generation catechized in a vague acceptance of all points of view as not only equally protected legally but as equally valid, apologetics can only wear the stale scent of a bygone era.

Yet the strength of the evidentialist tradition as enunciated by Warfield, Hodge, and Montgomery is its acknowledgement of the benefits even of frail probabilities in the defense of the faith. Unlike modern foundationalist claims to absolute certainty through the correct epistemological procedure, these apologists have recognized the modest and limited yet nevertheless crucial task performed by apologetics. Despite criticisms of this apologetic school, Cornelius Van Til also insisted upon the need for presenting arguments and evidences for the Christian claims. With Warfield he affirmed that "the Christian faith is not a blind faith but is faith based on evidence."[5]

In my own perspective the rivalries between these two schools are largely moribund. To be sure, there are important differences between evidentialism and presuppositionalism that should not be overlooked. Everything that God says is true simply because the God who reveals the truth is the source of all reality. Neutrality is a myth. All facts are interpreted from within the horizon of one's settled assumptions. The unbeliever does not stand midway between belief and unbelief but is actively engaged in suppressing the truth in unrighteousness. Yet just as we never know what will be said from the pulpit or in a conversation over coffee that is used by the Spirit to trigger repentance and faith, we cannot predict how our arguments and evidences might be used to clear the path to a better opportunity for hearing that good news. To be sure, human beings are reluctant to rethink their entire worldview—more so when it challenges autonomy at its root. Nevertheless, anomalies can throw a wrench into the machinery of our prejudices and force us at least to take more seriously that which we had previously dismissed without intellectual warrant. Perhaps it is time to provoke new conversations between these rival apologetic schools, but only if it is in the greater service of actually defending the faith to outsiders and helping believers respond appropriately to their doubts. However, a great deal of capital has been squandered on in-house debates over *how* to engage unbelievers when, given our shared consensus, our apologetics should be investing that intellectual energy on actual engagements with unbelievers and with non-Christian thought.

In my own apologetics conversations, appeals to evidences for the resurrection often yield predictable results with tough-minded skeptics. After listening to their alternative accounts of what happened to Jesus after his death, I attempt to show the implausibility of their arguments—and (with a good dose of presuppositionalism!) the *a priori* assumptions of their worldview that render miracles impossible by definition. In many of these instances, I discern that my interlocutor is confused, thrown back on his or her heels a bit, forced to pause and retrench. Perhaps he or she is retreating only to regroup for another assault. Yet confident in God's sovereign grace, I am hopeful that at the very least my conversation partner will be forced to recognize that he or she no longer opposes the gospel because of the reasons initially offered (viz., that it requires a sacrifice of the intellect) but because he or she remains *fideistically* committed to his presuppositions. Like the rich young ruler, such a person may walk away sorrowful yet confident in his own righteousness or rightness, but he has hopefully had some of his pretensions undermined. This is what Calvin means by offering arguments to "shut the mouth of the obstreperous."[6] That this procedure does not yield repentance and faith hardly vitiates its importance. In God's providence, it may just be that through these means the Spirit is breaking down his sinful autonomy, bringing to the surface the utter foolishness of one's unbelief, and therefore preparing one by such "law-work," as the Puritans would call it, for hearing the gospel.

Faith comes by hearing the good news announced. Good arguments can yield assent, but only good news can yield trust. Yet precisely because this faith, certain as to its object, is nevertheless constantly assailed by doubts, the Christian no less than the non-Christian should be equipped with arguments and evidences that can be used by the Spirit to lend support and encouragement in that struggle of faith seeking understanding.

Endnotes

1 All biblical quotations are from the English Standard Version (ESV).
2 Henry Chadwick, ed., *Lessing's Theological Writings* (Palo Alto: Stanford University Press, 1967), 53–56, 105–16.
3 Ibid., 51–53.

4   Cornelius Van Til, *The Defense of the Faith* (Philadelphia: Presbyterian and Reformed Publishing Co., 1967), 100.

5   Cornelius Van Til, *My Credo* (Phillipsburg, NJ: Presbyterian and Reformed, 1972), 21. It would seem that a lack of appeal to evidences is due less to Van Til's system than to the division of labor in those earlier years at Westminster Seminary: "I would therefore engage in historical apologetics. (I do not personally do a great deal of this because my colleagues in the other departments of the Seminary in which I teach are doing it better than I could do it.) Every bit of historical investigation . . . is bound to confirm the truth of the claims of the Christian position" (quoted by Thom Notaro, *Van Til and the Use of Evidence* [Phillipsburg, NJ: Presbyterian and Reformed Publishing Co., 1980], from Van Til's *The Defense of the Faith*, 199).

6   *Institutes*, I. vii. 4.

The Core Resurrection Data

The Minimal Facts Approach

Gary R. Habermas

The majority of my professional studies have been on the subject of Jesus' resurrection. This event is of central importance in Christianity, for establishing theological foundations as well as practical applications to real-life situations. So it was used in the New Testament. Here we want to visit the foundation of resurrection data and ascertain if it is secure.[1]

The Minimal Facts Method

Throughout my publications my emphasis has been to build a case for the resurrection of Jesus from the bottom up, like a brick wall. Each brick represents a historical fact. But in no case do any of these facts rest upon the overall reliability or inspiration of Scripture.[2] This is a legitimate path in itself, but it is not the chief one that I pursue in this essay or elsewhere.

Rather, I have employed here what I have termed the "minimal facts methodology."[3] This approach uses only those data that have two primary characteristics: (1) Each fact is multiply attested by subfacts that carefully establish its historicity. (2) Due to this strongly established groundwork, each of these facts is generally accepted as historical by an exceptionally large majority of the critical scholars who study this subject, whatever their discipline or theological outlook. For these two reasons, these individual data provide the "bricks" to build my argument. I will limit the discussion almost exclusively to the facts that enjoy such an excellent foundation.

How does this angle differ from the traditional methods usually employed in apologetic arguments, which are almost always based on a trustworthy or inspired Scripture? These efforts usually argue to a generally reliable Bible as a whole and then from this basis to items in the Bible. The assumption seems to be that if the *overall* text is trustworthy, then separate items under that umbrella are also true, in a "top-down" manner.

Although I will not critique this view in the present context, the minimal facts method builds in the opposite direction and is much tighter. Beginning from the bottom up, it utilizes *only* those facts that are *individually* substantiated for multiple reasons, thereby allowing more common ground. Each of the six major facts that we will employ below can be established by separate strands that are *themselves* also established in the same critical manner. This results in a single, firm argument. The minimal facts method differs from the reliability approach by being far more specific and more carefully grounded.

I frequently emphasize the second of the two requirements above—that contemporary critical scholars grant the historicity of each fact. But I have often said that the first argument is far more important, chiefly because it evidences the ground level of the entire argument, which rests upon it. Further, scholarly acceptance is more fickle and may even change. What basis, then, exists for the historicity of the resurrection? What are the individual bricks of the argument? How is the argument composed? And how are those bricks themselves supported? That there is such a foundation is assumed by many, but it is almost never delineated, at least not in detail. This is the topic for this essay. I will list those data that ground the best evidence for Jesus' resurrection.

The Factual Basis for Jesus' Resurrection

Usually I present a minimal list of 10 or 12 facts surrounding the end of Jesus' life.[4] Scholars almost always allow additional data beyond these. Thus, no scholar grants *only* these facts. In spite of this, I will limit this present discussion to an even smaller list—just six of these dozen, so as to better view the basis for each. Since researchers virtually always allow far more than these, more common ground is engendered by a case that is built on even fewer facts. Our purpose is to list the various strands of data in support of these half-dozen events. How does such a case for the resurrection look even when the historical evidence is reduced to this self-imposed, bare-bones level?[5]

Jesus died due to the process of Roman crucifixion.

That *Jesus died* because of Roman crucifixion is confirmed by a wealth of information. This fact is almost never questioned by critical scholars.

1. Many ancient texts, both Christian and non-Christian, record the death of Jesus, often providing details. These include (a) the unanimously acclaimed, pre-Pauline passage in 1 Corinthians 15:3 (see below). (b) Several other highly respected, early confessional reports also date earlier than the New Testament writings in which they appear.[6] (c) The Gospel narratives unanimously proclaim Jesus' death by crucifixion.[7] (d) About 10 non-Christian texts,[8] plus (e) several early Christian references also mention Jesus' death, sometimes with details.[9]

2. Many medical studies have addressed the general cause of death due to crucifixion. The majority of physicians report that the victims died of asphyxiation, complicated by other medical factors, caused by the arms being extended and fixed overhead while the weight of the body hung below. Assuming such a position for more than a few minutes may cause the individual to begin asphyxiating, due to the pressure on the lungs from the intercostal, pectoral, and deltoid muscles.[10]

3. Ancient sources report that final blows to crucifixion victims, such as broken legs and chest wounds, guaranteed their deaths.[11] Further, if Jesus had been alive when the spear had pierced his pleural cavity, an obvious sucking sound would have alerted his executors that he had not yet died. The predominant medical view is that the weapon punctured Jesus' heart, insuring his death.[12]

4. Arguably the most influential argument for Jesus' death by crucifixion was published by liberal critical scholar David Strauss over a century ago. Had Jesus failed to die on the cross, we could no longer account for the disciples' *belief and proclamation* that he had been raised. But their teaching of the resurrection is acknowledged by virtually all scholars as a minimum requirement for the apostolic preaching. The insuperable problem is that a crucified but still living Jesus would have been in gruesome shape: beaten, bloodied, severely limping, pale, unwashed, and obviously requiring medical assistance.

Though alive, Jesus obviously would not have been raised from the dead.

The problem is that the resulting contradiction would have left the disciples without a gospel to preach and thus cannot account for the birth of the church. There would be no grounding for the oft-repeated teaching that believers would someday be raised just like Jesus. A crucified, obviously stricken person would hardly have inspired Christian theology![13]

It is therefore no surprise that few critical scholars challenge the fact that Jesus died due to Roman crucifixion. Marcus Borg asserts that Jesus' execution by the Romans is "[t]he most certain fact about the historical Jesus."[14] Even more strongly, John Dominic Crossan states: "That he was crucified is as sure as anything historical can ever be."[15]

Once a persecutor of Christians, Paul became a believer because of an experience that he believed was an appearance of the resurrected Jesus.

Although this occurrence happened after that of the other apostles, Paul's experience was recorded at an earlier date. Unquestionably, Paul had a drastic turnaround from his former days as both an exceptional young scholar and chief persecutor of the church (Gal 1:13–14; Phil 3:4–7; 1 Cor 15:9). But just a few years later, Paul was *converted and transformed* because he was absolutely sure that he had met the risen Jesus.

1. There is an amazing unanimity among even skeptical scholars that Paul certainly had an experience that he thought was an appearance of the risen Jesus. As an eyewitness, Paul provides the strongest testimony to this occurrence, as noted by atheistic philosopher Michael Martin,[16] and Jesus Seminar member Roy Hoover adds: "Paul's testimony is the earliest and the most historically reliable evidence about the resurrection of Jesus that we have." He adds: "The most important evidence about the resurrection with which Paul provides us is . . . a direct claim that he has seen the risen Jesus."[17] (a) Paul reports his eyewitness testimony to a resurrection appearance of Jesus in 1 Corinthians 9:1 and 15:8–11 (cf. Gal 1:16). (b) Non-Pauline

confirmation of this testimony also appears three times (Acts 9:1–9; 22:1–11; 26:9–19).[18]

2. The other apostles confirmed Paul's experience and his teaching that Jesus' resurrection was an indispensable part of the gospel message. (a) Paul made at least two trips to Jerusalem to counsel with the apostolic leaders in order to inquire of them regarding the gospel message that he was preaching. We will hold our comments regarding Paul's first trip (Gal 1:18–20) until below. In his second trip to Jerusalem (2:1–10), Paul met with the chief apostles, namely Peter, James the brother of Jesus, and John. Paul specifically explained that the purpose his coming was to identify the nature of the gospel that he was preaching since he wanted to be absolutely sure that he was correct (2:2). The other apostles approved Paul's message (2:6–10) without adding any other requirements (2:6b). Paul's gospel message clearly included Jesus' resurrection (Gal 1:1; 2:20; 1 Cor 15:1–5).

(b) Additional substantiation that the other apostles confirmed Paul's gospel message is the subject of Acts 15:1–31. Scholars are undecided whether this is the same event as narrated in Galatians 2:1–10. If so, then it backs Paul's own report. If not, this may have been a *third* trip to Jerusalem by Paul, all for express purpose of checking his central proclamation! Regardless, multiple sources report that the content of Paul's gospel teaching had been confirmed by the leading apostles. This is crucial, of course, for they were the very same witnesses who originally experienced the risen Jesus.

Critical scholars acknowledge the approval of Paul's gospel message by the other major apostles. Hans Dieter Betz speaks for many when he notes, "The positive result consists of the fact that his gospel and mission were officially acknowledged by the Jerusalem apostles . . . a recognition of Paul and his gospel as theologically valid."[19]

The disciples had already experienced what they also thought were actual appearances of the risen Jesus.

Few facts are better established in current studies than that the disciples reported their *experiences that they were sure were appearances of the risen Jesus.* Many arguments support this contention.

1. Many ancient, critically attested texts, both Christian and non-Christian, record the apostolic teaching that their experiences were none other than Jesus' resurrection appearances. (a) As we will see below, by far the major example is the pre-Pauline text recorded in 1 Corinthians 15:3–8. (b) Other major support for the disciples' experiences is embedded in the early preaching passages in Acts and other creedal texts.[20]

(c) The Gospel narratives contain several individual resurrection traditions[21] and have been receiving increased critical attention. (d) Although not as valuable, a non-Christian source referring to Jesus' resurrection appearances is Josephus's disputed text in *Antiquities* 18:3. Another hint is provided by Tacitus (*Annals* 15:44), who mentions the Christian teachings that emerged after Jesus' execution. Gnostic writings theologize about Jesus' resurrection and exaltation after death.[22] (e) Other helpful reports are also located in the extra-New Testament writings of Clement of Rome (*Corinthians* 42), Ignatius (*Smyrneans* 3), and Justin Martyr (*First Apology* 50).

These writings make up a striking array of early teachings regarding Jesus' resurrection appearances, reported as experiences that occurred both to groups as well as to individuals. Such arguments account for the recognition by critical scholars that Jesus' death and the disciples' experiences are probably the two most widely accepted facts reported in the New Testament. Norman Perrin notes that "the more we study the tradition with regard to the appearances, the firmer the rock begins to appear upon which they are based."[23]

2. Very strong indications that the other apostles were also preaching and teaching about their own resurrection experiences comes from Paul, who was well aware of the appearances to Peter, the Twelve, the 500, James, and to all of the apostles (1 Cor 15:3–7). Paul's trips to Jerusalem to meet these others face-to-face furthered his knowledge of their experiences. It is very possible that he met still other early believers who had had similar experiences (15:6). As a result, Paul declared that the other apostles preached the same message that he did regarding Jesus' resurrection appearances (1 Cor 15:11,14–15). So Paul knew of these others' appearances and agreed with their testimony, completing the circle of confirmation from them to him, and vice versa.

As before, critical scholars rarely deny that Paul knew of the resurrection appearances to other apostles and agreed with them. Luke Timothy Johnson provides such an instance: "Paul insists that he proclaimed to his communities what he also had received, and that his preaching was in agreement with the other apostles."[24]

3. Although it is not as unanimously recognized as the other data here, the majority of contemporary scholars accept the historicity of the empty tomb.[25] This event is supported by strong arguments such as (a) the Jerusalem location for the burial, since the report could be checked out rather readily by either friend or foe, (b) the embarrassment caused by the women being the chief witnesses, (c) the multiple attestation from three or four ancient sources, (d) the implications that Paul knew of the empty tomb, and (e) the enemy attestation provided by the Jewish leaders.[26] The significance of these data is shown by ancient historian Michael Grant's assertion that "the historian . . . cannot justifiably deny the empty tomb. . . . But if we apply the same sort of criteria that we would apply to any other ancient literary sources, then the evidence is firm and plausible enough to necessitate the conclusion that the tomb was indeed found empty."[27]

If Jesus' tomb was later discovered to be empty, this strengthens further the case for the resurrection appearances, for it makes it more likely that whatever happened to Jesus involved his body. It also complicates considerably the formulation of naturalistic theories.

The apostles' proclamation of the resurrection dates from an exceptionally early time after Jesus' death.

Many of the apostolic and other sources for Jesus' appearances mentioned in the previous argument date from *a remarkably early time*. In fact, there never was a time in early Christianity where Jesus was preached as anything but raised from the dead.

1. Although this point is quite detailed and cannot be argued here,[28] (a) the pre-Pauline creedal text in 1 Corinthians 15:3ff is recognized by scholars to be an exceptionally early account of Jesus' resurrection appearances. There are a half-dozen markers indicating that this material is not Paul's[29] but predates him. For instance, Paul introduces this tradition by saying that he "delivered" to his listeners

what he had already "received" from others (15:3), using the equivalent Greek words for the technical rabbinic terms for passing on tradition. Further, (b) this material probably can be traced to eyewitness sources and includes more checks and balances than what is provided by almost any other ancient text.

When and from whom did Paul receive this material? Briefly, most scholars who answer this issue postulate that Paul probably got it from the chief apostles in the early to mid-30s AD, when he visited Jerusalem and met with Peter and James the brother of Jesus (Gal 1:18). Very helpfully, the term that Paul used (*historēsai*) is best translated as "to inquire or examine" and the context indicates that he was discussing the nature of the gospel.[30] Dunn states that we can be "entirely confident" that this tradition was formulated "*within months of Jesus' death.*"[31]

Even skeptical scholars generally concede this early time frame. Many examples could easily be provided.[32] Gerd Lüdemann dates the elements in this creedal text to "not later than" a maximum of two to three years after Jesus' crucifixion.[33] The Jesus Seminar even judged it most likely that "the components of the list reported there were formed prior to Paul's conversion."[34]

This creed is incredibly valuable not only for its early composition but also for the crucial report of Jesus' appearances to many key leaders as well as several groups, including 500 at once. This argument by no means relies on knowing the precise date when the material arrived in this form, or when Paul received this material, or exactly who passed it to him. Actually, as indicated in the above scholarly citations, the creed itself is not as important as its content—those data that became the creed—which we can assuredly date to immediately after Jesus' death.

Therefore, even this minimal scenario is sufficient to establish the point here. The resurrection appearances were proclaimed *immediately*. Hardly a commentator will ever dispute this fact.[35]

This traditional material obviously predates the composition of 1 Corinthians in the mid-fifties AD. Paul preached the same message a few years earlier in Corinth (15:1–2). Further, the apostle also states clearly that he received the content of this gospel message from someone else (15:3). The result is the almost unanimous critical approval that Paul received the data at an early date. Since he was an apostle and eyewitness, it follows that he received it from someone whom he deemed to be a trustworthy source.

2. But this particular text is not the only early source for this event. A majority of scholars also think the many sermon summaries in Acts, cited above, emerged at an early date. An example is Gerald O'Collins, who states that the Acts "incorporate resurrection formulae which stem from the thirties."[36] Each of these concise traditions includes the gospel message of the deity, death, and resurrection appearances of Jesus. In ancient times two sources even a full century or more after a report is often a luxury. As ancient historian Paul Maier reminds us, "Many facts from antiquity rest on just one ancient source, while two or three sources in agreement generally render the fact unimpeachable."[37] But rather incredibly, we have here more than a half-dozen texts, from independent sources, dating to perhaps a mere five years after Jesus' death!

3. If all this were not enough, Paul's epistles of 1 Corinthians and Galatians, which we have used here, are dated by scholarly consensus from the early to the mid-50s AD,[38] or just about 25 years after the crucifixion. Some scholars date Galatians even earlier. Mark is generally dated from AD 65–75.[39] Together we have numerous early sources dating from just five to 40 years after Jesus' crucifixion. To this total we add Matthew and Luke from perhaps 10 to 20 years after that, John and Clement about 10 to 15 years later, and Ignatius's writings at another 15 years.

In short, we have mentioned almost 10 independent sources here, and more if we try to separate the creedal texts from the thirties. All of these sources attest to Jesus' death and resurrection appearances! Such source richness is almost unheard of in the ancient world.

James, the brother of Jesus and a skeptic, was converted after experiencing what he also thought was an actual appearance of the risen Jesus.

The *conversion of James*, the brother of Jesus, followed his previous life of skepticism. Then he thought he met the risen Jesus. How do we know this?

1. More than one source reports that James, the brother of Jesus, was an unbeliever and apparently even rather cynical regarding Jesus' public ministry (John 7:1–5). Amazingly, Jesus' brothers even sought to remove him from the public eye because they thought he was insane (Mark 3:21). We also have multiple sources recording that, a few years later, James had become the leader of the early church at Jerusalem (Gal 1:18–19; Acts 15:13–21). In between these two times, the early creedal statement reported that another special event occurred: the risen Jesus appeared to his brother James (1 Cor 15:7).

2. Critical scholars learn about James' skepticism not only from the multiple independent sources that make this claim but also from applying the criterion of embarrassment. In light of his high position of leadership in the Jerusalem church, it is exceptionally unlikely that these early church documents would charge James with disbelieving the Savior, especially when he was Jesus' own brother, unless it were true.[40] So these scholars almost always claim that the texts are accurate. For such an embarrassing item to be remembered over several decades, it is likely that James's unbelief was rather staunch.

An indication of the firm critical conviction regarding James's conversion is Reginald Fuller's comment that even without the report in 1 Corinthians 15:7, "We should have to invent" the appearance to James. Otherwise it is difficult to account for both James's postresurrection conversion and his quick promotion to a major church leadership position.[41]

Not surprisingly, most skeptical scholars agree with this majority position. Lüdemann declares: "Because of 1 Cor 15.7 it is certain *that* James 'saw' his brother."[42] Helmut Koester shares this conviction: "That Jesus also appeared to . . . James . . . cannot very well be questioned."[43]

The disciples were utterly transformed by their conviction that they had seen the risen Jesus, even being willing to die for this belief.

The entire New Testament and earliest chapters of church history testify to the *transformation of the apostles*. Since there was no Christian faith apart from Jesus' resurrection, their metamorphosis was due directly to their convictions regarding this event.

1. The Gospels record that, prior to Jesus being crucified, the apostles abandoned and denied him. They panicked and fled. Afterwards they hid.[44] At least two critical criteria are evident here. We have multiple sources for these phenomena, all of which agree on this general scenario. Additionally, embarrassment is evident as well, for it is unlikely that these Christian texts would lampoon their leaders by charging that they had abandoned their Lord during difficult times, especially in order to protect themselves, unless this is precisely what had happened.

But we are told that seeing Jesus alive again radically modified the remainder of his disciples' lives, even to the point of their willing martyrdom.[45] The rest of the New Testament also witnesses to the life investments made by these followers, all rooted in their changed lives. This can be seen in their evangelism, teaching, and social involvement.

2. Extrabiblical sources confirm the preaching of the apostles (Clement of Rome, *Corinthians* 42; Barnabas 5) as well as their willingness to die for their faith (Ignatius, *Smyrneans* 3). Secular reports of Christian commitment are found in Tacitus (*Annals* 15:44) and in the edited citation by Josephus (*Antiquities* 18:3), and are implied in Mara Bar-Serapion's letter to his son (British Museum). Pliny records later, firsthand accounts of persecution that took place during his own governorship in Bithynia and testified that true believers did not recant of their faith (*Letters* 97).

The deaths of several key apostles are also recorded. Clement of Rome records both the martyrdoms of Paul and Peter (*Corinthians* 5), just 30 to 35 years after the events. Differing recountings of the violent killing of James, Jesus' brother, are provided by both the Jewish historian Josephus (*Antiquities* 20:9:1) and Hegesippus (in Eusebius, *Ecclesiastical History* 2:23). The deaths of Peter, Paul, and James the brother of John are also mentioned by Eusebius (*Ecclesiastical History* 2:9; 2:25). It is highly significant that of the four major apostles who met to confirm the gospel in Galatians 2, the martyrdoms of all but John are known from first-century extrabiblical literature.

That Jesus' disciples were transformed to the point of their willing deaths, due to their faith in Jesus' resurrection, is disputed by virtually no one. Admittedly, transformations often occur, usually for religious or political causes. The basic requirements are that those who are willing to die both genuinely believe the teachings and hold them as central tenets.

But the chief similarities to Jesus' disciples stop here, due to a crucial *qualitative* difference. Very much *unlike* other cases, the disciples suffered not only for their *belief* in Jesus' cause but *precisely because of their experiences after Jesus' death.* They were utterly convinced that they had seen him alive again. In short, their transformation was not simply due to their *beliefs*, like those who have died for other causes, but was strictly the result of their perceptual experience with the risen Jesus. So here is the key: they alone were in the best positions to know whether they had really seen Jesus after his death. Their answer to that question was their passionate change, since, apart from the resurrection experiences, there would have been no transformations or martyrdoms.

Critical scholars acknowledge that the disciples' resurrection experiences transformed their lives. Ben Meyer states: "That it was the Easter experiences which affected [the disciples'] transformation is beyond reasonable doubt."[46] Johnson agrees: "Christianity was birthed by the resurrection faith."[47]

The Value of the Minimal Resurrection Facts

Even this severely reduced list of just six historical facts has inestimable value in a historical case for Jesus' resurrection. As we said at the outset, these data and the material that backs them up are recognized by the great majority of critical scholars who treat this subject. This scholarly agreement exists precisely because of the strength of the arguments. Therefore, the most likely conclusions to which these facts lead ought to be acknowledged.

These minimal facts alone can provide a powerful defense of Jesus' resurrection. On the one hand, the data that establish these six historical facts are capable of producing the best refutations of the naturalistic alternative theories against the resurrection. That each hypothesis is met by several strong roadblocks[48] perhaps explains why the naturalistic approaches are held by comparatively few scholars today.[49]

On the other hand, this brief list of minimal facts also includes the most convincing evidences for the resurrection appearances of Jesus. Besides Jesus' death, each of the other items points to his resurrection. From more than one strand of eyewitness testimony, both singly and in groups, to exceptionally early reports, to the conversion of skeptics, all of which produced believers who were in the proper place to know whether the risen Jesus had appeared to them yet were willing to die for this event, creates quite a case. That each of these evidences is both multiply attested and often confirmed from more than one angle increases the depth of the considerations, especially when the case could be expanded by bringing in additional well-recognized data.

Conclusion

It is simply amazing that these minimal historical facts are so multifaceted. The resulting barrage of arguments both contrary to the alternative suggestions as well as supporting the resurrection appearances is incredible. The failure of the naturalistic theories combined with the arguments favoring the disciples actually seeing the risen Jesus indicate that the latter is the best explanation of the data.

We have said that virtually all recent scholars, whatever their ideological positions or discipline, acknowledge the historicity of these six facts. This is certainly significant, for it reflects the force of the data.

Contemporary critical scholars have repeatedly shown their respect for material such as this. One of the "secure facts" that E. P. Sanders places "almost beyond dispute" is that after Jesus' death, "his followers saw him."[50] Fuller pushes a bit further: "Even the most skeptical historian" must "postulate some other event" that is *not* the disciples' faith but "the cause of the Easter faith." He thinks that the "irreducible historical minimum" here is "a well-based claim of certain disciples to have had visions of Jesus after his death as raised from the dead."[51] So an experience beyond the disciples' faith is necessary to explain what really happened.

Of course there are disagreements about many details. Stated succinctly, this is the crux of the matter: the known evidence to which virtually all scholars agree strongly favors the thesis that the original disciples observed Jesus after his death. Since alternative theses have failed to account viably for these experiences in natural terms, as most scholars also agree, the best conclusion is that the early believers actually saw the risen Jesus.[52]

In short, there is a better option than just raising other questions that move us away from this central thesis. Why concentrate on the texts or issues that are less clear? Rather, critical scholars should focus on the data that they admit *can* be known.[53] My thesis has been that the minimal facts are sufficient to argue convincingly that Jesus' resurrection is by far the best historical explanation for what we know. Other questions remain to be researched, but this minimal foundation seems secure: after Jesus died by crucifixion, he appeared to his followers.

Endnotes

1 This volume honoring for my good friend John Warwick Montgomery is a wonderful place for an essay on Jesus' resurrection since this historical event appears so prominently in his publications. Without producing a full-length defense of the resurrection (as much as some of us would have greatly enjoyed such a treatment!), his works touch often on this topic. For examples, see Montgomery's writings *Where Is History Going?* (Grand Rapids: Zondervan, 1969), 29–36; *The Shape of the Past: A Christian Response to Secular Philosophies of History* (Minneapolis: Bethany, 1975), 138–45; *History and Christianity* (Downers Grove: InterVarsity, 1964, 1965), 72–80 along with the discussion in the appendix.

2 A much overlooked and often neglected aspect of critical research needs to be carefully noted here. Critical scholars do *not* object to the use of Scripture texts, as long as there are *good reasons* these particular portions should be cited. This is the chief point at which so many misunderstand this method. This also explains why critical scholars themselves most regularly use biblical citations. Even though I will not usually be able to provide here more than a few hints of these reasons, I will generally cite only those texts that, on critical grounds, have a good claim to being historical reports.

3 An overview of this methodology can be found in Gary R. Habermas, "Evidential Apologetics," in Steven B. Cowan, editor, *Five Views on Apologetics* (Grand Rapids: Zondervan, 2000), 99–100, 186–90.

4 These lists appear in a variety of my publications, for example: *The Historical Jesus: Ancient Evidence for the Life of Christ* (Joplin, MO: College Press, 1996),

158–61; with J. P. Moreland, *Beyond Death: Exploring the Evidence for Immortality* (Wheaton: Crossway, 1998; Eugene, OR: Wipf and Stock, 2003), 113–15.

5   A less detailed listing is found in Habermas, "Evidential Apologetics," 106–16. From a different angle, including more critical attestation, see Gary R. Habermas, *The Risen Jesus and Future Hope* (Lanham, MD: Rowman and Littlefield, 2003), 15–31.

6   These texts include Luke 24:34; 1 Cor 11:26; Rom 4:25; Phil 2:8; 1 Tim 2:6; 1 Pet 3:18, along with the Acts sermon summaries (2:22–36; 3:13–16; 4:8–10; 5:29–32; 10:39–43; 13:28–31; 17:1–3, 30–31 in particular).

7   Matt 27:26–56; Mark 15:20–47; Luke 23:26–56; John 19:16–42.

8   Though they differ in historical value, the non-Christian texts that mention the death of Jesus include Tacitus (*Annals* 15:44), Josephus's disputed text (*Antiquities* 18:3), the Talmud (*Sanhedrin* 43a; cf. 106b), Lucian of Samosata (*The Death of Peregrine* 11–13), Mara Bar-Serapion (from a Syriac letter in the British Museum), Thallus (from a Julius Africanus fragment), the so-called lost Acts of Pilate (Justin Martyr, *First Apology* 35). Gnostic works include the *Gospel of Truth* (20:11–14,25–29), the *Gospel of Thomas* (45:1–16), and *Treatise on Resurrection* (46:14–21). The *Toledoth Jesu* is a much later writing. For further details and evaluation of these texts, see Habermas, *The Historical Jesus*, chap. 9.

9   By date, see Clement of Rome (*Corinthians* 7; 12; 21; 49), Ignatius (*Trallians* 9; *Smyrneans* 1), Barnabas (5), and Justin Martyr (*First Apology* 32, 35; 50; *Dialogue with Trypho* 47; 108). Reference notations for the apostolic fathers follow J. B. Lightfoot, editor, *The Apostolic Fathers* (Grand Rapids: Baker, 1891/1971).

10 For various angles on crucifixion and death by asphyxiation, see especially William D. Edwards, Wesley J. Gabel, and Floyd E. Hosmer, "On the Physical Death of Jesus Christ," *Journal of the American Medical Association* 255 (1986); Robert Bucklin, "The Legal and Medical Aspects of the Trial and Death of Christ," *Medicine, Science and the Law* (1970), 14–26; Pierre Barbet, *A Doctor at Calvary* (Garden City: Doubleday, 1953); Joseph Zias and Eliezer Sekeles, "The Crucified Man from Giv`at ha-Mivtar: A Reappraisal," *Israel Exploration Journal* 35 (1985); Joe Zias and James H. Charlesworth, "Crucifixion: Archaeology, Jesus, and the Dead Sea Scrolls," in *Jesus and the Dead Sea Scrolls*, ed. James H. Charlesworth (New York: Doubleday, 1992), especially 281–82; Vassilios Tzaferis, "Crucifixion—the Archaeological Evidence," *Biblical Archaeological Review* 11 (1985), especially 9 (reprint); Hershel Shanks, "Scholar's Corner: New Analysis of the Crucified Man," *Biblical Archaeological Review* 11 (1985); Alexander Metherell and Lee Strobel, "The Medical Evidence," in *The Case for Christ* (Grand Rapids: Zondervan/Harper Collins, 1998), chapter 11.

11 See the excellent studies by Martin Hengel, *Crucifixion* (Philadelphia: Fortress Press, 1977), 70; S. Legasse, *The Trial of Jesus* (London: SCM, 1997), 116, 131; and James D. G. Dunn, *Jesus Remembered* (Grand Rapids: Eerdmans, 2003), 781. Other relevant details can be found in the sources in the previous note above.

12 For medical details of the chest wound, see Edwards, Gabel, and Hosmer, "Physical Death"; J. E. Holoubek and A. B. Holoubek, "Execution by Crucifixion: History, Methods, and Cause of Death," *Journal of Medicine* 26 (1995): 1–16; Bucklin, "Medical Aspects"; John Wilkinson, "The Incident of the Blood and Water in John 19.34," *Scottish Journal of Theology* 28 (1975); Frederick T. Zugibe, *The Cross and the Shroud* (Cresskill, NJ: McDonagh, 1981), especially 118–30.

13 David Friedrich Strauss, *A New Life of Jesus*, second edition; no translator provided; two volumes (London: Williams and Norgate, 1879), 1:408–12. Recent scholars who still think that Strauss's critique was decisive against the swoon theory include A. E. Harvey, "A Short Life After Death," review of *The Anastasis: The Resurrection of Jesus as a Historical Event*, by J. Duncan M. Derrett, in *The Times Literary Supplement*, No. 4153 (1982); Pheme Perkins, review of *The Anastasis: The Resurrection of Jesus as a Historical Event*, by J. Duncan M. Derrett, in *The Catholic Biblical Quarterly* 45 (1983): 684–85; T. S. M. Williams, review of *The Anastasis: The Resurrection of Jesus as a Historical Event*, by J. Duncan M. Derrett, in the *Journal of Theological Studies* 36 (1985): 445–47; cf. Otto Merk, review of *The Anastasis: The Resurrection of Jesus as a Historical Event*, by J. Duncan M. Derrett, in *Gnomon-Kritische Zeitschrift für die Gesamte Klassische Altertumswissenschaft* 59 (1987): 761–63. A careful critique of the swoon theory is found in Habermas, *The Historical Jesus*, 69–75.

14 Marcus Borg, *Jesus: A New Vision: Spirit, Culture, and the Life of Discipleship* (San Francisco: Harper Collins, 1987), 179.

15 John Dominic Crossan, *Jesus: A Revolutionary Biography* (San Francisco: Harper Collins, 1994), 145.

16 Michael Martin, *The Case Against Christianity* (Philadelphia: Temple University Press, 1991), 81; also p. 89.

17 Roy Hoover, "A Contest between Orthodoxy and Veracity," in Paul Copan and Ronald K. Tacelli, eds., *Jesus' Resurrection: Fact or Figment? A Debate Between William Lane Craig and Gerd Lüdemann* (Downers Grove: InterVarsity Press, 2000), 129 and 130–31, respectively.

18 Regarding natural challenges to Paul's experience, see Habermas, *The Risen Jesus and Future Hope*, 49–50, endnote 157.

19 Hans Dieter Betz, *Galatians: A Commentary on Paul's Letter to the Churches in Galatia* (Philadelphia: Fortress, 1979), 96, 100.

20 Specifically, see Acts 1:1–11; 2:32; 3:15; 4:10; 5:30–32; 10:39–43; 13:30–31; 17:2–3,30–31. Another early tradition that reports a resurrection appearance is Luke 24:34.

21 See Mark 16:1–8; Matt 28:9–20; Luke 24:13–51; and John 20:14–21:23. Most scholars conclude that Mark is the earliest and most authoritative Gospel and that Mark ended his Gospel at 16:8. Clearly, Mark still knew of Jesus' resurrection appearances, as indicated by Jesus' predictions (8:31; 9:9; 9:31; 10:33–34; 14:27–28), the angel who reported the resurrection, the empty tomb itself, and the mention of Peter, along with the projected appearance in Galilee (16:4–7, which is tied back to 14:28; cf. 1 Cor 15:5).

22 Such as *The Gospel of Truth* (25:25–34), *The Treatise on Resurrection* (44:27–29; 45:14–23; 46:14–21; 48:10–19), *The Gospel of Thomas* (opening prologue, 45:15–17), and *The Apocryphon of John* (1:5–12).

23 Norman Perrin, *The Resurrection According to Matthew, Mark, and Luke* (Philadelphia: Fortress, 1977), 80.

24 Luke Timothy Johnson, *The Real Jesus* (San Francisco: Harper Collins, 1996), 118.

25 From a survey of recent scholars, I have argued that about 75 percent accept the empty tomb. See Gary R. Habermas, "Resurrection Research from 1975 to the Present: What Are Critical Scholars Saying?" in *Journal for the Study of the Historical Jesus* 3 (2005): 140–41.

26 For a summary of these arguments along with further critical attestation, see Habermas, *The Risen Jesus and Future Hope*, 23–24.

27 Michael Grant, *Jesus: An Historian's Review of the Gospels* (New York: Collier, 1992), 176.

28 I have argued this case often. See the details, for examples, in *Historical Jesus*, 152–57; *Beyond Death*, 128–30; Gary R. Habermas with Antony G. N. Flew, *Resurrected? An Atheist and Theist Dialogue* (Lanham, MD: Rowman and Littlefield, 2005), 3–7; Gary R. Habermas, "The Resurrection Appearances of Jesus," in R. Douglas Geivett and Habermas, eds., *In Defense of Miracles: A Comprehensive Case for God's Action in History* (Downers Grove: InterVarsity, 1997), 262–75; Gary R. Habermas, "Why I Believe the Miracles of Jesus Actually Happened," in Norman L. Geisler and Paul K. Hoffman, *Why I Am a Christian: Leading Thinkers Explain Why They Believe* (Grand Rapids: Baker, 2001), 117–19; Gary R. Habermas, "The Case for Christ's Resurrection," in Francis J. Beckwith, William Lane Craig, and J. P. Moreland, *To Everyone an Answer: A Case for the Christian Worldview: Essays in Honor of Norman L. Geisler* (Downers Grove: InterVarsity, 2004), 182–84; Gary R. Habermas and Michael R. Licona, *The Case for the Resurrection of Jesus* (Grand Rapids: Kregel, 2004), 51–53.

29 For one such list of eight "linguistic items" in this text, see Pinchas Lapide, *The Resurrection of Jesus: A Jewish Perspective* (Minneapolis: Augsburg, 1983), 97–99.

30 See William Farmer's study of the term *historeō* as employed in Gal 1:18, in relation to the nature of Paul's inquiry while visiting the apostles in Jerusalem: "Peter and Paul, and the Tradition Concerning 'The Lord's Supper' in 1 Cor 11:23–25," *Criswell Theological Review* 2 (1987), especially 122–30. Paul Barnett agrees that this basic meaning also best explains its use by Herodotus, Polybius, and Plutarch (*Jesus and the Logic of History*, New Studies in Biblical Theology [Grand Rapids: Eerdmans, 1997], 41).

31 Dunn, *Jesus Remembered*, 855, his emphasis.

32 For a list of skeptical scholars who agree, see Habermas, *The Risen Jesus and Future Hope*, 18 and the corresponding endnotes.

33 Gerd Lüdemann, *The Resurrection of Jesus*, translated by John Bowden (Minneapolis: Fortress, 1994), 38.

34   Robert W. Funk and the Jesus Seminar, *The Acts of Jesus: The Search for the Authentic Deeds of Jesus* (San Francisco: Harper Collins and the Polebridge Press, 1998), 454.

35   John Meier states, "From the very beginning of Christian preaching about Jesus.... [t]here was no period when" this teaching did not include Jesus'"life, death, and resurrection" (*A Marginal Jew: The Roots of the Problem and the Person* [New York: Doubleday, 1991], 1:118). Reginald Fuller proclaims that "there was no period" when the resurrection was not the central proclamation of the church (*The Formation of the Resurrection Narratives* [New York: Macmillan, 1980], 48).

36   Gerald O'Collins, *Interpreting Jesus* (London: Geoffrey Chapman, 1983), 109.

37   Paul L. Maier, *In the Fullness of Time: A Historian Looks at Christmas, Easter, and the Early Church* (San Francisco: Harper Collins, 1991), 197.

38   An example is Helmut Koester, *Introduction to the New Testament*, two vols. (Philadelphia: Fortress Press, 1982), vol. 2, *History and Literature of Early Christianity*, 103–4.

39   Ibid., 164–71.

40   John Meier, *A Marginal Jew: Mentor, Message, and Miracle* (New York: Doubleday, 1994), 2:70.

41   Fuller, *The Formation of the Resurrection Narratives*, 37.

42   Lüdemann, *The Resurrection of Jesus*, 109.

43   Helmut Koester, *History and Literature of Early Christianity*, 84. For a list of other skeptical scholars who agree with this assessment, see Habermas, *The Risen Jesus and Future Hope*, 22 and the sources.

44   Matt 26:56,69–74; Mark 14:50,66–72; Luke 22:55–72; John 18:25–27.

45   See the examples in Acts 2:41–47; 4:1–4,8–21,29–31; 5:17–32,40–42; 7:54–60; 12:1–2; 1 Cor 15:9–11; 1 Tim 3:16. On the apostles' willingness to die for their convictions, see John 21:18–19; Acts 7:57–60; 12:1–3; 21:13, 25:11; Rom 14:8; 1 Cor 15:30–32; 2 Cor 4:7–14; 11:23–32; Phil 1:20–24; cf. 2 Pet 1:13–15.

46   Ben Meyer, *The Aims of Jesus* (London: SCM, 1979), 60.

47   Johnson, *Living Jesus*, 6.

48   For some examples, see Habermas, *The Risen Jesus and Future Hope*, 10–12, 16–17, 29–30. See especially Habermas and Licona, *The Case for the Resurrection of Jesus*, chapters 5–9.

49   For my survey of the scholarly minority who hold natural theses in comparison to other resurrection researchers, see Gary R. Habermas, "Mapping the Recent Trend Toward the Bodily Resurrection Appearances of Jesus in Light of Other Prominent Critical Positions," in *The Resurrection of Jesus: John Dominic Crossan and N. T. Wright in Dialogue*, edited by Robert B. Stewart (Minneapolis: Fortress, 2006), 78–92.

50   E. P. Sanders, *The Historical Figure of Jesus* (London: Penguin, 1993), 10–13; cf. 280. Sanders confesses that he does not know exactly how the disciples saw Jesus.

51   Fuller, *The Formation of the Resurrection Narratives*, 2, 169, 181–82.

52   In "Mapping the Recent Trend Toward the Bodily Resurrection Appearances of Jesus," I have argued that the predominant scholarly position at present, by a fairly large margin, is that the risen Jesus not only appeared to his followers, but that he did so in a bodily manner (see especially 90–92 for the final conclusion of the argument). For each step of the historical argument, along with far more data than we could mention here, see my publications listed above.

53   For a nonexhaustive list of more than 50 New Testament scholars, theologians, historians, and philosophers who recognize each of these six facts, see Habermas, *The Risen Jesus and Future Hope*, 50–51, endnote 165.

Apologetics, Persuasion, and Pastoral Care

Ross Clifford

One of Professor Montgomery's most beloved apologetic texts is 1 Peter 3:15–16, "Always be prepared to give an answer to anyone who demands it, but do so with gentleness and respect." Gentleness and respect at least imply that apologetics is more than persuasion, and that it interconnects with pastoral considerations. Yet surprisingly, written material on pastoral care and apologetics is scarce. The exception is the genre that concentrates on the deprogramming of those who have been caught up in the web of emotionally and/or physically "dangerous" cults. This is a specialist field, and it is fair to say that the jury is still out on the benefits of such "exit" counseling (Robbins, 1986; Browley and Richardson, 1983). In the controversial movie *Holy Smoke*, Hollywood actress Kate Winslet plays a powerful and earthy role that depicts the "negative" side of deprogramming.

For our more general pastoral care focus we should initially turn to biblical paradigms for the formation of helpful pastoral models in relationship to apologetics.

The shepherd metaphor is one of protection of the flock. The shepherd guides, feeds, and cares for his sheep. It also pictures the carer seeking out the lost (Luke 15:1–7). The model is the good shepherd: God in Christ. The good shepherd lays down his life for his sheep, including some not yet in the fold (John 10:1–21). Jesus' command to Peter was to continue this calling of equipping and protecting, in his command to "Feed My Lambs" and "Teach My Sheep" (John 21:15–16). It's a ministry the apostles commanded the leaders of the church to maintain (Acts 20:28; 1 Pet 5:2) and is particularly relevant to apologetics. From this metaphor the apologist appreciates that his role is in both negative apologetics (teaching the flock about heresy) and positive apologetics (reaching out in creative ways to engage the lost).

Jesus as healer is a prominent theme in the New Testament. In this context the motifs of forgiveness, purged conscience, and release from shame are significant (Heb 9:11–15). Pastoral care to those who have made lifestyle and truth-claim decisions that they now regret frequently involves such healing. While pastoral care has historically been related to the "cure" of souls, which may imply a one-time or short-term intervention, healing in pastoral care usually implies a more gradual change and ongoing structures of support. So for apologists it is not just a matter of saving a New Ager or a Mormon. It is also about being available for such a person as they face radical issues and changes, including possible separation from friends and loved ones when they commit their life to Christ.

A prophetic voice is not divorced from pastoral care. Old Testament and New Testament leadership included prophetic utterance. Care for the family of God involved confronting moral and social justice failures in the life of the individual and of the community (Amos 5; Matt 5:21–32). Prophetic insight also involved a message of judgment for those who thought and lived outside of God's boundaries. One does this with a sense of care for people's eternal destiny. The exercise of prophetic warnings is of particular importance for the apologist in a religiously pluralistic world.

With the current interest in Trinitarian theology, there has been a stress on the doctrine of the Trinity being the grammar by which we understand pastoral care. The Greek term *perichoresis* (mutual interpretation or indwelling) is of particular significance here. It envisages close relations in the Trinity but not to the detriment of the personhood of the Father and of the Son and of the Holy Spirit. However, the persons of the Trinity do not simply enter into a mutual relationship but are constituted by one another in relations. The implication for pastoral care is that William Temple's "principle of fellowship" and "the sanctity of personality" are two foundational concepts. In the context of apologetics it envisages a strong relational emphasis and supportive structures in the church ("principles of fellowship"), as we seek to reach people for Christ ("the sanctity of personality"). Good apologists will link individuals to a redeemed, vibrant Christian community.

Now the Church plays a primary role in pastoral care and apologetics. Through its preaching and teaching ministry, people ought to be shown a worldview that protects them from doctrinal confusion, understands "spiritual warfare," and equips one in apologetically sharing with others. Here faith is nurtured and sustained through the richness of the shepherd metaphor and the prophetic model. For the Church to fulfil its role, pastors need to be acquainted with worldviews, apologetics, theology of cults and alternative religious movements. Such training is not viewed as essential in many seminaries, and it should be. Michael Green says it best:

> It would be advantageous if much of the training was on the job, rather than in the classroom, and if it took place under competent practitioners rather than under theoretical academics. Both have their place, and both are needed if we are to prepare people properly for the increasing challenge of ministry in a largely non-Christian society.
>
> Furthermore, there needs to be a major concentration on apologetics and evangelism in the classroom. Tutors need to be recruited who are not only able to teach, but to take students out with them, and practise these two disciplines. I have made it a rule for my students . . . that nobody should graduate from the course without having been out with me in evangelising, and standing up to the objections of those who did not believe the Christian faith. . . .
>
> The sad thing is that few colleges today teach apologetics or evangelism, and even fewer have their instructors go out with their students into the chill winds of the agnostic world to learn by doing. When you do that, it transforms a college! . . .
>
> The study of Augustine would be revolutionised if students appreciated that the barbarians are at our gates today, just as much as they were at the gates of Rome in the fifth century. His priorities for Christian ministry make sense today! The study of Gnosticism could spring to life if it were seen as a major precursor of the New Age. Arianism would mean a lot more if it were related to the tenets of the Jehovah's Witnesses. And a doctrine like justification by grace through faith could be enormously sharpened if it were contrasted with the legalism of so many contemporary

cults—not to mention the assumptions of many church members! The church has a right to expect this sort of training from its theological colleges.

(McGrath and Green, 1993, 170–71)

The Church also has a role in creating support groups. Support groups can help build self-esteem and provide resources for living and social companionship. Cults and New Age movements often appeal to those who are experiencing a sense of personal inadequacy, are struggling with life, or are lonely. Further, the overall fellowship of the Church is an outworking of the communal nature of the Trinity. Many who are spiritually searching today have a real desire to belong.

When assisting someone who is considering joining or is coming under the influence of an alternative religious movement, again, apologetic teaching and warning are norms. However, these should not happen in an environment that is divorced from the deep emotional, psychological, demonic, and sociological factors that may be involved. Apologetics often takes place in a *complex tapestry*. There may be strategic issues bubbling away below the surface such as loneliness, adolescent problems, and dissatisfaction with life. Pastoral care and apologetics is much more than sharing good doctrine. Here one must be prepared to take time to ascertain the person's world, to put themselves in their shoes, and to evidence a real empathy. In this setting, pastoral care and apologetics are seeking to help the person work through the theological and personal issues involved. It is working toward the person being able to reach their own responsible decision as one also uses good apologetic tools.

Pastoral care for cult members won to Christ through apologetics is essential. Again the teaching/feeding imagery of the prophet and shepherd are to the fore. Also applicable is the healing motif, as ex-cult members may have to deal with a sense of anger, betrayal, and resentment toward the cult. They may blame the cult and others for the path they have followed. This has to be balanced with a reminder of the person's own freedom to make the decisions they have made. Real freedom may have been restricted by psychological or manipulative factors, but that is not necessarily so. In any event, as the person examines their own choices and life, the Christian discipline of confession for sin and guilt is an integral strand in pastoral care. It is integrated with the grace of forgiveness. For ex-cult members a debrief—"wrap-up talk"—is often beneficial. At the appropriate time it helps the person remember why decisions were made, what factors influenced the process, and why they have now determined to leave the cult or religious movement. The naming of these processes and the subsequent reframing assists in this difficult life transition.

The *family* has an important part to play in pastoral care and apologetics. A particular pastoral care focus will be the Christian family of the one who has chosen to commit himself to a non-Christian worldview or to abandon Christ. For some families the issue will be the real disappointment felt by them for the decision that has been made. Other families may be dealing with changed circumstances produced by someone joining a dangerous or fringe religious movement. The family member attracted to such a cult may have removed himself from an intimate family relationship. Saliba indicates Kübler-Ross' analysis of the feelings of dying patients has, with modification, helpful insights here. Kübler-Ross lists five stages the dying pass through: denial and isolation; anger; bargaining; depression; acceptance. In cult cases apologists/carers should help families overcome their strong emotions of "disbelief, grief, guilt and anger" (Saliba, 1995, 216). Encouraging the family to tell their stories associated with the transition and loss can be one expression of pastoral care. Families need assistance to learn how to handle these stages which will allow them to more helpfully reach out to their "lost" loved ones.

A sensitive but equally important task is an analysis of the dynamics of this particular family's life. This is certainly so where the member has limited their involvement with the family. Family Systems Theory may assist here. Individuals are sought to be understood in the context of the family. The evaluation of family relationships, school, work, and cultural preferences may help in unfolding why a family member has made a decision to join a particular religious group. This pastoral measure is not only preventative as far as other family members are concerned but may also engage the family in a new dynamic that is attractive to the family member who is now distant but is being reached for Christ.

Education also plays an important part for families. An understanding of the Christian worldview in contrast to other worldviews can form the basis for dialog as the family shares together. Families that read together C. S. Lewis's Narnia books and other such gems are going to interact over many important worldview issues.

Finally pastoral care and apologetics will embrace Martin Luther's *"the duties of humanity,"* i.e., the care of the sick, dying, and impoverished. In crisis situations of facing sickness or death, many seek or allow pastoral care. The opportunity may even be unsolicited. Here there is a real place for sensitive apologetics. The skill of listening is strategic, and one must avoid manipulation.

I vividly recall a very difficult non-Christian woman attending my church for prayer after she was diagnosed with cancer. Prior to this time she had resisted all attempts for us to share the gospel. A few days later I was visiting her in intensive care in hospital. In God's order of things her doctor was someone who attended my church. Together we stood by her bed, aware that she had hours left to live. I asked her if she wanted me to share the gospel message with her. She cried out, "I'm not sure about Jesus." A brief apologetic took place, and she repented and committed her life to Christ. Days later I was conducting the funeral. Very few were present, as she had been hard to please and had few friends. Her former husband was present, and he informed me that a miracle had taken place. Just after we left her, he had visited to say his farewells. He said, "She took my hand and apologised for all the wrongs she had committed in the marriage." He said, "It was a miracle. I couldn't believe the change in her words and demeanour. We parted friends." Clearly she had been converted and transformed by the grace of God. Apologetic ministry and the "duties of humanity" go hand in hand.

"The duties of humanity" can be broadened to incorporate general pastoral care for the community at large. For example, instructing parents in an open forum of ways of protecting their children from religious groups that are abusive—to ensure parents have the resources, or know where to obtain resources on groups and to give advice on raising children that, while promoting respectful behaviour, are also aware of the dangers of uncritical support for authority, structures, and institutions. Critical thinking in young people is a protection from the advances of abusive groups. Also open forums are a wonderful venue for apologetically presenting the Christian worldview and how that impacts individual and community life.

In conclusion, Professor Montgomery is a renaissance man. As Mohler states, he "has developed one of the most varied resumes in the evangelical world" (Mohler, 1989, 39). He is equally at home in theology, jurisprudence, historiography, library science, ethics, law, and apologetics. His work is interdisciplinary, which is in itself justification for reflecting on pastoral care in the light of apologetics.

Yet there is another reason for so doing. Montgomery's view of knowledge does not divorce one discipline from another. For example, for Montgomery just as the legal rules of evidence help us to justify whether an ordinary statement is true, so they can claim to justify whether Christ arose. And as Christianity is an historical religion, there is no justification in detaching the theology of the gospel from an historical investigation (Clifford, 2004, 253).

Therefore, as we honour Professor Montgomery at this time, it is appropriate for all those committed to apologetics to take the injunction of "gentleness" and "respect" seriously by combining the disciplines of apologetics and pastoral care.

References

Browley, David, and James Richardson, eds. *The Brainwashing/ Deprogramming Controversy: Socological, Psychological, Legal and Historical Persepectives*. New York: Edwin Mellen Press, 1983.

Clifford, Ross. *John Warwick Montgomery's Legal Apologetic: An Apologetic for All Seasons*. Bonn: Verlag für Kultur und Wissenschaft, 2004.

Collins, Gary R. *Family Shock: Keeping Families Strong in the Midst of Earthshaking Change*. Wheaton: Tyndale House, 1995.

Enroth, Ronald M. *Churches that Abuse*. Grand Rapids: Zondervan, 1992.

Goodliff, Paul. *Care in a Confused Climate: Pastoral Care and Postmodern Culture*. London: Darton, Longman and Todd, 1998.

Ingleheart, Glenn A. *Church Members and Nontraditional Religious Groups*. Nashville: Broadman Press, 1985.

Kirkwood, Neville A. *Pastoral Care to Muslims: Building Bridges*. New York, London, Oxford: The Haworth Pastoral Press, 2002.

McGrath, Alister, and Michael Green. *Springboard for Faith*. London: Hodder and Stoughton, 1993.

Mohler, Richard A. "Evangelical Theology and Karl Barth: Representative Models of Response." Thesis (Ph.D). The Southern Baptist Theological Seminary, 1989.

Robbins, Thomas. "Goodbye to Little Red Riding Hood." Update 10/2, June 1986, 5–18.

Saliba, John A. *Perspectives on New Religious Movements*. London: Geoffrey Chapman, 1995, chap.7.

Scott, B. J. M. "Pastoral Care in Multi-Faith Areas," in *Dictionary of Contemporary Religion in the Western World*. Christopher Partridge, ed. Leicester: InterVarsity Press; Downers Grove: InterVarsity Press, 2002, 49–54.

Tidball, Derek J. *Builders and Fools: Leadership the Bible Way*. Leicester: InterVarsity Press, 1999.

Christianity for the Technically Inclined

RISK ASSESSMENT, PROBABILITY, AND PROPHECY

James Dietz

Every day our physical safety is affected by the probability of failures associated with the machines we use. Designers of machines for use with the public follow probabilistic approaches in determining whether a machine is safe to use. If we accept this as a rational approach to self-preservation (and we do), then it seems reasonable to apply the same probabilistic criteria to the analysis of the Bible.[1]

Risk Assessment and Machines

An example of public safety and the consequences of machine failure comes from the use of public transportation, in particular trains and subways. In modern railroading, equipment on the trains and equipment on the ground communicate to form a sophisticated collision-avoidance system. If these systems fail to perform their function, trains can collide with deadly consequences.

Elements of these sorts of collision avoidance systems (called signaling in railroad jargon) date back to 1829. At that time, hand signals, flags, and lanterns were used on the B & O Railroad.[2] As time has advanced, machines have taken the place of humans in railroad signaling. Not only have machines replaced humans, but also the machines themselves have become complex.

When everything in a signaling system is working correctly, trains do not collide. Designers of signaling systems must also consider what happens when things break. One approach to this is to begin by making a list of every possible failure that can occur. Then, for every failure, assess two things. First, assess the severity of the consequences of the failure. Second, assess the probability of the occurrence of the failure. With these two pieces of information, one then determines whether the risk associated with each failure is acceptable or whether the machine must be redesigned in some way.[3]

The basic process is a formalized method of doing that which we do every day. We look at the consequences or rewards of a situation and evaluate the probability of occurrence. Consider the case where you spot a one hundred dollar bill in the middle of a highway. One considers the reward ($100) and the probability of success (no cars are in sight). As the reward changes (say $1) or the probability of success changes (rush-hour traffic), one makes a different evaluation as to whether to run into the street.

The basic process for our railway failure analysis is illustrated in the table below (see Appendix II for a more detailed view). Find the column for the severity, find the row for the frequency, and assess the risk associated with each conceivable failure by noting the region where the row and column intersect.

Risk Assessment		Severity			
		Really bad (e.g.; many deaths)	Bad (e.g.; death)	Minor Injuries	Everything's OK
Frequency	Occurs all the time	1	2	3	3
	Occurs sometimes	2	2	3	4
	Very rarely occurs	3	3	4	4
	Virtually never occurs	4	4	4	4

Where: 1 = Correct this as soon as possible!
2 = Correct this reasonably soon!
3 = This could be a problem. Caution!
4 = Acceptable risk.

Risk Assessment and Christianity

How is train safety relevant to discussions of Christianity? The first point is that our very lives are affected by probabilistic calculations, and we expect to survive on the basis of those calculations.[4] In our example, we board trains and travel from place to place with every expectation of reaching our destination. Whether we are aware of it, our expectations of surviving the trip without a collision are realistic, based on probabilistic calculations performed by the designers of public transportation systems.[5] If we use these analytical tools to evaluate life-and-death issues in the secular world, it would be hypocritical or prejudiced to discredit or fail to use the same tools in the investigation of theology.

The second point is to consider how an investigation into the truth of Christianity fits into the risk-assessment matrix. Consider the severity of the issue. In addition to affecting us in the here and now, Christianity states that there is life after physical death, and the nature of that life is dependent on whether one is truly a Christian. Not only is one's individual eternal destiny affected but also the eternal destiny of loved ones and others whom one might have affected. This corresponds to the most severe column of the risk-assessment matrix. Now consider the probability. In the technical risk assessment, the probabilities were related to the frequency of failures. In the Christianity risk assessment, the probabilities are associated with whether Christianity is true.[6] Using only the most severe column and modifying the row definitions for this discussion, consider the following table:

Christianity Risk Assessment		Severity
		Eternal Destiny
Probability	Christianity is very likely to be true.	1
	Christianity may well be true.	2
	Christianity probably isn't true.	3
	Christianity is very likely not to be true.	4

Where: 1 = Detailed investigation into Christianity is needed as soon as possible!

2 = Detailed investigation into Christianity is needed reasonably soon!

3 = I won't dismiss Christianity, but there isn't sufficient reason to investigate it now.

4 = Christianity isn't relevant to me. Maybe I'll go to a
restaurant tonight.

Probability

There are different approaches to assessing the probability associated with the truth of Christianity. In this essay we'll be considering prophecy (more on that later). To do that, some math is involved (but less than half a page).

Consider an event E1. Now consider that the probability of E1 actually happening is P1. We can write an equation for the probability of E1 as:

$$P(E1) = P1$$

Now consider that there are a several independent events E1 through En, with corresponding probabilities of P1 through Pn. We can write an equation for the probability of all these events occurring simultaneously as:

$$P(E1...En) = (P1 * P2 * P3 * ...P4)$$

As long as the events are independent, you derive the probability that they occur simultaneously by multiplying the probabilities of each event.[7] For a simple case, consider several events that each have the same probability Pe. The probability of all those events occurring simultaneously is:

$$P = Pe^n, \text{ where n is the number of events}$$

Prophecy

There are many prophecies in the Bible, that is, cases where a particular thing was predicted in advance of its actually occurring. Consider five criteria to use in evaluating prophecies and fulfillment.[8] They are:

1. Clarity: The prophecy must not be ambiguous.
2. Prior Announcement: The prediction must clearly be made before the fulfillment.

3. Independence: The prophet must not be able to cause the prophecy to occur.
4. Likelihood: The prophecy can't be just a good guess.
5. No Manipulation: The one fulfilling the prophecy cannot be manipulating the circumstances.

The discussion in this essay will be restricted to an evaluation of Old Testament prophecies concerning Jesus and those prophecies which are indicated to have been fulfilled in the New Testament.[9] Appendix I provides a basic list of 25 such prophecies.

A reading of the prophecies demonstrates the first criteria (clarity), the fourth criteria (likelihood), and the fifth criteria (no manipulation) of the set. As a result of the time difference between the writing in the Old Testament and the time of Jesus' life, these examples meet the second criteria (prior announcement) and third criteria (independence).

There is no clear basis for assigning individual probabilities to the individual prophecies. So one could consider some reasonable typical number. For argument's sake, say that there's a one in four chance (or 25% probability) for each prophecy to be true in Jesus life and person. That is, there is 25 percent probability that some prophecy would actually happen by random chance.[10]

Using the numbers above, the probability that all of these prophecies would be fulfilled in one person is:

$$\left(\frac{1}{4}\right)^{25} = \frac{1}{10^{15}} = 10^{-15}$$

So there is an extremely small probability that these prophecies could have all been fulfilled by random chance. Since there are actually more than 25 prophecies, this calculation is conservative. And the 25-percent probability for each individual prophecy is certainly conservative.[11] So one would conclude that the fulfillment of Bible prophecies offers objective grounds for believing the Christian truth claims.[12]

Back to Risk Assessment

On the basis of fulfilled prophecy, it's reasonable to eliminate at least the last two rows of the proposed Christian Risk Assessment Matrix. That leaves us with the following, depending on one's personal evaluation:

Christianity Risk Assessment—Reduced		Severity
		Eternal Destiny
Probability	Christianity is very likely to be true.	1
	Christianity may well be true.	2

1. Detailed investigation into Christianity is needed as soon as possible!
2. Detailed investigation into Christianity is needed reasonably soon!

Recap

A risk-assessment matrix is a formalized way of evaluating risk. One considers the consequences of an event and compares that to the probability that the event will occur. If the severity of the consequences is low and the probability of the event is low, then one can ignore the risk. Conversely, if the severity of the consequences is high and the probability is high, then one must not ignore the risk. This is a rational approach to risk assessment and one that is codified through formal standards and used for public safety.

The severity of the consequences associated with Christianity is high. A probabilistic evaluation of prophecy shows that Christianity is very likely to be true. Analyzing this data by using the same risk assessment approach that is used to assure that public transportation is safe, one is left with the conclusion that Christianity must be seriously investigated, and soon! Footnote 13 offers accessible resources for any reader who wants to investigate Christianity and investigate further evidence for its truth.[13]

Appendix I—Old Testament Prophecy and New Testament Fulfillment

Lists of fulfilled prophecies can be found in various sources. A short list of 38 prophecies about Jesus is found in the Thompson Chain-Reference Bible.[14] Twenty-five prophecies from that list are duplicated below, to correspond to the probability calculation in this essay. Note that some of the greater prophecies (e.g., virgin birth, resurrection) are not in the list below so that the reader does not have to accept or analyze the testimony for those miraculous events prior to evaluating the argument herein (although there is no studied reason not to include them). If there are prophecies in the list below that a reader finds objectionable for some reason, other prophecies can be used to make up the 25. Note that the Bible contains many more prophecies that are not directly related to historical events about Jesus.

	Prophecy Reference	Fulfillment Reference	Subject
1	Gen 18:18; 17:19; 28:14	Matt 1:2, Luke 3:34	Promised offspring of Abraham, Isaac, & Jacob
2	Gen 49:10	Luke 3:33	Of the tribe of Judah
3	Isa 9:7	Matt 1:1	Heir to the throne of David
4	Mic 5:2	Matt 2:1	Place of Birth
5	Dan 9:25	Luke 2:1–2	Time of birth
6	Jer 31:15	Matt 2:16	Slaughter of infants
7	Hos 11:1	Matt 2:14	Escape into Egypt
8	Isa 9:1–2	Matt 4:12–16	Ministry in Galilee
9	Isa 53:3	John 1:11	His rejection by the Jews
10	Zech 9:9	John 12:13–14	His triumphal entry
11	Ps 41:9	Mark 14:10	Betrayed by a friend
12	Zech 11:12	Matt 26:15	Betrayed for 30 pieces of silver
13	Zech 11:13	Matt 27:6–7	Money returned for a potter's field
14	Ps 27:12	Matt 26:60–61	False witnesses accused him
15	Isa 53:7	Matt 26:62–63	Silent when accused
16	Isa 50:6	Mark 14:65	Struck and spit on
17	Ps 69:4	John 15:23–25	Hated without cause
18	Isa 53:12	Matt 27:38	Crucified with sinners
19	Ps 22:16	John 20:27	Hands and feet pierced
20	Ps 22:6–8	Matt 27:39–40	Mocked and insulted
21	Ps 109:4	Luke 23:34	Prays for his enemies
22	Zech 12:10	John 19:34	His side to be pierced
23	Ps 22:18	Mark 15:24	Soldiers cast lots for his clothing
24	Ps 34:20	John 19:33	Not a bone to be broken
25	Isa 53:9	Matt 27:57–60	Buried with the rich

Appendix II—Failure Modes and Effects Criticality Analysis[15]

For those who would like more depth on the approach to risk assessment, the tables below provide more precise definitions. Feel free to skip this page. There are variations on these tables within the safety community, but the versions below illustrate the concept.

Hazard Severity Categories		
Description	**Category**	**Definition**
Catastrophic	I	Multiple fatalities; multiple serious injuries; system or equipment loss; or severe environmental damage
Critical	II	Fatality; severe injury or severe occupational illness; or major system, major environmental, or major equipment damage
Marginal	III	Minor injury or minor occupational illness; or minor system or minor equipment damage (damage that can be repaired with minor disruption to service)
Negligible	IV	System, environmental, or equipment damage that does not significantly reduce safety; injuries or illness that do not require first aid or medical attention

Hazard Probability Levels		
Description	**Level**	**Likelihood**
Frequent	A	Very High—likely to occur frequently (Many times per year)
Probable	B	High—Likely to occur occasionally (Once per year)
Occasional	C	Medium—Likely to occur under unusual circumstances (Once per 1–10 years)
Remote	D	Low—Likely to occur over lifetime of the system (Once per 10–100 years)
Improbable	E	Very Low—Could occur, however, not likely over the lifetime of the system

Hazard Risk Index Matrix				
Hazard Probability Level	**Hazard Severity Category**			
	Catastrophic I	Critical II	Marginal III	Negligible IV
Frequent—A	1	1	2	3
Probable—B	1	1	3	4
Occasional—C	1	3	4	4
Remote—D	3	4	4	4
Improbable—E	4	4	4	4

Hazard Risk Assessment		
Risk Index	**Description**	**Criteria**
1	Unacceptable	Must be mitigated with engineering and/ or administrative controls to a Risk Index of 3 or 4 as soon as possible.
2	Undesirable	Should be mitigated with engineering and or administrative controls to a Risk Index of 3 or 4 within a reasonable period of time (one year).
3	Acceptable with controls	Should be verified that the procedures or controls cited are in place and periodically checked.
4	Acceptable as is	No action to mitigate mishap is required.

Endnotes

1 John Warwick Montgomery, *Tractatus Logico-Theologicus* (Bonn, Germany: Verlag für Kultur und Wissenschaft, 2002), 128–31. In the *Tractatus*, Montgomery establishes the underlying approach of evaluating probability and prophecy. This present essay adds the concept of technical risk assessment both to intrigue the technically inclined and to demonstrate the relevance of the method to those who employ technical risk assessment concepts.

2 *Elements of Railway Signaling* (General Railway Signal, 1979), 6.

3 For readers who would like more detail on this methodology, the Reliability Analysis Center, in Rome, NY, offers a publication titled *Failure Mode, Effects, and Criticality Analysis* (FMECA). They can be reached at rac@rome.iitri. com.

4 Kenneth Ross and Bruce W. Main, *Risk Assessment and Product Liability* (For the Defense, 2001, and Web article at www.bowman-brooke.com/a

-risk_assess.htm). In this article, Ross and Main discuss the need formally to conduct and document a risk assessment to improve product design, reduce accidents, and curb liability exposure. The authors describe that this process is becoming commonplace in many industries.

5   And yet we periodically hear of train crashes. One might consider separating these crashes into four categories: (1) nonautomated systems with human error, (2) legacy systems that were not designed to today's evolving standards and are awaiting replacement, (3) improperly analyzed designs, and (4) the one-in-a-billion set of circumstances.

6   Blaise Pascal, *Pensées*, translated by A. J. Krailsheimer (New York, NY: Penguin Books), 121–25. Pascal, born in 1623, was, along with Fermat, a founder of the mathematical theory of probability (E. T. Bell, *Men of Mathematics* [New York: Simon and Schuster, 1937], 86). In "Pascal's Wager," Pascal, in the *Pensées*, argued that if you believe in God, then if you are correct, you win everything; and if you are incorrect, you lose nothing. Diminish your passions against belief and follow in the path of believers. What have you got to lose?

7   Paul L. Meyer, *Introductory Probability and Statistical Applications* (Reading, MA: Addison-Wesley, 1970), 36–44.

8   John Warwick Montgomery, *Evidence for Faith* (Dallas: Probe Ministries, 1991). The first four criteria for evaluating prophecy are from the essay "Truth via Prophecy" by John Bloom. In *Tractatus Logico-Theologicus*, 128–30, Montgomery addresses these points and adds the fifth point.

9   Ibid. Essays in *Evidence for Faith* also address other types and aspects of prophetic fulfillment. These are significant but outside the scope of this essay.

10 John Warwick Montgomery, *Tractatus Logico-Theologicus*, 129–30. In *Tractatus*, Montgomery starts with an arbitrary average probability of ½, and concludes that the number is too high. So he uses an average probability of ¼.

11 In safety related analysis, a probability of 10 E-9 is considered to be safe enough for events with even the most severe consequences. There is no analytical formula that derives 10 E-9 as the right number. It is based on minimizing death but is nevertheless subjective. Should this same number be used in the evaluation of the truth claims of the Bible? Apart from an answer to that question, 10 E-9 is used in the graph below to illustrate the relationship between the number of events and the average probability. Our example (25 prophecies, 0.25 average probability, and 10 E-15 total probability) is shown as a single reference point. The 'x' axis only goes up to 40 prophecies. While this is suitable for this discussion, there are many more prophecies, especially those not directly related to Jesus.

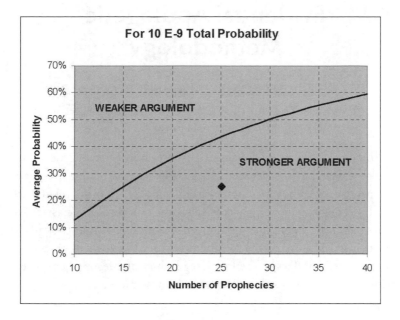

12 Another area of probabilistic study is that of confidence levels and confidence intervals. This sort of analysis is done when analyzing medical trials and opinion polls, where data is sampled. More work could be done to illustrate how this area of probability theory could be used to demonstrate confidence in the truth of Christianity.

13 For additional resources regarding the truth of Christianity from philosophical, historical, legal, and scientific points of view, consider the Canadian Institute for Law, Theology & Public Policy Web site at www.ciltpp .com. For additional resources regarding Christian theology, consider the Wisconsin Evangelical Lutheran Synod Web sites at www.wels.net and www. whataboutjesus.com.

14 Frank Charles Thompson, *Thompson Chain Reference Bible*, New International Version (Grand Rapids, MI: Zondervan Bible Publishers, 1983), 1567–70. Included in this Bible are various resources such as a list of prophecies about Jesus.

15 US Department of Defense, MIL-STD-882D, *Standard Practice for System Safety* (US Department of Defense, 10 February 2000). This standard describes the process of failure modes and effects criticality analysis. The earlier version, MIL-STD-882C, provides more examples of the process.

Evidential Apologetic Methodology

THE MONTGOMERY-BAHNSEN DEBATE

Gary R. Habermas

This essay[1] addresses several matters pertaining to apologetic methodology. Thus, it is concerned chiefly with the particular processes and practice of apologetics, not with epistemology or other related areas. I will begin by introducing briefly some aspects of the classic disputes between evidentialists and presuppositionalists that took place during the last third of the twentieth century. Then I will propose a number of rejoinders to the late Greg Bahnsen's presuppositionalist critique of evidentialist John Warwick Montgomery's system.[2]

Some Background

Longtime observers of the relevant issues in late-twentieth-century apologetic methodology will probably be aware of discussions between two of the chief positions, presuppositionalism and evidentialism.[3] About three or four decades ago, the classic protagonists of each view were probably Cornelius Van Til and John Warwick Montgomery, respectively. Other scholars like Gordon Clark and Clark Pinnock were also regularly involved in the dialogues, arguing for one side or the other. Time and again volleys were fired, sometimes striking their intended mark and sometimes not. Over the years other participants also got involved.[4]

At the close of the twentieth century, however, the discussions proceeded in new directions. As is so often the case in ongoing dialogues, additional issues have taken center stage while some of the older ones have receded into the background. Perhaps foremost among the new trends is that the discussions have been significantly less pointed in recent years. Even more importantly, the two sides (along with other apologetic methods) have unquestionably moved closer together, finding some significant agreement on several issues that used to be more divisive.[5] Steve Cowan concludes that there is "a growing consensus that the various apologetic methods are not as polarized as they once seemed ... apologetic methodologists of various schools have been willing to concede views that they once would have opposed."[6]

Still, we must add quickly that there are many important issues yet to resolve.[7] For example, questions concerning the central apologetic strategy of any methodology would certainly be significant. So when Bahnsen,[8] one of presuppositionalism's ablest defenders, challenged a number of John Warwick Montgomery's principal pillars, it is not surprising that some of his criticisms also questioned evidentialism in general.[9] So even though it was written just after the zenith of the earlier discussions between Van Til and Montgomery, Bahnsen's essay raises a number of significant issues that still need to be addressed today.

The exceptional length of Bahnsen's treatment, however, makes it closer to the size of a small book than an essay. This factor absolutely requires that I only respond to a few key issues. With this in mind, my twofold approach in the present critique will be both to address several of Bahnsen's claims against evidentialism and to challenge a few key issues regarding his own resulting apologetic system.

Bahnsen's Critique of Montgomery's Apologetic System: Select Challenges

In at least three important areas, Bahnsen takes great exception to Montgomery's entire apologetic approach. (1) He strenuously objects to what he considers to be Montgomery's reliance upon a long outdated positivistic methodology. Time and again, Bahnsen mentions Montgomery's appeal to data that can be neutrally observed,[10] brute facts that are inseparable from their meanings,[11] and the claimed objectivity of our knowledge.[12] Critiques regularly appear to take a taunting stance, almost whenever Montgomery's views are discussed. Bahnsen repeatedly attacks each of these aspects from the perspective of Scripture and contemporary epistemology, with some reference to philosophy of science.

(2) Further, Bahnsen questions Montgomery's reliance on probabilistic argumentation, denouncing such an approach as philosophically misguided, apologetically unworkable, and unbiblical.[13] Throughout, Bahnsen finds that Montgomery's appeal to this concept is completely misplaced.

(3) Bahnsen also attacks Montgomery's tiered evidential argument that progresses from the trustworthiness of the New Testament, to the historicity of Jesus' resurrection, to Christian theism.[14] Bahnsen charges that each of Montgomery's premises is defective and that his conclusion does not follow.[15]

These are some of the examples where we must be selective in our response. Any one of these three topics could well occupy us for an entire essay or even a book. I will make only a brief reply to each.

1. Bahnsen is certainly correct that contemporary philosophy has moved far beyond the positivism of the mid-twentieth century. We could also add a further point here. Virtually all recent historians and philosophers of history also reject the view that historical occurrences are self-interpreting, brute facts. Facts derive their meanings from their contexts, along with other considerations. Among these are human factors, which always enter into the process of historiography since there are usually multiple perspectives. Prejudices, biases, and ordinary preferences affect our interpretations in all areas.

Montgomery is well aware of the dynamic interactions between data and theories, between the naïve understanding of facts being "self-interpreting" and the Peircian concept of abduction and all that goes with proper theological theorizing. Montgomery has at least 40 references in his classic article "The Theologian's Craft" that more than carefully stave off the inference that he holds to a static view of facts being "self-interpreting." Rather, he holds, with the likes of Stephen Toulmin and C. S. Peirce, among others like Ian Ramsey, that "the theological model works . . . like the fitting of a boot or a shoe." Continuing, Ramsey relates further:

> In other words, we have a particular doctrine which, like
> a preferred and selected shoe, starts by appearing to meet
> our empirical needs. But on closer fitting to the phenomena the shoe may pinch. When tested against future slush

and rain it may be proven to be not altogether watertight
or it may be comfortable—yet it must not be too comfortable. In this way, the test of a shoe is measured by its ability
to match a wide range of phenomena, by its overall success
in meeting a variety of needs. Here is what I might call the
method of empirical fit which is displayed by theological
theorizing.[16]

So the often contradictory interpretations of facts must be viewed
against the data that we possess, as a creative intermix between induction and deduction that Peircian abduction typifies, as the "inference to the best explanation." The theoretical virtue in view here, as
Ramsey tells us, is "empirical fit." Montgomery is fully aware that the
human subject of experience has proclivities, presuppositions, hopes,
fears, and a long list of dreams and apprehensions that can, in some
measure, affect even one's perceptions to a significant, and sometimes
even telling, extent. The "empirical fit" virtue of theories, however, is
then translated—and this is the glory of Montgomery's insight, and
perhaps his key insight—into the "empirical fit" of the various interpretations (shoes) about Jesus of Nazareth, which is tested against
the data concerning his person, work, sinlessness, miracles, and resurrection. Only a divine Christ properly fits the historical data concerning Him.

I think Bahnsen missed this vital distinction about Montgomery's
use of abduction, but with reason: Montgomery could have done
a better job integrating his presentation of the craft of theological
theorizing into his views of Scripture, the testing of sets of historical
facts, the weighing of apologetic theories, and in related areas. All
too often, Montgomery provides excellent pointers but avoids giving
a detailed defense, as with the resurrection of Jesus.

Thus, we are still capable of ascertaining many historical events of
the past. Historians across a wide spectrum of views agree on many
of these matters.[17] In order to arrive at the data, we need to counter the subjective element, even though it cannot ever be completely
eradicated.[18] I have argued that these and related tenets are normal
fare, acknowledged by the vast majority of evidential apologists.[19] So

I have no problem with at least the general point made by Bahnsen here.

Still, is it the case that Montgomery subscribes to the older, positivistic schema? More importantly, does he do so in precisely the way that Bahnsen charges?[20] I think not. It is true that Montgomery regularly emphasizes the objective aspect of historical facts, perhaps even too much in light of the subjective element that we just mentioned. But to say that Montgomery is unaware that biases like those we have mentioned always affect the writing of history, or that such prejudice is always present, or that he disallows the influence of these subjective factors seems to ignore the presence of several decisive comments.

For example, although he appreciates the "rigorous standards for historical investigations," Montgomery specifically critiques positivism as follows: "The attempt to turn history into a science on a par with physics or chemistry was doomed to failure. . . . The Positivists made the mistake of believing that historical studies could attain the same degree of objectivity as scientific studies." A key reason such objectivism fails, Montgomery points out, is that our "philosophies of life have always, and will always, produce different interpretations of history. The Positivists did not recognize this, and spoke as if one could enter on historical work with complete objectivity." He also objects to the positivistic insistence on reducing history to objective laws when humans are "unique, free, and gloriously unpredictable."[21]

Moreover, in a chapter on historiography, Montgomery notes several problems with constructing a philosophy of history. The first of these is the part played by human nature, which "is always present at the outset of an investigation . . . prior to engaging in any specific investigation." These standards come from the historian's "general philosophy of life." The historian's view of reality, then, can make one "incapable of adequately interpreting" events.[22]

So Montgomery makes clear that subjective and other elements can certainly skew one's study of historical events. He makes this point a number of times, especially regarding the unbeliever's ability to discern the nature of reality. If, for instance, a researcher is convinced that human nature is not sinful, his "historical study will suffer in the gravest possible degree."[23]

It seems to me that many of Montgomery's comments on this subject would make a presuppositionalist proud, indeed![24] A fair interpretation, then, would be to understand Montgomery's references to objective facts, especially the many times where he simply utilizes these or similar terms without much explication, in light of his clearer explanations. Undeniably, Montgomery's statements have drawn an outcry.[25] But he has also been clear that the relevant terms should definitely not be equated with the way that positivists have used them.

I will simply mention in passing another relevant issue here. It will be pointed out below that presuppositionalism is not a monolithic position. One may get the impression from some presuppositionalists that admitting that there are no neutral viewpoints is sufficient to make one a presuppositionalist of the Van Til-Bahnsen variety. But this is not so. Virtually all commentators today freely admit the import of one's predispositions, or similar perspectives.[26] But we will see that it does not follow that such an admission makes one a presuppositionalist of this or another variety.

2. Regarding the related subject of using probability as a guide for historical research, I will simply add some comments. Bahnsen expresses much skepticism concerning the use of the inductive method,[27] but is he prepared to discard the method in every aspect of life? Or is he only objecting to its use in theological matters? The former would clearly seem to be unjustified, since it is the basis of the sciences that we rely upon daily, such as with the assessment and treatment of disease or in legal matters.

But if Bahnsen's chief concern is the application of probability to matters of faith, Montgomery could begin by pointing out that historians qua historians are limited to the use of their own tools in the process of uncovering the past. In other words, if we ask a historical question, the certainty of the answer cannot proceed beyond the inductive nature of the historical enterprise itself.[28] Although perhaps an overstatement, J. Oliver Buswell even goes as far as to say, "There is no argument known to us which, as an argument, leads to more than a probable (highly probable) conclusion."[29]

But, the apologist could continue, this is not the entire picture. In addition to the probabilities supplied by historical and other inductive arguments, there is also the ministry of the Holy Spirit, Who, as J. Oliver Buswell notes, provides "far more" than probabilities, as He convicts, regenerates, and energizes persons.[30] The work of the Holy Spirit might come in the form of moving beyond the lack of "absolute certainty in terms of historical method," closing the gap and bringing "absolute certainty."[31] Or it might be more a case of taking the historical facts and applying a personal faith decision.[32]

Thus, on the Christian understanding, historiography as a discipline can only yield some level of probability since this is simply the nature of its limits. But believers need not rely on this basis alone. Of course, Bahnsen is certainly correct that the New Testament speaks of events such as Jesus' resurrection as having occurred, not as probably having occurred.[33] But, then again, the New Testament also tells us that the Holy Spirit convicts believers of their salvation, thereby witnessing to the truth of the gospel message.[34] So there is certainly more to the story than history alone![35]

Interestingly, in the recent volume on apologetic methodology referred to above, all five writers, including the two evidentialists, subscribed to the view that the Holy Spirit provides such knowledge and certain assurance to the believer.[36] Very helpfully, Craig differentiates between "knowing" and "showing" Christianity to be true. Knowledge of the truth of Christian theism is due to the work of the Holy Spirit's witness in the believer's life. But showing Christianity to be true has to do with the presenting of evidences, some of which, like historical arguments, are probabilistic.[37]

So Bahnsen ought not object that other apologists are unbiblical in using probability arguments in contrast to Scripture's proclamation that historical events really occurred. One response, as we have said, is that Bahnsen's critique of probabilistic research does not allow that this is as much as the discipline of history can yield. Further, direct assurance may be provided by the Holy Spirit, proceeding beyond what history can contribute. I think recent apologists generally agree that the witness of the Holy Spirit provides believers with such absolute assurance.[38] Thus, Scripture may be referring either to the combination of history plus the Spirit's witness, or to the latter alone. Or, it could simply be using normal, nontechnical language when referring to human knowledge of past events.

3. I will not respond in detail to whether Montgomery actually succeeds in his six-premise apologetic argument from Scripture, to Jesus' resurrection, to the truth of Christian theism. Perhaps it was never Montgomery's purpose to do anything but *state* the argument, along with defending it against some initial objections. To my knowledge, Montgomery never develops his argument beyond these contexts, and certainly not in a lengthy treatise.[39] So for Bahnsen to address and examine it as a developed case is perhaps to miss the point.

Further, even if Bahnsen thinks that Montgomery's inductive argument is less than compelling, the worst that can be said is that we need additional or better data (assuming that such exists). So the chief issue here is whether there is such evidence, not whether Montgomery marshals it in all of its detail. As I said, his treatment suggests that such was not even his purpose. The principle I am suggesting here is well known in logic, and is called the principle of charity. Namely, we ought to strengthen our opponent's argument so that we are responding to its strongest form.[40] The principal idea here is plain—if an argument can simply be patched up or arranged differently, then the critique may fail on that grounds alone. I am suggesting that Bahnsen should have addressed the argument as if the appropriate details had been included.

In sum, we have considered briefly three of the chief areas where Bahnsen critiques Montgomery (namely, the claimed use of positivistic methodology, probability and his six-step evidential argument). In all three instances Montgomery can reassert his positions. Perhaps some clarification is needed, as in pinpointing in even more detail how he has already allowed for the presence of subjective factors in historiography. Or Montgomery might present a further treatment of the work of the Holy Spirit specifically regarding apologetics. Some of his other arguments could also be further evidenced, although Montgomery could simply say that it was not his purpose to develop a case in any great detail, referring to texts where similar points have long been made. But I do not think that Bahnsen's critique dismantles Montgomery's overall approach, much less the evidentialist apologetic method as a whole.

Bahnsen's Presuppositionalist Method and Positive Apologetics

One major concern that clearly emerges from reading published works from the Van Tillian presuppositional school of thought is that they seldom even attempt to develop positive evidences for Christian theism. A simply amazing phenomenon here is that, while Van Tillian scholars *clearly* acknowledge the need to do so, they very rarely ever attempt it.

For example, Van Til states that it is important to "engage in historical apologetics." But he explains that he does not do so because his colleagues in his seminary "are doing it better than I could do it." Still, he adds a few suggestions on how such an effort should be done.[41]

Now what is wrong with such a response? Is not modesty a laudable asset? The oddity of the matter, however, is when Van Til's key pupils, such as Bahnsen and Frame, say exactly the same thing. The end result is that the three main proponents of this brand of presuppositionalism have all commended positive evidences, but backed away from actually producing them. The similarities of the responses may be surprising.

For example, Bahnsen acknowledges Van Til's approval of historical evidences, listing some of Van Til's caveats about doing so.[42] Likewise, Bahnsen himself endorses historical evidences.[43] But to my knowledge, Bahnsen never develops a case himself, either in his lengthy response to Montgomery, or elsewhere.

Frame is even more straightforward. He recognizes that the Bible frequently makes use of historical evidences, holding that they are crucial in arguing a case for Christian theism. He even states: "I am happy to salute the evidentialist tradition," complimenting many authors, including Montgomery, Craig, J. P. Moreland, and myself for developing various sorts of evidential arguments.[44] Yet Frame admits that presuppositionalists have failed by not producing evidences for Christianity. He even goes as far as to say, "Unfortunately, there has been very little actual analysis of evidence in the Van Tillian presuppositionalist school of apologetics." Then he adds, "I hope this gap in the Reformed apologetic literature will soon be filled, though I cannot fill it, at least not here and now."[45] Elsewhere he speaks similarly, acknowledging this tendency as a weakness in presuppositionalism, but again noting that he is not the one to do anything about it.[46] And while discussing historical evidence for the resurrection of Jesus, Frame starts out by saying, "I shall not add much to the voluminous literature showing the credibility of the biblical witness to this great event."[47]

So these three scholars, perhaps the most influential Van Tillian presuppositionalists, each clearly acknowledge the critical need of providing positive Christian evidences. But for some reason there appears to be a curious but rather extreme reluctance to be the one to take such a step. So, during perhaps the last 30 years, in spite of many comments and advice concerning how the evidential enterprise should be conducted, few examples have been provided by their school.

Why, it may be asked, could not these presuppositionalists simply make the same move that I suggested Montgomery made? Namely, do not these scholars also have the option of laying out a basic, outlined historical case and conclude that it was simply not their purpose to present the evidence in great detail? The differences should be clear. We just saw that even presuppositionalists like Frame admit that he recommends the works of evidentialists who *have* developed strong historical arguments for Christian theism. However, such is clearly *not* the case with Van Tillian presuppositionalists, as Frame himself realizes. So the issue here is not only whether a particular scholar—say Montgomery or Bahnsen—develops such a case in detail. The problem is that such arguments are the very mainstay of the school of evidentialist apologetics as a whole, while Frame asserts that there is a "gap" in the Van Tillian camp here. So the latter cannot defer to other members of their own group to do a more complete job of historical apologetics, precisely since no Van Tillian examples apparently exist!

Perhaps presuppositionalists may simply retort that since evidentialists have already produced the necessary historical works, there is no more need to do so. But even this would seem to miss the mark for at least three reasons. (1) Presuppositionalists, like evidentialists, clearly pursue defensive apologetic efforts to answer Christianity's critics, with both groups producing many exemplary instances.[48] But presuppositionalists do not defer to evidentialist defensive arguments. Rather, they develop their own. Accordingly, why should the publication of many positive cases by evidentialists alleviate the need for presuppositionalists to produce positive arguments from their own perspectives? In other words, since presuppositionalists regularly originate their own defensive moves, they should produce the evidential (offensive) side, as well, especially since they both have conceded the need to do so, plus they apparently have particular concerns that are seldom dealt with by evidentialists.

2. Since presuppositionalists quite frequently correct the way evidentialists do historical apologetics,[49] this seems to beg for them to show us how it should be done! Is this not the normal response to those who constantly scold, correct, and offer suggestions without ever attempting to perform the task themselves? Correctives are welcome if they assist the Christian community to develop better offensives, but the challenges alone tend to make one wonder what a presuppositionalist historical argument would even look like.

3. If Van Tillians constantly need to "borrow" the evidentialist research here without producing their own, they open themselves to another, much more serious critique—it would then appear that their apologetic method is incomplete, offering only part of the picture.[50] Thus, if a positive apologetic is both crucial and biblical, to produce only defensive critiques of other systems without establishing one's own is a serious omission. And if such a positive apologetic virtually never appears, then in what sense is Van Tillian presuppositionalism a complete apologetic *system*?

At any rate, what we observe is that at least some Van Tillian presuppositionalists, of whom Bahnsen is perhaps the best example, continually want to tell evidentialists and other apologists how they *ought not* do historical evidences, countering that it should be done in a very specific manner. But they almost never produce the details themselves!

So we return to our original question. Why is there such a broad gap here in the Van Tillian camp? George Mavrodes, who has influenced Frame,[51] takes the next step and asks why Reformed thinkers as a whole so frequently devalue positive evidences? He answers his own inquiry: "Maybe it represents a deep ambivalence in Reformed thought, a tendency to oscillate."[52]

Could it be that certain Reformed theological commitments are responsible for this lack of positive apologetics? Might not treasured theological and/or biblical stances be placed above evidential ones? This would be intriguing since the latter are also found in the same Scripture, and we have seen that presuppositionalists freely acknowledge the presence and importance of evidences. Perhaps these theological or biblical commitments, for example, play such a key role that they prevent Van Tillians from developing specific evidential stances. I think that this is apparent enough to address it in the next section below. Are there other reasons? It would appear that whatever it is must be something major, or we would not witness this almost unanimous absence of positive evidences in Van Tillian works.

Or perhaps this lack is due to philosophical commitments. For instance, Bahnsen's seeming philosophical and/or religious skepticism, at least at points, might help us to understand why neither he nor other prominent presuppositionalists ever try to establish a major, positive case for Christianity.[53] Examples of Bahnsen's skepticism are not too difficult to produce.

For example, in order to challenge Montgomery and/or to avoid the thrust of the latter's arguments, Bahnsen makes many (sometimes rather unnerving) points on behalf of the nonbeliever's possible responses. Thus, there are continual references to unbelievers having even *better* arguments than Montgomery's or unbelievers not needing to be convinced by the evidence Montgomery produces.[54] Specific instances include the improbability of Christ rising from the dead when argued according to Montgomery's probabilistic standards,[55] or even Bahnsen's defense of naturalistic theories against Jesus' resurrection, done in the name of critiquing Montgomery![56] These last stances, in particular, are exceptionally objectionable, especially from one who complains regularly that we need apologetic approaches that are more biblical! Further, Bahnsen questions whether we can know Jesus' worldview, or even what kind of God ensues from Montgomery's arguments. Bahnsen insists that "the resurrection of Jesus does not infer His deity and His deity does not infer His truthfulness."[57]

Now I wish to be quick to point out here that no one who knew Greg Bahnsen would ever question his commitment to God or ever suggest that he believed any of these counter arguments. It must also be acknowledged that Bahnsen was proposing these unbelieving alternatives, not because he thought that they had any chance of being true but because he wanted to point out how Montgomery's approach championed "an alien epistemology."[58] Thus, Bahnsen thought that, *by Montgomery's standards*, we end up with an unbiblical scenario.

But as much as I appreciate Bahnsen's zeal, I think his approach as exhibited in these sorts of challenges to Montgomery is very wide of the mark for at least three reasons, which we draw from the comments immediately above. (1) Bahnsen almost gives the impression that he is more interested in winning a debate with Montgomery than winning hearts. Why would he *ever, under any circumstance,* want to provide some "leads" for unbelievers concerning how they might argue in order to preserve their unbelief? Although his chief point was to argue against what he thought was the unbiblical nature of Montgomery's evidentialist methodology, what price is Bahnsen willing to pay? I will not pursue this further, except to say that, in my opinion, raising objections on behalf of the unbeliever to the historicity of Jesus' resurrection, Jesus' view of God, His deity, or the truthfulness of Jesus' message is definitely not the way to argue against a fellow evangelical, even if we object to their methods! The response almost seems to be one of burning the message along with the messenger![59]

(2) To bring us back to the topic of this section, I am suggesting that we have perhaps uncovered at least one philosophical reason why the Van Tillian presuppositionalist fails to produce viable treatments of the evidence, in spite of specifically admitting the importance of doing so. Their (sometimes extreme?) skepticism concerning what they perceive to be unbiblical, manmade attempts to establish Christianity is so far-reaching that they simply fail to leave themselves many options for their own responses! It sometimes seems that Bahnsen has attempted to so denude the evidential playing field, that he has virtually no positive grounds on which he could possibly justify the Christian message, even if he intended to do so, except to proclaim it as true on its own grounds.[60]

Since evidentialist attempts to show that Jesus rose from the dead do not seem to please Bahnsen very much, at least as argued by Montgomery, I want to know how Bahnsen is going to respond to the exact same issues? Further, how is he going to refute the same naturalistic theories that he raises? Is he going to cite historical facts? How, if not the way an evidentialist does?[61] Surely, he will not simply state that the unbelievers are wrong because the New Testament says so and leave it there?[62]

I agree that Scripture states that unbelievers are absolutely wrong, as well as lost, but on what *factual* grounds are the unbeliever's naturalistic theories mistaken? Bahnsen needs to be reminded that just because he has raised questions, this *does not* mean that he has refuted Montgomery's argument! As we have just seen, attempting to build a positive argument is much tougher than simply asking questions.

(3) This brings us to perhaps the key issue that Bahnsen wants to discuss. What about the biblical teaching on this subject? Does the New Testament ever argue in a manner close to that presented by Montgomery? Does Scripture present a case that utilizes evidential-type considerations? Unquestionably, Bahnsen thinks that Montgomery's approach is unbiblical. But I think that Bahnsen has gone to such great extents to argue his points that he fails to come to grips with numerous biblical passages which he is forced either to ignore or to provide less than likely interpretations. This is troubling enough that I have devoted the next section to the issue.

I have said in this section that presuppositionalists of the Van Tillian persuasion are quite clear that historical evidences are biblical, important, and ought to be pursued. Yet one finds perhaps not a single, detailed example where their best-known representatives take their own challenge. They provide many suggestions, assertions, and outright dismissals of the work of others (like Bahnsen's critique of Montgomery), but virtually no detailed examples of their own historical spadework have been forthcoming. I have suggested that their theological, biblical, and/or philosophical commitments might militate against their own efforts here. Bahnsen's seeming philosophical and religious skepticism serves as a detailed example. As a result, I suggested that these commitments likewise dismiss certain Scripture texts that express positions unlike their own.

Scripture

Bahnsen castigates Montgomery's apologetic use of Scripture.[63] But in the process, Bahnsen struggles with the clear meaning of several texts, both ones he specifically mentions, as well as some others. For the sake of brevity, I will largely limit this discussion to passages regarding Jesus' resurrection, as Bahnsen does himself. Further, we must necessarily be very selective in our treatment here, which is nothing more than a cursory look at a few texts.

Bahnsen charges, "in fact there is no scriptural evidence at all that the apostles or anybody else urged the people to go prove the resurrection by inductive research."[64] While such a careful choice of words may perhaps be accurate, strictly speaking, it does not do justice to the plain meaning of several New Testament texts. And Bahnsen especially strains to make sense of those passages where Jesus clearly presented sensory evidence that He had risen from the dead.

For example, Bahnsen states that the best example of resurrection faith is not the case of doubting Thomas, but Abraham, who believed "[a]gainst all empirical probability or inductive reasoning."[65] Five items need to be briefly mentioned.

1. Even if Abraham is the believer's chief example of faith in Scripture, it is a bit anachronistic to call this Old Testament saint our "example of resurrection faith." Regardless, to say that Abraham believed "[a]gainst all probability or inductive reasoning" is rather badly to miss some key texts. On many occasions God specifically spoke to Abram (cf. Gen 12:1–3; 13:14–17; 22:1–2). Although we are not told the exact sense in which this occurred, these were clearly personal and meaningful communications. In another instance, precisely because Abram asked God for assurance of His promises, he was directly given a sign that God would do all that He had promised (Gen 15:8–21). Later God and two angels even visited Abraham and spoke directly to him (Gen 18:1–33). Abraham also witnessed God's very visible, physical, and supernatural judgment on Sodom and Gomorrah (Gen 19:1–29). On still another occasion,

an angel spoke to him twice (Gen 22:11–18). Incredibly, and *in spite of all these manifestations*, Abraham *still* suffered several crises of his faith.[66]

Even this brief survey shows that it is inaccurate for Bahnsen to say that Abraham's faith was established apart from and even "against" any data obtained from his sense experiences. Rather, Abraham's faith was clearly augmented at *many* points by direct, even miraculous, contact with God. This also means that Abraham was the recipient of many inductively derived data. His faith was definitely not produced in a vacuum! Further, also contrary to Bahnsen's assertion, on a few occasions Abraham's faith was not even established when the empirical data were directly in front of his eyes, such as laughing when God stood in front of him (Gen 17:15–17)!

2. Still, citing Abraham does not justify virtually ignoring the significant account of doubting Thomas's faith being generated by Jesus' resurrection appearance (John 20:24–28). Even though Jesus told Thomas that it would have been better if he had believed *without* requiring the appearance (20:29), it still remains that Jesus chose to appear to Thomas and present His resurrected body for inspection *after* the disciple said that he would not believe without empirical justification for doing so. It is also significant that this appearance led directly to the apostle's faith.

3. Further, the appearance to Thomas was not an isolated incident. The resurrected Jesus also showed Himself on other occasions, evidencing His bodily resurrection from the dead in more than one way. In these contexts, Jesus did not indicate any problem or hesitation in allowing (and even suggesting) physical contact and other sense data regarding His resurrected body. This included being seen by the women, who held His feet (Matt 28:9), as did Mary Magdalene holding on to Him after her return trip to the empty tomb (John 20:17). Jesus also showed His body and its scars to His disciples in order to calm their doubts, even eating in front of them as a further indication of His actual, time-space presence (Luke 24:36–43; cf. John 20:19–20). Just a very few years after the Gospel of John was written, Ignatius affirms that, on this occasion, the disciples both touched Jesus' body and believed in Him (*Smyrnaeans* 1:9–12).

4. Paul tells us that Jesus appeared several times to His followers, including to a group of at least 500 persons at once, which also carries some strong apologetic implications, especially since we are told that most of these witnesses were still alive. Responding to Montgomery's statement that the intent of Paul's report was to affirm that these witnesses could still be interviewed, Bahnsen scoffs, asserting that Paul made this statement to believers, who presumably would not need such assurance.[67]

But Bahnsen misses the point here, and, once again, by a large margin. For starters, he both overlooks and underestimates several texts that express much doubt and lack of recognition of the resurrected Jesus, even by the disciples themselves. After all, the resurrection of an individual before the end of the age was contrary to Jewish expectations (John 11:23–24), besides the incredible nature of a dead man returning to life, which makes the questions quite understandable! Further, throughout Scripture, believers regularly express even severe doubts on other matters, making strong charges and requesting assurance or other answers.[68] To miss the fact that believers also suffer doubts and need assurance is a grave miscalculation.[69] Further, the majority of commentators acknowledge that Montgomery's position is clearly correct—Paul's point was precisely that many of the eyewitnesses to the resurrected Jesus could still be checked out.[70]

5. Bahnsen closes his essay by paraphrasing (in terms of his own methodology) Jesus' teaching that "if men will not hear Moses and the prophets neither will they believe the most compelling, factual demonstration!"[71] But even here, he fails to make his contextual point against the use of empirical evidence.

Jesus obviously did not mean that His statement in Luke 16:31 should be taken without exception—that an empirical, "factual demonstration" should never be used and will never lead anyone to saving faith. If so, He never would have appeared after His own resurrection to the women and disciples, repeatedly using empirical evidence to answer their questions and to reassure them, even bringing at least Thomas to faith. But we also have additional demonstrations of the incorrectness of Bahnsen's position, provided by the cases of Paul and James, the brother of Jesus. Both of these apostles were also converted from their previous positions of skepticism and unbelief by resurrection appearances of the risen Lord Jesus (1 Cor 15:7–8). Once again, we have two more examples of the biblical use of sense data to induce belief or assurance. These are the sorts of reasons evidentialists do not shy away from using the historical evidence for Jesus' resurrection!

On an often-repeated, related charge by Bahnsen, why is it at all relevant that most unbelievers will fail to be convinced by Montgomery's apologetic approach?[72] Even in the Gospels, do not unbelievers regularly walk away in unbelief from Jesus Himself? And when Paul debated the philosophers in Athens, why did only a few become believers (Acts 17:32–34)?[73] Further, what about those unbelievers who heard or debated Bahnsen—like atheist Gordon Stein? Did they become believers?[74]

But this brings up an additional problem for Bahnsen regarding his understanding of Luke 16:31. That *anyone* came to Christ after a debate or dialogue concerning Jesus' resurrection seems to be counter to Bahnsen's approach, especially when the same author (Luke) explains that, rather than being atypical instances, apologetic approaches featuring the resurrection were Paul's customary method of presenting the gospel message.[75]

We could go on and on here. But I will very briefly mention just one other sort of evidential consideration from Scripture. We often get the impression from Van Tillian presuppositionalists that Scripture should stand on its own, and should not be tested or judged, as in compiling evidences to show that Scripture is trustworthy or inspired.[76]

However, throughout the biblical text, believers are constantly even *commanded* to test God's revelation by means of various checks and balances in order to see that it is truthful. For example, God's people were told to examine potential prophets and their predicted events to ascertain if their words really did come from God. Thus they would know if God had truly sent them (Deut 18:21–22). God Himself passed the test of fulfilled prophecy.[77] Further, God proposed that other "gods" be tested similarly (Isa 41:21–24; 44:7). God even called on Israel to be a witness to His mighty historical confirmations (Isa 44:6–8; 52:6).

Further, miracles also attested the truth of God's teachings. Without thinking that he was challenging God's authority, Elijah boldly proclaimed that the God who produced fire was the one, true God. And God responded (1 Kgs 18:20–45). Jesus used His miracles to answer John the Baptist's doubts (Luke 7:18–23). Moreover, Jesus proposed that His resurrection would be the chief sign of His identity (Matt 12:38–40; 16:1–4). Peter (Acts 2:22–24; 1 Pet 1:3–4) and Paul (Acts 17:31) both agreed that Jesus' resurrection confirmed His teachings.

In at least these ways, both believers and unbelievers were told to examine history to ascertain if God had indeed spoken. Apparently God did not think that such evidential checks and balances were out of line or that they somehow failed to take Him at His word. After all, it is God who even commanded the testing!

We will not lengthen this discussion of evidences and Scripture.[78] We have only looked very briefly at two areas—a few resurrection passages and some texts that instruct believers and unbelievers to test and examine God's revelation. I have argued, at least regarding the first, that Bahnsen has revealed a selective choosing of Scripture texts in order to argue his presuppositional case against Montgomery. Here, too, Bahnsen has failed to establish that case. Evidentialists may not always argue properly, but the fact that they utilize an evidential basis to argue for the truth of Christianity is far from condemning. This is especially so when, on several occasions, Jesus; presented His resurrected body to assuage doubt and to cause faith; and God, the Author of Scripture, challenged His people to check out both fulfilled prophecy and miracles in order to determine the truth of His revelation.[79]

Conclusion

Greg Bahnsen is very critical of John Warwick Montgomery's apologetic methodology. I responded initially to charges involving three pillars in Montgomery's works: his "positivism," probabilism, and his extended argument for Christian theism. Then I addressed two major problem areas regarding presuppositionalist apologetic systems of the Van Tillian variety, including Bahnsen's position. The initial inquiry concerned why detailed historical arguments for Christianity are so seldom forthcoming from the chief proponents of this variety of presuppositionalism, even though it is openly conceded that such endeavors are crucially important. Second, we explored various scriptural examples of what I will simply call evidential-like statements. The latter also involved Bahnsen's challenges to Montgomery. I now conclude that it is possible both to defend strongly an evidentialist methodology against Bahnsen's complaints and to pose some serious objections to his variety of Van Tillian presuppositionalism on its own grounds.

Endnotes

1 An earlier edition of this essay was published as Gary R. Habermas, "Greg Bahnsen, John Warwick Montgomery, and Evidential Apologetics," *Global Journal of Classical Theology*, vol. 3, no. 1 (March 2002).

2 Throughout, I will be assuming some background knowledge, including definitions of these viewpoints and some of the chief issues involved. Those who desire more information concerning these options should consult the texts listed in notes 3–4, 23 below.

3 Those who wish to study how related issues were dealt with throughout the Christian era, including both similar and dissimilar responses by Christian scholars, could consult works such as the following: L. Russ Bush, ed., *Classic Readings in Apologetics: A.D. 100–1800* (Grand Rapids: Zondervan, 1983); Avery Dulles, *A History of Apologetics* (New York: Corpus Instrumentum; Philadelphia: Westminster, 1971); John K. S. Reid, *Christian Apologetics* (London: Hodder and Stoughton, 1969); Bernard Ramm, *Varieties of Christian Apologetics* (Grand Rapids: Baker, 1979). Twentieth-century concerns are treated in Gordon R. Lewis, *Testing Christianity's Truth Claims* (Chicago: Moody, 1976).

4 Two of the works that drew some of the battle lines on these issues were E. R. Geehan, ed., *Jerusalem and Athens: Critical Discussions on the Theology and Politics of Cornelius Van Til* (Philadelphia: Presbyterian and Reformed, 1971) and Ronald Nash, ed., *The Philosophy of Gordon H. Clark* (Philadelphia: Presbyterian and Reformed, 1968).

5 This is amply illustrated by the fairly recent volume *Five Views on Apologetics*, ed. Steven B. Cowan (Grand Rapids: Zondervan, 2000). The presuppositionalist position is argued by John M. Frame while the evidentialist position is defended by Gary R. Habermas. William Lane Craig argued the classical position, and the late Paul D. Feinberg took a view that was closer to evidentialism. Kelly James Clark supported the view of Reformed Epistemology, sharing some aspects (but not others) with the presuppositionalist view. As editor Cowan remarks, however, one of the striking features of this volume

is not only the important areas of agreement between the contributors (375–76), but even the converging nature of their positions (380–81).

6　Ibid., 380–81.

7　As Cowan also realizes (ibid., 376–81).

8　My critique is made more difficult precisely because Greg passed away several years ago (in 1995), in the prime of his academic career. I wish to make plain at the outset that Greg and I were friends. We met in 1977 at the annual conference of the Evangelical Philosophical Society. Many years later, I invited him to lecture at Liberty University. While here, he addressed the LU Philosophy Club at my home. On several occasions over almost 20 years, Greg and I discussed various issues in apologetics. Sometimes we were in agreement, like the time we discussed over dinner an historical approach to the resurrection of Jesus. I deeply respected his friendship, his scholarly training, and accomplishments, as well as his commitment to our Lord. However, this does not keep me from concluding that he was mistaken in many of his critiques of evidentialism.

9　Greg Bahnsen, "A Critique of the Evidentialist Apologetic Method of John Warwick Montgomery" (1974) available from Covenant Media Foundation (1–800–553–3938), published at www.cmfnow.com/articles/pa016.htm.

10　Bahnsen, "A Critique," 2, 11–14, 16–17, 20, 26, 28, 31.

11　Ibid., 16, 22.

12　Ibid., 11, 13, 28, 31–32, 38.

13　This topic is predominantly treated in ibid., 17–24.

14　As found in Montgomery's volumes *The Shape of the Past: A Christian Response to Secular Philosophies of History* (Minneapolis: Bethany, 1975), 138–45; *Where Is History Going? Essays in Support of the Historical Truth of the Christian Revelation* (Grand Rapids: Zondervan, 1969), 31–36. Bahnsen lists the steps on page 11 of "A Critique."

15　Bahnsen, "A Critique," 11–16.

16　Ian Ramsey as quoted in John Warwick Montgomery, "The Theologian's Craft," in *The Suicide of Christian Theology* (Minneapolis: Bethany, 1970), 278.

17　See Ernst Breisach, *Historiography: Ancient, Medieval, and Modern*, 2nd ed. (Chicago: University of Chicago, 1994), 408; C. Behan McCullagh, *Justifying Historical Descriptions* (Cambridge: Cambridge University, 1984). Although older, Christopher Blake offers some fruitful commentary in the essay "Can History Be Objective?" in *Theories of History*, ed. Patrick Gardiner (New York: Macmillan, 1959), 331–33.

18　I treat some of these issues in detail in "Philosophy of History, Historical Relativism, and History as Evidence," in *Evangelical Apologetics*, ed. Michael Bauman, David Hall, and Robert Newman (Camp Hill, PA: Christian Publications, Inc., 1996) and Appendix 1, "Historiography," in *The Historical Jesus: Ancient Evidence for the Life of Christ* (Joplin: College Press, 1996).

19　Gary Habermas, "Evidentialism," in Cowan, *Five Views*, 94–95.

20　Bahnsen, "A Critique," 4, 28, 40, cf. p. 22.

21　Montgomery, *The Shape of the Past*, 73–74.

22　Ibid., 14–16.

23 Ibid., 16. For other relevant comments concerning the affects on, and lack of, an objective historiography, see ibid., 145–52; *Where Is History Going?*, 183–87; John Warwick Montgomery, *History and Christianity* (Downers Grove: InterVarsity, 1964, 1965), 75–80.

24 See Bahnsen's comments in "A Critique" on the affects of sin (3) and one's presuppositions (10) on our historiography. In the first reference, however, he is still not pleased with Montgomery's position.

25 Even a brief listing of relevant responses, both pro and con, would be lengthy. Some examples are as follows: Ronald VanderMolen, "The Christian Historian: Apologist or Seeker?" *Fides et Historia*, vol. 3, no. 1 (Fall 1970); Ronald H. Nash, "The Use and Abuse of History in Christian Apologetics," *Christian Scholar's Review* 1, no. 3 (Spring 1971), 217–26; Ronald VanderMolen, "'Where Is History Going' and Historical Scholarship: A Response," *Fides et Historia*, vol. 5, nos. 1–2 (Spring 1973), 109–12; Earl William Kennedy, "John Warwick Montgomery and the Objectivist Apologetics Movement," *Fides et Historia*, vol. 5, nos. 1–2 (Spring 1973), 117–21. But Montgomery was not without his own supporters: Paul D. Feinberg, "History: Public or Private? A Defense of John Warwick Montgomery's Philosophy of History," *Christian Scholar's Review* 1, no. 4 (Summer 1971), 325–31; Steven A. Hein, "The Christian Historian: Apologist or Seeker?—a Reply to Ronald J. VanderMolen," *Fides et Historia* 4, no. 2 (Spring 1972), 85–93.

26 I have even listed this as a tenet that is generally accepted by evidentialists (Habermas, *Five Views* in Cowan, 94–95).

27 Bahnsen, "A Critique," 17–24, 31–32.

28 Of course, many other apologists have also made similar claims, even from theological positions closer to Bahnsen's. Some examples prior to the discussions between Montgomery and Van Til include Edward John Carnell, *An Introduction to Christian Apologetics* (Grand Rapids: Eerdmans, 1948), 113–15; and James Oliver Buswell, *A Systematic Theology of the Christian Religion* (Grand Rapids: Zondervan, 1962), 1:72–101.

29 Buswell, *Systematic Theology*, 1:72.

30 Ibid., 1:74, 100–1.

31 As Carl F. H. Henry states during a dialogue in Montgomery's *History and Christianity*, 105.

32 As Montgomery responds in the same dialogue (ibid., 107).

33 Bahnsen, "A Critique," 21–22.

34 See Rom 8:14–16; Gal 4:6; 1 John 3:24; 4:13.

35 For a detailed explanation, see Gary R. Habermas, "The Personal Testimony of the Holy Spirit to the Believer and Christian Apologetics," in *Journal of Christian Apologetics* 1, no. 1 (Summer 1997), 49–64.

36 Cowan makes a similar point on page 376. For the views of the contributors, see Craig (28–38), Habermas (61–63, 96–98), Feinberg (158–60), Frame (78, 209–10), and Clark (83–85, cf. 271–74).

37 Craig, ibid., 28–45, 51–54.

38 Although Van Tillian presuppositionalist Frame offers some qualifications, he agrees with several of the chief features of Craig's distinction between knowing and showing the truth of Christianity (ibid., 78).

39 Probably the longest passage is found in Montgomery's *Shape of the Past*, where the entire treatment occupies a total of about seven pages. Of that, the outlined argument itself only takes about one page (138–39), followed by about five pages of answers to some objections (140–45). In *Where Is History Going?*, the whole argument is stated in just over one page (35–36). Of course, Montgomery returns to various points, especially the reliability and/or the inspiration of Scripture, throughout his writings.

40 For an example, see Charles W. Kegley and Jacquelyn Ann Kegley, *Introduction to Logic* (Columbus: Charles E Merrill, 1978), 20, 211.

41 Cornelius Van Til, *The Defense of the Faith* (Phillipsburg: Presbyterian and Reformed, 1980), 199. Thom Notaro points out the same in *Van Til and the Use of Evidence* (Phillipsburg: Presbyterian and Reformed, 1980), 19–20.

42 Bahnsen, "A Critique," 3–5.

43 Ibid., 10–11.

44 See Frame's statements in Cowan, *Five Views*, 228–30, 132–35, 358. For other instances, see Frame's volumes *The Doctrine of the Knowledge of God* (Phillipsburg: Presbyterian and Reformed, 1987), 353–54, 379; and *Apologetics to the Glory of God: An Introduction* (Phillipsburg: Presbyterian and Reformed, 1994), 60, 71, 85–86, 145–47.

45 Frame, *Doctrine and Knowledge of God*, 352.

46 Frame in Cowan, *Five Views*, 358.

47 Frame, *Apologetics to the Glory of God*, 145.

48 One example where Bahnsen argues defensively against Islam is found on pages 7–8 of "A Critique."

49 For some of Frame's cautions concerning positive arguments by evidentialists, see Frame in Cowan, *Five Views* 132–37, 357–63.

50 This is one of my chief critiques of the Van Tillian presuppositionalist school. See Habermas in Cowan, 238–41, 343–44.

51 Frame in Cowan, *Five Views*, 79, 222.

52 George Mavrodes, "Jerusalem and Athens," in *Faith and Rationality: Reason and Belief in God*, ed. Alvin Plantinga and Nicholas Wolterstorff (Notre Dame: University of Notre Dame, 1983), 197–98.

53 Again, I am speaking specifically of the Van Tillian variety of presuppositionalism here. Ronald Nash, being much more influenced by Gordon Clark (who himself had grave differences with Van Til!), is a very different sort of presuppositionalist. Among his many volumes, Nash has written an apologetics text, entitled *Faith and Reason: Searching for a Rational Faith* (Grand Rapids: Zondervan, 1988). While Nash spends significantly more time on philosophical issues than historical ones, yet as I remarked in a review of this book, he helps to answer the question we are addressing here—why at least some presuppositionalists do not write more books on evidences (Gary R. Habermas, "A Reasonable Faith," *Christianity Today*, June 16, 1989).

54 Bahnsen, "A Critique," 12–14.

55 Ibid., 21.

56 Ibid., 14–15.

57 Ibid., 15–16.

58 Ibid., 18.

59 There is also the matter of several rather strong comments directed against both Montgomery and his position ("A Critique," 11, 21, 28, 31, 32).

60 I can hear the immediate and often-repeated protest that this misrepresents the Van Tillian presuppositionalist's argument. While I do *not* subscribe to the position that presuppositionalists simply assume the truth of the Christian message, as per the older evidentialist critique, their lack of a positive apologetic comes back to haunt them again and again (see endnote 62 below). I will only refer the interested reader to my detailed objections to Frame's system at this point. (See Habermas in Cowan, *Five Views* especially 238–44, 338–41.)

61 A presuppositionalist often responds that it is the evidentialist's philosophical and theological foundations that they most object to—areas such as one's starting point, view of man, the noetic affects of sin, the theological system being used, and so on. But how, precisely, will the presuppositionalist deal with specific refutations of specific factual charges against the historicity of the resurrection, if not similarly to the evidentialist? Once again, the presuppositionalist must do more than *assert* an answer. She must work out the factual data, line by line, and it must be consistent with her own system, too!

62 Bahnsen states that "God's word is self-attestingly authoritative" ("A Critique," 9), but with little or no elaboration. But such a pregnant proclamation simply begs for some examination, both by him as well as by others. Is this said to the believer only? Or is this meant as a proclamation to the unbeliever? Does this describe Bahnsen's apologetic approach, or does he propose at least a few positive evidences for the truthfulness of Christianity? If so, how will he set them forth, given that he seems to have stripped apologetics of its usual tools of the trade? He needs to explain in detail how this is going to help us establish Christianity by anything other than a proclamation. Beating us over the head with a comment something to the effect that if natural man will not accept this proclamation then none other will be forthcoming not only falls prey to the above discussion about the lack of a positive apologetic but also tends to show further that an unwarranted skepticism is present. I will return in the next section to the issue of whether Bahnsen's is the approach set forth in Scripture, as he declares. But I am getting too far ahead of myself here. I will simply once again register my desire to have a straightforward answer to the question of whether positive apologetic arguments are possible, as well as a few details on how this would look in a Van Tillian framework. In the meantime, I will refer the reader to a more detailed discussion of circularity in the writings of Frame, who spells out the sense in which he makes what appears to be a related comment: "The Bible is the Word of God because it says so." (See Frame's *Apologetics to the Glory of God*, 14; cf. 136 and the discussion in these contexts.) For my critiques of what I think is a viciously circular argument, see Habermas in Cowan, *Five Views*, 241–48, 343–44. Frame responds kindly in the same volume, 354–59, where he also makes some very intriguing concessions, i.e. that his statement above "is not an apologetic argument in a serious sense" (356), that presuppositionalism has failed to offer positive arguments for Christianity (357), and that presuppositionalism may not be a complete apologetic system (357). It is unclear whether Bahnsen

would have agreed with his colleague Frame. But I think these problems are crucially serious objections to the Van Tillian apologetic method. Readers can make their own judgments after reading the dialogue between Frame and myself.

63 Bahnsen, "A Critique," 9, 42–43.

64 Ibid., 42–43.

65 Ibid., 43.

66 Examples include Gen 12:11–20; 15:8; 17:15–17; 20:1–7.

67 Ibid., 42.

68 For examples of the startling variety here in addition to those already mentioned in the resurrection texts in the Gospels, see Job 3:11; 6:8–9; 7:11; 10:3,18–19; 13:3,22; 14:19; 19:7; 23:4–5; 27:2; 30:20; Pss 35:13–14; 44:17–26; 73:12–14; 74:1,9; 82:2; Jer 12:1–2; 15:18; Lam 3:44; Isa 57:11; 59:2; Luke 7:18–30; 2 Cor 12:7–10.

69 For many other details regarding this issue, see Os Guinness, *Doubt* (Batavia: Lion Publishing, 1976); Gary R. Habermas, *Dealing with Doubt* (Chicago: Moody, 1990); Gary R. Habermas, *The Thomas Factor: Using Your Doubts to Grow Closer to God* (Nashville: B&H, 1999).

70 For instance, in a standard critical work on the subject, Reginald Fuller makes this clear (*The Formation of the Resurrection Narratives* [New York: Macmillan, 1971], 27–29). Ulrich Wilckens is another of the majority of scholars who agrees on this (*Resurrection: Biblical Testimony to the Resurrection: An Historical Examination and Explanation* [Edinburgh: Saint Andrew, 1977], 15).

71 Bahnsen, "A Critique," 43.

72 For this and related comments, see ibid., 12, 15, 21, 38–39.

73 Incidentally, that even a few philosophers became Christians after hearing Paul speak, using Jesus' resurrection as the chief evidence of his theistic claims (Acts 17:31), is one of many examples where straightforward presentations of the evidence led to conversions (see below, too).

74 This is not an informal fallacy of the *ad hominem tu quoque* variety, since I am not charging Bahnsen with failure to abide by his own challenge. Rather, I am simply arguing by analogy in pointing out that the observation he makes about Montgomery is not true of any apologist, including Jesus or Paul, and thus fails to count against Montgomery's position.

75 Intriguingly, we are even told that debating and presenting the resurrection was Paul's most frequent evangelistic approach, and again people believed (Acts 17:2–4). I wish to note here very clearly that whenever persons come to the Lord through apologetics or any other method, such was always and unequivocally the result of the Holy Spirit's power, not the overpowering nature of the historical evidences, human preaching, or witnessing.

76 Frame seems to acknowledge that he has moved a bit from the Van Tillian camp on this subject (Frame in Cowan, *Five Views*, 357–58), but the old vestiges are still apparent in some of his comments (*Apologetics to the Glory of God*, 14; *Doctrine of the Knowledge of God*, 130; Frame in Cowan, 218–19). For other good examples, see also Richard L. Pratt, *Every Thought Captive: A*

Study Manuel for the Defense of Christian Truth (Phillipsburg: Presbyterian and Reformed, 1979), 2–6; Notaro, *Van Til,* especially 46–47.

77 Isa 41:25–29; 42:9; 44:24–28; 46:10; 48:5, 14.

78 For more details, see Habermas in Cowan, *Five Views,* 245–47.

79 I also wish to be clear that I do not think that Scripture presents an exclusively evidential apologetic approach. Thus I hold that evidentialism is a viable way to argue but not the only way to do so. I also think most evidentialists agree here. For more details, see ibid., 98–99.

The Role of Public Debate in Apologetics

Dallas K. Miller

Today's postmodern world presents many challenges to the Christian apologist. From early Christian times, defenders of the faith have used public debate as one of their apologetic tools. Some Christians today, however, are insisting that we must abandon public debate in our apologetics. One author characterizes public debate as illegitimately using "power" over one's opponent. He asks, "How can any medium of power convey the gospel of grace?"[1] This line of thinking illustrates a total misunderstanding of how public debate is used in the New Testament and how it can be used to fulfil the mandate of 1 Peter 3:15: "Always be prepared to give an answer to everyone who asks you to give the reason for the hope you have."[2] The twentieth century is replete with examples of Christians effectively using public debate. In this chapter we will review some of the most prominent debates in the twentieth century and focus on the high profile debates engaged in by Dr. John Warwick Montgomery.

In 1948, before the age of television, philosopher and Catholic priest Fredrick C. Copleston squared off against agnostic Bertrand Russell on the issue of God's existence in a BBC radio broadcast, which gave the British public an opportunity to hear philosophical, theological discussion between two of the brightest minds of that generation.[3] In May 1985, another public debate took place between the twentieth century's foremost atheistic philosopher, Anthony G. N. Flew of England, and Dr. Gary Habermas, an evangelical apologist and specialist on the resurrection of Jesus Christ. "The Historicity of the Resurrection: Did Jesus Rise from the Dead?" was held before two expert panels and a live audience of 3,000; it operated under the strict rules of formal debate, with an affirmative statement by Habermas and a negative statement by Flew followed by the formal rebuttals of each participant, a head-to-head session, a question-and-answer period, and discussion.[4] The value of the Habermas-Flew exercise lies in the importance placed by the organizers on the makeup of the two panels, one consisting of five philosophers from various American universities and colleges whose task it was to render a verdict on the subject matter of the debate, and the second consisting of five professional debate judges (including theologians James I. Packer, Charles Hartshorne, and Wolfhart Pannenberg) who assessed the argumentation technique of the debaters: 10 experts, not all necessarily Christian believers, voting overwhelming in favour of the side taken by Habermas.[5]

The ministry of Dr. William Lane Craig stands as another example of the effectiveness of debate in apologetics. Since the 1980s Dr. Craig has participated in dozens of public debates against leading non-Christian scholars on a wide range of theological topics, employing an erudite, concise style always focussed on biblical ethics and the person of Jesus Christ.[6] "Atheism versus Christianity: Where Does the Evidence Point?" is the debate most representative of Dr. Craig's style and effectiveness; it was argued in 1994 against Frank Zindler, president of American Atheists, at Willow Creek Community Church in Chicago before a live audience of 8,000, and on radio.[7] Craig ultimately brought the debate to a conclusion by focussing not on the many unsupported assertions of his opponent but on the teachings, life, death, and resurrection of Jesus Christ as proof for the validation of Christianity. The audience voted overwhelmingly (98%) in favour of Craig as winner of the debate. To be sure, *vox populi* is not the same as *vox Dei* since a majority cannot define truth; however, analyzing debates like Craig's illustrates the value of public debate as an apologetic tool.

Copleston, Habermas, and Craig demonstrate how debate has been used positively for apologetic purposes in the twentieth century. Their work has solid biblical precedent. The most telling use of debate in a public format for an apologetic purpose can be seen in the ministries of Paul and those around him. Shortly after his conversion and before he had received his new name, Saul (with the encouragement of Barnabas) spent time in Jerusalem "speaking boldly in the name of the Lord. He talked and debated with the Grecian Jews" though they tried to kill him.[8] In his ministry throughout the book of Acts, we see Paul unafraid publicly to defend and proclaim the faith in the synagogue (Thessalonica, Ephesus) or before political leaders (Felix, Festus, Agrippa), often in a format that we would identify as public debate. Apollos, as well, exemplifies the scriptural debater. A Jew from Alexandria in Egypt and an aid to Paul's ministry, Apollos was a "learned man, with a thorough knowledge of the Scriptures" who spoke with fervour and taught about Jesus accurately (although, until he became a student of Aquila and Priscilla, he did not have a complete knowledge of Christ); he took guidance from mature Christians, was encouraged by the Ephesian church leaders to go to Achaia,[9] and was well received by believers in Corinth (as Paul made clear when he mentioned Apollos as one of four accepted teachers in that city).[10] The most striking description of his ministry is found in Acts 18:28: "For he vigorously refuted the Jews in public debate, proving from the Scriptures that Jesus was the Christ."

With this general and biblical background of debate, we approach the survey that is the subject of this paper. The apologetic career and ministry of Dr. John Warwick Montgomery, spanning five decades, is well-known through his writings and the writings of others.[11] However, no research has been conducted on the apologetic value of the series of nine public debates in which he participated with some of the most prominent and vociferous critics of biblical faith. This chapter will review the debates and provide background, summary, and a profile of lessons apologists can learn from Montgomery's debating style.

Madalyn Murray O'Hair (Atheist) Versus John Warwick Montgomery

Aired live from a Chicago radio station in 1967, this debate took place when Madalyn Murray O'Hair—founder of American Atheists and strident critic of Christianity in America—was at the peak of her popularity and on a zealous mission to rid America of all references to God, religion, and Christianity.[12] Her lobbying and litigation had been instrumental in the 1963 United States Supreme Court decision to outlaw prayer and Bible reading in public schools. The O'Hair-Montgomery interaction did not follow formal debating rules (such as an affirmative statement of a proposition by one debater and the response of a negative statement by the other) but consisted of a full exchange between the two followed by phone-in questions.

It was a highly emotional dialogue in which O'Hair (though often sidetracked with issues of a political nature, the Vietnam War, and tax-exempt status for churches) brought forth three accusations through her critique of Christianity and Scripture. She posed that there is no evidence Jesus existed as a historical figure, that the history of the church has been a history of oppression and slavery, and that the Christian view of sexuality is harmful and sexual liberation is what young people need as an ethic.

In support of her position that Jesus was not a historic figure, O'Hair cited no authority and declared the New Testament authors to be inaccurate historically and simply expressions of religious faith. When Montgomery quoted scholars regarding the historicity of the New Testament documents, O'Hair raised her voice, interrupted, or dismissed his statements as simply his opinion. Repeatedly throughout the dialogue, O'Hair accused Montgomery of offering no proof and no evidence that the four Gospels have come down to us in valid format. Of course the essence of Montgomery's apologetic style is to focus on exactly this issue, providing historic evidence for the validity of the Gospels and arguing that Jesus' resurrection proved his divinity—a subject on which Montgomery had already lectured and published groundbreaking work. Montgomery's arguments showed the basics of history and historic principles were lost on Mrs. O'Hair, who asserted with no supporting evidence that reference to the Gospel writers was worthless since scholarship does not recognize them. O'Hair's closed-minded display in refusing to allow Professor Montgomery to answer her concerns on the textual authority revealed that she was not interested in inquiry or freedom of thought but only in attempting to bully Montgomery verbally, the moderator, and any callers who did not agree with her ill-defined view of atheism.

O'Hair also accused the church and followers of Jesus Christ of being hypocritical and oppressive to blacks and women. Throughout the dialogue, O'Hair referred to the Inquisition, the support of slavery by the church in the southern United States, and the oppression of women as proof that Christianity is untrue, is worthless, and should be eliminated from America. Montgomery replied that the Bible does not teach slavery and that, in fact, Galatians 3:28 states the exact opposite and is a biblical foundation for the absolute equality of all human beings. Jesus did not advocate the Inquisition, and his teachings and ethics are completely contrary to anything along those lines. Professor Montgomery quoted a nineteenth-century rationalist in rebutting O'Hair's mischaracterization of the biblical ethic:

> The character of Jesus has not only been the highest pattern of virtue, but the strongest incentive to its practice, and has exerted so deep an influence, that it may be truly said, that the simple record of three short years of active life has done more to regenerate and to soften mankind, than all the disquisitions of philosophers and than all the exhortations of moralists.[13]

In relying on W. E. H. Lecky, someone who was not a Christian, Montgomery tried to show that it was the ethics of Jesus that were at issue; that Mrs. O'Hair needed to deal with the life of Jesus and his teaching, not the failures of his followers. Montgomery stated that examples of believers who are not following the Christian ethic are simply poor examples and that their failure to meet the appropriate standard is not proof the Christian religion is false. According to Montgomery, O'Hair was committing the fallacy of "guilt by association."

O'Hair's third attack against the Christian faith concerned the stifling of sexual freedom. Young people should be able to participate in sex freely and without inhibition when nature tells them they are ready; they should have their first sexual experience whenever they feel like it—when girls are about 13 or 14 years of age, and boys 15 or 16. O'Hair provided no justification for this proposition except to say that we should let nature take its course as it does in all other animal species. Montgomery replied that this type of evolutionary ethic is nothing but the naturalistic fallacy of confusing the "is" with the "ought." We are human beings distinct from the rest of nature, and unlike the rest of the animal world, we are capable of making decisions concerning our own natural environment. With this ability to make decisions, particularly in the area of sexual ethics, Montgomery argued that anyone without absolute moral grounding is left with whatever nature or culture dictates. This "moral relativism" is dangerous and causes one to separate the sexual experience from that of commitment—most disastrous to family life and social order, according to Montgomery.

The debate and following phone-in segment illustrated that O'Hair was out of her depth in attacking religion in general and Christianity in particular. She had no understanding of arguments from the perspective of history and was volatile and emotional when faced with an argument she could not address (virtually every one Dr. Montgomery put forward). Montgomery was commended by one of the callers for being so restrained and acting like a gentleman; however, throughout the debate he did attempt, in vain, to get Madalyn Murray O'Hair to face the historic question of Jesus Christ in deciding the religious question.

Thomas J. J. Altizer (Death of God) Versus John Warwick Montgomery

The 1960s saw the spawning of new and bizarre theological trends. One that caught the attention of the American media was the Death of God movement led by a small group of theologians including Thomas J. J. Altizer, William Hamilton, and Paul Van Buren. Altizer believed that God had actually died—that he ceased to exist as a transcendent, supernatural being at the death of Christ—but that he had become immanent in the world as universal humanity and that he continued to speak in exaggerated and dialectical language with reference to romanticism and mysticism. Dr. John Warwick Montgomery was invited to debate and dialogue with Altizer on February 24, 1967, at the Rockefeller Memorial Chapel, Chicago.[14] Raymond D. Fogelson of the University of Chicago moderated the debate, which began with Professor Altizer putting forth his position (described by Dr. Montgomery as brief and concise and not simply a rehashing of his previous writings). Montgomery then followed with a comprehensive and devastating critique of the Death of God theology, particularly Altizer's brand.[15]

The Altizer-Montgomery debate has been criticized by some evangelical attendees as an example of the side of orthodoxy (Montgomery) winning the argument but losing the soul (that is, the opportunity to evangelize Altizer). However, consideration of the debate on audio or through transcript reveals this interchange as a model for young apologists to study, with a view to emulating Montgomery's style in defending the faith against heretical positions. The crux of this debate is the importance of holding to a Christocentric apologetic. In order to illustrate Montgomery's approach, the following extensive exchange shows how Montgomery persistently came back to the historic Christ as the key to responding to Altizer's error:

> *Montgomery*. It's also the position of the orthodox Christianity of the first century that declared that on the basis of the *de facto* resurrection of Jesus Christ from the dead à la the Tallyrand story, they had a basis for affirming that Jesus Christ is the same yesterday, today, and forever. I'm still calling for a resurrection on your part, or a deferral to the One who did rise from the dead.
>
> *Altizer*. I really don't know how to reply to that, except that I can't conceivably imagine how such a question could ever be asked by a Christian.
>
> *Montgomery*. It seems to me Thomas asked it.
>
> *Altizer*. Yes, I think he's your model here.
>
> *Montgomery*. And most good exegetes of the Gospel of John point out that it reaches its climax in Thomas' affirmation, *Ho kyrios mou kai ho theos mou* ("My Lord and my God"). The Gospel of John begins with the incarnation—the Word became flesh—and comes to its climax with Thomas' affirmation of faith. Immediately following is John's statement that these things have been written that you might have life through believing in the name of Christ. It seems to me that you've got to ask yourself whether you're going to bring your theology into line with the primitive theology of the Christian faith, or whether you're going to continue to create a religion on the basis of your own inner experience. . . .
>
> *Altizer*. I'm afraid there aren't any easy answers, Mr. Montgomery.

Montgomery. You don't present *any* answers. I'll listen to any old answer.

Altizer. I'd be un-Christian if I presented an answer that would satisfy you.

Montgomery. That's interesting because that's about the criticism that the early Christians received. They went around actually proclaiming something—that God had come into the world in Jesus, that He had died for people's sins, and that He had risen again for their justification. Paul cites people who saw the resurrected Christ and says that over 500 were still alive—the implication being that if you don't believe it, go and ask one of them. The early Christians were so blamed definite that they turned the world upside down. But contemporary theologians, such as yourself, I'm afraid, are so indefinite that they're leaving the world in the mess in which they find it.[16]

Joseph Fletcher (Situation Ethics) Versus John Warwick Montgomery

San Diego State College hosted well-known proponent of situation ethics Joseph Fletcher and Professor John Warwick Montgomery in a February 11, 1971, debate asking, "Is situation ethics true or false?"[17] The format allowed formal statements of position and a rebuttal from each participant, with plenty of opportunity for questions from the audience of 1,600. The debate's popularity was indicative of the social and ethical tumult of North American society in the 1960s and early 1970s; its topic was timely and important, and the two debaters concise in representing their respective positions in a clear contrast of the choices available to a society seeking a basis for its ethical and moral system.

Professor Fletcher's opening affirmative statement in favour of situation ethics was replete with stories and so-called ethical dilemmas that he used to back up his theory. He summarized his view of situation ethics as follows:

I think that there are no normative moral principles whatsoever which are intrinsically valid or universally obliging.
I would contend that we may not absolutize the norms
of human conduct or, if you like theological rhetoric, we
may not make idols of any finite and relative rules of life.
Whether we ought to follow a moral principle or not
would, I contend, always depend upon the situation. This
is, of course, a reasonably straightforward statement of ethical relativity. If we are, as I would want to reason, obliged
in conscience sometimes to tell white lies, as we often call
them, then in conscience we might be obliged sometimes
to engage in white thefts and white fornications and white
killings and white breakings of promises and the like.[18]

Fletcher then placed situation ethics in the larger context of ethical options, of which only three are available to humans—legalism,
antinomianism, and situation ethics. Since legalism lies on the right
of the spectrum and antinomianism on the left, the only possible
legitimate middle ground is situation ethics, Fletcher said. A pithy
conclusion by Fletcher was, "We ought to live by the law of love and
never by any love of law."[19]

In his reply Dr. Montgomery went further than simply to respond
to Professor Fletcher's oral presentation. Montgomery presented a
prepared text wherein he went to the heart of Fletcher's writings and
distilled, in six points, situation ethics from Fletcher's perspective:

I.   Only one thing is intrinsically good, namely, love: nothing
     else.
II. The ultimate norm of Christian decisions is love: nothing
     else.
III. Love and justice are the same, for justice is love distributed.
IV. Love wills the neighbour's good whether we like him or not.
V.   Only the end justifies the means: nothing else.
VI. Decisions ought to be made situationally, not prescriptively.[20]

Montgomery began his critique with a devastating question, to
the delight of the audience: "How can we trust the situation ethicist
if he is adamant that the end justifies the means?" In other words,

if the situation ethicist is so convinced of his position and wants to be sure his neighbours are completely convinced of situation ethics, could he not lie according to principle V? In the restatement of an age-old conundrum, Montgomery took the wind out of the sails of the situation ethicist by asking, "If a situation ethicist, holding to the proposition that the end justifies the means in love, tells you that he is not lying, can you believe him?"[21] Dr. Montgomery pointed out that Fletcher committed the "category mistake" in confusing the identification of justice with love and that Fletcher totally misapplied the ethics of Jesus in failing to recognize Christ's strong opposition to lying in John 8:44. He carefully dissected Fletcher's inappropriate use of the word *love* and illustrated how he improperly applied the term *law*.

In addition to highlighting the inconsistencies and fallacies of Fletcher's system, Montgomery went on to illustrate the societal devastation that would occur if societies adopted situation ethics. Montgomery was indeed prescient in his analysis at this point. In fact, the postmodernism of the twenty-first century has created artificial absolutes that are the fruit of the situation ethics theory of the 1970s. That homosexual politics has created the so-called "gay rights" norms of our time, defining as politically incorrect and in some cases illegal the condemnation of homosexual behaviour, illustrates what Montgomery predicted:

> Unfortunately, arbitrary absolutes are a most dangerous commodity, for the love of one moment can become the hate of the next; and blind zeal for racial justice in the America of the 1970s may not differ motivationally from blind zeal for racism in the Germany of the 1930s.[22]

What is required as an ethical basis, argued Montgomery, is a system that properly stands as a justification for "absolute human rights" in the eye of ethics and law. Montgomery then relied on Wittgenstein to show that a human or man-made system of ethics is bound to fail because of the problems of the human predicament and the limitations and prejudices common to all. The standard for ethics and "absolute human rights" is derived from the transcendent, historic Christian faith. This transcendent word from God establishes permanent ethical values and is advantageous over any other ethical system, including situationalism, for four reasons: (a) love is expressly defined in terms of God's nature as revealed in Scripture and justified in terms of his very being; (b) absolute moral principles are explicitly set forth in Scripture, informing love and guiding its exercise; (c) final judgment on evil is assured, so no man ultimately gets away with evil; and (d) a remedy for the root problem in the human ethical dilemma (man's selfishness) has been provided.[23]

Julian J. Steen (Humanist) Versus John Warwick Montgomery

On February 5, 1969, Julian Steen, well-known American humanist and the dean of the Chicago School of Adults, faced off against Dr. Montgomery at DePaul University in Chicago.[24] Catholic theologian Robert Campbell acted as moderator, and several hundred students attended the debate, which asked, "Is man his own God?" Dr. Montgomery led off with his position from a written paper that eventually became the primary essay in his book *Christianity for the Tough-Minded.*[25] He structured his argument around (a) the unreality of the major theistic positions of pantheism, humanism, and agnosticism and (b) the reality of the biblical God as seen in the world, in his personhood, in Christ, and in human experience. Dr. Steen recited the humanist manifesto as his position and stated repeatedly that, as a humanist, he was concerned only about things that went on in this world, leaving issues relative to the "next world" to theologians and spiritualists. Steen's presentation was diffuse and rambling and failed to answer arguments presented by Dr. Montgomery or questions asked by the students at the end of the debate. His concern about building a better world focussed on the two main social problems he felt needed to be addressed: thermonuclear war and overpopulation. He cited the Vatican as the number one threat to solving the second problem and believed that, if people just worked harder at loving one another, we would solve the first. If there was any message of salvation from the world's problems coming out of Steen's message, it was his advocacy of world government through the United Nations. He displayed extreme difficulty in arguing why a humanist's values are superior to any other ethical system and failed to address Montgomery's trenchant analysis.

This debate reveals a consistent aspect of humanists: their closed-mindedness despite pride in using the scientific method and freedom of thought. While Steen emphasized that Jesus was a Jew, and he felt he should be revered as a prophet by the Jewish people today, he expressed the oft-used line that Jesus was a great moral teacher but not God and that he never claimed to be God. His debate with Montgomery revealed that his research was sadly lacking and his knowledge of the New Testament nonexistent and that he was blindly dedicated to the humanist manifesto. This debate, along with others in the series, illustrates so well how the Christian position, when clearly presented by a skilful academic, can overwhelm the critic. Much of Steen's content was ineffective and diffuse and did not address the debate topic.

Mark Plummer (Australian Atheist) Versus John Warwick Montgomery

Mark Plummer, lawyer and president of the New South Wales Humanist Society, debated Dr. Montgomery in Sydney, Australia, in February 1986.[26] Mr. Plummer claimed that since gods and goddesses do not exist, the Christian concept of God is irrelevant. He argued that modern science has demonstrated the Bible to be unhistorical and that the universe has evolved and exists without the need for God. The problem of evil illustrates that the Christian concept of God is impossible: if God is all loving, he must wish to abolish evil, and if God is all powerful, he must be able to abolish evil; therefore, God cannot exist because evil continues to exist. The majority of the world does not believe in the Christian concept of God, Plummer said, and for that reason God cannot exist. The Christian concept of God, according to the Bible, is full of contradictions and immoral acts, and therefore the universe is better off if this type of God does not exist. Throughout the debate, Plummer often alleged that American evangelists are detrimental to the social health of Australia, and the debate degenerated into an anti-American rant during much of his presentation. He mixed Christianity with American politics and sadly misinterpreted portions of Scripture, twisting scriptural terms to his own humanist ends.

Dr. Montgomery argued that the concept of a Christian God exists and that the life, death, and resurrection of Jesus Christ is the primary evidence for that claim. He asked Plummer properly and consistently to apply the "scientific method" in his presentation by starting simply to read the text of Scripture rather than make wild and illogical assertions—such as Plummer's repeated use of the term *apple eating* in reference to the story of Adam and Eve, a term Montgomery noted was never found in Scripture. Fallacies such as guilt by association and refusal to deal with the evidence for Christianity plagued virtually all of Plummer's presentation, and he failed to provide any rationale or basis explaining why his own value system as an atheist would be superior to anyone else's. Montgomery met him on his own terms and told the debate audience that humanism takes the best of human values and holds them high. Christianity can underpin humanism with an absolute value system that gives it a solid foundation. In presenting the case for Christianity, Montgomery established the New Testament documents as historically valid and illustrated the veracity of what the witnesses said in those documents. The question of whose value system can be maintained by the facts was answered by Montgomery's presentation of the legal/historical case for Christianity; he was the only participant who provided any evidence to answer the debate question.

Montgomery concluded by reminding the audience that debates are a dangerous forum for seeking religious truth and urging them not to be concerned with what Plummer, or even what he himself, said but to look instead at the primary evidence and check out the claims for Christ. Montgomery indicated a concern about Plummer's position, not so much for the answers or criticisms he gave but rather for his evasions and his refusal to look concretely at the New Testament documents for the evidence of Christ.

Dr. G. A. Wells (Sceptic) Versus
John Warwick Montgomery

Known for his radical thesis on the origins of Christianity, retired University of London professor G. A. Wells debated Dr. Montgomery on the topic "Jesus as Man, Myth, or God" on February 10, 1993, in London, England.[27] Wells argued that the New Testament records must be placed in chronological order, giving rise to questions regarding the consistency and credibility of the New Testament writers. Wells found no source for the early life of Jesus and believed any early Christian writings contradicted the later record of Jesus as a teacher and a miracle worker who died under Pilate. He found contradiction within the Gospel writers themselves, and the ethical teaching of Jesus to be objectionable in many instances. Professor Montgomery responded by addressing many of Professor Wells's specific attacks on Christianity. He answered the question of why the identity of Jesus is so important and discussed his opponent's reasoning as academically unsound. Montgomery profiled the legal/historical argument for Christianity and showed a divine picture of Jesus, at the end challenging the observers of the debate to consider what they should do with the evidence.

The question arose as to why Paul did not include any biographical or ethical details about Jesus, and Montgomery pointed to the purpose of that apostle's writings: to profile the work of Christ on the cross. Paul single-mindedly focussed on the death and resurrection of Jesus and the importance of this substitutionary work; his omission of the biographical details of Jesus and his miracles is no criticism of the Christian faith but rather a matter of emphasis. Professor Wells labelled as a "contradiction" the recording of any event expressed differently from one New Testament author to another, but Dr. Montgomery challenged his definition of the word; these were not contradictions but simply different versions of the events. Montgomery cited a late nineteenth-century lawyer who addressed the issue of the apparent contradictions and differences among the New Testament writers, Edmund H. Bennett, a former dean of the Boston School of Law:

What would have been my joy and confidence had I found
four such letters, in four different papers, written by four
different persons, giving an account of the same transac-
tion? And although in a close comparison of these four
accounts some variations should have been found as to the
particulars of that event, would that overthrow all belief in
the truthfulness of the accounts? Nay, would it not rather
furnish stronger proof of their integrity? Had all four accounts been exactly alike, the suspicion would have been
irresistible that one was copied from the other, or that all
were taken from one and the same original. But substantial
uniformity with circumstantial variety is one of the surest
tests of truth in all historical narratives.[28]

Here Bennett illustrates that, in the law, fact finding includes the
skill of looking carefully at the testimony of various witnesses; focussing on different aspects of an event does not equate to a contradiction. Montgomery highlighted the importance of debating this issue
dealing with Jesus Christ's claims: claims that he is the incarnation
of God Almighty, claims about eternity, claims on people's lives, and
claims concerning issues such as eternal salvation and life on earth.
These are questions everyone needs to address.

The problem with following Professor Wells's approach, according to Montgomery, was that Wells did not deal directly with the
primary source material, namely, the New Testament records. He
focussed on nineteenth-century and early twentieth-century German critical material, which undermines the authenticity of the New
Testament and purports to arrogate the judgment of the theologians,
almost 20 centuries later, over that of the eyewitnesses. The proper
approach is to deal with the records themselves and look at their integrity: are the New Testament documents trustworthy? According
to the best historical standards, Montgomery declared, the New Testament records come through as reliable. Citing the work of English
historian Chauncey Sanders in establishing three tests that establish
the authenticity of classical records,[29] Montgomery concluded:

On the basis, then, of powerful bibliographic, internal, and
external evidence, competent historical scholarship must

regard the New Testament documents as coming from the first century and as reflecting primary-source testimony about the person and claims of Jesus.[30]

Again, Professor Montgomery used a legal-historic approach by citing the work of Frank Morrison in his book *Who Moved the Stone?*[31] Morrison started writing his book to disprove the claims of Christianity but became a committed Christian after much research convinced him that the Jesus of the New Testament actually lived, died, and rose again. In asking what happened to the body, Morrison rejected two of the three possible parties that may have handled it; the Jewish religious leaders and the Romans would have acted against their own interest in removing and disposing of the body. The disciples, as the only other group that might have done anything with Christ's body, went out and proclaimed the life, death, and resurrection of Jesus—a message that caused their own deaths. It goes against all human understanding that the disciples would have disposed of the body and then gone out and died for something they knew to be untrue. Following Morrison's argument, Montgomery concluded that, according to high standards of legal and historic scholarship, the New Testament records are accurate in portraying that Jesus claimed to be God and proved his claim by dying and rising from the dead.

Dr. Lester Grabbe (New Testament Critic) Versus John Warwick Montgomery

"Did Jesus rise from the dead?" was the question debated on February 21, 1995, between Dr. Montgomery and Professor Lester Grabbe, dean of theology and humanities, before several hundred observers at Grabbe's home University of Hull in England.[32] According to Professor Grabbe, the New Testament offers a collection of testimonies about an encounter with the living Jesus after the crucifixion and a set of reports about an empty tomb—insufficiently substantiated information to infer the resurrection of Jesus. Grabbe argued that (a) no direct, but only indirect, testimony exists of anyone witnessing the actual resurrection event; (b) all claims to the events surrounding the resurrection (such as the crucifixion and the empty tomb) came from believing Christians, much of this testimony late and contradictory; and (c) the only firsthand evidence of someone seeing the resurrected Christ came from Paul (1 Cor 15), with no corroborating details or background information about how and when this took place. As a serious historian, Grabbe said, too many unknowns and too many alternative explanations led him to answer "no" to the question about Jesus' rising from the dead.

Montgomery did not respond point by point to Dr. Grabbe's concerns in his reply but rather laid out his own argument. If Jesus did in fact rise from the dead, he said, the implications are staggering. Christianity is then a technically and philosophically meaningful religion, as (according to 1 Cor 15) it becomes disconfirmable. Competing religious claims can be effectively tested since the resurrection is the verifying event. The position of Jesus Christ is established and allows transcendental assertions about values and a value system that is not based only on human opinion. Finally, Christ's resurrection establishes a sufficient basis for a proper eternal foundation; we can finally get things right in terms of handling issues of death and of life hereafter.

Montgomery, in disclosing the shortcomings of Grabbe's critique, contended that an individual making a commitment to Christianity on the basis of the evidence has a right to present that evidence. Grabbe, however, insisted that Christians are biased and cannot adequately examine the evidence or articulate a position on behalf of the resurrection. Underlying Professor Grabbe's position was the same view of the miraculous espoused by the eighteenth-century philosopher David Hume, who defined miracles out of existence in an attempt to do away with the greatest miracle of all—the resurrection of Jesus Christ. In response to Grabbe, Professor Montgomery cited the work of Thomas Sherlock, master of the Temple Church in London, whose 1729 book, *The Tryal of the Witnesses of the Resurrection of Jesus*, examined the type of evidence required to prove that Jesus rose from the dead. According to Sherlock, the requirement is eyewitness evidence that a person was alive at point A, dead at point B, and then alive again at point C—exactly the evidence Montgomery himself was presenting and arguing.[33] Taking a historical perspective of this issue involves two stages, according to Montgomery: determining what the evidence on the issue is and recognizing the implications of that evidence. With respect to determining the evidence, Montgomery went through the historical argument in detail, citing many authorities to show that the New Testament documents clearly present sound evidence for the life, ministry, death, and resurrection of Jesus Christ. Concerning the implications, Professor Montgomery used the legal approach to determine the validity of that testimony and found that the primary source material reveals testimony that is credible, was subject to rigorous cross-examination by hostile witnesses, was close to the events, and was written by eyewitnesses to the events.

John Naland (Atheist) Versus John Warwick Montgomery

John Naland, United States diplomat and atheist, wrote a 1989 magazine article for the *Free Inquiry*, criticizing the New Testament as a source of reliable information about the life of Christ. Because the documents are not reliable, Naland argued in his article, then we truly know nothing about Jesus of Nazareth. That same year Mr. Naland was invited to dialogue with Dr. Montgomery on the *John Ankerberg Show* in a series titled, "Did the Resurrection Really Happen?"[34] The televised debates were produced and graciously moderated by Mr. Ankerberg, who was able to interject clarification of the issues throughout the discussions and to provide detailed information harmonizing the Gospel accounts.

Mr. Naland held that the New Testament documents are contradictory—sometimes with too little evidence to determine what actually happened, and other times with too many facts causing confusion in determining what happened. Naland made several outrageous allegations with no supporting documentation—for example, equating Paul's conversion on the Damascus road to either heat stroke or epilepsy, and questioning whether the Scriptures handed down to us could be the works of the New Testament writers since all books were burned when Christianity was declared the official religion of the Roman Empire in AD 312!

Montgomery responded that these allegations were mere speculation and had no evidential basis. Upon Naland's complaints about differences between the Gospel accounts at the time of the resurrection (such as the number of women at the tomb, whether angels or men attended the tomb, and to whom Jesus appeared after the resurrection), Montgomery issued a reminder to consult the primary source documents and view them as four different perspectives of the same event—complementary, not contradictory. Naland's expectation of a comprehensive, minute-by-minute, detailed account of every event was answered by Montgomery's rebuke. The New Testament account was not an exhaustive, encyclopaedic version with a complete transcript of what happened, and Naland had a rather arrogant personal criteria regarding what God should have included in the New Testament documents to make an individual believe—a demand Naland did not make on any other historical documents. Montgomery went on to claim that the New Testament, viewed as one would view any other historic record, must be accepted as primary source, firsthand documentation written by eyewitnesses presenting Jesus claiming to be God Almighty.

The exchange was informative in that Naland himself realized the seriousness of the issue. At one point he asserted that, if this is the most crucial event in world history, we should have clear information about what happened. Perhaps the evidence for the gospel presented by Professor Montgomery in this debate has caused Mr. Naland to think more seriously about the pivotal event in human history.

Shabir Ally (Muslim) Versus John Warwick Montgomery

Shabir Ally, an imam from Toronto and one of the leading advocates for the Islamic faith, engaged questions on the identity and resurrection of Jesus with Dr. Montgomery at the Inns of Court Law School in London on October 17, 2003.[35] A pleasant and eloquent speaker who often publicly takes on opponents of Islam, Mr. Ally led off the debate: according to Muslims, Jesus is a prophet of God, and according to Christians, Jesus is the God of the prophets. Ally posed two questions: Did Jesus really die at the crucifixion? Did he really appear to disciples after his alleged death?

Ally claimed that, in ancient times, people did not know the difference between clinical death and brain death, and they were not sophisticated in understanding human anatomy. He cited historic examples of individuals hanging on a cross but not dying and asserted that, since Pilate expressed surprise over Jesus' quick death, he must have been on the cross only a few hours and was likely not dead when taken down but protected by the centurion guarding the tomb. Ally allowed that Jesus could have died later from shock and dehydration but that his death on the cross was no certainty, especially since the Gospel writers tried too hard to make it look as though he died in this fashion. Because Jesus did not actually die, the post-resurrection experiences are not reliable. Ally observed that the Gospel writers from Mark onwards enlarged and embellished the story of the postresurrection appearances. Without establishing evidential basis or logical analysis, Ally judged that the lack of definite proof of Christ's death invalidated accounts of his rising from the dead and his appearing to the disciples. Thus, we have no proof that Jesus is the God of the prophets and must conclude that he is a false messiah. Even so, based on the Koran Ally found value in Jesus as, if not a saviour, at least a prophet.

Montgomery responded that Ally filtered everything through the Koran, allowing the Koran to sit in judgment on the historicity and claims of Jesus in the New Testament. This position is *a prioristic* and starts with the Koran as God's final authority, which Ally imposed upon the New Testament. Montgomery used the example of one of Mr. Ally's books, in which he reviewed all the passages in the Gospel of John dealing with Jesus and declared them wrong because they contradicted the Koranic view of Jesus. Montgomery criticized this approach as very bad scholarship and noted that, in order to suggest a semblance of respectability in his argument, Ally quoted liberal New Testament critics in support, all critics who hold a naive acceptance of higher criticism of the New Testament, eschewing such scholars as F. F. Bruce or N. T. Wright who hold to the historicity of the New Testament. Ally avoided referring to direct eyewitness testimony recorded in the New Testament, an important point in analyzing the Muslim position in relation to the debate topic. The New Testament records were written by eyewitnesses within a generation of the events and were in circulation when hostile witnesses of the events could easily have challenged and destroyed the message of the New Testament if the material had not been accurate. To refute Ally's main contention that Jesus did not actually die a crucifixion death, Montgomery cited the eyewitnesses, who recorded that blood and water came from Christ's side when he was pierced with a spear, and paired this with modern scientific evidence from an article in the *Journal of the American Medical Association* titled, "On the Death of Jesus Christ":

> Clearly, the weight of historical and medical evidence indicates that Jesus was dead before the wound to his side was inflicted and supports the traditional view that the spear, thrust between his right ribs, probably perforated not only the right lung but also the pericardium and heart and thereby ensured his death. Accordingly, interpretations based on the assumption that Jesus did not die on the cross appear to be at odds with modern medical knowledge.[36]

Montgomery finished off his response by outlining two clear options facing the audience. They could accept the Islamic position as put forth by Mr. Ally and recognize its basis as speculation outlined by Mohammad, who wrote the Koran 600 years after the event. Alternatively, they could choose the historic evidence of the testimony of eyewitness or close associates, who wrote down the events before a generation had passed.

Conclusion

Montgomery's debating style and content are reminiscent of the apostle Paul's when, in Ephesus, he spoke boldly and argued persuasively. Montgomery's debate opponents often responded like Paul's listeners, who were "obstinate and refused to believe." Without a doubt, the debates in which Dr. Montgomery participated are a worthy study for any young apologist who is looking to perfect his or her skills. I submit four lessons that can be gleaned: One must know the opponent's arguments, recognize and challenge the underlying philosophy of the opponent, ensure the presentation is a Christocentric apologetic, and, finally, be sure to differentiate sociological criticisms against the church from theological arguments against the biblical faith.

With respect to preparation, Dr. Montgomery has always gone the extra mile in learning and understanding what the opponent is really saying. As an example, in the Altizer-Montgomery debate he quoted and critiqued Altizer's graduate work and pointed out, from his doctoral dissertation written only 12 years before the debate, that clearly Altizer had once accepted the orthodox Christian faith. By showing Altizer's rapid theological decline, he was effective in exposing his dependence on Enlightenment thinkers and illustrated how, when Altizer left the orthodox faith, he gave up objective truth because he adopted a "dialectical logic." The strategy of knowing an opponent's arguments well is based on Paul's example of knowing and quoting Stoic poets (Acts 17).

Montgomery was effective in pointing out faulty reasoning and gaps in logic by recognizing and challenging the underlying philosophy of his opponents. For example, in the debate on the Muslim view of Jesus, Montgomery proved Shabir Ally could not look objectively at the evidence for the New Testament faith, no matter what facts were presented to him, because of his presuppositional bias in favour of the Koran. Again, Montgomery dealt with Altizer's religious syncretism and avoidance of any biblical criteria for judging theology:

> Without a firm criterion for determining what is true and
> what is false religious belief—without a firm historical
> check on the Christ of faith—this kind of satanic error is
> not merely possible, but inevitable. Man is an idol-making
> animal, and he will build Christ to fit his own image or his
> most cherished dreams of egotistic autocracy when theo-
> logians are so misguided or foolish as to give him the tools
> for doing so.[37]

This approach is helpful in responding to a host of attacks on the Christian faith, from higher criticism to postmodernism. As an apologist, one needs to understand not only the gospel but also the dangers that entice people to build their own religious systems. Identifying the underlying philosophy of a person who criticizes the Christian faith allows the apologist then to apply properly the biblical gospel.

Today's intellectual climate is characterized by a tendency to abandon the laws of logic, yet a skilful apologist must go back to the historic Jesus as the focal point. The only effective response continues to be the Christocentric apologetic. The temptation is great to try to answer all of the charges levelled against the Christian faith, but in the debates Montgomery was careful to focus his time and energy on the important accusations, and respond to the critic by continually going back to the Jesus of Scripture, as we see practiced consistently by the New Testament "apologists." Arguing endlessly about the existence of God may be intellectually gratifying, but the good apologist deals with those arguments quickly and then moves to the Christ of Scripture as soon as possible (John 14).

Finally, arguments in almost every one of these nine debates against the Christian faith dealt with ethical questions such as the Inquisition. Montgomery illustrated the importance of differentiating between the New Testament ethic as the standard proclaimed by Jesus, and the occasional failure of his followers to uphold this standard. The best example of Montgomery's dealing with this problem is his counter to Altizer's accusation that Christians supported slavery:

> You confuse sociology with theology. You see a situation
> in the South which is a mess sociologically. And you see
> churches that have deviated from the historic Christian
> proclamation and who still claim to be in accord with it.
> But instead of bringing their false theology up against the
> historic Word and the Christ who is objectively present
> in history, and whose words are objectively presented in
> Scripture, you dump the whole business. You manifest the
> Hegelian dialectic in your own person in that you're tossing out baby and bath water. In Scripture it says that there
> is neither Jew or Greek, neither bond or free, and that we
> are all one in Christ Jesus. Thus any Christian who claims

segregation to be Christian is un-Christian. The way to handle this is not to toss out the Christian faith, but to apply the Christian faith.[38]

Oftentimes when Christians are confronted with these inconsistencies in spiritual practice, they are left flat-footed and are unable to respond. The value of Montgomery's approach lies in his exemplification of how to distinguish between sociological/psychological problems and theological issues, and then focussing attention on the main issues, disallowing the opponents of Christianity to sidetrack the apologist from the key thrust of defending and proclaiming the faith.

For young apologists at the beginning of the twenty-first century faced with a host of postmodern attacks on the Christian faith, sitting at the feet of expert apologists is important. One can do no better than to study the debates of Dr. Montgomery in audio, video, and written formats to learn the skills necessary to present biblical faith "boldly" and to "argue persuasively" for the gospel of Jesus Christ.

Endnotes

1 John G. Stackhouse, *Humble Apologetics* (New York: Oxford University Press, 2002), 219.

2 All biblical references are given in *New International Version*.

3 The debate has been published in several sources and continues to serve as an ideal portrayal of the "contingency argument" for the existence of God. See Al Seckel, ed., *Bertrand Russell on God and Religion* (Buffalo, NY: Prometheus Books, 1986).

4 The debate and responses of the panel of theologians and the debate specialists are all fortunately recorded for the public in an excellent book: Terry L. Miethe, ed., *Did Jesus Rise from the Dead?* (San Francisco, CA: Harper and Row, 1987). For a helpful review of Flew's journey from atheism to theism that the 1985 debate helped influence, see "My Pilgrimage from Atheism to Theism: A Discussion Between Antony Flew and Garry R. Habermas," *Philosophia Christi* 6 (2004): 197–211.

5 Ibid., 8.

6 Dr. Craig's own Web site contains actual transcripts of 11 of those debates for complete public access online at www.leaderu.com/offices/billcraig.

7 Willow Creek Association, *Atheism Versus Christianity: Where Does the Evidence Point?* (Grand Rapids, MI: Zondervan, 1994), videotape, ISBN 0–310–24579–6.

8 Acts 9:27–29.

9   See Acts 18:24–28.

10 1 Cor 1:12.

11 For a complete reference to the writings of Dr. John Warwick Montgomery, see Will Moore, *Bibliography of Dr. John Warwick Montgomery's Writings* (Edmonton, AB: Canadian Institute for Law, Theology and Public Policy, 2003); see also www.jwm.christendom.co.uk.

12 See John Warwick Montgomery and Madalyn Murray O'Hair, *Great Chicago Air Show* (Edmonton, AB: Canadian Institute for Law, Theology and Public Policy), live audiotape recording; available online at www.ciltpp.com.

13 W. E. H. Lecky, *History of European Morals from Augustus to Charlemagne II*, 2nd ed. (London: Longmans, Green, 1869), 88.

14 See John Warwick Montgomery and Thomas J. J. Altizer, *Death of "The Death of God"* (Edmonton, AB: Canadian Institute for Law, Theology and Public Policy), live audiotape recording; available online at www.ciltpp.com.

15 See Montgomery's presentation and the moderated exchange with Altizer in John Warwick Montgomery, *The Suicide of Christian Theology* (Minneapolis, MN: Bethany Fellowship, 1969), 121–22.

16 Ibid., 154.

17 See John Warwick Montgomery and Joseph Fletcher, *Situation Ethics* (Edmonton, AB: Canadian Institute for Law, Theology and Public Policy), live audiotape recording; available online at www.ciltpp.com. This debate is also available in written format: John Warwick Montgomery and Joseph Fletcher, *Debate on Situation Ethics* (Minneapolis, MN: Bethany Fellowship, 1972).

18 Montgomery and Fletcher, *Debate on Situation Ethics*, 15.

19 Ibid., 24. This new morality propagated by Dr. Fletcher under the name of situation ethics is also presented in his initial work titled *Situation Ethics* (1966) and a further work titled *Moral Responsibility* (1967).

20 Montgomery and Fletcher, *Debate on Situation Ethics*, 25.

21 Ibid., 32.

22 Ibid., 43.

23 Ibid., 44.

24 See John Warwick Montgomery and Julian J. Steen, *Is Man His Own God?* (Edmonton, AB: Canadian Institute for Law, Theology and Public Policy), live audiotape recording; available online at www.ciltpp.com.

25 John Warwick Montgomery, *Christianity for the Tough-Minded* (Minneapolis, MN: Bethany Fellowship, 1973), 21.

26 See John Warwick Montgomery and Mark Plummer, *The Great Australia Atheism Debate* (Edmonton, AB: Canadian Institute for Law, Theology and Public Policy), live audiotape recording; available online at www.ciltpp.com.

27 See John Warwick Montgomery and George Albert Wells, *Jesus: What Evidence?* (Edmonton, AB: Canadian Institute for Law, Theology and Public Policy), live audiotape recording; available online at www.ciltpp.com. See also Wells's books: *The Jesus of the Early Christians* (1971), *Did Jesus Exist?* (1975), and *The Jesus Myth* (1998).

28 Edmund H. Bennett, *The Four Gospels from a Lawyer's Standpoint* (Boston: Houghton Mifflin, 1899; reprint, *Simon Greenleaf Law Review* 1 [1981]).

29   Chauncey Sanders, *Introduction to Research in English Literary History* (New York: Macmillan, 1952), 143.

30   A similar argument can be found in John Warwick Montgomery, *History, Law and Christianity*, 2nd ed. (Edmonton, AB: Canadian Institute for Law, Theology and Public Policy, 2002).

31   Frank Morrison, *Who Moved the Stone?* (Downers Grove, IL: InterVarsity Press, 1981).

32   See John Warwick Montgomery and Lester Grabbe, *Jesus' Resurrection: What Historical Evidence?* (Edmonton, AB: Canadian Institute for Law, Theology and Public Policy), live audiotape recording; available online at www.ciltpp .com.

33   Thomas Sherlock, "The Tryal of the Witnesses of the Resurrection of Jesus," in *Jurisprudence: A Book of Readings*, ed. John Warwick Montgomery (Strasbourg, France: International Scholarly Publishers, 1980), 339.

34   See John Warwick Montgomery and John K. Naland, *Did the Resurrection Really Happen?* (Edmonton, AB: Canadian Institute for Law, Theology and Public Policy), live audio and video recordings; available online at www .ankerberg.com.

35   See John Warwick Montgomery and Shabir Ally, *Who Was Jesus? Did He Rise from the Dead? A Muslim-Christian Debate* (Edmonton, AB: Canadian Institute for Law, Theology and Public Policy), live audiotape recording; available online at www.ciltpp.com.

36   William D. Edwards, Wesley J. Gabel, and Floyd E. Hosmer, "On the Death of Jesus Christ," *Journal of the American Medical Association*, 255 (March 21, 1986): 1455–63.

37   John Warwick Montgomery, *The Suicide of Christian Theology* (Minneapolis, MN: Bethany Fellowship, 1969), 173.

38   Ibid., 151.

John Warwick Montgomery as Evangelical, Evidential, and Confessional Lutheran Apologist

Craig Parton

Summarizing the contribution of any important thinker can be dangerous business. It is especially dangerous in this case when the life and work of the subject is, God willing, far from over.

While volumes like this tend to honor a revered teacher on his one hundred fifth birthday and are composed by students and colleagues who want to say *something* before the funeral, that is hardly the case here. Dr. Montgomery's legendary Scottish genetic makeup makes it a good bet that he will outlive most (all?) of the contributors to this volume. He continues to write, lecture, and debate (let alone lead frenetic tours of the glorious Alsace region of France each summer at the International Academy of Apologetics, Evangelism, and Human Rights). For the record, he can also consume impressive amounts of Alsatian wine at dinner at my expense, park his vintage Citroën about anywhere he pleases within the confines of the city of Strasbourg, render spellbound students ranging from high school level to housewives to Ph.D.s, and be equally at ease whether discussing Wittgenstein,[1] Luther,[2] Bach,[3] or Sherlock Holmes.[4]

How does one "categorize" someone who is a rare American member of both an elite gastronomical academy in Paris[5] and culinary and wine society in the Alsace,[6] founded the first Christian law school that integrated theology, law, and apologetics, is a member of the Sherlock Holmes Society of England, argues cases of international import involving religious liberty and human rights before the International Court of Human Rights in Strasbourg,[7] debated the likes of the infamous atheist Madalyn Murray O'Hair, death-of-God theologian Thomas J. J. Altizer, and liberal Bishop James Pike, has disturbingly annoying (and generally disturbingly operable) robots roaming the confines of his house in the Alsace, at last count had 10 earned degrees (including advanced degrees in law, history, philosophy, and theology) from such diverse institutions as Berkeley,

University of Chicago, Essex, Cardiff, and Strasbourg, published over 45 books and 100 articles in five languages,[8] is the editor of an international journal of classical theology and apologetics,[9] has done the definitive treatment on the history of efforts to locate Noah's ark as well as personally led two expeditions up Mt. Ararat in search of the ark,[10] whose fascinating footnotes make better reading than most author's books, who considers exercise a remnant of the fall,[11] and only drinks water on pain of death and considers it to be a threat to cultured living?

With such an interesting and encompassing scholarly background and reputation for utterly engaging public lecturing, and with the honed polemical ability of an English barrister (which he is) and American attorney licensed to practice in California, Virginia, and Washington and before the Supreme Court of the United States, surely the name of John Warwick Montgomery is a household word within both his own Lutheran church and more widely within the Christian church militant.

Strangely, and disturbingly, significant segments of the Christian church in general (with notable and enthusiastic exceptions to be sure) are tragically stone ignorant of Montgomery's colossal impact for the gospel of Jesus Christ in the modern secular era and the value of his work in equipping the next generation of *fides defensors* to "contend earnestly for the faith once delivered." Why is that the case?

Menace to Liberals and Mystery to Moralists

We might well first ask what it is about contemporary American Christianity that has resulted in its being intimately knowledgeable about the latest contribution of Tim LaHaye to the Left Behind grocery store pabulum or right on top of the health-and-wealth preaching of the well-coiffed televangelists and their surgically improved trophy wives but largely clueless concerning the fruitful efforts of an extraordinary apologist who has been toiling in the vineyards since the time of C. S. Lewis. Besides the obvious geographical fact that Montgomery has lived in Europe now for almost two decades, two driving forces keep his impact in the shadows of contemporary American Christianity:

First are the devastating consequences of theological liberalism within mainline Christian denominations (Dr. Montgomery has often commented that one is better off not having *any* contact with Christianity rather than having contact with Christianity as presented by theological liberalism). Liberals are anything but liberal when it comes to studying the sources establishing the intellectual defensibility of orthodox Christianity and so their lack of familiarity with the defense of the Christian faith found in the books, articles, and debates of Dr. Montgomery is not surprising.[12] Underlying liberalism are two basic assumptions: First, Christianity is not about objective, propositional statements of truth but is a call to a new life and to social action. Second, liberals believe that Christianity is really not qualitatively different from other religions. Little wonder, then, that liberal Christians have had little interest in defending Christian orthodoxy. When there is no orthodoxy, that leaves little to defend.[13]

Second, American Christianity is now most interested in preaching evangelical moralism, giving tips on getting a purpose-driven life, and exercising and eating the way Jesus did. As such, it has not been attracted to a serious, scholarly, and objective presentation of the case for Christianity within a growing context of secularism but instead has stressed "Jesus in the heart" to the exclusion of the head. In its charismatic mutation especially, evangelicalism has not integrated itself into culture and has spawned both separatist and pietistic variants.[14] Anti-intellectual and corporate-oriented American evangelicalism (growth is good for any business and the church is really a business, and growth in numbers and money means God surely is blessing that church) has also not taken the defense of the Christian faith sufficiently seriously and so has not familiarized itself with the work of solid apologists like the unknown trinity of Wilbur Smith, Edward John Carnell, and John Warwick Montgomery.[15]

But even more astounding is how Dr. Montgomery's own church body has accomplished simultaneously avoiding, ignoring, and being irritated with his work at a time when its rediscovery is most needed. While it was largely due to the contributions of thinkers like Montgomery and Robert Preus in the late 1960s and early 1970s that his own church body (the Lutheran Church, Missouri Synod) accomplished the unheard of feat of successfully diverting its seminary from continuing down the path of theological liberalism,[16] Lutherans by and large have never figured out Montgomery. Of course, that assumes Lutherans have even heard of him. Most have not.

Any French-speaking Lutheran without a German surname, and without degrees from Synod-blessed schools,[17] comes with a large dosage of suspicion within the confines of the Amish-like society known as the Missouri Synod (as well as the other theologically orthodox Lutheran Synods like the Wisconsin Evangelical Synod based, oddly enough, in Wisconsin, and the Evangelical Lutheran Synod, out of that thriving metropolis of Mankato, Minnesota). Lutherans, incredibly, have accused him of either being a *liberal* (he teaches all manner of Christians[18] and is not a beer drinker) or a *synergist* (surely he must believe that arguments win people into the kingdom for otherwise why would he write so many books that invite the non-Christian to weigh the evidence for the truth of the claims of Christianity and that advocate "evidence that demands a verdict"?).[19]

Montgomery was a veritable menace to liberal and so-called "moderating" Lutherans in the confrontation over inerrancy within the Lutheran Church, Missouri Synod. In his distinctive fashion, Montgomery called out the leaders of the compromising movement by name, documenting how they were arguing that Scripture has errors and contradictions and yet were utterly ignorant of the best responses to these supposed errors and contradictions that were in many cases articulated centuries earlier.[20]

The monumental and innovative contributions of Professor Montgomery to the apologetic task and defense of the faith are seen in his ability to integrate his training as a theologian, historian, philosopher, and lawyer with an unswerving commitment to the centrality of the saving message of Jesus Christ contained in a totally reliable Scripture.

That impact is best understood in seeing John Warwick Montgomery as being an *evangelical, evidential, and confessionally Lutheran apologist.*

Evangelical Apologist

John Warwick Montgomery's life and work are above all *evangelical*—that is, their sum and substance are a commitment to the intellectual defensibility of the gospel, the complete trustworthiness of the record in which that gospel is found and the aggressive presentation of that saving gospel to all men by calling for their personal commitment to the Jesus who saves.

Being evangelical in manner and flavor does *not* mean that Montgomery can in any way be understood as a *sociological* evangelical. Hardly. By formal theological commitment, training, and temperament, he is best understood first as a confessional Lutheran.[21] By that we mean that his roots are in Luther's Reformation and doctrine of the freedom of the Christian man, rather than in American evangelicalism's moorings traced best to revivalistic Wesleyan Methodism and pietistic and moralistic Arminian "decide for Jesus and then work with God to save you" theology.

If the truth be known, American Evangelicalism has long had a love-hate relationship with John Montgomery.[22] He is indeed actually best known in evangelical circles, having taught, spoken, and lectured in the hallowed halls of its best teaching institutions for almost 50 years. But because he is so theologically solid in the Reformation tradition and because he is so enthusiastically and contagiously *Lutheran*, evangelicalism has never quite known what to do with him.[23]

Few know evangelicalism better than Dr. Montgomery since he has his Christian origins in evangelicalism. It was as an undergraduate at Cornell that he first came into contact with a serious orthodox and evangelical theology.[24] Montgomery's conversion took place through the human instrument of evangelicalism as an undergraduate at Cornell. Being a classics major, Montgomery then immediately went about determining which expression of Christianity most clearly mirrored the canonical documents that serve as the basis for the Christian position. In order to do that, he set the Greek text of the New Testament alongside the 39 Articles of the Anglican Church of England, the Reformed Heidelberg Catechism, and the Lutheran Augsburg Confession. Result? He promptly became a confessional Lutheran. Why? He concluded that Lutheranism adhered most closely to the controlling texts and that it valued faithfulness to those texts more than it did adhering to any procrustean notion of philosophical or logical consistency. More importantly, Lutheranism emphasized the doctrine of justification as the central doctrine on which the Church rises or falls. Montgomery concluded at the very beginning of his career that his central academic contributions would be committed to the defense and proclamation of the facticity of the gospel of Jesus Christ and the complete and total reliability of the Scriptures in which that gospel is situated.

It is fitting that the early Lutherans were actually called "evangelicals." The term *evangelical* comes from the Greek word *euangellion*, or *evangel*. It simply means "good news," or in the common English contraction, "gospel." The Lutherans in sixteenth-century Germany were originally called "Evangelicals" because of their primary emphasis on Christ's atoning death and resurrection. That was appropriate because if Lutheranism does anything right, it gets the gospel right. Thus the gospel has become the focus of all of Montgomery's writing, lecturing, and debating. No lecture on human rights, or on gastronomy, or on Sherlock Holmes, or on analytical philosophy, or on the music of J. S. Bach, is delivered without the implications for the gospel boldly proclaimed and defended at the highest levels of scholarship.

Montgomery's evangelical focus is particularly evident in his public presentations. Three things one can *always* be sure of with respect to a Montgomery lecture: First, he is always prepared as one would expect a trial lawyer to prepare to address a jury. He has the keen awareness to respect his audience enough to deliver wonderfully and engagingly on whatever the topic might be, and regardless of whether there are 600 people, 60 people, or 6 people. Second, the case for the truth of the gospel of Jesus Christ (Christ's perfect life, atoning death, and verifiable resurrection) finds its way into the presentation in a way that is never contrived, always clear, and unfailingly defensible, and emphasizes the *extra nos*[25] character of that case. Third, the presentation is at such a high level of scholarship that one could confidently invite non-Christians to attend. It is the same confidence one has when recommending that someone read Lewis's *Mere Christianity*[26]—the trust that comes with knowing that the non-Christian will be respected, not talked down to and not subjected to "in group" Christian lingo. Modern-day American evangelicalism, which is often a mile wide and an inch deep, would so gloriously benefit from a rediscovery of Montgomery's work and its focus on the centrality of the gospel as the intellectual reference point in dialogue with unbelief.

But as important as the gospel is (what the Reformers called the "Material Principle of all theology"), Montgomery saw immediately and early in his career that a gospel contained in a text with errors and contradictions was intellectually indefensible. If the texts which give us the gospel (that is, the Holy Scripture—the "Formal Principle of all theology") cannot be trusted in what they say on what the temple in Jerusalem looked like, how can it be trusted when it speaks of the heavenly Jerusalem? Montgomery saw the logical failings being engaged in by the so-called neoorthodox theologians and "mediating evangelicals" of his own church body as they sought to maintain an *inerrant* gospel residing in an *errant* Scripture. He launched a series of polemical broadsides at the logical errors and utterly unscientific and fallacious manner in which neoorthodox theologians and the seminaries they had infected were abandoning the doctrine of inerrancy for weasel words like *infallibility* and *partial inerrancy*.[27]

What American evangelicals need is a recovery of total confidence in the gospel[28] and the recovery of a vigorous and intellectually defensible grounding of that gospel in a similarly totally reliable Scripture. In Dr. Montgomery they have a sure and tried native son who can guide them in that critical endeavor.

Evidential Apologist

Similarly, Montgomery's approach to the defense of the saving gospel and the record that contains it has been unashamedly, vigorously evidential and fact driven from the beginning of his career. His best-known and most popular book boldly set out the "historical-legal" apologetic approach that sets him apart from all contemporary apologists. That important work[29] presents a set of tests to determine the reliability of the New Testament Gospels. Montgomery has then built upon the test to establish the reliability of the New Testament

Gospels and established a wider ranging evidential progression that proves the case for Christianity under legal standards of evidential probability.[30]

The flow of Montgomery's defense of the faith is built on his training as an English barrister and American attorney. In his argumentation, presuppositions are kept to the bare minimum. The least quantum amount of data is *assumed* (only presuppositions of form, such as assuming the objectivity of the external world, the inferential operations of induction and deduction, the meaningfulness of language, the validity of the law of noncontradiction) so that the maximum amount of data is capable of being *discovered*. This stands in stark contrast to the various Calvinist presuppositionalists who seek to show that Christianity makes sense *if* certain fundamental content-laden assumptions are first accepted.[31] In the historical-legal apologetic presented by Montgomery, the inquirer is invited to investigate the claims of Christianity contained in the New Testament documents as he would any other work of antiquity and to apply probability reasoning and the widely accepted canons of legal evidence in doing so.

The colossal import of Montgomery's specifically legal emphasis in apologetics comes in at least three areas: First is the concept of probability reasoning; second is his use of the principle of the "burden of proof"; and finally is his insistence that a *verdict* be rendered and that the historical case takes one beyond mere intellectual acknowledgment of the claims of Christ into the very presence of the Transcendent God who has become man via the mystery of the incarnation.

With respect to probability reasoning, Montgomery is unique in his reliance on the position that the case for Christianity is ultimately a case based on establishing the facticity of certain events (as opposed to arguing that Christianity is true because it is necessarily the most "logical" system). *If certain central events did not occur, Christianity is a sham. Period.* Since Christianity is fact centered, one must understand the nature of factual assertions. Facts never rise to the level of didactic proof. There is always the possibility of error. Thus, the case for Christianity is never apodictically certain because 100-percent certainty only comes in matters of pure logic or pure mathematics. One weighs probabilities, looks at the evidence as a lawyer would in presenting evidence to a court or jury, and then a decision must be rendered. One must never demand of religious claims a level of factual certainty not demanded in any other domain.[32]

Second, Montgomery stresses that the "burden of proof" is actually on the Christian to establish the case for Christianity. This has gigantic practical implications. First, Christians will see the importance of bringing the case for Christ into the marketplace and stressing arguments that can be checked out. On more than one occasion he has remarked in public when discussing one of his numerous— and infamous—debates, that he seeks to win the person in the audience who truly does not know which side they are on but is "sitting on the fence."

This emphasis on the Christian assuming the burden of proof means that Dr. Montgomery's apologetic is more interested in focusing on positive, fact-driven arguments for the case for Christianity than it is in tearing down the weaker arguments of other world religions. Compare this approach to that of Francis Schaeffer, who once opined that if he had one hour in a train with a non-Christian he would spend the first 55 minutes tearing down the false beliefs of the person and the last 5 minutes on the positive evidence for Christianity.

As a trained trial lawyer, Montgomery knows that as a plaintiff with the burden of proof, the key is to the return of a favorable verdict. The law recognizes this fact since even an executive pardon must be "accepted" to be effective.[33] The mere acceptance of facts is not enough when confronted with the claims of Christianity. If the factual case is solid—which trial lawyers have concluded for centuries is indeed the situation based on the overwhelmingly solid evidence— then personal commitment to those facts is central. As our Lord Himself says, "He who believes in Me will live, even if he dies."[34]

Montgomery has addressed precisely why lawyers have been more inclined to do apologetics than dentists and engineers. The primary reason is not because Scripture itself is so intertwined with law. The main reason is the manner in which the Christian truth claims cry out for verification. Montgomery has dedicated his energies to establishing that the biblical witnesses are not subject to the hearsay objection as to their testimony but stand the test of the most rigorous cross-examination.[35] Whether applying the parol evidence rule or the principles of the ancient document rule, the biblical documents are, simply put, the best-attested works of all antiquity.[36]

Confessional Lutheran Apologist

Ultimately Montgomery's apologetic is evangelical and evidential *because* it is confessionally Lutheran in its central incarnational focus on the perfect life and atoning death of the One who suffered under Pontius Pilate. Being Lutheran in focus, his approach is centered in the gospel of Jesus Christ. His early lectures in Lutheranism and the defense of the biblical gospel[37] spell out an apologetic approach from which he has never wavered and which has, instead, grown and matured in quality like a Lafite-Rothschild Bordeaux.[38]

Above all, John Montgomery has remained a faithful proclaimer of Christ crucified to all men. This unfailing commitment to the truth of the Christian faith as expressed in the confessional documents of the Lutheran Reformation, to Luther's freedom of the Christian man in Christ who has indeed set us free from the law of sin and death, and to the lordship of Christ over all intellectual and cultural life, sets him alone among apologists of our day. It flows so directly out of his primary commitment to the insights of the Lutheran Reformation.

What sets him apart from other serious confessional Lutherans is that he is not only an apologist and a contagiously zealous defender of the faith, but he is an *evangelist*. Lutherans would do well to remember this and to see that there is utterly no tension between being a serious follower of the insights of the Lutheran Reformation *and* a zealous advocate of Christ crucified to unbelievers *and* a proclaimer of "many infallible proofs" that demand a personal verdict. One illustration will suffice of how that life has been lived out as an evangelical, evidential, and confessional apologist.

Dr. Montgomery was founder and dean of The Simon Greenleaf Law School in California in the 1980s. I rapidly discovered that Montgomery's courses—whether on jurisprudence, evidence, or legal literature—were really a synthesis of Western philosophy, law, theology, and apologetics all superbly integrated into a coherent package of interrelated ideas. Though a student in the apologetics program, I took a fair number of law classes for the sole purpose of being around that kind of unified approach to knowledge. It was utterly magnetic.

The school was in the process of obtaining critical accreditation from the state of California. For months extremely diligent efforts were in the works to prepare for the arrival of the state bar examiners. The examiners were to spend a week at the school, doing the legal equivalent of a proctology exam. Everything was reviewed, from curriculum to teaching qualifications and abilities to library resources to finances to administration. I did not have direct concern over the process since I was studying theology and apologetics with the likes of Walter Martin, Harold Lindsell, and Rod Rosenbladt— the cream of the apologetic crop. The law curriculum was only of interest to me because Montgomery taught in both the apologetics and law departments and was dean of the school.

The examiners were a mixed lot, to be sure, and apparently there was a tremendous amount of skepticism, even hostility, among some of them concerning the concept of a "Christian" law school. I came to class in the middle of what was obviously a very important week for the school and for Dean Montgomery personally.

Before class began, and certainly when no accreditation overseers were present, Dr. Montgomery recounted to our class that he had been up the night before to the wee hours of the morning with the state bar examiners. One of that group in particular had really played his "hostility" cards about Christianity in general and about the facticity of the gospel in particular. The subjects raised went to the heart of why the school had come into being. It would have been understandable if Montgomery had kept his own cards close to his vest; no one, especially his board of trustees, would have faulted him (or even known) if he had steered the discussion to other safe harbors. Montgomery's comment to the class went something like this: "After the rest of the examiners finally left, I was alone with this one fellow. A terrific opportunity to preach the gospel presented itself. I took full advantage of that opportunity. If he becomes a Christian, I really don't give a hang whether we get the accreditation." I don't know whatever has become of that state bar examiner. I do know that the school got the accreditation.

An Apologist for All Seasons

That is John Warwick Montgomery—defender of the faith to all men and for all seasons. The sum and substance of his life, the raison d'être for the degrees, the books, the debates, and all the rest of the colossal contribution to the defense of the faith is not some esoteric and "upper story" intellectual chess game done at the expense of human souls. It has been a life lived *sub crucis*—under the cross and dedicated to the aggressive defense and presentation of Christ crucified for sinners and raised again for our justification.

For that, I tip my glass, light up a fine Dominican cigar,[39] and toast the health and continued prosperity of a true doctor and defender of the Church militant.

Endnotes

1 See Montgomery, *Tractatus Logico-Theologicus* (Bonn, Germany: Science and Culture Publishers, 2002). This theological *magnum opus* by Montgomery mirrors in structure what many consider the most important work of philosophy in modern times done by the great 20th century analytical philosopher, Ludwig Wittgenstein. Elsewhere I have described Montgomery's *Tractatus* as the "apologetical equivalent of Bach's *Mass in B Minor*." See Parton, *The Defense Never Rests: A Lawyer's Quest for the Gospel* (Saint Louis: Concordia Publishing House, 2003), 136.

2 Montgomery's commitment to the insights of the Lutheran Reformation are better known within evangelicalism than they are within his own Lutheran church, a fact discussed in more detail elsewhere in this article. Suffice it at this point to say that it is widely thought that his volume on the issue of Scripture's total reliability and authority (*Crisis in Lutheran Theology*) was perhaps the single most important and comprehensive work to lance the boil of doubt concerning scriptural authority that lay festering within the Lutheran Church, Missouri Synod. His volume dedicated solely to the work of Martin Luther has such fascinating chapters as "Luther, Libraries and Learning." See Montgomery, *In Defense of Martin Luther* (Milwaukee: Northwestern Publishing House, 1970).

3 See videotape no. 120 titled "Bach: The Fifth Evangelist," found in the series by Montgomery titled "Christianity on Trial." Available through the Canadian Institute for Law, Theology and Public Policy in Edmonton, Alberta, Canada. See www.ciltpp.com.

4   Montgomery, *The Transcendent Holmes* (Ashcroft, British Columbia: Cala-
    bash Press, 2000). Here one learns of Holmes's evolving religious position,
    which includes a refutation of the popular notion–which Montgomery shows
    to be utterly unsupportable—that Holmes ended up in Tibetan Buddhism.

5   L'Académie Internationale des Gourmets et des Traditions Gastronomiques,
    where he has the rank of Académicien, seat number 41 of 50, dedicated to the
    French translator of Apicius, Bertrand Guégan.

6   La Confrérie St-Etienne, where he has attained the highest rank of Master
    on the basis of three sets of tests. For a fuller discussion of the connection of
    gastronomy to metaphysics, see Montgomery, "Transcendental Gastronomy,"
    published in *Christianity Today*, November 22, 1974.

7   Montgomery's critical work on the general topic of human rights is *Human
    Rights and Human Dignity* (Grand Rapids: Zondervan, 1986). His legal
    role in the critical case vindicating the freedom to preach Christ Crucified
    in Greece but outside the dominion of the Orthodox Church is chronicled
    in *The Repression of Evangelism in Greece* (Lanham, MD: University Press of
    America, 2001). That work, in addition to being dedicated to his son Jean-
    Marie and daughter-in-law Laurence, is inscribed as follows: "For My Lay
    Clients and Their Missionary Organisations Endeavoring, as Did Saint Paul,
    to Preach the Gospel in Greece."

8   For a complete catalog of the writings, debates, videotapes, film, and lectures
    of Dr. Montgomery, see the pamphlet titled "Bibliography of Dr. John War-
    wick Montgomery's Writings," published by the Canadian Institute of Law,
    Theology and Public Policy. www.ciltpp.com.

9   See *Global Journal of Classical Theology*, published by Trinity Seminary and
    College of Newburgh, Indiana, and London, England. The journal has a
    strong emphasis on apologetics and classical and Reformation theology.

10 Montgomery, *The Quest for Noah's Ark* (Minneapolis: Bethany Publishing
    House, 1972). The book is worth the price for the hilarious pictures of Dr.
    Montgomery and his particularly greasy mountain climbing guides.

11 When confronted about the importance of jogging or exercise, his response
    typically is to cite former Chancellor Hutchins of the University of Chicago:
    "Whenever I feel the need to exercise, I lie down until the feeling passes."

12 See Parton, "Why Liberals Didn't Understand Passion Play 2000," published
    in the *Global Journal of Classical Theology*, vol. 4, no. 1 (February 2004).

13 For a fuller discussion of liberalism's devastating impact on American Chris-
    tianity, see the section titled "Protestant Liberalism: A Christianity Without
    a Cross," in *The Defense Never Rests*, 53 ff.

14 Michael Horton, "The New Gnosticism," *Modern Reformation* (July/August
    1995): 4–12.

15 Both Carnell's *Introduction to Christian Apologetics* (Grand Rapids: Eerdmans,
    1948) and Smith's *Therefore Stand* (Boston: W. A. Wilde & Co., 1945) were
    instrumental to the development of Montgomery's own unique apologetic
    contributions while an undergraduate at Cornell.

16 Montgomery, *Crisis in Lutheran Theology* (Minneapolis: Bethany Publishers,
    1973), volumes 1 & 2, 2nd ed. Happily, though, the best apologetic show on
    radio bar none is now produced by the Lutheran Church, Missouri Synod;

and it has had Montgomery on as a guest on a regular basis. One illustration of their apologetic and theological acumen will suffice: They devoted a series of one-hour programs to discussing each chapter of Montgomery's *Tractatus Logico-Theologicus*. See www.issuesetc.org.

17 His master's in sacred theology from Wittenberg University apparently does not count.

18 Montgomery held a faculty position at the charismatic-oriented Melodyland School of Theology (appropriately located across the street from Disneyland) as well as the evangelical Trinity Evangelical Divinity School in Illinois. He currently is distinguished professor of theology and law for Trinity College and Seminary in Indiana. In addition, he has taught for numerous campus evangelical groups at universities across the country, including Campus Crusade, InterVarsity, and The Navigators, lecturing as recently as February 2006 for Campus Crusade at UCLA on "Why Human Rights Are Impossible Without Religion."

19 "Synergism does not come about when unbelievers are expected to accept persuasive, objective evidence for the truth of the Bible or its gospel message, any more than it is synergistic for evangelists to call for decisions for Christ. Apologists (and evangelists) operate outside the house of salvation; they are not pastors or systematic theologians interpreting the conversion experience after it has come about. Synergism exists only when, following conversion, the justified man is led to believe that in any way whatever (rational, moral, volitional) he contributed to his own salvation." Montgomery, "The Holy Spirit and the Defense of the Faith," *Bibliotheca Sacra: A Journal of the Dallas Theological School* 154, no. 616 (October-December 1997): 387–95.

20 See Montgomery, *Crisis in Lutheran Theology*.

21 As a "confessional" Lutheran, Montgomery "holds to the validity of the Ecumenical Creeds of Christendom" and to the Reformation's commitment that "the Holy Scriptures, as originally given, are correct, reliable, and sufficient to provide the church and the world with perspicuous revelational truth" and that "the central answer to human need is a personal, living relationship with Jesus Christ." See Montgomery, *Christ Our Advocate: Studies in Polemical Theology, Jurisprudence and Canon Law* (Bonn, Germany: Culture and Science Publishers, 2002), 10. For those who were wondering, he is also an ordained clergyman in the Lutheran Church, Missouri Synod, and still eligible for a call to a church. Any takers?

22 One may find amusement in pondering what it was like at the charismatic Melodyland School of Theology in Anaheim when Dr. Montgomery taught there in the late 1970s along with now sainted and then highly polemical Walter Martin. Dr. Rod Rosenbladt, described by J. I. Packer as a "living embodiment of Luther," was also a member of the faculty at the time. We do know that because of Montgomery's influence that school became the first theological seminary in the world to adapt a doctrinal statement with built-in hermeneutic commitments. Those commitments are a template for any modern-day seminary or college that wants to get its epistemology right from the get-go and desires that real teeth be set in place to combat the twin cancers of neoorthodox and postmodern deconstructionist hermeneutical

approaches. For that doctrinal statement, see Montgomery, *Faith Founded on Fact: Essays in Evidential Apologetics* (Nashville: Thomas Nelson Publishers, 1978), 225 ff. Virtually the same doctrinal statement became the foundation for the later Simon Greenleaf School of Law, for which Montgomery served as dean in the 1980s.

23 As further evidence that God has a sense of humor and that he goes wherever doors for the gospel open, Dr. Montgomery was featured on a series of television programs for Trinity Broadcasting Network (the one and same TBN of Paul and Jan Crouch fame). The result was the show *Christianity on Trial*, which is, to put it charitably, a "study in contrasts" with the normal TBN offerings on such important topics as raising one's poodle from the dead.

24 The impact of Herman John Eckelmann on Montgomery at Cornell is incalculable. Montgomery later edited a set of essays in honor of Eckelmann, all authored by Cornell graduates. See *Evidence for Faith: Deciding the God Question*, ed. J. W. Montgomery (Dallas: Probe Books, 1991). The essays sprung out of The Cornell Symposium on Evidential Apologetics, which took place in Ithaca, New York, in 1986.

25 *Extra nos* simply means "outside of us," and it is Luther's characterization of the gospel. This is evidenced by Montgomery's debates, where he is often quick to make clear to the audience that the debate is not about the personalities of the debaters but about an objective and *extra nos* truth fully capable of being investigated by the serious inquirer.

26 Montgomery sent Lewis the monograph that became the basis for one of his earliest (and still most popular), works: *History and Christianity* (Minneapolis: Bethany Publishers, 1964). Lewis, in a letter to Montgomery in August 1963, said that Montgomery's work "did me good and I shall constantly find them useful. . . . I don't think it could be bettered." Ibid., 6–7.

27 Montgomery's central articles on inerrancy and the complete reliability of Scripture are found in *The Suicide of Christian Theology* (Minneapolis: Bethany Publishers, 1970), esp. the article "Inductive Inerrancy," at pp. 356 ff; *Crisis in Lutheran Theology*, vol. 1, esp. the articles "Inspiration and Inerrancy: A New Departure" and "Lutheran Hermeneutics and Hermeneutics Today," 15–77; *God's Inerrant Word: An International Symposium on the Trustworthiness of Scripture*, ed. J. W. Montgomery (Minneapolis: Bethany Publishers, 1974), esp. the articles "Biblical Inerrancy: What Is at Stake?" and "Lessons from Luther on the Inerrancy of Holy Writ," 15–42 and 63–94 respectively; *Ecumenicity, Evangelicals and Rome* (Grand Rapids: Zondervan, 1969), esp. the article "The Approach of New Shape Roman Catholicism to Scriptural Inerrancy: A Case Study for Evangelicals," 73–93; and *Faith Founded on Fact*, esp. the article "The Fuzzification of Biblical Inerrancy," 215 ff.

28 See Parton, "Whatever Happened to the Gospel?" in *Defense Never Rests*, 9 ff.

29 Reprinted now as *History, Law and Christianity* (Edmonton, Alberta: Canadian Institute of Law, Theology and Public Policy, 2002). The three-part test for establishing the reliability of the gospel records are the *bibliographical test* (deals with how good the manuscript tradition is from which we get the present text), the *internal evidence test* (answers whether the authors had the

means, motives, and opportunities to be accurate eyewitnesses of the events or whether they make factual errors), and *external evidence test* (determines if any other historical materials confirm or deny the biblical material).

30 The outline of the historical-legal argument is as follows: (1) The Gospels are reliable historical documents or primary source material. All scholars (even non-Christians) admit that Matthew, Mark, and Luke were written within 50 years after Christ's death and John within 65 years after Christ's death. The objector can check this out in any encyclopedia. (2) In the Gospels, Christ claims to be God in human flesh (Matt 11:27; 16:13–17; John 10:30; 12:45). (3) In all four Gospels, Christ's bodily resurrection is described in great detail. Christ's resurrection proves His claim to Deity. (4) If Christ is God, whatever He says is true. (5) Christ stated that the Old Testament was infallible (Matt 5:17–19) and that the coming New Testament (written by apostles or close associates of apostles) would be infallible (John 14:26–27; 16:12–15; Acts 1:21–26). This material is a summary of the analysis found in Montgomery's *The Shape of the Past: A Christian Response to Secular Philosophies of History* (Minneapolis: Bethany Publishers, 1975). See also his article "The Jury Returns: A Juridical Defense of Christianity," found in *Evidence for Faith: Deciding the God Question* (Dallas: Probe Ministries, 1991), 319 ff.

31 Probably the best-known presuppositionalists are Cornelius Van Til and Greg Bahnsen of Westminster Seminary. More shrill is Calvinist presuppositionalist Dr. R. J. Rushdoony (whom Montgomery invited to address the student body at Simon Greenleaf at one point), who labels as "blasphemy" any attempts to prove the existence of God, since "God is the necessary presupposition of all proof." R. J. Rushdoony, *The Institutes of Biblical Law* (Nutley, NJ: Presbyterian and Reformed Publishing House, 1973), 127. For an amusing look at how *any* "content" can legitimately be the basis of a presupposition if the test is "logical or internal consistency," see Montgomery's "Once upon an *A Priori*: Van Til in Light of Three Fables," published in *Faith Founded on Fact*, 107 ff. Bahnsen confronted Montgomery (unsuccessfully and with hilarious running commentary by Montgomery all captured on tape) during the question-and-answer session following the lecture Montgomery gave at the Evangelical Theological Society, the results of which are *must* listening. See the tape titled "Presuppositionalism-Evidentialism Revisited—a Careful Examination of the Epistemological/Methodological Issues Dividing These Two Schools of Thought," available from the Canadian Institute for Law, Theology, and Public Policy (www.ciltpp.com).

32 For further work in this area, see the second and third propositions of Montgomery's *Tractatus Logico-Theologicus*, 23–128.

33 *United States v. Wilson* 32 U.S. 150, 161(1833) ("Thus a prisoner cannot be forced to accept a pardon, whether conditional or not. The pardon recipient always has the choice of rejecting the offer of clemency and suffering the consequences of the judicially imposed sentence. . . . Either the prisoner accepts the pardon or commutation as conditioned or he rejects it. The choice is clear and there is no in-between.")

34 John 11:25 NASB.

35 Montgomery, *The Law Above the Law* (Minneapolis: Bethany Publishers, 1975). See esp. 84 ff. dealing with legal reasoning and Christian apologetics.

36 Montgomery's *The Law Above the Law* deals with these issues, as does his work *Law and Gospel: A Study in Jurisprudence* (Oak Park, IL: Christian Legal Society, 1978), esp. 34–37. For a current treatment, see Parton, *The Defense Never Rests*, esp. the section titled "A Lawyer's Case for Christianity: An Apologetic for the Tough-Minded," 73 ff.

37 This foundational and critical material is contained in a series of lectures delivered at Bethany College in Mankato, Minnesota, at a time when sainted Robert Preuss presided as president of the college. See Montgomery, "Lutheranism and the Defense of the Christian Faith," *Lutheran Synod Quarterly* 9, no. 1 (Fall 1970): 1–56. For a contemporary discussion, see Parton, "Why Distrust of Evidential Apologetics Is Not Lutheran," *The Defense Never Rests*, 63 ff.

38 I reference Chateau Lafite ("premier des premiers") because it heads the list of First Growths, or Premiers Crus, pursuant to the official classification of Medoc and Graves of 1855. See *The Oxford Companion to Wine*, ed. J. Robinson (Oxford, England: Oxford University Press, 1998), 245.

39 Strangely, Montgomery's marvelous work on the freedom of the Christian life, as well as his careful study of the life and work of Sherlock Holmes, has yet to lead him to a more sanctified view of cigar smoking and tobacco use in general. I leave him with that challenge in his remaining decades and pray he will overcome his apparently scarring exposure to Calvinistic cigar smoking in particular, which one can only assume resulted from an unfortunate visit or two to Grand Rapids. That solid *non-Calvinistic* apologists have benefited from tobacco is simply undeniable (witness Lewis, Tolkien, Dorothy Sayers, Charles Williams, and the Lutheran J. S. Bach—the list is impressive in depth of contribution to the defense of the faith), and I have in other places noted the theological parallels of cigar smoking and the retention of the highest Christology. See Parton, "Martin Chemnitz and a Smoked Theology," in *Logia: A Journal of Lutheran Theology*, Reformation 2005, vol. 14, no. 4. Perhaps I might suggest to the doctor that he begin with a mild cigar known as the "Credo Magnificat." It is produced by a *French-owned* company and uses tobacco from the Dominican Republic and a Latin theological title (the "perfect storm" for the professor—a cigar that is international, solidly theological— even Lutheran in central focus, and French). The name itself is a particularly wonderful example of confessing the incarnation. The evangelical uses of such a glorious gift are obvious.

Christianity Needs More Lutheran Apologetes

Alvin J. Schmidt

The Roman Catholic scholar Avery Cardinal Dulles in his comprehensive book *A History of Apologetics* (2005) makes only a few passing references to Lutherans as Christian apologetes. Regarding Martin Luther, he says Luther "constructed no formal system of apologetics," primarily because that would have "run counter to his idea of the relations between faith and reason."[1] While this assessment of Luther is partly true, one can, however, argue that Luther was an ardent apologete in his defense of *solus Christus, sola gratia, sola fide,* and *sola Scriptura.*

Dulles gives a bit more credit to Philip Melanchthon as a Lutheran apologete, and he also notes that John Gerhard, Abraham Calov, and David Hollaz were somewhat apologetically oriented; but, for the most part, he does not see Lutherans during the Reformation era or even in the "age of orthodoxy" as apologetes. Regarding apologetics today, Dulles does devote some attention to Wolfhart Pannenberg, the Lutheran evidential apologete, for his contributions. But he makes only passing reference to John Warwick Montgomery, whose publications in evidential apologetics have been rather prolific during the last several decades, especially in regard to underscoring the empirical, historical fact of Christ's physical resurrection.

Although I cite a few Lutherans below in the church's history of apologetics, it can hardly be denied that Christianity since the Reformation could have used a lot more Lutheran apologetes than it has had. This is especially true in America where Christian apologetes have mostly been non-Lutherans, Reformed, or Evangelicals.

Biblical and Church History Precedence for Apologetics

St. Paul told the Christians in Philippi he had been "appointed for the defense [*apologia*] of the gospel" (Phil 1:17),[2] and St. Peter urged the Christians, "Always be ready to give a defense [*apologia*] to everyone who asks you a reason for the hope that is in you" (1 Pet 3:15). Both Paul and Peter knew the gospel not only needed to be proclaimed but also defended. The early church fathers knew this, too. Thus, we find Quadratus in about AD 124 defending the Christian faith to Hadrian, the Roman emperor. A generation later the church was blessed by having Justin Martyr (c. 100–166), a philosopher layman, who vigorously defended Christianity against pagans and against a Jew named Lucius Trypho. He also penned an apology of Christianity to the Roman senate about five years before he died. Aristides (second century), another Christian layman, wrote a lengthy defense to the Roman emperor defending Christianity, telling him why Christians rejected the pagan gods of the Greeks and Romans. He also reminded the emperor that Christ had died, but on the third day he rose bodily from the dead and later ascended to heaven. Tatian (110–172), a student of Justin Martyr, greatly influenced by his mentor, wrote *Oratio ad Graecos* ("Words to the Greeks"). This book defended Christianity and denounced Greek philosophy and mythology, declaring the latter as incompatible with Christian teachings and values.

In about AD 177, Athenagoras addressed Emperor Marcus Aurelius and his son Commodus, rebutting pagan accusations against Christianity. In addition, he wrote *On the Resurrection of the Dead*, and he was the first to defend the doctrine of the Trinity. Also in the latter part of the second century, Theophilus, bishop of Antioch, wrote a work named *Apology*, written for Autolycus (second century) in defense of the Trinity. This was the first Christian document to use the Greek word *trias* (triad) for the three-persons Godhead. Around the end of the second or early third century, Minucius Felix, a Christian lawyer, in his book *Octavius*, defended Christianity so successfully against the pagan critic Caecilius that he became a Christian. And from about AD 195 to about 210, Tertullian (c. 160–c. 220), a North African lawyer, defended Christianity in a number of his writings. He fervently defended the nonconforming behavior of his fellow Christians vis-à-vis pagan Roman practices and customs. He titled one of his works *Apology*, written in about AD 197.

Not far removed from Tertullian's time, Origen (184–254) entered the apologetics arena. He defended Christianity in his book *Contra Celsum*, a publication that countered the pagan Celsus's work *Alethes Logos* ("True Doctrine"). Origen defended Christian theology ranging from Christ's virgin birth to His resurrection. He also contended that Christians, in spite of their rejecting many Roman values and practices, were nevertheless benefiting Rome by their higher morality and praying for the welfare of the state.

After the Roman coemperors Constantine and Licinius had signed the Edict of Milan in 313, giving Christianity legal status and relative peace, numerous other apologetes took to the task of defending the Christian message. Eusebius of Caesarea (c. 280–339), the father of church history, best known for his *Ecclesiastical History* and *The Life of Constantine*, not only was an historian but also an apologete. Noteworthy is his work *Demonstration of the Gospel* (now only partly extant), which argues for Christianity's veracity. And, as a contemporary of Eusebius, Athanasius of Alexander (c. 295–373) penned *The Treatise Against the Pagans* and another titled *The Incarnation of the Word of God*. Both volumes put forth a strong defense of Christianity.

In the early fifth century St. Augustine (354–430) emerged as one of the church's great apologetes. His *The City of God* not only defended Christianity's presence in the Roman culture, but it also argued that Christianity, which led many Romans to abandon pagan gods, was not the cause of Rome's decline. Two other prominent apologetes during Augustine's time were Cyril of Alexandria (d. 444) and Theodoret of Cyrrhus (c. 393–c. 457)

The Christian apologetes during the first five centuries were not the only defenders of Christianity. Others, not cited during these centuries because of space limitations, also defended the foundations of Christian theology. Similarly, a number of apologetes defended Christianity in various ways during the Middle Ages and centuries after.

The following is a partial list, beginning with the seventh century: John of Damascus (c. 674–c. 750), Theodore Abu Qurrah (c. 740–c. 820), Peter Damian (1007–1072), Anselm (1033–1109), Peter Abelard (1079–1142), Thomas Aquinas (1225–1274), Raymond

Lull (c. 1235–1316), Ricoldo de Monte Croce (1242–1320), John Duns Scotus (1266–1308), Nicholas of Lyra (1270–1349), Dionysius the Carthusian (1402–1471), Nicholas of Cusa (1401–1454), Girolamo Savonarola (1452–1498), Martin Luther (1483–1546), Philip Melanchthon (1497–1560), Martin Chemnitz (1522–1586), David Chytraeus (1531–1600), Leonhard Hutter (1563–1616), John Gerhard (1582–1637), Hugo Grotius (1583–1645), Abraham Calov (1612–1688), Johann Quenstedt (1617–1685), Robert Boyle (1627–1691), Richard Bentley (1622–1742), Blaise Pascal (1623–1662), John Locke (1632–1704), Gottfried Wilhelm Leibniz (1646–1716), David Hollaz (1647–1713), William Paley (1743–1805), G. K. Chesterton (1874–1936), Benjamin Warfield (1851–1921), Cornelius Van Til (1895–1987), C. S. Lewis (1898–1963), Francis Schaeffer (1912–1984), Carl F. H. Henry (1913–2003), Wolfhart Pannenberg (1928–), Paul L. Maier (1929–), John Warwick Montgomery (1931–), Norman Geisler (1932–), and Josh McDowell (1939–).

This chronological list of Christian apologetes from the early Middle Ages to the present day, which is not exhaustive, together with those apologetes in the church's early years, indicates that defending Christianity's biblical teachings has spanned the entire existence of the Christian church. At the same time it is important to note that many of the apologetes took different tracks. They corroborate Avery Dulles's observation, namely, that "each age has its own style of apologetics."[3] Some defended Christianity by accenting the historicity of Christ's miracles; some accented the higher morality of Christians vis-à-vis the pagan Romans; some argued there was no conflict between faith and reason; some tried to persuade unbelievers of God's existence; some contended against the teachings of Muhammad and Islam; and some, such as the presuppositional apologetes, argued it is necessary to presuppose the existence of God before one could engage in defending the truths of Christianity; still others—the evidential apologetes—took the track of arguing that Christianity's biblical evidence, such as Christ's miracles and the greatest miracle of all—His bodily resurrection—was (and is) the best way to counter and overcome the doubts of the skeptics regarding Christianity's veracity, as well as the existence of God. It is the evidential apologetes of which John Warwick Montgomery is an eloquent spokesman and to whom this volume is dedicated.

Promoting Evidential Apologetics

Christian apologetes tend to take one of three tracks. One is the classical approach, which largely employs rational arguments to convince skeptics that God exists, or that given biblical accounts are not contrary to reason. Another is the presuppositional method that assumes skeptics, like all people, have unrecognized presuppositions— one being that God exists. This presupposition, its proponents say, makes possible for a person to think and reason, and thus there is no need for the apologetes to convince the skeptic that God exists but rather for him to use this presupposition to persuade skeptics that the Bible is true since it is inspired by God.

The third approach is evidential apologetics. Proponents of this method hold it is important that apologetes present the biblical evidence—Christ's miracles and especially His bodily resurrection— as historically reliable facts from which the Holy Spirit can bring skeptics to faith in Christ's atoning work. Since Christ's miraculous works and His resurrection are recorded as facts in the New Testament documents, shown by scholars to be historically reliable, the skeptic can conclude that those miraculous phenomena were indeed the work of God, in fact, that Christ is God Himself. This conclusion is especially true of Christ's resurrection, for no man could raise himself from the dead, even if he had performed some lesser miracles.

Evidential Christian apologetics is not new. St. Paul used this method when he tried to persuade the doubters in the Corinthian church who said Christ had not risen bodily from the dead. He told them the risen Lord had been seen by Cephas, James, all of the apostles, by himself, and by some 500 people, many of whom were still living (1 Cor 15:4–6). In effect, Paul told the doubters they could ask those eyewitnesses whether Christ had in fact risen from the dead.

The evidential method was also used by Jesus when He responded to two disciples of the imprisoned John the Baptist, who one day came to Jesus asking whether He really was the promised Messiah.

Jesus told them to tell John that He had healed the blind, the lame, the deaf, and the lepers (Matt 11:4–5). In short, Jesus pointed to the empirical evidence of His miraculous works from which John could conclude He was indeed the Messiah. Jesus did not tell John's disciples simply to have "faith" that He was the Promised One, apart from pointing them to empirical evidence.

Evidential Apologetics Versus Fideism

Montgomery often castigates fideism, namely, believing something to be true without any evidence or saying that evidence is not important for a Christian's faith. Fideism, in reality, is blind faith. Evidential apologetics, as Montgomery has so ably demonstrated with strong biblical support, asserts that the Christian faith is founded on evidence, on historically reliable facts. One of his many books is titled *Faith Founded on Fact* (1978), another is *Evidence for Faith* (1991).

Christians who are given to fideism sometimes cite the words Christ spoke to Thomas, namely, "Thomas, because you have seen Me, you have believed. Blessed are those who have not seen and yet have believed" (John 20:29). Using the latter sentence in support of blind faith ignores the context of what Jesus had just done in the presence of Thomas and the other disciples. Jesus saw no problem in giving Thomas the evidence he demanded, that is, to see and feel His crucified wounds. Moreover, when Jesus gave Thomas the evidence of showing His wounds, it brought forth the greatest confession of faith recorded in the Bible, "my Lord and my God."

Thomas's confession was founded on the fact of his having seen the risen Christ. His saying "my Lord and my God" was indeed an expression of faith, but seeing the resurrected Christ was not. That was an observable, historical phenomenon, similar to all other occurrences in human history.

But what do the words, "Blessed are those who have not seen and yet have believed," really mean? The answer is simple. Jesus had in mind all those (including us today) who had not seen the risen Lord but who believed the reports of those (the disciples, for example) who did see Him after He rose from the dead. He did not mean that merely believing He rose from the dead was all that mattered. If that were true, He would not have shown Himself to His disciples and many others for a period of 40 days; nor would He have asked Thomas to see and touch His preresurrection wounds. Similarly, He would not have said, as He did another time, "Behold My hands and My feet, that it is I Myself. Handle Me and see, for a spirit does not have flesh and bones as you see I have" (Luke 24:39).

It should also be noted the epithet of "Doubting Thomas" that history pinned on him is unfortunate, for he did all Christendom a huge favor by asking for the empirical evidence of Christ's physical resurrection. He showed the world one need not be a fideist to be a Christian. From his experience, Christians can be confident that Christ's postresurrection appearances were not phantoms or apparitions that made it merely look as though He had risen from the dead. Moreover, Jesus, showing His wounds to Thomas, tells Christians that He did not expect Thomas, or others after him, to accept His resurrection on blind faith. At no time did Christ ever promote fideism.

Thomas likely said to himself, if I am going to take Christ's Great Commission seriously, I want to make sure when I teach and preach that Christ rose from the dead, He really did rise, rather than merely believing He rose from the dead without any visible, concrete evidence. Although I have never heard any evidential apologete or critic of fideism mention it, the label of "Doubting Thomas" is also unfortunate in that it has the connotation of fideism, implying Thomas should have believed in Christ's resurrection without any factual evidence.

Fideism often manifests itself in different forms. The following is an example that I as a professor experienced in the classroom at a Lutheran college in the late 1960s. I perceived that my students—all of them Lutherans and some products of Lutheran parochial schools—did not understand the relationship between faith and the resurrection of Christ. So I wrote the following statement on the blackboard: "The resurrection of Jesus Christ is true because my faith tells me so." Then I asked the students (about 25 of them) whether this statement was true or false. All but one said "true." The response of most students was clearly one of fideism; thus it required my telling them that it is not one's faith that makes Christ's resurrection true, but rather it is the historical fact of His resurrection that makes one's faith true and valid.

The students had an erroneous understanding of faith, and as I interact with Lutherans in Bible classes and in other contexts, I find many misunderstand what is meant by faith, quite similar to the students. Apparently, our Lutheran pastors have not done a good job in defining the concept of faith. Although confessional Lutheran pastors do not deny the historicity of Christ's physical resurrection, they have not adequately distinguished His resurrection as an historical event from faith in its benefits. Pastors need to teach and preach that the resurrection of Christ happened in history and that as an event it has nothing to do with faith, no more than the one-time existence of Christopher Columbus or Martin Luther is a matter of faith. They need to teach it is only the benefits of Christ's resurrection that are received by faith, but the phenomenon of His rising from the dead is totally independent of any Christian's faith. It can be expressed in the following manner: If I say, "I will some day rise from the dead," that is a matter of faith. But whether Christ rose from the dead is not a matter of faith. That is an event that happened in history.

Two Questions Fideists Never Ask

Was it the faith of the disciples that convinced them Christ had risen from the dead? The answer, of course, is an unequivocal NO. Simply put, they were convinced because they had seen Him and interacted with Him during the course of 40 days, from Easter to Ascension Day. It was because they had seen Him and even eaten with Him after His resurrection (Luke 24:42; Acts 10:41), not because of their faith. So convinced were they of this factual experience that they later as martyrs signed their testimony in blood, so to speak.

This simple question of what convinced the disciples all too often has not been asked by pastors in catechetical classes, Bible classes, or sermons. Thus, many Lutherans, like my students noted above, have a fideistic understanding of Christ's resurrection, quite at variance with what the New Testament teaches.

Does any passage in the New Testament ever say that a person's faith makes Christ's resurrection true? The answer again is NO. Here it is well to remember what the New Testament does say. Luke in the book of Acts states Christ "presented Himself alive after His suffering by many *infallible proofs*" (Acts 1:3, emphasis added). The Greek word for "infallible proofs" is *tekmeriois*, a word that, according to Aristotle, meant an argument or evidence was "irrefutable."[4] Note there is no mention of faith in Acts 1:3. Also, in Acts we read that Matthias, the successor to Judas, was chosen because he was "a witness with us of His resurrection" (Acts 1:22). In Acts 2:32 Peter says that of Christ's resurrection, "we are all witnesses." And on one occasion, when Peter and John taught and preached the resurrection of Christ, the authorities commanded them to stop their evangelizing. What was their response? "For we cannot but speak the things which we have *seen* and *heard*" (Acts 4:20, emphasis added). Still another example from Acts informs us the apostles "gave witness to the resurrection of the Lord Jesus" (Acts 4:33). Notice in these references the use of the word *witness*, a courtroom term pointing to evidence that the apostles saw, not what they believed.

When Paul told Festus and King Agrippa about Christ having risen from the dead, he said, "This thing [Christ's resurrection] was not done in a corner" (Acts 26:26). Again, the appeal was to the known knowledge and evidence (not faith) of Christ's resurrection. And as noted above, Paul told the skeptics in Corinth the risen Christ had been seen by the 12 apostles, by James, by himself, and by some 500 brethren, many of whom were still alive.

Divorcing faith from the Bible's factual evidence in history, a distinguishing mark in today's liberal theology, not only is biblically wrong, but it also ignores the insightful observation of Germany's Lutheran theologian, Wolfhart Pannenberg. According to him, "If . . . historical study declares itself unable to establish what 'really' happened on Easter, then all the more, faith is not able to do so, for faith cannot ascertain anything about events of the past that would perhaps be inaccessible to the historian."[5]

Alvin J. Schmidt

Fideism, Liberal Theology, and the Lack of Lutheran Apologetics

Although I have mentioned some Lutheran apologetes above, ranging from Melanchthon to Hollaz, for the most part, these men were not evidential apologetes, at least not in terms of defending the resurrection of Jesus Christ as an historical phenomenon. This particular apologetic tack was not necessary during their time, for the Age of Enlightenment (18th century), which produced radically liberal theologians who began doubting divine revelation and the historicity of the biblical miracles, including the resurrection of Christ, had not yet arrived.

With the *Weltanschauung* of the Age of Enlightenment (18th century) that cast doubts on the authenticity of biblical miracles and Jesus' divinity, Germany, the land that produced Martin Luther who restored the gospel, now produced radical theologians who undermined much of what Luther had preached and taught. Men like Gotthold Ephraim Lessing (1729–1781), Immanuel Kant (1724–1804), David Strauss (1808–1874), F. C. Baur (1792–1860), Albrecht Ritschl (1822–1889), and Martin Kähler (1835–1912), all of whom rejected much of the historical accuracy of the New Testament. Lessing argued that even if the physical resurrection of Christ were historically true, it could not impart eternal truth, such as life and salvation, because it would be merely an accident of history. To him this was an "ugly ditch" (history on one side and faith on the other) over which he could not cross. Ironically, Lessing was the son of a Lutheran pastor. Similarly, Kant, also a Lutheran layman, saw historical events as incapable of imparting any eternal truth, for he spoke of two realms, the phenomenal and noumenal. The phenomenal is the empirical world in which we experience and know its real happenings and events, while the *noumenal* is the nonempirical realm, where things cannot be known by the human senses. Strauss declared the Jesus of the Bible was not the same as the Jesus of history; the former was merely a portrayal of the early church's faith, which was different from Jesus as a person in history, not seen through the eyes of faith. Truth, including the truth of Christ's resurrection, could only be found in the person's faith, not in history. Baur dismissed the New Testament's miracles and argued that Jesus' ethical teachings were the core of Christianity's teachings. Ritschl saw faith as the essence of Christianity; miracles and the resurrection of Christ were not historical phenomena. Kähler introduced the concepts of *Geschichte* and *Historie* in 1892. According to this dichotomy, Christ's resurrection did not occur in *Historie* but in the realm of *Geschichte* (suprahistory), where "events" are only accessible by faith. In this realm, scholarly, scientific examination of historical events is not possible, as it is in *Historie*.

All these radically liberal theologians had two things in common. One, they no longer saw the New Testament as a reliable historical document, as the apostles saw it when they conscientiously recorded the miraculous acts of Jesus, including His bodily resurrection. Two, they posited a Jesus of faith and a Jesus of history. The former laid the foundation of modern fideism. Contrary as this twofold division is vis-à-vis the New Testament, it enabled liberal theologians to have their Christian cake and eat it, too. Fideism permitted them to deny the biblical miracles as factual phenomena while ostensibly allowing them to retain the aura of scholarly or scientific respectability, enabling them still to retain their Christian identity, which for some reason, ironically, they were not willing to forfeit. Many liberal theologians still feel that way.

In spite of the massive inroads liberal theologians have made as a result of the Enlightenment by placing the miraculous works of Jesus outside the parameters of history into the realm of faith, Lutheran theologians, both in Europe and America, basically failed to respond as apologetes to this heretical maneuver. With the exception of a few American Lutherans like Theodore Graebner, Alfred Rehwinkel, John Klotz, and Paul Zimmermann in the Lutheran Church-Missouri Synod (LCMS), who argued mostly against the theory of evolution, there were no Lutheran apologetes who argued against the theology that said Christ's resurrection occurred in *Geschichte* or in suprahistory. Only two Lutheran evidential apologetes of note have argued against this radical theology, and then only since the 1960s. These two Lutherans are Wolfhart Pannenberg and John Warwick Montgomery. One could also cite Paul L. Maier, whose publications, which reflect archaeological findings, strongly underscore the historical foundations of Christianity, although his works do not directly address the suprahistory, fideistic position of liberal theology.

Strange as it may seem, before the days of Pannenberg, Montgomery, and Maier, one finds Francis Pieper (1852–1931), a highly influential conservative theologian in the Lutheran Church, Missouri Synod, not favoring Christian apologetics. In his *Christian Dogmatics* (three volumes), first published in German between 1917 and 1924 but available in English since 1950, he wrote, "The arguments supplied by the science of apologetics—and there is a great wealth of them—cannot change the human heart, cannot produce an inner acceptance of the Gospel."[6] His negative view of apologetics is further expressed in his words, "The best apology of the Christian religion is its proclamation."[7]

While most LCMS pastors have been opposed to liberal theology as a whole, ironically, they have not really been bothered by the presence of fideism, really the product of liberal theology. In fact, it is not difficult to hear some LCMS pastors making fideistic statements. Here is a relatively recent example from a highly conservative former LCMS pastor: "Faith means believing something is true without the benefits of the five senses. If the senses (feeling, tasting, seeing, smelling, or hearing) are involved, the belief is no longer based on faith, but on fact."[8] This statement could easily have been uttered by Paul Tillich (1886–1965), the well-known liberal theologian of the 1950s and 1960s. In one of his books, Tillich wrote, "The truth of faith cannot be made dependent on the historical truth of the stories and legends in which faith has expressed itself. It is a disastrous distortion of the meaning of faith to identify it with the belief in the historical validity of the Biblical stories."[9]

One has to ask this former LCMS pastor, "What about Thomas? Did he not want to use at least two senses (sight and touch) to make sure Christ had risen from the dead?" Given this pastor's reasoning, Thomas's confession of "my Lord and my God" evidently was not a confession of faith.

Given Francis Pieper's long-standing influence, which continues to the present time in the seminaries of the LCMS, where students still are required to read his three volumes in dogmatics, it is not surprising that fideism has not been countered apologetically in the circles of the LCMS. It is also interesting to note that to this day neither of the synod's two seminaries (Fort Wayne and St. Louis) has a required course in apologetics in their curricula.[10]

When one ventures outside of the LCMS to other Lutheran bodies, the absence of apologetes, defending the historical resurrection of Jesus Christ, is even more pronounced. This, of course, is easy to understand, given that the Evangelical Lutheran Church in America (ELCA), formed in 1988, has totally capitulated to higher-critical, liberal theology. Evidential apologetes in the ECLA would be an amazing anomaly.

Faith and the Role of the Holy Spirit in Apologetics

Christian apologetics is sometimes criticized by some who say that it ignores the role of the Holy Spirit, as it seeks to persuade unbelievers on the basis of evidence to become Christians. This criticism reflects a wrong understanding of Christian apologetics, for when apologetes point non-Christians to the biblical facts that happened in history, the Holy Spirit is invariably operative. Also, when the biblical facts of Christ's life, death, and resurrection are defended, God's Word comes into play. And when God's Word is present, the Holy Spirit is also present seeking to create faith in the hearers by moving them to accept the benefits (eternal life and salvation) of Christ's death and resurrection

When a Christian believes in the merits and benefits of Christ's death and bodily resurrection, it is the result of the Holy Spirit having worked faith in the person through the Word of God, preached, read, or received in baptism. The Holy Spirit was also active when Thomas confessed, "My Lord and my God." For as St. Paul says, "No one can say that Jesus is Lord except by the Holy Spirit" (1 Cor 12:3). Thus, when Christ gave Thomas the empirical evidence he wanted, the Holy Spirit was at work prompting him to believe when Jesus said, "Do not disbelieve, but believe" (John 20:27 ESV).

The New Testament also presents other examples of how the Holy Spirit moved individuals to come to faith upon seeing the evidence of miracles. For instance, when the apostle Peter in Joppa raised Tabitha from her death, "many believed on the Lord" (Acts 9:42).

And when Elymas (a sorcerer) tried to prevent Sergius Paulus (a proconsul) from becoming a Christian, Paul invoked the Holy Spirit, which resulted in the sorcerer's becoming blind. Seeing this miraculous act, the proconsul was "astonished at the teaching of the Lord" to believe (Acts 13:7–12). Thus, evidential apologetics by pointing to the Bible's miraculous events does not supplant or preempt the role of the Holy Spirit, but rather it brings the full force of God's Word to bear on unbelievers so the Holy Spirit might bring them to faith. Evidential apologetics also strengthens the faith of those who already believe, for it shows them that their faith in the benefits of Christ's resurrection is founded on fact, not on blind faith.

Fideism and the Concept of Faith in Non-Christian Religions

Given that today's concept of faith is commonly understood as believing in something not founded on factual evidence—and thus fideism—one wonders whether this unbiblical understanding of faith would have become what it is today had Christian theologians been better apologetes by rejecting the concept of fideism when it first reared its ugly head.

When one examines non-Christian religions, whether Islam, Hinduism, Sikhism, Shintoism, or Mormonism, it is readily apparent the word *faith* is used in the sense of fideism. The so-called "faith" of non-Christian religions is not the response to miraculous phenomena such as the acts performed by Jesus Christ or His rising from the dead, which moved Thomas to say, "My Lord and my God," or Peter to affirm, "For we did not follow cunningly devised fables ... but we were eyewitnesses of His majesty" (2 Pet 1:16). Not a single non-Christian religion can point to that kind of historically factual foundation of their basic religious teachings.

Had Christian pastors from the outset taught their parishioners that their faith is founded on facts, the concept of faith might never have come to include the beliefs of non-Christian religions, as it now is used and understood when people and the media say, "the faith of Muslims," "the faith of Hindus," "the faith of Mormons," or "people of faith" when speaking about people of non-Christian religions.

Not only is the concept of "faith" used in regard to what members of non-Christian religions believe, no matter how bizarre those beliefs might be, but it also used as a synonym for any religion. Thus, we hear about "the Islam faith," "the Hindu faith," "the Buddhist faith," and so forth. It has even become part of today's American political language, for example, when President George W. Bush speaks of "faith-based initiative" programs, a concept intended to provide economic support to needy individuals, primarily by members of different religious bodies.

Using the English word *faith* as a synonym for any religious group slights Christianity, for it ignores that the New Testament, which first gave the word *faith* (*pistis* in Greek) a religious meaning, did not use this word in reference to non-Christian religious bodies. Giving *pistis* a religious meaning, applicable only to Christianity, was an exclusively Christian innovation.[11] This observation is confirmed by the scholar Dieter Lührmann, who says, "'Faith' as a category of Greek religious language did not exist."[12]

Second, it slights Christianity in that the ancient Greeks also did not use *pistis* as a synonym for religion or for a body of religious knowledge, as the New Testament does, for instance, when Luke writes that many Christians were "obedient to *the faith*" (Acts 6:7, emphasis added). In a similar manner Paul says, "In latter times some will depart from *the faith*" (1 Tim 4:1, emphasis added). The New Testament has additional examples of equating faith with given Christian knowledge.

Third, the present use of *faith* slights Christianity by misrepresenting it, for it implies Christianity is similar to all non-Christian religions, namely, that its teachings, like theirs, are also based only on "faith," without any historically factual foundations. Thus, all religions are placed on the same level of credibility or authority. This is demonstrably false! Christianity is the only religion whose faith is linked to historical facts. For instance, faith in the physical resurrection of Jesus Christ (as noted above) rests upon the historical fact that he did indeed rise from the dead, not in the faith of his disciples. In short, the Christian concept of faith is not a faith in faith itself. Christianity is not a religion that stands independent of historical facts or referents. Unfortunately, that is how many in our culture, including many religious and political leaders, speak of faith today. Believing in something for which there is no evidence is not faith but fideism. In biblical theology of orthodox Christianity that is the absence of faith.

Finally, using the term *faith* in regard to non-Christian religions also slights Christianity in that it lends support to their teachings. Thus, recognizing the powerful effect of language, Christians need to make concentrated efforts to stop using the term *faith* when they are referring to non-Christian religious groups. Instead, they should say, "the Islamic religion," not "the Muslim faith," "the Mormon religion," not "the Mormon faith," and so on. Similarly, Christians should stop using the term *interfaith* when referring to religious events in which non-Christian religious groups are represented. Nor should Christians say "people of faith" when talking about members of non-Christian religious groups.

Giving Unintentional Support to Fideism

As already noted, confessional Lutheran pastors, unlike liberal theologians, do not deny that Christ's resurrection occurred as an event in ordinary human history. But many pastors give unintentional support to fideism, or they are not troubled when a parishioner makes a fideistic statement, for example, "I *believe* Christ's resurrection happened," rather than say, "I *know* Christ's resurrection happened." These pastors would find it strange if a parishioner said, "I *believe* Abraham Lincoln was assassinated," rather than say, "I *know* Abraham Lincoln was assassinated." But when the word *believe* is used in reference to Christ's resurrection, it seems quite acceptable, thus revealing that fideism is not seen as a problem by many pastors. It seems so long as one uses the word *faith* all is well, and therein lies a great deal of the problem, commonly not recognized as a problem.

The Need to Recover the Classic Lutheran Definition of Faith

Given that fideism has made pervasive inroads in today's culture and in the thinking of many Christians, including many Lutherans, it is time to recover the classic Lutheran definition of faith. The Augsburg Confession (1530) states faith consists of believing "the history [and] also the effect of history, namely, this article of the forgiveness of sins—that is, that we have grace, righteousness, and forgiveness of sins through Christ" (Article XX). Briefly stated, a Christian's faith is not a subjective experience divorced from factual evidence in history, for instance, the bodily resurrection of Christ. Informed confessional Lutherans have always insisted that faith consists of *notitia* (knowledge), *assensus* (assent), and *fiducia* (trust) in the promise of God in Christ.

This threefold understanding of faith needs to be recovered and taught by Lutheran pastors in Sunday school classes for the youth, confirmation classes, adult Bible classes, and preached in sermons. Only then will the tendencies of many Lutherans to lapse into fideism come to an end when they, for example, are asked about the veracity of the Bible's miracles and Christ's resurrection. Instead of saying, "I believe them to be true," they will respond, "I *know* them to be true, for the New Testament documents, which report them, have been shown to be true and reliable."

Conclusion

Given that confessional Lutheran theology's concept of faith has since the Reformation era defined faith not only consisting of *assensus* (assent) and *fiducia* (trust) but also *notitia* (knowledge), Christianity would be well served if more confessional Lutheran apologetes entered the arena of modern apologetics. To say a Christian's faith is based on factual knowledge runs counter to the current liberal understanding of faith as believing in something that is beyond the scope of historical examination. Thus, Lutherans, if they are true to their heritage, must of necessity reject all forms of liberal theology and its heretical fideistic understanding of Christ's miracles and His physical resurrection. Lutherans with Job can boldly say, "I *know* that my Redeemer lives" (Job 19:25, emphasis added), rather than "I *believe* my Redeemer lives." That is why Christianity, which is being undermined by today's liberal theology, needs more confessional Lutheran apologetes in the mould

of John Warwick Montgomery. May our gracious God bring it to pass!
Soli Deo Gloria!

Endnotes

1   Avery Cardinal Dulles, *A History of Apologetics* (San Francisco: Ignatius, 2005), 146.
2   All biblical citations in this chapter are from the New King James Version unless otherwise noted.
3   Avery Cardinal Dulles, *Apologetics and the Biblical Christ* (Paramus, NJ: Newman, 1971), 4.
4   Aristotle, *The Art of Rhetoric*, trans. John Henry Freese (New York: G. P. Putnam's Sons, 1926), I, 2.16–18. See also Aristotle's *Prior Analytics*, trans. Hugh Tredennick (Cambridge, MA: Harvard University Press, 1938), II, 27:70.
5   Wolfhart Pannenberg, *Jesus—God and Man*, trans. Lewis I. Wilkens and Duane A. Priebe (Philadelphia: Westminster, 1969), 1109.
6   Francis Pieper, *Christian Dogmatics* (St. Louis: Concordia, 1950), 1:65.
7   Ibid., 109.
8   Jack Cascione, "Wise Men Act on Faith," *Christian News* (January 5, 1998), 24.
9   Paul Tillich, *Dynamics of Faith* (New York: Harper and Row, 1957), 87.
10 Concordia Theological Seminary, Fort Wayne, Indiana, does offer an elective course titled "Modern Apologetics." It was first introduced in 1976 at my request when I served on the faculty of the seminary at that time.
11 Alvin J. Schmidt, "Polytheism: The New Face of American Civil Religion," *The Anonymous God: The Church Confronts Civil Religion and American Society*, ed. David L. Adams and Ken Schurb (St. Louis: Concordia, 2004), 207–9.
12 Dieter Lührmann, "Faith," in *The Anchor Bible Dictionary*, ed. David Noel Freedman (New York: Doubleday, 1992), 2:751.

TOUGH-MINDED
CHRISTIANITY

Part V

LAW, ETHICS, SOCIETY

Environmental Education, Ethics, and Evidential Apologetics

Mary Hurn Korte, Ph.D., D.C.A.
Department of Natural Sciences
Concordia University, Wisconsin

One of the greatest challenges of teaching an environmental science course is the need to address the issue of environmental ethics. Since the early 1960s, when ecology was usually understood only by biologists, the general public has become increasingly attuned to and interested in ecology, numerous global and local environmental issues, and the development of environmental ethics. Some state agencies such as the Wisconsin Department of Public Instruction now require that environmental science be taught in all preservice teacher education programs licensed by the state. The roots of such requirements were laid almost four decades ago with passage of the first environmental education legislation in the United States.

On October 30, 1970, the first environmental education law was signed by President Richard Nixon. One of the consequences of this law was the creation of the Office of Environmental Education (OEE). After the Department of Education was established in 1979, the OEE was moved to the newly created department. Monies were awarded to fund enterprises such as the development of environmental education curricula and professional development in environmental education for teachers and educational professionals. Funding for provisions of the original act was cut in 1981; however, a decade later, the 101st Congress passed a new National Environmental Education Act (NEEA) which President George Bush signed into law on November 16, 1990, to achieve the following goals: (1) promote public understanding of environmental issues, including global environmental concerns, and (2) encourage students to pursue careers in environmental studies. The NEEA of 1990 established a new Office of Environmental Education under the auspices of the U.S. Environmental Protection Agency (EPA). One of the mandates of the 1990 NEEA was that the EPA make public environmental education a top priority of the Environmental Education Division. As a result, the EPA has awarded grants to fund environmental education projects, established internships for college students, made fellowships available to in-service teachers, recognized excellence in environmental education through awards for exemplary models of environmental education, recognized students in grades K–12 for outstanding environmental-awareness projects through the "President's Environmental Youth Awards" program, and established a National Environmental Education Advisory Council, a Federal Task Force on Environmental Education, and a National Environmental Education and Training Foundation. This level of federal commitment reflects a public concern about the environment and an acceptance of the assumption that humans *should* care for the environment. However, the proposed rationales for the assumption that humans should embrace an environmental ethic range from the purely utilitarian and pragmatic to the truly ethical and altruistic.

The author of a well-known collegiate environmental science textbook acknowledges that a fully developed stewardship ethic must be based upon "[e]thical principles [that] are justified by reference to some philosophical or theological basis. This is the foundation for an ethical system."[1] Although Wright recognizes the need for a philosophical or theological base for an environmental or stewardship ethic, he does not address the problem of identifying what such a base should be nor does he offer a method by which the truth claims of competing bases can be tested. However, he does ask, "To whom is the steward responsible?" He suggests that a person who has religious convictions might answer that the steward is ultimately responsible to a "higher being" or to God because God is the owner of the world and all that it encompasses. Wright suggests that, in contrast to theists, other people might answer that the steward is ultimately responsible instead to present and future generations of mankind. He presupposes that "well-established ethical principles" do exist as regards human interests and behavior; however, he does not identify any specific principles or contemplate how or by whom any such "well-established" principles were or could be established in fact. Wright recognizes that ethical violations often occur and concludes, "However, there is no firmly established ethic that deals with care for natural lands and creatures for their own sake. Most of our ethic concerning natural things really deals with how those things serve human purposes; that is, our current ethic is highly anthropocentric."[2]

From his conclusion, one understands that Wright does not believe that prevailing environmental ethics have been firmly and absolutely established for the purpose of serving God through Christian stewardship of the natural world. There is a fundamental difference between Wright's inability to identify what the basis of an environmental ethic should be and a Christian's confidence that an environmental ethic, as well as all ethics, can only be based on the authority of God's revelation in Holy Scripture. Unless the basis for an ethical system stands outside of that ethical system, the system has no abiding, all-encompassing, or absolute moral authority: it merely reflects the personal preferences of the creator(s) of that system. As such, the creators of the system are not themselves bound by their own system. "Unless the measuring rod is independent of the things measured, we can do no measuring."[3] Neither are common sense and practical considerations a rational basis for determining the content of an environmental ethic or religious truth because if they were reliable sources of self-evident truth, then all people and cultures would reach a consensus as to the appropriate content of an environmental ethic and have the same religious convictions.[4]

Even though most people are not aware of the biblical mandate to care for creation, the global consensus appears to be that some type of environmental stewardship ethic should be established not only at local levels but also at the international level. Even fewer people in today's secular, pluralistic, postmodern world understand that the Christian Bible is the only religious text that has been shown through an apologetic based on well-established legal methods of evidence verification and witness evaluation to be a transcendent revelation from God to man. Additionally, the Bible is the only religious text that has been documented by using standard historical methods of academia to be a reliable historical account of an actual event.[5] Accordingly, the Bible should be regarded as the only authoritative foundation for any environmental ethic. Christian teachers must understand that it is necessary to base any environmental stewardship ethic on a revealed, absolute ethic. Furthermore, they must be prepared to defend such an assertion logically and be equipped to teach their students to do the same. Gaining a thorough knowledge of evidential-legal apologetics is the best preparation for this task.

Christians can trust the historical reliability of Scripture and thereby find absolute answers in God's Word. Wright must be content to formulate only a relative, anthropocentric, descriptive environmental stewardship ethic whereas a Christian can depend on biblical authority to establish firmly an absolute, Christocentric, prescriptive environmental stewardship ethic. If an environmental ethic has been transcendently revealed to mankind, then it would be true for all men, in all cultures, and in all times. Furthermore, if such an authoritative ethic has been revealed, then it is incumbent upon us to discover the source and content of that revelation. Montgomery's evidential-legal apologetic is the tool with which Christians can defend the assertion that an authoritative ethic has indeed been revealed to mankind in the Holy Scriptures.

The French verb *environner* (to surround) serves to remind us that "the environment" encompasses every single factor that surrounds and affects biological organisms, including humans, be it a physical aspect of the natural world or a system of ethics and social structures—cultural, religious, philosophical, theological, technological, economic, political, aesthetic, or legal.[6] Therefore, an "environmental" ethic is actually all encompassing and should prescribe for humanity "that which ought to be," not only in the natural world but also in human societies and cultures. An environmental ethic should not merely describe "that which is" as determined by human logic, personal preference, or sociopolitical consensus but should establish "that which should be" according to God's will as revealed in Scripture. Some environmentalists have pointed out that "for an increasing number of environmental issues, the difficulty is not to identify remedies. Remedies are now well understood. The problem is to make them socially, economically, and politically acceptable."[7] For Christians, the authority of Scripture, once properly understood, makes remedies both acceptable and imperative.

Because many environmental problems must be remedied and avoided in the future, instruction in environmental science and environmental ethics should be included in the curriculum of Christian schools from prekindergarten through post-secondary institutions. All students should be taught not only *how* but also *why* Christians are called to practice wise environmental stewardship and make ethical decisions regarding their relationship to the world of nature. In their study of environmental ethics, students must also learn how to defend the reliability of Scripture because God's Word must be the well-established, firm foundation that dictates and encompasses all axioms of any environmental ethic. Otherwise, no universally applicable environmental or stewardship ethic can be established because, as in the latter days of Israel's judges when "everyone did as he saw fit" (Judg 21:25, NIV), each person will continue to do as he or she sees fit whether that is taking care of God's creation or misusing His bountiful gifts. All of creation *is* a gift from God; therefore, the earth's resources should be used wisely by Christians as they serve God and their neighbors. Integration of faith and knowledge is an important dimension of Christian education: environmental education is particularly well-suited for this task if teachers understand how to approach the subject from the perspective of a Christian philosophy of environmental stewardship rather than from the perspective of a secular, pragmatic, utilitarian philosophy of resource conservation or environmental preservation. Pauls summarized the contrast between a Christian philosophy of environmental stewardship and a secular philosophy of environmental preservation thusly:

> Secular approaches to the environment are diverse, but usually share a common theme: since secularism holds that God does not exist or cannot be known, this earth is all there is. It must be maintained and defended because there is no other source for life. Therefore, preservation—sometimes militant preservation—of the earth is necessary. Note how quickly a secular approach makes a god out of the planet. The Triune God is no longer the maker and preserver of all things; rather, the earth is. A feminized "Mother Earth," not God the Father, becomes the source

of life and help. Rather than caretakers, people are often portrayed as enemies of nature.[8]

A secular philosophy of environmental ethics will ultimately fail because not all people will care what happens to the earth and its natural resources either in the immediate present or in the distant future. There will also be disagreement among people as to the content of, and authority for, an environmental ethic. As Lewis noted:

> The moment you say that one set of moral ideas can be better than another, you are, in fact, measuring them both by a standard, saying that one of them conforms to that standard more nearly than the other. But the standard that measures two things is something different from either. You are, in fact, comparing them both with some Real Morality, admitting that there is such a thing as a real Right, independent of what people think, and that some people's ideas get nearer to that real Right than others.[9]

Consequently, the evidential-legal apologetic as developed by John Warwick Montgomery, which establishes the authority of Scripture and integrates faith with knowledge, is the only sure way to identify that standard of morality upon which to construct an environmental ethic. Unless faith is integrated with knowledge and the Bible is defensible as a true, transcendent revelation, the "glue of common vision and common commitment, common standards and values, disappears ... [and] we become very concerned that no one set of commitments, values, or standards is allowed to prevail in the public arena."[10] Relativism and postmodernism triumph in the culture, at least superficially and temporarily, as the "religious dimension of life, including also ethical postures based on religious views, become identified as 'sectarianism.'... Therefore, the quest for knowledge [is] dissociated from the quest for God, and the love of wisdom is no longer the ally of love of God, as it was for more than a thousand years."[11]

In 1967, Lynn White Jr. published an influential landmark paper titled "The Historical Roots of Our Ecological Crisis" in the AAAS journal, *Science*, in which he asked, "What did Christianity tell people about their relations with the environment?"[12] White claimed that the global ecological "crisis" can be traced to biblical roots because he believes that Scripture teaches that "God planned all of [creation] explicitly for man's benefit and rule: no item in the physical creation had any purpose save to serve man's purposes. . . . Especially in its Western form, Christianity is the most anthropocentric religion the world has seen."[13] He charged that the Judeo-Christian heritage established a dualism between man and nature and that by destroying pagan animism, which tended to unite man and nature, Christianity made it possible for Western man to degrade the land, be "indifferent to the feelings of natural objects," disregard the "spirits *in* natural objects," and ignore the rights of nonhuman species because it "insisted that it is God's will that man exploit nature for its proper ends."[14]

In contrast, many Christians believe that there is a scriptural imperative to be good stewards of creation. White himself acknowledges that his assessment of the guilt Christianity must bear for the world's ecological problems will be unacceptable to many Christians, and he concedes that in addition to Christians, many "post-Christians" share the exploitative treatment of the environment. He concludes his indictment of the supposed "Christian arrogance" vis-à-vis nature and nonhuman species by condemning

> distinctive attitudes toward nature which are deeply
> grounded in Christian dogma. The fact that most people
> do not think of these attitudes as Christian is irrelevant.
> No new set of basic values has been accepted in our society
> to displace those of Christianity. Hence we shall continue
> to have a worsening ecologic crisis until we reject the
> Christian axiom that nature has no reason for existence
> save to serve man.[15]

To counter charges that Christianity is responsible for the ecological problems of modern society, environmental science, ethics, theology, and apologetics must be taught holistically in Christian schools. Environmental degradation in non-Christian cultures may also be discussed to expose the fallacy of Lynn White's thesis.[16] However, merely establishing the fact that Western civilization or Christianity is not the only culture or religion to have despoiled the environment cannot be used to identify an authoritative foundation on which *to found* an environmental ethic. That task requires evidential-legal apologetics to establish the authority of Scripture. Professors and students should understand environmental issues, know how to respond to charges made by radical environmentalists against Christianity, and be able to defend an environmental ethic based on the authority of a revealed scriptural ethic and a proper understanding of man's relationship to the Creator and the creation. Because environmental science is a broad field that includes not only ecology but also such diverse fields as political science, economics, engineering, sociology, business, philosophy, and history, this is true not only for biologists but also for professors of all academic disciplines, including the other natural sciences such as chemistry, geology, and physics.

Students should learn that environmental scientists investigate problems using experimentation and epidemiology. Just as importantly, students should be taught to understand that valid differences of opinion exist even among experts in their respective disciplines regarding experimental design, data manipulation and interpretation, and application of scientific discoveries. They must learn that modern science is descriptive and cannot tell us anything about ethics. Science cannot answer the grand "Why?" questions of the universe. For example, questions concerning transcendent relationships lie outside the realm of science. Science does not reveal one final truth—only closer and closer approximations to truths about the physical world of matter and energy.

Knowledge of science and scientific apologetics does enable Christian professors to counter the claims of evolutionary naturalism. For example, examples of intelligent design, specified complexity, and irreducible complexity can easily be integrated into environmental science courses from the level of organisms through ecosystems. The second law of thermodynamics, for example, as illustrated by energy transfers in food chains, can be used to establish the impossibility of an infinitely old universe in the absence of a transcendent Creator and Sustainer.[17] Although a scientific apologetic can demonstrate only theism, not Christianity, it may be a useful method of breaking down the resistance to theism rampant in a culture that believes the only way to discover truth is through methodological naturalism and worships at the altar of scientism. Moreover, if fully naturalistic evolution were the explanation for man's existence as a top predator, then each person would be fully justified in his or her preference to use, or abuse as the case may be, the earth and other creatures as he or she sees fit. An organism that has evolved by random chance, with no purpose or design, has no moral obligation or responsibility to be a wise steward or to consider the needs of those weaker than itself. Self-preservation and personal advantage are completely justifiable in a world in which survival of the fittest, differential reproduction, and contributions to future gene pools of the species are the ultimate goals of existence.

Students should study examples of environmental problems and proposed remedies from countries with different cultural and religious heritages in order to build the necessary perspective for today's global, secular, and pluralistic world. Students should be educated so that they understand why remedies for environmental problems must be innovative and sophisticated, often taking into account different cultural norms, ethical systems, religious expectations, and technological capabilities. They should discover that science does not offer one "best" solution but presents competing solutions that must be weighed with regard to risks and benefits, competing societal needs, and different systems of ethics. Consequently, it is important for students to be taught how to evaluate the truth claims of competing ethical systems on which different systems of environmental ethics could be built.

In a book titled *Western Man and Environmental Ethics*, White responded to critics of his 1967 paper and wrote that mankind "shall not cope with our ecologic crisis until scores of millions of us learn to understand more clearly what our real values are."[18] Although White phrased the problem as something "far more than simply rethinking and revising our economic and political systems,"[19] what is actually needed is a search for truth in order to discover how humans should act toward nature and on what ethical grounds they can defensibly base an environmental ethic. The necessary search for truth reveals our need for a revealed ethic. As White observed, artifacts of a society, including its political, social, and economic patterns, are shaped primarily by what the mass of individuals in that society believe, at the sub-verbal level, about who they are, about their relation to other people and to the natural environment, and about their destiny. Every culture, whether it is overtly religious or not, is shaped primarily by its religion.[20]

In the above quote, White does not consider either man's relation to the Creator or man's responsibility to search for an authoritatively revealed source for all ethical decisions. However, neither does he completely denounce Christianity, nor should he be vilified on all counts for, although his theology may be of a liberal persuasion, he acknowledges that "in its doctrine of the Holy Spirit, Christianity fortunately makes provision for continuing revelation. Or, to phrase the matter in a more orthodox way, it recognizes the progressive unfolding of truths inherent in an original deposit of revelation."[21]

White's solution for finding a viable religious-ecological ethic is that modern Christianity must elucidate an acceptable and equivalent alternative to animism that will eliminate the man-nature dualism, which he believes is the religious root of modern ecological problems. He also questions whether an environmental ethic based on pragmatic concerns for the welfare of mankind is an ethic at all and correctly concludes that any ethic or value system based on self-interest can be easily discarded if those interests change. What White does not realize is that the only enduring solution to the problem is to base all ethics and value systems, including environmental ethics, on the authority of a transcendently revealed Scripture, which teaches that the earth and all living organisms, including man, were created to glorify their Creator. In Colossians 1:16 we are told that Christ is supreme: *all* things were created by Him and *for* Him.

Although when Odysseus returned from Troy he hanged a dozen slave women for suspected misconduct and unfaithfulness during his absence, he was nevertheless considered to be a hero by the Greeks of his time. They considered that he had the right to do so because the women were property, and the disposal of property was a matter of personal choice. The Greeks had a well-developed system of ethics, but their ethics did not extend human rights to slaves. Since then, ethics have been extended in many areas, the most important of which is human rights. However, only in the twentieth century were ethical considerations widely extended to include nonhuman species and the land itself.

In 1933, public expenditures of the New Deal indicated to Aldo Leopold, a professor at the University of Wisconsin, that the public might be persuaded to pay for the "ecological debt" incurred by private exploitation and abuse of the land. He campaigned to educate the public that it was far wiser to prevent than to remediate environmental deterioration. In 1949, Leopold published *A Sand County Almanac* in which he proposed a *"land ethic"* that affirms the rights of plants, animals, and land to continued existence in a natural state. Leopold's land ethic *presupposes* that man is ethically responsible not only to other human beings but also to the larger community of nature. *A Sand County Almanac* has sold over 1,000,000 copies and is the environmentalist "bible." Written more than 50 years ago, it outlines a contemporary environmental ethic. However, it assigns *a priori* intrinsic rights to land, nonhuman species, and ecosystems. What is not commonly questioned by environmentalists is the source of those rights. The land ethic implies these assumptions: (1) each generation has its own responsibility for environmental stewardship; (2) although we may claim ownership of land by legal title, we are only brief tenants on the land; (3) we will carve out an inheritance of land for future generations by default, if not by choice; (4) we may choose to abuse land and its resources or live so that physical and spiritual affluence are in harmony; and (5) humans are an integral part of the land and its ecosystems.[22]

Leopold's land ethic was built on the work of author and essayist Ralph Waldo Emerson; transcendentalist author Henry David Thoreau; and conservationist John Muir, organizer of the Sierra Club in the 1890s and a sharp critic of Christianity. As early as 1836, Emerson published an essay in *Nature* in which he criticized widespread economic development at the expense of nature, and in his *Journals*, published in 1840, he wrote about the "balance of Man and Nature," charging that "Nature" was being endangered by trade, economics, and technological advances of the time such as railroads.[23] Thoreau is best known as the author of *Walden*. He characterized urban society as deceitful in contrast to the truth of nature and wilderness. In *Journal* 3 of January 1861, Thoreau wrote, "Most men, it seems to me, do not care for Nature and would sell their share in all her beauty, as long as they may live, for a stated sum—many for a glass of rum. Thank God, men cannot as yet fly, and lay waste the sky as well as the earth!"[24] It is well-known among environmentalists that Emerson, Thoreau, and Muir argued in essentially religious terms that man has a responsibility to act ethically in his relationship with nature; Leopold's contribution was that he stated his arguments in scientific terms. A unique aspect of Leopold's land ethic was his assertion that land contributes to culture because land can be cultivated to yield an aesthetic harvest—the beauty of the biotic community is one of land's most valuable qualities.

Approximately 75 years before Leopold, Charles Darwin had forecast that ethics extending beyond the sphere of human relationships would develop as a result of an evolutionary-historical ethical sequence. Darwin's forecast rested on his theory of descent with modification, better known as evolution by means of natural selection. According to evolutionary naturalism, humans are only accidental products of blind, random forces that did not have them in mind. A corollary of evolutionary naturalism is that because humans and other organisms are all merely products of chance and necessity, all species, therefore, have equal rights. This reasoning is foundational for the animal rights and animal liberation movements.

Some extremists even see humans not as creatures made in the image of God but as a plague on nature. Darwin anticipated White when he railed against the "anthropocentric" character of Christianity and the "tyrannical mandate" of Genesis. Many people are unaware of the philosophical connections among atheism, Darwinism or other forms of evolutionary naturalism, radical environmentalism, and the animal liberation[25] movement; therefore, students in Christian schools must be made aware of these connections and be prepared to debate the merits of a Christian philosophy of environmental stewardship apologetically based on the authority of Scripture vis-à-vis secular philosophies of environmental ethics or animal liberation. Peter Singer, vegan philosopher and founder of the animal liberation movement, claims that Christian attitudes to animals are rooted in Judaism and ancient Greece and that callousness to animals is based on the creation account in Genesis. He believes that the "enlightened" treatment of nonhuman species only emerged as philosophers broke away from orthodox Christian teachings.[26] Singer integrates Darwinism with animal liberation as follows:

> Intellectually the Darwinian revolution was genuinely revolutionary. Human beings now knew that they were not the special creation of God, made in the divine image and set apart from the animals; on the contrary, human beings came to realize that they were animals themselves. . . .
>
> With the eventual acceptance of Darwin's theory we reach a modern mentality, one which has since then changed in detail rather than in fundamentals. It can no longer be maintained by anyone but a religious fanatic that man is the special darling of the whole universe, or that other animals were created to provide us with food, or that we have divine authority over them, and divine permission to kill them.[27]

To address claims of both Darwinists and animal liberation activists, it is especially imperative that environmental education in Christian schools integrates environmental science with theology and apologetics. Conversely, professors of theology would do their students a great service if they would teach them how to integrate theology with environmental science. Ideally, a science curriculum should integrate a study of anatomy and physiology, genetics, creation-evolution, and environmental science with apologetics and theology. Much of the invective voiced against Christianity by secular environmentalists, fully naturalistic evolutionists, and animal liberationists is based solely on Genesis 1:28 which states, "God blessed them [man and woman] and said to them, 'Be fruitful and increase in number; fill the earth and subdue it. Rule over the fish of the sea and the birds of the air and over every living creature that moves on the ground" (NIV). The significance of the preceding verses, Genesis 1:26–27, is ignored: "Then God said, 'Let us make man in our image, in our likeness, and let them rule over the fish of the sea and the birds of the air, over the livestock, over all the earth, and over all the creatures that move along the ground.' So God created man in his own image, in the image of God he created him; male and female he created them" (NIV). Because they fail to include Genesis 1:26–27 in their analysis, critics of Christianity fail to recognize the importance of man's creation *in the image of God.*

Created in the image of God, man is obligated to exercise dominion over the environment and nonhuman species as God's steward with the same loving concern with which God cares for man. Genesis 2:15 summarizes man's relationship with the earth: "The LORD God took the man and put him in the Garden of Eden to work it and take care of it" (NIV). The Hebrew word *abad,* translated by the NIV as "work," may also be translated as "till," which, as any successful farmer knows, implies careful tending and preparation of the soil in order to cultivate crops. In other words, Adam was to be a tiller and gardener, not a plunderer, of the land: he was to serve as a steward who managed the land and its resources according to God's will. Similarly, the Hebrew word *shamar,* translated as "take care of," implies that one is to watch over, protect, and look after another's welfare vigilantly. The dominion entrusted by God to Adam and his descendents does not authorize man to exploit, pollute, abuse, or squander the earth's biotic or abiotic resources. To the contrary, man has a divinely appointed duty to care for the environment and use earth's bountiful resources to serve God and his fellowman in a spirit of humility as evidenced by King David in Psalm 8:3–9 (NIV):

> When I consider your heavens, the work of your fingers, the moon and the stars, which you have set in place, what is man that you are mindful of him, the son of man that you care for him? You made him a little lower than the heavenly beings and crowned him with glory and honor. You made him ruler over the works of your hands; you put everything under his feet: all flocks and herds, and the beasts of the field, the birds of the air, and the fish of the sea, all that swim the paths of the seas. O LORD, our Lord, how majestic is your name in all the earth!

Human rule over nature and nonhuman species is solely a function of man's blessed position as God's designated steward on Earth, and we exercise that function correctly only when we strive to fulfill our potential as made in the image of God with diligence, obedience, and humility as befits beings redeemed by the blood of Christ. The very incarnational nature of Christianity establishes a Christocentric concern for the environment and man's responsibility to treat it with care and love just as Christ first loved us. Jesus modeled for us the attitude we should have as environmental stewards: "For even the Son of Man did not come to be served, but to serve, and to give his life as a ransom for many" (Mark 10:45 NIV). Likewise, man's authority over nature must be exercised in accordance with Jesus' teachings about authority as recorded in Luke 22:25–26: "Jesus said to them, 'The kings of the Gentiles lord it over them; and those who exercise authority over them call themselves Benefactors. But you are not to be like that. Instead, the greatest among you should be like the youngest, and the one who rules like the one who serves'" (NIV).

Every Christian should embrace environmental stewardship and humane treatment of nonhuman species as one of his or her many vocational callings. At the same time, each person must exercise dominion out of his or her responsibility of office, not out of greed, pride, or human ego. The distinction between exercising dominion over creation as a responsibility due to man's office as God's divinely appointed steward rather than as a personal right deserved due to individual merit is essential if one is to practice environmental stewardship in the fullest sense. It is certainly true that people do not always act as they should, and this includes actions that have environmental impacts. Nevertheless, this is a problem of human self-centeredness, not a problem of biblical theology. As Lewis has noted:

> Atheists naturally regard the co-existence of man and the
> animals a mere contingent result of interacting biological
> facts; and the taming of an animal by a man as a purely
> arbitrary interference of one species with another. The
> "real" or "natural" animal to them is the wild one, and the
> tame animal is an artificial or unnatural thing. But a Christian must not think so. Man was appointed by God to have

dominion over the beasts, and everything a man does to an animal is either a lawful exercise, or a sacrilegious abuse, of an authority by Divine right.[28]

Christian professors must be able to show students that ultimately environmental problems cannot be addressed, much less solved, without an absolute, revealed ethic. This requires a discussion of how one can know whether or not an absolute ethic has been transcendently revealed to man. Furthermore, if an absolute ethic has been revealed, then it is incumbent upon man to discover and adhere to the content of that revelation. The key question becomes, "*Has* a transcendent, absolute ethic that dictates the content of an environmental ethic been revealed to mankind?" If the answer is "no," then environmental ethics are moot. Even though a consensus may be reached by the majority, each person is ultimately free to follow his or her personal convictions, if any, regarding environmental ethics.

Without a transcendent mandate to care for creation, an individual is free to use natural resources wisely and sustainably or unwisely and wantonly according to his or her own conscience and desires. It becomes a matter solely of personal choice coupled with utilitarianism; however, a useful choice for one person can be detrimental to another as illustrated by Garrett Hardin's model of the "tragedy of the commons." In this model, a "commons" is any resource to which a population has free and unmanaged access. The opposite of a commons is privately owned or publicly managed property. The "tragedy of the commons" occurs when resources such as clean air, clean water in a river or lake, or wildlife are considered to be common property and free to be used by anyone as he or she sees fit. Commons are often overharvested and/or polluted. This happens because individuals maximize their use of a common resource until the cumulative effect of so many people either depletes the usable supply or degrades the quality of the resource. Examples of resources that have been exploited include species such as whales, ocean fish, fur seals, buffalo, sea otters, and passenger pigeons. Countless other examples of overharvested species could be named. Even Native Americans, so often extolled by environmentalists as living in harmony and peace with nature, were often eager to sell "Brother Beaver's" pelt to fur traders for a few trinkets so that fashionable European ladies could sport fur-trimmed hats. Moreover, their willingness to do so can hardly be attributed either to Christianity or God's command in Genesis that Adam and his descendents should exercise dominion over the earth. Hardin noted, "The fundamental error of the sharing ethic is that it leads to the tragedy of the commons."[29] Sharing is suicidal and counterproductive in Hardin's world in which "distribution systems, as with individual morality, good intentions are no substitute for good performance."[30]

Hardin's "lifeboat ethics" approach to environmental problems also illustrates the difficulty inherent in competing views of environmental ethics. In this analogy, lifeboats adrift at sea represent the various countries of Earth. Some lifeboats are richly stocked; some lifeboats are poorly provisioned. Some lifeboats are overcrowded; some lifeboats have plenty of room for all aboard. "Continuously, so to speak, the poor fall out of their lifeboats and swim for a while in the water outside, hoping to be admitted to a rich lifeboat, or in some other way to benefit from the 'goodies' on board. What should the passengers do? This is the central problem of 'the ethics of a lifeboat.'"[31] In Hardin's ethical system, to be generous is to be suicidal. He states, "We may be tempted to try to live by the Christian ideal of being 'our brother's keeper,' . . . so we take all the needy into our boat. . . . The boat is swamped, and everyone drowns. Complete justice, complete catastrophe."[32] With regard to population, Hardin believes that each "human being born constitutes a draft on all aspects of the environment—food, air, water, unspoiled scenery, occasional and optional solitude, beaches, contact with wild animals, fishing, hunting—the list is long and incompletely known. . . . *Every life saved this year in a poor country diminishes the quality of life for subsequent generations.*"[33] His "final solution" to the human population problem is that in "the foreseeable future survival demands that we govern our actions by the ethics of a lifeboat. Posterity will be ill-served if we do not."[34]

Because environmental problems are global and pollution does not respect international borders, a global consensus is necessary to solve environmental problems including those posed by the tragedy of the commons and the dilemma of lifeboat ethics. However, if the Old Testament documents are a reliable transcendent revelation, then the fall recorded in Genesis explains the "tragedy of the commons." If the New Testament documents are reliable, then Christ has unambiguously told us how to answer the question posed by the dilemma of lifeboat ethics: "Jesus said, 'Feed my lambs. . . . Take care of my sheep. . . . Do you love me? . . . Feed my sheep'" (John 21:15–17 NIV).

The question then may be logically asked, "Would it be Jesus' will that all lifeboats sink, killing all aboard?" The most probable answer is "no." The same Jesus who took on human flesh, suffered and died on the cross to redeem fallen humanity, rose from the dead, and promises all believers eternal life would not will such human suffering. Scripture reveals the solution to this seeming paradox: men and women must live as responsible stewards of God's creation according to a biblically based environmental ethic.

Because the answer to the question, "*Has* a transcendent, absolute ethic that dictates the content of an environmental ethic been revealed to mankind?" is yes, environmental education must be integrated with knowledge about the source and dictates of this transcendent, absolute ethic. Only a transcendent, absolute ethic provides a logically defensible justification for any other ethical system; however, an absolute ethic must be revealed to man by God, not revealed by human reasoning. Christians believe that the Triune God has revealed an absolute ethic to man through His Word and Jesus, the Word made flesh. It is important to teach students how to defend this assertion, and an evidential-legal apologetic is the best defense.

Many environmentalists agree with Lynn White's thesis that Christianity is the root cause of the world's current environmental problems. Christianity is vilified in many environmental science textbooks because, according to a preponderance of authors, "Christianity bears a huge burden of guilt"[35] in their view for all of our twenty-first-century environmental problems. This accusation can be countered with an evidential-legal apologetic that effectively demonstrates that Scripture is an authoritative revelation from God to man. Revelation 4:11 teaches that all things were created to glorify God, not man: "You are worthy, our Lord and God, to receive glory and honor and power, for you created all things, and by your will they were created and have their being" (NIV). Psalm 19:1 tells us, "The heavens declare the glory of God; the skies proclaim the work of his hands" (NIV). Genesis 2:15 warns that man is accountable to God for how he exercises his rule over nature: "The LORD God took the man and put him in the Garden of Eden to work it and take care of it" (NIV). Unfortunately, Genesis 3:17 records the sad truth that man failed to protect Eden from the encroachment of Satan, and therefore God cursed Earth because of man's sin: "Cursed is the ground because of you; through painful toil you will eat of it all the days of your life. It will produce thorns and thistles for you, and you will eat the plants of the field" (NIV). Biblical Christianity gives man a threefold responsibility as a steward of the earth: to guard the earth against degradation, to cultivate the earth so as to increase its fruitfulness, and to restore its beauty and fruitfulness where these have been damaged by sin (Gen 1:26; Pss 115:16; 8:3–6). Establishing the authority of Scripture with an evidential-legal apologetic can answer the false charges against Christianity made in the sixties by White and which are made even today by many environmentalists.

In *Tractatus Logico-Theologicus*, Montgomery successfully argued that apart from a revelation from God there is no foundation for any system of ethics.[36] Therefore, apologetics must be integrated with environmental science courses when discussing the land ethic. Without a revealed absolute ethic, there is neither justification for Leopold's land ethic nor for any other environmental or stewardship ethic. It is impossible to derive absolute principles or inalienable human rights, much less nonhuman rights, from human reasoning alone because humans are not transcendent or omniscient. According to Montgomery, the infinite cannot be located in the finite. Therefore, a transcendent source outside of the world is required to reveal an absolute ethic to man. Since there are many claims to transcendence, men and women must determine which claim is valid.

The land ethic extends human rights to nonhuman species and the land. If human rights rest on a revealed and absolute ethic, then any rights that are an extension of human rights, such as the rights ascribed by Leopold's land ethic, rest on the same revealed and absolute ethic. Understanding the justification for human rights is the foundation for understanding the justification for the land ethic. Group or cultural consensus is inadequate to determine or assign human rights. As Montgomery teaches, "But the fact alone that 'many heritages' agree on goals or policies doesn't necessarily make them right. The naturalistic fallacy again raises its ugly head. Fifty million Frenchmen can *still* be wrong!"[37] He has also pointed out that there is no assurance that a consensus is true goodness; the *vox populi* can be the *vox diaboli* just as easily as it can be the *vox dei*, and an absolute ethic must be revealed transcendently. Religions do not teach the same thing, nor do their adherents worship the same god(s). It may be that no religion is true; it is certain that they cannot all be true. Aztecs routinely practiced human sacrifice; Christians believe that Jesus was sacrificed once for the sin of all mankind.

Likewise, the utilitarian ethic of Jeremy Bentham, which evaluates the moral "rightness" or "wrongness" of an act based on a determination of whether the act causes suffering, is an insufficient basis on which to establish a system of environmental ethics. In some ways, Bentham's philosophy foreshadowed the animal liberation movement. He understood that race does not give one person the right to inflict pain or suffering on someone of a different race based on skin color, and he anticipated Singer's ethic vis-à-vis animal rights when he considered the proposition that in some future time, variables such as an organism's appendages, integumentary system, or its *os sacrum* would not be an acceptable basis on which to differentiate the rights of nonhuman species from rights of human beings. Bentham noted, "The question is not, Can they *reason?*; nor, Can they *talk?*; but, Can they *suffer?*"[38]

Neither consistency nor elegance is a reliable truth test. Madmen can devise internally consistent, even elegant, ethical systems. The human rights of Jews were consistently abrogated by the Nazis; an "elegant final solution" was devised to deal with the "Jewish problem," and this was perfectly consistent within the ethics of Nazism because it applied equally to all Jews. During the Nuremberg trials, Nazi lawyers argued that laws were only a product of society and that their laws could not be judged by *ex post facto* laws. They maintained that each society has the authority to make its own laws and establish its own ethics and that ethics established by a society are valid only for that society. Since all ethics and laws are relative to the society that created them, one society's ethics cannot be judged by another society's ethics.

The Nazi argument reflected the nineteenth-century theory of legal positivism, which was based on the proposition that laws are developed in a particular social context and are simply the reflection of a particular society. By appealing to an absolute ethic that transcends manmade law of any particular society or time, the Allied prosecution successfully argued that there is a Higher Law by which the Nazi war criminals could be judged. Hitler's *abschließende Lösung des jeweiligen Problems* was, and is, judged to be a crime against humanity. "If no set of moral ideas were truer or better than any other, there would be no sense in preferring civilised morality to savage morality, or Christian morality to Nazi morality. In fact, of course, we all do believe that some moralities are better than others."[39]

The truth of ultimate claims is determined by its correspondence to reality; therefore, one cannot decide on an ethical system in advance of the facts. Decision-making in religion parallels ordinary life, and we do not need 100-percent certainty or absolute proof to make a decision in fields such as law, medicine, or science. In fact, 100-percent certainty is unattainable except in analytic statements; therefore, man must make the most probable decision based on the best available evidence. Christianity is the only religion founded on an event, Christ's empty tomb, that occurred in real time and which can be researched by established historical and legal methods. The truth of historical claims can be determined without revelation, and Christ's death, the empty tomb, and Christ's resurrection can be investigated historically. If it is determined that claims surrounding these events are most probably true, then Christ must be interpreted based on His revelation of Himself as God.

As Montgomery has successfully shown in numerous books and papers, more evidence exists for the authenticity of the Gospels as primary source documents than for any other document that has come down to us from ancient history. Because the Gospels include eyewitness accounts of Christ's empty tomb and these accounts can be verified by an abundance of historical evidence and legal reasoning, it is only logical to accept Christ's own explanation for His empty tomb. Jesus foretold His resurrection and offered it as proof that He was who He claimed to be: God incarnate. Furthermore, as God incarnate, Jesus taught that all Scripture is the Word of God.

Because Christ taught that all Scripture is profitable for instruction, inerrant, and revealed by God, we may confidently conclude that *Scripture must be the basis of all ethics*, including human rights and the extension of human rights to animals, plants, and the land as proposed in Leopold's land ethic or in any other environmental ethic that has been or may be proposed by man. In the absence of biblical authority, there is no ethical basis on which to establish an environmental stewardship ethic; however, God has given man a firm command, "Do not pollute the land where you are. . . . Do not defile the land where you live and where I dwell" (Num 35:33–34 NIV), and a clear warning, "The time has come for judging the dead . . . and for destroying those who destroy the earth" (Rev 11:18 NIV).

Works Cited

Bentham, Jeremy. "An Introduction to the Principles of Morals and Legislation." As quoted in *The Rights of Nature* by Roderick Frazier Nash. Madison, WI: University of Wisconsin Press, 1989.

Cunningham, William P., Mary Ann Cunningham, and Barbara Woodworth Saigo. *Environmental Science: A Global Concern.* Dubuque, IA: McGraw-Hill, 2003.

Enger, Eldon D., and Bradley F. Smith. *Environmental Science: A Study of Relationships, Seventh Edition.* Dubuque, IA: McGraw-Hill, 2000.

Hardin, Garrett. "Living on a Lifeboat." *BioScience* 24 (1974): 561–68.

Leopold, Aldo. *A Sand County Almanac.* New York: Oxford University Press, 1949.

Lewis, C. S. *The Problem of Pain.* New York: HarperSanFrancisco, Harper Collins, 1940.

_____. *Mere Christianity.* New York: HarperSanFrancisco, Harper Collins, 1952.

_____. *Christian Reflections.* Grand Rapids, MI: William B. Eerdmans, 1995.

Montgomery, John Warwick. *Human Rights and Human Dignity.* Edmonton, Alberta, Canada: Canadian Institute for Law, Theology, and Public Policy, 1995.

_____. *Tractatus Logico-Theologicus.* Bonn: Verlag für Kultur und Wissenschaft, 2002.

Pauls, Timothy J. "Toward a Distinction Between Lutheran and Secular Approaches to Education." *Logia* XI, no. 2 (2002): 43–46.

Singer, Peter. *Animal Liberation: A New Ethics for Our Treatment of Animals.* New York: Avon, 1973.

White, Lynn, Jr. "The Historical Roots of Our Ecological Crisis." *Science* 155 (1967): 1203–7.

_____. "Continuing the Conversation," in *Western Man and Environmental Ethics: Attitudes Toward Nature and Technology,* ed. Ian G. Barbour. Boston, MA: Addison-Wesley, 1973: 55–64.

Wright, Richard T. *Environmental Science, Ninth Edition.* Upper Saddle River, NJ: Pearson Education Inc., 2005.

Endnotes

1 Richard T. Wright, *Environmental Science, Ninth Edition* (Upper Saddle River, NJ: Pearson Education, 2005), 11.

2 Ibid.

3 C. S. Lewis, *Christian Reflections* (Grand Rapids, MI: William B. Eerdmans, 1995), 73.

4 John Warwick Montgomery, *Tractatus Logico-Theologicus* (Bonn: Verlag für Kultur und Wissenschaft, 2002), 23.

5 Ibid., *passim.*

6 William P. Cunningham, Mary Ann Cunningham, and Barbara Woodworth Saigo, *Environmental Science: A Global Concern* (Dubuque, IA: McGraw-Hill, 2003), 17.

7 Ibid.

8 Timothy J. Pauls, "Toward a Distinction Between Lutheran and Secular Approaches to Education," *Logia* XI, no. 2 (2002): 43.

9 C. S. Lewis, *Mere Christianity* (New York: HarperSanFrancisco, Harper Collins, 1952), 13.

10 Carlson, Edgar M. "Perspectives of Lutheran Higher Education and Lutheran Cooperation." In *Seventy-five Years of LECNA: The Pursuit of Opportunity: Papers and Proceedings of the 75th Anniversary Meeting,* January 29–30, 1985, by the Lutheran Educational Conference of North America, 37–38.

11 Ibid., 38.

12 Lynn White Jr., "The Historical Roots of Our Ecological Crisis," *Science* 155 (1967): 1205.

13 Ibid.

14 Ibid.

15 Ibid., 1207.

16 Numerous examples may be cited such as deforestation and soil erosion in Buddhist China, soil salinization and over-irrigation in the lower Nile region in pre-Christian Egypt, deforestation and land degradation in pagan Greek and Roman lands, air and water pollution in atheist Communist Eastern

Europe, degradation of resources in Hindu India, crop failure due to soil degradation in Mayan cultures, or encroaching desertification in Islamic nations.

17 Montgomery, *Tractatus*, 119.

18 Lynn White Jr., "Continuing the Conversation," in *Western Man and Environmental Ethics: Attitude Toward Nature and Technology*, ed. Ian G. Barbour (Boston, MA: Addison-Wesley, 1973), 55.

19 Ibid., 56.

20 Ibid., 57.

21 Ibid., 60.

22 Aldo Leopold, *A Sand County Almanac* (New York: Oxford University Press, 1949), *passim*.

23 Eldon D. Enger and Bradley F. Smith, *Environmental Science, Seventh Edition* (Dubuque, IA: McGraw Hill, 2000), 21.

24 www.walden.org/Institute/thoreau/writings/Quotations/Conservation.htm.

25 Readers must not confuse animal liberation with animal welfare (the humane treatment of animals). Animal liberation is a radical movement that seeks to free all nonhuman species from the tyranny of human "exploitation," which according to animal liberationists is any use designed to benefit the human species such as food, clothing, pharmaceuticals, medical research, goods containing animal by-products, or entertainment. Furthermore, animal liberation demands complete equality between animals and humans: animals are not to be regarded as property but as persons both legally and morally.

26 Peter Singer, *Animal Liberation: A New Ethics for Our Treatment of Animals* (NY: Avon, 1975), 193.

27 Ibid., 215–16.

28 C. S. Lewis, *The Problem of Pain* (NY: HarperSanFrancisco, Harper Collins, 1940), 142.

29 Garrett Hardin, "Living on a Lifeboat," *BioScience* 24, no. 10 (1974): 562.

30 Ibid.

31 Ibid., 561.

32 Ibid., 562.

33 Ibid., 565.

34 Ibid., 567.

35 White, "Historical Roots," 1206.

36 Montgomery, *Tractatus, passim*.

37 John Warwick Montgomery, *Human Rights and Human Dignity* (Edmonton, Alberta, Canada: Canadian Institute for Law, Theology, and Public Policy, 1995), 101.

38 Jeremy Bentham, "An Introduction to the Principles of Morals and Legislation," as quoted in *The Rights of Nature*, by Roderick Frazier Nash (Madison, WI: University of Wisconsin Press, 1989), 23.

39 Lewis, *Mere Christianity*, 13.

Political Correctness: Blessing or Curse?

Robert S. Ove

Political correctness is a deceivingly complex topic especially when we examine Holy Writ for some suggestions. We could call someone a "damned fool," which some would complain was insensitive and not politically correct. It is, however, biblically accurate if that person is an atheist. "The *fool* has said in his heart 'there is no god'" (Pss 14:1; 53:1). If he does not believe in God, then as far as Scripture tells us he has damned himself. On the other hand, we are admonished *not* to judge others (see Matt 7:1; Luke 6:37). So it may come down to our motive. If we were making such a rash statement out of disgust or anger, then it would not be acceptable, but if our motive were concern and love for that person in order to bring his heart around to let God find him, then it might be called acceptable "tough love." We are commanded to "admonish" (see Col 3:16; 1 Thess 5:12). It is so easy to cross the line between admonishing and judging just as it is so easy to turn political correctness into a grudging command instead of a sensitive state of mind and heart and a loving concern for the welfare of others. One of the central issues I intend to demonstrate in this essay is that the motive is more important than the letter of the law. "He has made us competent as ministers of a new covenant-not of the letter but of the Spirit; for the letter kills, but the Spirit gives life" (2 Cor 3:6 NIV). That sums up my purpose.

When I agreed on the topic of political correctness, or "PC" as I will call it to save space, we had all heard the term for decades and could have been part of the many who began using it derisively; but when I received this suggested assignment, I had to do research other than biblical. I am not the scholar that my friend John Montgomery is and wondered why he gave someone so low on the academic scale the privilege of submitting an essay in honor of his seventy-fifth birthday. He is a prime example of someone who not only follows the letter of PC but most importantly also exemplifies its spirit in his life and writings.

I doubt all the questions related to PC will be answered in these few pages. It may, in fact, raise more than it answers. In addition to some selected quotes, I have made use of the Bible, and I have also made liberal use of personal experiences in this essay, which I felt were relevant to the subject of PC.

There is no unanimity as to whether PC is succeeding in its goal of increased sensitivity and awareness or how it started originally. It apparently grew haphazardly over the past four or five decades. The only thing that is obvious is that it did not migrate from the top down. It started as a grass roots movement perhaps motivated originally by feelings of guilt. It was initiated by sensitive, social-minded people with the best of motives and intentions. From there it made a devious detour both for good and not so good. There is some evidence that it has always been with us in one form or another throughout human history and with the same mixed reviews.

Every age—every decade—has its standards of social correctness accepted by the majority of people or at least the leaders of society, even though it may have been only grudging acceptance in some cases by either side.

Overview of This Essay

First, I would like to show the necessity for some societal change. Then I will offer some of the positive goals of the movement: philosophical, biblical, and personal. Next I will give an example of rigid PC regulations and the response from those it was intended to help. Following this key example, I will give some overall negative reactions to the movement with responses, including some perceived indications of its origins. Then I will show some abuses generated from affirmative action or caused by overzealous proponents of PC. The confusion caused by PC was also a great factor in those who view it negatively. Some examples will follow of oversensitivity, which really benefited only a few and created a natural human resistance to *any* PC regulations. Then I will deal more specifically with the implications of PC for the Christian church, including the extremes of present and past treatment of and by Christians in church and mission fields, before my conclusion. I found it difficult at times in this essay to be objective and not cynical, which may be apparent to the reader.

Societal Norms That Needed Changing in Recent Times

Before the era of PC we could publicly ridicule blacks, women, Jews, Indians, Roman Catholics, Italians, or whoever else we felt disposed to insult, without fear of retribution from the WASP majority. It was more likely that we would get support and even additional invective or demeaning comment from those who shared our prejudices. It was a divisive time in which we openly separated ourselves into exclusive, isolated camps (KKK, Gentiles-only golf clubs or men-only clubs, for example). Unjust treatment of these minorities seemed acceptable.

Most people were unconscious of offending others and were surprised to discover it, but of course others did not care at all. It seemed that a Sunday sermon was insufficient to accomplish any basic improvement in social sensitivity. It became more and more apparent that the minorities were becoming less likely to endure silently plus their numbers and influence were growing. As friendly contacts were made between various ethnic groups (often through the church), both sides became painfully aware of a need for change, and it appeared that it was not going to occur quickly enough (if at all) to maintain peace. This led to an appeal for legislation and other regulations to correct the situation before it got out of hand. There was obvious injustice in the status quo. Of course, one thing led to another, and finally PC came to include a far wider scope than just race, ethnicity, and religion and much more than just verbal usage. It invaded almost all areas of life in the English-speaking world

Good Intentions of PC

A Ph.D. student in Victoria, British Columbia, studying in this area (my son, Peter Ove) said: "PC got its start from what are commonly called the New Social Movements. Over the past 30 years or so, these movements have fought for equality and equity among the marginalized in North American society—this is something worth maintaining—it was intended to be an enormously liberating movement. It originated from people, not from politicians."

But was it liberating in practice? In many cases it no doubt was, especially at the beginning. It began to make people aware of the hurt and injustice they had caused and were still causing others.

Rev. Wayne Weisenbuhler, a former bishop of the Rocky Mountain Synod of the ELCA and now professor at the Wartburg Seminary in Dubuque, Iowa, felt that "a Christian should not need PC restrictions. We should *want* to treat others with sensitivity and make sure they are treated with equality in our society. But unfortunately not all society is Christian."

His point was that it should be *voluntary*—from the heart. Christians should not have to be subject to stifling regulations that do not always produce the intended result. As Christians, he suggested later, we should follow the summary of the second part of the Ten Commandments quoted by Jesus from Lev 19:18: "Love your neighbor as yourself" (Matt 19:19; 22:39; Mark 12:33; Luke 10:27,29,36 NIV). That should be the only rule needed for a Christian's relationship with others because *love* is the fulfilling of the law. This is spelled out in much of the New Testament, in Paul's letters (Rom 13:9–10; 15:2; Gal 5:14; Eph 4:25) and especially in the three epistles of John. The frequency of this subject found in the epistles and Gospels emphasizes its importance to any Christian and should be a foundation for all PC. The regulations should only be a reminder to those who had failed in their words, actions, or motivations.

My own parents were excellent examples of voluntary PC. In my sapling years back in the dark depression ages of the 1930s, a black family lived across the street from us. I played with their children, but when I asked my mother why they were a different color, she said, "They are just Danes turned inside out." (She used a common practice among Danes of self-deprecation.) I had a babysitter who was Italian. Some of my relatives were shocked at this, especially with all the available Danes in Racine, but my parents accepted everyone as they were and used no insulting terminology in their conversations at or away from home. They did not even condemn *non-Lutherans*, which was quite a concession back in pre-WWII days: My mother told me that when I went out to eat with a Roman Catholic friend on Friday, I should *not* order meat so as not to offend him. My parents were sensitive to other's feelings long before PC became an issue, and it was a natural thing based on their Christian faith. Some of it must have rubbed off on me. I dated a Jewish girl in high school and a black girl in college. I had a long romance with a Japanese girl there also. But when I married a girl of Austrian descent, my aunt Agnes had not advanced quite that far. She said to me at the wedding in hearing distance of the bride, "She is a nice girl, but we have so many nice *Danish* girls here in Racine!" In my first job teaching Apaches in New Mexico, I had no feeling of superiority or condescension. I felt this personal illustration was appropriate even in a formal essay because of its relevance.

PC started as a good idea, a means of correcting injustice and creating a more comfortable atmosphere, but it seems to have gotten out of hand. No specific guiding rules were established. Only obscure legislation and sporadic office memos such as the one quoted below sufficed, so it was open to abuse. Following is an example of how stultified it became in an attempt to be sensitive.

A Concrete Example of Petrified PC Followed by a Reaction

Below is a memo from the acting assistant secretary for civil rights to the Office for Civil Rights Senior Staff specifically pointed at the language reference to persons with a disability. The main problem is the transparent artificiality, which dampened much of the intended sensitivity. Excerpt from paper, "The Pitfalls of Political Correctness: Euphemisms Excoriated" by Dr. Kenneth Jernigan (copyright © 1994, 1999 by the National Federation of the Blind).

> As you know, the October 29, 1992, Rehabilitation
> Act Amendments of 1992 replaced the term "handicap"
> with the term "disability." This term should be used in all
> communications.

OCR recognizes the preference of individuals with disabilities to use phraseology that stresses the individuality of all children, youth, and adults, and then the incidence of a disability. In all our written and oral communications, care should be given to avoid expressions that many persons find offensive. Examples of phraseology to avoid and alternative suggestions are noted below.

- "Persons with a disability" or "individuals with disabilities" instead of "disabled person."
- "Persons who are deaf" or "young people with hearing impairments" instead of "deaf people."
- "People who are blind" or "persons with a visual impairment" instead of "blind people."
- "A student with dyslexia" instead of "a dyslexic student."

In addition, please avoid using phrases such as "the deaf," "the mentally retarded," or "the blind." The only exception to this policy involves instances where the outdated phraseology is contained in a quote or a title, or in legislation or regulations; it is then necessary to use the citation verbatim.

That is what the memorandum requires; and if it were an isolated instance, it might be shrugged off and forgotten. But it is not. Later I will add some additional attempts at codifying PC. Proponents of PC have not changed the essence but only the terminology: It has become more and more the standard practice, and anybody who objects to the use of PC terminology is subject to sanction. But what if the supposed victims of insensitivity didn't agree?

Response to the Above Regulation

Well, we of the National Federation of the Blind do object, and we are doing something about it. At our recent national convention in Dallas we passed a resolution on the subject, and we plan to distribute it throughout the country and press for action on it. Here it is:

Resolution 93–01

WHEREAS, the word blind accurately and clearly describes the condition of being unable to see, as well as the condition of having such limited eyesight that alternative techniques are required to do efficiently the ordinary tasks of daily living that are performed visually by those having good eyesight; and

WHEREAS, there is increasing pressure in certain circles to use a variety of euphemisms in referring to blindness or blind persons—euphemisms such as hard of seeing, visually challenged, sightless, visually impaired, people with blindness, people who are blind, and the like; and

WHEREAS, a differentiation must be made among these euphemisms: some (such as hard of seeing, visually challenged, and people with blindness) being totally unacceptable and deserving only ridicule because of their strained and ludicrous attempt to avoid such straightforward, respectable words as blindness, blind, the blind, blind person, or blind persons; others (such as visually impaired, and visually limited) being undesirable when used to avoid the word blind, and acceptable only to the extent that they are reasonably employed to distinguish between those having a certain amount of eyesight and those having none; still others (such as sightless) being awkward and serving no useful purpose; and still others (such as people who are blind or persons who are blind) being harmless and not objectionable when used in occasional and ordinary speech but being totally unacceptable and pernicious when used as a form of political correctness to imply that the word person must invariably precede the word blind to emphasize the fact that a blind person is first and foremost a person; and

WHEREAS, this euphemism concerning people or persons who are blind—when used in its recent trendy, politically correct form—does the exact opposite of what it purports to do since it is overly defensive, implies shame instead of true equality, and portrays the blind as touchy and belligerent; and

WHEREAS, just as an intelligent person is willing to be so designated and does not insist upon being called a person who is intelligent and a group of bankers are happy to be called bankers and have no concern that they be referred to as persons who are in the banking business, so it is with the blind—the only difference being that some people (blind and sighted alike) continue to cling to the outmoded notion that blindness (along with everything associated with it) connotes inferiority and lack of status; now, therefore,

BE IT RESOLVED by the National Federation of the Blind in convention assembled in the city of Dallas, Texas, this 9th day of July, 1993, that the following statement of policy be adopted:

We believe that it is respectable to be blind, and although we have no particular pride in the fact of our blindness, neither do we have any shame in it. To the extent that euphemisms are used to convey any other concept or image, we deplore such use. We can make our own way in the world on equal terms with others, and we intend to do it.

I used this lengthy example because it illustrates so well two totally different viewpoints of PC, and it is central to my thesis.

Another example of how confusing and misguided PC can become and how it may not be appreciated by those it was intended to address: In a lecture at the Smithsonian Institute that I heard about, when I visited there as a contributing member, an Indian speaker asked everyone in the mixed audience how many were born in this country. All the hands shot up. "So," he said, "then we are *all* Native Americans!" He said he preferred to be called by his tribal name or just plain Indian. Even those terms have morphed into "Indigenous People" "Amerindians," or in Canada: "First Nations" or "Aboriginal Peoples." Evidently the supersensitivity of some has not helped or even been appreciated by those it was intended to address. The

Smithsonian took note of this in naming their museum, "National Museum of the American Indian."

Here in Albuquerque a Hispanic professor from the University of New Mexico Psychology Department (who wished to remain anonymous) was interviewed to determine what term he preferred, and he said he liked to be called "Chicano," yet that is used as a derisive term by some. *Hispanic* has largely been replaced with *Latino* except in the local paper. Much confusion has been created in PC by trying to be sensitive to other's feelings without asking their opinion. It has made us uncomfortable communicating with minorities.

I called a member of my church in Ogden, Utah, "black" a few years ago. She corrected me immediately. She said, "I'm not black, I'm brown!" She obviously did not want to play the game.

My African-American friend, Rev. Clint Lewis, a former member of my congregation in Cheyenne, Wyoming, said that even he was confused. First he was Negro, then colored, then a person of color, then black, then African-American, then Afro-American. He said he didn't care. He thought he was just an American and resented being singled out and made to feel different. All do not share his feelings, but enough do to make one uncomfortable when initiating conversations with minorities.

A derisive comment came from Andy Rooney, the TV personality, with which Rev. Lewis might agree:

> I am sick of "Political Correctness." I know a lot of black people, and not a single one was born in Africa; so how can they be "African-Americans"? Besides, Africa is a continent. I don't go around saying I am a European-American because my great, great, great, great, great, great grandfather was from Europe. I am proud to be from America and nowhere else. And if you don't like my point of view, tough!

The fact that he is still on the air indicates that he has many who support those feelings, including his sponsor.

Following an era of laisez-faire, we were suddenly forced to watch every word (the words changed so frequently it was difficult to know the current usage) and action for fear of retribution, as the OCR example above hinted. This was sometimes in the form of a lost job or promotion or business opportunity, a scholarship or a lost election for those who were not minorities and acted without considering the consequences of inadvertently using some non-PC terms despite the discomfort and even resentment of many minorities who decried its use. It could leave a person in a limbo between the new supersensitive approach, the people who resented it and one's "old buddies" (or the electorate) who still carried on their ancient prejudices in secret. One had to decide which group to offend because even unintentional words can affect one's future.

At the ELCA headquarters in Chicago in 1997, I applied for a return to Nepal under the Board of World Mission. I was grilled on my relations with my former seminary students. I made a dire mistake. I called them my "boys," which was what my old dean in seminary called us. Immediately someone attacked me and said, "They are *not* boys. They are *men!*" In other words, he assumed that "boy" was a "put down" and not a term of endearment. I had stumbled into a PC error with just *one word*. It could have been a factor in the church not endorsing me for a return to Nepal.

Definitions and Negative Reactions to PC

We find an attempt to define PC more narrowly in Wikipedia, the Free Encyclopedia:

> The term (PC) is often used in a manner that implies, first,
> that there are a significant number of people who make
> conscious political choice of the words they employ in
> their speech and writing, with the intention of influencing
> broader usage and, through that, social outcomes; second,
> that this group is roughly equivalent to the political left,
> or some large sector of the left; third, that these conscious
> political choices of words constitute a single phenomenon,
> designated as "political correctness"; and fourth, that these
> usages are enforced in a manner that is often repressive to
> freedom of speech.

Then we have this definition from "Political Correctness Home Page" (no author listed)

"Political Correctness" is the name given to a set of political policies that have been promoted in Australia, New Zealand, Britain, the United States, and Canada since the 1960s. These policies are constantly changing, and what is "politically correct" in 1970 may no longer be "politically correct" in 2000. People become aware of "Political Correctness" when they or someone else fall victim to it.

But an even less supportive definition came from Bill Lind in a speech delivered at the American University. He states: "The term *political correctness* originated as a joke in the comic strips—PC had its true origins as a Marxist movement where equality was not only stressed, but all the force of law was behind it."

Now we will turn to some additional unfavorable comments on PC voiced from additional sources. These seemed to be in the vast majority in my research. It was difficult to find positive statements on PC: "As civilizations decline, they become increasingly concerned with form over substance, particularly with respect to language" (from "The Pitfalls of Political Correctness: Euphemisms Excoriated" by Dr. Kenneth Jernigan, copyright © 1994, 1999 by the National Federation of the Blind; extensively quoted above).

This concern of form over substance is especially true with respect to PC. The OCR memo above is a typical example.

PC is used in most available sources as a derogatory term to criticize what are seen as misguided attempts to impose limits on language and the range of acceptable public debate. While it frequently refers to a linguistic phenomenon as Jernigan states, it is often extended to cover political ideology and behavior as in "affirmative action" legislation (hiring and firing, membership in clubs, purchase of real-estate, etc.), and an overweening attempt not to change another person's or group's politics, religion, or customs.

From Wikipedia, the Free Encyclopedia, we read these additional comments:

The term (PC) is generally employed to mock either
the idea that carefully chosen language can encourage,
promote, or establish certain social outcomes and relationships, or the belief that the resulting changes benefit

society. This mocking usage often targets certain forms of identity politics, including gay rights, feminism, multiculturalism and the disability rights movement. For example, the use of "gender-neutral" job titles ("firefighter" instead of "fireman," "chairperson" instead of "chairman," etc.), the use of the expression "differently abled" rather than "disabled," or the systematic use of "Native American" rather than "Indian," are all sometimes referred to as "politically correct" to characterize proponents as overly sensitive or even coercive.

As was indicated above, PC was also mocked by some of the disabled and the Indians who rejected it.

I should give an example involving the "sensitive" treatment of Indians in the *Albuquerque Journal* (8/8/05). The front page had a huge article in which the use of Indian names for sporting teams was condemned and teams with those names (there were almost a hundred, including my alma mater) would not be allowed to compete in the same league as the more PC teams. Some tribes were happy to see this change, but some were openly hostile to this new regulation. There was no unanimity.

We are selective in our use of PC, however. Some tribes could complain freely about the use of Indian names for football teams, but they would laugh if I complained about the use of the name "Vikings," who were my ancestors, since Scandinavians could be conceived of as a minority, or the use of "Fighting Irish" for Notre Dame.

Who Is a Minority?

One interesting question I received from a member in my Cheyenne congregation who was Finnish. He said, "There are many blacks and Hispanics here in Cheyenne, and they are called a minority, but there are only a handful of us Finns. Am I not a minority?" Being considered a minority, then, is a state of mind based on a traditionally accepted social level usually established by *non* minorities rather than something endemic to one's nature. It is based on color of skin, language accents, dress, physical condition, or other peculiarities that set a person or group apart in a negative way.

Misunderstandings Between Blacks and Nonblacks

Black people were forced to create a new jargon to survive since slavery days when they couldn't let on to the white community what they were really thinking if they wanted to survive. It was a habit that still continues.

In the 1950s, Martin Luther King, addressing a mixed group in Los Angeles, used the names *Mary* and *Joseph* to indicate "pure, innocent whites." The blacks caught the implication and laughed, but the whites were confused and didn't know what it meant. They were puzzled and even offended by the laughter. I heard this from another black pastor friend, Massey Kinard, whom I roomed with in Washington, DC, more than 20 years ago. Because he was black, he understood the implication.

One black woman in the early days of "integration" was asked by Dr. Franklin Clark Fry, former president of ULCA, how she was treated in the women's group in her Lutheran congregation. She used terminology familiar in the black community and said that no one cut her with a knife, but they sometimes used a razor. Fry was shocked by this seeming reference to violence, but what she meant is that, in former days, when someone insulted a person, there was no doubt that person was abused; they felt the stab wound. But when a person is cut with a razor, sometimes they don't realize it until later when they feel the blood. In other words, the new insults were so subtle you might miss them until you caught on later. Hearts had not changed, just language.

One example of the razor that I didn't realize until I was in a Spanish class: the Lone Ranger's faithful sidekick was named Tonto, which in Spanish means "stupid"!

Affirmative Action

Another form that PC took was in the law of "affirmative action," which was intended to assure that a proportionate number of minorities were represented with respect to job availability. It has undoubtedly proven to be a great help in improving employment opportunities for minorities, but it has created backlash among those it was meant to benefit but who had already crossed the line and succeeded on their own ability against all odds.

One black musician in the Cleveland Symphony resented affirmative action because he wanted to be able to say he was chosen because he was the best musician and wasn't hired just because he was black.

Jackie Robinson would not have been as proud of his rise to sports fame if he were chosen just to fill out a quota.

Clint Lewis, whom I have referred to before, was asked to be our congregation's delegate to our synod meeting. He called me aside and asked seriously because of the quotas being encouraged by synod, "Do they really want *me*, or am I just the sample Nigger?" Those who had made it on their own resented being lumped together with those who according to the law only "made it" because of their ethnicity or color.

Abuse of PC for Personal Advantage

An example of how the quota system and antidiscrimination laws affected job relations: was someone fired or not hired for any reason other than their ability, training or experience or the quality of their work? Some minorities have taken unfair advantage of the fear of litigation and threaten to sue if not hired or are fired. Neither side is sure where they stand. In this case it creates even more hostility, or at least an uncomfortable atmosphere for the innocent minorities who did not abuse the new movement's "liberating" influence. We are called on as Christian "peacemakers" to bring reconciliation and not just take sides as PC "advocates" for the disadvantaged whether their case is valid or not. We can lose credibility if we fight for an obviously unjust cause.

At the beginning it was a subtle thing. The items that made the news back in those days were when the Roman Catholic Church and the Boy Scouts were charged with refusing to hire gays. The gays usually lost, at least in contests with religious groups, but it made others wary. It was casting shame on some who refused gays for any reason. It went beyond the "don't ask, don't tell" policy adopted by the military. In the earlier pre-PC days you could lose your job for being gay. The then president, Dwight D. Eisenhower, in executive order 10450, stated, "No pervert, gay or lesbian shall be hired by this government." But today one could lose one's job or be sued if one *refused* to hire someone who was gay or fired him for that reason.

Who Has the Right to Complain?

Programs like the Bill Cosby and Oprah Winfrey shows helped create a favorable view of minorities and so corrected abuses. How different those shows were from *Amos and Andy* or Jack Benny's chauffer, Rochester. If one is in a minority group, it can give one an advantage to speak out, as when Bill Cosby pointed out the failings of his own people. I've heard my friend Clint speak in a black congregation where he castigated black fathers for not being good examples to their children.

A minority person has the right to say things about those within his group that outsiders don't. When I served as a teacher of the Chiricahua Apaches, I had no right to tell them to get over the terrible hurts and injustices of the past and move on. Only they had the right to forgive and forget.

Extreme Accommodation of Minorities

Although Christians are in the overwhelming majority, and the US is filled with time-honored customs like a crèche at Christmas on the courthouse lawn or prayer in the public schools, they are eliminated if even one person objects, as for example Madeline Murray O'Hair, who challenged these practices in the courts. Others do, however, under the right of free speech, run down or ridicule the Christian faith whenever they are so inclined and are protected by the law of free speech, so care must be taken not to offend other people's faith or culture but accept peacefully insults directed at us Christians. Confusion reigned in two cases before the Supreme Court at the end of the past term in 2005. In *McCreary County vs. American Civil Liberties Union of KY*, the court ruled by a 5–4 vote that two courthouses in Kentucky could not display framed copies of the Ten Commandments on their walls, while a 5–4 majority decided in *Van*

Orden vs. Perry that it was constitutional for a six-foot monument inscribed with those same Ten Commandments to remain standing on the capital grounds in Austin, Texas.

The enforcement of PC is too subjective and even the courts can't determine definitively if PC has been violated.

One teacher living in the so-called Bible belt almost lost his job because a Bible was lying on his desk. It is odd that in another school in the Northwest, a Taoist teacher could have his literature displayed on his desk without complaint. If he were asked to remove it, he might well have sued for discrimination.

And what of those who demand to wear distinctive religious clothing in France? French refuse all signs of one's faith in the classroom. At least they are consistent!

PC Impact on the Christian Church— Feminist Accommodation

There are feminists who carry PC to extremes by calling God "He-She" or "Mother-Father." One clergywoman preaching at a United Church of Christ conference in California back in the 1970s said, "You could put a Band-Aid on Jesus' wounds compared to all the suffering of women down through the ages." A number of the constituency, both men and women, walked out.

"Man does not live by bread alone" became "people do not live on bread alone" in the 1996 NIV Inclusive Language Edition of the Bible, Matthew 4:4. That does not seem too extreme, but a former bishop of the ELCA, Dr. James R. Crumley, criticized the "inclusive language edition" in a synod meeting in the 1980s because it was not faithful to the original Greek. His complaint was that there was danger of having to rewrite the Bible for every shift in societal norms.

Women were frequently enrolling in seminary in the US and Canada just to prove that a woman was equal to the task. This was a complaint of the professors at the Lutheran seminary in Saskatoon, Saskatchewan. Many were turned down after four years of study because their only calling was to prove that a woman could do it. All the seminaries finally started questioning the motivation of women before enrolment. There never was a question that women could pass the academic requirements or that they might be spiritually motivated!

PC Sensitivity Related to Other Cultures

Paul Raffaele wrote an article for the *Smithsonian* titled "Out of Time" (April 2005). He said he was trying to keep out all outsiders (especially missionaries) to prevent them from destroying the culture of an isolated tribe in Brazil, though he *was* bringing in modern medicine. He wanted to keep them healthy but in spiritual darkness like museum pieces. The tribes often killed one another and there was fear from within, but he wanted to freeze their culture at a certain point in time as an anthropological curiosity and forget the centuries of development other civilized nations have gone through. He had a point in that the intrusion of the "outsiders" often took the form of farmers encroaching on tribal land and government military forcing their way in to find drug producers.

In the article "Born into Bondage," also in the September 2005 *Smithsonian*, Paul Raffaele seems to reverse himself. In the above example, he was trying to preserve the traditional customs of the tribe he was reporting on, as violent as they might be, but in this article he abhors the time-honored traditional practice of slavery in Africa, more specifically in Niger: "The families of slaves have been held for generations and their captivity immutable." And quoting from an African, Zangaou, whom he interviewed, "It's woven into our traditional culture," he mentions another African, Moustafa, who "in boyhood was steeped in his *tribal* tradition with slaves to wait on him hand and foot."

So Raffaele was very selective in the customs that must be preserved. Well-intentioned scientists can do as much damage as missionaries, regardless of their denomination, ever could.

Extreme Reversals

The opposite extreme of Raffaele's first example took place with our indigenous people back in the late 1800s. Many were taken from their homes and sent by the US government to a school in Carlisle,

Pennsylvania (and other specified schools in this country), in an attempt to make them "darker skinned white people." The purpose was completely to destroy their culture and even their language. I had several of those "guinea pigs" more than 50 years ago in my Whitetail community on the Mescalero reservation in New Mexico. Today, however, the government is trying to give the Indians back their language, customs, and religion and almost force it upon them to make up for past sins! The government was just beginning to make these changes when I was serving in the Whitetail community more than 50 years ago. What extremes society goes to! We need to find middle ground acceptable to all. Humans change for better or worse every year. The best method of positive change is putting the Spirit of Jesus Christ in people's hearts rather than a rulebook or memo in their hands. The underlying motive must be love, which stands as a balance between restricting every move and encouraging complete freedom. I should add that the motive for the Carlisle school, no matter how misguided, was still love for the people! This would seem to indicate that circumstances and enlightened understanding must accompany the motive of love. It is encouraging to see the ancient Apache customs being practiced again with the blessing of the churches in Mescalero, just as we use a Christmas tree, which comes from an ancient pagan practice attributed to our European ancestors.

In Conclusion

One can hope that a Hegelian synthesis will resolve this present attempt at overreacting to an obvious injustice in our society—the injustice of hurting those who differ from us in any way, and most often were in a minority, though sometimes, as I have pointed out, the majority can be hurt with impunity (a revenge motivation, I presume). Some have always felt free to hurt or insult certain others before the emphasis on PC, and while PC did get some to start thinking and becoming more sensitive, history has proven that old habits are hard to break and humans don't like to be forced to do anything and resent any attempt to change bad attitudes even if God Himself orders them to do so! Hearts need to be changed and not just rules enforced to bring external conformity. Perhaps the move for PC was necessary to start reversing the abuses of the past, but in some cases it has gone to unfortunate extremes that could destroy the very changes meant to liberate people. The main reactions to PC I heard were not against the original intent but rather against the ridiculous artificial extreme to which it was sometimes carried and the selfish use to which it was put by the unscrupulous.

An article by Michael Barone, "Cultures Aren't Equal" in the August 2005 issue of *US News,* indicates what might be a turning point. Multiculturalism has been the shibboleth of not only mainline churches but also governments. We could hope for a gradual return to sanity, but life is not like that. It often takes some major, often violent, event to precipitate change. Barone writes about the recent British experience of the bombers who had lived as citizens in Briton for many years and yet turned against it in such a violent way. He says, "A civilization that feels guilty for everything it is and does will lack the energy and conviction to defend itself. Tolerating intolerance, good hearted people are beginning to see, does not necessarily produce tolerance in return." It may be time to stop groveling and making a god out of multiculturalism and, as Pamela Bone says in that article, "Perhaps it is time to say, you are welcome (in our country), but this is the way it is here."

Certainly no *Christian* should ever be ashamed of our gospel. It's not the only way because "I" say so, but because *God* says so, and there is only *one* God! We want to let others know that it is not *we* who are intolerant; it is God Himself! We should be able to say to all who move to our (Briton, Australian, New Zealand, Canadian, USA) shores, "We will respect you as individuals, but we are mostly Christian here, and we hope you will learn our rules and accept them."

God was never very politically correct in the way we have come to understand the term. We know the motivation of the whole PC movement originated mostly in the minds of Christians and was intended for the good of all, and we hope that in future generations a better, more open, accepting society will be created. We should not give up just because of the quirky trail it seems to be taking. We should not be pessimists about what God can do in this world, but rather in retrospect of man's efforts we should not put much faith in ourselves. As I quoted, "The letter kills, but the Spirit gives life." Our optimism should be in God alone as we follow His command to love our neighbor as ourselves. His Word and His Spirit should guide Christians unashamedly. We should grow in sensitivity politically, socially, and spiritually. But a Christian's motives should accord with God's intention. Even if we err, there must be forgiveness. God save us from ourselves!

We should continue our attempts to improve society, realizing that we can face failure if we leave out the God factor. No matter how well intentioned we are, history has shown that man alone has fallen far short of not only God's goal but even our own goal. We fail because (1) human beings tend to resist being forced to do anything; (2) humans traditionally have gone to ridiculous extremes to live up to the letter of the law or on the other hand want to resist all change; and (3) too much effort has been spent to change the rules and insufficient efforts have been made to change human hearts. So let our governmental leaders continue creating well-thought-out legislation based on sound moral principles, and let clergy and other religious leaders work to change human hearts. Let our motive be our Lord's command to love our neighbor as ourselves, for love is the fulfilling of the law.

Planting a Rawlsian Garden

PROPER FUNCTION, THE PROBLEM OF EVIL, AND "THINKING BEHIND THE VEIL"

Edward N. Martin

Weeds are flowers too, once you get to know them.
—Eeyore in Winnie the Pooh *by A. A. Milne*

When it comes to the problem of evil, there are *defenses*, and there are *theodicies*. A defense is an attempt to show that the propositions "God exists" and "evil exists" are not logically incompatible. Defenses are relatively easy to fashion. A theodicy, or a justification of the ways of God to men, as Milton put it, is the attempt to tell a story that even the atheist will grant is probably true *given Theism*, or at least, not irrational to believe, *given Theism*. Theodicies are a relatively difficult undertaking. For it is simple to see that God might have reasons concerning the patterns of goods and evils he permits in our lives that we cannot even fathom. Perhaps more modest, and still saying something more than a mere defense, is to give *theodical suggestions*, or parts of a potential theodicy that may work together with other suggestions, ultimately, to give a viable theodicy. The best theodical suggestions are, I think, housed within what John Hare calls a *disjunctive theodicy*.[1] A disjunctive theodicy is one that says that the reason for evil E is either good G1 or G2 or G3 or . . . Gn . . . or, some good that we cannot even fathom but of which God is perfectly aware. Some of the suggestions I give in this essay fall squarely within a soul-making theodical framework. Too often we pair this theodicy together with various liberal philosophical theologians (such as John Hick) and miss the importance of the rich resources within the theodicy itself. I propose that we not overlook the continuing importance of this theodical method, for this method seems in line, in its essential parts, with the New Testament conception of the development of Christian character and the theological virtue of *hope*. Consider Paul's sentiment in the book of Romans:

[W]e also rejoice in our sufferings, because we know that
suffering produces perseverance; perseverance, character;
and character, hope. (Rom 5:3–4 NIV)

Obviously, for suffering ultimately to produce character and hope
for the believer there has to be a human mechanism (or set of mechanisms) whereby the intrinsic evil of suffering can "produce" this se-
quential process, from suffering to perseverance to character and
finally to hope.

What ought we to say, however, for the nonbeliever? Is there a
structure in place in the human psyche or the human epistemic belief processes such that suffering can, in some way, produce *hope* for
this person as well? The *hope* in view here need not be true, conscious, Christ-focused eschatological hope, or a true instantiation of
the theological virtue of hope (which takes knowledge of Christ as
personal Savior as a necessary condition for obtaining). Although
Paul was addressing believing Christians in Romans 5, perhaps there
is a sort of "first level" of hope, a proto-hope, possibly shared in by
any conscious human being, whereby even the nonbeliever can get a
foretaste or shadow of the true hope that we find in Christ. I believe
indeed that there is.

In this essay I shall look at various theodical suggestions that arise
from an investigation of the intersections of the study of the soul-
making theodicy, virtue, belief, warrant, and allied topics. I want to
show that because of the necessary conditions for seeking and obtaining the various virtues, and because of the nature of our belief-
forming, belief-revision, and belief-defeater mechanisms, there are a
wealth of theodical resources, within theism generally and Christian
theism particularly, significant enough to defeat the potential defeaters that the problem of evil might raise for theism.

I. Preparing the Soil: Kant, Time, and Hope

A discussion of the virtue of hope leads at least to a mention of the
temporal dimensions of human existence. Hope has a future orientation; we do not hope for what is past, but we hope in the present for
that which will be (or may be) realized in the future. Faith also has a
future orientation. And though admittedly the temporal dimensions

of faith and hope are not altogether coextensional, still from our current temporal vantage point, being decidedly preeschatological, the present, future, and even past, horizons of the virtues of hope and of faith do intersect significantly. For the Christian, our present and future faith is based on historical realities in the past: God having actually become incarnate and having borne our iniquities in his body on the cross and having resurrected from the dead "for our justification" (Rom 4:25). Keep in mind, though, what passage follows this Pauline thought: Romans 5:1–5, which culminates in our key verse, above, that suffering produces hope. So, in a word, Christ gave (past) believers their *object of* both faith and hope by his decisive actions.

The unbelieving person does not have this ontological rooting in the past to enliven, make sure, give "full assurance" of one's faith (cp. 1 Thess 1:5). Yet, in any philosophy that exhibits a concept of hope and faith in the possibility of future realization of renewal of life (resurrection) and the fusing of one's desert for happiness with virtue through a universal judgment and restoration of creation, there would be a tacit acknowledgement that God is somehow centrally in the picture. And interestingly, this is the picture we get from Immanuel Kant. Kant himself stated in the first Critique:

> All the interests of my reason, speculative as well as
> practical, combine in the three following questions:
>
> 1. What can I know?
> 2. What ought I to do?
> 3. What may I hope?[2]

Kant summarizes his famous and expansive speculative, moral, and practical project in these three questions. In question three Kant speaks of some sort of eschatological hope. Question 2, the question of moral action, leads to question three. The question "at once theoretical and practical," is that of hope, "for all hoping is directed to happiness."[3] But in order for Kant's moral project to work, he needs his famous "postulates of pure practical reason" to be the case, namely, God and immortality. That is, there must be a Pure and Wise Being powerful enough to create and sustain both the world and moral and rational beings within that world. God must also resurrect people to an immortal life and judge them equitably, enabling those who are worthy of happiness to enjoy virtue and happiness in a consciously unending way. (One wonders of the theistic worldviews that are available, which one or ones would be consistent and theoretically rich enough in their concept of God and the afterlife to supply the right view for Kant. For Kant, and for us, Christianity is the obvious choice.) So, is Kant trying to make us read between his difficult German lines and see that if he presupposes God's existence for his moral project, and if his moral faith leads to a practical hope, then it follows (by transitivity) that by presupposing God we therefore (ought to) have hope in God? It appears that there is, then, a sort of first-level hope that we find in Kant's famous question, "What may I hope?"

Kant's moral philosophy is predicated on the moral principle that *ought implies can*, and, by contraposition, that *cannot implies ought not*, that is, practical reason commands us to follow the categorical imperative, but we find ourselves (throughout this life) unable to put our inclinations in order and to overcome the radical evil we find in our wills, that is, a propensity to do what is wrong, even when we know better. But the law would not oblige us if it were not possible for us to fulfill it: "cannot" (we cannot fulfill the moral law *simpliciter*) implies "ought not" (we are not obligated to fulfill the law). Therefore, Kant reasons, we must presuppose or assume or "postulate" that there is in the noumenal realm (beyond or outside time and space) a holy and just Author of us who will resurrect, judge, and preserve us. But Kant has said (as cited above) that hope always tends toward one's happiness. He expands this point: happiness is the fulfillment of all of one's desires extensively (many types of desire), intensively (the magnitude or intensity of desire), and protensively (the duration of the desire).[4]

So, if Kant has it right, a sort of first-order hope is accessible to a rational mind to discover and understand. An interesting account of this sort of hope, from a different perspective, comes to us in C. S. Lewis's spiritual autobiography *Surprised by Joy*. Lewis speaks of the boarding school that he attended as a boy and how memories of that experience are important to his present hope and faith: "Life at a vile boarding school is in this way a good preparation for the Christian life, in that it teaches one to live by hope. Even, in a sense, by faith; for at the beginning of each term, home and the holidays are so far off that it is as hard to realize them as to realize heaven." Lewis goes on to explain the temporal dimensions of going off to school with so many months to go before end of term would finally come:

> Tomorrow's geometry blots out the distant end of the term as tomorrow's operation may blot out the hope of Paradise. And yet, term after term, the unbelievable happened . . . [six weeks became one week, then one day, then] the almost supernatural bliss of the Last Day punctually appeared. It was a delight that tingled down the spine and troubled the belly and at moments went near to stopping the breath.

Lewis says,

> In all seriousness I think that the life of faith is easier to me because of these memories. To think, in sunny and confident times, that I shall die and rot, or to think that one day all this universe will slip away and become memory (as Oldie [Lewis's cruel schoolmaster] slipped away into memory three times a year, and with him the canes and the disgusting food, the stinking sanitation and cold beds)— this is easier to us if we have seen just that sort of thing happening before. We have learned not to take present things at their face value.[5]

Kant and Lewis help us see that time and hope are inextricably bound together and that there is a sort of spiritual or supernatural sense to hope that even the nonbeliever can experience and, in time, actually, or at least hope to, appreciate. However, notice that the temporal dimensions of human existence and finitude alone cannot solve our problems. Kant himself situates his theological-sounding claims within morality. We, too, are driven to look to morality and theological-sounding claims in order to situate the problem of evil. But it is important to see that the concept of hope arises for moral beings in general. What we gather from this point is that it is reasonable to believe that if God has created us, then God has given resources to all people on an ontological level shared by all—Christians would say on the level of the *imago Dei*—that are altogether powerful for, and relevant to, dealing with the problem of evil. We shall turn now and investigate how suffering and hope are indeed inextricably linked one to the other.

II. A Bit on Moral Theories: Groundwork for the Metaphysics of Theodicies

When we talk about the virtue of hope, we talk about virtue, and virtue is decidedly a moral category. It will be helpful, then, to discuss ethical views and the importance of freedom to theodicy.

Since suffering is what sets in motion this chain of implications in Romans 5, we know that suffering plays a key role in this process. It is the door, the enzyme, the first domino to fall, the trigger mechanism that can lead the human heart and mind ultimately to *hope*. Notice the word *can* here. In reading Romans 5:1–5, one might consider that Paul is saying that suffering *will most definitely produce* perseverance, character, and hope. But this is not so; experience has falsified that claim. What is missing, of course, is the work of the *will*. No virtue, no good habit, no right interpretation of God's allowance of evil will happen unless the person in question uses his will rightly, unless he allows the will to function properly. And the so-called freewill defense comes to bear here—claiming that God cannot *both* create beings who causally bring themselves always to act freely and rightly *and* have beings whom *God causes* always to act freely and rightly.[6] The result? In order to have a world with moral good, it may be necessary also to have a world with significant types of evil, amounts of evil, and particular evils that not even an omnipotent being can avoid while at the same time getting the moral goodness in the world produced by these freewilled agents. It is an empirical question as to whether the freewilled agents will in fact always choose to do rightly; sadly, in our world, we have sometimes chosen not to act rightly. The point is that the process of soul making assumes an indeterministic, agent causation account of human freedom, and most soul-making theodicists use the freewill defense (or freewill theodicy) as part of their artillery against the problem of evil.[7]

It might be helpful to take a transcendental approach here, that approach offered by Kant in his various Critiques. The transcendental argument-type one might employ would be to observe an X and to ask: *what conditions must be met for the very possibility of the instantiation of X?* The strength of this approach for theodicy is that it allows for two important steps in properly expressing a theodicy. First, the theist is allowed to start with basic knowledge claims that both sides of the debate can agree upon. Call this set of claims that he starts with "common background knowledge." Background knowledge is important because if both parties agree to it, one can ask about the transcendental grounds for those things to be the case. Second, taking the transcendental approach allows the theist to proceed past basic (shared) common background knowledge to "tell the theodical story" with a goal in mind of supplying sets of *plausible* or *not irrational* sufficient conditions for God's permission of evils. Many theodicists, for example, have started with basic background assumptions such as the following:

1. There is a vast amount of moral and natural evils in the world.
2. There is a vast amount of moral and natural goods in the world.
3. For a great many evils (whether moral or natural), when critically investigated over time, we very often recognize the outweighing good served by God's permission of these evils.[8]
4. For some evils (whether moral or natural), when critically investigated over time, we do not recognize the outweighing good served by God's permission of these evils.

The following could be added as well, I think, to our list of common background knowledge. This point refers to cognitive function and will play an important part in what follows.

5. Our cognitive mechanisms (including our powers of induction, deduction, *a priori* reasoning, abduction, modal thinking, counterfactual thinking, risibility,

belief-forming, belief-revising, and belief-defeating mechanisms) are wonderfully complex and *prima facie* (and I believe *ultima facie*) justify our belief that they exhibit intelligent design.[9]

What are some sets of sufficient conditions that could *plausibly* give rise to worlds in which the above agreed-upon realities are true? We have already heard from Kant and remarked that he thinks the answer is clear: the plausible worldview must include the existence of a wise and just Author who embodies or actualizes the postulates of pure practical reason (the existence of God and immortality), and who shows how His actions are causally beneficial to us in the eschaton. Interestingly, Kant acknowledges that such a wise and just Author (God) would thus have to be omnipotent, omniscient, omnipresent, and eternal.[10]

So, what is the inference to the best explanation regarding 1–4? To begin to answer this question, let us look at the framework within which the soul-making theodicy is usually given. The theist must include, as part of his presentation, a good bit of ethical theory by which to explain and help understand providence, the nature of virtue, suffering as a possible extrinsic good, and God's duties as Creator, Providence, Savior, and Judge. It is important in this context to notice what 3 and 4, above, say:

3. For a great many evils (whether moral or natural), when critically investigated over time, we very often recognize the outweighing good served by God's permission of these evils.

4. For some evils (whether moral or natural), when critically investigated over time, we do not recognize the outweighing good served by God's permission of these evils.

Three does *not* say, "We very often recognize the outweighing good served by *these evils*." Rather, as Stephen Wykstra points out, it is *God's permission of these evils* that serves the outweighing good.[11] This distinction shows that our considered ethical framework needs to be a deontological-aretaic framework rather than *merely* a means-to-ends consequentialistic framework. After all, God may permit certain evil states (e.g., hangover pain) that are the consequence of well-known patterns of behavior (overconsumption of alcohol) and be morally justified in doing so. The evil itself doesn't necessarily give rise to a greater good. In fact, the world may be a worse place, over-all, with episodes of heavy drinking than not. But again, this doesn't render morally doubtful God's permission of such. There is plenty of room here, then, in Christian defenses and theodicies, for a concept of divine *justice*, justice as fairness or justice as desert. Evils often occur in our world that could well be allowed by God simply due to (1) the principle that widespread moral freedom (which sometimes results in misuse of that freedom) is a very great good, and (2) the principle that God sometimes may shape the patterns of allowed goods and evils according to certain principles of justice, for exam-ple, reflecting God's righteousness and holiness.[12] What follows from this point is that the theist can be among the first to say that there being evil in the world really is evil and evil doesn't necessarily make the world a more pleasant place than the world otherwise would have been. But the presence of evils can still be justified through the theist's theodical story that grows up in the richness of a deonto-logical soil. The grounding for the metaphysics of theodicies, then, is a deontological/aretaic environment, dealing with people made in the image of God, who are significantly morally free and who have marvelous belief mechanisms, sometimes seeing the justification for evils, and sometimes not.

III. How Does Your Garden Grow?
Proper Function, Warrant, and Belief

Some recent developments in the area of *epistemology* are also, I believe, of great relevance to theodicy. Recent work by Alvin Plant-inga and others holds that epistemic justification or "warrant" hinges on the idea of the "proper functioning" of one's cognitive mechanisms in the environment in which one was designed to function, aimed at truth (forming true beliefs), in the absence of significant epistemic defeaters, overriders, or undercutters.[13] We form a belief in a circum-stance, such as "my shoe is on fire," and we are led to believe this by means of possession of a properly functioning belief-forming apparatus (our minds), which functions according to a "design plan." Plantinga says that the apparatus must also be functioning in the environment in which it is "designed" to function at peak capacity (on Earth, say, rather than in the fiery atmosphere of Alpha Centauri). If these conditions are met, then we are justified or warranted in that belief that "my shoe is on fire." (Thankfully, at this time, this is a false belief and one that I properly do not possess.) The terms I have employed here, *design plan*, *designed*, and the like, have been carefully selected so as not to beg the important question of etiology of these epistemic mechanisms. Darwinian evolutionist and theist alike could speak of the "design plan" of a tulip, which might entail the flower's "way" of reproduction and propagation, its genetic constituents, and whatever teleological (or seemingly teleological) systems may be enjoyed by the tulip (such as having reproductive faculties, genetic endowments, tulip-like traits, causal powers of movement and growth, etc.). Evolution might be said to have "designed" such a system. I feel that the naturalists strain credulity to speak in such a way, but for our purposes we can allow such talk to remain worldview neutral. However, it should be noted: teleological talk is at home in the theistic universe—since God is a creator and a purposeful agent—but it *prima facie* seems a very strange member in a nontheistic universe indeed.

Theists hold that our belief-forming mechanisms are created by God not only to provide us the ability to form true beliefs about ourselves and our environment but also to lead us, at some opportune moment, to freely believe in God. Part of Plantinga's religious epistemology, which he has developed over the last 40 years, is to argue that minds have to be operating *in the environment* in which God designed the mind to function and form true beliefs. We may ask: how do our belief-forming mechanisms operate in our environment in such a way that they cooperate with God's work in our hearts, working as a necessary but not sufficient component for fully human rational thought and consciousness? For obviously there was a time in each of our lives when we did not believe in God. However, through various experiences and the prodding and effectual call of the Holy Spirit upon our lives, we came to put our trust in God for salvation. It is not irrational, but eminently rational, to think that if our belief-forming mechanisms had not been functioning properly in the past, and were not functioning properly now, we might well have not "seen" God, seen that spiritual object of worship and awe (according to Christian theism) that the properly functioning mind was designed to "see" or "perceive."

One false conclusion to draw from this last point would be that since nonbelievers do not "see" God and have not put their faith and trust in Him, they must not have properly functioning belief-forming mechanisms. However, this would be a faulty inference. According to Ephesians 4:23, it is the "*spirit* of the mind," not the mind *itself*, that is renewed in salvation. The spirit or helmsman over the human mind is evidently *the will*, not the mind itself. My claim here is that the mind is functioning properly or largely properly in the nonbeliever; however, the will is not allowing the evidence of creation, the written Word of God, and the voice of God within, to convict properly and lead to a repentant heart that longs to know and "see" God again and again. What the mind is designed to "see," the heart is designed to will to desire time and time again. Augustine spoke wisely when he said, in the opening lines of *Confessions*, that "our hearts find no peace until they rest in you [the Lord]."[14]

The experience I would like to focus on here that gives rise to religious and moral awareness in humans is the experience of pain and suffering. Every human individual has experienced great pain on many occasions in his life, and that pain, among its many useful qualities, has one in particular that makes it perhaps unique. This property is the virtuous property of being able completely to take hold of and sustain our attention until such pain should be eradicated, or the dimensions of the pain are understood. For example, if my wife puts a cool and refreshing drink on my desk while I am not looking, I may leisurely discover the source of this blessing later on in the day. However, if my left big toe is beset with a terrible cramp, I turn all of my attention to eradicate or alleviate this painful condition. Indeed, pain is God's "megaphone" by which God awakens the soul, again and again, from its dogmatic slumbers.

My claim here would be that part of our "belief-forming mechanisms," those mechanisms with which God has so outfitted us to form beliefs upon experiencing certain cognitive or psychological states in this life, is the same part that gives rise to an awareness of a state we might call "exasperation by evil."

If indeed we are "naturally outfitted," with our minds so constructed, whether Christian or pagan, when we experience an evil situation sufficiently dreadful to give rise to feelings and beliefs of exasperation, then we should conclude that it is therefore "natural" to cry, as the psalmist did, "How long, O LORD? How long?" (e.g., Ps 13).

Our belief-forming mechanisms naturally lead us to form such beliefs as these when we experience what we might perceive to be debilitating or soul-destroying evil. Suppose we say that when in a pain state, which is sufficiently long-lasting and violent, I form the belief that there is no loving heavenly Father who loves me. Call this a "D-belief," or "a belief formed by the doubt belief mechanism," and the formation of such a belief "D-belief formation." So far, we are saying that both a Christian and pagan are outfitted to form such a belief and to do so by God's design. It is therefore "natural" to form doubt beliefs, or D-beliefs, concerning God's existence. To appreciate what I am up to here, I do want to point out a few important ideas. First, it seems safe to infer that the Christian believer must have cognitive mechanisms and experiential and background knowledge sufficient to defeat any D-belief. However, as part of my analysis, I am breaking down the act of belief formation and the mechanisms important to such formation of beliefs into some of the important component parts. By so distinguishing between the different belief mechanisms, I am not meaning to imply (and probably would rather want to deny) that many of the belief-forming mechanisms we enjoy definitely do not work simultaneously or in tandem to produce their intended effects. This beliefs-giving-rise-to-other-beliefs process has a sort of narrative and diachronic way about it that is hard to pin down but is known to us all.

Second, let me add that this model I'm presenting is also consistent with the person who is so certain of God's existence and goodness that she does not doubt the existence and goodness of God at all, even in the midst of exasperating evil. While I have perhaps never met someone who would fall into this category of human persons who are able not to doubt (*posse non dubitare?*), still such is possible.

In such an instance, we could say that the person is either so resolute and assured of God's goodness that D-beliefs never come to his
mind; or, that these beliefs never come *consciously*, on that occasion,
to his mind (but they are there, nonetheless); or, that the person's D-
belief formation mechanism is not functioning properly (or, in general, his mind simply lacks some part of the design plan that usually
functions so that D-beliefs are formed in those circumstances). I do
not mean to build an auxiliary hypothesis into my model here that
causes it to be unverifiable and resilient to testing. But the experience
of the formation of D-beliefs is so well verified in common experience (and in the literature of the world) that such exceptions would
seem exceptionally rare. Perhaps it is proper even to view Jesus' actions of praying in the garden before His arrest, or crying in exasperation on the cross, as an episode of forming D-beliefs, in a natural
way, when one experiences the pangs of exasperating evil.

IV. Fending Off Enemies: Defeaters and Doubt

Let us assume without argument that any activity that leads to
moral maturity necessarily leads to soul maturity, or "soul-making,"
and that any activity that leads to the appearance or improvement of
a virtue (according to Christian morality) is a type of moral maturity.
Gaining virtues, then, necessarily leads to soul maturity. We should
also recognize that there are virtues of the intellect: there is undoubtedly a deontological aspect of belief. We have a right to hold certain
beliefs given what we know, and we have a permission to believe certain things so long as we don't have sufficient reasons against such
beliefs. The considered view of the Clifford-James-Plantinga debate
about the rationality of religious belief is that belief in God is, sometimes, properly basic, and if we are created by God with the goal
that we should freely worship God, then it is both eminently rational
and warranted to believe in God when our cognitive faculties, functioning as God designed them to function in a congenial epistemic
environment, and aimed at forming true beliefs, involuntarily form
beliefs in us that imply that the theistic God exists. For example,
"God is pleased with how I have acted in circumstance C." But we
would not be rational, and we would not be warranted in our belief,

if we formed the belief, "The Great Pumpkin is pleased with how I have acted in circumstance C." For, among other things, there are no good reasons to believe that the Great Pumpkin exists and has the ability to create people with the faculties that they in fact have. Even better, we do not naturally form belief in the Great Pumpkin when we see a beautiful sunset or the starry host above us or the moral law within us. Sometimes such beliefs *are* naturally formed in those circumstances, though, concerning God.[15]

Forming a belief and holding that belief, even in the face of seemingly contrary evidence, is a complex and wonderful cognitive process each of us often goes through. Especially important to this process is our belief-defeating, or defeater, mechanism. What is a *defeater*? A defeater D for person H for a belief B is another belief of H such that, given H's cognitive system C, and the use H has made of C, D makes it rational, *prima facie* and *ceteris paribus*, to give up belief B. Defeaters come in at least two kinds: those that either (a) rebut B, or (b) undercut B. Also, there are rationality defeaters and warrant defeaters.[16] Our focus here is on rationality defeaters. To rebut or to have a "rebutting defeater" of B is for H to have a D that shows that it is no longer rational to believe B because what H comes to learn (this other belief D) is in fact inconsistent with B. For example, Fred believes that 1 is not equal to .999...(repeating). Then Joe, his math teacher, shows him the proof for why 1 = .999...(repeating). Fred understands the proof and sees that it is a valid and sound argument. This proof is a rebutting defeater for Fred's previous belief, and it would be rational for Fred to give up the previous belief.

To have an "undercutting defeater" is somewhat different: it is to have a reason for not believing B, but where the exact nature of the case concerning B or not-B is not yet determined. D in this circumstance is a reason that neutralizes your previous evidence or grounds for believing B. Suppose your friend, who is a specialist in literature, and especially Lewis Carroll, stays at your house for a week. Later on, a sheet of paper is found under the bed that, according to your wife, is complete gobbledygook. Still later, your friend calls and wonders if you found any papers in his room because he lost one of them, apparently during the visit. Your friend says, "It will say 'page 123' in the upper right corner if it is mine." You look at the paper your wife found, and find it marked "page 123" in the upper right corner. You are sure this must be your friend's lost sheet. However, you don't know if the friend has actually written something intelligible on the paper (perhaps mathematical or logical symbols, or another language, or whatever), or whether he was reading Lewis Carroll and intentionally trying to write gobbledygook. On the paper it reads, "'Tis brilldunk, and the slozzy traves slep huppily on the weeb." You recall your friend saying something at breakfast about "slup" being the past participle of "slep," and you figure that the paper (perhaps!) is not gobbledygook after all. It's hard to tell, but this example is probably an example of an undercutting defeater. Your previous grounds (your wife's testimony) for thinking that the paper contains gobbledygook has been successfully undercut by the rest of your belief set. But the paper may still contain gobbledygook for all you know; it's not clear yet.

Some defeaters are not rationality defeaters, Plantinga says, but warrant defeaters.[17] Bertrand Russell's clock example might be an example of this kind of defeater. You walk into a room and wonder what time it is. You look at the clock on the wall, which reads 4:05. You therefore form the belief, "It is 4:05." However, as you stay awhile, you realize that the clock's hands are not moving; apparently the batteries are dead. This new knowledge about the improper functioning of the clock would give you a reason for undercutting or neutralizing any positive reason for believing it is 4:05 *on the basis of what this clock tells*. Would it be rational to give up your previous belief that it is now a few minutes after 4:05? It's not clear; it depends on what else you know. (Suppose you also know that it feels to you to be about teatime; it seems about three hours after lunch, and you know you ate at one o'clock, and so forth.) It is interesting that, as in this case, a broken clock would still tell the time correctly exactly two times a day! But because of the relative frequencies involved, it's much more probable that the clock told the incorrect time at the time at which you first looked at it. However, it *could be* that the clock did tell the correct time just when you looked. Russell's example of a defeater, then, is a pre-Gettier Gettier counterexample.

Of course, there can be defeater defeaters, and defeater defeater defeaters, and such things *ad infinitum*. Our interest with defeaters will be to ask: what does God naturally build into our belief-forming and belief-defeating mechanisms to rebut or undercut D-beliefs in God?

What about going through periods of doubt? Upon reflection I think we can safely say that going through doubt can in fact lead to significant soul maturation. If doubt makes one more courageous, or more persevering, then clearly this kind of doubt is soul-making. The doubt itself may be intrinsically neutral; the event in the world that caused the doubt may be intrinsically evil; but that to which the doubt leads, if it leads to a virtue, could itself make the doubting into an extrinsic good. That is, the doubt in such a case would have served some outweighing good, if the outcome were intimately causally tied up with the doubt and could not, in some sense, have been obtained without it. Some doubt could also of course be perceived to be soul-destroying. We shall say more on this below.

Severe doubt can be a form of suffering, and doubt about the most important things may indeed be most vexing and soul-disturbing. If St. Paul is correct in Rom 5:1–5, then severe doubt can lead to hope, and hope does not disappoint us. Forming doubt beliefs, or "D-beliefs," then, is part of the natural process of soul-maturation, and, importantly, is *not essentially sinful*. It is not morally blameworthy to form a belief such as, "I doubt whether God exists and cares about me and my pain." It may well be that the human epistemic system is properly functioning when we *do* form such beliefs, since the doubt mechanism that we have is a centrally important part of our overall cognitive apparatus. I shall say more on this point just below. So, it may be morally permissible to *form* D-belief, if one does so naturally and spontaneously, during intense and prolonged suffering.[18] However, it is *not* morally permissible, one could hold, to *maintain* and *harbor* D-belief in the nonexistence of God due to evil, *if there were reasons, that is, undercutting or rebutting defeaters, that would defeat (neutralize or turn the tide of) the force of that doubt.*

A person's remaining in doubt without making use of positive reasons for God's goodness and existence would be misusing the good aspects of one's own existence and defeating the overall purpose of the natural formation of D-beliefs. First, then: what might be the overall intentions of God in giving us our doubt mechanisms? Second: does the nonbeliever have accessible to his consciousness at least undercutting defeaters for the natural formation of D-beliefs, namely, the belief that there is not a good God?

First, why did God give us doubt mechanisms? God Himself is the author of these mechanisms. What good do they serve? We know that God's creative activity always tends to secure *goods* which otherwise would not have been present. We must view this tendency, of course, deontologically: sometimes God's goodness to us in a circumstance implies pain or punishment. Also, we accept as a moral principle that to will some end necessarily implies willing the *means* to that end. Thus, if God wills some good end by allowing us to *form* D-beliefs, we know He also wills some means to that end. It would not be surprising if those means were some sort of *defeater* to this ability of the mind to *sustain* D-beliefs. We also hold that God's excellent beneficence is dead set, *ceteris paribus*, against any evil that does not bring about a greater good, or is highly likely to bring about a greater good, at some time in the life of humans. Yet we see that upon severe suffering, Christians as well as nontheists may form the belief, "I'm doubting whether God exists because of this evil situation." What, then, is the *intended good*, in God's good design of the human belief-forming mechanism, in programming humans *naturally* to form D-beliefs?

There are clearly many beneficial purposes that doubt mechanisms serve. One chief reason comes from considerations in human epistemology. Since roughly half of all propositions are false in any possible world, there is a need to be able critically to ferret out which of any two contradictory propositions is in fact true. Doubt plays an important role in that process for any being that is significantly less than occurrently or dispositionally omniscient. Also, doubt and wonder seem to go together, and so doubt seems to be a logically necessary condition for discovery and invention. There is a joy to freely discovering our own world. Doubt plays a part in the scientific method and may be a necessary concomitant of a free being who is not omniscient but who undertakes any scientific enterprise. Thus, the intention of D-Beliefs, the soul-making theodicist maintains, is manifold, but perhaps one of the most important reasons for the existence of doubt beliefs would be that a person consciously comes justifiably to believe, by experiencing harsh evils, that *he cannot secure a truly happy life on his own steam.* (Remember here that hope, for Kant, is always directed toward one's happiness, but God is necessary to secure a lasting, true happiness. Thus, one discovers through experiencing harsh evils that one's hope does not lie in oneself but must be outwardly directed.) This is the first stage in what we commonly call *conversion*. To see that one cannot live this life on one's own steam means to come to see, taste, and acknowledge that one is not an island unto himself, but rather a dependent being whose existence is frail and evidently upheld by another. This "another" is an outside source who has been merciful *enough* not to destroy one for the sinful attitudes, thoughts, and actions he has harbored, entertained, or committed, but also merciful enough *not* to allow the person to continue in the illusion that human beings are independent and that human happiness consists in a life of seeking only one's selfish human projects and ends.

V. Pruning D-Beliefs Through Undercutters: What Reasons Has the Unbeliever?

Does the nonbeliever have a sufficiently robust defeater to undercut the belief, "there is not a good God," which is formed naturally when he undergoes severe suffering? I believe the answer is affirmative. But to understand why, at least in part, we must examine our question in the context of the recent debate on the evidential argument from evil. William Rowe is famous for his presentation of various forms of this type of argument. His foundational argument, dating from 1978, takes the following form:

1. There exist instances of intense suffering which an omnipotent, omniscient being could have prevented without thereby preventing the occurrence of any greater good.
2. An omniscient, wholly good being would prevent the occurrence of any intense suffering it could, unless it could not do so without thereby preventing the occurrence of some greater good.

Therefore,

3. There does not exist an omnipotent, omniscient, wholly good being.[19]

Rowe claims that the argument is valid and then tries to show that it is also sound. To show soundness, he argues in this way. First, he maintains that we have *good reasons* for thinking that the first premise is true. Second, he states that the second premise is true. And we see that the conclusion follows from the premises. So, using the principle of the preservation of degree of belief, we have therefore *good reasons* for thinking that the conclusion is true. If we have good reasons for thinking premise one is true, know that the second premise is *true*, and the conclusion is a deductive consequence of the two premises, then we conclude that we have *good reasons* to accept the conclusion of the argument.

What are the *good reasons* for accepting premise (1)? Suppose we call the set of all goods we know of "G," and the set of all possible goods "G*." I shall assume that G is a proper subset of G*. An omniscient being would know of all conceivable goods that could come to pass. But that is not all, we should add, that an omniscient being would know. That being would also know all the possible connections between events in a world, and the relationship of the properties of those events with the properties associated with all present, past, and future events, as well as *our reactions and internal dialogue and feelings toward* the events we are aware of. Of course, we should also add that part of omniscience includes knowledge of the way in which humans and nonhuman animals react to evil: the way in which they experience evil, benefit from evil, are not affected by it or are crushed by it (and to what degree those agents are responsible for suffering, and whether they make the right sort of response to evil). According to Rowe, we have good reason to accept (1) because of all the goods G we know of (all the goods we can conceive of, whether or not they are known to have become actual), we can see that G does not contain any good or set of goods which justify God in permitting the examples of evils Rowe gives, E1 and E2.[20] And so Rowe concludes that probably G* does not contain any goods taken singly or jointly that justify God in permitting E1 and E2. The "good reason," then, for accepting premise (1) is the inductive step of Rowe's empirical argument from evil. So Rowe moves inductively from the "goods we know of" to "all possible goods."

This inductive move itself is not justified, and the literature on the evidential argument from evil since Rowe's original formulation substantiates this claim. By 1996, Rowe admits that this earlier form of the argument from evil, in fact, is a weak argument.[21] The point here is that even though we might naturally *form* the belief, "There is not a good God," there are significant epistemic defeaters that keep us from *habituating* that belief, harboring that belief, becoming obdurate in that belief. First, no one is justified, being less than omniscient, to suppose that they might know the reasons why God has allowed this particular severe suffering to exist. Wykstra treats a similar point to my own here: whether someone is justified in making a claim of the form, "It appears that p." (This would be similar to forming the belief, upon suffering, that "there is not a good God.") As Wykstra points out, a human being H would be justified in making an "appears" claim (it appears that p) in some conscious situation s only if

> it is reasonable for H to believe that, given her cognitive faculties and the use she has made of them, if p were not the case, s would likely be different than it is in some way discernible by her.[22]

If this principle is right, and I'm inclined to believe it is, then the person who forms a D-belief should see that she is not justified to *retain* this D-belief because to do so entails that she can see that if there *were* a good God, then God would not allow this severe suffering to exist. A significantly less than omniscient being could not know the reasons God permitted the said suffering to occur, even though God would know the reasons. So the inference from the initial naturally formed belief, upon suffering, "there is not a good God," to having justification for harboring this belief, is not justified; in fact, that initial belief is *defeated by this undercutting defeater*.

The form of Rowe's evidential argument from evil (and many other evidential arguments from evil) is, in essence:

(1) There are gratuitous evils.

(2) If God exists, then there are no gratuitous evils.

Therefore,

(3) God doesn't exist.[23]

However, Rowe suggests that the theist's best move against his 1978–79 version of the evidential argument from evil may well be to employ the "G. E. Moore shift." By instituting this "shift," one sees there is an equally logically rigorous argument lurking here.[24] One must only negate premise 1 and 3 and switch them, giving:

(~3) God does exist.

(2) If God exists, then there are no gratuitous evils.

Therefore,

(~1) There are no gratuitous evils.

Since premise (2) is the same in both arguments, how one decides which argument will hold sway is by pitting premise (1) against (~3) and asking: which one has the most appeal? If a person gets to the stage, of course, of having had a life that allowed rational reflection of this nature, for him the answer seems obvious: since good precedes evil, and evil (if Augustine is right) is parasitical on good, and being is convertible with goodness, my existence is a good to me, a gift to me. I did not have to be, but here I am. I also find that my life is a life worth living, and if it is not, it is through no fault of anyone else but my own. My good life owes a great deal of its goodness to the grace from others, primarily from God. What is the explanation for my being and for these gracious benefits I have received so freely? It comes from another person, or process, which led me here to my current state. If it is a person, then I should investigate the matter and be thankful to have received such a precious gift from this (or these) person(s).

In part, the epistemic question that confronts us is, "Which one comes first: good or evil?" Proper function or malfunction? People intuitively strongly side with good as having a priority over evil in the categories of temporality (which came first?) and causal dependence (which depends on which for its existence?), and perhaps in several other ways. Clearly proper function comes first; malfunction seems subsequent to, dependent on our definitions or intuitions about proper function. I think these considerations give us reasons to believe that God Himself has provided undercutting defeaters that keep formation of a D-belief from rationally moving on to harboring of a D-belief. There is, of course, the interpretation that the person places upon his experience. This interpretation may agree with the natural formation of beliefs, remember the good gifts one has received, and find an undercutter to one's D-belief; or, it may not. Unfortunately, the person may decide freely to harbor D-belief. The latter, however, would be no fault of God's. It is the clear witness of Scripture that God has provided such evidences as make His existence and power clearly known to all people.[25]

The famous religious skeptic David Hume agrees as spoken through his character Philo in *Dialogues Concerning Natural Religion*: if one does one's theism first, and then looks at the patterns of evil in this world, one

> might, perhaps, be surprised at the disappointment, but
> would never retract his former belief if founded on any
> very solid argument; since such a limited intelligence must
> be sensible of his own blindness and ignorance, and must
> allow that there may be many solutions of those phenom-
> ena which will forever escape his comprehension.[26]

That is, if one has justification or reasons or good arguments for believing in God, and then turns to consider the rational issues surrounding evil, "the traditional problem of evil reduces to a noncrucial perplexity of relatively minor importance."[27]

VI. A Rawlsian Precultivation Thought Experiment: Thinking "Behind the Veil"

There are other rational considerations that theodicists in general would do well to keep on the theodical playing field. In going back to Kant's transcendental approach, if we know certain things to be likely true or eminently rational (where "rational" for a human means being consistent with the belief that a properly functioning mind aimed at truth would form), we can ask, "What are the conditions for the possibility of the truth or rationality of these things?"

To begin to develop this second-order, reflective stage, we can say the following. Each human person, in order to transcend the evil that besets him, must seek succor in one who is sufficiently strong to deliver him from the present evil and pain. In short, one is led by experiencing tragedy to consider a relationship with the living God who desires to deliver us from these circumstances. One finds through the experience of almost insurmountable evils what one is really made out of, that this life in the flesh is fleeting and transient, and that certain decisions (about morality and spirituality) in this life are indeed the decisions that demand our deepest and most resolute attention. This second stage, whereby we can come to warranted conclusions about evil, God, and existence, might be described as a belief-stage whereby we go behind what John Rawls has called the "veil of ignorance."[28] Imagine a situation in which you, as a benevolent rational spectator, consider characteristics of the world to be created, without knowing exactly what *your* human existence in that world would be. Here we come to believe that God must have a certain nature if He created us as beings who on the one hand share many of the attributes that we naturally attribute to Deity or Godhood (spiritual-, moral-, and self-consciousness, rationality, language use, communication, relation, affection, mathematic ability, having projects, building our own characters consciously, etc.), and yet who suffer greatly in this life.

The Gestalt experiment I bring up here using Rawls' veil of ignorance is a rational inquiry into the type of world a God who is all-good, all-powerful, and all-knowing would make. Figuring that the following four possibilities are presented to a benevolent human inhabitant-to-be in the world to be selected, what world would you choose to be the case?

1. A world in which no one suffers.
2. A world in which humankind suffers but God does not suffer.

3. A world in which humankind does not suffer but God does suffer.

4. A world in which both humankind suffers and God suffers.

We must bear in mind here at least two items. First, the point of the freewill defense is that even the omnipotent God cannot actualize just any world that He wishes: if there is a world W in which a finite moral agent H created by God freely actualizes some state of affairs S at time t, then God cannot both create H in W and make H freely actualize S at t. If H actualizes S at t, it is up to H and not God that S obtains. In a world in which there are many humans trying to make their souls, it is *probable* (in some sense of probable) that humans (who are indeterministically free) will sin and sometimes freely do wrongly. Also, there is the fact that some evils are *logically necessary conditions* for the mere possibility of certain goods. For example, for Smith to gain the property, "courageously bearing pain," Smith must obviously *bear pain*. Not even an omnipotent being can get Smith to have the attribute of courageously bearing pain without Smith's bearing pain. But notice that *courage* is one of the virtues. It turns out that all the virtues, except perhaps love, have evils as logically necessary conditions for possibly obtaining, at least for finite agents. (God is, from eternity, maximally virtuous without any evils being logically necessary conditions, or conditions *simpliciter*, for any divine virtue.) To acquire virtues, according to Christian and Aristotelian ethics, one must persevere through a danger (to acquire the *habit* of courage), or live through significant pressure (to acquire the *habit* of fortitude), or overcome temptations (to acquire the *habit* of self-control), and so forth. In short: to acquire virtues, one must acquire good *habits* through encountering significant evils. A virtuous character is one that can, in time, help to turn an intrinsic evil into (or largely into) an extrinsic good. In the Christian view of things, the virtuous character, who has "love" as a binding agent over all that it does (cf. Col 3:14), is able to help turn "suffering," with God's grace, into perseverance, giving rise to Christian habits of long-suffering, self-control, and the like, which in turn produce *hope* of gaining a truly happy life.

I dare say that our sense of justice would preclude the mind behind the veil of ignorance to choose either 2 or 3. Therefore, there remains for consideration option 1 or 4. In light of what we have said just above, and in light of the claim of Romans 5, that suffering is a necessary, in fact, logically necessary, condition for obtaining a good character which in turn is necessary for securing *hope* (that is, longing for lasting happiness and assurance of future beneficial experiences for the conscious mind), then it seems we are led to elect *option 4* over option 1. But is it even logically possible for a perfect being *to suffer?* For to suffer is to change, and to change implies being in time. These are deep and complex issues. According to purveyors of perfect being theology, God's properties that are constitutive of his metaphysical and moral highest possible excellence, would have a relationship to X (what x is: an event, a property, a habit, a character trait, or a metaphysical quality or relation or state) that would be consistent with maximal excellence and ultimate metaphysical stature. I believe it is coherent that a perfect being could suffer: one could employ the concept of "value-neutral change," as discussed by Thomas Morris. God can be conceived to change, for example, not talking to Abram in 2500 BC, then talking to him in circa 2000 BC, then ceasing to talk to him again shortly thereafter. God is neither increased nor decreased through this episode, *pace* Plato, in his metaphysical or moral stature.[29] It is not irrational to include in one's doctrine of God this concept of value-neutral change; and if one did include it, this would entail that God could, in some sense, suffer along with His creatures. Plantinga says the following about God's capacity to suffer:

> As the Christian sees things, God does not stand idly by, coolly observing the suffering of his creatures. He enters into and shares our suffering. He endures the anguish of seeing his son, the second person of the Trinity, consigned to the bitterly cruel and shameful death of the cross. Some theologians say God cannot suffer. I believe they are wrong. God's capacity for suffering, I believe, is proportional to his greatness; it exceeds our capacity for suffering in the same measure as his capacity for knowledge exceeds ours. Christ

was prepared to endure the agonies of hell itself; and God, the Lord of the universe, was prepared to endure the suffering consequent upon his son's humiliation and death. He was prepared to accept this suffering in order to overcome sin, and death, and the evils that afflict our world, and to confer on us a life more glorious than we can imagine. So we don't know why God permits evil; we do know, however, that he was prepared to suffer on our behalf, to accept suffering of which we can form no conception.[30]

It is reasonable to believe that behind the veil we would choose a world in which both creator and creature experienced pains and evils commensurate with their metaphysical stature. Christian theism is the only monotheism on offer that explicitly maintains that God indeed has taken such actions—leveling the playing field with respect to what God expects humans to suffer and what he himself is willing to suffer—where that suffering of God was *in fact on our behalf*. This shows that God is interested in us—that he acts decisively and gracefully toward us. Dorothy Sayers draws this conclusion:

> For whatever reason God chose to make man as he is—limited and suffering and subject to sorrows and death—He had the honesty and courage to take His own medicine. Whatever game He is playing with His creation, He has kept His own rules and played fair. He can exact nothing from man that He has not exacted from Himself. He has Himself gone through the whole of human experience, from the trivial irritations of family life and the cramping restrictions of hard word and lack of money to the worst horrors of pain and humiliation, defeat, despair, and death. When He was a man, He played the man. He was born in poverty and died in disgrace and thought it well worthwhile.[31]

So, for Christians, one of the defeaters of doubt beliefs that are naturally formed is the belief that Jesus knows our pain and Himself bore like pain in His body on the cross. There is an unquantifiable kinship of spirit that happens between those who have suffered in like manner or who have suffered in something approaching that degree. Jesus' suffering was undeserved; if any particular instance of suffering in a human was deserved, then it was deserved and the problem is dissolved. If it was undeserved, then there may be a kinship with Christ that defeats the doubt belief. If an all-good God would allow such suffering, then His permission may alone be sufficient since it opens up the possibility of a deeper relationship with the greatest conceivable being, which itself is a morally sufficient reason for God's permission of the suffering. But what of the person: what of his free will to elect to suffer in such a way? What would the person "behind the veil" *have chosen*, not knowing what degree of suffering he would have been called upon to suffer? It is ludicrous to see anything other than that, at least in this world, with these types of personal characteristics, people choose risk, even great risk, of significant injury or even loss of life, for the possibility of experiential success or the "rush" of obtaining certain goals or completing or participating in certain projects. People would clearly, behind the veil, choose worlds of type 4. Being less than omniscient, however, when suffering does come our way in this life, we find that indeed it does trigger in us a desire for our happiness; in reality, it opens us up to the sort of *hope* of which Kant spoke.

VII. Weeds Make Haste, but Sweet Flowers Do Grow: D-Beliefs Defeaters

We have held, then, that forming D-beliefs in God is not essentially sinful. What, though, of maintaining D-beliefs? Here, the theodicist may posit the existence of another type of, as it were, "defense mechanism" in the human belief-forming mechanism that, it is being held, is a function created by God. The defense mechanism is the forming of M-beliefs and Meta-M beliefs. M-beliefs, or memory beliefs, are formed and retained when a human with a properly functioning belief apparatus experiences life in all of its convolutions, twists and turns, as well as in everyday life and living. Meta-M beliefs are warranted beliefs that are formed or synthesized on the basis of M-beliefs. Meta-M theistic beliefs are the beliefs that show the positive cumulative weight of *reasons for* belief *and trust* in God (cf. Rom 1:18ff).

Meta-M beliefs are the natural defense mechanisms against D-beliefs. For is it not true that what get the Christian believer through doubts and valleys are the certitudes of seeing glimpses of God's face, of the mountaintop experiences of seeing God's healing and miraculous hand at work in one's life? Is it not a miracle that sinful human individuals are brought to see their vileness, to confess it, and to put their trust in Christ Jesus for the forgiveness of their sins? Is there not a whole array of intellectual reasons, testimony, and other evidences whose cumulative effect is the conclusion that there is an eternal God who cares for us and holds us within His careful watch? We conclude that Meta-M beliefs are one of God's built-in defense mechanisms in humans to defeat D-beliefs. We simply must *remember* that God, who is awesome, made us many promises that fly in the face of the present evil—promises that say, "If you bear the pains of this life, and believe in Me and My promises, you will enter into My rest." The same psalmist who cried, "How long, O Lord?" completes the psalm by saying these words significant in this context:

> Look on me and answer, O LORD my God. Give light to my eyes, or I will sleep in death; my enemy will say, "I have overcome him," and my foes will rejoice when I fall. But I trust in your unfailing love; my heart rejoices in your salvation. I will sing to the LORD, *for he has been good* to me. [Meta-M beliefs here overcome the D-beliefs] (Ps 13:3–6 [NIV])

So, for the believer, there is another type of asymmetry that surfaces as we ruminate on the *causes of* good and evil things in life. Suppose that Jones has tasted the goodness of God and formed the warranted belief that indeed it was God who has graciously shared good things to make Jones's life overall pleasant for a time. Jones reflects on the wonder of existence: why he exists and how something so wonderfully complex and intricate such as his life among a vast cosmos could have come to be. Through reading and being invited to church, he comes to understand God's creative activities, man's sinfulness, and God's redeeming activities and promise of an ultimate restoration of all things, "having the hope of eternal life" (Titus 3:7 NIV). God has shown Himself to be gracious and merciful and has given hope that the future will reveal all the more the depth of God's goodness and love of us.

Suffering then comes to Jones, and what is he to think? He finds himself, when the suffering gets excruciating, forming the belief that God is not good. He entertains this belief; but what saves him from harboring this belief? As the psalmist said, Jones believes, I will sing of God's love, for God has been good to me. In a word, we have something much closer to Basil Mitchell's *Stranger* than to R. M. Hare's *blik*: we have justification for believing in God, that He is good and loving, even in the midst of seemingly unjustified suffering.[32] Lewis's point bears mentioning here:

> To love involves trusting the beloved beyond the evidence, even against much evidence. No man is our friend who believes in our good intentions only when they are proved. No man is our friend who will not be very slow to accept evidence against them. Such confidence, between one man and another, is in fact almost universally praised as a moral beauty, not blamed as a logical error. And the suspicious man is blamed for a meanness of character, not admired for the excellence of his logic. . . . To believe that God—at least *this* God—exists is to believe that . . . you are no longer faced with an argument which demands your assent, but with a Person who demands your confidence.[33]

It is *prima facie* much more difficult, then, to show the nonexistence of something than to show the existence of some x. If we once have seen the goodness of God, and have good reasons to believe that God is steadfast in His character, does things for purposes (oftentimes for reasons that outstrip our relatively puny abilities to understand), and ultimately intends good for His creatures, then when severe suffering comes, and doubts appear in consciousness, we like the psalmist must allow our Meta-M beliefs to defeat our D-beliefs on each such occasion.

But consider also the situation of the nonbeliever. It must be maintained that it is not morally and intellectually justifiable to maintain and harbor a D-belief. Does the nonbeliever have sufficient resources of data by which to construct coherent Meta-M beliefs that are sufficient to defeat the invasive doubt beliefs whose implication is that God does not exist? Clearly the nonbeliever, too, according to the theodical story of the Christian theist, has been shown that God is, that He is to be worshipped and adored rightfully, and that He is a rewarder of those who diligently seek Him. He also knows in his heart that many people suppress this truth about God and do not deem God worthy of receiving such worship and adoration. However, what follows, if Christianity is true, is that the nonbeliever does have warranting grounds for trusting and *hoping* in something greater than himself. First, he is indelibly created in God's image. He knows full well that if naturalism were true, then no person would be justified *knowingly* that for *any* belief that the brain would happen to form, that that belief would in fact be true. But the thoughts concerning naturalism itself would not be known to be true; the objective probability of such a belief would be unknown or inscrutable. Thus, naturalism is not metaphysically robust enough to explain what we indeed *know* about the inner workings of the human epistemic apparatus and what confidence we rightly place upon its current more-or-less proper functioning and its current actual production of largely true beliefs.[34] Second, he has hope, Kant says, that there must be a higher harmonization of things to fulfill this absolute law. The person knows that the moral law demands absolute obedience from him and that the actors behind good actions be rewarded and the perpetrators of bad actions be punished, yet such does not perfectly happen in this life. Therefore, Kant reasons, there must be a holy and just Being who will bring about this eschatological reality and make things right.

There are many other significant rational considerations, besides what going "behind the veil" has told us, about God and evil. I note just four below:

1. A caring, saving God would appear only once in history to save humankind as we know it (He would not make no appearance, because He cares; not more than one, because two or more epiphanies would cause equal numbers of claims

of superior and authoritative revelations of God). Think of Leibniz's "least action" principles here: why have two or more incarnations when one would be needful (cf. Anselm) but sufficient?[35]

2. If God revealed Himself, there would be a textual aspect to that revelation (because that is the most effective way in this world to preserve thoughts the longest without corruption by opinion and false report).

3. God would not necessarily eradicate evil at that exact point when it got to be too much to bear for any single human individual (for we would inductively learn this, and transfer all "bearing" of pain to God immediately upon suffering, which would defeat the end of soul-making and successful diachronic good character formation).

4. God and humans would be called upon in this life to bear pain commensurate with their metaphysical stature (this concerns the *amount* of evil borne and the effect of humans and God bearing evils).

The Rawlsian thought experiment shows us that God, if He exists, would likely create a world in which *both* man and God suffer. What this means, when added to point four (4), just above, is that God would bear an amount of pain and suffering in this world commensurate with the pain and suffering of any human individual. We know that the Passion Week of Christ, the time of the active and passive humility of Christ, meant for Jesus a most excruciating amount of pain and suffering. I have heard of only a few stories of torture and difficulty that begin to approach the agonies of Calvary and the Passion Week that our Lord bore in His body on the cross. I am not saying here that by using this Rawlsian thought experiment, the sufferings of Christ suddenly become clear for the nonbeliever. Clearly they do not. Rather, I am saying that there are significant rational tools by which we can get the nonbeliever to acknowledge that his sense of justice agrees with the Christian story, this story that a good theodicy will no doubt tell and bring to light, in a way consistent with the conclusions that the nonbeliever can come to acknowledge using the "steam" of his reason alone.

Thus, significant evils show themselves to be a rich potential of important *extrinsic goods* in a moral universe in which *we* (*both* theists and atheists) are commanded (by our conscience) to overcome the naturally formed D-belief by using another naturally formed set of beliefs: *M-beliefs* (memory beliefs), and the facts surrounding our awareness of our possession, undeservingly, of a good "life worth living" seen in one's existence formed by the recombination of those M-beliefs.

One epistemological criticism is obvious and demands an answer. Could not the atheist simply respond, "I could just as well say that D-beliefs are the 'natural defense mechanism' against wishful thinking as expressed in 'Meta-M theological beliefs'"? Perhaps so. But Lewis and Plantinga's argument from reason against naturalism helps here: for if naturalism is true, then we could never muster a sufficient justification for thinking that our belief-forming mechanisms were in fact reliable. How can an intrinsically nonintentional, nonreliable, non-goal-directed process produce a wonderfully tuned, intentional, reliable, goal-directed mechanism that spontaneously and involuntarily produces within us largely *true* beliefs? People cannot but rely on their belief-forming mechanisms for all of their thoughts; but again, in effect all of us are saying, "I cannot do this [e.g., thinking] on my own steam; I acknowledge these belief mechanisms come from some other intelligent source outside myself." Truly, God is the vine; we are the branches. Apart from Him, we cannot even think anything justifiably, for we find ourselves groundless without Him. But if we abide in Him, as the transcendental Word from beyond who is also immanent, Immanuel, God with us, we will bear much fruit. Only in Him, as John W. Montgomery summarizes, do we find in perfect fulfillment what our heart longs for: a true value system by which to act; an integrated personhood by which to have peace; a genuine fellowship among which to have importance yet to situate ourselves as one part within the "one body"; an assurance of personal purpose in life by which to have hope; and a fulfillment that is ultimate by which to enjoy table fellowship with the Royal Gardener in the true Garden, at once being restored and, one day, restored and everlasting.[36]

VIII. Conclusion: Yielding a Harvest Pleasing to God

I have given some theodical suggestions, many of which could be situated within a soul-making theodicy. St. Paul says that hope is made possible by suffering. Character and hope development are important ends for the Christian; indeed, these ends are among the most important for us.

If we should suffer exasperating evil, we may find ourselves naturally forming D-beliefs, such as that God does not love us or that He is not good. But, in light of God's purpose for us—to bring us into a loving relationship with Him—God would not leave us without a sufficiently robust defeater for this naturally formed D-belief. We overcome these D-beliefs through Meta-M theological beliefs: we remember God's past goodness and grace to us, and this rightfully defeats the D-belief and gives us reason to *hope* in His deliverance, as even He has suffered—on our behalf—and was delivered from such pains through death and resurrection.

The unbeliever, too, is aware of past goodness and grace toward him by someone or other; thus, he has an undercutting defeater to defeat his D-beliefs. It appears, in fact, that for the Christian, forming D-beliefs about God during suffering gets rebutted by our knowledge of God's past good and loving actions toward us. The nonbeliever in the same circumstance has, we might hypothesize, a different type of defeasibility to his retention of D-beliefs. For the nonbeliever, when he forms D-beliefs about God during unremitting suffering, also knows full well about the good life that, one day, he will call *God's* past goodnesses toward him. He is the recipient, after all, of a life that has been potentially a life better to have been lived than not; how he has actualized his life is largely and most significantly up to him. If God wishes to show His grace to him, that is grace and not justice, so God could not be faulted for not so intervening if He wished.[37] Thus, the nonbeliever has an undercutting defeater against any D-belief that he should entertain.

Reason gives some insights that can be useful in a theodicy to get the nonbeliever to form the belief that he cannot obtain a lasting happy life on his own steam. The result of our Rawlsian thought experiment was the belief that God would favor those worlds in which both God and humans suffer evil. A further belief, possibly formed here, would be that God and humans in this envisaged world would suffer to an extent commensurate with one's own internal metaphysical stature. God does not remain coldly aloof from His world but enters into humanity through His divine Son, takes His own medicine, and plays by the rules that He lays down for us to follow, too.

The results for the soul-making theodicist from our study are twofold. First, evil is shown to be an extrinsic good because when God wills that we ought to mature morally, he simultaneously also wills the *means* to that end. The means for acquiring the property (e.g.) of "courageously bearing pain" is clearly the human *bearing pain* of some sort as a logically necessary condition.[38] Second, we form D-beliefs in the face of evil, which shows, in effect, that we are concerned with human *being* (because one person is caring for another, etc.). But this clearly shows that we value *persons*, meaning that, again, we necessarily will the means to the end of *building* the character ("souls") of people. But if this is so, it acts as a powerful reason to show that we will that evil should exist, since it is a necessary condition for the building of persons. We cannot ultimately complain, therefore, about evils—even deep evils, since these make possible the most treasured virtues and the deeds of heroism, sacrifice, tenacious resiliency to evil, purity of heart in the midst of temptations—since they are necessary conditions for the maturity of persons.[39] Would Frodo and Sam have had opportunity to become the deeply faithful and hopeful people (or *Hobbits*) they were had it not been for *some deep evils of one kind or another* to be overcome (in this case, the evil heart of Sauron and the foul deeds of his minions)?

We believe God has a good reason for the evils that He allows. When we become exasperated with evil, we form D-beliefs, which are not sinful but natural to form and in line with our design plan. But God's past goodness to His human creatures, of which it is reasonable to believe any sound rational human mind would be sufficiently aware, warrants the formation of Meta-M beliefs that *rebut* or *override* the harboring of D-beliefs. That is, past goods overcome present evils and cause us to *hope*, if we persevere, to enjoy the promise of a happy future existence.

It is important *in excelsis* to understand that in the "G. E. Moore" shift argument mentioned in this essay, the human is confronted with two propositions and is asked to consider which is more likely:

1. God exists.
2. Gratuitous evils exist.

There are *a great many evidential lines of argumentation in favor of the theistic God!* What of the best forms of the cosmological argument? What of the most recent teleological arguments from probability and fine tuning? What of the arguments of intelligent design, which Antony Flew says are the evidential strands that recently pushed him from atheism to theism (or Deism)? And what of Norman Malcolm's and Alvin Plantinga's modal ontological arguments? Don't these seem so close to being sound as to compel belief in God? What of the historical unbreakable data about the resurrection of Jesus Christ from the dead? What about the argument from consciousness, intentionality, human freedom, truth, and the success of our belief-forming mechanisms? Taken jointly and cumulatively, all of these evidential paths only strengthen each other and make belief in God probable. The fact is, quite apart from these considerations in this paper, there is a great deal of evidence in favor of (1), above; and if we do our theism first, (2) will not ever be seen to be more probable than (1). What I have focused on in this paper is a situation in which a person with no knowledge or familiarity with the formal aspects of these traditional arguments for God's existence is confronted with the problem of evil. *Even in that case*, I have attempted to show, God has not left us without a clear mark of His good effects upon us, even at the ground level of our belief formation and belief defeat.

Perhaps if I have contributed anything to the continuing debate on theodicy, here it is to give some reasons that even a seasoned Christian will form D-beliefs about God's goodness when evil strikes in his life. God deserves all of our worship and desires to give us a true, lasting happiness. To bring us to worship Him properly and to accept His gracious gift of happiness *freely*, He allows enough pain and suffering so that we form a virtue of *faith* given by His free gift and maintained by the proper functioning of our belief mechanisms over the long haul. God uses evil as a logically necessary willed *means* to the end of soul making, to bring us more and more into the image of Christ and to make us fit vessels for eternal fellowship with Him. The first logical step on the road to Christlikeness, I have maintained, is for a person to form the belief "I cannot secure a lasting happiness on my own steam." God is too merciful to allow us to continue in the illusion that we can solve all of our own problems. But He calls us to be those who keep the garden well. And this is the answer to the Wisdom-Flew Garden Parable: there is a Gardener, and a Royal one at that, who offers us the condescension of cooperation in the task of keeping the garden He loves:

> And when the garden is in its full glory and the [earthly] gardener's contributions to that glory will have been in a sense paltry compared with those of nature. Without life springing from the earth, without rain, light, and heat descending from the sky, he could do nothing. When he has done all, he has merely encouraged here and discouraged there, powers and beauties that have a different source. But his share, though small, is indispensable and laborious.[40]

We will grow the virtue of *love* as we keep the Lord's commands, and we will cultivate the virtue of *hope* as we persevere doing what is right and good, in spite of the ever-present reality and awfulness of evil.[41]

Endnotes

1   See his "The Problem of Evil," in John W. Montgomery, ed., *Evidence for God* (Dallas: Probe Ministries International, 1991), 231–52. Two or so significant differences in my theodicy versus Hick's, spawned by theological differences, are my belief in soteriological exclusivism, judgment of heaven or hell, and nonuniversalism (the belief that there will be some souls that in fact do not come freely ultimately to bow the knee and worship God). Also, I take a middle position between Augustine and Hick on the original state of humans. I believe *pace* Augustine that Adam was not created perfect in the sense of morally perfect (*thoroughly made*). Adam would not be considered as created absolutely morally perfect, for moral perfection in a finite being has significant moral *experience* through which one has lived and made free choices *as a necessary condition*, which is not the case for Adam according to the traditional Genesis account. And yet *pace* Hick I think Adam was not created immature, but that he was properly functioning as he arrived on the scene, was free to

sin or not to sin, and then, if he exercised his will rightly, he would have grown morally and spiritually. God would then have given him another stage, and another, and another, leading him on to perfection. Unfortunately, our first father, at some time after being created, freely sinned.

2 Immanuel Kant, *Critique of Pure Reason*, trans. Norman Kemp Smith (New York: St. Martin's Press, 1965), 635 [A 805].

3 Ibid., 636.

4 Ibid.

5 C. S. Lewis, *Surprised by Joy* (New York: Walker and Company, 1955), 53–55.

6 Alvin Plantinga is famous for his rigorous and compelling Free Will Defense. See *The Nature of Necessity* (Oxford: Oxford University Press, 1974), chap. 9; *God, Freedom and Evil* (Grand Rapids: Eerdmans Publishing Company, 1974).

7 E.g., Hick says that the "Irenaean Intuition" is that it is much better to produce free-willed agents who come to have their own moral characters, through overcoming various temptations and the like over time than to be created by God with a ready-made virtue that has not been so earned. See John Hick's reply to C. Robert Mesle, in *John Hick's Theodicy*, ed. C. Robert Mesle (New York: St. Martin's Press, 1991), 115–34.

8 Note the distinction here between an evil having a God-justifying reason for its permission, and *God's permission* having a God-justifying reason for the permission of that evil. Sometimes God allows evils because they make possible, and perhaps even likely, a greater good.

9 I consider C. S. Lewis's and Alvin Plantinga's argument against naturalism from human cognitive function to spell decisive problems for naturalism and in turn to point strongly toward theism. Being created in the image of God, e.g., would surely include these properties if God intended by creating us that we would freely turn to worship Him (for we would have to know x to worship x). See Lewis, *Miracles*, chaps. 3, 4, 13; Plantinga, *Warrant and Proper Function* (New York: Oxford University Press, 1993), chap. 12; and, Victor Reppert, *C. S. Lewis's Dangerous Idea* (Downers Grove: InterVarsity Press, 2003). I have argued in a similar fashion in Martin, "On Behalf of the Fool: G. E. Moore and Our Knowledge of the Existence of Material Objects," *Sorites* 2 (1996): 41–53.

10 Kant, *Critique of Pure Reason*, 642 [A815].

11 Stephen Wykstra, "The Humean Obstacle to Evidential Arguments from Suffering: On Avoiding the Evils of 'Appearance,'" *International Journal for Philosophy of Religion* 16 (1984), 73–93. Reprinted in R. M. Adams and M. M. Adams, *The Problem of Evil* (New York: Oxford University Press, 1990), 138–160, 141.

12 Ibid.

13 Alvin Plantinga, *Warrant and Proper Function* (New York: Oxford University Press, 1993).

14 St. Augustine, *Confessions*, trans. R. S. Pine-Coffin (Harmondsworth: Penguin, 1961), 21.

15　The example of Great Pumpkinism is from Plantinga. See his "Reason and Belief in God," in *Faith and Rationality*, ed. Alvin Plantinga and Nicholas Wolterstorff (Notre Dame: University of Notre Dame Press, 1983), 16–93, 74.

16　For our purposes, suppose that a belief, as Plato taught us, is a mental assent to a proposition. For more on defeaters, see Plantinga, *Warranted Christian Belief* (New York: Oxford University Press), 359–66.

17　Ibid., 359.

18　Or it would entail God's lack of omnigoodness. Many are of the opinion that if x is not omnigood, x is not *God*; I think for theoretical reasons this opinion is right: God is essentially omnigood. But upon experiencing intense suffering, we *may* be more prone to doubt God's *goodness* rather than His existence, thinking (apparently) that He exists but does not appear (in that situation) to be essentially omnigood. Thanks to David Baggett for making me consider this alternative here.

19　William L. Rowe, *Philosophy of Religion: An Introduction* (Belmont, CA: Wadsworth, 1978), 87.

20　Rowe's E1 refers to a hypothetical fawn who is burned to death in a forest fire; E2 to a five-year-old girl in Michigan in 1986 who is brutally raped and murdered.

21　William Rowe, "The Evidential Argument from Evil: A Second Look," in Daniel Howard-Snyder, ed., *The Evidential Argument from Evil* (Bloomington: Indiana University Press, 1996), 263. Rowe's "second look" includes his giving there another evidential argument from evil couched in Bayes' Theorem that avoids the inductive step.

22　Wykstra, "Humean Obstacle," 152.

23　A "gratuitous" evil is one for which there is not a morally sufficient reason for God to permit. Some theorists have maintained that it may be gratuitous evils are actually necessary conditions for having a world of soul making. See William Hasker, "The Necessity of Gratuitous Evils," *Faith and Philosophy* 9 (1992): 23–44.

24　William Rowe, "The Problem of Evil and Some Varieties of Atheism," *American Philosophical Quarterly* 16 (1979): 335–41; reprinted in Adams and Adams, *Problem of Evil*, 133–34.

25　I'm thinking here of Rom 1:18–20 for starters; Rom 2:14–15 is important here, too, as well as Ps 19:1–6.

26　David Hume, *Dialogues Concerning Natural Religion* (Indianapolis: Hackett Publishing Company, 1980), 68. This quotation is from Part XI, paragraph 2.

27　Nelson Pike, "Hume on Evil," *Philosophical Review* 72 (1963): 180–97; reprinted in Adams and Adams, *Problem of Evil*, 52.

28　John Rawls, *A Theory of Justice* (Cambridge: Harvard University Press, 1973).

29　See Thomas V. Morris, *Our Idea of God* (Downers Grove: InterVarsity Press, 1991), 127–28. Plato's famous argument for immutability in a perfect being (God) is: if God were to change, it must be a change for the better or for the worse. If God changes for the better, then He was not previously perfect. If

He changes for the worse, then He ceases to be perfect. Therefore, God cannot change. See *Republic* Bk. 2 (381b).

30 Alvin Plantinga, "Self Profile," in Peter van Inwagen and James Tomberlin, *Alvin Plantinga* (Dordrecht: Reidel, 1985), 36.

31 Dorothy Sayers, *Christian Letters to a Post-Christian World* (Grand Rapids: Eerdmans Publishing Company, 1969), 14. Cited in Phillip Yancey, *Where Is God When It Hurts?* (Grand Rapids: Zondervan, 1977), 161–62.

32 Cf. the discussion in Lewis's Socratic Club at Oxford with Antony Flew, I. M. Crombie, Basil Mitchell, and R. M. Hare titled "Theology and Falsification," first printed in Antony Flew and Alasdair MacIntyre, eds., *New Essays in Philosophical Theology* (New York: Macmillan, 1955), 96–130.

33 C. S. Lewis, "On Obstinacy in Belief," in *The World's Last Night and Other Essays* (New York: Harvest/HBJ, 1960), 26.

34 For more on this argument from reason against naturalism, see Plantinga, *Warrant and Proper Function* (New York: Oxford University Press, 1993), chap. 12.

35 In this context, it is no surprise to the rational mind, I am claiming, to understand or accept that God would have "a chosen people" to whom He intimately revealed Himself as Creator, Savior, Providence, and Judge.

36 John Warwick Montgomery, *Tractatus Logico-Theologicus* (Bonn: Verlag fur Kultur und Wissenschaft, 2002), 183ff. Proposition 6.

37 This seems to be a minimal duty that a Creator God may have toward His moral creatures that He creates; but even here, thinking of Dostoyevsky's "dear kind God" little girl example (in *The Brothers Karamazov*), God of course also has the idea of *compensation* open to those who truly suffer lives that are better not to have been lived than otherwise. Also, with respect to the goods served by God's permission of such evils, there may be other avenues that outstrip our knowledge but that are *pellucidly clear and intended* by the omniscient and omnibenevolent God to apply in such relatively few circumstances of the serious human sufferer of intense and long-lasting pain or suffering.

38 You could of course say that the human could just seem to be in pain. But seeming to be in pain and being in pain are indistinguishable and therefore functionally equivalent in human experience. Also, God would not be a deceiver on such a vast scale in a world so that almost universally our belief-forming mechanisms would tell us that we were experiencing pain daily, when in actuality there was *no* pain in that world.

39 Thanks to Keith Yandell for this point. See his "Evil and Tragedy," *International Journal for Philosophy of Religion* 36 (1994), 1–26; 25.

40 C. S. Lewis, *The Four Loves* (London: Fontana, 1963), 107–8.

41 I am indebted to John Warwick Montgomery, David Baggett, and Melanie Martin for their pruning in earlier drafts of this paper.

The Natural Law Foundations of Lord Denning's Thought and Work

Andrew Phang

Prologue

It is a great honour for me to present this essay to Professor John Warwick Montgomery on the occasion of his seventy-fifth birthday. We celebrate his life; we also celebrate his immense capacity for interdisciplinary work (as witnessed, *inter alia,* by the fact that he holds 11 earned degrees from a number of jurisdictions and disciplines) as well as his prodigious output of scholarly writing (at last count some 45 books—in five languages—and more than 100 scholarly articles).

This essay was a paper delivered at Buckingham University on 23 January 1999 in a symposium celebrating the one hundredth birthday of one of the greatest English judges of the twentieth century, Lord Denning; and it was subsequently published in *Denning Law Journal* 159 (1999). The full (and much lengthier) version of this paper was subsequently published online (in two parts) in the *Global Journal of Classical Theology*. I am grateful to the *Denning Law Journal* for permission to republish the (first-mentioned) essay in this work.[1]

The occasion on which this paper was delivered was itself one that will be forever etched in my memory. Although not everyone agreed with Lord Denning's views, we did hold one thing in common—that he was a man of outstanding intellect who cared deeply for others. Everyone, myself included, had a "Denning story"—stories of the warmth and kindness of the man, often displayed to others at whom society would not take a second look. This was the measure of the man—of his greatness as well as of his care and concern for others. Sadly, Lord Denning passed away some six weeks later, on 6 March 1999. Had he lived to greet the new millennium, he would literally have been witness to three centuries. Sadly, this was not to be. However, his legacy in his writings, judgments, and (above all) care and concern for others lives on as a legacy that few will match in the legal (or, indeed, any other) sphere.

I. Introduction

There is a constant tension in the law between certainty on the one hand and fairness on the other. While they are not necessarily incompatible with each other, there are numerous occasions when conflicts do occur. Not surprisingly, therefore, the focus in English and (probably) Commonwealth law is on the former. This explains, in large part, the rule-oriented and positivistic nature of law in these various legal systems.[2] The primary concern in this regard is with the maintenance of the objective and, consequently, of stability, eschewing any descent into the vagueness and subjectivity that a contrary approach might entail. There is, in other words, no necessary connection as such between the law on the one hand and morality on the other. While there is much merit in this approach inasmuch as it avoids unnecessary uncertainty once the applicable legal rule(s) have been identified, it loses force if it can be demonstrated that the law is premised on an objective set of higher-order morality.

Lord Denning's thought and work (as encompassed within both his legal judgments and extrajudicial writings and lectures) in fact evince an approach that is based on the assumption that there are in fact objective and universal values. His is a *natural law* approach, which is premised in no uncertain terms upon a religious foundation—or, to be more precise, on a Christian foundation. For him religion and law are inextricably connected together in a symbiotic relationship. There is, to Lord Denning, a higher (and objective) law, against which all legal rules and principles have to be measured. The objection from subjectivity and relativity does not, therefore, bother him. And this approach is evident throughout his thought and work. In the sphere of binding precedent or *stare decisis*, for example, Lord Denning always championed fairness at the expense of certainty, although the doctrine itself was concerned more with the latter than the former.[3] And such an approach also characterised his activist approach toward the interpretation of statutes.[4] In the sphere of substantive law, he was a constant advocate of fairness, even if this meant that the existing legal rules had to be either circumvented or even abrogated altogether. All this was, of course, anathema to the general approach embodied in the Commonwealth in general and England in particular.[5] Indeed, Lord Denning has been criticised (on occasion even trenchantly) precisely because of his alleged iconoclasm.[6] One oft-cited criticism has been that his approach has engendered excessive uncertainty in the law—an uncertainty that has undermined the adjudicative process as well as the attainment of justice. The present essay argues otherwise; its purpose is threefold. I will first outline Lord Denning's ethical and religious beliefs. I will then briefly explore how his ethical and religious beliefs are manifested (in the process of *application*, in particular) in the law. Finally, I will attempt to assess not only the influences on but also (and more importantly) the possible justifications for Denning's beliefs.

II. Lord Denning's Ethical and Religious Beliefs

In General

As already mentioned, the stock criticism of Lord Denning's thought and work has centred on their perceived arbitrariness and the alleged uncertainty that results.[7]

As I shall attempt to demonstrate, these "popular" perceptions of Denning's thought and work could not be further from the truth. Denning, as already mentioned, *perceived his thought and work to be based on the objective truth to be located in the religious foundations of Christianity*.[8] It is, however, perhaps ironic to note that Denning himself always claimed to be wary of theory and endorsed experience and practice instead.[9]

Turning to Denning's specific enunciations of his beliefs, in a brief typescript titled "What Life Has Taught Me,"[10] Lord Denning commences by stating that "[t]he most important thing that life has taught me is to believe in God." He then proceeds to state that this belief is due both to his upbringing and to his experience "in going through life."[11]

Insofar as the experiential aspect is concerned, he says that "[m]y experience as a lawyer and as a judge has verified what I was taught about God." To him, law and religion are inextricably connected: "The aim of the law is to see that truth is observed and that justice is done between man and man."[12] On another occasion Lord Denning observed that "without religion there can be no morality and without morality there can be no law."[13]

As to the question as to what constitute "truth" and "justice," Lord Denning is of the view that they are "eternal" and that they are the product of a person's *spirit*.[14] And as to how the "right spirit" is created in man, Lord Denning is of the view that "[t]hat is the province of religion"—in particular, the Christian religion. He elaborates thus: "religion concerns *the spirit* in man *whereby he is able to recognise what is truth and what is justice: whereas law is only the application*, however imperfectly, of truth and justice in our everyday affairs."[15]

Indeed, "the spirit in Man, when it reaches the highest and wisest plane, is but the reflection of the spirit of God." And in an amazingly candid passage, Lord Denning states:

> I do know that in the great experiences of life, and indeed
> in the small ones too, such strength as I have is of God, and
> the weakness is mine. Need I enumerate the experiences?
> Take the hard things. When faced with a task on which
> great issues depend; when high hopes lie shattered; when
> anxiety gnaws deep; or when overwhelmed by grief; where
> can I turn for help but to God? Or take the joyful things: A
> hard task attempted or done; the happiness of family life;
> or the beauty of nature; where can I turn for thankfulness
> but to God? All experiences convince me, not only that
> God is ever-present, but also that it is by contact with the
> spirit of God that the spirit in Man reaches its highest and
> wisest plane.[16]

The "spirit of God" Denning refers to is probably a reference to the Holy Spirit, who is also described in the Bible, *inter alia*, as a "counselor."[17]

In an address to the Medico-Legal Society, Lord Denning elaborated on the concept of "justice"[18] by stating that it "is *what the right-thinking members of the community believe to be fair*."[19] The upshot of all this is that:

lawyers should be men of religion: and speaking generally that has always been the case in this country. It is the reason why the common law of England is so great. The law has been moulded for centuries by Judges who have been brought up in the Christian faith. The precepts of religion, consciously or unconsciously, have been their guide in the administration of justice.[20]

In a message given to the Quarterly Meeting of the Lawyers' Christian Fellowship held at the Law Society on 22 May 1950, titled "The Influence of Religion on Law,"[21] Denning L. J. (as he then was) observed that "[i]n the days when the Bible was first put into English the Judges laid down rules which were undoubtedly influenced by Bible teaching."[22] More importantly, perhaps, he points (in the same message) to "the more fundamental teaching of our Lord:"[23] "the Gospel of Love,"[24] that is, that one is to love God first and then our neighbour as ourselves.[25] However, "[t]his is a precept of religion, not of morals nor of law."[26] Denning was of the view, nevertheless, that "it is not unrelated to them,"[27] for "[i]n social organisation, love finds its primary expression through justice":[28] "The two—love and justice—are interdependent."[29]

Insofar as societal welfare is concerned, in a lecture delivered as far back as 1953,[30] Denning argued that "the Welfare State has come into being by a true application of Christian principles, but ... there is a danger of its being mishandled and abused by people who have no knowledge of those principles and seek only their own advantage."[31] Denning argues that the recapture of love and service through Christian principles is essential to combat such abuse.

In the Law

1. General

What precisely did Lord Denning stand for in the more explicitly legal realm? He was, in fact, a passionate advocate of many institutions that are traditional elements underlying the Rule of Law: for instance, the independence of the judiciary[32] and various freedoms (including freedom of the press[33]). One overarching theme centres, in fact, on the need to restrain the misuse of power.[34] He also advocated equality for women,[35] although here writers have argued that Denning's judgments (particularly in the sphere of family law) have fallen short of the mark.[36]

Although often perceived as radical, Denning did not advocate rampant activism. For example, referring to the reform of family law in 1977, he was of the view that any reform would be too complex and widespread for judges to handle, although he opined, "Judges can work on a minor scale within the existing law."[37]

In a later work Denning vigorously denied the charge of being politically motivated; he emphatically stated: "I deny the charge. Some decisions are fraught with political consequences—such as decisions about trade unions or local authorities or ministers. *Whichever way the case goes, one side or the other will say it is a 'political' decision. That is their way of saying that it is a policy decision with which they disagree.*"[38]

2. The Law of Contract

This area is the primary illustrative focus, although I hasten to add that constraints of space allow only a few areas of contract law to be considered.[39]

A more general observation by Lord Denning himself may be apposite before turning to the more specific areas of contract law proper. Denning observes that insofar as the law of contract was concerned:

> [T]he influence of the Church was immense: because
> the Church courts assumed jurisdiction in matters of
> conscience. Originally in English law a promise was not
> enforceable unless is [sic.] was hedged about with the
> formality of a seal. But the teaching of the Church was in
> favour of rejecting formalities and insisting on good faith.
> The just man is "he that sweareth to his neighbour and
> disappointeth him not, though it were to his own hin-
> drance."[40] If a man made a promise and did not keep it, the
> ecclesiastical courts would punish him for breach of faith.[41]

Unfortunately, however, contract law today has been secularized, with the emphasis on rationalism and individualism,[42] and this may well explain why courts have been unable to mediate objectively the tension, mentioned at the outset of this article, between certainty and technicality on the one hand and fairness on the other. As Professor Berman pertinently argues, a return to the objective religious foundations will enable a new and more coherent theory of contract law to be developed.[43] Denning would surely agree with this suggestion.

Turning to the more specific areas of contract law proper, the doctrine of consideration is familiar to all law students. Yet it is not without problems.[44] Indeed, a strict application of it often leads to injustice.[45] This is particularly so, perhaps, in the situation concerning the promise to take part payment in full discharge of a debt already owed. This has, in accordance with the leading authorities, notably that of the House of Lords in *Foakes* v. *Beer*,[46] been traditionally held not to constitute consideration. This being the case, the various exceptions that mitigate possible injustice become of signal importance. In this regard, the most significant exception is the doctrine of promissory estoppel, which has its origins in the seminal judgment of Denning J. (as he then was) in *Central London Property Trust Ltd.* v. *High Trees House Ltd.*[47] Briefly put, if one person makes to another an unambiguous representation that he or she will not enforce his or her strict legal rights, intending that other party to act on it, and that party does act on it, then the representor/promisor will not be allowed to resile from his or her promise if it would be inequitable to do so.[48]

The *High Trees* case is commonly hailed as a landmark in the common law of contract.[49] However, it was also a radical step forward. To Denning himself, the *High Trees* case "helped to narrow [the] gap" between the "strict rules and the social necessities of the 20th century,"[50] thus achieving justice in the process.

Leaving aside certain problematic aspects of the doctrine,[51] when all is said and done, however, Denning reminds us once again that the doctrine of promissory estoppel is based on *moral foundations*; it is a doctrine that aids in the attainment of justice and the avoidance of the technicality and injustice that have been encrusted around the doctrine of consideration. Indeed, of the doctrine of consideration, Denning says that "[i]t has been replaced by the better precept: 'My word is my bond,' irrespective of whether there is consideration to support it."[52] More significantly, perhaps, there are resonances of Christian principles when he proceeds to add thus: "Once a man gives a promise or assurance to his *neighbour*—on which his *neighbour* relies—he should not be allowed to go back on it. In stating the principle, and its extensions, the lawyers use the archaic word 'estoppel.' I would prefer to put it in language which the ordinary man understands: It is a principle of *justice and of equity*."[53]

Lord Denning was also very active in the sphere of implied terms, which he viewed as centring on the demands of what he termed "simple justice";[54] and he made no secret that in implying terms, courts were, in effect, "[filling] in the gaps."[55] To this end, his assertion, in *Liverpool City Council* v. *Irwin*, that the courts could imply terms whenever it was "reasonable" into the contract is not in the least surprising.[56] Although this general principle was rejected by the House of Lords,[57] Denning actually won a victory of sorts, for in the *Liverpool City Council* case itself, the House drew a distinction between "terms implied in fact" and "terms implied in law,"[58] the test of reasonableness and public policy applying to the latter, which constituted a broader category of terms implied in a particular *class* of contracts, even if this would be contrary to the actual or presumed intentions of the parties concerned. What was particularly interesting was the ambiguity of the language utilised,[59] which suggests that the House was not comfortable with the distinction, in particular, the criterion of reasonableness. Denning was nevertheless quick to seize upon this distinction and (naturally) gave it his full endorsement.[60] This was not a "full victory" as such, but it represented some headway, so to speak. What is particularly interesting about this distinction in general and the category of "terms implied in law" in particular is the focus on the concept of "reasonableness" that, in turn, correlates to Denning's idea of what is "justice."[61] And "justice" is, as we have seen, ultimately linked to Denning's own Christian values.[62]

Lord Denning is perhaps best known for his judgments geared toward aiding (in particular) consumers with respect to exception clauses. This was not, however, always the case. Denning, in fact, lamented his involvement in the decision of *L'Estrange* v. *Graucob*, which held that a contracting party is, in the absence of fraud or misrepresentation,[63] bound by exception clauses in a contract on appending his or her signature to it.[64]

But things rapidly and radically changed by the time Denning was appointed to the bench. The famous doctrine of fundamental breach as a rule of law finds its genesis with Denning himself.[65] It may, in fact, be said that the underlying impetus for Denning's approach toward exception clauses stemmed from the perception of the need to prevent abuse, which (in turn) is embodied in Christian doctrine.[66] However, this doctrine was finally (and decisively) rejected by the House of Lords in *Photo Production Ltd. v. Securicor Transport Ltd.*[67]

Notwithstanding the sounding of the death knell for fundamental breach as a rule of law in the *Photo Production* case,[68] Denning could take more than scant consolation in the enactment (in 1977) of the Unfair Contract Terms Act.[69]

On an even broader level is Lord Denning's controversial statement of principle with respect to inequality of bargaining power that he enunciated in *Lloyd's Bank Ltd. v. Bundy.*[70] Denning's statement of principle has often been read as embodying too general and vague a standard that only emphasises inequality of bargaining power and does away with the necessity for some form of wrongdoing on the part of defendant. It has therefore been rejected by the courts in no uncertain terms.[71] However, it should be noted that *prior* to enunciating the above statement of principle, Lord Denning in fact embarked on a fairly detailed survey of the existing law: in particular, the existing categories, all of which in fact involve some form of wrongdoing by the defendant.[72] It is true, however, that Denning does state that there is no real need for proof of "any wrongdoing."[73] However, it is suggested that this is itself inconclusive because Denning is utilising the concept of "wrongdoing" in the sense of the intention to bring distress to the other party, as opposed to a standard embodied in the law itself.

There is no reason in principle, in fact, why the courts should not adopt a broad approach analogous to that advocated by Lord Denning in *Lloyd's Bank Ltd. v. Bundy.*[74] I have ventured to suggest elsewhere that the development of the doctrine of unconscionability may be a viable alternative instead.[75]

Another area where Lord Denning thought that justice ought to be done pertained to contracts to confer benefits on third parties.[76] Indeed, in an extrajudicial context, he argues that the departure from the Christian ethic in the nineteenth century in favour of a philosophy of giving untrammelled reign to the concept of free will had now been discredited and that, therefore, "it is to be hoped that soon there will be restored the principle that a person who makes a solemn promise must keep it" and hence, there should be recognised contracts for the benefit of third parties.[77] Denning thus strenuously attempted to effect a change in the law in this particular context, but to no avail.[78]

Recent (and not so recent) events appear, however, to have vindicated Denning's views in this particular sphere of contract law.[79]

3. Other Areas

It will be seen that the basic (substantive) pattern underlying Denning's judgments in the law of contract is replicated in other areas of the law.

Constraints of space preclude an even cursory discussion, and the reader is directed to the various learned articles on specific topics in this volume (i.e., *Denning Law Journal* 159). However, it might be very briefly mentioned that Denning's various seminal contributions[80] have almost always been marked by his religious beliefs. For example, he viewed the law of negligence as embodying a moral element,[81] and *explicitly* refers to Christianity in the context of Lord Atkin's seminal "neighbour principle" enunciated in *Donoghue v. Stevenson*.[82] More generally, his views on sexual morality (though criticised[83]) are entirely consistent with Christian morality.

However, Denning has been often trenchantly criticised for his approach toward (in particular) trade unions in the sphere of labour law.[84] Even here, however, it could be argued (although this is not to state that he was invariably correct) that he was concerned to curb the *abuse* of power, thus preserving the rights of individual workers as well as the structure of the nation itself. This is not, of course, to state that Denning was always right. However, the other extreme should also be avoided, namely, the argument to the effect that Denning was irretrievably (and, worse still, irrationally) biased against trade unions.

Indeed, it may be said that Denning also brought a realistic and practical view to bear on the entire issue of submission to the authority of the State in a *balanced* fashion, for he was of the view that the State ultimately "derives its authority from God."[85] Equally well, Denning saw his general emphasis on the importance of individual freedom as entirely consistent with his adoption of Christian principles.[86]

But how is the balance[87] between individual freedom and societal order to be achieved? The answer has in fact been referred to above: through Christian principles. However, one may ask, why are Christian principles appropriate unless they embody objective truth? My answer is that they do, and this is a proposition that we shall be returning to below.[88]

Lord Denning's Attitude Toward Other Religions

What, then, about Denning's attitude toward other religions and religious groups? His basic philosophy is that there ought to be freedom of religion.[89] Indeed, his openness toward other religions is displayed, for instance, in his exhortation that "Christians and Jews should come together in the search for truth."[90] All this is despite the clear difference between Jewish and Christian beliefs, which Denning frankly and matter-of-factly acknowledges.[91] Indeed, in *Landmarks in the Law*, Denning devotes a significant portion of his book to the Jews.[92]

Insofar as *Christianity* is concerned, Lord Denning is firmly of the view that "[w]e have reached the point . . . that whilst the Christian beliefs still form the foundation of our way of life, as I trust they always will, they are not to be enforced by law[93] but by teaching and example."[94]

III. On Christian Influences and Apologetics

Introduction

Given the secular cast of societies in general and philosophy in particular, it is by no means unreasonable for the reader to ask why Lord Denning's natural law approach premised on Christianity should be persuasive in the first instance. Although constraints of space preclude an extended discussion, I shall attempt to set out (albeit in the briefest of fashions) some reasons as to why Lord Denning's stance is not in the least untenable. These reasons were never, explicitly at least, utilised by Denning, although I am sure that he would not disapprove of them. A brief note first on influences, however, would not be amiss.

The Influence of William Temple[95]

Denning does consistently refer to the work of the late Archbishop of Canterbury, William Temple.[96] Indeed, Denning once described Temple as "one of the greatest thinkers of the present century."[97]

To take but one instance, Denning recounts how Temple, in an address at the Inns of Court, commenced his message by saying, "I cannot say that I know much about the law, having been far more interested in justice."[98] Denning endorsed this view by criticising positivism and argued that people obeyed the law because they felt a "moral obligation" to do so.[99]

There is insufficient space and time to deal with William Temple's philosophy. But it is important at least to state that his philosophy was very consistent with Denning's: both were based on Christian principles, and it is no wonder, therefore, that Denning constantly cited Temple's work and philosophy. Indeed, I would add that Temple's work and philosophy are close (as I recently discovered) to the principles that I briefly allude to in the next section: in particular, with respect to the pervasively real (yet seemingly intractable) problem of how one is to reconcile the universal with the particular.[100] Another significant point Temple deals with (in my view at least) is the role of the Holy Spirit in the life of the individual.[101]

The Relevance of Christian Apologetics

In an age characterised by pluralism, Christianity is by no means an attractive option. Even the adoption of the classical natural law approach (perhaps best embodied within the work of Aquinas,[102] and which comes [it is suggested] closest to what Lord Denning would probably endorse) would necessarily entail a systematic defence of the Christian faith (popularly encompassed within the—perhaps semantically misleading—rubric of "Christian apologetics"), lest the embrace of Christianity and its underlying values be thought to be mere assertions without any rational basis whatsoever.

Constraints of space again preclude an even cursory discussion, but it is suggested that, as preliminary arguments, one would have to consider arguments centring on the existence of God,[103] the creation-evolution debate,[104] and (in a related vein) the issue of probabilities.[105] It should also be mentioned that these various issues and arguments are themselves also linked across disciplines.[106]

More directly, one would have to consider the claims of Christianity itself. These would include the arguments of C. S. Lewis with respect to the claims of Jesus,[107] arguments with regard to the authenticity of the Bible,[108] as well as the arguments demonstrating why Jesus was in fact resurrected from the dead.[109] It should also be mentioned that Christianity enables the seemingly abstract and universal concept of God to be objectively real, thus integrating the universal and the particular. This occurs in at least two related ways. First, as Jesus Christ claimed to have come from God the Father, to be the Son of God, indeed God Himself, but in the form of man (in order to die for sinners and to be thereafter resurrected from the dead and to ascend to heaven), we find that, if this claim be established, there is the confluence (indeed, unity) of both the infinite and particular in one Person. In addition, the universal and the particular meet inasmuch as the divinity of God (in Jesus Christ) is also testable, both through logic and historical argument.

On a practical level, it is suggested that the Holy Spirit is also part of the Godhead of the Trinity and provides the individualised guidance to each person *transcending* space and time. *Truth* is thus imparted in an *individualised* fashion, and we are no longer left with the frustration that stems from the absence of linkage between the universal and the particular that gives rise (in turn) to an inability to test an abstract belief and a contrasting resignation to (and even feeling of despair in) individual relativity. Indeed, in *Jesus Himself*, as we have already seen, the universal and the particular are also united.

Much more remains to be unpacked, but I hope to have made out an at least *prima facie* case for *consideration* of the Christian natural law alternative. More importantly, I hope to have demonstrated that

Denning's Christian natural law approach is by no means without any basis and that the charge of personal preference omits, amongst other things, to take into account the individualised guidance of the Holy Spirit that I am sure must have been an integral part of Denning's thought and work.

IV. Conclusion

The traditional (or at least popular) view of Lord Denning is that of a maverick: a judge who believes passionately in justice, but who often circumvents the law in order to achieve what he perceives to be justice in the case in hand. Put this way, the entire enterprise becomes a contradiction in terms, for the law should not be undermined if justice, the very object of the law itself, is to be achieved. But this argument presupposes that the law never goes wrong and, in the context of the common law and its methodology, this is a dangerous assumption to make: if nothing else, then because human beings are not infallible.

How, then, is the judge to know when (and when not) to depart from law that has somehow gone "wrong"?[110] This, in fact, entails the adoption of a natural law approach, which is to be contrasted with positivism, which does not contemplate any *necessary* connection between law and morality. However, the options available to positivism, insofar as the *legitimacy* of the law is concerned, are not particularly attractive—mere circularity or infinite regress—and it is, with respect, no answer to say that pragmatism demands that we have to arrive at a particular decision in any event. Any recourse to a pragmatic argument brings us dangerously close to (if not within the very depths of) personal preference. This is what led (in the main) to the demise of American Realism and is very much the cause of the woes facing critical legal studies. Neither is liberalism's recourse to frameworks of ground rules, persuasive.[111] This is simply the distinction between procedure and substance, and it is, with respect, woefully inadequate since the law is all of a piece.[112]

However, can the natural law argument be *justified?* Is it not subject to the same critiques canvassed in the preceding paragraph? It is submitted that it is not, provided it is premised on *Christianity.* Such a type of natural law is testable (both logically and historically) and has a functionality that lies, in the main, in the concept of the Trinity. The arguments are certainly at least as plausible as any on offer. And this is the approach that Lord Denning adopts. What appears like an arbitrary hunch is (in substance) a recourse not only to the value system underlying Christianity but also a receipt of supernatural guidance by the Holy Spirit. But this is *not* to state that such an approach *guarantees* even close-to-perfect results. If nothing else, it is also dependent on one crucial element that God does not control, and chooses not to, our freewill: our decision to submit the problems and questions to Him for a cooperative solution and not wanting to take the law, as it were, into our own hands.

Lord Denning's greatest contribution, in my view, was not merely "the law" which he left behind but, rather, the spirit of justice that was guided by a supernatural force. Denning never wavered from the conviction that this was always so. More importantly, he persevered right until his retirement, and has left a legacy of immeasurable proportions not only in the materials of the law itself but (more importantly) in the minds *and* hearts of not only those who are legally trained but also all those who are genuinely and passionately interested in justice. He brought a particularity and reality to the abstract concept of justice that tangibly demonstrated what it was all about.

In his reply to the various valedictory speeches made upon his retirement as master of the rolls, Denning ended thus: "I wish I could say, as a great man did once, 'I fought a good fight; I finished the course; I have kept the faith.'"[113] He can, and ought to, say it.

Endnotes

1   The full version of this highly abbreviated paper has now been published online (in two parts) as "A Passion for Justice—the Natural Law Foundations of Lord Denning's Thought and Work" in the (2005) 5(1) *Global Journal of Classical Theology* and (2006) 5(2) *Global Journal of Classical Theology* (available, at the time of writing, at www.trinitysem.edu/journal/5-1/3_Part_%20 1_%20Phang.htm and www.trinitysem.edu/journal/5-2/PhangPart2.htm, respectively). Insofar as this particular paper is concerned, I am grateful to Ms. Rosemary Dunhill, county archivist, Hampshire Record Office, and her staff for all their help in retrieving materials from the Denning archive; to Ms. Sheena McMurtrie, editor of the *Denning Law Journal*, for all her kind-

ness and assistance; as well as to Mr. Aqbal Singh for his comments and encouragement. All errors, however, remain mine alone.

2 See e.g., P. S. Atiyah and R. S. Summers, *Form and Substance in Anglo-American Law* (Clarendon Press, 1987); P. Devlin, *The Enforcement of Morals* (Oxford University Press, 1965) at chap. 3, esp. at pp. 44 and 51; and A. Phang, "Positivism in the English Law of Contract" (1992) 55 *M.L.R.* 102.

3 For an extended discussion by Lord Denning himself, see Lord Denning, *The Discipline of Law* (Butterworths, 1979) at Pt. 7. However, Denning was not against the doctrine of precedent because he championed subjective judicial fiat. On the contrary, he is at pains to point out that the doctrine is still important: see at p. 314.

4 See generally Denning, *supra* n.3 at pp. 9–22. See also Lord Denning, *The Closing Chapter* (Butterworths, 1983), at p. 97 *et seq.*, and where, *inter alia*, there is also biblical reference to adherence to the spirit, rather than the letter, of the law.

5 The position in the United States of America is far more substantive: see e.g., Atiyah & Summers, *supra* n.2.

6 And see Lord Denning himself: "The Way of an Iconoclast" (1959–1960) 5 *J.S.P.T.L.* (N.S.) 77 (this address by Lord Denning was also published in [1960] 3 *Sydney Law Rev.* 209).

7 The literature on this point is voluminous; and see generally the following excellent collections of essays: P. Robson and P. Watchman (eds.), *Justice, Lord Denning and the Constitution* (Gower, 1981) and J. L. Jowell and P. W. B. McAuslan (eds.), *Lord Denning: The Judge and the Law* (Sweet & Maxwell, 1984). The former collection is far more critical although the latter does not pull its punches either. See also Lord Wilberforce, "The Academics and Lord Denning" (1985) 5 *O.J.L.S.* 439 at p. 439.

8 See also Lord Edmund-Davies, "Lord Denning: Christian Advocate and Judge" [1986] *Denning L.J.* 41 at pp. 41 and 47.

9 See e.g., Lord Justice Denning, "The Independence of the Judges" in B. W. Harvey (ed.), 7 *Lawyer and Justice—a collection of addresses by judges and jurists to the Holdsworth Club of The University of Birmingham* (Sweet & Maxwell, 1978), 55–69 at pp. 56 and 62; and by the same author, *The Changing Law* (Stevens & Sons Limited, 1953), 15–16 as well as *The Family Story* (Butterworths, 1981), 240. Though cf. his article, "The Universities and Law Reform" (1947–1951) I *J.S.P.T.L.* (N.S.) 258 at pp. 268–69.

10 On file at the Hampshire Record Office.

11 See also A. T. Denning, "Why I Believe in God" (transcript of a talk delivered on the B.B.C. Home Service, Tuesday, 14 September, 1943 at 10.15 p.m.; on file at the Hampshire Record Office). All references hereafter will be to page numbers of the transcript itself. See also Lord Edmund-Davies, *supra* n. 8 at p. 41, where the learned Law Lord refers to Denning's Service as a churchwarden as well as member of the Parishional Church Council. Denning was of course also for many years President of the Lawyers' Christian Fellowship. See, further, Denning, *The Family Story, supra* n. 9 at pp. vi and 180–83.

12 See Denning, "Why I Believe in God" *supra* n. 11 at p. 2. See also Denning, *infra* n. 21 at p. 8.

13 See Lord Denning, "The Right Standards of Conduct" (1957) *Law Society's Gazette*, 609. This conviction is indeed often repeated in his extrajudicial writings.

14 See Denning, *supra*. n. 10 (emphasis added). See also Denning, "Why I Believe in God" *supra* n.11 at p. 2.

15 See Denning, *supra* n. 10 (emphasis added). See also Denning, "Why I Believe in God" *supra* n.11 at p. 3. See, further, by the same author, "Address Delivered by the Rt. Hon. The Lord Denning, Master of the Rolls, at the Annual Service on October 6th" (Lawyers' Christian Fellowship, 1977; on file at the Hampshire Record Office; hereafter referred to as "Address 1977").

16 See Denning, *supra* n. 10 (part of this passage is handwritten). See also Denning, "Why I Believe in God" *supra* n. 11 at p. 4.

17 See John 14:16,26; 15:26; and 16:7. See also Denning, "Address 1977" *supra* n. 15.

18 Interestingly, in his coat of arms, Denning took as his motto, "*Fiat justitia*" *viz.*, "Let justice be done," although he later found the actual origin of this motto to be rather dubious: see Denning, *The Family Story, supra* n. 9 at p. 172.

19 See Lord Denning, "The Freedom of the Individual To-day" (1977) 45 *Medico-Legal J.* 49 at p. 55 (emphasis added).

20 See Denning, "Why I Believe in God" *supra* n. 11 at p. 3. See also, by the same author, "The Influence of Religion" in *The Changing Law, supra* n. 9 at p. 109 (hereafter "Influence").

21 In pamphlet form (Bletchley Printers Ltd., 1950) (hereafter "The Influence of Religion on Law"). See also, by the same author, "Influence" *supra* n. 20.

22 See Denning, "The Influence of Religion on Law" *supra* n. 21 at p. 2.

23 Ibid., 3.

24 Ibid.

25 Citing from Luke 10:25–28: see ibid. See also *infra* n. 82.

26 Ibid.

27 Ibid.

28 Ibid.

29 Ibid.

30 See Sir Alfred Denning, *The Christian Approach to the Welfare State* (The 17th Shaftesbury Lecture, The Chaseton Press of H. Williams & Son, Ltd., 1953).

31 Ibid., 3.

32 See e.g., Denning, "The Independence of the Judges" *supra* n. 9 and, by the same author, "The Independence and Impartiality of the Judges" (1954) 71 *S.A.L.J.* 345.

33 See e.g., Sir Alfred Denning, *The Road to Justice* (Stevens & Sons Limited, 1955) at chap. 4 and, by the same author, "Law and Life in Our Time" (1967) 41 *Australian L.J.* 224 at p. 227 — although the learned judge correctly points to the need for *balance* so that the freedom not be abused.

34 And see generally Denning, "Restraining the Misuse of Power," in *Jubilee Lectures Celebrating the Foundation of the Faculty of Law, University of Birmingham* (Wildy & Sons Ltd., 1981) and, by the same author, "Misuse of Power"

(1981) 55 *Australian L.J.* 720. Reference may also be made to Lord Denning's more recent works: see e.g., *The Due Process of Law* (Butterworths, 1980) and *What Next in the Law* (Butterworths, 1982) especially at pt. 8.

35 See e.g., "The Rights of Women" in Denning, *The Changing Law, supra* n. 9 at pp. 79–98 and, by the same author, *The Equality of Women* (Eleanor Rathbone Memorial Lecture, Liverpool University Press, 1960).

36 See e.g., M. D. A. Freeman, "Family Matters" in chap. 4 of Jowell & McAuslan, *supra* n. 7.

37 See *"Denning and Scarman:* A conversation between Lord Denning, Master of the Rolls, and Lord Justice Scarman" (B.B.C. Broadcasting Corporation Transcript, Radio Three, Talks and Documentaries Department, recorded Wednesday 19 January 1977, Transmission: Thursday 3 March 1977, on file at the Hampshire Record Office), 9; Denning, significantly in my view, then proceeds to talk about consumer protection as well.

38 See Denning, *What Next in the Law, supra* n. 34 at p. 333 (emphasis added). See also, by the same author, *The Family Story, supra* n. 9 at p. 28.

39 The reader is directed to Professor Atiyah's perceptive overview published shortly after Lord Denning's retirement: see P. S. Atiyah, "Contract and Tort" in chap. 2 of Jowell & McAuslan, *supra* n. 7.

40 Citing from Psalm 15:4.

41 See Denning, *supra* n. 21 at p.7. See also, by the same author, "Influence" *supra* n. 20 at pp. 104–5.

42 See generally Harold J. Berman, "The Religious Sources of General Contract Law: An Historical Perspective" (1986) *Journal of Law and Religion* 4 (reprinted in chap. 7 of Harold J. Berman, *Faith and Order: The Reconciliation of Law and Religion* [Scholars Press, 1993]).

43 See Berman, *supra* n. 42.

44 And see the calls for abolition by the English Law Revision Committee in 1937 (Cmd. 5449). See also A. Phang, "Consideration at the Crossroads" (1991) 107 *L.Q.R.* 21.

45 The recent development in *Williams* v. *Roffey Bros. & Nicholls (Contractors) Ltd.* [1991] 1 Q.B. 1 has not, however, significantly mitigated such injustice; see, in particular, *Re Selectmove* [1995] 1 W.L.R. 474. See also A. Phang, "Acceptance by Silence and Consideration Reined In" [1994] *L.M.C.L.Q.* 336.

46 (1884) 9 App. Cas. 605, reaffirming the so-called rule in *Pinnel's Case* (1602) 5 Co. Rep. 117a.

47 [1947] K.B. 180.

48 This is, of course, a rough description: much more elaboration is required.

49 [1947] K.B. 180. See also Denning, *supra* n. 3 at pp. 197–223 (an extended account by Lord Denning himself).

50 See Denning, *ibid.,* 197.

51 E.g., the concept of detriment (which Denning eschewed: see e.g., *W. J. Alan & Co* v. *El Nasr Export and Import Co.* [1972] 2 Q.B. 189 at p. 213; but cf. Atiyah, *supra* n. 39 at p. 35 and A. B. L. Phang, *Cheshire, Fifoot and Furmston's Law of Contract—Second Singapore and Malaysian Edition* (Butterworths Asia, 1998) at pp. 202–5) and whether the doctrine could be used as a sword as well (which Denning also eschewed: see *Combe* v. *Combe* [1951] 2 K.B. 215

though cf., in a separate videotaped interview: M. Dockray, E. Lomnicka, S. Lee, and J. Fortin. *Review of The Denning Interviews* (video cassettes of interviews with Lord Denning of Whitchurch) (1985) 101 *L.Q.R.* 137 at p. 140 and the leading Australian High Court decision of *Walton Stores (Interstate) Ltd. v. Mäher* (1988) 164 C.L.R. 387.

52 See Denning, *supra* n. 3 at p. 223.

53 Ibid. (emphasis added).

54 See Denning, *supra* n. 3 at p. 33. See also ibid., 34 (reference to "reason and justice").

55 Ibid., 34.

56 [1976] Q.B. 319.

57 See [1977] A. C. 239. See also Atiyah, *supra* n. 39 at pp. 37–39.

58 Not explicitly: but the point has been since reaffirmed in a number of cases: see *Scally v. Southern Health and Social Services Board* [1992] 1 A.C. 294; *Spring v. Guardian Assurance plc* [1993] 2 All E.R. 273 at 296; and *Malik v. Bank of Credit and Commerce International S.A.* [1997] 3 W.L.R. 95 at 108–9.

59 See generally A. B. L. Phang, "Implied Terms Revisited" [1990] *J.B.L.* 394 and, by the same author, "Implied Terms in English Law—Some Recent Developments" [1993] *J.B.L.* 242.

60 See *Shell U.K. Ltd. v. Lostock Garage Ltd.* [1976] 1 W.L.R. 1187 at 1196–97.

61 See *supra* n. 19.

62 See e.g., *supra* n. 20.

63 See [1934] 2 K.B. 394. And on the last-mentioned point, see *Curtis v. Chemical Cleaning and Dyeing Co.* [1951] 1 K.B. 805.

64 See e.g., Denning, *supra* n. 13 at p. 610 and, by the same author, *The Family Story*, *supra* n. 9 at pp. 99 and 174–75.

65 The literature is voluminous. However, for excellent expositions of the doctrine of fundamental breach in the context of exception clauses, see the following works by Professor Brian Coote: "The Rise and Fall of Fundamental Breach" (1967) 40 *Australian L.J.* 336; "The Effect of Discharge by Breach on Exception Clauses" [1970] *C.L.J.* 221; "The Second Rise and Fall of Fundamental Breach" (1981) 55 *Australian L.J.* 788; and "Discharge for Breach and Exception Clauses Since Harbutt's 'Plasticine'" [1977] *C.L.J.* 31.

66 See *supra* n. 41.

67 [1980] A.C. 827.

68 Ibid.

69 See Lord Denning, "This Is My Life" [1986] *Denning L.J.* 17 at p. 25.

70 See [1975] 1 Q.B. 326 at 339.

71 See e.g., the House of Lords decision of *National Westminster Bank plc v, Morgan* [1985] A.C. 686 at 707–8 *per* Lord Scarman.

72 These include duress of goods, unconscionable transactions, undue influence, undue pressure, and salvage agreements: see generally [1975] 1 Q.B. 326 at 337–39. A notable omission is economic duress, but this is due to the fact that its modern beginnings can be traced to a couple of years after the decision in *Lloyd's Bank Ltd. v. Bundy* itself: see, in particular, *Occidental*

Worldwide Investment Corp. v. Skibs A/S Avanti (The Siboen and the Sibotre) [1976] 1 Lloyd's Rep. 292 (noted, J. Beatson, "Duress by Threatened Breach of Contract" (1976) 92 *L.Q.R.* 496).

73 See [1975] 1 Q.B. 326 at 339.

74 [1975] 1 Q.B. 326.

75 See e.g., A. Phang, "Undue Influence—Methodology, Sources, Linkages" [1995] *J.B.L.* 552 at pp. 570–74 and, by the same author, "Economic Duress: Recent Difficulties and Possible Alternatives" [1997] *R.L.R.* 53 at pp. 63–64, as well as "Tenders, Implied Terms and Fairness in the Law of Contract" (1998) 13 *J.C.L* 126 at pp. 137–40. This would also meet the objection that there is no element of wrongdoing involved.

76 And see Atiyah, *supra* n. 39 at p . 45: "Lord Denning has never had much love for the doctrine of privity."

77 See Denning, "The Universities and Law Reform" *supra* n. 9 at pp. 261–62. See also *supra* n. 41.

78 See, in particular, Lord Denning's dissenting judgment in *Scruttons Ltd. v. Midland Silicones Ltd.* [1962] A.C. 446 and his judgment in *Beswick v. Beswick* [1966] 1 chap. 538 (an approach that was rejected by the House of Lords: see [1968] A.C. 58).

79 See e.g., *The Eurymedon* [1975] A.C. 446 and *The New York Star* [1980] 3 All E.R. 257. There have been developments in the Australian and Canadian contexts as well: see e.g., the Australian High Court decision of *Trident General Insurance Co. Ltd. v. McNiece Bros. Pty. Ltd.* (1988) 165 C.L.R. 107 and the Canadian Supreme Court decision of *London Drugs Ltd. v. Kuehne & Nagel International Ltd.* [1993] 1 W.W.R. 1. In addition, and perhaps even more significantly, the U.K. Law Commission has recently published a *Report* containing proposals for *legislative* reform—the basic thrust of which is to allow third parties to avail themselves of the benefit of contracts under certain stipulated circumstances: see *Privity of Contract: Contracts for the Benefit of Third Parties* (H.M.S.O., Law Com. No. 242, Cm. 3329, July 1996). See also A. Burrows, "Reforming Privity of Contract: Law Commission Report No. 242" [1996] *L.M.C.L.Q.* 467. In an even more recent development, the Contracts (Rights of Third Parties) Bill has just been introduced in Parliament.

80 See e.g., *Nelson v. Larholt* [1948] 1 K.B. 339 at 342 (restitution) and *Candler v. Crane, Christmas & Co.* [1951] 2 K.B. 164 (liability for negligent misstatement: Denning's dissenting judgment, as vindicated by the House of Lords in *Hedley Byrne & Co. Ltd. v. Heller & Partners Ltd.* [1964] A.C. 465).

81 See Denning, *supra* n. 3 at p. 280.

82 [1932] A.C. 562 at 580. He observes that "Lord Atkin took the Christian precept as underlying the basis of his decision": see Denning, *supra* n. 21 at p. 7.

83 See e.g., R. Geary, "Lord Denning and Morality" in Robson & Watchman, *supra* n. 7, at pp. 74–86. The oft-cited decision in this regard is *Ward v. Braford Corporation* (1972) 70 L.G.R. 27 esp. at 35, *per* Lord Denning M.R. To be fair to Denning, however, in the same case, Phillimore L.J. echoed the same sentiments: see (1972) 70 L.G.R. 27 at 38.

84   See the excellent and fair-minded essay by P. Davies & M. Freedland, "Labour Law" in chap. 8 of Jowell & McAuslan, *supra* n. 7.

85   See Denning, "Influence," *supra* n. 20 at p. 117 (and citing Rom 13:1).

86   See Denning, *The Changing Law, supra* n. 9 at p. 3. See also Lord Edmund-Davies, *supra* n. 8 at p. 45.

87   See Sir Alfred Denning, *Freedom Under the Law* (Stevens & Sons Limited, 1949) especially at pp. 4–6.

88   See the section below entitled "The Relevance of Christian Apologetics."

89   And see generally Denning, *supra* n. 87 at pp. 35 and 45–48 and, by the same author, *supra* n. 33 at pp. 116–17 as well as *Freedom of Religion* (William Ainslie Memorial Lecture, delivered at St. Martin-in-the-Fields on 17 November 1955; The Cranbourn Press, 1955).

90   See Lord Denning, *Landmarks in the Law* (Butterworths, 1984), 328.

91   Ibid., 314.

92   See ibid., 309–29.

93   The leading case that holds that Christianity is not part of the law of England is the House of Lords' decision in *Bowman v. Secular Society Limited* [1917] A.C. 406.

94   See Denning, *supra* n. 87 at p. 47 and, by the same author, *supra* n. 33 at pp. 117–18. However, there were, in Denning's view, limits, particularly with respect to religious cults: see *The Road to Justice supra* n. 33 at p. 237.

95   See generally, F. A. Iremonger, *William Temple, Archbishop of Canterbury—His Life and Letters* (Oxford University Press, 1948); A. M. Suggate, *William Temple and Christian Social Ethics Today* (T. & T. Clark, 1987); C. W. Lowry, *William Temple—an Archbishop for All Seasons* (University Press of America, Inc., 1982); and J. Kent, *William Temple—Church, State and Society in Britain, 1880–1950* (Cambridge University Press, 1992). Reference may also be made to the introductory essay on Temple by Canon A. E. Baker in *William Temple, Religious Experience and Other Essays and Addresses* (James Clarke & Co. Ltd., 1958), 1–31 as well as to "Introduction" by R. Preston to the reissue (in 1976 by Shepheard-Walwyn) of Temple's *Christianity and Social Order*: see ibid., 5–26.

96   See *e.g.*, A. T. Denning, "The Traditions of the Bar" (1955) 72 S.A.L.J., 43 and, by the same author, *supra* n. 33 at pp. 1 and 34.

97   See Denning, "Influence" *supra* n. 20 at p. 107.

98   See Denning, *supra* n. 33 at p. l.

99   See generally ibid., 1–3. See also Lord Justice Denning, "English Law and the Moral Law" (1954) *The Listener* 332. But cf. the late Professor H. L. A. Hart who (particularly in the "Postscript" to the second edition of his classic work, *The Concept of Law* [2nd ed., Clarendon Press, 1994]) adopted a descriptive (as opposed to a prescriptive) approach in support of his positivist thesis: but cf. (in turn) A. Phang, "'The Concept of Law Revisited'" (1995) *Tydskrif Vir Die Suid-Afrikaanse Reg* 403.

100 See e.g., W. Temple, *Mens Creatix* (Macmillan and Co. Ltd./St. Martin's Street, London, 1st ed., 1917; reprint, 1949), 36, 318–20 and 364–66 and, by the same author, *Christus Veritas* (Macmillan & Co. Ltd., 1924), ix and 243–44; *Nature, Man and God* (Macmillan and Co. Ltd./St. Martin's Street,

London, 1st ed., 1934; reprint, 1953), 184, 245, 296–97, 299–300, 306–7, 318 and 354–55; and *Christian Faith and Life* (Student Christian Movement Press, 1931), 24, 53, and 110.

101　See, e.g., Temple, *Mens Creatix,* 342–43 and, by the same author, *Christus Veritas,* ibid., 155 and chap. 15; *Nature, Man and God,* ibid., 446; and *Christian Faith and Life,* ibid., chap. 6.

102　See e.g., R. J. Henle, S.J., *St. Thomas Aquinas: The Treatise on Law* (University of Notre Dame Press, 1993) and E. Gilson, *The Philosophy of St. Thomas Aquinas* (translated by E. Bullough, 1929, and edited by G. A. Elrington; Dorset Press Reprint). Cf. A. J. Lisska, *Aquinas's Theory of Natural Law: An Analytic Reconstruction* (Clarendon Press, 1996). But cf. W. Temple, "Thomism and Modern Needs" in W. Temple, *Religious Experience and Other Essays and Addresses* (James Clarke & Co. Ltd., 1958), 229–36.

103　These would include, *inter alia,* the cosmological argument as well as the argument from design. See generally e.g., J. P. Moreland, *Scaling the Secular City: A Defense of Christianity* (Baker Book House, 1987) and J. P. Moreland and K. Nielsen, *Does God Exist?: The Debate Between Theists and Atheists* (Prometheus Books, 1993). For a particularly accessible (yet nuanced) account (which comes down on the side of the existence of God), see R. Swinburne, *Is There a God?* (Oxford University Press, 1996).

104　See e.g., Phillip E. Johnson, *Darwin on Trial* (2nd ed., InterVarsity Press, 1993).

105　See generally the works cited at *supra* n. 103.

106　See e.g., Phillip E. Johnson, *Reason in the Balance: The Case Against Naturalism in Science, Law and Education* (InterVarsity Press, 1995) and C. S. Lewis, *Miracles* (Fount/HarperCollins, 1947; reissue, 1974).

107　See C. S. Lewis, *Mere Christianity* (Macmillan Publishing Company, rev. ed., 1952; 1st paperback ed., 1960), 55–56.

108　See e.g., F. F. Bruce, *The New Testament Documents: Are They Reliable?* (InterVarsity Press, 5th rev. ed., 1960).

109　See e.g., J. McDowell, *Evidence That Demands a Verdict,* vols. 1 & 2 (Here's Life Publishers, 1972 & 1979); J. W. Montgomery, *History and Christianity* (reprint: InterVarsity Press, 1971); Sir N. Anderson, *Jesus Christ: The Witness of History* (InterVarsity Press, 1985); S. Greenleaf, *The Testimony of the Evangelists: The Gospels Examined by the Rules of Evidence Administered in Courts of Justice* (reprint: Kregel Classics, 1995); Frank Morison, *Who Moved the Stone?* (Faber & Faber, 1958); R. Clifford, *Leading Lawyers' Case for the Resurrection* (Canadian Institute for Law, Theology & Public Policy, 1st Canadian ed., 1996); and N. L. Geisler, *The Battle for the Resurrection* (Thomas Nelson Publishers, 1989). It is of no mean significance that the vast majority of the authors cited in the present note are lawyers.

110　And see e.g., R. M. Dworkin, "Law, Philosophy and Interpretation" (1994) *Archiv Fuer Rechts- und Sozialphilosophie* 463 esp. at pp. 474–75 and, by the same author, "Objectivity and Truth: You'd Better Believe It" (1996) 25 *Philosophy & Public Affairs* 87.

111 The paradigm model, arguably at least, is to be found in the work of Professor John Rawls: see *A Theory of Justice* (Harvard University Press, 1971) and *Political Liberalism* (Columbia University Press, 1993).

112 And see, in the context of the law of contract, the incisive essay by Professor Atiyah, "Contract and Fair Exchange" (1985) 35 *University of Toronto L.J.* 1 (reprinted as Essay 11 in P. S. Atiyah, *Essays on Contract* [Clarendon Press, 1986]).

113 See "Valedictory Speeches upon the Impending Retirement of the Master of the Rolls" [1986] *Denning L.J.* 7 at p. 15. The passage of Scripture he cites from is 2 Timothy 4:7.

"Higher Law," Corporations, and Christian Lawyers

Bruce Burgess
B.A. (Hons.), LL.B. (Hons.), M.A. (Chr. Stud.), M.Th.

Introduction

It is some 30 years since John Montgomery's fabled philosophical hare presented the argument for the relativity of all law and morals, only then to be gleefully consumed by his more politically orientated dinner guest, the fox.

So began Montgomery's *The Case for "Higher Law"* (1975), in which he outlined the difficulties facing the modern-day lawyer in identifying any common moral dimension or "ethical norms" for the evaluation of the legal rules that govern us. Montgomery argued that any such universal moral framework must be free from the accusation of being acceptable for the society adopting it yet still being morally repugnant to a broader populace, as with regimes such as Marxist Russia or Nazi Germany. This moral framework must also be sufficiently specific; it must be more than a mere assertion of broad natural law principles whose character is so fundamentally vague ("tell the truth, keep your promises") as to be incapable of reduction to any system of rules permitting legal decisions or societal organisation to be based on them.

Montgomery's argument is for recourse to a "higher law" that sits beyond and above human law, to "revealed" biblical law and its ethical standards and relational precepts. According to Montgomery, the validity of the Bible as a transcendental source of this higher law is established through its historical facticity; only Christianity and its revelational source, the Bible, meet the test that God has come into our midst, in the person of Jesus Christ.[1] The call is put out to the modern lawyer ("jurisprudential son") to leave behind the unsatisfying husks of worldly legal systems and return to the house of the Father whose promise of the higher law of Scripture remains open to all (1975, 56–57).

This paper engages with Montgomery's work in the field of legal ethics through reexamining this same foundational issue of the interrelationship between law and morality but situating the discussion within the context of the world of the modern corporation. As the corporate world struggles to discern and define what is and is not "morally right," the argument presented here is that ethical principles emerging from a Christian worldview can indeed offer coherent answers and tangible assistance to those seeking to frame the moral parameters of corporate conduct and the corporate law that regulates it.[2]

The Rise of the Corporation

Historical analysis reveals that companies were originally created as a means of providing special privileges for certain charities and other benevolent organisations by giving them limited liability for their activities (Vermeesch and Lindgren 2001, 557–60). Now no longer primarily a charitable creature, the modern corporation has developed to the point where "business enterprises with limited liability are a feature of virtually all developed business systems" (Lipton and Herzberg 2001, 28).

The most significant benefit of incorporation is the protection it offers investors from risk through the legal fiction of the "corporate veil," which permits the corporation to exist (and be sued) as a separate legal entity from its shareholders (investors). As well as protecting the shareholder from personal liability for the acts of the corporation, the limited liability principle enhances the ease of raising capital, allows the enterprise to continue despite changing shareholders, enables management to run the company without constant shareholder involvement, and frequently provides opportunities for advantageous tax planning. These advantages are in essence subsets of the ultimate *raison d'être* of the modern corporation—it is an efficient vehicle for wealth creation. Whilst the making of profit in and of itself is commonly regarded as morally neutral (du Plessis, McConvill & Bagaric 2005, 356–57), it is the manner in which corporations make profits that gives rise to issues within the moral domain.

Corporations and Questions of Morality

The Myth of the Christian Legal System

One of the significant myths periodically raised about Western legal systems is that the law as a whole (and therefore corporate law as a component part) actually *does* have an innate moral code, and that code is Christianity.[3]

Certainly, historically, this was once the position. Cases such as *Williams' Case*[4] in England in 1797 (a blasphemy case about Paine's *Age of Reason*) and even *Darling's Case*[5] in Australia as late as 1884 (disturbance of a Salvation Army worship meeting) held that Christianity was part of the very law itself. This position was finally and dramatically dismantled in the English case of *Bowman v Secular Society*.[6] The case involved determining the validity of a bequest to a society whose main object was the propagation of anti-Christian doctrine. In the seminal passage, Lord Sumner concluded (at p. 464):

> My Lords, with all respect for the great names of the law-yers who have used it, the phrase "Christianity is part of the law of England" is really not law; it is rhetoric. . . . Best CJ once said in *Bird v Holbrook* (a case of injury by setting a spring gun): "There is no act which Christianity forbids, that the law will not reach; if it were otherwise, Christian-ity would not be, as it has always been held to be, part of the law of England"; but this was rhetoric too. Spring guns, indeed, were got rid of, not by Christianity, but by Act of Parliament. "Thou shalt not steal" is part of our law. "Thou shalt love thy neighbour as thyself" is not part of our law at all.

This watershed in the judicial expression of the relationship be-tween Christianity and the law no doubt reflected deeper social changes that had been taking place for some time. Commenting on similar changes seen within the American legal system, Walker ob-serves that "the twentieth century has witnessed biblical law being less understood and increasingly abandoned on both a personal and collective level in society. With the loss of biblical authority came the loss of biblical law as an authority" (1998, 216).

Despite the apparent dangers to ordinary citizens (particularly in dictatorial or totalitarian States) of this relatively recent moral relativism within the law, the likelihood in our pluralistic twenty-first-century society of a return by world legal systems to Christian biblical law appears to be somewhat remote. By way of example, the present situation in Australia is well summarised by Justice Anthony Mason (at p. 134) in the High Court decision of *Church of the New Faith v Commissioner for Pay-Roll Tax (Vic)*[7]: "Under our law, the State has no prophetic role in relation to religious belief; the State can neither declare supernatural truth nor determine the paths through which the human mind must search in a quest for supernatural truth."

The position now reached is that whilst the Christian heritage of our law is not disputed, and whilst many of the broad ethical principles that underlie Christianity are still contained in our law, it is no longer possible to assert that law either embodies Christianity itself or that it is appropriate to enforce adherence to Christian beliefs through legal process.

Whilst this position may be lamented by some Christians, it is surely a healthy development for the courts to formally recognise that faith entails a voluntary act of the mind and heart, rather than, to use the language of the modern corporation, enforced "legal compliance." As the writer to the Hebrews explains, when Christ came into the world, he did not desire sacrifices and offerings, although the (Judaic temple) law required them (Heb 10:5–8). Rather, having offered Christ as the sacrifice, God desires for people to draw near to him "with a sincere heart in full assurance of faith" (Heb 10:19–22 NIV). It is wholly appropriate that our courts recognise this position, rather than alienate people whose beliefs are other than Christian by enforcing laws reflecting a belief system to which the majority no longer adheres.[8]

The Amoral Corporation and "Minimum Moral Standards"

Although the law (including corporate law) no longer draws its moral content from Christianity, the questions remain as to what relationship does or should exist between corporate law and morality, and what role (if any) Christianity and Christian lawyers might still have in that discussion. It is worth noting at this point that corporations themselves are actually amoral. As Velasquez observes, "It makes sense to say that a corporation is morally responsible for a wrongful act only as an elliptical (and somewhat dangerous) way of saying that certain human individuals are morally responsible for that act" (1983, 1).

This is not to say that corporations operate in a moral vacuum—far from it. Recent events have demonstrated that the actions of corporations have far-ranging commercial and social implications that bring with them questions of moral accountability, where the underlying public opinion is that "what was done was wrong." Within Australia, corporate collapses and dubious behaviour such as that seen in the HIH group, the OneTel group, and James Hardie group continue to wreak social and financial havoc on those affected. Internationally, collapses such as Enron, WorldCom, and Parmalat and environmental disasters such as Bhopal (Union Carbide), Seveso, Italy (ICMESA), and Exxon Valdez (Exxon Mobil) have repercussions potentially lasting for decades. Tapping into the current of public dissatisfaction, the film industry has pilloried corporate ethics in recent films such as *The Insider* (1999), *The Bank* (2001), and *Enron: The Smartest Guys in the Room* (2005).

If, then, the conduct of corporations is routinely publicly perceived as being "right" or "wrong," to what extent is it appropriate for *corporate law* to be used as a means of enforcing "moral" corporate conduct? Some half century ago, Stumpf observed, "The law is concerned with *minimum moral standards*, whereas morality envisions the truly good or *ideal life*" (1966, 231). Stumpf's argument has been affirmed more recently by writers such as Finn (1989, 91), French and Granrose (1995, 82), and Mason (1990, 28–29).

The point can be illustrated by looking to an area of constant importance to the modern corporation: the law of negligence. In the famous English case of *Donoghue v Stevenson*,[9] a manufacturer was charged with negligence for distributing a ginger beer bottle containing a decomposed snail. Lord Atkin—incidentally, a committed Christian—sought to bring a moral (Christian) perspective to the law of negligence, whilst at the same time recognising that he would be ruling on a question of law not morality. The outcome was Lord Atkin's conclusion (at p. 580) that "the rule that you are to love your neighbour becomes *in law*, you must not injure your neighbour" (emphasis added).[10] The significant aspect to note here is that the broader moral principle was pared down in a legal context to a minimum moral standard; a positive obligation to love was reframed as a negative obligation not to harm.

Lord Atkin's judgment graphically illustrates a careful application of pared down moral principles of "neighbourhood" to a legal context. However, in recent times, developments in areas of law such as good faith, not engaging in misleading or unconscionable conduct, and unjust and unfair contract legislation are changing the landscape somewhat. Finn observes that such concepts are "rich in moral connotation" and indicate that "individualism has to accommodate itself to a new concern: the idea of 'neighbourhood'—a moral idea of positive and not merely negative requisition—is abroad" (1989, 92).

While such change in no way represents a return to a point from which law will enforce particular religious beliefs as legislated morality, it does signal a growing recognition both that there is now scope for law to reflect *more* than a bare minimum moral standard, and that it is appropriate for it to do so. The remainder of this paper illustrates how a Christian moral perspective on corporate law can assist law- and policy-makers to go "beyond the bare minimum," yet at the same time refrain from any attempt to (re-)legislate Christian belief itself.

Corporate "Virtues" and Christian Perspectives on Them

Through a veritable barrage of recent changes,[11] the law has taken up the cudgel of the vulnerable and the disadvantaged to protect them against unfair treatment. This tide of change represents what Finn describes as "a watershed period in the history of our common law" (1989, 88). Yet as Finn observes, a paucity of "doctrinal tools" to express these concepts leaves both legislators and the judiciary alike in something of a quandary as to how to talk about the undeniable moral concepts that underpin these recent developments.

One approach, adopted by Terry and Giugni,[12] is to speak in terms of ethical "virtues" that are now increasingly dominating the landscape of commercial law: "Underlying and shaping the rule of ethics, however, are a set of universal values including *honesty, integrity, fairness and respect for others.* The content of these values is essentially unchanging. They are not relative to swings of social mood or taste" (2003, 743).[13]

Whilst the notion of unchanging human universal values may be dubious when viewed historically or cross-culturally (Montgomery 1998, 73–78; Montgomery 2002 proposition 5.275), the virtues enunciated by Terry and Giugni may nevertheless be accepted as conservatively expressing the heart of the "watershed" occurring in modern corporate law,[14] and form a basis from which to proceed in considering how a Christian worldview can inform these principles.[15]

Fairness

To a degree, the concept of being *just* as a moral virtue becomes the notion of being *fair* in a commercial context. Sir Edward Pearce— a former member of the English Court of Appeal—remarked, "Abstract notions of justice are reduced to the search for 'fair play.' In a very practical sense that approach is to be applauded. 'Fair play' in reality is more comforting than 'justice' in theory."[16] Having said this, there are now numerous legal doctrines that freely appeal to the concept of justice as a prerequisite to acceptable corporate conduct. These include such developments as the doctrine of unjust enrichment, the Contracts Review Act 1980 (NSW) (which deals with unfair contracts), the unconscionable dealings principle in contract, and the general doctrine of unconscionability in equity.

For the Christian, doing justice in dealing with others goes beyond simply applying the minimum standards that are required to avoid acting illegally. As Marshall reflects: "Nor should justice be equated with legalism: it is not a simple totting up of legal precedent or an application of abstract legal principles. Justice is a drive to *make* things right, it is a movement toward good and lifegiving relationships. Justice must always include *kindness* (Matt 25:31ff) and *generosity* (2 Cor 9:9ff)" (1984, 54–55). In similar vein, Wolterstorff's consideration of the biblical notion of "shalom" peace (entailing right relationships with God, self, fellows, and nature) declares justice to be indispensable to shalom, because "shalom is an *ethical* community" (1983, 71, author emphasis).

Justice is a theme that flows through God's dealings with people through eternity.[17] More than that, it reflects the very character of God. As Moses told the Israelite people before chastening them for their unfaithfulness toward God, "The Rock, his work is perfect, and all his ways are just. A faithful God, without deceit, just and upright is he" (Deut 32:4 NRSV).

The divine purpose both to bring and embody justice is seen in Jesus' very first recorded words of public declaration of his mission to his world. Reading from the book of Isaiah, he announces that the prophecy of good news to the poor, the captives, the blind, and the oppressed has been fulfilled in the sight of the people who were there (see Luke 4:16–21). Jesus' message to the people is clear; not only does he bring justice, but also as the fulfilment of the prophecy declares, he *is* justice personified.[18]

On the occasion of his swearing in as chief justice of the High Court of Australia on 21 April 1995, Brennan expressed it this way:

> For the Christian, justice has a special and central signifi-
> cance: it is a divine imperative. Justice is not brought to the
> people either by populist clamour or by implementing the
> will of the powerful. It must be sought by careful reflec-
> tion upon the interests of the individual and of society as a
> whole and there must be an especial concern for the power-
> less, the socially insignificant, the weak minority.[19]

In sum, the Christian perspective on justice is holistic rather than instance specific. Whilst the Christian will have recourse to biblical teaching and narratives in forming a concept of what is just in a particular situation, of more significance is the Christian's drawing upon the very nature of God, embodied through the incarnation of his son Jesus on earth, to develop an overarching "worldview" of what is just (Marshall 1984, 51–56).

Armed with this understanding, the Christian is then well placed to present his or her personal response to issues of morality that arise in the context of corporate law. True, the Christian may not go so far as to suggest that the modern corporation in essence should be a vehicle for "making things right" in society. Nevertheless the Christian perspective on what is just or unjust is a valuable reference point for business leaders, legislators, and judges making assessments of what is "fair" in the corporate world and how far they should go in curbing corporate activity by which the powerful take advantage of the weak, the less informed, or the less well resourced.[20]

Honesty and Integrity

Modern corporate law is replete with requirements to act honestly and with "good faith," particularly in the area of director's duties owed to the company. To these notions, Terry and Giugni add the word *integrity*. At first sight, acting with honesty and integrity is a relatively simple affair; we must tell the truth. Yet as the courtroom oath to "tell the truth, the whole truth and nothing but the truth" suggests, truth and integrity have many shades of grey. Whilst Grenz argues that honesty forms part of the broader concept of integrity, he explains that for Christians the notion of integrity goes further: "Basically integrity has to do with authenticity. Persons of integrity are free from duplicity. With them, 'what you see is what you get.' Likewise, integrity has to do with the courage of conviction. Persons of integrity act on their beliefs even when this exacts a great personal cost" (1997, 229–30).

As Grenz notes (1997, 230), the value of the good reputation that comes from being a person of integrity is given biblical recognition by the Wisdom literature, quoting as an example: "A good name is more desirable than great riches; to be esteemed is better than silver or gold" (Prov 22:1 NIV). Similar attestations to the value of a good reputation and of dealing with integrity are found in popular management texts such as Clark and Jonson (1995, 42–55) and Covey (1989, *passim*).

Respect for Others

This is the last of the corporate "virtues" listed by Terry and Giugni. Interestingly, it is not directly expressed in any legislative or judicial announcements of which this writer is aware. Yet it represents something of a subtext for the various recent changes occurring in corporate law that give protection to the less powerful and call upon corporations to refrain from misleading, unconscionable, or oppressive conduct.

By contrast to the position within corporate law, the Christian faith is rich in imagery and teaching in this area. At its most fundamental level, Christ's "new commandment" for his disciples is the high watermark of respect for others: love one another in the way that I (Jesus) have loved you (John 13:31–35). Later in John's Gospel, Jesus explains to his disciples that he has loved them in the same way that God the Father has loved *him* (John 15:9–12). Jesus is pointing to the manner in which persons of the Trinity love one another as the model for how his followers should relate to one another (thus Carson 1991, 484–88).

Each person in the Trinity is distinct from the others, yet at the same time, together they constitute a cohesive whole. There is at the one time separate identity as well as relationship in and responsibility to the broader "community." What distinguishes this "corporate person," the Trinity, from all others is the extraordinary unity of purpose and love (including mutual respect but so much more as well) that its individual members exhibit for one another (Gunton 1993, 214–19; McGrath 1987, 119–37). In expanding on the "unitedness" that he sees as best expressed by the Greek term *perichoresis* (a sort of mutual coinherence of shared life), Moltmann describes the relationships this way: "Because of their eternal love, the divine persons exist so intimately with each other, for each other, and in each other that they themselves constitute a unique, incomparable complete unity" (1984, 166).

A diagrammatic expression of this unity appears below:[21]

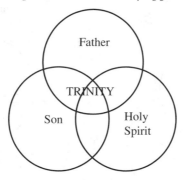

Boff has expounded the social justice implications of the trinitarian community to society at large:

From the *perichoresis*-communion of the three divine
Persons derive impulses to liberation: of each and every human person, of society, of the church and of the
poor. . . . Society offends the Trinity by organizing itself
on a basis of inequality and honours it the more it favours
sharing and communion for all, thereby bringing about
justice and equality for all (1988, 236).

This trinitarian model of community has potentially powerful applications to the manner in which corporations function in society
that will now be explored in more detail.

Corporations and Their Communities

Corporations and Their Internal Stakeholders

Whilst the *share*holders are the owners of a corporation, the *stake*holders are a broader group including the corporation's directors and
employees. These three kinds of stakeholders together represent the
internal "corporate community" whose collective conduct melds together to determine the acts undertaken by the corporation to which
they "belong." Together, they constitute the community that in a functional sense "is" the modern corporation, even as the various persons of
the Trinity together represent the spiritual community that is God.

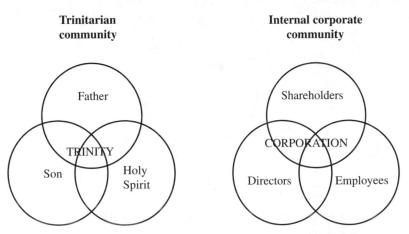

A uniquely Christian perspective is the notion that this internal community will function more successfully if its component parts mirror to a greater degree the kind of unity demonstrated by the Trinity, so that shareholders, directors, and employees alike are more unified in the direction in which they are heading and demonstrate heightened levels of mutual respect and care for one another. Thus, shareholders will be motivated not only by profit but also by a concern for the reputation of directors and the well-being of the employees who generate that profit. Directors (and management) will act honestly and in good faith, and will balance shareholder interests with the manner in which employees are treated.[22] Employees will recognise that their work is more than just to earn a personal wage; it is also for the purpose of creating shareholder wealth and should be done is a manner that minimises directors' exposure to legal liability.

The notion of limited liability can threaten such a unified community, particularly in the case of insolvency, where shareholders seeking accountability for their financial losses are faced with the corporate veil that presents the corporation as a separate legal entity. Statutory provisions that hold directors personally responsible for insolvent trading are to be applauded from a Christian perspective because they hold directors accountable for the unethical conduct of placing at risk the legitimate interests of the other stakeholders within the corporate community—both shareholders and employees alike.

Another area where real questions of equity arise is in relation to the position of employee wage, leave, and superannuation (pension) entitlements, particularly when a corporation becomes insolvent. Frequently, such entitlements rank behind secured creditors and costs of administration of the winding up, and their payment is by no means guaranteed due to the fact that the company's assets are deficient.

From a Christian perspective, these are matters that raise significant issues of justice and offend the principle of concern and respect for those within the corporation's internal community. While employees contribute at the most fundamental level to the well-being of the corporation, when insolvency occurs they are frequently in a position of helplessness, having no legal ability to protect entitlements that are their due. Christian concepts of justice provide protection for the weak. Christ was concerned for the poor (economically weak), as well as those oppressed in other ways (see Luke 4:16–22). From another perspective, Christ also tells the parable of the workers in the vineyard, each of whom is entitled to the wages that are agreed with the master (Matt 20:1–16).

Christian lawyers ought properly to contend for legislation that protects the rights of employees to be paid what they are due. Firstly, and most importantly, because this is just. But also, presenting the economic argument, because the contented worker is the more productive worker, whose energies are not diverted by concerns for the safety of their economic entitlements. This is another way of saying that the stakeholders together, as a corporate community, will function more effectively (and in all likelihood profitably) because there is a higher level of trust and mutual care where the law protects the weaker parties.

Corporations and Their Wider Stakeholders

Many commentators recognise that the true stakeholders of a corporation's community actually extend far more broadly to include such persons as parties to corporate transactions, trade creditors, customers and consumers, governments, and regulators, as well as society at large (du Plessis, McConvill and Bagaric 2005; Letza, Sun and Kirkbride 2004; OECD 2004). This is the broader external corporate community with which the corporation relates.

The nature of the external corporate community differs materially from the nature of both the trinitarian community and the internal corporate community because its component parts do not together in any sense "constitute" the corporation. Nevertheless, there are good grounds to contend that it is "right" for the corporation also to treat these broader stakeholders with appropriate care and respect, not the least because this is exactly what these persons expect (and, increasingly, require) of it.

One of the interesting observations made by Finn (1989, 90) is that "there is an evident change in the standards of conduct which the law is exacting from persons in their voluntary or consensual dealings with others." His argument is that whereas in the past the

Trinitarian community

Internal corporate community and its broader stakeholder (external corporate community)

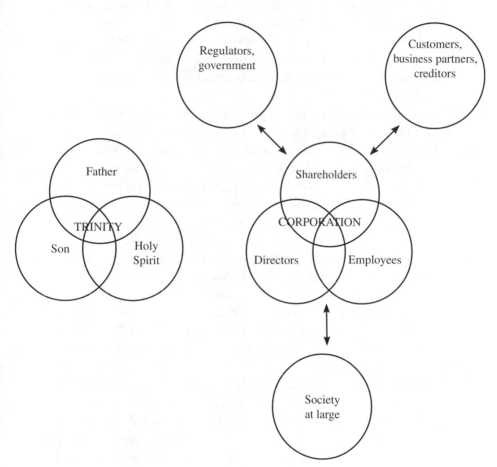

law would largely condone selfish behaviour and hard bargains as a reflection of the value of individual autonomy, now the law is more inclined to impose positive obligations on persons (including corporate persons) based on notions of broader moral obligations that persons in community owe to one another.[23]

Perhaps the most influential of all outworkings of this change on the Australian scene has been the introduction in 1974 of section 52 of the Trade Practices Act (Cth). The section reads simply enough: "A corporation shall not, in trade or commerce, engage in conduct that is misleading or deceptive, or is likely to mislead or deceive." And yet as any corporate lawyer will confess, section 52 is the first cause of action considered in mounting a challenge to objectionable corporate conduct. In words reminiscent of Finn, Terry and Giugni describe section 52 as imposing "a new business ethic, a new standard of commercial morality" that is "simply the most visible manifestation of a much wider trend in statutory and judge-made law" (1997, 481–82).

From the Christian lawyer's perspective, the rise of this new business ethic is to be applauded as an appropriate introduction of a broad-based ethic of corporate conduct that requires corporations to behave in a manner that is more considerate of the external stakeholders with which they interact, rather than allowing uninhibited hard dealings to go unchecked. Although not a direct reflection of the trinitarian model of community, these developments do strike blows for justice, fairness, honesty, and good faith—all of which are values intrinsic to a Christian perspective on relationships between persons and the "community" in which those persons function.

Another example of the changes that are occurring is the development of the duty of good faith. This concept is unremarkable in the United States, where for example section 1–203 of the Uniform Commercial Code that provides that "every contract or duty within this Act imposes an obligation of good faith in its performance or enforcement." [24] In Australia, while enjoying a measure of judicial support, [25] the doctrine has yet to be embraced by the High Court.

The perspective of the Christian lawyer is to applaud and support these developments. Why so? On the one hand, there is a strong argument that a commercial environment in which good faith and fair dealing are normative is a more efficient and cost-effective environment for corporate activity. Negotiations can become more streamlined because parties more clearly express what they really want and the reasons for wanting it. "Due diligence" investigations for corporate acquisitions or mergers can be scaled down because the need for independent verification of data provided by a vendor is lessened. The extraordinary lengths to which parties go to document transactions due to an unwillingness to place legal reliance on trust of the other party can be reduced so that documents can still comprehensively deal with the necessary issues without engaging in obsessive levels of pedantry or detail.

If these are the "commercial reasons" to support good faith and fair dealing within the corporation's external community, the other basis is that they embody Christian principles of relationship discussed earlier in this paper. The strength of the Christian perspective is that the principles of fairness, honesty, integrity, and respect for others presented by writers such as Terry and Giugni are not only consonant with biblical teaching, but they also deliver tangible benefits to the way that corporations carry on business. The biblical perspective therefore is self-validatory in a manner that extends beyond its godly authorship; the validation is seen in the way in which Christian principles applied in corporate practice can actually work to make the corporate world function more effectively than it currently does.

Corporations and Society at Large

As earlier parts of this paper have indicated, society does make moral judgments about the conduct of corporations. This section gives a brief legal and Christian perspective on two significant areas in which the "morality" of the corporation is brought under public scrutiny.

Corporate Ethics

Whenever corporate conduct adversely impacts the lives of people in significantly adverse ways, the issue of "unethical" corporate conduct looms large. Yet with the "involuntary redundancy" of the earlier Christian legal framework, there is now a significant difficulty to be faced; namely, that "in the business community there is not a body of accepted and recognised business ethics in the same sense as those which exist in the professions" (Holley 1996, 182). Consistent with the present difficulty of finding a doctrinal basis for the moral content to corporate law, so too the business community is now searching to find an acceptable doctrinal source for its codes of ethics.

The lack of prescription about ethical content reflects the reality that unethical people are rarely made to behave ethically through legislative injunction. In commenting on the dramatic increase in "black letter law" following the 1980s, Dalton observes, "This has only compounded the problems (a fact now recognised by the present Attorney-General). In reality, ethical corporate practice is beyond the limits of legal regulation" (1996, 179).

The consequence has been to adopt an approach under which corporations are, by and large, told in various ways that they need to "be ethical," but it is left to each corporation's own discretion to decide just what that means. For example, while corporations listed on stock exchange typically must disclose their corporate governance practices, the content of their ethical policies is generally not externally prescribed. It is into such discretionary environments of ethical standards that the Christian lawyer has much to offer.

Although this may seem a little surprising to other sections of the community, corporate lawyers and managers alike are well aware that the most common "first draft" authors of a corporation's ethical and corporate governance policies are lawyers! Compliance with the statutory or regulatory need to have such policies in place is often perceived as primarily a *legal* requirement, and as such the drafting of these policies is given to lawyers to do. Not infrequently, these policies take the form of a precedent that is then "tweaked" to suit the corporation in question.

Regardless of the appropriateness of this approach, in such circumstances Christian lawyers have a real contribution to make. Whenever they are involved in the drafting of policies that have some form of ethical dimension, they have the opportunity to draft in such a way that is more than perfunctory, more than the "minimum standard," but actually embodies high ethical standards reflecting more than dry satisfaction of a legal requirement. Whilst the final wording is of course determined by the corporation, preparing the initial draft is an opportunity for substantial influence.

Further, and probably even more importantly, the Christian lawyer has the chance to influence corporate culture by engaging with management or the board to discuss the relevant policy, and canvass its significance as being more than just a legal document, but rather a benchmark of ethical behaviour that they themselves can model for the corporation they lead. As Holley remarks, "The ethics of a business will comprise much more the ethics of the individuals within that business" (1996, 182).

The Corporation as a Social Citizen

The power of the corporation to influence both society at large and governments in particular has never been greater. Domestically, corporations routinely lobby governments to introduce legislation that assists doing business (that is, making profit) and limits public disclosure obligations. Internationally, the push for globalisation of trade to enhance available markets and profit-making opportunities is seen in multimillion-dollar campaigns for global trade agreements whose social implications may be problematic.[26]

Yet at the same time, the corporation is powerfully aware of the importance of public opinion as it affects the "bottom line":

> [T]o some extent, an expanded social responsibility will inevitably arise because the corporation perceives that it is in its own interests to pursue socially responsible policies. It may believe that such policies will attract favourable publicity and so increase sales—for instance, if it donates money to a worthy cause or adopts more favourable consumer policies (Berns and Baron 1998, 91).

Even if the corporation has nobler motives than this in making positive social contributions, there are at present various structural difficulties in its ability to do so. These include the fact that by law, directors must generally act at all times "in the best interests of the company," which has traditionally been seen as the pursuit of profit for shareholders, so that philanthropic acts of no direct benefit to the company may or may not survive judicial scrutiny.[27] Further, the majority of shareholders (at least in larger corporations) have little influence on corporate policy, both because this is largely dictated by decisions of the board and senior management and second because they have limited opportunity other than at annual general meetings to express their views on the corporation's actions. The power to vote directors in or out in no real sense communicates any clearly understood message about company policy, let alone the company's approach to issues of social responsibility. In addition, as Redmond points out, there is no broad consensus about whom this broader social responsibility is owed (creditors? employees? consumers? society at large?) (2005, 78–81).

What can a Christian perspective contribute to this difficult conundrum for the twenty-first-century corporation and its leaders? As observed earlier, the corporation's "culture" or "social ethic" is not so much determined by rules, regulations, or even legislation, but rather by the values held by the board and senior management and the manner in which they act upon them.

Into this reality, the Christian can offer two paradigms that may be of significant assistance in defining and shaping corporate culture. The first paradigm relates to the manner in which the corporation functions at a relational level. Earlier in this paper the argument has been made that the various persons who make up the corporation's *internal* community—shareholders, directors, and employees—do not function in isolation from, but rather in intimate corelation with, each other.

Looking to the mutual relationships found within the Trinity, the Christian contends that a corporate body of persons will function most effectively if its component parts treat each other with love, care, and respect. Further, as public opinion towards corporations progressively hardens, it is increasingly important for corporations to take into consideration the needs and views of the various persons who represent the external community as well.

Shriver notes that, whether from the (internal) perspective of the investor or the (external) perspective of those interested in making corporations more "socially accountable," these trends are significant:

> Whether by religious vision that centers on the plight of
> the world poor, a commitment to democratic "liberty and
> justice for all," or a new awareness of the finitude of planet
> earth, a sizable number of investors and other constituents
> of corporate responsibility movements believe that, if they
> are to be investors, they must do so for social purpose as
> well as for their own profit (1989, 245).

As Dalton's discussion of the growing importance of "ethical investment funds" in America in particular, but also in Australia, reveals, this trend toward recognition of socially responsible investment practices is growing at a prodigious rate (1996, 174–76). Tangible manifestations of such change include global "socially responsible" share indices, "socially responsible investment" (SRI) lobby groups, and prestigious international awards being given to ethical business leaders.[28]

While the trinitarian injunction to "love" one another in community may be too high a benchmark for the corporation (just as "loving our neighbour" is too high a standard in the law of negligence), the Christian paradigm that calls for genuine respect for, and a willingness to make a positive contribution to, the other aspects of the community with which the corporation interacts is apposite for the twenty-first-century corporation.

The individuals controlling corporations have a choice. Will they determine corporate social policy based solely on perceived corporate expediency (profit from good reputation), or also on the foundation of a genuine commitment to higher ethical principles of relatedness to the community?

The Christian lawyer's challenge is to encourage those in positions of influence in corporations to be socially responsible for the *right* motives—those that send a message to the employees and broader community that the internal codes of conduct, ethical policies, corporate governance statements, and contributions to "socially worthwhile causes" are not motivated by expediency—they reflect the genuinely held beliefs of those running the company about what the proper role and contribution of the corporation to its community should be. This creates a corporate culture founded on integrity, and, ironically, is likely to create the kind of company with which desirable employees, trading partners, and customers will want to be associated. It is the closest thing to living out a corporate equivalent of the biblical injunctions to "look not only to your own interests but also to the interests of others" (Phil 2:4 NIV) and to "let love be genuine" (Rom 12:9 ESV).

If a trinitarian paradigm of community is the first contribution that Christian thinking brings to developing an ethical corporate

639

culture, the second is the model of virtue ethics. The approach of virtue ethics is to focus not on "What should I do?" but rather on "Who should I become?" (Keenan 1998, 84). From a moral perspective, the Christian's main aim is to "develop a vision and to strive to attain it. Inasmuch as that vision is who we ought to become, then the key insight is that we should always aim to grow" (Keenan 1998, 85).

In language reminiscent of the Christian tradition, most larger corporations now have a "vision" or "mission" statement. Most statements of this kind are developed by a small number of senior managers, perhaps with the input of an outside consultant, and are then publicised to the employees and wider audiences at a later date. Such a process neglects two of the three "persons" of the internal community affected by them—shareholders and employees.

Adopting an approach similar to that used by virtue ethicists (and which resonates with Terry and Giugni's list of virtues), there would seem to be a better way. As a starting point, ask the question, "What kind of corporation do we want to become?" Seek to identify those virtues that are important to all the persons of the internal community, and plan the corporate vision around those. Corporate strategy then becomes an outworking of the way in which the company will go about becoming the kind of corporate citizen that embodies those virtues.

Radically, seek input about corporate values from all stakeholders within the corporation's internal community. Involve directors, management, and employees. Perhaps hold sessions with the shareholders to discuss and ultimately to vote to adopt the company's vision statement (and maybe statement of corporate virtues as well!). Ideally, seek the views of the corporation's external community as well.

These suggestions are intentionally idealistic, in the sense that they are aspirational in character. Yet is it not highly probable that such a corporation would have a greater internal unity, sense of purpose, and broader community respect after embarking upon such a process? The corporation would more closely resemble a trinitarian model of community. And, as a pleasant incidental consequence, there is strong evidence to believe that such an organisation will become more financially successful in the longer term as well (GovernanceMetrics International 2005; Holley 1996, 186; Mbare 2004).

Implications for Christian Lawyers

Where, then, does the individual Christian lawyer stand in the midst of this discussion of corporations, morality, and ethical conduct?

The capacity of the Christian lawyer to influence corporate conduct in the context of broader corporate decision and policy making in areas such as ethical policies, corporate governance statements, codes of conduct, and a corporation's understanding of itself and its social responsibilities has already been canvassed. Certain lawyers may also have the opportunity to have input into corporate law as it is promulgated and interpreted by the legislature, judiciary, and regulatory authorities. Yet Christian lawyers can also have an impact, both in the context of how they relate to and treat the people with whom they work, and in response to specific ethical issues as they arise in the daily operation of business.

Relating to Others in the Workplace

Christian lawyers working either with or within corporations need to model Christlikeness to the persons with whom they come in contact (Phil 2:1 16). This entails genuine care for their wellbeing, being patient and forgiving, considering their human frailties and tendencies to unpleasant conduct (the outworking of the fallenness of the human condition), and demonstrating a concern for principles of justice, integrity, and honesty.

Whilst each Christian must filter what this means in a corporate context and in their particular workplace situation, as Mason observes:

> Honesty, good faith, respect for the worth of individuals, restitution of benefits unjustly received, fair compensation for wrong done, these are Biblical principles and no less so because non-Christians also hold them to be valid. Christianity can teach how better to recognise the need for these and other values and, hopefully, assist in applying them to particular cases (1990, 29).

Specific Ethical Issues

The corporate world can be tough. Decisions are routinely made under extreme pressure. The negotiation of corporate transactions often occurs in a concentrated period of time, where nerves are frayed and bodies tired. In this environment, there are strong structural temptations to engage in behaviour that is expedient and, sometimes, less than ethical.

The following are examples of corporate conduct that is of questionable or objectionable ethical character.[29]

+ Using legal devices to disentitle employees from financial entitlements or disempower them in labour negotiations.
+ Lying (for example, overstating or misrepresenting a company's position on various issues in the context of a negotiation).
+ Allowing a new employee who has left a competitor to pass on confidential information from that competitor.
+ Engaging in serious price discounting or anticompetitive conduct to put a competitor out of business, then raising prices above precompetition levels once the competition is gone.
+ Using consultants to take advantage of a drafting "loophole" that allows a provision which clearly does not reflect the legislative intention to be exploited to deliver a financial advantage to the client.

While some of this conduct is illegal, some of it is not. Most of it is difficult to prove. In the pressure of such an environment, in which some see such conduct as "just business," Christian lawyers have an important role to play. Yes, they may influence corporate conduct through the character of their interactions with others. Sir Gerard Brennan, however, has suggested another dimension that goes even beyond these matters. It is revolutionary, profoundly challenging to the Christian lawyer, and perhaps somewhat shocking to those who are accustomed to corporate lawyers keeping strictly to their principal roles of drafting documents, negotiating agreements, and providing legal advice.

Brennan proffers the striking suggestion that the role of the commercial lawyer is to be the corporate client's *moral* adviser:

> Because the moral purpose of much commercial law is
> known to or ascertainable by commercial lawyers alone, the
> commercial lawyer becomes by default the moral as well
> as the legal adviser of the client. There is nobody else to be
> the moral adviser. The role sits uneasily on a lawyer's shoul-
> ders. Yet it must be accepted if professional advice is to
> avoid the reproach of being the solvent of the client's moral
> responsibility. . . . If [the lawyer] perceives that it is within
> the client's legal power to impair the rights of a third party
> whom the legislature has ineffectually tried to protect or
> to exercise that legal power in a way which is unjust, surely
> the moral dimension must be pointed out. But the moral
> decision is not for the lawyer to make: that decision is for
> the client (1989, 105).

As Brennan points out, for many lawyers, this is an uneasy role. On the one hand, there is concern not to transgress the limits of one's practising certificate and thereby invalidate one's professional indemnity insurance. However, provided the lawyer follows Brennan's advice and allows the client to make the decision on the issue, this should hardly be a concern. The more significant source of unease may be a lack of confidence on the part of the lawyer in being able to discern, much less articulate, what is in fact moral or ethical in the context of corporate conduct.

It is here that the Christian lawyer has a tremendous advantage. True it is that Christian lawyers can hardly advocate that the corporation "live" in its community in a Christian way because the lawyer in question happens to have a Christian belief system. However, he or she *can* nevertheless advocate Christian ethical approaches to corporate clients in their decision- and policy-making, knowing that these principles have a long history of making positive contributions to society, that they are part of a coherent overall moral code (as set out in the Bible) *and*, most importantly, that they can help to enhance both the internal and external corporate community's assessments of the "corporate culture" of that corporation. Apart from the inherent moral value of Christian ethical perspectives, they provide tangible commercial benefits in areas as diverse as employee and union relations, corporate reputation, customer service, and trust and integrity with business partners.

Certainly, Christian lawyers must refrain from pious moralising, lest they be discounted as irrelevant at best and insubordinate at worst. As with the way in which Christians are encouraged to share their Christian hope generally, they should share moral perspectives with gentleness and respect.[30] From personal experience, a generous dose of good humour is normally also well received!

Christians ought not to presume that the (corporate) world is against all that Christians stand for. There are many ethical people of great integrity within the business community, and many others who are willing and open to be persuaded to follow ethical paths if a reasonable case can be mounted for doing so. There is much scope for Christians to influence the world of business in a way that assists corporations to make positive contributions to all of their stakeholders (both internal and external), if they will only have the courage to seek to live out their Christian faith in this most practical of ways.

Conclusion

At the Inaugural Australasian Christian Legal Convention held in Melbourne in 2001, Brennan again spoke of the contribution the Christian lawyer can make to the community at large:

> And while Christian values cannot demand public acceptance if a majority of the community otherwise determine, their inherent worth to the community has been demonstrated through the centuries by the civilizing influence of the church and by the Christian foundation of our legal system. There is no reason why the Christian's voice should not be heard and, if Christian principles command majority support, they will be accepted (2001, 7).

Now is the time for Christian lawyers to be reevaluating the contributions they can make in the world of corporate legal practice. A degree of self-examination is needed, to see that their own personal conduct does not disenfranchise them from having a voice in the corporate world. As Kelly remarks in speaking of the church in general, "We have some repentance to do before our secular culture. If we appear to be more concerned with our rights than with the temporal and eternal well-being of the very people with whom we do not agree, we will have little to say to them" (1998, 200). Returning to Montgomery's biblical analogy, if Christians seek to engage with the prodigal jurisprudential son about the benefits of the higher law offered by the Father, they must ensure their attitude and conduct is not that of the elder son, pouting outside the boardroom (feast) with righteous indignation.

Christian lawyers also need to be open for the conversation to move both ways. There are various areas of corporate conduct from which Christian communities may learn, without risk of becoming "secularised" in the process. As but one example, corporations generally have documented and professionally implemented employee appraisal, disciplinary, and, if necessary, dismissal procedures. These provide a measure of fairness and justice in dealings with employees. By contrast, Christian churches and organisations are notorious for not even documenting job descriptions, for being short on process when it comes to evaluating the performance of people in ministry, and for being woefully ill at ease when it comes to dealing with conflict (despite clear biblical teaching in this area—see for example Matt 18:15–20).[31]

In seeking a "voice at the boardroom table," particularly in relation to issues having a moral dimension, Christians must strive to be identifiable as persons whose conduct exemplifies Christian principles and Christlike behaviour. This will include demonstrating through actual *conduct* the impact of their Christian beliefs: that each person deserves the respect due to someone made in the image of God, that Christians are willing to take stands for Christian concepts of justice and integrity, and that the Christian's view of and interaction with his or her community is one that reflects a trinitarian understanding of how persons best relate to one another. But more than that, Christians will seek to be people who are discernibly different, because they demonstrate in their lives and in their dealings with others the difference made by the fact that Christ himself dwells within them (Col 1:27).

And this great difference is the defining distinctive of the Christian moral perspective not only on corporate conduct but also on all human conduct. For the Christian view of life and the world is undergirded by a personal relationship with God, made possible by the life and saving work of God incarnate in the person of Jesus Christ, who showed his love for all humanity by sacrificing his own life so that all might live (Rom 5:1–2). This broader picture of the meaning of life cannot but influence Christian views of all moral and ethical questions, as it "gives us our stance towards the world and its creation, towards the value and significance of the human person ... towards what constitutes flourishing or perfection, towards success and failure. These are matters which in subtle ways colour understanding of the moral response" (MacNamara 1998, 153).

For Christians then, these two levels are in play: the level of our daily relationships with our fellow workers, clients, and colleagues in the corporate world and the second, deeper level of our faith in Jesus Christ. The extent to which Christian lawyers are given opportunity to interact on this second level will in all likelihood be governed by the quality and character of our interaction on the first.

Bibliography

Bagaric, M
2001   "A utilitarian argument: laying the foundation for a coherent system of law," *Otago Law Review*, 10:163–80.

Beasley-Murray, P
1995   *A call to excellence*, Hodder & Stoughton, London.

Berns, S & Baron, P
1998   *Company law and governance*, Oxford University Press, Melbourne.

Boff, L
1988   *Trinity and society*, translated by P Burns, Orbis, Maryknoll, New York.

Brennan Sir, G
1989   "Commercial law and morality," *Melbourne University Law Review*, 17:100–6.

2001   *Opening address: inaugural Australasian Christian Legal Convention*, viewed 22 November 2005, www.lcf.pnc.com.au/convention_papers3.htm.

Burgess, B
2005   "Christian mediation: a critical analysis of mediation from a Christian perspective in the context of secular approaches," MTh, Morling College, Sydney.

Carson, DA
1991   *The gospel according to John*, Leicester, InterVarsity Press and Eerdmans, Grand Rapids.

Clark, GL & Jonson, EP
1995   *Management ethics: theory, cases and practice*, Harper Educational, Melbourne.

Clarke, T
2004   "Introduction to part four," in *Theories of corporate governance: the philosophical foundations of corporate governance*, edited by T Clarke, Routledge, London, 117.

Covey, S
1989   *The seven habits of highly effective people: restoring the character ethic*, Simon & Schuster, New York.

Craddock, F
1990   *Luke*, John Knox Press, Louisville.

Dalton, JF
1996   "Boardroom ethics," in *Business ethics in Australia and New Zealand*, edited by K Woldring, Nelson, Melbourne, 173–82.

du Plessis, JJ, McConvill, J & Bagaric, M
2005   *Principles of contemporary corporate governance*, Cambridge University Press, Melbourne.

Finn, P
1989   "Commerce, the common law and morality," *Melbourne University Law Review*, 17:87–99.

French, W & Granrose, J
1995   *Practical business ethics*, Prentice Hall, Upper Saddle River, New Jersey.

GovernanceMetrics International
2005   *GMI governance and performance studies*, viewed 20 December 2005, www.gmiratings.com/(xif11tjberoigjb4x4ieg5ql)/Performance. aspx.

Grenz, SJ
1997   *The moral quest*, Apollos, Leicester.

Gunton, CE
1993   *The one, the three and the many: God, creation and the culture of modernity*, Cambridge University Press, Cambridge.

Holley, G
1996   *Management and the law*, Pitman Publishing, South Melbourne.

Keenan, JF
1998   "Virtue ethics," in *Christian ethics*, edited by B Hoose, The Liturgical Press, Collegeville, Minnesota, 84–92.

Kelly, D
1998   "The religious roots of Western liberty: cut them or renew them?" in *The Christian and American law*, edited by HW House, Kregel Publications, Grand Rapids, 177–207.

Letza, S, Sun, X & Kirkbride, J
2004   "Shareholding versus stakeholding: a critical review of corporate governance," *Corporate Governance: an international review*, 12:242–62.

MacNamara, V
1998   "The distinctiveness of Christian morality," in *Christian Ethics*, edited by B House, The Liturgical Press, Collegeville, Minnesota, 149–59.

Marshall, IH
1978   *The gospel of Luke: a commentary on the Greek text*, The New International Greek Testament Commentary, The Paternoster Press, Exeter.

Marshall, P
1984   *Thine is the kingdom: a biblical perspective on the nature of government and politics today*, Marshall Morgan & Scott, Basingstoke.

Mason, K
1990   *Constancy and change*, Federation Press, Leichardt.

Mbare, O
2004   "The role of corporate social responsibility (CSR) in the new economy," *Electronic Journal of Business Ethics and Organization Studies*, 9, no. 1, http://ejbo.jyu.fi/index.cgi?page=articles/0901_5.

McGrath, A
1987   *Understanding the trinity*, Kingsway Publications, Eastbourne, Surrey.

Moltmann, J
1984   "The unity of the triune God," *St Vladimir's Theology Quarterly*, 28, no. 3, 157–71.

Montgomery, J W
1975   "The case for 'higher law,'" in *The Law Above the Law*, edited by JW Montgomery, Bethany House Publishers, Minneapolis, 17–57.

1981   *The shaping of America*, Corrected ed., Bethany, Minneapolis.

1993   "Law & morality: friends or foes?" *Law and Justice: The Christian Law Review*, 122:87–106.

1994   *Law and gospel: a study integrating faith and practice*, Canadian Institute for Law, Theology and Public Policy, Christian Legal Fellowship, Edmonton, Alberta.

1996   "Should we legislate morality?" in *Christians in the public square: law, gospel and public policy*, edited by CEB Cranfield, D Kilgour and JW Montgomery, Canadian Institute for Law, Theology and Public Policy, Inc., Edmonton, Alberta, 69–79.

1998   "Why a Christian philosophy of law?" in *Christian perspectives on human rights and legal philosophy*, edited by P Beaumont, Paternoster Press, Cumbria, 73–93.

2002   *Tractatus logico-theologicus*, Verlag für Kultur und Wissenschaft, Bonn.

O'Brien, A & Vagg, M
2001   "Women, GATS and corporate globalisation," *Lysistra*, Winter, 18–9.

OECD
2004   *OECD Principles of corporate governance*, OECD, www.oecd.org/dataoecd/32/18/31557724.pdf.

Redmond, P
2005   *Companies and securities law*, Lawbook Co., Pyrmont, NSW.

Rush, M

1983   *Management: a biblical approach*, Victor Books, Wheaton, Illinois.

Sande, K

2004   *The peacemaker*, 3rd edn, Baker Books, Grand Rapids.

Schrock-Shenk, C, ed.

2000   *Mediation and facilitation training manual*, 4th edn, Mennonite Conciliation Service, Akron, Pennsylvania.

Stassen, G & Gushee, D

2003   *Kingdom ethics: following Jesus in contemporary context*, InterVarsity Press, Downers Grove.

Stumpf, SE

1966   *Morality and the law*, Vanderbilt University Press, Nashville.

Terry, A & Giugni, D

1997   *Business, society and the law*, 2nd edn, Harcourt Brace, Sydney.

2003   *Business, society and the law*, 3rd edn, Thomson Learning, Southbank, Victoria.

Velasquez, MG

1983   "Why corporations are not morally responsible for anything they do," *Business and professional ethics journal*, 2, no. 3, 1–18.

Vermeesch, RB & Lindgren, KE

2001   *Business law of Australia*, 10th edn, Butterworths, Chatswood.

Walker, L

1998   "The abiding value of biblical law," in *The Christian and American law*, edited by HW House, Kregel Publications, Grand Rapids, 208–24.

Wolterstorff, N

1983   *Until justice and peace embrace*, Eerdmans, Grand Rapids.

Endnotes

1   These arguments are developed further in Mongtomery (1993, 16–20).

2   This paper concentrates on the Western common law tradition in Australia, the United Kingdom, and the United States.

3   In America, Montgomery (1996, 71–73) cites Jerry Falwell of Moral Majority as one example of people having made assertions of this kind. In Australia, Mason (1990, 1) gives Howard Carter of the Logos Foundation and politi-

cian Eddie Hann as other examples, and the first chapter of his work explores the myth in more detail.

4   (1797) How St Tr 654 at 703.

5   (1884) 5 NSWR 405.

6   [1917] AC 416.

7   (1983) 154 CLR 120.

8   Montgomery presents this argument in detail in "Should we legislate morality?" (1996).

9   [1932] AC 562.

10 Lord Atkin was of course referring to the dialogue between Jesus and the lawyer in the context of the parable of the good Samaritan found in Luke 10:25–37. For further background to this decision—which was reached in part through after-church family discussions of Jesus' question "Who is my neighbour?"—see Montgomery (1993, 15–16).

11 The changes are well summarised by Finn (1989) and are ongoing. They cover developments affecting both contract law (unconscionable dealings doctrine, relaxation of the strict law of privity of contract, changes in the law of mistake, law of implied terms, growth of doctrine of "good faith," introduction of trade practices/antitrust legislation), as well as the law of equity (equitable estoppel, a general unconscionability principle, changes in the law of breach of confidence, and fiduciary duties).

12 Terry and Giugni are well-placed to opine on and summarise the current trends in this area of the law, holding and having held the positions of head of school and senior lecturer respectively at the School of Business Law and Taxation at the University of New South Wales.

13 By way of comparison, see Bagaric's (2001) utilitarian presentation of "universal" corporate morals.

14 For a consistent yet higher expression of suggested corporate morals that also includes a *positive* duty of benevolence "to assist others in serious trouble, when assistance would immensely help them at little or no inconvenience to ourselves," see du Plessis, McConvill, and Bagaric (2005, 343–62).

15 There are, of course, numerous other ethical "virtues" that are of central importance to the Christian faith apart from those considered here—these include love, kindness, humility, gentleness, patience, tolerance, unity, peace, joy, righteousness, and endurance. See the treatment by Stassen and Gushee (2003, 32–54) of these virtues in the context of a discussion of the traditional formulations of virtue espoused by Aristotle and Thomas Aquinas.

16 Cited in Terry and Giugni (1997, 15).

17 See, for example, Proverbs 21:15, Isaiah 1:16–17, Amos 5:15, 24, and Micah 6:8 (this last verse is the motto of Christian Lawyers Fellowships in both England and New South Wales).

18 Craddock (1990, 62) and Marshall (1978, 183–85) provide expanded treatments of these themes.

19 Cited in Terry and Giugni (1997, 13).

20 Also see Montgomery (1994, 21–23) for a helpful discussion of the interaction of the law of equity with Christian concepts of justice and mercy.

21 The interlocking circles (without words) appear on the front cover of McGrath's *Understanding the Trinity* (1987).

22 Note in this context du Plessis, McConvill, and Bagaric's discussion (2005, 374–81) of the growing impact within the field of corporate governance of "stewardship theory," which "acknowledges a larger range of human motives [other than self-interest] including orientation towards achievement, altruism and the commitment to meaningful work" (Clarke 2004, 117).

23 Finn lists the following areas as indicative of a higher level of "regard for others" reflected in commercial law: (1) enhanced duties of disclosure; (2) duties to provide independent advice or else to provide explanation; (3) duties to have regard to the legitimate interests or reasonable expectations of another; and (4) the advent of the unconscionability principle (1989, 90–97). Notable examples of (1) include the Cadbury Report 1992 in the United Kingdom and the Sarbanes-Oxley Act of 2002 in the United States.

24 See also Montgomery (1998, 79–80) for further discussion of the "good faith" notion in the American and French traditions.

25 See *Hughes Aircraft Systems International v Airservices Australia* (1997) 146 ALR 1, Renard Constructions (M.E.) *Pty Ltd v Minister for Public Works* (1992) 26 NSWLR 234 and *Alcatel Australia v Scarcella* (1994) 44 NSWLR 349.

26 See, for example, O'Brien and Vagg (2001) for a broader discussion of concerns about the impact of corporate globalisation.

27 For example, in *Parke v Daily News Ltd* [1962] Ch 927, in disallowing a voluntary payment to employees losing their jobs, Plowman J specifically held (at 967) that companies do not have a duty to take into account the position of employees in considering what is in the best interests of the company. Rather, he held that that duty is owed solely to shareholders.

28 In 2005, John Whitehead (United States), Adrian Cadbury (United Kingdom), and Dr. Karl-Henrik Robèrt (Sweden) were given the inaugural awards conferred by The Global Centre for Leadership and Business Ethics for their achievements in leadership, corporate governance, and social responsibility.

29 While the conduct listed has all occurred in Australia in the last 10 years, it is suggested that such conduct is not unique to this country.

30 1 Peter 3:16, and see also Montgomery (1981, 152–58).

31 For works providing biblical approaches to people and management issues, see Beasley-Murray (1995) and Rush (1983) and as to conflict, see Sande (2004) and Schrock-Shenk (2000). Indeed, Christian lawyers involved in mediating conflict in specifically Christian ways that emphasise relational restoration (as well as dealing with substantive issues in dispute) may in so doing also tacitly bear witness to others of the transformative potential of the greatest ministry of reconciliation, that performed by Christ himself; see 2 Corinthians 5:17–20 and Burgess (2005).

Muslim Immigration to Europe and Its Challenge for European Societies

HUMAN RIGHTS, SECURITY ISSUES, AND CURRENT DEVELOPMENTS

Christine Schirrmacher

The Present Situation—History and Background

Globalization is a subject of great significance for Europe, too. The world has moved closer together. This is true also for the Islamic world and Europe. New chances for the shaping of a shared future in the twenty-first century, as well as challenges, result from this situation.

North Africa is closely linked with France by virtue of its colonial past, as are Bangladesh, Pakistan, and India with Great Britain. Nearly 2 million Muslims live in Britain; in France about 6 million; in Germany 3.2 million. The immigration of Muslims to Germany began roughly 45 years ago when, in the post-War period, the recruitment of workers from southern (and southeastern) Europe and, later, also from Anatolia (Turkey) appeared to be the solution for an expanding labor market.

The first 10,000 Muslims came to Germany beginning about 1960. They were primarily male workers without families; women and children followed later. Through revolutions and wars (above all, the Iranian Revolution of 1979, the war in the Balkans, and the Iran-Iraq war from 1980 to 1988), through the influx of refugees and asylum-seekers, and by virtue of a higher birthrate compared with the Western population, the number of Muslim immigrants in Europe increased to roughly 16–20 million persons.

Even in the last 20 years, when this development was foreseeable, European countries found it difficult to consider themselves as countries "open to immigration." There was repeated failure to discuss cultural, social, and political as well as religious commonalities and differences, to consider the mistakes that were made, and to work out rules for life together in the future. The German society, for example, assumed all too naturally that these people would prefer the Western, secular way of life to their own tradition, would give up their religious-cultural roots over time, and would "assimilate" themselves. Today, it is clearly evident that in many parts of Europe a contrary development—a return to tradition and a retreat into a world of one's own—long since has begun.

Most of the Muslims who live in Europe today will remain; their number will continue to increase. The political or economic situation in their home countries frequently offers them no perspective for a return; their children and grandchildren have grown up in Europe, and they, too, will not return.

In view of this situation, several challenges result:

1. Social Aspects

Never before have so many people from the Islamic cultural sphere lived permanently in Europe. But are they also at home in Europe?

Many young people of the second and third generations speak too little German (or French, Spanish, or Dutch) to be successful in a vocation. What future do these young people face? Not a few of them retreat into their own world, their own language, the mosque, and the Turkish or Arab neighborhood.

Forced marriages and murders of honor occur precisely within the parallel society in which its members take justice into their own hands. At long last, the duty of speaking the language of the host country finally is being discussed openly in Europe. Without the command of the language, there is no integration; without integration, there is no vocational success and no shared future.

Neither the immigrants nor their host countries originally reckoned with a permanent life together. Both sides at first thought their coexistence would last only a few years. Especially the majority society concerned itself too little and not intensively enough with the cultural and religious peculiarities of the immigrants. The "other culture" was either admired uncritically or ignored and rejected. The knowledge about Islam among many people in Europe is still too undeveloped. Many Muslims, at first, wanted to become "Europeans" but then turned away in disappointment. Many make contact with a mosque that preaches distance and withdrawal and extols the nationalism from the home country and Islam as an identity as an alternative in a "godless" Western society. Then it is perhaps only a small step to a turn toward political Islam (Islamism) or even to extremism.

A New Situation for Both Sides

The situation is new not only for Europeans but also for the Muslim communities. They must undertake a new definition of their theological and political-social position here in the "diaspora" in a non-Muslim Western society. Many questions arise: Is it possible in non-Islamic countries to do without the amplification of the call to prayer by loudspeaker—in Muslim countries an everyday occurrence? May meat slaughtered by non-Muslims (and, of course, not *ritually* slaughtered by them) be eaten by Muslims—a situation that hardly ever will occur in Islamic countries? How are the Islamically based social conventions (no contact between young men and girls) to be adhered to in a liberal, pluralistic society in which only a few people still stand up for religious values? Is one's own son allowed to marry a German, non-Muslim woman who possibly judges the family of her husband to be "unbelievers"? All of these are questions that never arose in the Islamic land of origin, and they are questions to which the Muslim community must find answers—answers that can turn out to be quite different even within the Muslim community.

But even beyond the conduct of daily life, many questions arise in regard to religion: How can the Islamic faith be passed on to the younger generation that lives in the midst of a pluralistic, secularized society that often is not very much characterized by visible ethical and religious values? Many families begin to practice their religion for the first time in the diaspora, in the desire to preserve their cultural roots. Others observe the regulations more strictly than they did in their lands of origin. Especially in Turkish Islam in Germany, a conservative religion is thus "conserved" that hardly exists in this form in present-day Turkey.

And how does the Western majority society act? Does it understand the tall minaret, which perhaps towers above all the other buildings in the neighborhood, as a cultural enrichment or as a threat? Or perhaps in earlier years as an enrichment but today as a threat? Does it believe the peaceful declarations from the neighborhood mosque association, or does it consider the mosque to be the meeting place for "sleepers" and terrorists? Are the people who pray there those who practice their religion or those who form political cells? Is the headscarf worn as a personal confession of faith, or as a political symbol? Do European societies at all desire a coexistence with the immigrants? And do most immigrants today still desire integration? How far do the tolerance and freedom of democratic societies reach, and where does indifference or rejection begin?

2. The Political Challenge

Today, everyone is aware of what is meant under the subject of the "political challenge": Many people in Europe in the last 30 years considered the occupation with this political dimension in Islamic countries to be subject matter appropriate for some Near East experts. It was assumed for a long time that extremist efforts limited themselves to internal conflicts in countries like Algeria, Palestine, or Iran. Today, this view has changed fundamentally, and quite rightly so.

Whoever focuses one's attention only on countries such as Afghanistan as areas of refuge for extremist networks will no longer grasp the present-day situation in all of its implications. European metropolises also have become the scenes of terrorist attacks, among them Amsterdam, Madrid, or London, which for quite a long while has been considered to be the hub of international political Islam. With logistical and financial support from the Near and Middle East, Europe has become the area of refuge and action for extremist groups. Mosques and Islamic centers have become scenes of significant incidents. International Islamistic terrorism, long underestimated in regard to its significance and its claim to power, has not stopped before the gates of Europe but rather today—as dreadful as this conclusion is—has become an element of European reality. It is no longer the only goal of present-day extremist groups to pursue the conflict in and in the vicinity of Israel in the Middle East or to struggle against the regimes in their own Islamic countries they deem to be "open to compromise" or "un-Islamic." Horror and terror are carried into the Western world, too, in the name of Islam, and Muslims as well as non-Muslims are killed because they are representatives of the "godless West" or because they are "collaborators" with it.

Islamism as a Political Power

Of course, political Islam does not consist only of violence and terror. Violent extremism is only one wing of political Islam and, in terms of numbers, on the whole a small spectrum. That area of Islamism that pursues its goals by legal means, with a strategy, with financial resources stemming in part from foreign donors, with well-schooled personnel but not with less determination, is also to be counted as a form of political Islam. Politically motivated Islam exerts its influence over mosque associations and umbrella organizations, and this in two ways. First, it declares itself as organized Islam to be the spokesperson of "the" Muslims in Germany and employs titles such as "Zentralrat der Muslime," although this "central council" is likely to represent less than 1 percent of the Muslims in Germany. Altogether, from 5 to, at most, 10 percent of all Muslims in the country belong to one of these organizations, that is, a minority. Nevertheless, politically organized Islam formulates statements proclaimed to the public. Since the Muslim community has no membership status or hierarchy comparable to those in the churches, organized Islam thus appoints itself to be the partner in dialogue with the church and to be the contact organization for the state, although a majority of at least 90 percent of all the Muslims in Germany do not desire to be represented by one of these organizations.

Representatives of Islamism seek influence in universities and in politics, demand equality with the Christian churches and increased rights, or even demand adjustments in legislation (the law for the protection of animals had to be altered to allow special permission for the ritual slaughter of animals not previously numbed). Other points of contention carried before the highest courts in the last few years also include the question of the headscarf for women teachers with civil servant status, or the call to prayer broadcast by loudspeaker.

The preeminent goal is the recognition of Islam as a religion possessing equal rights in Europe and the acquaintance and pervasion of Western society with Islamic values. The second step is the establishment of Sharia, the Islamic order, first of all over the Muslim community. But, in addition, politically organized Islam also has an effect within the Muslim community through its desire to urge Muslims in Europe to adopt a stricter observance of Islam. If female teachers from organized Islam give instruction in religion in the public schools while wearing the headscarf, and if they thus display their traditional role that legally discriminates against women, then the pressure upon female students in this environment to wear the headscarf more frequently obviously becomes greater. Thus is a traditional, nonenlightened Islam fostered and carried into the parents' house.

Consideration of the background of political Islam, thus, is today neither "far-fetched" nor an offbeat intellectual field of activity but rather is of the greatest significance for European society. Neither scare tactics nor minimizing of the risk nor generalizing is appropriate here. A sober stocktaking is required.

Differentiation Creates Sobriety

If the background and motives of political Islamic groups, on the one hand, are recognized and analyzed soberly, then this will contribute to the sophisticated perception of the Muslim community and, in the end, to the avoidance of false judgments. If apolitical Muslim groups distance themselves emphatically from violence, terror, and Islamism—indeed, it is even more valuable if they find arguments in the Koran and the writings of Muslim theologians that reject the justification of a violent Islam—then this will serve to make more clearly discernible the differences existing between it and the peaceful majority in the Muslim community in Europe. Neither a resistance directed against Muslim neighbors and fellow citizens arising out of fear nor a minimizing of the political activities of the known groups will contribute to peaceful coexistence and the constructive shaping of a shared future.

Making an Accounting Is Required

Critical questions also must be allowed if the urgently necessary objective discussion is to take place, critical questions of the majority as well as of the minority society. Subjects of such questions could be the mistakes of the past, the failed integration, but also subjects such as forced marriages and so-called murders of honor. Both have existed in Germany for more than 40 years but until recently were of little interest to the majority of society. The fact that today there is rather an increase in murders of honor, and that there is still a large number of forced marriages of young Turkish girls in Germany, at the same time poses the question about the defense of European values, such as how women are to be protected and how European notions of the equality of men and women are to be established in an environment that, through the importation of antiquated traditions, fundamentally questions these values. Only a sober discussion of present problems will bring us a step forward.

3. The Question of Religion

In a time in which, in the West, the general mood is that religion has hardly any public significance anymore and, in the consciousness of many, is so characterized by the Enlightenment and secularization that it has only little to do with the European order of values, Islam appears as an exceedingly energetic, worldwide networked, and above all self-confident religion with an apologetically presented claim upon absolute truth.

In Islam, of course, we encounter not only a religion but also a social system that is clearly bound with religion and tradition. At the same time, religion is in a much greater measure an element of daily life, of public life, and of the family than is the case in general in Europe. The tradition woven closely together with Islam contains detailed rules in regard to clothing and food, feasts and holidays, the conduct of men and women, marriage and divorce, the relationship of Muslims to non-Muslims, and war and peace. Because tradition and faith are bound closely to each other, and the tradition is grounded in religion, the tradition retains a determinative power in daily life. For this reason alone, it is not easy to separate the political sphere from the religious one in a question such as the significance of the headscarf or the function of the mosque. With religion and tradition (which does not always have to be specifically Islamic), social and political aspects are bound together. Thus, the headscarf is for many Muslim women simply more than only a personal confession of faith, but rather also stands for recognition of the legal stipulations in Sharia concerning marriage and the family, and of the legally disadvantaged position of the woman. Thus, the significance of the headscarf altogether goes far beyond a personal confession.

By virtue of the fact that Islam raises the subject of religion anew, Western society, too, will have to ask itself what values it wishes to defend. Do the values of European society rest upon the foundation of a Jewish-Christian legacy? If so, must this Jewish-Christian legacy be preserved in order to be able to preserve Europe's central values? Or can the two be decoupled from each other? The sometimes heated debate, within the framework of a possible entry of Turkey into the European Union, about whether Europe is a "Christian club" definitely has shown that this question in the last analysis always maintains an unspoken presence in the course of the confrontation with Islam. European countries first must answer this question for themselves before they will be able to give an acceptable answer to Turkey.

Discernible is also the fact that Islam has gained in attractive power rather than lost. One today can no longer speak of the much-invoked "wearing down" of religion in the second and third generation. There is certainly the sphere of "secularized" Islam—Muslims who pursue the same forms of leisure-time entertainment as do European or German youth—but considered as a whole, Islam has remained a lively religion among the immigrants. Not, perhaps, in the sense that every individual Islamic religious regulation is observed to the last detail in every family but indeed in such a manner that Islam offers support and identity. It is, in part, the case that precisely young people—after their parents have lived a relatively enlightened form of Islam—again turn to a stricter observance of Islamic regulations.

Concrete Fields of Discussion

A sign of a detailed treatment of the subject of "Islam" would be a discussion about concepts and content that, in another religious-cultural context, could have a different meaning.

A. The Question of Human Rights

There is, for example, the discussion about human rights. Muslim organizations have emphasized repeatedly that Islam not only respects human rights but even has formulated more extensive catalogues of human rights than the West and is really the "author" of all human rights. At the same time, however, a second look at the contents of the human rights declarations in the Western and Islamic contexts reveals clearly that all the Islamic declarations place the Sharia as a preamble before any kind of human right. In practical application, this means that an apostate can no longer demand any human rights at all since he, according to the stipulations of Sharia, has committed a crime worthy of death and, thus, can no longer claim any religious freedom or other human rights. In the opinion of the vast majority of Muslim theologians, the right to religious freedom and human rights ends with the defection from Islam, even if the death sentence only rarely is carried out by courts but in most cases is done so by the offender's family or the society.

Here lies the real focus in the discussion between the Western and the Islamic understanding of human rights, and not in the superficial discussion of whether Islam recognizes human rights at all. If, however, there are reports from all Islamic countries about violations of human rights and limitations upon religious freedom, especially for converts, then these become understandable only in the context of the official Islamic definition of human and minority rights. Only on the basis of a detailed knowledge of the religion, culture, and legal system of Islam will it be possible to conduct this discussion at all in wider settings and in the public realm.

B. Suicide Attacks

Here is another example: The terror attacks from 2001 and the following years were condemned repeatedly from the Muslim side with the argument that the Koran emphasizes that the one who kills a human being has "killed the whole world" (Sura 5:32). Numerous Muslims emphasized that the attacks are in no way to be justified with the aid of Islam.

It is correct that the Koran (Sura 4:29), as well as Islamic tradition, disapproves of murder, just as it does suicide. Murder is one of the serious crimes listed in the Koran. The tradition explicitly condemns suicide: Whoever commits suicide out of the fear of poverty or out of despair will not enter Paradise.

Of course, those who carry out attacks in Palestine and other places do not consider themselves as those who commit suicide but rather first of all as martyrs, that is, as human beings who fight and die for the cause of Islam, for the cause of God. An attack that is carried out with the high probability of the attacker's own death is hardly ever interpreted as suicide but rather as Jihad, as commitment to the cause of God, as the final weapon against the wrongful oppression of the community of Muslims. The Koran promises martyrs entry into Paradise (Sura 4:74), without examination of their faith:

> I will let no action that one of you commits go unrewarded,
> whether it is done by a man or a woman. . . . And those who,
> for my sake . . . have suffered hardship, and who have fought
> and been killed, I will forgive them their bad deeds, and, as a
> reward from God, I will let them enter gardens in whose val-
> leys streams flow. With God, one is rewarded well (3:195).

The martyr, however, can expect Paradise (Sura 47:4–6). "And if you are killed or die for God's sake, then forgiveness and compassion from God are better than what you manage to do" (3:157).

C. The Question of Tolerance

Another example is the question of tolerance and of the concept of tolerance. A frequently expressed reproach made by Muslim apologists is that Islam accepts Christianity, but the Christians do not accept Islam. It is frequently pointed out in this connection that Muslim conquerors, in contrast to the Christian churches and crusaders, did not force Christians to choose between conversion to Islam or death. In addition, so the argument, Muslims accepted Jesus Christ quite fundamentally as a respected prophet and the Old and New Testaments as revelations, while Christians refused their recognition of Mohammed as well as of the Koran.

Here, too, a discussion about the concept of "tolerance" easily moves in the wrong direction without a detailed knowledge of Islam: What is understood under the term *tolerance* within Islam? In any case, not the recognition of another religion on an equal basis. The Koran already makes clear that Mohammed, to be sure, campaigned for the recognition of the new religion by Christians (and Jews) and urged Christians and Jews to become members of it, but in his later years, after the Christians of his time refused to follow him, he considered the Christian faith more and more to be blasphemy and the Christian revelation to be falsified. Christians in areas conquered by Islam, indeed, were permitted as a rule to retain their faith. But they became subjugated persons (Arabic: *dhimmis*—protected minorities), who paid taxes for their "unbelief" and had to endure many legal disadvantages, even persecution and death.

The Koran, indeed, certifies the Old and New Testaments as God's revelation, and Jesus is a respected prophet in the Koran. But He is respected only as a "herald of Islam," as a precursor to Mohammed who is only a human being and who brought salvation to no one. Jesus, according the Islamic position, was falsely revered by the Christians as God's Son, and thereby they distorted His "originally Islamic" message completely. The Christian revelation as a "falsified text" is given only very little respect in Islam, and the person of Jesus as it is represented in the Old and New Testaments, just as little.

Worrying is the fact that many Muslim organizations in Europe today urge that nothing "negative" be permitted to be published any more about Islam, since this would mean discrimination. In other words, everything not written from the Muslim point of view is to be prevented from being published (a development that is far more advanced, for example, in Great Britain thanks to the efforts of Islamic lobbyists). The point of departure for these considerations is the *dhimma* status assigned in the Muslim view to the Christians, that is, the status of the protected minority that is placed under Islam and is subjugated to Islamic law. Here, how "awake" Western society is will be very essential as it follows this development as well as to what extent it is ready to defend the freedoms of the press and speech established only after great effort.

D. The Question of Women

A further example is the frequently cited situation of women. Here, too, a detailed knowledge of Islam would lead to a better initial situation in the discussion and, finally, to more honesty in regard to the really controversial points. Muslim apologists emphasize that the woman in Islam enjoys equal status before God with men and, indeed, that Islam endows the woman with true dignity, freedom, protection, and respect. In the Western view, a woman with head-scarf and cloak is an "oppressed creature." What is right?

The Koran, indeed, speaks of the fact that man and woman were created equal before God, without giving an indication that the woman might be a creature of "less value." At the same time, the Koran speaks—and the Islamic tradition even more clearly—of the different duties assigned to the man and the woman, from which different rights are derived and, indeed, with which the legal discrimination of the woman is sanctioned. She is legally discriminated against in the law of inheritance (she inherits only half of what the man inherits), in witness rights (her testimony is worth only half as much as the testimony of a man), and in marital law (a divorce is made more difficult for her; in some countries it is almost impossible; in most countries polygamy is allowed for the husband). A foundation of Islamic marital law that is recognized everywhere is the wife's duty to be obedient and the man's right of discipline in regard to her that forbids her to make her own self-determined decisions against his objections (to leave the house, to maintain contacts with persons of whom he disapproves, and similar restrictions). If she does not render him this obedience, then, according to the opinion of the majority of theologians, he is permitted to resort to means of discipline in accord with Sura 4:34.

It is, thus, much more this marital law (polygamy, duty to obey, discipline, law of inheritance), which in the Islamic world, is interpreted in the vast majority of cases in a conservative sense (Turkey forms a certain exception to this rule), that stands much more in opposition to European conceptions of law than does a piece of clothing. But these controversial "women's questions" have appeared to the present only too seldom in public discussion.

Summary

It is not necessarily the case that the same content lies at the root of the same concepts. This cultural-religious content results rather from the specific cultural-religious-political context in which it originated. Concepts such as "tolerance" and "equality"—robbed of their occidental roots—cannot simply be transferred without problem to other cultures and religions and then, as a matter of course, also offer the same content.

The present debate about the foundations of this society, and about the confrontation with a quite different value system and religion, has in a sense forced itself upon us with all its might. This frightens us deeply and yet at the same time opens paths to a sound discussion, as long, then, as Western society is able to resist falling into panic and raising the barricades but rather is able to take stock soberly of the conditions in its countries and among the immigrants, and to seek constructive solutions. Perhaps the debate about "integration" also is so agitated because the cultural-social or religious peculiarities of Europe, which should be defended here, have been defined clearly only in rare cases. Does Islam perhaps make Western society's lack of goals and values particularly clear?

Most Muslims who live and think apolitically in Europe and are worried about the rights Islamic groups bit by bit successfully demand expect an answer from the state, whose task it is, on the basis of a detailed knowledge of Islam, to arrive at a reasonable demarcation over against political forces. There cannot be any double legal standard—either in regard to the position of women or in regard to the recognition of polygamy, for example—for only an agreement upon a shared legal and value system will be able to guarantee the preservation of our state in the long run. It is rewarding to argue and to struggle for these shared values and to defend anew Europe's foundations for society, church, and state.

Conference paper presented at Europe/International House, Pécs, Hungary, November 22, 2005, "Continents—Globalisation—Security," November 22–23, 2005.

The Sacred and the Secular

RELIGION IN THE STATE UNIVERSITY

George Wolfgang Forell

It is, indeed, an honor for me to be able to present the Sixth Annual Presidential Lecture at The University of Iowa where I have had the privilege of teaching for most of my academic career. When I was invited to give this lecture, the temptation was considerable to present something in the area of my current research, for example, Luther's ethics in his 1515/16 lectures on Paul's letter to the Romans, but I decided soon after the invitation arrived that I would try to deal with a more general question which has been in the background of all my work during the more than three decades I have taught here, namely, "How does one deal with the sacred in an essentially secular setting?" The first director of the School of Religion, M. Willard Lampe, had written that "religion, theoretically and practically, is inseparable from education; hence it should be taught, even in a tax-supported university, not indirectly or surreptitiously, but unapologetically, comprehensively, and in line with the best educational procedures."[1]

The first question this exhortation raises seems to be, what is this "religion" that we ought to study in the university? Virgilius Ferm, who once edited *An Encyclopedia of Religion*,[2] observed when dealing with this word, "the term religion belongs to that large class of popular words which seems acceptable as common coin of communicative exchange but which on closer examination fails to carry the imprint of exact meaning."[3] The customary efforts to explore the meaning of this word with the help of its Latin roots may lead to all kinds of intriguing speculations but do not make for precision.

Other definitions are so inclusive as to permit one to define everything of concern to human beings as religious. For some the term *religious* has for all practical purposes become coextensive with *human*. Whatever is specifically human is *ipso facto* religious.[4] Here "religion is the capacity of the human organism to transcend its biological nature through the construction of objective, morally binding, all-embracing universes of meaning."[5] "The only non-religious phenomena in the human sphere are those that are grounded in man's animal nature, or more precisely, that part of his biological constitution that he has in common with other animals."[6] In this context Max Mueller's understanding of religion as a "disease of language"[7] becomes comprehensible and may explain the decision of *The Oxford Dictionary of the Christian Church*[8] simply to ignore this troublesome term.

The situation has been further complicated by the fact that the word *religion* has taken on a negative meaning not only for those who claim to be enemies of the study of the subject because they consider it unworthy of serious consideration in a university or threatening the "wall of separation" between church and state but also in the writings of one of the most important theologians of this century. The Swiss theologian Karl Barth has a chapter in his massive *Church Dogmatics*, volume 1, part 2 with the title "The Revelation of God as the Abolition of Religion."[9] In chapter 2 of this volume Barth refers to religion as unbelief and writes: "Revelation does not link up with a human religion which is already present and practiced. It contradicts it."[10] (By the way, it is in the light of this point of view that we must understand the sympathy for atheism as practiced by Marxist communism on the part of Barth and his followers. To Barth the denial of "religion in general" or the God of the philosophers was not only excusable but actually praiseworthy. This explains among other things the fierce opposition of Barth to the Nazis and his relative tolerance of Stalinist Communism. The Communists were atheists, i.e., they objected to "religion." To Barth this seemed understandable and even commendable. The Nazis, on the other hand, were anti-Semites and hated Jews. Since for Barth the only true revelation is connected with the Jews, i.e., the Old and New Testaments, anti-Semitism is, indeed, revolt against God.)

Thus, not only people who consider themselves irreligious but also some who are devoted to their faith find the academic study of religion of doubtful value. I recall people standing at the doors of Macbride auditorium, here at The University of Iowa, handing leaflets to the students attending classes of the large course dealing with

Judaism and Christianity, trying to persuade them to drop the course because participation would threaten their faith.

By now it may be apparent that we could spend most of our time discussing the problems raised by the term *religion*. I have tried to show my hand by using the word *sacred* as defining the subject matter of religious studies. It is a word that has been given considerable prominence by the students of comparative religion associated with the *Religionsgeschichtliche Schule*. Professor Eliade used it to define the nature of religion in his seminal work *The Sacred and the Profane*,[11] but when defined as "the power, being, or realm understood by religious persons to be at the core of existence and to have transformative effect on their lives and destinies,"[12] even the term *sacred* seems rather vague.

I shall try to overcome this vagueness by identifying and addressing four aspects of religion and examining their relationship to the basic concerns of the university. But this proposal immediately opens another Pandora's box. What, indeed, are the basic concerns of the secular university? John Henry Newman defined this ideal University as "a place of *teaching* universal *knowledge*," and added, "This implies that its object is, on the one hand, intellectual, not moral; and, on the other, that it is the diffusion and extension of knowledge rather than the advancement." He immediately continued: "If its subject were scientific and philosophical discovery, I do not see why a University should have students."[13] But as this quotation indicates, Newman spoke of a quite different institution from the modern secular university. He was convinced that "[The University] cannot fulfill its object duly, such as I have described it, without the Church's assistance; or to use the theological term, the Church is necessary for its *integrity*."[14]

However, it is part of the charter of an American state university functioning in a pluralistic society that it fulfill its task without the assistance of any church. Professor Sinclair Goodlad suggests four types of expectations and goals commonly proposed for the secular university:[15]

> First, a socially defined goal of equipping individuals with the knowledge and skills suitable for given

occupations. . . . Second, . . . the social goals of the "consumers" of higher education—of students and perhaps more importantly of their parents—for the social status which a degree . . . is believed to confer, and for a "meal ticket"—a job qualification to be achieved as quickly and as efficiently as possible. Third, there are the personal goals of some students to achieve independence in criticism or to acquire a philosophy of life. Fourth, there are academic goals of unhurried and careful elaboration of theory supported by minutely detailed observation within the context of a discipline offering the support and respect of fellow scholars, and the possibility of "international visibility."[16]

It is obvious that this list is somewhat arbitrary. Several of the goals most cherished by some may seem irrelevant to others. In the secular university the very ranking of these goals is a problem. Students, faculty, parents, administration, regents, legislators, etcetera, see these goals differently and would assign varying priorities to them. Some considered marginal at best by faculty may justify the commitment of large sums of money by parents. In a pluralistic society, in contrast to the society Newman envisioned, the university "has no integrating or commonly accepted ethos, but tolerates an immense variety of beliefs, life styles, moral standards and forms of art."[17] But it is precisely because of the pluralistic character of the goals of the secular university that the study of religion in its broadest context is so useful, not because it provides simple answers to be adopted by everybody, but because it furnishes a broad context in the search for goals for all participants. If religion in all its forms is an effort at world-construction, in Peter Berger's phrase, "the audacious attempt to conceive of the entire universe as being humanly significant,"[18] the study and analysis of this extraordinary effort should be undertaken by the university. Regardless of one's own religious stance, the mere examination of this endeavor, regardless of its outcome, is bound to contribute to the development of communal and personal priorities.

We may now be ready to return to our examination of the various facets of religion: First we note a "cognitive aspect." All religions deal with certain propositions demanding assent. "Hear O Israel: The

LORD our God is one LORD" (Deut 6:4) is such a proposition. And so is, "God was in Christ, reconciling the world unto himself" (2 Cor 5:19) or "Allah is God and Muhammad is his prophet." Every religion enunciates statements that demand assent from its adherents. These propositions are part of the religious quest for a humanly significant universe. For some people, especially in the West, this cognitive aspect of religion seems preeminent. Religion is considered a system of beliefs that must be accepted. This understanding of religion is prevalent among the intellectual leadership of religious communities. But while theology or the theoretical elaboration of the religious system of meaning is important, it is not as important for the total religious community as theologians would like to think.

Secondly, and for many people in our culture by far the most important element of religion, is its moral aspect. Particularly for men and women influenced by Judaism, Christianity, and Islam, morality and religion are seen as substantially identical. Religion is considered a moral system, and morality is seen as virtually the same as religion. It is true, of course, that this has not always been the case. Plato was so offended by the morality of the gods of popular Greek religion that he banished them from his ideal state, and even Judaism, Christianity, and Islam have been reproached by some critics on moral grounds. Indeed the basic objection to Christianity by the political authorities of the Roman Empire was based on moral reasons; the Christian objection to emperor worship was considered unpatriotic. Be that as it may, religion is in the minds of many people so profoundly linked to ethics that the introduction of religious practices such as prayer and Bible reading is assumed to assure the improvement of morality.

Thirdly, religion has a profound emotional dimension; it involves some of the most deep-felt and penetrating sentiments of human beings. This fact led the nineteenth-century theologian Friedrich Schleiermacher to define religion as the "absolute feeling of dependence." He suggested that the variety of forms this feeling assumes among various ethnic groups and individuals explains the differences among human religions. Because of this emotional aspect of religion, all purely intellectual criticism may appear to the religious person irrelevant and immaterial. It may also help to explain the interdependence of art and religion resulting in music, literature, and visual arts so profoundly linked to a particular faith as to become almost incomprehensible without some understanding of the religious source. The emotional dimension can be so powerful that people even after they have abandoned the cognitive elements of their religion may remain attached to their faith because of nonrational feelings associated with emotions they may find as difficult to explain as to escape.

And this brings us to the fourth and last aspect of religion, the communal dimension. Religion is always the function of a community. It creates, maintains, and gives meaning to human communities. We observe that it is commonly involved in the rites of passage from birth to death. This function of religion explains the development of quasi-religious rites of passage even in societies officially atheistic. The present debate among our Jewish fellow citizens about the question, "Who is a Jew?" illustrates the communal dimension of religion very clearly. Recently Ari L. Goldman observed in *The New York Times*, "In the United States, it is difficult to pick up a Jewish journal, open mail from Jewish organizations, or hear a sermon in a temple or synagogue without encountering the words 'who is a Jew?'"[19] But various groups of Christians as well as Muslims are confronted by the same question. What constitutes membership in a religious community? Does it depend on assent to propositions, behavior according to certain moral standards, or the presence and awareness of certain feelings? Many people understand religion almost entirely in communal terms, as participation in the life of a religious community. Such participation may occur even though all the other aspects of religion discussed so far may be missing. While frequently ignored by theologians, the communal aspect of religion is for many people who consider themselves religious an essential, if not *the* essential, aspect.

Even though we have not been able to come to a precise definition of religion, we have observed the power and pervasiveness of the phenomenon. In recent years it has even returned to the book review sections of our most prestigious newspapers. For example, the front page of *The New York Times Book Review* of February 12, 1989, featured a long article by the novelist Dan Wakefield with the intriguing title, "And Now, a Word from Our Creator." He not only detailed the return of "God" and religion as a force in serious fiction but also reported the claim of at least one science writer, the author of *God and the New Physics*, that "it may seem bizarre, but in my opinion science offers a surer path to God than religion."[20]

While one may want to question the reliability of this observation, it illustrates the broad and pervasive interest in religion and in God in our time. How should the university deal with it? It is not unusual in an American state university simply to ignore it or treat it as an embarrassment, hoping that the inconvenient topic might go away. One sometimes has the impression that religion has taken the place occupied by sex in the nineteenth century. Everybody knew then that sex existed, but it was not mentioned in polite society. In many universities religion appears to suffer the same fate. The University of Iowa made an innovative decision more than 50 years ago to deal with the subject of religion in a straightforward and pluralistic manner. This pioneering venture has demonstrated two facts: (1) The university is a major resource to the study of religion, and (2) the study of religion is a valuable resource to the academic task of the university.

Because of the many dimensional character of religion as observed earlier, it can be most adequately investigated with the help of the broad resources in the social sciences and the humanities available in the university. The scholarly resources of a research university will enrich and deepen the study of religion. If, indeed, such study deals with epistemological problems, if it has to ask, "What can we know?" it is most likely to aid in finding an answer in conversation with others who have to ask the same question from different perspectives. Similarly, the moral question, "What must I do?" is clearly not an exclusively religious concern, and its profound religious dimension can be probed more adequately in the context of the university. Even the most specifically religious question in the Kantian triad, the eschatological question, "What may I hope for?" is best addressed in the context of all the humanities.

The same is true for the other aspects of religion mentioned before. To deal with emotions and feelings without the aid of psychology and especially the psychology of religion seems irrational, and to explore the artistic expressions of religious feelings isolated from the insights supplied by art and music history would make a comprehensive understanding very difficult. The communal dimension of religion is best understood in dialogue with sociology and anthropology as the works of sociologists of religion, quoted in this presentation, have demonstrated.

But if the assistance in the study of religion of the resources of the university is manifest, so is the aid the study of religion supplies to the many central endeavors of the university. It may be especially obvious in the humanities since no human culture can be understood in isolation from its religious setting, but it is helpful in the social sciences as well. Furthermore, students of law and of medicine would benefit in their work with men and women if they would see them against the background of their religious environment, making use of the comprehensive understanding of religion here proposed. The religious dimensions of the political conflicts from Sri Lanka to Ireland and from Armenia to Lebanon and the Sudan are obvious. The study of religion might have informed those who a few years ago approached the Ayatollah Khomeini with a cake and a King James Bible of the ineptness of such an overture. Indeed, I would be willing to argue that the absence of any understanding of the reality of religion, apart from Washington prayer breakfasts or the fulminations of the televangelists, is related to the failure of some of our leaders to comprehend the influence of religion as it affects the political lives of men and women everywhere in the world.

So far we have discussed the value of the study of religion at a secular university for religion as well as the university. One difficult issue has been avoided: how does this effort relate to the religious commitment of the people involved in this study? We have observed the subtle power of religion in the lives of human beings. Can it be approached in an objective and scientific manner without falsifying it? Is the very character of religious commitment so fragile, so idiosyncratic, that scholarly scrutiny is impossible? To answer this question one would have to analyze religious commitment with some care since it is a fairly complex phenomenon pertaining not only to people commonly regarded as religious but also to those whose commitment is apparently fiercely antireligious.

Two forms of religious commitment seem generally observable.[21] When dealing with this issue in the past, I have suggested that the first form of religious commitment apparent to everybody and affecting by far the largest number of people is commitment as the acceptance of a historical-cultural tradition. The tradition may be Hindu or Buddhist; it may be Zuni or Dobu. For most Americans it is generally Jewish or Christian. This commitment is a form of self-acceptance. It is the admission that this is the kind of man or woman I am. These are my antecedents; this is my history and my culture; this is how I came to be who I am. In a sense it is a commitment to a specific history and culture. Many people accept their religion as a bond to the past. To illustrate what this may mean specifically, I shall use the model of Christianity as an example since this is the tradition that has been the object of my research.

The historical-cultural commitment means in the instance of Christianity a commitment to the church as the guardian and herald of certain historical values. Here it is both a bridge to the past and an effort to find new ways of expressing these values creatively in the present. It is also a commitment to the Bible as the document that has shaped me and my people. It is a clue to Dante as well as Shakespeare, to Emerson as well as John Updike, to Goethe as well as Hesse, to Pascal and André Gide. Considering my particular situation in time and space, if I do not know the Bible, I will have trouble knowing myself. This book is important not only for what it meant at the time it was written but also for what it has continued to mean in every age that followed, from the rabbi's interpretation of the Talmud to Bultmann and Barth in our century. It is also a commitment to the validity of the religious experience. Even if I never shuddered in awe before the vastness of the universe and the beauty of holiness, this commitment means that I shall respect such experiences in others and be grateful for them—just as I respect the painter and the composer and appreciate their accomplishments, though I may not be able to paint or compose. The university is an excellent place where such a commitment can be examined, interpreted, perhaps deepened, changed, or even abandoned, on the basis of serious study and reflection. This process does not demand any belief in the supernatural and can be dealt with by anybody who wants to learn.

But there is also a religious commitment that involves the acceptance of a specific social-moral perspective. Persons so committed assert that religion and ethics belong together. They give assent in thought, word, and deed to the moral vision of their faith. This is in a sense a commitment to righteousness. While this is possible within the context of all religions, I shall again illustrate it from the point of view of the Christian faith. Here the church is seen as a moral and maternal community that both teaches and upholds these values and helps her children put them into practice. Here morality receives a dimension of significance that it does not have if approached from a purely prudential or rationalistic point of view. The Bible is seen not so much as the record of particular cultural tradition as a collection of sayings offering moral guidance. It is considered the "Good Book." This popular expression reflects the ethical connotations the Bible has for all those who read it in the light of this type of commitment. The Bible is the guide to the good life and the passages that contain clear moral exhortations are the favorite passages of those committed in this second sense. Religious experience is here seen primarily as moral experience and the person who has learned to live the good life in peace with the neighbor is the religious individual. Here, too, scholarly study can help clarify and deepen or critically evaluate this moral commitment by seeing it in a cross-cultural and historical context.

An element of religious reality does not belong in the secular university. Worship, however valuable to the individual or the community, should be left untouched. It could be examined from the outside, as in a course on liturgy in the school of music, but not practiced. Anything that demands ultimate commitment, total belief or unbelief, does not properly belong in the university. Here everything must be left open-ended, subject to further examination and revision. Those who claim to have found the ultimate answer are entitled to enjoy it and share it with like-minded friends. If these discoveries are brought to the university for study and evaluation they become forthwith penultimate and subject to critical analysis. This applies to final answers in all fields, and religion is no exception.

At this point it may have become more plausible why some friends as well as enemies of religion would like to keep the sacred out of the secular university. The sacred, "the power, being or realm understood by religious persons to be at the core of existence and to have transformative effect on their lives and destinies," is bound to be sensitive and controversial. But what right does the university have to avoid such issues? If they are examined "not indirectly or surreptitiously, but unapologetically, and comprehensively," they will aid the entire *universitas*, the association of masters and scholars leading the common life of learning, to clarify its complex and controversial goals—not because the study of religion supplies these goals ready-made and in a final form but because such study illustrates and encourages the perennial search.

Endnotes

1 M. Willard Lampe, *The Story of an Idea: The History of the School of Religion of The University of Iowa* (Iowa City, IA: University of Iowa Extension Bulletin, no. 806, September 1, 1963).

2 New York: The Philosophical Library, 1945.

3 Ibid., 646.

4 Cf. Thomas Luckmann, *The Invisible Religion* (New York: Macmillan, 1967).

5 The description of the Luckmann position in Peter Berger, *The Sacred Canopy* (New York: Doubleday, 1967), 177.

6 Ibid.

7 Max Mueller, *Essay on Comparative Mythology* (1856) as quoted in Berger, *Sacred Canopy*, 175.

8 F. L. Cross and E. A. Livingstone, eds., *The Oxford Dictionary of the Christian Church* (Oxford: Oxford University Press, 1978).

9 Karl Barth, *Church Dogmatics*, 2 vols. (Edinburgh: T. & T. Clark, 1956), 280 ff.

10 Ibid., 303.

11 Mircea Eliade, *The Sacred and the Profane: The Nature of Religion* (New York: Harcourt, Brace, 1959).

12 F. I. Streng in *Encyclopaedia Britannica*, 16:122 (15th edition).

13 John Henry Newman, *The Idea of a University*, edited with introduction and notes by I. T. Ker (Oxford: Clarendon Press, 1976), 5.

14 Ibid.

15 To the following see: Sinclair Goodlad, *Conflict and Consensus in Higher Education* (London: Hodder and Stoughton, 1976), 6 ff.

16 Goodlad, *Conflict and Consensus*, 6.

17 Ibid.

18 Berger, *Sacred Canopy*, 28.

19 *The New York Times*, National Edition, Monday, January 9, 1989, 9.

20 *The New York Times Book Review*, February 12, 1989, 1 and 20 ff.

21 To the following: "Varieties of Religious Commitment" in George W. Forell, *The Proclamation of the Gospel in a Pluralistic World* (Philadelphia: Fortress, 1973), 14 ff.

TOUGH-MINDED
CHRISTIANITY

~~~~~~

Part VI

TRIBUTE

~~~~~~

Personal Letter

To Dr. John W. Montgomery

I count it an honor to be asked to address you in celebration of your seventy-fifth birthday.

Few men have influenced my life as you have. For 26 years I have had a nationwide television program that defends and presents the Christian faith. The foundation of my ministry came from sitting under your teaching at Trinity Seminary and watching you in your many public debates with skeptics.

I consider you to be one of the clearest teachers and defenders of the Christian faith today. A statement you made on our television program exemplifies your challenge to all serious thinkers to investigate Jesus and His claims:

> There are innumerable religious claims in the world. Religions appear on the scene right and left. I come from California, "the land of the fruits and the nuts," and in California the number of religions probably exceeds the number of people. Now, it's one thing to make a religious *claim*. It's a totally different thing to demonstrate that claim. As in the field of law, anybody can file suit, but winning the case is a very different matter. And in the case of Christianity, we have claims that have to do with history, with historical fact; with certain events which, if they took place, the Christian faith is vindicated. If they didn't take place, it's false. And Christianity has been willing to put itself on the line in that respect across the centuries. At the very beginning, a rabbinic lawyer and convert to Christianity by the name of Paul said, "If Christ isn't risen from the dead, we are of all men most miserable." In other words, if the resurrection didn't take place, Christianity is false. If the resurrection did take place, Christianity turns out to be true. So, history is the field in which we can test the claims of Christianity.

Over the years I have watched you faithfully defend and present the historical evidence for the Christian faith in the classroom, as a guest on our television program, and in public debates with the "death of God" theologians, apostates such as Bishop Pike, and skeptics such as Madelyn Murray O'Hair.

Further, your numerous books and articles have influenced many lives.

May our Lord grant you many more years of presenting and defending the truth about who He is and what He has done for us.

Dr. John Ankerberg

Open Letter

I was for many years a colleague of Dr. Montgomery and have shared with him in the defense of the faith. He is a man of encyclopedic knowledge and unswerving commitment to orthodox Christianity. Once, while working on my dissertation, John brought to my attention a book that was very important to the discussion. I was impressed that his knowledge was so extensive, even in a field in which I was specializing. During our time together at Trinity Evangelical Divinity School, I was able to attend his famous debate at the University of Chicago with William Altizer of the "Death of God" movement. Montgomery completely demolished his arguments. In addition, Dr. Montgomery is one of the pioneers of historical apologetics and one of the foremost apologists of our time. His extensive knowledge, voluminous writings, and vigorous defense of creedal Christianity are virtually unparalleled in this field.

Norman L. Geisler
Dean, Southern Evangelical Seminary

Table Talks with John Warwick Montgomery

AN ESSAY IN HONOR OF
DR. JOHN WARWICK MONTGOMERY

James Lutzweiler

"John Warwick Montgomery," I replied. John Warwick Montgomery constituted one-third of my answer to a question. John Warwick Montgomery (hereafter JWM), Paige Patterson, and Terry Sanford, the late Duke University president and U.S. Senator from North Carolina, together make up the complete answer to the same question. The question was this: "If you could have lunch today with any three people of your choice, who would they be?" It's a question I often ask others, and one that I am asked myself on occasion by those to whom I pose it.

On 29 March 2005 I placed this question before JWM over lunch at The Athenaeum, an exclusive club in London where the Lutheran scholar is a member. He had kindly invited me there after I had proposed a get-together. Originally scheduled to meet on April Fools' Day, we both adjusted our calendars to meet earlier, a seemingly insignificant chronological (and perhaps even superstitious) detail. But in the overall scheme of things it was not an insignificant alteration. The end result was that I have three more days of reflection on the delightful occasion than I would have had, if we had met three days later. For those who don't care how long or intense their pleasures are, this will make no difference. Those who have sucked the marrow out of life will understand. William Wordsworth was one. In "Daffodils" sucked he:

> For oft when on my couch I lie
> In vacant or in pensive mood,
> They [= daffodils] flash upon the inward eye
> Which is the bliss of solitude.

> And then my heart with pleasure fills
> And dances with the daffodils.

So then, "Long live '*Carpe diem!*'" on the couch or on the divan, whether the flash upon the inward eye be daffodils or doctors of theology.

Before I put the question to JWM about whom he would like to dine with if he had three choices (sadly I was not one of them, but the rules of the inquiry are that it cannot be anyone presently at your table), we had already been deep in pleasurable exchange. It began the moment the vibrant academic walked in the door. I had arrived 10 minutes early, driven by faraway Vince Lombardi's *Green Bay Packer* maxim, "If you aren't 10 minutes early, you are 15 minutes late," and yet another, to wit, "People count the faults of those who keep them waiting." Having as many faults as I do, I did not wish to leave any of my doors, windows, vents, or even eyes of needles open wide enough for a penetrating mind like JWM's to drive a double-decker bus through, not to mention a caravan of camels.

Smiling and gripping my hand, JWM began instantly to show me around The Athenaeum. It was clearly a sanctuary of scholarship, one at which he himself had recently lectured on "Do Human Rights Need Religion?" to a group of distinguished members and guests that included the retired canon of St. Paul's Cathedral and author of the contemporary hymn "Christ Triumphant," the Rev. Canon Michael Saward, who also introduced him. Outside it was stately yet reserved. Inside it was very quiet and a plush, architectural beauty. Before heading to the resplendent dining room, he led me up a grand staircase at the bottom of which, he later pointed out, Charles Dickens and William Makepeace Thackeray had reconciled after 12 years of alienation. Harmony happens.

At the top of the stairs, JWM pointed out a book that he said contained the names of 50 or so Nobel Prize winners who were either presently or previously members of The Athenaeum. Surely we were gamboling all about in tall cotton, as folks have never quite yet said just that way around my own Southern staircase or anywhere else for that matter. But we were.

The room at the top of the staircase was the library. And what a library it was! I think he said it contained 80,000 volumes, mostly leather-bound collector's editions. It also contained about 80 bottles of various spirits on a freestanding table, apparently there for consumption by anyone so inclined. There was no bartender in sight, and I assumed the literati sort of just helped themselves, as the spirit and spirits moved. But I was too intoxicated on books to have my sensitivities numbed artificially. I walked around in a trance with JWM, a Ph.D. in theological bibliography with 18,000 books of his own, providing animated color commentary as my guide. I could have spent two weeks in this room right then and there. But lunch was waiting, and we wandered on toward it.

We descended the staircase and entered the dining room, taking our seats at a small table by a window overlooking the ghosts of *Titanic* victims, who had purchased their tickets a block away, and the pigeon-plastered statues of King Edward VII, American Revolutionary War General John Burgoyne, Lord Curzon, and Florence Nightingale that lined the street just outside. Seated at the table next to ours were a number of mucky mucks whose professional appearance but unknown identity gave them a pleasant air of Sherlockian mystery. I did not want to discover otherwise and let my imagination run amok.

"Whosoever will may come" does not apply at The Athenaeum. And even if it did, few would find the lunch tab of $128-plus that JWM picked up digestible. That tab included a bottle of Alsatian wine, which had quickly become a topic of discussion. Sensitive to my Southern Baptist associations, JWM, now a Frenchman, gingerly approached the question of quaffing a quart with him. With my own family's roots in Alsace-Lorraine and never having had a drop of this particular delicacy, I hastened to assure him quite piously and persuasively that the same Jesus who had once turned water into wine could certainly, upon request, convert this damnable stuff back into water—but hopefully not before passing it over my taste buds, and yet just before causing offense to one of my brothers. With that the order was placed and the bottle was ultimately liquidated, though I confess here that I forgot to request the Redeemer to reverse the miracle.

JWM segued from this exchange into a few of his experiences at the *Evangelical Theological Society*, where he had attempted to order wine at a banquet. In the first instance a waiter refused his request, after having been prompted to do so by a Baptist from Lynchburg, Virginia, who taught in a school operated by the son of the city's former biggest bootlegger. JWM, a Lutheran and very much a European, solved this problem in a succeeding year American-style by bringing his own bottle.

Once we had ordered, we began chattering like chapmonks [sic] over a wide range of subjects. While I had invited him to lunch with the intent of pumping him with questions till we both dropped exhausted, I found out that he made the conversation a two-way street. That is another way of saying that I found JWM to be a very good listener as well as a fine talker. He not only listened but made it a point to ask me questions as well. I have not always found such to be the case with scholars of his stature, many of whom seem to think that the most fascinating thing in life is whatever they are about to say next.

One of the questions I asked him was the question raised in the first paragraph of this tribute, to wit, "If you could have dinner with any three people from all of human history, exclusive of biblical characters, who would they be?" Without much hesitation at all he replied, "Luther, Augustine, and C. S. Lewis." He even went beyond the question to indicate whom he would not like to have dinner with, to wit, Calvin. Not altogether content with a simple diss of this Swiss, he added, "Nobody would want to have dinner with Calvin." Even though we both knew Al Mohler would crawl through sewers for a chance to feast with JC, *sans* Servetus, in Geneva, his point was well taken. He would later explain that it was fundamentalism's focus on Calvinism and Arminianism that kept him on the periphery of that movement.

JWM's answer of C. S. Lewis interested me more than the other two, and so I asked him why Lewis. He told me of an epistolary exchange he had had with Lewis some years back and how Lewis had commended him for a paper he had written. JWM had already written up this story in *Where Is History Going? Essays in Support of the Historical Truth of the Christian Revelation, with a Commendatory*

Letter by C. S. Lewis (Zondervan, 1969), which I consulted for details upon my return to the states. Of course Lewis is a very good
answer, whether one has ever received a letter from him or not.

When JWM asked me the same question about my choices, I replied, "Joseph Stalin, the poet Robert Service of *The Cremation of
Sam McGee* fame, and Scott Joplin who composed *Maple Leaf Rag.*"
Careful readers of these remarks will note that these are not the
same three I mentioned in the opening paragraph. Just as Heraclitus
said that no man can ford the same stream twice, I would argue that
no man can meet the same man twice. My answers differ depending on my mood and my companions and are in no way inherently
contradictory.

That Stalin was one of my answers evoked from him a story about
Harold Lindsell and Yuri Andropov. Andropov led the Soviet Union
from 1982 until 1984. Halfway through his administration those
"godless communist bastards" (J. Edgar Hoover's view, not JWM's
or mine) had allegedly shot down the commercial Korean airliner
Flight #007, a Boeing 747 that had also allegedly strayed into their
airspace. Whether for this transgression or others during Andopov's
previous reign as the head of Soviet Intelligence, Lindsell was driven,
proleptically *a la* Pat Robertson's Venezuelan flap, to utter an im-
precatory prayer on Andropov's pate. Not long thereafter Andropov
died, and Brezhnev's Bolshevik buddies began studiously to avoid
offending the Southern Baptist Lindsell.

I added to this murderous mix two Stalinist stories in which
JWM seemed to take relish. The first concerned one of those frequent midnight banquets in the Kremlin, one of which found Stalin
and Churchill as dinner companions. Churchill had come to Uncle
Joe to request the spilling of more Russian blood on behalf of British
chestnuts in WWII fires. Churchill, knowing that he himself had
militantly opposed the Russian Revolution in 1917 and was, therefore, on shaky ground, made it a point to express regret to Stalin
for his previous attempts "to strangle the Bolshevik baby" during the
War of Intervention. The confessing capitalist then asked the communist to forgive him. The ostensible atheist replied, "It is for God
to forgive," leaving Churchill baffled and filled with foreboding, notwithstanding the revelation in the memoirs of Clark Kerr, Britain's

WWII ambassador to the Soviet Union, that Stalin had told Kerr that he indeed did believe in God.

Since none of my choices for dinner companions were theologians or evangelicals, JWM was curious about my interest in Stalin. I explained this interest, in part stemming from my discovery in the past that Stalin had been a seminarian and how his mother had wanted him to be a priest in the Russian Orthodox Church. I told him how I had once sought additional information about Stalin by writing to his daughter, Svetlana. She had replied, and I shared her reply with him.

In my letter I had asked Svetlana for the whereabouts of a picture to which Stalin kept pointing, while he was on his deathbed. She replied that she did not know where it was because the NKVD came in right after his death and seized everything. She added, "Where it is now, only God knows." In parentheses she added the word "perhaps," as if to say, "The NKVD hid it so well that *perhaps* even God did not know!" If laughter aids digestion, that and our Alsatian libation were working together for good to the two of us who loved God and were called according to His purpose.

After communing about these saints and sinners of the past, we moved into the present. He told me about a former student and a leading churchman, both of whom wear household names in the publishing world today. He explained his relationship to both but how both had managed to avoid replying to initiatives that he had subsequently made toward them. I was startled at this apparent disrespect and invoked an exchange I had had recently with Jimmy Carter for contrast. JWM expressed some initial disdain for the liberal Plains poet laureate, disdain that changed to respect after I shared with him the following story.

President Carter had never been my student, of course, and owed me nothing. Yet on one occasion I took it upon myself to write a short essay concerning his frequent jabs at the Southern Baptist Convention. I entitled my screed "A Fond Farewell and Call to Jimmy Carter." It was published in a very obscure fundamentalist periodical (redundancy unavoidable); but nevertheless, it came to Carter's attention. That was because I sent him a copy. The essay was an irenic combination of warmth and warmongering, if such there can be. I did not expect to hear back from the president. However, one day I did; and in his kind reply he expressed appreciation for it. Since then we had had about a dozen exchanges, and JWM and I began pondering the meaning of how two of his former friends, who—unlike Carter—owed him responses, were unable to manage them. Without naming names the first initial of the one is "R" and his last initial can be found in a puzzle. The other fellow deserves to be ignored rather than damned, in keeping with the principle that people would rather be damned than ignored.

I further explained to JWM how my attack on Carter focused on his sympathies with people like Paul Tillich. JWM suggested that I should digest his own writings on Tillich, a project I have undertaken. I suggested to him that perhaps the reason Carter had quoted Tillich was because he may have used ghostwriters and that he himself was not as immersed in the duplicity of Tillich as others were. I mentioned in this connection how Billy Graham and Jerry Falwell had themselves used ghostwriters and how they were quite publicly embarrassed to discover that one of them was later revealed to be a homosexual. JWM had not heard of this scandal, and I was both pleased and displeased to share it with him in the shadows of the nearby Jerusalem Chambers where an alleged homosexual, King James, had set some translators to work producing a Bible that still goes by his name. Homosexuality happens. And irony.

It was not a large leap from Billy Graham and Jerry Falwell to fundamentalism in general. Our discussion of this subject was prompted in part by one of my earliest recollections of JWM, one from 40 years earlier. He had been quoted as saying that a fundamentalist was someone who could see through a keyhole with both eyes, a well worn witticism by now but at the time a fresh one that irked a fundy like me in no small measure. I later came to learn that his estimate was an understatement and that some (accent on "some") fundamentalists could see through the eye of a needle with both eyes. Some (accent still on "some") could even see through a pinhole. But to be balanced, thanks in part to JWM's provocation, I have also come to learn that some liberals can't see through a hole the size of the Grand Canyon, Crater Lake, or the Columbia River Gorge combined with both eyes wide open or even with all the eyes of liberaldom and a few Hindu gods thrown in for good measure. Neither group seems to have a corner on myopia, though I'd rather be able to see through pinhole nuances with one or one hundred eyes than not to be able to see through them at all.

This common discourse with respect to fundamentalism that served to bring JWM and me together again at *The Athenaeum* in the first place. I had met him 25 years earlier on one of his guided trips to the sites of the German Reformation. It was a marvelous trip, and I had dinner with him many times then, but only in group settings. The London lunch was a one-on-one affair, the best class ratio one can have. It came about more immediately in connection with a project I had underway and still have underway at this writing, namely, the creation of a biographical dictionary of the original contributors to *The Fundamentals*, those little booklets published by *Union 76* oilman and BIOLA bankroller, Lyman Stewart, between 1910 and 1915. I had made contact with JWM to see if he might be willing to write a sketch of one of these fellows. He not only consented to do the sketch of the almost forgotten English cricketer C. T. Studd but networked with me until I found Christoph Raedel in Germany who took on two sketches of the most obscure contributors himself.

Thus, this biographical dictionary, tentatively titled *The Faces of Fundamentalism*, will contain JWM's fine contribution to the history of fundamentalism. While JWM's darkened acquaintance E. J. Carnell had lightly lamented that "fundamentalism was not enough fun, too much damn, and no mentality," I have found it to be a source of great fun, not nearly enough damnation, and plenty of mentality—if the little known academic credentials and skills of the original contributors are any indication.

JWM told a tale that illustrates some of the fun with fundamentalism. He said he envisioned the day when even fundamentalists and the higher critics would beat their swords into plowshares and come to agreement on something. Puzzled at this prophecy, I queried him on what could possibly bring about this state of affairs. He replied that just as soon as the higher critics were able to redact the virtually problem-free text of the second chapter of John's Gospel into some variant that yielded a translation of "grape juice" rather than "wine," fundamentalists would embrace them like long lost cousins. Hilarity happens.

Damnation is quite another matter. Years earlier I had read and used as a textbook in a Wooddale Baptist Sunday School class JWM's book *Damned Through the Church*. I had used it to suggest to the class that infant baptism was one of those things that people erroneously counted on to save them. I was surprised to learn years later that JWM leaned toward or was wholeheartedly devoted to this doctrine of infant baptismal regeneration. At least that is what I recalled him saying. Naturally that would not be my view.

Nor, of course, were we in agreement on the mode of immersion. JWM views sprinkling as a method of immersion, and I only consider immersion as a method of immersion. I recall fuming at him one sleepless night in Leipzig because of his views. I thought I would write a tract and blast him like a good Tom Paine-ish pamphleteer and German reformer should. I still have my notes on that simmering meditation somewhere, yet here I am 25 years later writing a tribute to him instead of a tirade. Back then I wanted to immerse him in tar and feathers. Now all I want to do is sprinkle a little bit on him and immerse him in joy. And actually I have since even inched a little bit JWM's way, now fully embracing Mark Twain's view of the subject. When asked if he believed in infant baptism, Twain tittered, "Believe in it? Why man, I've seen it!" Sprinkling happens.

Notwithstanding JWM's addlepated aberriginal [sic] views on baptism (my sincere apologies for this gratuitous lick here, JWM, but I submit this in lieu of that longer Leipzig tract), Southern Baptists have savored and proliferated a quotation from him in the 1980s debates on inerrancy and liberal trends within the SBC. The sainted Harold Lindsell was one of them in his influential book *The Battle for the Bible*. The magnificent quote reads as follows:

> If I profess with the loudest voice and clearest exposition
> every portion of the truth of God except precisely that
> little point which the world and the devil are at that mo-
> ment attacking, I am not confessing Christ, however boldly
> I may be professing Him. Where the battle rages, there
> the loyalty of the soldier is proved, and to be steady on all

the battlefield besides, is merely flight and disgrace if he flinches at that point.

JWM attributed this quotation to Martin Luther. But when Bill Youngmark, my incalculably fussy and prissy archival associate, went looking for the quote in the original German, he couldn't find it precisely as JWM had it written out in his book, *The "Is God Dead?" Controversy*. After some prodigious research, Youngmark discovered JWM's confession that he had copied Ken Taylor rather than King James in his translation style, though JWM's paraphrase had not altered the substance of the quotation. When Youngmark wrote JWM seeking a solution to this difference, JWM, unlike some to whom he had written and been ignored, graciously and apologetically replied, teasing Youngmark for having nothing better to do than "to engage in the textual criticism of a single Luther quotation."

Differences such as these, of course, provoke debate, and so I brought up that general subject. Heaven and earth both know of JWM's debates with Madalyn Murray O'Hair, Thomas J. J. Altizer, *et al.* In fact it may have been his debate with Altizer that first brought him to my attention, when I was in college. In all events I asked him what gave him the greatest kind of a holy high: lecturing in the classroom, debating with opponents (like Altizer or in court, now that he is a lawyer), or writing a book. It did not take him long to answer. He cited a case he argued in court concerning religious freedom in Moldavia and made that his first choice of endeavors.

He segued from this Moldavian story to one about a losing lawyer who refused the kindness of JWM's directions about town after this opponent had lost a case to JWM. The loser protested that he was in a hurry to get to a prosecutor's convention in Paris and did not want JWM's help. JWM, invoking a Victor Hugo template, called him "a regular Javert," and pointed out how people hate lawyers whether they win or lose. He said, "They hate them, if they lose, for losing; and they hate them, if they win, for not winning enough."

Another topic that engaged our attention was the subject of his own personal manuscript collection. Being an archivist and preservationist, I had been anxious to learn what the ultimate disposition of JWM's papers would be upon his rejoining Luther and Lewis, if not Calvin, in the skies. I had visited with him by e-mail about this before going to London. He told me that his papers were presently at Syracuse University, where were also the papers of Thomas J. J. Altizer. He expressed some concern about how much they were being used, and I promised to explore this upon my return to the States. He threatened to sic the Mafia on me if I did not. I needed no such threat, of course, because of my own interest in them. But I did let him know that my ex-brother-in-law had Mafia ties in Chicago and perhaps we might provoke a Mafia war over manuscripts—and what a marvelous war that would be. When I returned to the states, I did explore the status of his papers with the result that they were shifted from Syracuse to Southeastern Baptist Theological Seminary in Wake Forest, North Carolina, where I am now their curator. Shift happens.

One purpose of gathering such papers is, of course, biographical. I encouraged JWM to write his autobiography. He assured me that he was working on one, while quipping, "I caused trouble while I was living; why not cause it when I am dead?" He told me that his Andropov-annihilating friend, Harold Lindsell, had chosen not to write an autobiography because "he knew too much," presumably preferring to annihilate only communist comrades and not any of his Christian colleagues. I protested that Lindsell should have written it and put it under seal for 25 or 50 years. Then I told him how Lindsell's contemporary, J. C. Massee, had gone to the pains of actually writing a tell-all history of fundamentalism and had shown it to Ralph W. Neighbour Sr. for review. The latter told him to burn it. He may have since it has never surfaced. It is no *Unsinngeschichte* to lament that fundamentalists have been too obsessed with *Heilsgeschichte* instead of St. John's kind of history, namely, "Write what you have seen."

Homer Simpson fleshes out the interminable topics we covered over the two hours we were together. The only time I saw pain creep across the brow of JWM was when he winced after I invoked the name of that lovable buffoon. He expressed a legitimate concern that Homer was making a mockery of religion. I assured him that from my perspective Simpson was for the most part mocking the kinds of things JWM and I would mock ourselves. I thought of asking him to bow his head right then and there, to repent, and receive Homer into his heart, as I softly sang the *Simpsons* theme song. But The Athenaeum just did not seem to be the right venue for an invitation, and so I bit my tongue along with the last of my pork loin and salmon. Besides, as the unapologetic apologist for the sitcom, I thought I might have convinced him of Homer's socially redemptive qualities with the vignette or two that I shared. Homer happens.

Our conversation continued into dessert, brought by our rather attractive Polish waitress. The multilingual Lutheran engaged her in a brief discussion about her pronunciation of "almond," one of the prospective components in the desserts. I cannot recall the point of dispute in this dialogue, but I do recall admiring her beauty, the elongated opportunity to do so being a by-product of her detention to discuss this no doubt critical nuance in phonics.

Dessert and dialogue being over, I asked JWM if he might possibly escort me to the librarian of The Athenaeum to do a bit of quick research among their holdings for the papers of William Bollaert, of whom more momentarily. He readily assented, and we made our way back to the second floor. As we walked down a corridor, he pointed out to me a number of framed cartoons lining the walls, one of which displayed a Christmas dinner among friends featuring for feathered fare a boiled owl, not your customary cuisine. We laughed heartily, and I told him of an experience I'd had in Michigan a few years earlier where a man had allegedly been sentenced to six months in jail and fined $5,000 for eating an endangered spotted owl. As this connoisseur of wildlife was being escorted out of the courtroom, the judge interposed a question concerning what a spotted owl tastes like—just for the record, of course. The fellow replied, "Your honor, it's about halfway between an American eagle and a California condor." We were howling once again in the otherwise totally quiet library corridor. I share all of these vignettes to emphasize that lunch with JWM is a dialogue, not a monologue, and a corollary thereof, to wit, that noisy professional librarians can ignore more rules than the U.S. Supreme Court.

To put the pleasure of this lunch with him in full context and a bit of bolder relief, I must share briefly how my morning hours had been spent that same day. They were spent at the Royal Institution of Michael Faraday fame and at Sotherans, a rare bookstore, both no more than one mile from The Athenaeum. I had begun my day at the former in search of the personal papers of the William Bollaert just mentioned. Bollaert was one of Faraday's assistant chemists, and his books were recommended reading for Charles Darwin, who also dined frequently at The Athenaeum. I had gone to Sotherans on my walk to The Athenaeum just to browse and to covet—conscientiously, of course—and, as it turned out, quite serendipitously.

I had written my M.A. thesis for North Carolina State University on a story about Texas that William Bollaert (who had once saved Faraday's eyesight in a laboratory accident with the result that Faraday enjoyed many more years of productive scientific endeavor) had recorded in his diary in 1842. Bob Tutt of the *Houston Chronicle* has called this story the "juiciest story in Texas history," and Kent Biffle of the *Dallas Morning News* has regaled his readers with my research into it on numerous occasions (incidentally, my research involved some real pinholes through which I saw with four eyes more clearly than I see through a glass darkly with only two).

Craving more of that kind of pleasant media attention, I had been on the prowl for more of Bollaert's papers for close to a decade to see if he had any single tidbit to add to his story. That "decade" is to say this is a front-burner passion of mine. The story, in brief, is popularly but erroneously known as "The Yellow Rose of Texas." In reality, it is about a mulatto girl from New Haven, Connecticut, with whom Santa Anna "kept company" in his tent on the afternoon of April 21, 1836, thus causing him to lose not only the little known Battle of San Jacinto but, along with it, close to a million sensational square miles of territory (all of Texas and parts of Oklahoma, Utah, Colorado, Nevada, and New Mexico). I had shared the details of this story with JWM during our lunch. It is a story that continues to enchant researchers and the public, and I was wishing to develop it further.

My trip to the Royal Institution, where Bollaert had once worked, proved disappointing. The curator had nothing of Bollaert's but a few of his generally available published books. I had already searched the National Archives in Kew Gardens and the Royal Geographical Society Archives earlier in the month, and the Royal Institution had been my last reasonable hope of finding more of his papers and diaries. With that end dead, the trail turned fully cold.

So I meandered down the street toward The Athenaeum and spotted Sotherans. I entered with the idea that I would just browse and not speak with anyone because I was not a serious buyer of their collector's items (one of them was an autograph letter of the amazing Antarctic adventurer, Ernest Shackleton, for only $1,500). However, I could not control the prospect that someone might speak with me.

Someone did. His name was Stuart Leggatt. Quite naturally, he asked if he might help me. An answer formed instantaneously in my mind. It was not "No." Instead I replied with a wild prayer of hope in my heart and on my lips, to wit, "You could help me, if you could only direct me to the papers of William Bollaert." His reply stunned me.

Said Stuart, "As a matter of fact a bookseller from Buenos Aires via France was just in here recently, and he had with him several diaries of Bollaert and some of the books from Bollaert's personal library that he was offering for sale. He wanted $16,000, and we thought that was too much, so we passed on them." Incredulous, I had to have him repeat what he said to make sure I was not dreaming or hearing a faulty wish fulfillment. He assured me that what he said was correct and that there was hope that the diaries might yet be located and available.

In short, Stuart did locate those diaries in another rare bookstore down the street (Maggs, where they had a King James autograph letter for $9,000, a Tolkien letter for $7,000, some Churchill marginalia for $7,000, and an Oscar Wilde autograph for $9,400—the transgender tale-teller trumping the translator, Tolkien, and 10 Downing Street), and I had a little bit to do with their tentative denouement, all of which amounts to another fascinating story involving the Newberry Library and the alleged Kingpin of Rare Booksellers in New Haven, Connecticut. I tell that bibliographic story in another place. But I provide this abstract of it here in order to give the reader an idea of just how extraordinarily pleasant my morning had already been by the time I made it to The Athenaeum for lunch with JWM, the Ph.D. in bibliography. In short, by high noon I did not think my day could get any better. But it did.

And so until further notice my favorite attraction in old London town is not Trafalgar Square or St. Paul's Cathedral or John Wesley's Chapel and home (where I had been microfilming the fascinating papers of Gipsy Smith for two weeks) or Bunhill Cemetery across Wesley's street (where I had been communing with the ghosts of Defoe, Blake, Bunyan, Watts, and Susannah Wesley each morning the week before) or Westminster Abbey, nor even the pervasive voluptuous visual art. Rather it is the conjuring up like a simple cud the recollection of my laughter-and-literature-laced lunch at The Athenaeum and the table talks between a bovine Baptist and the no-longer-to-be-abbreviated *bon vivant*, JWM, hereafter, John Warwick Montgomery.

Sermon: The Ascension

William Norman

Preacher to Lincoln's Inn, London

While he blessed them, he was parted from them, and carried up into heaven (Luke 24:51).

This world is not all there is. This universe is not all there is. Scientists now speak—in language to me scarcely intelligible—about parallel universes. So how much more readily should those who believe in spiritual realities hold on to the notion of heaven, a place or state beyond our imagining but none the less real. And the boundary between there and here is thin; for all we know the one may interpenetrate the other, the seen and the unseen, the temporal and the eternal.

Most of us do not pass through that thin veil until we come to die. The Scriptures tell us that a few have done so. There is the old story of Enoch, of whom it is said that he walked with God—and in these mysterious words, "He was not; for God took him," the writer of the letter to the Hebrews uses him as one of the examples of saints of old who exercised faith. Then there was Elijah, who was taken from this world in a whirlwind. Possibly there have been some such in modern times—some say that this is what happened to the Sikh saint, Sundar Singh.

There are others who have had extraordinary visions and have lived to tell of them. Paul says that he knew a man (he must mean himself) who was taken up to the third heaven—and he does not know whether he was in the body or out of it, and there he heard things that no mortal may repeat.

And there are examples too of the dead making themselves visible or audible to the living, in order to encourage or to warn. It does not happen often, but there are well-attested instances of it.

We are not encouraged to try to penetrate the veil between this world and the next; indeed we are warned strongly not to do so, for it is only too likely that we shall be deceived or even endangered. But that veil is thin.

So when Jesus rose from the dead, He was able to come and go between this world and the other, to appear and to disappear, and this He did, so Luke tells us, over a period of 40 days. But then it was time for Him to depart finally. So He gave His friends their last instructions, He bade them farewell, and then He was lifted up (we are not told that He went right up into the sky as in some depictions of the scene). He may only have been lifted a few feet from the ground, a cloud came down and hid Him, and when the cloud vanished, He was not there.

Well, some may say, is not this rather crude, this notion of Jesus going up? Does this suggest a primitive and naive understanding of the universe as consisting of three stories or decks—earth being the middle one and heaven the top one? But surely if Jesus wanted to indicate that He was leaving His friends and that they would not see Him any more in the same way, this was an appropriate way to do so. We cannot think, for instance, that it would have been more suitable for the earth to have opened and swallowed Him up. We are three-dimensional beings. We can only think in terms of up and down and sideways. Naturally we think of heaven as being up, knowing very well that this is a metaphor, a picture, and not to be taken literally. If Jesus leaves this earth and returns to heaven, and wants His disciples to know that this is what is happening, of course He must go up.

What then does it mean? First this: in His ascension Jesus goes from the here into the everywhere. As long as He is here, He is in one place at one time. This is so even when He shows himself to His disciples in His resurrection body. So He goes away, but He only goes away in order that He may not be limited as He is in His earthly life. He leaves His disciples to carry on His work; and though He is not visibly with them, He is spiritually present wherever they go. They are, as He tells them, to be His witnesses, starting in Jerusalem, then in Judaea and Samaria, and then to the ends of the earth. "If I do not go away, the Spirit cannot come to you. But if I go I will send Him to you." And so He did. The ascension is necessary for the gospel to be heard and received in all the world.

As someone has said, the ascension marks the end of the time of Jesus and begins the time of the church. Jesus departs from the here so that He may enter the everywhere. "Oh Jesus, why could You not have stayed? We did not want You to leave. If only You were here now, we could come to You and ask Your help in solving all our problems: Israel, Iran, the energy crisis, the water crisis, global warming, world trade, the European constitution. You would have answered the questions. Why could You not stay?" And of course Jesus never did answer that sort of question when He was here with us. His Father had given us free will; we used it to reject Him and in the end to crucify Him. The temptation to take over all the kingdoms of the world was one which He refused. This is not the way He operates. He works through us sinful and selfish and flawed human beings.

But because of His departure, His ascension, He can give us His Spirit. By His Spirit working in and through us, if we will only listen to Him, people can be brought into His kingdom, and if we allow the Spirit to guide us, and are humble enough to listen, we will find a way through. He leaves the here to enter the everywhere.

A second reason for the significance of the ascension is that Jesus goes as Man, or, to follow current fashion, as human, to the very presence of God. As we say in the Creed, He sits at the right hand of God—a phrase derived from several passages in the Epistles. The right hand, the place of honour and of power. Now, of course, as we use such language, we know that we are picturing something absurd. We think of God as an old man with a long beard sitting on a great throne somewhere high up above the clouds and Jesus sitting beside Him. It is difficult for us not to have some such picture in our minds when we use such phrases. But this is simply because of the weakness of language to convey meaning. We know that the picture is absurd, but the truth is still true—absolutely true and absolutely wonderful and heartwarming and encouraging. Wherever it is that this universe and all universes are ruled from, wherever is the centre and heart of the entire cosmos, there is Jesus Christ, a human being like ourselves.

Do not allow our sophisticated contemporaries to deprive us of faith in this glorious truth. The letter to the Hebrews, which is, looked at from one point of view, an extended commentary on the ascension, uses the picture of the Jewish high priest entering the holy of holies in the temple, which He did only on one day in the year and only with great trepidation and after observing the most detailed rituals. And Hebrews says Jesus is *our* high priest. He has entered a temple not made with hands but the highest heaven of which the earthly temple is just a shadow. And, I quote, "We have not a high priest who cannot be touched with the feeling of our infirmities, but was in all points tempted as we are, yet without sin. Let us therefore come boldly to the throne of grace, that we may obtain mercy and find grace to help in time of need" (Heb 4:15–16). The ascended Christ—one of us—on the throne of the universe.

The ascension means that Christ is universal, and it means that Christ, as Man, is exalted. What else does it mean?

It means that in one sense we who believe in Him and are by faith united with Him can already ascend with Him. This is what the collect for Ascension Day prays, that we may in heart and mind thither ascend and with Him continually dwell. We find this notion especially in the letter of Paul to the Ephesian church. "Blessed be the God and Father of our Lord Jesus Christ, who has blessed us with all spiritual blessings in heavenly places in Christ" (Eph 1:3). Yes, we are here in the world; and, yes, we have all the joys and difficulties of work and family and the world situation. But we are also already with Christ in the heavenly places in heart and mind, and so whatever happens to us, we can look at it all from the point of there, the supersensual, the eternal viewpoint—and that may not solve the problem at all, but it does give us hope. It makes all the difference. Christ is risen and ascended, and we are already by faith with Him there, as well as He being with us here.

Christ everywhere, Christ exalted, we with Him in heavenly places, all that is part of the meaning of ascension. But before He arrived there, He had to pass through a very dark place indeed. In the upper room Jesus says to His disciples, "Where I am going you cannot come, not now, but you shall come hereafter." "Hey," Peter exclaims, "no, I want to come now straight away. I will lay down my life for You." "Will you?" asks Jesus. "Truly I say, the cock shall not crow before you have denied Me three times." In other words, you are not ready to go with me now, but you will be, in time, later. For the death and burial and resurrection and ascension are all part of one great movement. And if we are really with Jesus in His resurrection and ascension, we must also be with Him in His death. This includes our literal death, yes, but also all those little or greater decisions which we have to make against our own inclinations and against our own apparent interests, for conscience's sake, for love's sake, for our friends' sake, for our enemies' sake.

May the risen and ascended Christ give us grace by the Spirit whom He sent into the world at His ascension, to follow the way He has set for us, to follow Him through whatever rough or smooth places our path lies, to that place where in heart and mind we have already ascended, so that in the end, where He is we may be also.

Original Hymn Reflecting Montgomery's Apologetic

The plan of God is sure,
eternal in its scope.
It offers to the human race
its one enduring hope.

The truth of God breaks through,
revealing to the wise
His saving purposes, long hid
from unbelieving eyes.

The Son of God on earth,
child of the virgin's womb,
He lived and died, the perfect man,
resurgent from the tomb.

The church of God includes
the faithful in all lands;
both young and old, both rich and poor,
secure in God's good hands.

The reign of God is near,
peaceful and just its goal.
As Father, Son, and Spirit rule
a universe made whole.

Words ©   MICHAEL SAWARD 2004

Bibliography

Compiled by Will Moore

Notes: (1) "Mss." indicates that the item has never been published. (2) Some articles have been published in more than one journal. Not all journals are cited. (3) Many articles have been anthologized. The numbers in round brackets at the end of entries indicate the book(s) in which the articles appear. See "Books—Written/Edited" for the list of books by number. (4) Articles that are listed after a book include only the articles that have not appeared previously in a journal.

1956

"A Hermeneutic Case Study: Jonah and Leviathan," Mss., 1956

"Place of Conversion in the Life of a Christian," Mss., 1956

"An Historical Study of the 'Dignus Est Agnus' Canticle," Mss., 1956

1959

The Writing of Research Papers in Theology (1959; 1996)

"The Colonial Parish Library of Wilhelm Christoph Berkenmeyer," *Papers of the Bibliographical Society of America*, vol. 53, 2nd Quarter, 1959 (33)

"The Chronicles of Narnia and the Adolescent Reader," *Religious Education*, Sept./Oct. 1959 (29)

"Born of the Virgin Mary," *The Lutheran*, December 23, 1959

1960

A Union List of Serial Publications in Chicago-Area Protestant Theological Libraries (1960), editor

1961

"God's Devil," *Chiaroscuro*, 4, 1961 (25)

"Some Comments on Paul's Use of Genesis in His Epistle to the Romans," *Bulletin of Evangelical Theological Society*, April 1961

"How Muslims Do Apologetics," *Muslim World*, vol. 51, no. 2, April 1961; July 1961 (35)

"Ascension Perspective," *Cresset*, May 1961 (17)

"Can We Recover the Christian Devotional Life," *Christianity To-day*, Sept. 25, 1961 (17)

"Eros and Agape in Pico of Mirandola," *Concordia Theological Monthly*, Dec. 1961 (17)

1962

A Seventeenth-Century View of European Libraries: Lomeier's De Bibliothecis, *Chapter X* (1962) [M.A. thesis, U. of C. Berkeley, 1958]

Chytraeus' *On Sacrifice: A Reformation Treatise in Biblical Theology* (1962) [S.T.M. thesis, Wittenberg U., 1960]

The Libraries of France at the Ascendancy of Mazarin: Louis Jacob's Traicté Des Plus Belles Bibliotheques, *Part Two* [Ph.D. dissertation, U. of Chicago, 1962]

Shape of the Past: An Introduction to Philosophical Historiography (1962, rev. 1975)

"Introduction," *The Christian Idea of History* by D. C. Masters (1962)

"Cause and Cure of Sin," *Resource*, 1962

"Wisdom as Gift," *Interpretation*, vol. XVI, no. 1, Jan, 1962 (17)

"Count How Much?" [Book Review], *Christianity Today*, Jan 5, 1962 (17)

"Over Against Words of Angels and Devils" [Book Review], *Christianity Today*, Feb. 16, 1962

"Luther and Libraries," *Library Quarterly*, vol. XXXII, no. 2, April 1962 (16)

"Mazarin: homme d'état et collectionneur, 1602–1611" [Book Review], *Library Quarterly*, vol. XXXII, no. 2, April 1962

"A Normative Approach to the Acquisition Problem in the Theological Seminary Library," *Summary of Proceedings of the Sixteenth Annual Conference of the American Theological Library Association*, June 12–15, 1962

"Surmount the Temptation" [Book Review], *Christianity Today*, Aug. 3, 1962

"Barth in Chicago," *Dialog*, Fall 1962 (17)

"Shirer's Re-Hitlerizing of Luther," *Christian Century*, Dec. 12, 1962 (16)

1963

"Cross, Constellation, and Crucible: Lutheran Astrology and Alchemy in the Age of the Reformation," *Transactions of the Royal Society of Canada*, 4 ser., I, 1963 (16, 22)

"Sixtus of Siena and Roman Catholic Biblical Scholarship in the Reformation Period," *Archiv fur Reformationgeschichte*, LIV, 2, 1963 (13)

"Choice Books on the Holy Spirit," *Christianity Today*, Jan 4, 1963

"The Fourth Gospel Yesterday and Today," *Concordia Theological Monthly*, April 1963 (17)

"The Law's Third Use: Sanctification," *Christianity Today*, April 26, 1963 (10, 17)

"Karl Barth and Contemporary Philosophy of History," *Bulletin of Evangelical Theological Society*, May 1963 (14)

"God Plus Three" [Book Review], *Christianity Today*, July 19, 1963 (14)

"Christian: Do It Yourself" [Book Review], *Christianity Today*, Aug. 30, 1963 (17)

"Le Traite" [Book Review], *Library Quarterly*, vol. XXXIII, no. 4, Oct. 1963

1964

History and Christianity (1964) (14)

"Where Is History Going?" *Religion in Life*, Spring 1964 (14)

"Jesus Christ and History," *His*, Dec. 1964, Jan.–Mar. 1965 (7, 14, 53)

1965

"Renewal and Contemporary Theology," *United Evangelical Action*, April 1965; in *Why . . . in the World?*" ed. H. C. Warner (1965) (17)

"On Taking a European Theological Doctorate," *Christianity Today*, Jan. 15, 1965 (17)

"Faith, History, and the Resurrection," *Christianity Today*, March 26, 1965 (7, 14)

"Inspiration and Inerrancy: A New Departure," *Bulletin of Evangelical Theological Society*, vol. 8, no. 2, Spring 1965; in *Evangelicals and Inerrancy*, ed. R. Youngblood (1984) (10, 17)

"Robert M. Grant" [Book Review], *Bulletin of Evangelical Theological Society*, vol. 8, no. 3, Summer 1965 (17)

"Justification: The Doctrine of Karl Barth and a Catholic Reflection" [Book Review], *United Evangelical Action*, Aug. 1965 (13)

"Evangelical Unity in the Light of Contemporary Eastern Orthodox—Roman Catholic—Protestant Ecumenicity," *Springfielder*, vol. 30, Autumn 1965 (13)

"Guest Editorial," *Bulletin of Evangelical Theological Society*, vol. 8, no. 4, Autumn 1965

"History with Style" [Book Review], *Christianity Today*, Nov. 5, 1965 (17)

"Why Churches Decline," *Christianity Today*, Dec. 3, 1965 (17)

1966

The "Is God Dead?" Controversy (1966) (17)

"Towards a Christian Philosophy of History," in *Jesus of Nazareth: Saviour and Lord*, ed. C. F. H. Henry (1966) (14)

"Lutheran Hermeneutics and Hermeneutics Today," *Aspects of Biblical Hermeneutics: Concordia Theological Monthly, Occasional Papers*, no. 1 (1966) (10, 16)

"'Sensible Christianity Seminar' Bibliography" [Annotations by Ken Harper], Mss., 1966

"Frontier Issues in Church History," *Bulletin of Evangelical Theological Society*, vol. 9, no. 2, Spring 1966 (14)

"Charles Nodier" [Book Review], *Library Quarterly*, vol. 36, no. 1, Jan 1966

"Theological Doctorates," *Christianity Today*, Feb. 18, 1966

"The Place of Reason in Christian Witness," *His*, Feb. 1966; March 1966 (35)

"Second Thoughts on 'Secular City'" *Christianity Today*, Feb. 18, 1966

"How to Decide the Birth-Control Question," *Christianity Today*, March 4, 1966; in *Birth Control and the Christian*, ed. W. O. Spitzer and C. L. Saylor (1969) (38)

"Justified by History [The Reformation and World Evangelism]," *Christianity Today*, April 29, 1966 (17)

"Pike's Peregrination" [Book Review], *Christianity Today*, April 29, 1966 (17)

"Agent 666: Bishop Pike and His Treasure Hunt," *Sunday School Times*, April 30 and May 7, 1966 (17)

"Morticians of the Absolute," *Springfielder*, Spring 1966; in *The Meaning of the Death of God*, ed. B. Murchland (1967) (17)

"Gospel According to LSD," *Christianity Today*, July 8, 1966 (17, 25)

"Current Theological Trends in the L.C.M.S.," *Lutherans Alert— National*, Aug./Sept. 1966; Oct. 1966 (10)

"Bibliographical Bigotry," *Christianity Today*, Aug. 19, 1966; Sept. 30, 1966; & Nov. 11, 1966 (17)

"The Theologian's Craft," *Journal of American Scientific Affiliation*, Sept., 1966 (17, 28)

"Freedom and the Gospel," *Christianity Today*, Sept. 30, 1966 (17)

"The Christian Church in McNeill's *Rise of the West*," *Evangelical Quarterly*, Oct./Dec. 1966 (14)

"'Death of God' Becomes More Deadly," *Christianity Today*, Dec. 9, 1966 (17)

1967

The Altizer-Montgomery Dialogue (1967) (17)

Crisis in Lutheran Theology, vol. 1 (1967, 1973)

"Theological Issues and Problems of Biblical Interpretation Now Facing the Lutheran Church Missouri Synod"

"A Critic Criticized"

Crisis in Lutheran Theology, vol. 2 (1967, 1973), editor

"The Problem of Leisure," *Christianity Today*, Jan 20, 1967

"Inductive Inerrancy," *Christianity Today*, March 3, 1967 (17)

"The Waning Death-of-God Tumult," *Christianity Today*, May 26, 1967

"Vidler at Strasbourg," *Christianity Today*, May 26, 1967 (17)

"Down with Kookishness," *Eternity*, July 1967

"Dialogue on the New Morality," *Christianity Today*, July 21, 1967 (17)

"Luther's Missionary Vision [Luther and Missions]," *Evangelical Missions Quarterly*, vol. 3, no. 4, Summer 1967 (16)

"Tillich's Philosophy of History," *Gordon Review*, Summer 1967 (14)

"The Inspired Word" [Book Review], *Eternity*, Sept. 1967 (13)

"Kirchentag 1967," *Christianity Today*, Sept. 1, 1967 (17)

"The Approach of New Shape Roman Catholicism to Scriptural Inerrancy: A Case Study for Evangelicals," *Bulletin of Evangelical Theological Society*, vol. X, Fall 1967 (13, 27)

"95 Theses," *Christianity Today*, Oct. 27, 1967 (16, 17)

"A Day in East German Luther Country," *Evangelize*, Oct./Nov. 1967 (16)

"The Relevance of Scripture Today," *Christianity Today*, Nov. 10, 1967 (17)

"Altizer and Rome," *Christianity Today*, Nov. 24, 1967 (13, 17)

1968

Es Confiable el Cristianismo? (1968)

"Gordon Clark's Historical Philosophy," in *The Philosophy of Gordon Clark*, ed. R. Nash (1968) (14)

"The Relevance of Scripture Today," in *The Bible: The Living Word of Revelation*, ed. M. C. Tenney (1968) (17, 28, 47)

"Confessional," in *Spectrum of Protestant Beliefs*, ed. R. Campbell (1968)

"The Bishop, the Spirits, and the Word," *Christianity Today*, Feb. 16, 1968

"The Suicide of Christian Theology and a Modest Proposal for Its Resurrection," *Bulletin of Evangelical Theological Society*, Spring 1968 (17)

"Cryonics and Orthodoxy," *Christianity Today*, May 10, 1968

"Frederick Herzog" [Book Review], *Bulletin of Evangelical Theological Society*, vol. 11, no. 3, Summer 1968 (17)

"Fresh Spirit Lifts European Scholars," *Christianity Today*, July 5, 1968 (17)

"Evangelicals and Archaeology," *Christianity Today*, Aug. 16, 1968

"France in Flame," *Christianity Today*, Aug. 16, 1968 (17)

"Soderblom: Ecumenical Pioneer" [Book Review], *Evangelical Missions Quarterly*, Fall 1968 (13)

"Source of Our Faith," *Bible Study*, Oct./Dec. 1968

"Automating Apologetics in Austria," *Christianity Today*, Nov. 8, 1968 (12)

"Reproduction Restudied," *Christianity Today*, Dec. 6, 1968

"Dissecting Courage," *Christianity Today*, Dec. 6, 1968 (17)

"Remythologizing Christmas," *Christianity Today*, Dec. 20, 1968 (17)

1969

Computers, Cultural Change, and the Christ (1969)

Ecumenicity, Evangelicals, and Rome (1969)

Where Is History Going? Essays in Support of the Historical Truth of the Christian Revelation (1969)

"The Christian View of the Fetus," in *Birth Control and the Christian*, eds. W. O. Spitzer and C. L. Saylor (1969) (28, 38)

"Missouri Compromise I," *Christianity Today*, Jan 17, 1969 (10)

"Change for the Better?" [Book Review], *Christianity Today*, March 14, 1969 (17)

"Missouri Compromise II," *Christianity Today*, March 28, 1969 (10)

"Is Man His Own God?" *Journal of Evangelical Theological Society*, vol. 12, pt. 2, Spring 1969 (17, 21, 28)

"Missouri Compromise III," *Christianity Today*, June 6, 1969 (10)

"Demos and Christos," *Christianity Today*, July 18, 1969 (17, 47)

"Searching the Reins," *Christianity Today*, Aug. 1, 1969 (47)

"Professionals Discuss Contemporary Theology," *Christianity Today*, Sept. 26, 1969 (17)

"A Critique of G. Ernest Wright's *The Challenge of Israel's Faith*" [Book Review], *Journal of Evangelical Theological Society*, vol. 12, pt. 4, Fall 1969 (17)

"The Failure of Current Theology," *His*, Nov. 1969; Dec. 1969; Jan 1970; Feb. 1970

"Missouri Turns a Corner," *Christianity Today*, Nov. 7, 1969 (10)

"The Bible and Science," *Journal of American Scientific Affiliation*, Dec. 1969

1970

Damned Through the Church (1970)

In Defence of Martin Luther (1970)

Suicide of Christian Theology (1970)

"Evangelical Social Responsibility in Theological Perspective," in *Our Society in Turmoil*, ed. Gary Collins (1970) (47, 56)

"Tractatus Logico Theologicus" [Part I; Part II to be completed.] Mss., 1970

"God's Country?" *Christianity Today*, Jan 30, 1970 (17, 47)

"Marcuse," *Christianity Today*, April 24, 1970 (17)

"The War on the Womb," *Christianity Today*, June 5, 1970

"Paris Theatre: The Cinema," *Christianity Today*, July 17, 1970

"Patton," *Christianity Today*, Oct. 23, 1970

"Lutheranism and the Defense of the Christian Faith," *Lutheran Synod Quarterly*, vol. XI, no. 1, Fall 1970

Part 1, Should Christianity Be Defended? (35)

Part 2, The Apologetic Thrust of Lutheran Theology (35)

Part 3, How to Validate the Gospel Truth in Our Time: Is Man His Own God?" (17, 21, 28)

"A.M.A. Symposium: When Does Life Begin?" *Journal of American Medical Association*, vol. 214, no. 10, Dec. 7, 1970 (28, 38)

1971

"Once Upon an A Priori," in *Jerusalem and Athens*, ed. E. R. Geehan (1971) (35)

"The Apologetic Thrust of Lutheran Theology," in *Ditt Ord Aer Sanning*, ed. S. Erlandsson (1971) (35)

"Christian World of C. S. Lewis" [Book Review], *Revue d'Histoire de Philosophie Religieuses*, LI, 2, 1971 (29)

"Paris Theatre: The Stage," *Christianity Today*, Jan 15, 1971

"Making Sense out of History," *His*, March 1971

"The Current Muddle over History," *His*, April 1971

"The Last Days of the Late, Great Synod of Missouri," *Christianity Today*, April 9, 1971 (10)

"Where Is History Going?" *His*, May 1971

"Ark Fever," *Christianity Today*, July 2, 1971 (19)

"A Question of Credentials," *Christianity Today*, Aug. 27, 1971

"Neither Marx Nor Jesus," *Christianity Today*, Oct. 8, 1971 (47)

"The Speck in Butterfield's Eye: A Reply to William A. Speck," *Fides et Historia*, vol. IV, no. 1, Fall 1971.

1972

La Mort de Dieu (1972)

The Quest for Noah's Ark (1972, rev. 1974), editor

Situation Ethics: A Dialogue Between Joseph Fletcher and John Warwick Montgomery (1972)

"Arkeology 1971," *Christianity Today*, Jan 7, 1972 (19)

"Having a Fuddled Easter?" *Christianity Today*, March 31, 1972 (35)

"Technology and Eschatology," *Christianity Today*, June 23, 1972 (35)

"How Scientific Is Science?" *Christianity Today*, Sept. 29, 1972 (35)

"Jesus Returns to France," *Eternity*, Oct. 1972

"Unbridgeable Chasm: Gospelism or the Scriptural Gospel?" *Affirm*, vol. II, no. 7, Dec. 1972 (10)

"How Not to Find the Ark," *Christianity Today*, Dec. 22, 1972 (19)

1973

Christianity for the Tough Minded (1973), editor

Cross and Crucible: Johann Valentin Andreae (1586–1654), Phoenix of the Theologians, vols. 1 and 2 (1973) [Th.D. dissertation, U. of Strasbourg, 1964]

How Do We Know There Is a God? (1973)

International Scholars Directory (1973), editor

Principalities and Powers: A New Look at the World of the Occult (1973, rev. 1975)

Verdamnt durche die Kirche? (1973)

"An Exhortation to Exhorters," *Christianity Today*, March 16, 1973 (35)

"Episcopal Futurity and Futility," *Christianity Today*, March 16, 1973

"Last Judgment for Missouri," *Christianity Today* June 8, 1973

"The French Contribution I: Goldmann," *Christianity Today*, Sept. 14, 1973

"The London Stage," *Christianity Today*, Dec. 7, 1973

1974

God's Inerrant Word: An International Symposium on the Trustworthiness of Scripture (1974), editor

"Biblical Inerrancy: What Is at Stake?"

Jurisprudence: A Book of Readings (1974, rev. 1980), editor

Myth, Allegory, Gospel (1974), editor

"The Apologists of Eucatastrophe"

"The Quest for Absolutes: An Historical Argument," Mss. 1974 (28)

"East Side, West Side," *Christianity Today*, March 1, 1974 (47)

"The Exorcist: An Interpretation of the Film," *Trinity Journal*, Spring 1974 (25)

"Lessons from Luther on the Inerrancy of Holy Writ," *Westminster Theological Journal*, Spring 1974 (27)

"An Anti-Ecumenical Devil?" *Christianity Today*, May 24, 1974 (25)

"Exorcism: Is It for Real?" *Christianity Today*, July 26, 1974 (25)

"To Help You Understand 'The Exorcist,'" *Incite*, Aug. 1974 (25)

"From Enlightenment to Extermination," *Christianity Today*, Oct. 11, 1974 (33, 47)

"The Occult: Demonology," *Christian Ministry*, Nov. 1974 (25)

"Transcendental Gastronomy," *Christianity Today*, Nov. 22, 1974

1975

Como Sabemos que Hay un Dios? (1975)

The Law Above the Law (1975)

"Legal Reasoning and Christian Apologetics," *Christianity Today*, Feb. 14, 1975 (31)

"Fetus and Personhood," *Human Life Review*, Spring 1975 (38)

"Is Theology Dying?" *Christianity Today*, May 9, 1975 (35)

"Washington Christianity," *Christianity Today*, Aug. 8, 1975 (33, 47)

"Ecumenical Whooping in Strasbourg," *Christianity Today*, Nov. 7, 1975 (35)

"Dialogue on Marriage, Divorce, and Abortion," *The Jurist*, Winter 1975 (38)

1976

Demon Possession: A Medical, Historical, Anthropological and Theological Symposium (1976), editor

"Not Suffering Witches to Live [Witch Trial Theory and Practice]"

"Commentary on 'Hysteria and Demons, Depression and Oppression, Good and Evil'"

The Shaping of America (1976)

"Chemnitz on the Council of Trent," in *Soli Deo Gloria: Festschrift for John H. Gerstner*, ed. R. C. Sproul (1976)

"Encounter in Florence," *Christianity Today*, Jan 30, 1976; March 26, 1976; & April 9, 1976 (35)

"Should We Export the American Way?" *Christianity Today*, April 23, 1976 (47)

"Why Lutheran?" *Christian News Encyclopedia*, vol. I, June 7, 1976

"If You Can't Beat 'Em, Separate from 'Em," *Christianity Today*, July 2, 1976 (47)

"The Revolution: Christian in Spite of Itself," *Christianity Today*, July 16, 1976 (47)

"Will an Evangelical President Usher in the Millennium?" *Christianity Today*, Oct. 22, 1976 (47)

1977

Weltgeschichte Wohin? (1977)

"The Millennium," in *Dreams, Visions, and Oracles,* ed. C. E. Amerding and W. W. Gasque (1977)

"Scott H. Hendrix, *Ecclesia in Via*" [Book Review], *Christian Scholars Review,* vol. VII, no. 2/3, 1977

"Mass Communication and Scriptural Proclamation," *Evangelical Quarterly,* vol. 49, no. 1, Jan./March 1977 (35)

"Questions for Potential Lutheran Faculty and Pastoral Candidates," *Christian News Encyclopedia,* vol. 2, Jan 10, 1977

"Do We Have the Right to Die?" *Christianity Today,* Jan. 21, 1977 (47)

"Survey of Evangelical Apologetes" [Book Review], *Christianity Today,* April 1, 1977 (35)

"Dr. Johnson as Apologist," *Christianity Today,* April 15, 1977 (35)

"Whatever Happened to Noah's Ark?" [Book Review], *Christianity Today,* June 3, 1977

"Whither Biblical Inerrancy?" *Christianity Today,* July 29, 1977 (35)

"Hitler—a Career," *Christianity Today,* Oct. 21, 1977 (47)

1978

Faith Founded on Fact: Essays in Evidential Apologetics (1978)

Law and Gospel: A Study in Jurisprudence (1978, 1995)

"What Is Sin?" *Alternate,* 1978

"Thielicke on Trial," *Christianity Today,* March 24, 1978; June 23, 1978; Sept. 8, 1978

"Testamentary Help in Interpreting the Old and New Testaments," *Christianity Today,* May 5, 1978

"Christian Apologetics in Light of the Lutheran Confessions," *Concordia Theological Quarterly,* vol. 42, no. 3, July 1978

"Luther, Anti-Semitism, and Zionism," *Christianity Today,* Sept. 8, 1978 (47)

"Israel vs. the 'Religious Enticers': Before Rulers and Kings for a Testimony," *Inspiration,* vol. 1, no. 4, Sept./Oct. 1978

"A Report on F.E.E.T.," *Christianity Today,* Dec. 15, 1978

"Science, Theology, and the Miraculous," *Journal of American Scientific Affiliation,* vol. 30, Dec. 1978 (35)

1979

Children's Story of Noah's Ark, Mss. (1979)

"Why Has God Incarnate Suddenly Become Mythical?" in *Perspectives on Evangelical Theology*, ed. K. S. Kantzer and R. H. Gundry (1979) (47)

"The Case for 'Higher Law,'" *Pepperdine Law Review*, vol. 6, no. 2, 1979 (31)

"Open Doors in the Middle East," *Christianity Today*, March 2, 1979

"Presenting the Prince of Peace," *Christianity Today*, March 23, 1979

"Savourless Salt: A Social Curse," *Christianity Today*, Oct. 19, 1979

"Brief for the Plaintiffs/Appellants in James E. Brown v. National Distillers & Chemical Corp.," Mss., 1979

1980

"Abortion: Courting Severe Judgment," *Christianity Today*, Jan. 23, 1980 (38)

"Strasbourg: The Capital of Human Values," *Human Rights*, Spring 1980 (41)

"The Reasonable Reality of the Resurrection," *Christianity Today*, April 4, 1980 (47)

"Truth in Transition: A Case Study," *Christianity Today*, April 18, 1980

"France Take Care Not to Lose Your Soul," *Christianity Today*, Nov. 21, 1980 (47)

"Clergy Malpractice," *The Priest*, Dec. 1980

1981

Slaughter of the Innocents: Abortion, Birth Control, and Divorce in Light of Science, Law, and Theology (1981)

"Abortion and the Law: Three Clarifications," in *New Perspectives on Human Abortion*, ed. Hilgers, Horan & Mall (1981) (38)

"The Limits of Christian Influence," *Christianity Today*, Jan 23, 1981 (47)

"Could You or Your Pastor Be Sued?" *Christian Life*, May 1981

"Believing the Bible Breeds Revival," *Christianity Today*, May 8, 1981

"Getting Hold of Our Feelings," *Christianity Today*, Oct. 2, 1981

"The Trial of Jesus" [Book Review], *Simon Greenleaf Law Review*, vol. I, 1981/82

"Human Rights After Helsinki" [Book Review], *Simon Greenleaf Law Review*, vol. 1, 1981/82

"Jacques Ellul" [Book Review], *Simon Greenleaf Law Review*, vol. 1, 1981/82

1982

"Jesus Takes the Stand: An Argument to Support the Gospel Accounts," *Christianity Today*, April 9, 1982 (47, 52)

"School Prayers: A Common Danger," *Christianity Today*, May 7, 1982 (47)

"'Born Againism': An Evangelical Innovation?" *Christianity Today*, Oct. 22, 1982

"Jaworski" [Book Review], *Simon Greenleaf Law Review*, vol. 2, 1982/83

"On Being a Christian and a Lawyer" [Book Review], *Simon Greenleaf Law Review*, vol. 2, 1982/83

"Whitehead" [Book Review], *Simon Greenleaf Law Review*, vol. 2, 1982/83

"Anti-Gnostic Essays" [Book Review], *Simon Greenleaf Law Review*, vol. 2, 1982/83

"Human Rights Today" [Book Review], *Simon Greenleaf Law Review*, vol. 2, 1982/83

1983

The Marxist Approach to Human Rights: Analysis and Critique (1983) [M.Ph.L. thesis, U. of Essex, 1983]

1985

"The Rights of Unborn Children," *Simon Greenleaf Law Review*, vol. 5, 1985/86 (47)

1986

"Defending the Biblical Gospel" Study Guide (1986, 1997)

Human Rights and Human Dignity (1986, 1995)

"Millennium," in *International Standard Bible Encyclopedia*, rev. ed., vol. 3, ed. G. Bromiley (1986)

"Legal Reasoning and Christian Apologetics," Mss., Feb. 3, 1986

"Is the Bible Only Reliable Spiritually?" *Moody*, March 1986 (47)

"Simon Greenleaf," *Eternity*, Nov. 1986

"A Glaswegian Triumph" [Book Review], *Simon Greenleaf Law Review*, vol. 6, 1986/87

"A French Exposé of the Moonies" [Book Review], *Simon Greenleaf Law Review*, vol. 6, 1986/87

"More Conceptual Chaos than Clarity" [Book Review], *Simon Greenleaf Law Review*, vol. 6, 1986/87

1987

"Law and Justice," in *Applying the Scriptures*, ed. K. Kantzer (1987) (47)

"The Emperor's Clothes," *Moody*, April 1987 (47)

"Simon Greenleaf's Appellate Brief Defense of 'The Athens 3'," *Simon Greenleaf Law Review*, vol. 7, 1987/88

"Law and Literature" [Book Review], *Simon Greenleaf Law Review*, vol. 7, 1987/88

"The Soft-Headed Generation" [Book Review], *Simon Greenleaf Law Review*, vol. 7, 1987/88

"The Consequences of Consequentialism" [Book Review], *Simon Greenleaf Law Review*, vol. 7, 1987/88

"A Convert Speaks Out on Human Rights" [Book Review], *Simon Greenleaf Law Review*, vol. 7, 1987/88

1988

Jesus Christ: Was He a Liar, a Lunatic, a Legend, or God? Mss., 1988

"The World-view of Johann Valentin Andreae," in *Das Erbe Des Christian Rosenkreuz* (1988)

"LCMS Charismatic Found Not Guilty," *Christian News*, Jan 25, 1988

1989

"Religion and Human Rights," Mss., 1989

1991

Evidence for Faith: Deciding the God Question (1991, 2004), editor
"The Jury Returns: A Juridical Defense of Christianity" (47)
Wohin Marschiert China? (1991)

1992

"The Strange Decline of American Evangelicalism," *New Oxford Review*, Sept. 1992
"Eugen Drewermann's Trivialization of Theology," *New Oxford Review*, Oct. 1992
"What Can Be Learned When a Christian Institution Falls from Greatness," *Christian News*, Oct. 5, 1992
"The Bishop and the Muslims," *New Oxford Review*, Nov. 1992
"The New Archbishop of Canterbury," *New Oxford Review*, Dec. 1992
"Holmes in Tibet," *Sherlock Holmes Journal*, Winter 1992

1993

"Introduction," *Human Rights and Eastern Europe*, by Richard Hörcsik (1993)
"Harry Dickson, Le Sherlock Holmes Américain," in *France in the Blood: A Practical Handbook of French Holmesian Culture*, ed. Philip Porter and Catherine Cooke (1993)
"Holmes Vinaire," in *France in the Blood: A Practical Handbook of French Holmesian Culture*, ed. Philip Porter and Catherine Cooke (1993)
"What to Do with a Guilty Client," SUARA, 1992/93
"Marriage in Church After Divorce," *Ecclesiastical Law Journal*, Jan. 1993
"An Invitation to Injustice," *Christian News*, Jan. 18, 1993

"Trust Me?" *New Oxford Review*, Jan./Feb. 1993

"Anglican Priestesses," *Christian News*, Feb. 1, 1993

"The Search for Absolutes: A Sherlockian Inquiry," *Christian Legal Journal*, vol. 2, no. 3, Spring 1993 (47)

"A Lawyer's Case for Christianity," *Christian Legal Journal*, vol. 2, no. 3, Spring 1993 (47)

"Law and Christian Theology: Some Foundational Principles," *Christian Legal Journal*, vol. 2, no. 3, Spring 1993 (47)

"Can a Scientist Pray?" *New Oxford Review*, April 1993

"Did Jesus Exist?" *New Oxford Review*, May 1993; *Christian News*, Sept. 13, 1993

"God and Other Law-Makers," *Beyond Culture Wars*, May/June 1993 <www.alliancenet.org/pub/mr/mr93/1993.03.MayJun/ mr9303.jwmlawmakers.html>

"When Is a Jew Not a Jew?" *New Oxford Review*, June 1993

"Gorgan Theology," *New Oxford Review*, July/Aug. 1993

"New Light on the Abortion Controversy?" *New Oxford Review*, Sept. 1993

"Fido in Heaven," *New Oxford Review*, Oct. 1993

"Lessons from the Amish," *New Oxford Review*, Nov. 1993

"The Virgin Birth: A Problem?" *New Oxford Review*, Dec. 1993

1994

Giant in Chains: China Today and Tomorrow (1994)

Law and Morality: Friends or Foes? (1994)

"Law and Justice," in *God and Caesar*, ed. Michael Bauman and David Hall (1994)

"Holmes, the Law, and the Inns of Court," in *Back to Baker Street: An Appreciation of Sherlock Holmes and London*, ed. Roger Johnson and Jean Upton (1994)

"How Lawyers Reason," Mss., 1994

"Human Dignity in Birth and Death: A Question of Values," *International Journal of Value-Based Management*, vol. 7, 1994 (47, 52)

"Je*sus in the Dic*tion*ary," *New Oxford Review*, Jan./ Feb. 1994

"There Goes Hell and the Second Coming," *New Oxford Review*, March 1994

"Dracula or Jesus?" *New Oxford Review*, April 1994

"On the Reliability of the Four Gospels," *New Oxford Review*, May 1994

"Philosophy Revisited," *New Oxford Review*, June 1994

"Back to the Sixties?" *New Oxford Review*, July / Aug. 1994

"The Religion of Dr. Johnson," *New Oxford Review*, Sept. 1994

"The Famous in France: Why They Believe," *New Oxford Review*, Oct. 1994

"Otto von Habsburg and the Christian Renaissance of Europe," *New Oxford Review*, Nov. 1994

"Yuletide Feasting," *New Oxford Review*, Dec. 1994

1995

Jésus: La Raison Rejoint l'Histoire (1995)

"Legal Hermeneutics and the Interpretation of Scripture," in *Evangelical Hermeneutics*, ed. Michael Bauman and David Hall (1995)

"Jesus and the Bell Curve," *New Oxford Review*, Jan./Feb. 1995

"School Prayer Born Again?" *Christian News*, Feb. 27, 1995

"The American Law Degree," parts 1–3, *Malaysian Law News*, February–April, 1995

"Christianity's Unique Intellectual Opportunity," *New Oxford Review*, March 1995

"Will the True Biblical Scholar Please Stand Up?" *Christian News*, March 27, 1995

"Defining Rights in General and Human Rights in Particular," Mss., June 16/21, 1995

"The American Law Teaching Experience," *Law and Justice: The Christian Law Review*, no. 126/127, Trinity/Michaelmas, 1995

1996

Christians in the Public Square (1996)

"Neglected Apologetic Styles: The Juridical and the Literary," in *Evangelical Apologetics*, ed. Michael Bauman *et al* (1996)

"Pourquoi aimons-nous Sherlock Holmes?" in *Sherlock Holmes et la France: Une étude en bleu, blanc, rouge* (1996)

"Hermeneutics, Legal and Theological: An Exercise in Integration," Mss., April 1, 1996

"Whose Life Anyway?" *Nexus: A Journal of Opinion*, vol. 1, no. 2, Fall 1996 (52)

"The O. J. Simpson Trial," *Barred: The Law Society's Monthly Magazine*, Oct. 1996

"The Alleged Myth of the Mafia," *Law and Justice: The Christian Law Review*, no. 130/131, Trinity/Michaelmas, 1996 (52)

1997

"The Descent of Evangelicalism: Origins of the Specious," *Modern Reformation*, Sept./Oct., 1997 and "Response to David Neff," *Modern Theology*, vol. 7, no. 3, May/June 1998

"The Holy Spirit and the Defense of the Faith," *Bibliotheca Sacra*, vol. 154, no.616, Oct./Dec. 1997

1998

"The Incarnate Christ: The Apologetic Thrust of Lutheran Theology," *Modern Reformation*, vol. 7, no. 1, Jan./Feb., 1998

"Defense of Apologetics," *Christian News*, Feb. 9, 1998

"When Is Evangelicalism Illegal?" *New Law Journal*, vol. 148, no. 6835, April 10, 1998 and *Fulcrum*, no. 52, Sept./Dec., 1998

"The Criminal Standard of Proof," *New Law Journal*, vol. 148, no. 6836, April 24, 1998

"Beggars Can and Should Be Apologists," *Christian News*, June 8, 1998

"A Lawyer's Defense of Christianity," *Faith and Thought*, no. 24, Oct. 1998 and "A Rejoinder to Prof. Millard," *Faith and Thought*, no. 26, Oct. 1999

"Advocacy, Classical Rhetoric, and Legal Ethics," *Law and Justice*, no. 138/139, Trinity/Michaelmas, 1998 (52)

"Why a Christian Philosophy of Law?" in *Christian Perspectives on Human Rights and Legal Philosophy*, ed. Paul R. Beaumont (1998)

1999

"Een Bijbelse Fundering Voor Mensenrechten En Voor Menselijke Waardigheid," *Beweging*, Nummer 1, Maart, 1999

"A Review of Brian Tierney's *Rights, Laws and Infalliblity in Medieval Thought*" [Book Review], *Fides et Historia*, vol. 31, Winter/Spring 1999 (52)

"If God Is Love and All-Powerful, Why Does He Not Bring Peace on Earth?" *The Call*, vol. 6, issue 3, March 1999

"A Lively Exchange on Evidentialism and Presuppositionalism," *Philosophia*, vol.1, no.4, April 8, 1999

<www.trinitysem.edu/philosophia.html>

"A Review of Norman L. Geisler's *Baker's Encyclopedia of Christian Aplogetics*" [Book Review], *Global Journal of Classical Theology*, vol. 1, no. 3, 7/99 (52)

"A Review of Jean-Marc Berthoud's *Une Religion sans Dieu: Droits de L'Homme et Parole de Dieu*" [Book Review], *Global Journal of Classical Theology*, vol. 1, no. 3, 7/99

"Lord Denning (1899–1999): An Appreciation," *Faith and Thought*, no. 26, Oct. 1999

"Canon Law as the Juridic Reflection of Theological Norms," *Law and Justice*, no. 142/143, Trinity/Michaelmas, 1999 and "A Rejoinder to Bishop Jukes," *Law and Justice*, Trinity/Michaelmas, 2000 (52)

"Editor's Introduction [Dangerous Eschatology]," *Global Journal of Classical Theology*, vol. 2, no. 1, 12/99

"A Critique of Certain Uncritical Assumptions in Modern Historiography," *Global Journal of Classical Theology*, vol. 2, no. 1, 12/99

"Foreword" to *Engaging the Closed Mind* by Dan Storey (1999)

2000

The Transcendent Holmes (2000)

"Justification Through the Ages: *Justitia Dei* by Alister McGrath" [Book Review], *Modern Reformation*, vol. 9, no. 2, March/April, 2000 (52)

"Greek Opposition to Evangelism," *Religion-Staat-Gesellschaft: Zeitschrift fur Glaubensformen und Weltanschauungen*, 1/2, 2000 (52)

"Christian Education and Worship in State Schools," *Law and Justice*, Hilary/Easter, 2000 (52)

"Editor's Introduction [Political Correctness, Child Abuse, and the Threat to Christian Scholarship]," *Global Journal of Classical Theology*, vol. 2, no. 2, 2000

"Book Review of *Christian Justice and Public Policy* by Duncan B. Forrester," *Global Journal of Classical Theology*, vol. 2, no. 2, 2000 (52)

"Can Blasphemy Law Be Justified?" *Law and Justice*, Trinity/Michaelmas, 2000 (52)

2001

The Repression of Evangelism in Greece: European Litigation vis-à-vis a Closed Religious Establishment (2001)

"Prophecy, Eschatology, and Apologetics" in *Looking into the Future: Evangelical Studies in Apologetics*, ed. David W. Baker (2001) (52)

"Luther and Canon Law," *Bibliotheca Sacra*, April-June, 2001 (52)

"Editor's Introduction [The Oberammergau Passion Play 2000—Anti-Semitic?]," *Global Journal of Classical Theology*, vol. 2, no. 3, 2001

2002

Christ Our Advocate: Studies in Polemical Theology, Jurisprudence, and Canon Law (2002)

"Modern Theology and Contemporary Legal Theory: A Tale of Ideological Collapse"

"Justice Denied: Church Property Disputes Under Current American Law"

"Church Remarriage After Divorce: A Third Way"

History, Law, and Christianity (2002)

Tractatus Logico-Theologicus (2002)

"John Gerhard: Theology and Devotion" in *Not Omitting the Weightier Matters: Essays in Honour of Robert E. L. Rodgers* (2002)

"Rozwazania nad 'Ius et Lex,'" in *Ius et Lex* (2002)

"Subsidiarity as a Jurisprudential and Canonical Theory," *Law and Justice: The Christian Law Review*, No. 148, Hilary/Easter, 2002 (52)

"How Many Holmeses? How Many Watsons?," *The Baker Street Journal*, vol. 52, no. 2, Summer 2002

"The Un-Apologist [G. K. Chesterton]," *Christian History*, vol. 21, no. 3, 2002

"The Human Embryo Cloning Danger in European Context," *Philosophia Christi*, vol. 4, no. 1, 2002 (52)

"Editor's Introduction [Boa and Bowman's *Faith Has Its Reasons: An Apologetics Handbook*; the "Open Theism" Debate]," *Global Journal of Classical Theology*, vol. 3, no. 1, 2002

"Editor's Intoduction ["Men in Black II" and Apologetics]," *Global Journal of Classical Theology*, vol. 3, no. 2, 2002

2003

"'Breath of Life' Needs the Spirit Who Convicts and Saves" [Play Review] *The Christian Lawyer*, Spring 2003

"Life Can Be Difficult if You Are Bessarabian Orthodox: *Bessarabian Orthodox Church v. Moldavia* before the European Court of Human Rights," *Law and Justice: The Christian Law Review*, no. 151, Trinity/Michaelmas, 2003

"Editor's Introduction ["Ararat," the Armenians, and Missionary Doctor Clarence Ussher]," *Global Journal of Classical Theology*, vol. 3, no. 3, 2003

"Defending the Hope that Is in Us: Apologetics for the 21st Century," www.bucer.de/theologyconsultation/Docs/JWMENGLISH.pdf:1–11

Heraldic Aspects of the German Reformation (2003)

2004

"Die Verteidigung der Hoffnung in uns—Apologetik für das 21. Jahrhundert" in *Europa Hoffnung geben*, ed. Thomas Meyer and Thomas Schirrmacher (2004)

"Computer Origins and the Defense of the Faith," *Perspectives on Science and Christian Faith: Journal of the American Scientific Affiliation*, 56/3, Sept. 2004

"Did Jesus Die for E.T. as Well as for *Homo Sapiens?*," *Faith and Thought: Bulletin of the Victoria Institute*, no. 36, Oct. 2004

"Editor's Introduction [Refuting Richard Packham's Broadside Against Our Legal Apologetic]," *Global Journal of Classical Theology*, vol. 4, no. 1, 2004

"Editor's Introduction [Matthew 18:15–17 and Romans 8:28—Their Neglect in Evangelical Circles]," *Global Journal of Classical Theology*, vol. 4, no. 2, 2004

"Editor's Introduction [Saint-Exupery's *Little Prince*]," *Global Journal of Classical Theology*, vol. 4, no. 3, 2004

The Church: Blessing or Curse? (2004)

Hat die Weltgeschichte einen Sinn? (2004)

"An Historical Study of the Dignus Est Agnus Canticle," *Concordia Theological Quarterly*, vol. 68, no. 2, April 2004

"The Life of Paul Luther, Physician," *Lutheran Forum*, vol. 38, no. 3, Fall 2004

2005

"Editor's Introduction [Thornton Wilder's *Bridge of San Luis Rey*]," *Global Journal of Classical Theology*, vol. 5, no. 1, 2005

"Einleitung," in *Ein Maulkorb für Christen?* ed. Thomas Schirrmacher and Thomas Zimmermanns (2005)

"Robert Preus Remembered," *Christian News*, Dec. 12, 2005

2006

"Encounter in Florence," *Life in the Spirit*, vol. 14, no. 5, Sept./Oct. 2006

"Legal Evidence for the Truth of the Faith," *Modern Reformation*, vol. 15, no. 2, March-April 2006

"Witnesses, Criteria for," *New Dictionary of Christian Apologetics*, ed. Campbell-Jack and Gavin J. McGrath (2006)

"Editor's Introduction [The *Da Vinci Code* Movie]," *Global Journal of Classical Theology*, vol. 5, no. 3, 2006.

"The Film of the *Da Vinci Code*," *Christian News*, July 10, 2006

2007

"Slavery, Human Dignity, and Human Rights," *Evangelical Quarterly*, vol. 79, no. 2, April 2007

"Defending the Hope That Is in Us: Apologetics for the 21st Century," in *Reasons for Faith: Essays in Honor of Bob and Gretchen Passantino*, ed. Chad Meister (2007)

"The Apologetic Thrust of Lutheran Theology," in *Theologia et Apologia: Essays in Reformation Theology and Its Defense Presented to Rod Rosenbladt*, ed. Steven P. Mueller (2007)

"Can the Gospel Writers Withstand the Scrutiny of a Lawyer?" in *The Apologetics Study Bible*, ed. Ted Cabal (2007)

"Editor's Introduction" [The Irrationality of Richard Dawkins' Evolutionary Atheism], *Global Journal of Classical Theology*, vol. 6, no. 1, 2007

Forthcoming

Nineteen articles for the *Encyclopedia of Christian Civilization*, ed. George Kurian (Blackwell, 2008)

"C. T. Studd," in *The Faces of Fundamentalism*, ed. James Lutzweiler and B. Dwain Waldrep

"Pain in Theological Perspective," *Faith and Thought: Bulletin of the Victoria Institute*

"Tolkien: Lord of the Occult?" *Tolkien and Religion*, ed. Paul Kerry

The Bessarabian Church Case Before the European Court of Human Rights (Verlag für Kultur und Wissenschaft)

Christian Faith: Its Truth and Relevance (Verlag für Kultur und Wissenschaft)

"A New Approach to the Apologetic for Christ's Resurrection by Way of Wigmore's Juridical Analysis of Evidence," *Festschrift for Irving Hexham*, ed. Ulrich Van der Heyden and Andreas Feldtkeller

Autobiography (Canadian Institute for Law, Theology, and Public Policy)

Books Written or Edited

1. *The Writing of Research Papers in Theology* (1959, 1996)
2. *Union List of Serial Publications in Chicago-Area Protestant Theological Libraries* (1960), editor
3. *A Seventeenth-Century View of European Libraries: Lomeier's De Bibliothecis*, Chapter X (1962), editor

4. *Chytraeus' On Sacrifice: A Reformation Treatise in Biblical Theology* (1962), editor

5. *The Libraries of France at the Ascendancy of Mazarin: Louis Jacob's* Traicté Des Plus Belles Bibliotheques, Part Two (1962), editor

6. *The Shape of the Past: An Introduction to Philosophical Historiography* (1962, rev. 1975)

7. *History and Christianity* (1964)

8. *The "Is God Dead?" Controversy* (1966)

9. *The Altizer—Montgomery Dialogue* (1967)

10. *Crisis in Lutheran Theology*, vols. 1 & 2 (1967, 1973)

11. *Es Confiable el Cristianismo?* (1968)

12. *Computers, Cultural Change, and the Christ* (1969)

13. *Ecumenicity, Evangelicals, and Rome* (1969)

14. *Where Is History Going? Essays in Support of the Historical Truth of the Christian Revelation* (1969)

15. *Damned Through the Church* (1970)

16. *In Defence of Martin Luther* (1970)

17. *The Suicide of Christian Theology* (1970)

18. *La Mort de Dieu* (1972)

19. *The Quest for Noah's Ark* (1972, rev. 1974), editor

20. *Situation Ethics: A Dialogue Between Joseph Fletcher and John Warwick Montgomery* (1972)

21. *Christianity for the Tough Minded* (1973), editor

22. *Cross and Crucible: Johann Valentin Andreae, Phoenix of the Theologians*, vols. 1 & 2 (1973)

23. *How Do We Know There Is a God?* (1973)

24. *International Scholars Directory* (1973), editor

25. *Principalities and Powers: A New Look at the World of the Occult* (1973, rev. 1975)

26. *Verdamnt durch die Kirche?* (1973)

27. *God's Inerrant Word: An International Symposium on the Trustworthiness of Scripture* (1974), editor

28. *Jurisprudence: A Book of Readings* (1974, rev. 1980), editor

29. *Myth, Allegory, and Gospel* (1974), editor

30. *Como Sabemos que Hay un Dios?* (1975)

31. *The Law Above the Law* (1975)

32. *Demon Possession: A Medical, Historical, Anthropological and Theological Symposium* (1976), editor

33. *The Shaping of America* (1976)

34. *Weltgeschichte Wohin?* (1977)

35. *Faith Founded on Fact: Essays in Evidential Apologetics* (1978)

36. *Law and Gospel: A Study in Jurisprudence* (1978, 1995)

37. *Simon Greenleaf Law Review*, vols. 1–7 (1981/82–1987/88), editor

38. *Slaughter of the Innocents: Abortion, Birth Control, and Divorce in Light of Science, Law, and Theology* (1981)

39. *The Marxist Approach to Human Rights: Analysis and Critique* (1983)

40. *"Defending the Biblical Gospel" Study Guide* (1986, 1996)

41. *Human Rights and Human Dignity* (1986, 1995)

42. *Evidence for Faith: Deciding the God Question* (1991, 2004), editor

43. *Wohin Marschiert China?* (1991)

44. *Giant in Chains: China Today and Tomorrow* (1994)

45. *Law and Morality: Friends or Foes?* (1994)

46. *Jesus: La Raison Rejoint L'Histoire* (1995)

47. *Christians in the Public Square* (1996)

48. *Incotro se Indreapta istoria?* (1996)

49. *Conflict of Laws* (1997)

50. *The Transcendent Holmes* (2000)

51. *The Repression of Evangelism in Greece: European Litigation vis-à-vis a Closed Religious Establishment* (2001)

52. *Christ Our Advocate: Studies in Polemical Theology, Jurisprudence, and Canon Law* (2002)

53. *History, Law, and Christianity* (2002)

54. *Tractatus Logico-Theologicus* (2002)

55. *Heraldic Aspects of the German Reformation* (2003)

56. *The Church: Blessing or Curse?* (2004)

57. *Hat die Weltgeschichte einen Sinn?* (2004)

58. *Christ as Centre and Circumference: Essays Apologetic and Cultural in Support of Historic Christian Faith* (2009)

General Editor

Evangelical Perspectives

Tom Skinner, *How Black Is the Gospel?* (1970)
Richard V. Pierard, *The Unequal Yoke* (1970)
Vernon C. Grounds, *Revolution and the Christian Faith* (1971)
Merville O. Vincent, *God, Sex, and You* (1971)
Edwin Yamauchi, *The Stones and the Scriptures* (1972)
Raymond F. Surburg, *How Dependable Is the Bible?* (1972)
David O. Moberg, *The Great Reversal* (1972)

Simon Greenleaf Law Review

vol. 1 (1981/82)–vol. 7 (1987/88)

Videotapes
1988–1992

"Christianity on Trial" with Dr. Charles Manske

#101 Ideologies in Conflict
1. Islam and Christianity
2. Gods of the New Age
3. The Challenge of Marxism
4. Reincarnation or Resurrection

#102 Social Crises
1. The War over Human Rights
2. Hooked on Drugs
3. What Is Killing Our Youth?
4. Racism in the Church

#103 Medical Ethics: When Life Begins
1. When and How Does Life Begin?
2. Slaughter of the Innocents
3. Abortion
4. Fetal Tissue Implantation: Is Man Playing God?

#104 Death and Aids
1. Who Controls Death
2. Death on Demand?
3. The AIDS Epidemic—How Should Christians Respond to the AIDS Epidemic
4. Should AIDS Be Reported?

#105 Christian Apologetics
1. Can the Resurrection Be Proven?
2. When God Came into the World
3. Secular Humanism
4. The Forces of Evil

#106 Science and Religion in Conflict
1. Bible Inerrancy
2. Does Archaeology Support the Scriptures?
3. Do You Believe in Miracles?
4. Scientific Apologetics

#107 God and Evil
1. How Do We Know God Exists?
2. God and Modern Science
3. The Problem of Evil (Part 1)
4. The Problem of Evil (Part 2)

#108 Incarnation at Bethlehem
1. The Virgin Birth
2. Fairy Tales and the Gospel
3. The True Meaning of Christmas
4. Fulfilled Prophecy and the Truths of the Christian Faith

#109 Verdict for a Divine Jesus
1. The Case for the Triune God
2. The Meaning of Christ's Death
3. Legal Evidence for the Christian Faith (Part 1)
4. Legal Evidence for the Christian Faith (Part 2)

#110 Jesus' Death and Resurrection as Historical Fact
1. The Nature of the Case for Christianity
2. The Bible Confirmed by Archaeology

#117 War
1. Understanding War in Muslim Countries
2. Can War Be Fought Justly?
3. God's Miracles in Warfare
4. The End of Marxism

#118 Luther's Faith and Reforming Work
1. How the Reformation Came About
2. How Do We Get to Heaven?
3. Luther and the Scriptures
4. Who Was Martin Luther?

#119 The Reformation and Its Influence
1. The Heroism of the Reformation
2. The Invention of Printing and the Spread of the Gospel
3. Luther vs. Modern Secularism
4. The 20th Century: Age of Extermination

#120 Celebrating Christmas and Easter
1. Who Was Handel's Messiah?
2. Bach: The Fifth Evangelist
3. Luther on Birth, Death, and Christmas
4. Easter Special from South Africa

Film

Christianity—Fact or Fiction? (1960)
Mid America Films, Des Moines, Iowa 50265

Theses and Dissertations Centrally Addressing JWM

Anderson, Hyle R. "The Apologetic Approach of John W. Montgomery as Viewed from the Perspective of the Lutheran Confessions." M.Div. thesis, Concordia Theological Seminary, 1979.

Batts, Martin. "A Summary and Critique of the Historical Apologetic of John Warwick Montgomery." Th.M. thesis, Dallas Theological Seminary, 1977.

Boa, Kenneth. "A Comparative Study of Four Christian Apologetic Systems." Ph.D. diss., New York University, 1985.

Bush, Luther Russell, III. "An Inquiry into the Relationship between the Critical Problems of Historical Knowledge and Historical Explanation and the Methodological Formulation of a Christian Philosophy of History." Ph.D. diss., Southwestern Baptist Theological Seminary, 1975.

Hein, Steven A. "The Apologetic of John Warwick Montgomery: Its Theology, Historiography, and Method." B.D. thesis, Concordia Theological Seminary, 1971.

Liefeld, David R. "Lutheran Motifs in the Writings of John Warwick Montgomery." Th.M. Thesis, Westminster Theological Seminary, 1986.

Luck, William F. "The Resurrectional Argument for the Existence of God: An Analysis." M.A. thesis, Trinity Evangelical Divinity School, 1973.

McRoberts, Kerry D. "Faith Founded on Fact: The Apologetic Theology of John Warwick Montgomery." M.C.S. thesis, Regent College, 1998.

Mohler, Richard Albert, Jr. "Evangelical Theology and Karl Barth: Representative Models of Response." Ph.D. diss., Southern Baptist Theological Seminary, 1989.

Phillips, W. Gary. "Apologetics and Inerrancy: An Analysis of Select Axiopistic Models." Th.D. diss., Grace Theological Seminary, 1985.

Rook, Stephen D. "Historical Objectivism: The Apologetic Methodology of John Warwick Montgomery." M.A. thesis, Harding Graduate School of Religion, 1986.

Winn, Richard. "The Concept of History in the Thought of John Warwick Montgomery and Wolfhart Pannenberg." M.Div. thesis, Concordia Theological Seminary, 1978.

An Afterword in Honor of John Warwick Montgomery

Howard Hoffman

It is indeed a privilege to compose a postlude for this celebration of writings in honor of an accomplished scholar and mentor who is one of the clearest expositors of the Christian faith and one of its ablest defenders. What is the significance of Montgomery's work for the layperson? It is largely the same for the layperson as for the theologian. As Lead Belly used to sing, "We're in the same boat, brother!"[1] In our post-Christian era, Christianity is under continuous and often vicious attack, from without and from within. Militant atheists allege that Christianity is not only false but also evil. Liberal theologians try to redefine Christianity as something derived from their personal and political preferences, rather than being based on its historical, prophetic, and evidential foundations. We are in great need of a clear presentation of the gospel of Jesus Christ and its defense. John Warwick Montgomery has done both for decades, as a "good and faithful servant" (Matt 25:23).

Montgomery's scholarship and apologetics have meaning for the layperson indirectly through his salutary influence on Christian theology and Christian leaders, and directly by being available through his lectures, articles, and books. (See the bibliography in chapter 6.6, his Web site, the Web site of the Canadian Institute for Law, Theology and Public Policy, and the links at the end of the Wikipedia article on Montgomery.[2]) Montgomery has shown us that Christianity is to be believed because it is true, as based on historical and contemporary evidence.

My Beginnings

I was nurtured by kind Christian parents and a small-town mainline Protestant church with sound orthodox theology. I was taught John 3:16 and knew, therefore, that God loves me just as God loves every human being.[3] I learned that I should believe in Jesus Christ, that I should place my trust in Him rather than in myself for the sake of my eternal destiny. Sin was not an abstract concept. Sin was not insufficient self-righteousness or inadequate self-esteem. The Bible teaches that "sin is the transgression of the law" of God (1 John 3:4 KJV). Was I divine and thus morally perfect like God, already suitable to dwell with Him forever, or was I a sinner? Even a young child can know the answer to that question.

I knew that I did not always keep God's law in both thought and deed, even when I tried diligently to do so. Paul told us that "all have sinned, and come short of the glory of God" (Rom 3:23 KJV). I was in the same needful state as everyone else because sin separates us all from Him. I knew that we all need a Savior who can wash away our sins and cover us with His righteousness. Paul teaches, "God was in Christ, reconciling the world to Himself" (2 Cor 5:19 NKJV). I knew that one should be good out of gratitude for God's free gift of salvation, not to curry favor and receive salvation as barter. One cannot purchase God's grace. One should treat all people with love and respect because one should trust, obey, and emulate Christ. Critics should not use the genetic fallacy (a fallacy of irrelevance) to dismiss lightly what I have to say because of early influences, especially in light of Dr. Montgomery's *magna opera*.

My "Great Awakening"

When I became a teenager in 1956, I began to read literature sent out by mainline Protestant denominations to church members, especially for young persons of my age group.

I "discovered" in those liberal publications that one could pick and choose which parts of the Bible to accept and which to reject, based upon one's preferences, if one were to emulate the liberal clergy in the hierarchy. Being a Christian seemed to consist primarily of the correct political positions, which seemed always to be theologically and politically left and often Marxist. The attempt to merge Christianity and Marxism seemed preposterous to me, even as a teenager, because Christianity is based on God's revelation and the historicity of the life and work of Christ, not on one's political preferences or Marxist materialism. The assertions of any "higher-archy" that the essence of Christianity consists of left-wing politics (or, for that matter, middle-of-the-road or right-wing politics) seemed bizarre to me, and still does since there is no historical or biblical foundation for such a view.

The most bizarre teachings were found in the extremely far-left United Methodist Church magazine *Motive* (1941–1971), which contained little Christian teaching but instead preached a fervent message that the key to salvation was radical left-wing politics. The referent of salvation was culture; the salvation of individual souls apparently was unimportant. *Motive* pointed out social injustice but demanded that this be addressed by radical left political solutions rather than by following Christ. *Motive* had considerable influence on many young people, for example, a bright young lady who is currently an important liberal U.S. senator and in 2008 was a leading candidate for her party's nomination for the presidency of the United States—Hillary Clinton.[4]

Ideas Have Consequences

Traditional Christianity stands in stark contrast to the preaching of *Motive* magazine then and liberal theology before and since. Christian ideas have eternal consequences.[5] Although some of the church leaders believed in the incarnation, atonement, resurrection, and deity of Jesus Christ and in His miracles, others regarded these as nonhistorical since sophisticated people were giving up such beliefs. To them the miracles were myths, that is, "higher truths." It seemed to me that accepting and rejecting parts of Holy Scripture should not be justified by mere preference. Their fast and loose gerrymandering was, and still is, a form of self-deification. Those who do so are arrogating God's role because they presume to have a standard higher than Scripture by which to judge its teachings.

I read materials from other mainline denominations also, especially articles by the Episcopal Bishop James Pike. Brilliant and well educated, Pike was orthodox (and quite conservative) when he began his church career in the 1940s, but during the 1950s and 1960s he was in the process of jettisoning all of the fundamental doctrines of Christianity. Doing so severely damaged not only his personal and professional life but also those of his family and his mistresses. His rejection of Christian teachings also destroyed the real basis for his pursuit of social justice. How his persistent rejection of the truth led to his destruction is a truly tragic story.[6] Francis Schaeffer asked, "Who is responsible for the tragedy of Bishop James A. Pike? His liberal theological professors who robbed him of everything real and human. We cannot take lightly the fact that liberal theological professors in any theological school are leaving young men and women with a handful of pebbles, nothing more." Pike's downfall has been variously and naively attributed to external circumstances, such as a variety of administrative and largely nontheological dysfunctions within the Episcopal Church.[7] Except for the virtual absence of discipline within the hierarchy of the Episcopal Church, such assertions ring hollow.

Consider what Pike said. Schaeffer tells us of his last visit with Pike: "I will never forget the last time I saw him as Edith and I were leaving the Center for the Study of Democratic Institutions. He said one of the saddest things I have ever heard: 'When I turned from being agnostic, I went to Union Theological Seminary, eager for and expecting bread; but when I graduated, all that it left me was a handful of pebbles.'"[8] Pike's rejection of the authority of Scripture left him little reason to resist his egotism, narcissism, self-aggrandizement, dishonesty, womanizing, marital infidelity, heavy smoking, and alcoholism, which contributed to his multiple personal tragedies. His rejection of Christianity and adoption of an unoriginal mishmash of theological errors left him without a solid foundation for his worldview, and he became his own and only theological authority.[9] Still searching, he then slid down the slippery slope of spiritism, aided by charlatans such as Arthur Ford, and died a premature and tragic death.[10]

That some church leaders believed in a personal God and others did not seemed to me to be an untenable contradiction, especially since these officials presumed to speak for clergy and laity alike. When the laity objected to the liberal redefinition of Christianity, the reaction of the officials was always hostile and arrogant. The dissenting laypersons were supposed to keep their wallets open but their mouths shut. Like the Red Queen in Wonderland, the church officials seemed to be saying, "All ways here are my ways!"[11] It was disturbing to me, even as a teenager, that liberal theology was seriously damaging the Christian church. The mainline denominations seemed to be a maze of shifting inconsistencies.

By the end of high school, I decided that liberal theology had only the social gospel to offer but had destroyed the basis for that also. The most important problems of man are eternal, but the liberal church hierarchy seemed concerned only with the temporal. Social justice was important, but I could not see how remedying social injustice could be substituted for the foundation for such remedies, that is, the authority of the written Word, the Bible, and the living Word, Jesus Christ.

Human Rights?

Consider the consequences of extensive financial and political support by my previous mainline denomination and far-left religious organizations like the World Council of Churches for Robert Mugabe in Zimbabwe, beginning in the 1960s, which helped him defeat moderate and nonviolent black opposition parties and thus helped create the human rights disaster that exists there today.[12] Mugabe gradually substituted Marxism for his Christian roots. His corrupt and ever-worsening rule is characterized by brutal political repression, torture, and murder of political opponents, widespread starvation, 80 percent unemployment, and an inflation rate greater than 8,000 percent. For years he has curtailed or stopped the distribution of food from aid agencies. Instead, he has seized control of the food and used it as a political weapon by distributing it as bribes only to people who agree to support him. Recently (June 2008) Mugabe suspended the relief efforts of CARE International.[13] On 27 June 2008 Mugabe "won" reelection in a one-man race by his usual dishonest and repressive methods.[14] The financial aid and "moral" support of liberal church organizations has greatly helped Mugabe to create a Marxist "worker's paradise" but has not thereby furthered the social gospel of Jesus Christ. Montgomery's efforts in behalf of human rights have set a far better example.

I was being offered lots of human opinions (often inconsistent with one another). But I could find those anywhere! Like many members of mainline Protestant denominations, I began to attend church less. I studied literature, philosophy, the sciences, and medicine, searching for clearer answers to the important questions of life and its meaning but found no ultimate and consistent answers. I then discovered the books and lectures of a Christian theologian named John Warwick Montgomery, who helped me return to my roots as a Christian.

The Theologian's Craft

A theologian is one who studies the nature of God. In his essay, "The Theologian's Craft: A Discussion of Theory Formation and Theory Testing in Theology,"[15] Montgomery confirms that "we can say very simply that the theologian is one who engages in forming and testing theories about the Divine." Theology cannot be based on mere existential subjectivism. The subject-object distinction is as essential for the theologian as for the scientist or anyone searching for truth. The universe and the Scriptures are distinct from the person who studies and interprets them. Theology is not merely a "language game" requiring no verification. A careless and superficial interpretation of Ludwig Wittgenstein, substituting his later work for his earlier work, rather than considering both together as he intended, has sometimes erroneously been used to portray and misuse theology as an arbitrary and isolated language game.

Montgomery demonstrates in detail that theological theories must fit the facts within a structured system, very much analogous to scientific theories: "First, theories do not create facts; rather, they attempt to relate existent facts properly."[16] As do Karl Popper and Wittgenstein, Montgomery utilizes the concept of theories as "conceptual fabrics" or "nets" by which we "catch" (explain) the world.[17] For our beliefs to be justified, they must be based on facts as interpreted within theories and as models that represent reality. As Robert Nozick states, "A belief is the appropriate kind of response to a fact then, because unlike an arbitrary item like a twitch or a sound or a flag signal in an (arbitrary) code, a belief represents and states a fact within a structured system of representing other facts; in that way a belief *means* or *refers to* the fact it states and believes in."[18]

One utilizes four primary sources: the Holy Scriptures, Christian church tradition, Christian experience, and reason. Reason is a necessary tool but gives us no data about the universe or Scripture. Reason enables us to understand and interpret both. Personal Christian experience is important and is emphasized in many Protestant churches but is not sufficient to establish a firm knowledge of God. Christian church tradition is also very important and is emphasized in Roman Catholicism but cannot serve as our final theological authority. Montgomery points out that the assertion that "even an infallible Bible requires an infallible interpreter suffers from the fallacy of infinite regress; one can always ask, Then how can the Church itself function without a higher-level interpreter? Moreover, no Divine mandate can be produced to justify the authority of the Church as interpreter of Scripture" (p. 282).

The ultimate source of theological authority is the Bible. Using historical and legal evidence, Montgomery makes an extremely strong case that the Bible is reliable. I recommend the new edition (2002) of his *History, Law, and Christianity*, an excellent presentation of the truth of the gospel.[19] This concise volume is the Montgomery book that one should read first as an introduction to his evidential apologetic. Although Montgomery's apologetic and this volume are primarily addressed to the tough-minded seeker after truth, he does not neglect the tender minded. He discusses in detail the artistic level of the theologian's craft, which appeals to the heart of man.[20] He integrates the three levels of the craft of the theologian and the apologist (defender of the faith), that is, the scientific, the artistic, and the holy.[21]

The Triune Nature of God

Is God triune? Does the theological theory of the Trinity fit the facts? Fact number one: There is a person named the Father, who is identified in Holy Scripture as God. "Grace to you and peace from God our Father and the Lord Jesus Christ" (1 Cor 1:3 NKJV). (See also 1 Cor 8:6.) "You, O LORD, are our Father, our Redeemer from of old is your name" (Isa 63:16 NIV).

Fact number two: There is a person named the Son, Jesus the Christ, also identified as God. "In the beginning was the Word, and the Word was with God, and the Word was God. He was with God in the beginning. Through him all things were made; without him nothing was made that has been made" (John 1:1–3 NIV). In this passage, "the Word" (the Logos) is Jesus. Jesus Himself also claimed divinity explicitly. For example, when being questioned by some Jewish religious leaders who were disputing Him, "Jesus said to them, 'Truly, truly, I say to you, before Abraham was, I am'" (John 8:58 ESV). By quoting Exodus 3:14, Jesus referred to Himself with the same language used by YHWH God of the Old Testament to refer to Himself. His opponents immediately and clearly understood His claim, "So they picked up stones to throw at him [as punishment for blasphemy], but Jesus hid himself and went out of the temple" (8:59 ESV).

Fact number three: There is a person named the Holy Spirit who is also identified as God. As the Father sent the Son, the Son promises to send the Holy Spirit. Jesus says, "I will send him to you . . . when he, the Spirit of truth, comes, he will guide you into all truth" (John 16:7,13). Peter specifically identifies the Holy Spirit as God in Acts 5:3–5. "Now the Lord is the Spirit" (2 Cor 3:17). These three persons are mentioned together in more than 60 Bible passages, such as, "As soon as Jesus was baptized, he went up out of the water. At that moment heaven was opened, and he saw the Spirit of God descending like a dove and lighting on him. And a voice from heaven said, 'This is my Son, whom I love; with him I am well pleased'" (Matt 3:16–17 NIV).

Fact number four: There is only one God! The Sh'ma Yisrael: "Hear, O Israel: The LORD our God, the LORD is one" (Deut 6:4 NIV). "This is what the LORD says— Israel's King and Redeemer, the LORD Almighty: I am the first and I am the last; apart from me there is no God" (Isa 44:6 NIV). "I am the LORD, and there is no other; apart from me there is no God" (Isa 45:5 NIV). "For there is one God" (1 Tim 2:5 NIV). It follows that there is one God and only one God who exists in three Persons: Father, Son, and Holy Spirit.

Montgomery presents a powerful case for the resurrection of Jesus Christ, which is a cornerstone of the Christian faith. The Bible tells us that God the Father raised Jesus from the dead ((Acts 17:30–31; 1 Thess 1:10), that the Son raised Himself from the dead (John 2:19–22), and that the Spirit raised Jesus from the dead (Rom 1:4). That the three persons are the one God renders these assertions consistent and further establishes the triune nature of God.

It is common to hear an objection from people that they have come close to acceptance of the Christian concept of God but have difficulty in accepting His triune nature, that is, the Trinity. One should point out to them that God has explicitly told us of His triune nature in Scripture. One should also point out to them that they hold a *sub rosa* presupposition or assumption that they would understand the nature of God if He were not triune. This presupposition or assumption is unjustified. Since God is infinite, we finite created beings cannot comprehend His nature better by an *a priori* restriction as to what we will allow Him to be. We must instead humbly accept what He has told us about Himself as sufficient for us in this life: There is one God in three Persons.

Montgomery Contra Liberal Theology

Montgomery shows us clearly and in detail that the two most fundamental errors of liberal theologians are: (1) their acceptance of unsound criticisms of the Bible based on outmoded methods of poor scholarship, and their consequent rejection of its reliability and authority, and (2) their uncritical acceptance of the presuppositions of naturalism and consequent *a priori* rejection of all biblical miracles and fulfilled prophecies. Some liberal theologians reject theism entirely but claim to remain Christian by redefining it as a new secular religion. Others still believe that God created and sustains the universe and everything in it but do not believe in the miracles and fulfillment of prophecies told in the Bible. This, of course, is deism, but most of these theologians call themselves Christians rather than deists and remain in the church. They have an exceedingly strange concept of God. That is, they believe God can create the universe out of nothing and sustain it but that He is not capable of effecting any other miracles or prophecies, which is patently absurd.

One does not have to be a conservative Christian to recognize the obvious failures of liberal theology. The philosopher and foremost Nietzsche scholar Walter Kaufmann, who was hostile to Christianity, wrote, "The central shortcoming of liberal Protestantism lies in its attitude toward truth . . . , a radical disregard for history and philology . . . in accord with the fashions of the day which they swallowed uncritically. . . . In the case of the New Testament, they ended up . . . by reconstructing Jesus in their own image, in flat defiance of the texts and all historical probability."[22] Montgomery frequently observes that in liberal Protestantism one finds more autobiography than theology. Montgomery teaches fidelity to the texts when interpreting them as ordinary historical documents and also as revelations from God, and he carefully distinguishes these two activities as bases for what we know about Jesus of Nazareth.

Liberal theologians accept the specious presuppositions of the so-called "Higher Bible Criticism." Although this school of criticism began primarily in German universities, it quickly spread to the U.S. and England and became widely accepted. Kaufmann elucidates: "In this genre interpreters for the past hundred years have not been satisfied to deal with evident contradictions: they have searched for contradictions, hunted for them, and not infrequently invented them. And one of the axioms of this so-called Higher Bible Criticism . . . is that whenever two statements are inconsistent in any way they must have been written by different authors. The absurdity of this axiom is covered up by the fancy name of *Quellungscheidung*: discrimination of sources."[23] Kaufmann and Montgomery have pointed out that the "Higher Critical" method would prove in exactly the same manner that single-authored works such as Goethe's *Faust* were written by multiple authors.

Liberal theologians accept the primacy of the hypothetical Q source (German *Quelle*: source) as a real source of information about Jesus that antedates and disagrees with the Gospels, when this is merely conjecture. Not even a fragment of Q has ever been found. There is no definite historical or documentary evidence for Q. As biblical scholar Eta Linneman points out in referring to the alleged existence of Q, "This is the stuff of fairy tales."[24]

As Kaufmann says, "The so-called Higher Criticism . . . bears the stamp of the second half of the nineteenth century. It was one of the myriad forms of popular Darwinism, an attempt to understand everything in terms of evolution and—a widely prevalent confusion—progress." This popular Darwinism was admixed with the equally unwarranted Hegelian view that the religion of Israel developed "from primitive naturalism into lofty ethical monotheism." Kaufmann also refutes in detail the mistaken notion that the first five books of the Old Testament were mosaic (authored by multiple persons) rather than Mosaic (authored by Moses).[25]

Montgomery and Kaufmann both go into detail beyond the scope of this essay in revealing the unwarranted assumptions and poor scholarship of the school of Higher Biblical Criticism. Montgomery's view is clearly expressed by Kaufmann, who sums up: "The Higher Criticism must be understood as a revolt against the long-unquestioned authority of the Old Testament, and some of its chief exponents were clearly motivated in part by the wish to debunk the book and its god. Really, some Higher Critics seem to be saying, this god is not so great or mysterious—we don't mind calling him Yahweh to make clear that he is no better than Jove or Aphrodite—and as for the book, any one of us could have done much better."[26] Montgomery has wryly added that this is why God did not choose such arrogant and presumptuous types to be the authors of Scripture!

Substitutions for Holy Scripture

To salvage Christian symbols, rituals, churches, morals and ethics, and Jesus as an example to be emulated, liberal theologians make heroic efforts to find foundations for Christianity other than the Bible. Montgomery discusses these in detail. He offers a clear account of the nineteenth-century modernists' error of substituting a naïve, nonhistorical, and nonbiblical faith in man's essential and ever-improving goodness for belief in Scripture. He explains that the modernists were creatures of their time and were thus trying to conform with the general optimism and notions of inevitable evolutionary progress of man prevalent in the West during the nineteenth century.

The horrors of World War I ended that illusion. Karl Barth saw clearly that bankrupt nineteenth-century liberal theology offered no solution for humankind's fundamental needs; it could not heal the rift between man and God. As theologian David Wells emphasizes, liberalism "always incorporates modernity into its theology, not simply as an external pole of reference for that theology, but as its internal substance. It imagines, as Barth noted earlier in the century, that we can call God by shouting man in a loud voice." [27] Barth realized that man is a sinner in need of redemption by a divine Savior who is Jesus the Christ.

However, Barth also accepted the destructive "higher criticism" of the Bible. To save the orthodox foundations of Christianity from destructive attack, he placed the miraculous events, such as the resurrection of Christ, into a special realm of history (suprahistory, *Geschichte*) which is not subject to historical investigation, but which instead consists of revelational events separate from the ordinary historical events (*Historie*) in the Bible. Barth's valiant but misguided attempt to save Christian faith via an unstable dialectic was doomed to failure. Barth substituted transcendence for Scripture. He retained the transcendence of God but lost the immanence of God, who had entered real history in the incarnation and atoning sacrificial physical death of Jesus Christ on the cross. Montgomery retains both in his theology.

Bultmann's Dilemma

Like the nineteenth century liberal Protestant theologians and Barth, Rudolf Bultmann accepted the destructive "higher criticism" of the Bible and a naturalistic worldview, asserting, with an air of finality, "For modern man the mythological conception of the world, the conceptions of eschatology, of redeemer and redemption, are over and done with."[28] However, Bultmann rejected the neoorthodoxy of Barth. Bultmann contended that rejection of the historicity of the Bible need not undermine Christian faith. What is essential is the content of the Christian message, which is the personal existential experience of Christ. One can remove Christianity's mythological (i.e., miraculous and prophetic) elements and still retain the content.

Hence, his dilemma. If God's miracles of the incarnation and resurrection of Jesus Christ are myths that must be discarded and if the powers of sin and death have not been miraculously conquered, then what has Bultmann to offer us? In his answers to Karl Jasper's criticisms, he asserts (of Jaspers), "He is as convinced as I am that a corpse cannot come back to life or rise from the grave." Bultmann then queries, "But how am I, in my capacity as pastor, to explain, in my sermons and classes, texts dealing with the Resurrection of Jesus in the flesh . . . ? And how am I, in my capacity as theological scholar, to guide the pastor in his task by my interpretations?"[29] How indeed? If one accepts the metaphysical assumptions of naturalism and accordingly demythologizes Christianity, there is nothing left but one's ethical and moral preferences based only on fallible human opinion.

Where did Bultmann find such an unsound basis for Christian faith? He answers the question thus: "I have endeavored throughout my entire work to carry further the tradition of historical-critical research as it was practiced by the 'liberal' theology and to make our more recent theological knowledge fruitful for it. In doing so, the work of existential philosophy, which I came to know through my discussion with Martin Heidegger, has become of decisive significance for me. I found in it the conceptuality in which it is possible to speak adequately of human existence and therefore also of the existence of the believer."[30] He reemphasizes that "the hermeneutic principle which underlies my interpretation of the New Testament arises out of the existential analysis of man's being, given by Martin Heidegger in his work, *Being and Time* . . . , [which] is not a speculative philosophy, but an analysis of the understanding of existence that is given with existence itself."[31]

Bultmann placed his faith in Heidegger and his *Sein und Zeit*, rather than the Word of God. Bultmannians ignore the fact that their faith is founded on the sand, nay, the quicksand of Heideggerian personal existential experience and have a Christianity without adequate foundation. Bultmann says, "Let those who have the modern world-view live as though they had none."[32]

Wittgenstein's Fly-bottle

Montgomery aptly employs Wittgenstein's metaphor of entrapment in the "fly-bottle" to illustrate the confused situation of theologians who substitute their naturalistic presuppositions and personal preferences for Holy Scripture as a foundation for a redefined secular "Christianity." The nineteenth-century modernist theologians substituted man's essential goodness and inevitable ascending evolutionary progress for Scripture. Rejecting that naive illusion, Barth substituted transcendence. Rejecting nineteenth-century modernism and neoorthodoxy, Bultmann substituted Heideggerian personal existential experience. Rejecting nineteenth-century modernism, neoorthodoxy, and Bultmannian existential experience, Tillich substituted ontology and "Being-itself" for Scripture. Thus, they all end up in the fly-bottle, creating a new but false "Christianity" with no salvation and no sound basis for morality.

Montgomery has rightly noted that liberal theology transmutes the gold of Christianity into a plumbian chameleon that sits on the latest cultural or philosophical trend and becomes virtually indistinguishable from it. The path into the fly-bottle is paved with good intentions, but one cannot get back out unless one knows how one got in. Otherwise, there is a great deal of energetic buzzing about in the fly-bottle and lots of erudite theological treatises are generated, but no progress is made in getting out. Liberal theologians are there entombed and, as it were, entomed.

Wittgenstein said, "What is your aim in philosophy?—To shew the fly the way out of the fly-bottle."[33] A major aim of Montgomery in theology is "to shew the theologian the way out of the fly-bottle!" His expert guidance is simple: reverse course and trust in the truth and authority of Holy Scripture "so that we may no longer be children, tossed to and fro by the waves and carried about by every wind of doctrine, by human cunning, by craftiness in deceitful schemes. Rather, speaking the truth in love, we are to grow up in every way into him who is the head, into Christ, from whom the whole body, joined and held together by every joint with which it is equipped, when each part is working properly, makes the body grow so that it builds itself up in love" (Eph 4:14–16 ESV).

The late liberal theologian Robert W. Funk wrote in 1966, "As evidence that Barth and Bultmann were negotiating a significant turn in the history of the tradition, it might be observed that many of the newer theological modes, which appear to forecast the shape of the second half of the century, are traceable, directly or indirectly, to one or the other of them. It is astonishing, for example, that so many of the new 'radical' theologians are of Barthian parentage."[34] This seem astonishing only if one considers the "orthodoxy" in Barthian "neo-orthodoxy" but ignores the new dialectic in "neo." Barth severed the orthodoxy that he taught so brilliantly from its biblical foundation and married it instead to transcendence.

Funk may have vaguely sensed the early cracks in the foundations in wondering, "Is it possible that Barth seized the gravity of the issue already in 1919?" The implications of neoorthodoxy were there to see, however, and H. Richard Niebuhr saw them 37 years before. Jon Diefenthaler notes, "As early as 1929 he was convinced that Barth had gone too far in his *Epistle to the Romans*. His wholly transcendent God was too remote from human experience."[35] Funk continues, "And Bultmann has also spawned a variety of new theological movements, some of which, at least, are in the theological vanguard." Funk does not see the slippery slope here, and stops abruptly with, "It is not our aim here to indulge in prediction." Funk, of course, eagerly slid down that slippery slope into the fly-bottle to become one of the radical theologians that he was astonished about earlier.

Montgomery shows that the logical and actual outcome of liberal theology is the death of God, which is not astonishing but is inevitable. If Barthian "wholly other" transcendence is followed out completely to its logical conclusion, God floats infinitely far away into an unfathomable mist and disappears forever. Similarly, the ever-internalized God of Bultmann disappears forever into the deep, dark, dank interior of Heideggerian personal existentialism. Tillich was correct in teaching that our proper ultimate concern is God only. However, God is not "Being-itself" as vaguely defined by Tillich. If one is consistent with Tillich and applies (as did his student Thomas J. J. Altizer) his Protestant principle to all religious assertions, then even the assertion that God is Being-itself is negated, and God again disappears completely. These muddy streams of theological error merged in the 1960s into a stagnant, dead-end pond called the "Death of God" movement, a movement that is now moribund, due largely to the contemporaneous and subsequent analyses of its failings by Montgomery. Two of the best books for those who want to get out and stay out of the fly-bottle are Montgomery's magnificent concise logical tract on theology and William Lane Craig's "signature book" on "reasonable faith."[36]

Shibboleths: Tolerance and Diversity

Our era is post-Christian. There are a variety of worldviews in the marketplace of ideas to choose from. Attacks on traditional orthodox Christianity are continually increasing in number and virulence. Ted Turner has asserted that "Christianity is a religion for losers."[37] He is likely unaware of the irony that his assertion is soteriologically correct! As it is written, "There is none righteous, no, not one" (Rom 3:10 KJV). Anyone who is morally perfect would not need Christianity.[38]

Currently, science writer Richard Dawkins asserts unconvincingly that Christians live under "The God Delusion."[39] Chris Hedges calls conservative Christians "American Fascists"[40] in his wildly exaggerated book of the same name. Our era is much like the first century in the history of Christianity. When Sam Harris attacks Christianity by setting up and knocking down straw men in his "Letter to a Christian Nation," he seems to believe that the U.S. is such a nation, but this is an exaggeration.[41] In our modern and postmodern era, diversity in our culture is wonderful, as long as diversity does not include theism, especially Christianity!

A. C. Grayling describes theists as "those who persist in wanting to have an invisible friend, who continue believing in fairies at the bottom of the garden." He hopes that they eventually will have their ideas banned from the marketplace of ideas and will do their believing "in private, where such proclivities belong along with wearing the opposite sex's underwear." That analysis of theism leads one to wonder where he developed such an intense interest in "wearing the opposite sex's underwear."[42] He doth protest too much, methinks.[43] Does he perhaps want theism banned from culture by the thought police? It is indeed a shame that we Christians are not tolerant like these folks. It seems reasonable to expect that Professor Grayling's next treatise, perhaps his philosopher's stone, his *magnum opus*, will be *Grayling's Philosophy of Cross-Dressing*.

Reading Dawkins, Hedges, Harris, and Grayling motivates me to plead for a return to civil discourse! Edmund Burke famously and wisely taught us that what is in our hearts is primary and cannot be replaced by the laws of a particular political system; he said, "Manners are of more importance than laws. . . . Manners are what vex or soothe, corrupt or purify, exalt or debase, barbarize or refine us, by a constant, steady, uniform, insensible operation like that of the air we breathe in."[44] An eminent philosopher recently published an excellent concise essay, "Manners," which articulates the same vital lesson: "Manners are central to the true morality . . . , the softener of conflict. Without them society itself would be impossible." He rightly states that people "have to put civility at their heart, because nothing else— certainly not the blunt instrument of law nor the despairing council of social apartheids—can do nearly as well." He adds that "the point of manners is, fundamentally, consideration . . . , graceful treatment of others." By coincidence, the philosopher who wrote these wise words on good manners has the same name as the other person who equated believing in God with a proclivity for "wearing the opposite sex's underwear." It would benefit the rude writer greatly to read the sagacious words of the philosopher, who traces the tradition of "the well-mannered person" back to Castiglione and to "the 'great-souled individual' central to Aristotle's idea of ethics."[45]

Coming Full Circle

It is ironic that liberal theology and The New Atheism offer us the same empty solutions to the universal problems of our human situation, and there is almost nothing new in either. The attacks on traditional Christianity from within and without have more in common than they differ. The attacks from within are more dangerous, being a quisling fifth column, which claims that it will save Christianity by redefining it. The attacks from without are easier to identify and oppose. What does liberal theology offer us? No one has summarized the answer better than theologian H. Richard Niebuhr: "In its one-sided view of progress which saw the growth of the wheat but not that of the tares, the gathering of the grain but not the burning of the chaff, this liberalism was indeed naively optimistic. A God without wrath brought men without sin into a kingdom without judgment through the ministrations of a Christ without a cross."[46]

Montgomery offers us instead the rational conviction of the utter uniqueness of the personal salvation found in the Christian message. And for that we honor him with our reflections. We remember also what Montgomery consistently teaches: the social gospel of correcting injustice and relieving human suffering is based on the evangelical gospel which offers eternal salvation through God's grace. The best and only basis for the social gospel is transformation of the human heart by faith in Jesus Christ.[47]

Endnotes

1 "We're in the Same Boat [God's Boat], Brother," by Huddie "Lead Belly" Ledbetter: "We're in the same boat brother / And if you shake one end / You gonna rock the other." From *ChickenBones: A Journal for Artistic and Literary African-American Themes*. See www.nathanielturner.com/wereinthesameboatbrother.htm.

2 For these Web sites, see respectively www.jwm.christendom.co.uk, www.ciltpp.com, and hen.wikipedia.org/wiki/John_Warwick_Montgomery.

3 "For God so loved the world, that he gave his only begotten Son, that whosoever believeth in him should not perish, but have everlasting life" (KJV). The most well-known verse in the New Testament tells us explicitly that what one believes is absolutely essential, not only temporally but also eternally.

4 www.frontpagemag.com/Articles/Read.aspx?GUID={1FDE94D2-EE3E-411C-9ACC-ABC598B8760B}. Edward Klein asserts (in his book, *The Truth About Hillary*) that *Motive* magazine has been a great influence on Hillary Clinton. In his review of Klein's book, Richard Poe writes (in *FrontPage Magazine*): "*Motive* was gleefully vulgar; it editorialized that words like f-ck, b-tch and sh-t should be printed 'intact.' Photo features included a birthday card for Ho Chi Minh and a picture of a pretty coed with an LSD tablet on her tongue. . . . Advice was dispensed on draft dodging, desertion, and flight to Canada and Sweden. . . . *Motive* devoted an entire issue to a radical lesbian/feminist theme, which emphasized the need to destroy 'our sexist, racist, capitalist, imperialist system.'" According to Klein, Hillary became an avid reader of *Motive*. She told *Newsweek* in 1994, "I still have every issue they sent me." The last issue of *Motive* (1972) was not under church sponsorship, having been hijacked by radicals. Available online at: www.rainbowhistory.org/lmotive.htm. A favorable but superficial review of *Motive* (containing a

mock obituary for God) appeared in 1966 in *Time*: www.time.com/time/printout/0,8816,836518,00.html.

5 Richard M. Weaver, *Ideas Have Consequences* (Chicago: The University of Chicago Press, 1948). The latest (1984 paperback) edition has a new foreword by the author. Weaver offers a brilliant analysis of the consequences of man's choices, especially his choosing to evict the transcendent from his worldview.

6 John Warwick Montgomery, "Agent 666: Bishop Pike and His Treasure Hunt," and "James A. Pike," in *The Suicide of Christian Theology* (Minneapolis: Bethany Fellowship, 1970), 47–61, 231–32.

7 George S. Lockwood at titusonenine.classicalanglican.net/?p=644.

8 Francis Schaeffer, *The Complete Works of Francis A. Schaeffer: A Christian Worldview, Volume Four, A Christian View of the Church*, 2nd ed. (Wheaton, IL.: Crossway, 1985), 357–58.

9 David M. Robertson, *A Passionate Pilgrim: A Biography of Bishop James A. Pike* (New York: Knopf, 2004). Pike attended Union Theological Seminary but did not complete the requirements for the B.D. degree and was not graduated, but falsely reported to his employer, Columbia University, that he had earned that degree. See pp. 61, 72. Reviewed ("Lost Shepherd") by Ian Hunter, in *Touchstone: A Journal of Mere Christianity*, www.touchstonemag.com/archives/article.php?id=19–02–045-b.

10 William Stringfellow and Anthony Towne, *The Death and Life of Bishop Pike* (Garden City, NY: Doubleday, 1976). Reviewed by Richard John Neuhaus, from the Web site of the Carnegie Council for Ethics in International Affairs, http://www.cceia.org/archive/worldview/1976/10/2763.html/_res/id=sa_File1/v19_i010_a018.pdf. See also Charles Templeton, *An Anecdotal Memoir: Inside Television at CTV*, 1966, www.templetons.com/charles/memoir/tv-ctv.html.

11 *Alice in Wonderland* script, Disney movie version, scifiscripts.name2host.com/cartoon/AliceScript.htm.

12 Mark D. Tooley, "The Religious Left's Monster," 2 April 2007, *FrontPage Magazine.com*:
www.frontpagemag.com/Articles/ReadArticle.asp?ID=27631.
See also: www.aluka.org; www.amnesty.org/en/region/africa/southern-africa/zimbabwe;
www.layman.org/layman/news/news-around-church/will-ecumenical-groups.htm;
www.parade.com/dictators/2008/profiles/robert-mugabe.html;
www.speroforum.com/site/article.asp?id=4175.

13 www.citizen.co.za/index/article.aspx?pDesc=67468,1,22.

14 Heidi Holland, *Dinner with Mugabe* (New York: Penguin, 2008) and Martin Meredith, *Mugabe: Power, Plunder, and the Struggle for Zimbabwe* (Philadelphia: Perseus, 2007).

15 Montgomery, "The Theologian's Craft," in *The Suicide of Christian Theology* (Minneapolis: Bethany, 1970), 267–313. I also recommend an independent essay of the same title by theologian David Wells, i.e., "The Theologian's Craft," in John D. Woodbridge and Thomas Edward McComisky, *Doing*

Theology in Today's World: Essays in Honor of Kenneth S. Kantzer (Grand Rapids: Zondervan, 1991), 171–94. Wells concisely states (p. 172), "For theology is the sustained effort to know the character, will, and acts of the triune God as he has disclosed and interpreted these for his people in Scripture, to formulate these in a systematic way in order that we might know him, learn to think our thoughts after him, live our lives in his world on his terms, and by thought and action project his truth into our own time and culture. It is therefore a synthetic activity whose center is the understanding of God, whose horizon is as wide as life itself, and whose mission echoes the mission of God himself, which is to gather together in Christ a progeny as numerous as the stars above" (Gen 15:1–6; Gal 3:6–16).

16   Montgomery, "Theologian's Craft," 273.

17   Ibid., 271–75.

18   Robert Nozick, *The Examined Life: Philosophical Meditations* (New York: Simon & Schuster, 1989), 96.

19   John Warwick Montgomery, *History, Law and Christianity* (Edmonton, Alberta: Canadian Institute for Law, Theology and Public Policy, 2002).

20   John Warwick Montgomery, editor and contributor, *Myth, Allegory and Gospel: An Interpretation of J. R. R. Tolkien, C. S. Lewis, G. K. Chesterton, and Charles Williams* (Minneapolis: Bethany Fellowship, 1974).

21   Ross Clifford, *John Warwick Montgomery's Legal Apologetic: An Apologetic for All Seasons* (Bonn, Germany: Verlag für Kultur und Wissenschaft, 2004), 185–89.

22   Walter Kaufmann, *Critique of Religion and Philosophy* (Princeton: Princeton University Press, 1958), 288–89. "In sum, liberal Protestantism has courted reason by rewriting history in defiance of reason and evidence" (p. 311).

23   Ibid., 377.

24   Eta Linneman, *Biblical Criticism on Trial*, English translation by Robert W. Yarbrough (Grand Rapids: Kregel, 2001), 20. Originally published in 1990 as *Bibelkritik auf dem Prüfstand: Wie wissenschaftlich ist die "wissenschaftliche Theologie"?* by VTR, Nuremberg, Germany. For additional views, see Paul Rhodes Eddy and Gregory A. Boyd, *The Jesus Legend: A Case for the Historical Reliability of the Synoptic Jesus Tradition* (Grand Rapids: Baker, 2007); Robert L. Thomas, ed., *Three Views on the Origin of the Synoptic Gospels* (Grand Rapids: Kregel, 2002); Robert L. Thomas and F. David Farnell, *The Jesus Crisis: The Inroads of Historical Criticism into Evangelical Scholarship* (Grand Rapids: Kregel, 1998).

25   Kaufmann, *Critique of Religion and Philosophy*, 378–96.

26   Ibid., 383–84. "The Higher Critics have not literally destroyed the texts, but they have taught several generations to see only the potsherds."

27   David Wells, "The Theologian's Craft," 179.

28   Rudolf Bultmann, "Demythologizing: Controversial Slogan and Theological Focus—Jesus Christ and Mythology" (1958), in Roger A. Johnson, ed., *Rudolf Bultmann: Interpreting Faith for the Modern Era* (Minneapolis: Augsburg Fortress, 1991), 292.

29 Karl Jaspers and Rudolf Bultmann, *Myth and Christianity* (Amherst, NY: Prometheus, 2005), 66. This edition contains a new and very helpful introduction by R. Joseph Hoffmann.

30 Rudolf Bultmann, "Lebenslauf" ("Autobiographical Reflections") in *Existence and Faith: Shorter Writings of Rudolf Bultmann*, selected, translated, and edited by Schubert M. Ogden (New York: Meridian, 1960), 288. Bultmann taught at the University of Marburg (1921–1951), and the atheistic existentialist philosopher Martin Heidegger taught there also (1923–1928). The brilliant and charismatic Heidegger had serious moral failings (marital infidelity and support of Nazism) but had a Svengali-like influence on many intellectuals, e.g., Hannah Arendt.

31 Rudolf Bultmann's foreword to John Macquarrie, *An Existentialist Theology* (London: SCM Press, 1955), vii.

32 Rudolf Bultmann, "Demythologizing," in *Existence and Faith*, 328. Bultmann cites (as analogous) 1 Cor 7:29–31: "From now on, let those who have wives live as though they had none, and those who mourn as though they were not mourning, and those who rejoice as though they were not rejoicing, and those who buy as though they had no goods, and those who deal with the world as though they had no dealings with it. For the present form of this world is passing away." We should live good lives here on earth being in the world, but also remember that we are not of the world and are preparing for the eternal kingdom of God to come. We cannot repose in the temporal. "Therefore, if anyone is in Christ, he is a new creation. The old has passed away; behold, the new has come"(2 Cor 5:17 ESV). Bultmann accepts a naturalistic metaphysic inconsistent with the Christian worldview but arbitrarily says that we should live the latter.

33 Ludwig Wittgenstein, *Philosophical Investigations*, 3rd ed., translated by G. E. M. Anscombe (Oxford: Blackwell, 1953), 309. "Shew, fly! Don't bother me! For I belong to somebody!"—"having been bought with a price. So glorify God in your body" (1 Cor 6:20); "do not become slaves of men" (1 Cor 7:23). See also Garth Hallet, *A Companion to Wittgenstein's "Philosophical Investigations"* (Ithaca: Cornell University Press, 1977), 383.

34 Robert W. Funk's introduction to Rudolf Bultmann, *Faith and Understanding*, vol. 1 *(Glauben und Verstehen, I)*, translated by Louise Pettibone Smith (New York: Harper & Row, 1966), 12–13.

35 Jon Diefenthaler, *H. Richard Niebuhr: A Lifetime of Reflections on the Church and the World* (Macon, GA: Mercer University Press, 1986), 38. Diefenthaler adds, "Niebuhr welcomed the revolt against the anthropocentrism of nineteenth-century religious thought" (ibid.).

36 John Warwick Montgomery, *Tractatus Logico-Theologicus*, 3rd rev. ed. (Bonn: Verlag für Kultur und Wissenschaft, 2005). Available from: the Canadian Institute for Law, Theology and Public Policy in Edmonton, Alberta, Canada. William Lane Craig, *Reasonable Faith: Christian Truth and Apologetics*, 3rd ed. (Wheaton: Crossway, 2008).

37 Robert Goldberg and Gary Jay Goldberg, *Citizen Turner: The Wild Rise of an American Tycoon* (New York: Harcourt Brace, 1995), 424.

38 "But now the righteousness of God has been manifested apart from the law, although the Law and the Prophets bear witness to it—the righteousness of God through faith in Jesus Christ for all who believe. For there is no distinction: for all have sinned and fall short of the glory of God, and are justified by his grace as a gift, through the redemption that is in Christ Jesus, whom God put forward as a propitiation by his blood, to be received by faith. This was to show God's righteousness, because in his divine forbearance he had passed over former sins" (Rom 3:21–25 ESV). "The Lord is my strength and my song, and he has become my salvation; this is my God and I will praise him, my father's God, and I will exalt him" (Exod 15:2 ESV).

39 Richard Dawkins, *The God Delusion* (New York: Mariner, 2008).

40 Chris Hedges, *American Fascists: The Christian Right and the War on America* (New York: Free Press, 2007).

41 Sam Harris, *Letter to a Christian Nation* (New York: Knopf, 2006).

42 A. C. Grayling, writing in *New Humanist* 122(6), November/December 2007: http://newhumanist.org.uk/1667.

43 With apologies to Gertrude. The allusion is, of course, to William Shakespeare's *Hamlet*, Act III, scene 2, 222–30.

44 Edmund Burke, "Three Letters Addressed to a Member of the Present Parliament, on the Proposals for Peace with the Regicide Directory of France: Letter 1, On the Overtures of Peace," in *The Works of the Right Honourable Edmund Burke*, vol. 5 (1815; reprinted Charleston, SC: BiblioBazaar, 2007), 213.

45 A. C. Grayling, "Manners," in *The Heart of Things: Applying Philosophy to the 21st Century* (London: Orion Books, 2006), 18–20.

46 H. Richard Niebuhr, *The Kingdom of God in America* (1937; reprinted Middletown, CN: Wesleyan University Press, 1988), 193. This edition has a new and perceptive introduction by Martin E. Marty.

47 Diefenthaler, *H. Richard Niebuhr*, 94. Niebuhr "contended that hard times had come upon the social gospel because the twentieth-century phase of the movement tended to ignore the stark realities of human sinfulness and to become almost completely identified with liberal Protestantism. The new generation of leadership had forgotten what Jonathan Edwards knew too well, that 'true virtue' required that God first accomplish a 'second birth,' a conversion of the human heart and will. Niebuhr's intention was not to condemn the social gospel, but to transplant it back into that soil of evangelicalism from which it had emerged in the nineteenth century." Montgomery has consistently maintained the same position.

Name Index

Subject Index

Scripture Index